The System of Japanese Society

A Historical Sociology of Work and Employment

The System of Japanese Society

A Historical Sociology of Work and Employment

Eiji Oguma

TRANS
PACIFIC
PRESS

The System of Japanese Society: A Historical Sociology of Work and Employment
Translated from the first Japanese edition,
Nihon shakai no shikumi: Koyō, kyōiku, fukushi no rekishi shakaigaku,
published in 2019 by Kōdansha, Japan.

English edition © 2024 Eiji Oguma
Published by Trans Pacific Press Co., Ltd.

Trans Pacific Press Co., Ltd.
PO Box 8547
#19682
Boston, MA, 02114, United States
Telephone: +1-6178610545
Email: info@transpacificpress.com
Web: http://www.transpacificpress.com

Copyedited by Miriam Riley, Armidale, NSW, Australia
Layout designed and set by Ryo Kuroda, Tsukuba-city, Ibaraki, Japan
Cover designed by Henry Adrian

Distributors

World
Independent Publishers Group (IPG)
814 N. Franklin Street,
Chicago, IL 60610, USA
Email: frontdesk@ipgbook.com
Web: http://www.ipgbook.com

China
China Publishers Services Ltd.
718, 7/F., Fortune Commercial Building,
362 Sha Tsui Road, Tsuen Wan, N.T.
Hong Kong
Email: edwin@cps-hk.com

Japan
MHM Limited
3-2-3F, Kanda-Ogawamachi, Chiyoda-ku,
Tokyo 101-0052
Email: sales@mhmlimited.co.jp
Web: http://www.mhmlimited.co.jp

Southeast Asia
Alkem Company Pte Ltd.
1, Sunview Road #01-27,
Eco-Tech@Sunview
Singapore 627615
Email: enquiry@alkem.com.sg

The publication of this book was supported by a Grant-in-Aid for Publication of Scientific Research Results (Grant Number 22HP6007), provided by the Japan Society for the Promotion of Science, to which we express our sincere appreciation.

Library of Congress Control Number: 2024908667

Cover Photo: Recruitment examination for public service staff of the Tokyo Metropolitan Government, 1952 (*Mainichi Shimbun*).

ISBN 978-1-920850-43-2 (paperback)
ISBN 978-1-920850-44-9 (eBook)

Contents

List of Figures vi

List of Tables vii

About the Author viii

Preface ix

Introduction 1

1 The Dual Structure of Japanese Society 23

2 The Japanese-style Employment System and Its Characteristics 73

3 Implanted Bureaucracy: The Origins of 'Japanese-style Employment' 121

4 The Formation of Norms 171

5 Democratization and Equality of '*Shain*' (Company Employee) 223

6 High Growth and the Completion of the Japanese-style
   Employment System 287

7 A New Dual Structure 339

8 Japan's Employment System and Dual Structure 385

Notes 407

Bibliography 459

Index 495

Figures

1.1 Trends by employment status (1984–2022) 28

1.2 Trends in the 'seniority-based wage' group (1982–2022) 33

1.3 Career paths for new graduates of four-year universities by year 36

1.4 Labor participation rate for women 15–64 years old
(2021, selected countries) 43

1.5 Labor force participation rate for 65-year-olds or more
(2002, 2022, selected countries) 51

1.6 Trends by social group organization rates in Japan (1972–2017) 60

1.7 Trends by employment status (1953–1983) 62

1.8 Employees in private enterprises by firm size (1956–1979) 63

1.9 The Japanese labor market model (1954) 71

2.1 Incidence of over-qualification (selected countries) 80

2.2 Women's share of management positions (selected countries) 90

2.3 Female labor force participation rate by age grade (2022) 91

2.4 A model of the international comparison of differences
in hiring practices 97

2.5 Size of previous company of workers who switched companies (2020) 102

2.6 Strictness of employment protection in regular contracts
(2019, selected countries) 103

3.1 The three-tier structure of the pre-war civil service 132

5.1 The average Densan 'livelihood' wage, January 1947 237

5.2 Wages by age category and company size (1946) 243

5.3 Correlation between age and wage of workers with 0 years of service
(1965, manufacturing industry) 244

5.4 A ranking scheme introduced by Nippon Light Metal (1953) 259

5.5 Wages by age and years of service (1954) 267

6.1 High school and university enrolment rates (1950–2022) 290

6.2 Trends in the number of Japanese universities (1955–2020) 304

6.3 Competence ranking system at Nippon Kōkan (1966) 322

6.4 Employee categories and occupational categories
at Nippon Kōkan (1966) 323

7.1 Hiring trends at Toyota Motor Company (1962–1980) 344

7.2 Absolute percentage of votes in general elections (1952–1990) 352

7.3 Net migration to the three major metropolitan areas and regional income gap ratio (1955–1997) 353

7.4 Personnel evaluation form for a worker at Misawa Homes Co., Ltd. (1987) 361

8.1 Collective agreement coverage (selected countries) 394

8.2 Wage gap by establishment size (selected counties) 395

8.3 Unionization trends in Japan (1947–2019) 397

8.4 Employees in private enterprises by firm size (1956–2022) 398

Tables

1.1 Relative share of the 'seniority-based wage' group (1982–2022) 33

3.1 Correspondences between official rank and positions (1886) 133

3.2 The Japanese government salary schedule (1886) 137

3.3 Mitsubishi salary schedule (1917) 145

3.4 Konishiroku (Konica) qualification scheme 146

3.5 Ishikawajima Heavy Industries Promotion Selection Criteria Table (1) 149

3.6 Ishikawajima Heavy Industries Promotion Selection Criteria Table (2) 152

3.7 Ishikawajima Heavy Industries Promotion Selection Criteria Table (3) 153

4.1 Rules for years-in-rank on active duty in the Ordinance on the Promotion of Army Officers (1874) 177

7.1 Increasing trends in management positions at Nippon Kōkan (1957–1977) 357

7.2 Cumulative timeline of the introduction of competence ranking systems 358

About the author

Eiji OGUMA is professor at the Faculty of Policy Management, Keio University. His socio-historical works on modern Japan cover national identity, colonial policy, post-war democratic thought, the 1968 student movement and Japan's employment system. He has been awarded seven major prizes for his work, including the Suntory Prize for Social Sciences and Humanities, the Mainichi Publishing Culture Award and the Japan Sociological Society Encouraging Award, as well as one prize for documentary filmmaking in Japan. His major publications in English are *A Genealogy of 'Japanese' Self-Images* (2002) and *The Boundaries of 'the Japanese'*, vols. 1 (2014) and 2 (2017), all published by Trans Pacific Press.

Preface

My theme has been 'What is Japan?' As a researcher who was born and raised and has family in Japan, I have a responsibility to Japanese society. This has not changed over time.

I once published an English book on the genealogy of Japanese discourses on the self-image of the 'Japanese' that took the form of discourses in academic articles of ancient history and anthropology since the nineteenth century. Later, I published a two-volume book about how the Japanese legal and educational systems have established the boundaries of the 'Japanese' between Koreans, Taiwanese and Okinawans. After the Fukushima Daiichi nuclear accident in 2011, I joined the anti-nuclear movement and made a documentary film about it. I also wrote a book on the oral history of my father, a former Japanese soldier who was interned in a Soviet labor camp in Siberia and who was a co-plaintiff in a lawsuit by a former Korean Chinese/Japanese soldier, a Korean who had lived in Manchuria and had been conscripted to the Imperial Japanese army, demanding compensation from the Japanese government (the book was also translated into English, but the Chinese version has a larger readership). My best-known work in Japan may be a book that analyzes the relationship between the war experience of World War II and postwar democracy. Topics have thus shifted, but the theme remains the same: 'What is Japan?' My overarching concern is identifying what people are bound to in Japanese society. My approach has also remained consistent. In order to relativize the current Japanese society, I look back at its history, compare it internationally, and analyze it using sociology.

This book is a study of Japan's employment system and the dual structure of society. I had worked for six years in a Japanese company before entering graduate school and have personally experienced many of the employment practices described in this book. My father, however, was a small business owner who was almost self-employed. Therefore, the lifestyle into which I was born and in which I was raised was different from the practices and lifestyles in large Japanese companies. The employment practices I experienced in Japanese company were foreign to me, even though they were from the same country. My father's small business was overwhelmed by competition from larger companies and closed down in 1996. I have been pondering this issue ever since, trying to unravel the true nature and historical origins of the Japanese-style employment system and to analyze how this system has created a dual structure that excludes the self-employed and microenterprises.

As reviewed in this book, there are many studies on the Japanese-style employment system. I am dissatisfied with them, however. Most were conducted by economists and management researchers, based on temporary observations and interviews, and theoretical analysis. They had never experienced for themselves what it was like to work for a Japanese company. Furthermore, they were focused on elucidating the employment system of large corporations and not the dual structure it created. My research departs from the different experiences and interests of these researchers. The Japanese edition on which this book is based was published in 2019 and sold about 80,000 copies in Japan, including the electronic version. It was read with much interest, not only by researchers, but also by people working within the Japanese-style employment system and in positions excluded from the system. I believe this is because my writing was based on empathy for the experiences of working people.

This book is based on the Japanese edition. However, the Japanese edition included many explanations of employment practices and social security systems in Western Europe and North America for Japanese readers. The current state of employment practices in Japan was not included in the Japanese edition because it was not necessary for Japanese readers. There were also many descriptions that did not require explanation for Japanese readers but cannot be understood by the average English-speaking reader without additional explanation. Therefore, of the nine chapters, the Introduction and chapters 1, 2 and 8 were newly written. In addition, many additions and corrections were made to chapters 3 through 7. In particular, some descriptions of the status of women in Japanese society have been added. Graphs and tables have been newly created, and statistical figures have been brought up to date. In effect, this is a new book.

This book is a study of the historical process by which the Japanese-style employment system has been formed and the dual

Preface

xi

structure it creates. Such a study will provide all researchers and students interested in Japanese society in English-speaking settings with essential knowledge for understanding Japan. Even if you are not interested in Japan itself, if you are interested in labor, sexism and inequality, and how they are structured in a society, you will find much to learn in this book. The book takes a case study of a society in the Far East and describes how a complex historical process involving a variety of actors led to the formation of the structure of the current society. Even though Japan is a specific subject, universal insights can be gleaned from this case study.

Stephen Robertson, who translated this book, did an impossible job with machine translation, drawing on his knowledge of Japanese history and the nuances of historical documents. Miriam Riley, the editor, checked the data, pointed out logical flaws and corrected the sources. I must apologize to them for the extra work they had to do as a result of their excellent work, which aroused my desire to revise and improve the contents. Yuko Furuya Uematsu of Trans Pacific Press appreciated the value of this book and took on the challenge of the publishing project. Yoshio Sugimoto paid attention to the Japanese edition of this book and recommended it for publication. Needless to say, without their help, this book would have never seen the light of day.

Introduction

The proliferation of non-standard workers and the dualization of the labor market are becoming issues of global concern. In 2016, the International Labor Organization, in a report entitled *Non-standard Employment Around the World*, described the Japanese labor market in the following terms:

> Japan has a highly dualistic labour market with a large proportion of workers, particularly women, employed in non-standard jobs. These jobs, while often referred to as "part-time", do not necessarily involve shorter working hours, but are nonetheless characterized by lower pay, fewer career prospects and less job security. Japanese unions, which are enterprise-based, have traditionally limited their membership to regular employees, viewing non-regular workers as a buffer to protect the "lifetime employment" of regular workers.[1]

The Japanese dual labor market is thus inhospitable to women. At the same time, some observers have also advanced the criticism that Japan's 'lifetime employment' system leads to the dominance of older men, which in turn exacerbates social stagnation. The 21 June 2018 issue of the *Nihon Keizai Shimbun*, Japan's newspaper of financial record, carried an article under the headline 'Keidanren, that terrible, homogeneous group'.[2] The gist of the article was that all nineteen vice presidents of Keidanren (the Japan Business Federation) were Japanese men, the youngest of whom was sixty-two years old, who had only ever worked for that corporation. According to the article, in other words, they were all 'people who had been utterly steeped in the Japanese corporate system of workplace seniority, lifetime employment and career advancement within a single firm'.

However, such criticisms of 'lifetime employment' in the Japanese context are made, perhaps unknowingly, within the framework of Japan's collective norms. The above article, listing the names of famous Japanese universities, states that twelve of nineteen of the members, including the chairman, are graduates of the University of Tokyo and other famous universities. However, while specifying their alma maters, nothing is mentioned regarding their undergraduate faculties or majors. That is, it is the names of the schools that are seen as a problem, rather than what they studied. This indicates that the Japanese business community, including critics of its employment practices, believes that what matters is the university from which one graduated and the length of tenure at a single company, rather than one's specialization or professional qualifications. This will have a negative impact on the development of professional human resources in Japan by hindering the evaluation of professional skills.

In other words, the Japanese-style employment system has engendered the situations so often highlighted as problems in Japanese society: the relative exclusion of women and foreign nationals, inequalities vis-à-vis non-regular workers, and the difficulty in acquiring highly specialized personnel. These problems have been consistently pointed out since the 1990s, when the Japanese economy entered a period of stagnation. It has also been noted that the cause of these problems lies in the employment system, prompting repeated calls for systemic reform. However, little progress has been made either in resolving these problems or in reforming the employment system. Why is this? How did the collective norms that are at the root of these problems and that define the Japanese-style employment system come into being? This book investigates these questions. Further, exploring the process by which these dominant norms were constructed will also provide a useful comparative perspective for reexamining the state of employment and inequality in other countries.

Furthermore, this book argues that this employment system has created a dual structure of the labor market and has been a defining factor of Japanese society as a whole. As will be discussed in Chapter 1, this system covers less than 30% of working people in Japan.[3] Nevertheless, it defines the dual structure of Japanese society, and this structure is extremely stable. To present the overall structure of Japanese society as defined by this system is another aim of this book.

Hereafter, 'Japanese-style employment system' is used to refer to the employment practices realized among regular employees of Japanese large companies, and 'Japan's (or the Japanese) employment system' is used to refer to the employment system in Japan, including

Introduction 3

non-regular workers outside of the 'Japanese-style employment system'. This is because the 'Japanese-style employment system' does not cover all employment in Japan.

Research objective and literature review

This book has two objectives. One is to investigate the history of the formation of the Japanese-style employment system, and the other is to present the overall structure of Japanese society as defined by this system. A literature review of previous studies is a necessary part of achieving these objectives. Let us begin with the review of previous studies on the history of the Japanese-style employment system.

The history of the Japanese-style employment system and the reasons for its emergence have been taken up by a wealth of previous studies. However, the basic arguments of these studies were largely already formulated by the 1980s, when the Japanese economy was the focus of considerable global attention. Writing in 1991, Jeremiah J. Sullivan and Richard B. Peterson summarized the English literature on the Japanese-style employment system to that point as follows.[4]

Most studies suggest that while the characteristic pattern of the Japanese-style employment system can be found in the inter-war period, it only became entrenched between the end of World War II and the period of rapid economic growth in the 1960s.[5] Nevertheless, some studies also point to the existence of earlier cultural origins, such as in the Japanese family system, that date to the Edo period (1603–1868).[6] Sullivan and Peterson identified four distinct explanations for the emergence of Japan's employment system. The first of these was the Cultural Model, which sees the influence of a culture of familism and communalism that emphasizes harmony, as well as the history of merchant houses and rural communities in the Edo period.[7] The second was the Control Model, which attributed the cause to Japanese managers' attempts to compromise with the labor movement through the provision of job security and seniority-based wages.[8] The third was the Economic Model, which argued that the employment system was based on economic rationality and that it contributed to the growth of the Japanese economy by enabling the retention of workers and the accumulation of skills through the development of internal labor markets in companies.[9] The fourth explanation was the Motivation Model, which positioned the employment system as something that increased workers' motivation and strengthened their creativity and commitment.[10] In previous studies written in Japanese by Japanese researchers, many management and economics researchers took the Economic Model, while many labor historians took the Control Model.[11] Of these models, the Cultural Model tends to trace the origin of the Japanese-style employment system back to the culture of the Edo period, whereas the others tend to view the system as having its origins in Japan's heavy industry during the inter-war period but only becoming widely established in the immediate aftermath of Japan's defeat in World War II, when the labor movement was at its most radical, and after the late 1950s, when Japan was experiencing rapid growth.

In hindsight, all of these explanatory models have their own limitations. While we cannot ignore residual cultural influence, this hardly explains the full reason for the existence of the contemporary employment system. Although the Economic Model and Motivation Model were both advocated by economists on the premise that the Japanese-style employment system is beneficial to economic growth, they found less and less support among researchers as the Japanese economy stagnated after the 1990s. Finally, the Control Model, although advocated by labor historians who had studied negotiations between labor and management, still fails to explain the persistence of this employment system since the late 1980s, when the Japanese labor movement became less radical and the number of labor disputes plummeted.[12] In other words, these models were defined by the state of affairs that prevailed up to the 1980s.

Research that has taken place since the 1990s is referred to in the notes accompanying the chapters of this book. As a basic trend, researchers since the 1990s appear to have shifted their attention to how the employment system is confronting its limitations such as gender inequality and how it is being transformed.[13] While some research has been carried out on the history of the Japanese-style employment system, for the most part this has taken the form of detailed historical

Introduction

studies that basically follow the arguments of research conducted in the 1980s and earlier.[14] Presumably, this is because it is sufficient to study the period up to the 1960s to look at why and how Japanese-style employment was formed, no matter how evaluations of Japanese-style employment and labor relations have changed since the 1990s, and as a result it has not been considered necessary to make any major changes to the four explanatory models that had been proposed by the 1980s.

In contrast, this book distinguishes itself from previous studies on the following three points.

First, this book shows that the Japanese-style employment system has remained fundamentally unchanged since the 1990s. Many studies in the last thirty years have cited factors such as the increase in non-regular employment in Japan to argue that the country's employment system is changing.[15] Researchers who studied the situation of non-regular workers did not analyze the overall situation of working in Japan.[16] As this book shows, however, this increase in non-regular employment is a phenomenon that is occurring *outside* the employment system, and the system itself has not undergone any significant change. Previous studies have focused only on trends among employed workers while ignoring the overall picture of employment, which includes the self-employment sector, whose decrease offset the increase in non-regular employment.[17] A few researchers noted the relationship between the increase in non-regular workers and the decline in self-employment, but did not analyze it as part of the structure of Japanese society.[18] This has resulted in their misinterpretation of the increase in non-regular employment as a change in the employment system.

Second, this book points to the influence of governmental bureaucracy as the historical origin of Japanese-style employment system. Long-term employment and seniority-based wages are not exclusively characteristic of Japan, but are common in the career-based system that prevailed in European bureaucracies as we will see in Chapter 2 of this book. In Japan, the ranking system, which is a characteristic of the career-based systems of bureaucracy, spread to the private sector through the privatizing of state-owned enterprises, where it became established in the form of in-house ranking systems. Meanwhile, unlike

Western Europe and North America, Japan did not have a history of strong occupational organizations and craft unions and a cross-firm qualification system never took shape. In addition, as will be discussed in chapters 3 and 4, although the spread of the bureaucracy's influence to the private sector is also present in the US and Germany, the characteristics of Japanese bureaucracy were different from those of the other countries. As a result, postwar Japanese workers tried to gain upward mobility in their in-house ranking systems through the enterprise union movement. Ironically, its success allowed management to control the labor movement inside firms, which resulted in the accumulation of skills and the retention of workers inside companies. The Control Model, Economic Model and Motivation Model described above focus on the process of labor-management negotiations that took place after the formation of the prototypical expression of the Japanese-style employment system before World War I under the influence of the bureaucracy, as well as on the improvements in motivation that occurred as an unintended consequence.

Why has this bureaucratic influence been overlooked? The fact is that scholars of the history of the employment system in Japan have been economic, business and labor historians who have mainly studied the wage systems and labor-management negotiations of large private-sector manufacturing companies, especially among blue collar workers, for which an abundance of records exist pertaining to business administration and labor-management negotiations. Andrew Gordon, for example, researched the labor-management relations in Japanese heavy industry from the 1850s to the 1980s, and argued that the Japanese-style employment system took root as a result because the Japanese factory workers and labor unions sought 'regular raises' of wages 'granted to salaried, white-collar employees'. Although I agree with his argument, as for the origin of the 'regular raises' of the salaried white-collar employees, he only wrote that Japanese management 'apparently looked for clues to the more prestigious government bureaucratic organizations [...] where hierarchies of rank and pay were already in place'. He did not explore the issue further, stating that 'to identify the origins [...] is barely to begin our story', and concentrated his research on how the Japanese-style employment system, which had already existed in government bureaucratic organizations (or in the white-collar divisions of large private companies), expanded to blue-collar workers.[19] Thus, Gordon suggested that the system originated in the bureaucracy, but did not explore the topic.

While labor historians such as Gordon have promoted the Control Model, economic and business historians who studied the management of white-collar workers have advocated the Economic Model and Motivation Model. However, these researchers have not examined the personnel practices of government agencies and their impact on private companies. Since government agencies do not engage directly in economic activities, explaining their personnel practices from the standpoint of economic theory would be difficult, to say the least. This may be why economic and labor historians have (most likely unconsciously) avoided focusing on government agencies. Although the personnel system used by the Japanese government has been studied by scholars of public administration and administrative history, these researchers have been less interested in how the practices of government agencies have affected the private sector.[20] In other words, the history of the impact of government agencies' personnel practices on the Japanese-style employment system represents a lacuna across several academic disciplines.

Third, this book argues that the employment system has created a dual structure in the labor market and become a defining factor of Japanese society as a whole. As Chapter 1 of this book shows, long-term employment and seniority wages in Japan are largely limited to employees of large companies, who account for only about 27% of 'working people' in Japan.[21] However, as we will see in Chapter 2, the fact that no cross-firm qualification system for evaluating human resources was ever formed in Japan means that it is impossible to evaluate personnel who move between firms, thereby limiting lateral mobilities of workers between companies. Accordingly, workers in Japanese companies fall easily into two groups, namely workers in large companies, where seniority-based wages are realized through in-house personnel evaluations, and workers in small and medium-sized enterprises (SMEs), who cannot move into large companies. As a result, the Japanese labor market is divided into three types of workers: large company type employees, with long-term employment and seniority-based wages; SME type employees, with regular employment but without long-term employment or seniority-based wages; and informal employment type workers, which includes non-regular workers, the self-employed and contributing family workers.[22] As shown in Chapter 1, these three types are estimated to account respectively for 27%, 27% and 46% of Japan's working people.

What I refer to as the Japanese-style employment system is by and large only realized in the large company type. Even so, the effects of this system are felt by Japanese society as a whole. For example, as we will see in Chapter 2, the principal way to enter the large companies is to be hired as a new graduate immediately upon graduating from a prestigious university, but no importance is attached to the attainment of a master's or doctoral degree. This process forms a hallmark of educational competition in Japan. Moreover, as will be seen in Chapter 1, the public social security system established by the Japanese government provides adequate pensions for those who are employed long-term in large companies, but not for those in the SME or informal employment types. This dictates the state of the elderly in Japan and the disparity between urban and rural areas. Beyond making it difficult for workers to move between large companies, the Japanese-style employment system is also unable to appreciate the value of women as employees once they have left a large company. This has a significant impact on the state of women in Japan. Hence, in this book I argue that the Japanese-style employment system prescribes the entirety of Japanese society as a system. This is why the book goes into so much detail in describing how the employment system relates to the historical background of education and social security, as well the dual structure formed by the three types defined above. This point differentiates the book from previous studies, which have generally restricted their focus to the employment practices of large corporations.

As sated earlier, the research objective of this book is not only to investigate the history of the Japanese-style employment system, but also to elucidate Japanese society as a structural system. The reason that it takes the history of the formation of the employment system as

Introduction

9

its main subject is that the employment system defines the structural system of Japanese society as a whole. It is in these respects, then, that this book differs from the historical studies of the employment system carried out by economists and labor historians.

Next, I will review what kind of research has been conducted on the structure of Japanese society in relation to employment.[23] There are two branches of this research. The first is the work of Japanese economists of the 1950s, and the second is the international comparative studies of social security systems in the 2000s, influenced by Espin-Andersen's welfare regime theory.

As we will see in Chapter 1, Japanese economists in the 1950s argued for the existence of a dual structure in Japanese society, especially in the labor market. Some of these economists independently proposed concepts almost identical to those of underemployment and the informal sector, which later became established in studies of developing countries.[24] Labor economist Shōjirō Ujihara further argued that the employment system of large firms was a factor in the formation of this dual structure.[25] The research in this book is based on their works.

However, these Japanese economists studied Japan in contrast to Western countries based on Western economic theories, including those of Karl Marx. As a result, they tended to position Japan's distinctive phenomena as the result of delayed modernization. These theories have been largely ignored since the 1970s, when it was thought that the dual structure should have been eliminated as Japan's modernization progressed with the rapid economic growth of the 1960s. This was inevitable because these economists themselves considered Japan's dual structure to be a result of its delayed modernization. Even as Japan's economic stagnation and widening inequality became more noticeable in the late 2000s, the dual structure theory of economists in the 1950s was largely ignored.[26]

In the 2000s, much attention was paid to the application of Espin-Andersen's welfare regime theory to Japan. Espin-Andersen, a Danish sociologist, classified the social security systems of Western countries into three regimes: the liberal regime typical of the United States, the social democratic regime typical of Scandinavian countries, and the conservative regime typical of Germany. According to him, the main factor in the formation of these regimes is party politics. He claimed that a liberal regime emphasizing market competition is formed in a society with a strong political party supported by management, a social democratic regime in a society with a strong social democratic party supported by workers, and a conservative regime in a society with a strong Catholic conservative party.[27] He also argued that women's labor participation and fertility rates decline in conservative regimes.[28] This theory attracted the attention of Japanese researchers, especially political scientists studying the comparative politics of social security and female researchers interested in gender equality, and attempts were made to apply this theory to Japan.

These attempts of Japanese researchers, however, did not work. First, Japanese political parties did not represent a particular class as Western parties did, and the differences in claims on social security between parties were unclear.[29] Japanese scholars have attempted to place Japan in the same conservative regime as Germany, but as we will discuss in this book, Japan has a very weak tradition of occupational organizations such as artisan unions, which was the social foundation of German conservatism. In addition, Germany had high social security spending as a percentage of GDP and a high unemployment rate from the 1970s onward, while Japan had consistently low levels of both. Espin-Andersen also introduced the concept of employment regimes and analyzed how governments responded to the rise in unemployment in the 1970s.[30] According to his analysis, the US left it to the automatic adjustment of the market, while in Sweden, the public service sector hired large numbers of women as care workers, thereby reducing unemployment and enhancing social security at the same time. Germany, on the other hand, by enhancing social security, let the elderly and women retire from the labor market, thereby stabilizing the family order while maintaining the employment of male workers. Japan, however, does not fit into either of these categories. As discussed in Chapter 1, the labor force participation rates of the elderly and women are high in Japan.

Japanese researchers who were inspired by the welfare regime theory positioned the low unemployment rate in Japan in the 1970s as a result of public works projects undertaken by Japan's conservative government at the time for political reasons.[31] According to them, the creation of jobs through public works was a functional substitute for social security. However, even after public works spending was cut in the late 2000s, Japan's unemployment rate remained low. Various studies attempting to position Japan in terms of welfare regime theory were conducted until the early 2010s but have become less common since then.

One reason for the failure of these attempts is that many of the researchers who conducted these studies were comparative political science and social security researchers. They tended to overestimate the coverage of the Japanese-style employment system in the Japanese labor market. Reading their studies, one gets the impression that most Japanese workers in the twentieth century enjoyed long-term employment and seniority-based wages, while the rest were employed in public works projects carried out in rural areas. Of course, they are aware that there were many self-employed agricultural workers in Japan in the past, and that the number of non-regular workers has increased rapidly since the 2000s. However, they were still researchers of social security and politics, and were not familiar with the Japanese employment system and the historical background of its formation. Furthermore, as will be discussed in Chapter 7, they overlooked the fact that public works projects in the 1970s had more to do with the increase in the number of micro-manufacturers through the construction of the transportation network than with the direct increase in employment by the actual projects.

What these two research trends – economists in the 1950s and political scientists and social security researchers in the 2000s – have in common is a disregard for history. Economists and comparative political scientists tend to explain the present in terms of theory. However, the practices and institutions that exist in a society are not simply determined by the degree of modernization or the number of seats held by labor or conservative parties. Although it is a trend that is not reviewed in this book, some management studies have analyzed the differences in employment systems in different countries theoretically.[32] In one such study by British researcher

David Marsden, the employment systems of the US, Japan, the UK and Germany are classified into four types based on two axes. Japan is classified as the 'competence/rank' rule, in which 'job demand' is based on the 'production approach' and 'the focus of enforcement criteria' is 'function/procedure-centered'.[33] I basically agree with the classification, because as discussed in Chapter 2, the Japanese-style employment system is characterized by an in-house ranking system in which management assesses the competence of individual employees.

However, theorists such as Marsden do not explain why such an employment system took hold in Japan.[34] Sanford Jacoby, a scholar of American labor history, commented on economics' theoretical explanation of how American employment practices were formed as follows. 'These newer theories give us an elegant explanation [...]. But the theories tend to be ex-post-facto rationalizations of postwar American practices'. According to Jacoby, they do not tell us why those practices have not always existed, if they are so theoretically efficient and rational, or why their features are so different in other industrial nations. In the real world, for either employer or employee, 'their actual choices are constrained by social, cultural, and even political considerations'. Even if they are rational, what is rational depends on the social conditions in which they are placed and on their rivalries. Only a study of history can tell us what social conditions dictated their practices and in what rivalries they formed these practices. Jacoby concludes his comment by stating, 'Several of these theoretical problems are attributable to the lack of a historical perspective'.[35]

I agree with Jacoby's views. In Chapter 1, I estimate the coverage of the Japanese-style employment system and outline the Japanese employment regime and dual structure formed by the influence of this system. Chapter 2 outlines the characteristics of the employment system that defines Japanese society and presents hypotheses on its formation. Subsequent chapters 3 through 7 examine the historical process of the formation of the Japanese-style employment system. Thus, this book focuses on the historical process, rather than theoretical analysis of management studies or economics. This is because this book takes the approach of historical sociology that the employment system is not necessarily something that can be explained

Introduction 13

by economic theory, nor by the fact that it lags behind modernization; rather, it is a system of collective norm-bundling of practices that are historically formed.

Research methodology

This book's major research objective is to clarify the historical process by which the system of collective norms that defines the structure of Japanese society was constructed. This is because the Japanese-style employment system and the social structure defined thereby are themselves systems of collective norms. It is not necessarily a system stipulated in laws, and nor is it something that can be explained in terms of economic rationality.

As noted above, Japanese and US economists, considering the Japanese-style employment system as economically rational, have tried to elucidate it using explanations that correspond to Sullivan and Peterson's Economic and Motivation Models. For their part, labor historians advocated the Control Model to explain the employment system in terms of management and collective bargaining. And yet none of these explanations are able to account for the persistence of this system even in the aftermath of Japan's economic stagnation and the deradicalization of the labor movement. Even so, it would not be appropriate to explain the existence of the employment system in terms of the survival of a culture that has persisted since the Edo period, if for no other reason than the fact that the category of 'culture' should not be treated merely as a dustbin in which to toss anything that defies rational explanation.

Sociologists have discussed culture as a historically constructed system of collective norms. A classic example is Max Weber's *The Protestant Ethic and the Spirit of Capitalism*.[36] Originally an economist, Weber pointed out that agricultural laborers in the eastern Germany of his day were behaving in ways that could not be explained by economics. Even when wages were paid on a piece-rate basis, once they had earned what they needed to live on for that day, they did not want to work any further. This might seem like irrational behavior, but if one might die tomorrow, it is foolish to spend today working for tomorrow's need. In a society where one cannot know what will happen tomorrow, what would instead be irrational would be to try to pay piece-rates to increase labor efficiency. This would only be rational behavior in a society characterized by a shared belief that the future will continue in a stable fashion. In other words, what is economically rational depends on the collective norms that a society shares. From this realization, Weber came to believe that behavior oriented to the accumulation of capital would only be found in societies that shared a norm based on a particular vision of the future. He went on to examine views of the future among various Christian denominations, arguing that capitalism emerged from societies that believed in Calvinism.

It is worth pointing out that the German word *Ethik*, which is included in the title of Weber's book, is the German translation of the ancient Greek word 'ethos' (ἔθος), which refers to norms that are acquired experientially through the accumulation of daily actions. These norms are mastered through communal living and have nothing to do with phenotypical markers such as skin color or physical characteristics. At the same time, however, as these norms represent a historically accumulated legacy in any given society, they cannot be changed overnight.

Since Weber, sociologists have discussed systems of social norms in various ways. In 1965, American sociologist Jack P. Gibbs identified three basic dimensions to which all concepts of norms could be subsumed: '(1) a collective evaluation of behavior in terms of what it *ought* to be; (2) a collective expectation as to what behavior *will* *be*; and/or (3) particular *reactions* to behavior, including attempts to apply sanctions or otherwise induce a particular kind of conduct'.[37] French sociologist Pierre Bourdieu used the term 'habitus' to refer to an internalized set of norms and expectations unconsciously acquired by individuals through experience and socialization as embodied dispositions. Bourdieu claimed that habitus is both structured and structuring, not only the product of our position in the social structure, but something that also shapes our thoughts and practices, thereby reproducing the social structure.[38] On the other hand, Peter Berger and Thomas Luckmann introduced the term 'social construction' to theorize the creation of a social system whose constituent members

Introduction   15

gradually create concepts or mental representations of each other's actions, and argued that these concepts eventually become habituated into reciprocal roles that over time become institutionalized within the system.[39]

According to these sociological theories, norms determine human practice while at the same time are constructed through practices and interactions. Examples might include things like handwriting, the way we walk or the way we hold a pen. Such behaviors are not genetically determined from birth but become entrenched through the accumulation of daily actions and interactions with others (e.g., cautions from parents and teachers). Once entrenched, however, they begin to dictate our day-to-day behavior, and are difficult to change. Human societies are defined by such systems of collective norms, which their members hold in common. They may not be genetically determined or have existed since ancient times, but people's daily actions and interactions do accumulate to form tacit rules. These are not necessarily explicitly codified in laws or other regulations, but in many cases, they hold more sway than explicitly stated rules. Even so, they are not immutable, but change with the further accumulation of people's actions.

Nor do these norms exist by virtue of their economic rationality. Rather, as Weber argued, the definition of what constitutes rational behavior is determined by the norms shared by the society. In the context of microeconomics and utilitarianism, people rationally prefer actions that maximize utility. However, the Japanese-style employment system has persisted despite the fact that it has lost claim to economic rationality. Sociologists believed that human behavior, which defies explanation by microeconomics, can also be explained by a historically constructed system of norms. Weber's research methodology involved the use of statistics to discuss overall trends in a society while subjecting religious texts to individual analysis to explore that society's underlying principles. Likewise, Bourdieu also used a combination of quantitative statistical analysis and qualitative analysis of interview texts. Esping-Andersen, who proposed three types of welfare regimes, also referred to party politics as well as the historical process of society as factors in the emergence of different regimes, and used both welfare and employment statistics and historical process descriptions in his analysis.

This book follows a similar approach. On the one hand, it uses statistics to describe the dual structure of Japanese society of each period. On the other, it qualitatively examines the recollections of managers and workers during each period, as well as contemporary documentary records from personnel systems in government agencies and companies, as well as labor unions and governments. My goal in this examination of documentary records and memoirs, however, is not to probe the intentions of specific actors, such as business owners or labor unions, nor to determine what influence they exerted in shaping employment practices. Rather than exploring such direct influences or causal relationships, I am interested in the norms they share in common within the same social context. Accordingly, my investigation centers on how government agencies, business owners, labor unions and other actors all appear to have shared the same discourses and narratives, even when they had no direct relationship with each other. That they did so indicates that they also shared the same norms, just as how people who share the same grammar will share the same way of speaking.

Weber analyzed the texts of the sect founded by sixteenth century French theologian John Calvin as a way of exploring the norms defining German society at the start of the twentieth century. Certainly, these texts represented a discourse that was shared by many people in twentieth century German society. Yet, Weber never demonstrates any causal relationship between these sectarian texts and the society under consideration. From the standpoint of someone who emphasizes causal inference, this may appear to be a methodological flaw. Then, would we be able to detect a direct causal relationship between the United States Declaration of Independence or the Gettysburg Address and their impact on US society in the twenty-first century? Could we say that the norms expressed in these texts do not define US society simply because we cannot detect such causality?

In contrast, sociologists (though perhaps not all of them) would think as follows. For a group of people to share the same discourses and the same narratives means that they have constructed a society

Introduction   17

in which they share the same norms. Although the norms themselves cannot be observed, the fact that they share the same discourses and the same narratives can be investigated by analyzing written records and conversations. This is also the methodology adopted by Michel Foucault's archaeology of discourse,[40] which has had a significant impact on historical approaches within sociology. I used this same methodology to investigate the genealogy of Japan's collective identity from the nineteenth to the twentieth century, based on the researches of the discourses of Japanese self-images and boundaries of the Japanese.[41]

In part of this book, I note the similarity between the personnel files kept by a government agency in the 1890s and those of a Japanese company in the 1970s, without showing any direct causal relationship. I also cite materials in which HR managers in Japanese firms in the 1960s speak of personnel systems they tried to introduce modeled metaphorically on Japanese military hierarchies from the 1930s. The reason I cite these sources is not to prove a direct causal relationship between these actors; rather, by observing how they share the same discourses, I aim to show how these actors continue to construct the same norms, regardless of their mutual temporal distance and the fact that they have no direct relationship with one another. This is based on a methodology that uses the analysis of these discourses to investigate the nature of their collectively shared norms, how these have constructed the employment system and their effects on the dual structure of Japanese society.

At the risk of repeating myself, this book examines the system that defines not only employment, but also the whole society including education, social security, politics, identity, gender inequality and lifestyles in Japan. Although its emphasis is placed on employment practices, these do not in themselves represent the object of this study. I am instead concerned with the elucidation of the system of collective norms that represent the tacit rules of Japanese society. In terms of both its research objectives (i.e., the elucidation of collective normative systems) and its research methodology, this study represents an exercise not in economics or labor history, but in historical sociology. The purpose of this book is to describe these normative systems, rather than to uncover particular historical facts. Accordingly, in addition to conducting my own research on particular facts, as illustrated in the notes to each chapter, I have also drawn extensively on previous studies on economic history, labor history, administrative history, social security history and history of education.

The use of previous historical research as a secondary source has been a well-established practice in historical sociology since Weber's day. Theda Skocpol, who has served in the American Political Science Association and the Social Science History Association, endorses the effective use of secondary sources by historical sociologists, since their goal is not to uncover particular historical facts, but to provide a comprehensive analysis of a society by describing its long-term history and by making international comparisons with other societies.[42] Certainly, this book also brings to light the particular historical fact, hitherto neglected by economic and labor historians, of the impact of bureaucracy on the Japanese-style employment system. Even so, its main purpose is not to elucidate particular historical facts but rather to analyze the process of construction and transformation of collective social norms, including by means of international comparisons. In a case like this, relying on facts already uncovered by previous historical researchers can be an effective method.

To clarify my objective and methodology, I will review works of the social anthropologist Chie Nakane. Identifying the collective norms of a society is also an object of anthropological investigation. Nakane argued that Japanese society is characterized by the predominance of tangible relationships in 'frames' (*ba*) such as in workplaces or villages where people work together as a group. In her view, Japanese society lacks horizontal (*yoko*) solidarities of identity, such as craft unions or castes, that would cut across these frames, and it is rather the hierarchical and vertical (*tate*) relationships between superiors and subordinates that form the basic principle constituting society.[43] The book also positions the lack of a craft union tradition as one of the social backgrounds for the formation of the in-house ranking system in Japanese companies. Nakane's assertions, consequently, are in some respects similar to those advanced in this book. Something lacking

Introduction 19

in her study, however, is the perspective that norms are historically constructed. Thus, Nakane falls back on the claim that the Japanese characteristics she describes have existed since ancient times.[44] Her theory also fails to explain why a Japanese company with tens of thousands of employees would engender a solidarity of identity that extends beyond the tangible sphere of contact. Generally speaking, Nakane inadvertently goes too far in generalizing, both spatially and temporally, anthropological findings from ethnographic surveys at the village level. Nakane's book thus verges on offering a theory of Japanese culture based on the essentialist claim of its existence since ancient times.

While theories of Japanese culture have discussed employment practices since as early as the 1960s, most such discussions are little more than *a posteriori* historical projections of practices that only became common after Japan's postwar period of rapid economic growth.[45] They are better seen as nationalist products intended for popular consumption rather than scholarly achievements, and have been the subject of critical analysis by sociologists in their own right.[46] Unsurprisingly, this book does not make the claim that Japanese employment practices are an expression of an essential 'Japanese culture' that dates back to ancient times. Rather, I argue that they have been constructed as a normative system in the course of a historical process from the nineteenth to the twentieth century under the influence of bureaucracy, a universal factor found everywhere in the world. My goal with this book is to show that what is seen as characteristic of Japanese society, rather than being an element of ancient or even Edo-period culture, has in fact been constructed in the course of modern and contemporary history.

Organization of this book

The book is arranged as follows.

Chapter 1 describes the present dual structure of Japanese society that has resulted from the Japanese-style employment system. It shows how those who enjoy seniority-based wages and long-term employment in Japan account for only about 27% of the working people and demonstrates the extreme stability of this dual structure, noting that an increase in non-regular employment has been accompanied by a decline in the self-employment sector. I also posit the theory that this dual structure is engendered by the closed nature of the internal labor markets of large companies in Japan, which hinders workers' mobility.

Chapter 2 sketches an outline of the Japanese-style employment system and compares it with those of Western Europe and North America. Here, after demonstrating that the Japanese-style employment system has not changed significantly in the twenty-first century and that its various characteristics are derived from the absence of cross-firm standards for professional qualifications, I offer two hypotheses regarding the historical origins of the Japanese-style employment system. The first is that one consequence of the historical absence in Japan of the strong craft unions and occupational organizations that influenced employment practices in North America and Western Europe was that the labor movement developed in a different form. The second is the influence of the career-based system found in European-style bureaucracy.

Chapters 3 and 4 explore the origin of the Japanese-style employment system, which I trace to the Meiji period that began in 1868. Here, I describe the nature of this origin, as well as how the employment system gave rise to its characteristic practices, including the mandatory retirement system, regular personnel transfers and the periodical bulk recruitment of new graduates. This employment system was strongly influenced by the Japanese bureaucracy through the privatization of state-owned enterprises. In view of this, I also describe the history of Japan's bureaucracy while touching on bureaucracies in Germany and the US, and the extent of their influence on the private sector, for the sake of comparative analysis.

Chapter 5 discusses the period from Japan's wartime defeat to the 1950s, and then Chapter 6 takes up the period of high growth that took place in the 1960s. During this period, the Japanese-style employment system, which had existed in only limited scope among upper-echelon employees before the war, now underwent a massive expansion in conjunction with the rise of the labor movement. This was also the period when the employment system spread to blue-collar workers.

However, it was also a time when the business community, the government, labor unions and other actors were seeking alternatives to this employment system. Furthermore, I describe how such exploratory attempts were frustrated before eventually converging to become the employment system that continues to this day.

Chapter 7 describes the period from the 1970s to the 2010s as the background leading up to the present situation, which is characterized by the dual structure outlined in Chapter 1. By the late 1970s, the problems of Japanese-style employment were already manifesting in various ways. A 'new dual structure' of regular employees and non-regular workers was also starting to emerge. In this chapter, I identify these problems while sketching out the process by which they have been carried over into the twenty-first century. Finally in Chapter 8, after rechecking the characteristics of the Japanese employment system and its dual structure, I will analyze how and why this employment system and dual structure arose, and clarify the academic contributions of this book.

1 The Dual Structure of Japanese Society

In this chapter, I describe the present state of Japanese society based on various statistics mainly from the 1980s to 2010s. I lay out the following arguments.[1]

Those capable of securing long-term employment and seniority-based wages account for only about 27% of 'working people' in Japan, a group that includes regular employees in the public service sector and at large companies.[2] While non-regular employment is increasingly common, the total number of regular employees has not decreased significantly. The increase in non-regular employment has come at the expense of the self-employed and family workers, whose share of the total number of working people is decreasing. Furthermore, only about half of regular employees are likely to secure seniority-based wages or long-term employment. In other words, it is estimated that about 27% of Japanese working people enjoy seniority-based wages and long-term employment, about 27% work for small and medium-sized enterprises (SMEs) as regular employees but cannot secure seniority-based wages or long-term employment, and about 46% are in what we may call 'informal employment type', which is made up of self-employed, family workers, and non-regular workers. This means that there are three types of working people in Japan: 27% are 'large company type' employees, 27% are 'SME type' employees, and 46% are 'informal employment type' workers. This structured employment regime has been very stable since the 1980s, as can be evidenced by government statistics.

The fact that we can observe this employment regime suggests that what Japanese economists in the 1950s called a 'dual structure' has been maintained in the twenty-first century. However, whereas the focus in the 1950s was on the dual structure formed by large companies on the one hand and SME workers and the self-employed on the other, attention since the 1990s has shifted to the dual structure of regular employees vs. non-regular workers. Even so, this change took place as

23

a result of the introduction by SMEs of the Japanese-style employment system for core employees and the decrease of the self-employment sector (self-employed and family workers) which has been offset by the increase of non-regular workers, so the dual structure itself has remained unchanged.

This dual structure in employment is also linked to a dual structure in social security, and the present state of poverty and inequality in Japan reflects division arising from this structure. In saying so, however, I am not arguing that the lives of those on the lower tier of Japan's dual structure are necessarily precarious. Those who have spent their entire lives living in their hometowns and who are self-employed or are employed by SMEs, together with their families account for 36% of Japan's population, and 78% of residents outside the three major metropolitan areas (Tokyo, Osaka and Nagoya). Although these people have low incomes, they may be well-off in terms of local social capital.

However, once we exclude the 27% of the population accounted for by large company-type employees and their families who enjoy stable employment and salaries, and the 36% who enjoy the support of local social capital, about one-third of the population left over consists of those unable to secure long-term employment and seniority-based wages who are also marginalized from local social capital. We can surmise that the increasing visibility of inequality and poverty in Japanese society in the twenty-first century is the result not only of the increase of non-regular employees, but also the increasing number of those who are disadvantaged in terms of both employment and social capital.

The stability of this dual structure may be attributed to the fact that the overall structure is determined by the closed nature of the employment system in Japan's large companies, and the fact that this system has remained unchanged. The objective of this chapter is to lay the groundwork for our examination in the following chapters by firstly presenting the overall structure of Japanese society and secondly showing that the Japanese-style employment system is a determinant of this structure.

In this chapter, I use the term 'employment regime' to refer to a labor market structure that is defined by the employment system of large companies.[3] The three types of Japanese workers presented in this chapter correspond to the employment regime, and the structural disparity including social security and social capital corresponds to the dual structure here. The Japanese-style employment system defines the employment regime, and the employment regime defines the dual structure of society.

No decline among regular employees

As noted in the Introduction, many studies on the Japanese-style employment system since the 1990s have claimed that this system is changing. One such shift that has been highlighted is an increase in the number of non-regular workers, which reached 21 million and 38.3% of the total employees in the Labor Force Statistics of 2018.

The Japanese definition of 'non-regular worker' is confusing. Regular employees in Japan are full-time permanent workers, but full-time permanent workers are not necessarily regular employees.[4] A 2016 report by the International Labour Organization on *Non-standard Employment Around the World* states that 'Labour market statistics in Japan are based on employers' classifications, thus the category of "part-time" is a reflection of how they are classified by their employer, rather than the number of hours they work'. As a result, 'in practice, the term "part-time worker" is sometimes used as a generic term to designate non-regular employees, some of whom actually work full time' sometimes without a fixed-term contract.[5] More precisely, the Japanese 'Labor Force Survey' divides 'employees' who are not executives into 'regular' and 'non-regular', though the latter includes sub-categories of '*Paat*' (i.e., housewife part-time workers), '*Arubaito*' (i.e., student and young part-time workers), 'Dispatched workers from temporary agencies', 'Contract employees', 'Entrusted employees' and 'Other'.[6] A 2011 report by the Japan Institute for Labour Policy and Training (JILPT), a research institute affiliated with the Japanese government's Ministry of Health, Labour and Welfare (MHLW), states, 'Consequently, a "Non-regular Employee" is an employee who does not meet one of the conditions for regular employment'.[7] In other words, the term 'non-regular worker' is an umbrella term that refers to employed workers who are referred to as 'non-regular.'

Classification of occupations in labor force surveys or wage censuses is itself a product of the history of employment practices in a country.[8] The '*paat*' and '*arubaito*' are legally part-time workers with the same status. In the context of the 1980s in Japan, '*paat*' represents housewife part-time workers, and '*arubaito*' represents student part-time workers. In the Wage Census and Monthly Labor Survey conducted by the Japanese government, employers fill out a survey form about the status of their workers, so the classification was probably adopted to make it easier for employers to understand. Since the 1990s, '*paat*' are not necessarily housewives and '*arubaito*' are not necessarily students or youth, but these classifications continue to be used in government surveys and statistics. The fact that employers classify and report their workers as 'regular' and 'non-regular' to the surveys also contributes to the lack of clear objective criteria for classification, resulting in some workers being classified as '*paat*' even though they are full-time workers as the 2016 ILO report stated.

The Japanese non-regular worker is characterized by low wages, gender inequality, ease of dismissal, and inequality in social security. According to the Labor Force Survey, non-regular employees accounted for 36.7% of the workforce in 2021, of which 70.5% were part-time workers (49.3% were '*paat*' and 21.2% '*arubaito*'), 13.3% 'contract employees' with fixed-term contracts and 6.8% 'dispatched workers'. According to the 2020 Health and Labor White Paper, wages converted to hourly wage in 2019 compared to full-time regular employees were 66.1% for full-time non-regular workers and 55.8% for part-time non-regular workers.[9] The Labor Force Survey shows that the number of non-regular workers was 20.7 million in 2021, 68.4% of whom were women. As we will see in chapter 2 and 7, the rules governing dismissal in Japan are based on labor-management norms and legal precedents from the 1970s, rather than being explicitly prescribed by law, and these dismissal rules do not apply to non-regular workers even if they are not on fixed-term contracts. Many studies of the dual labor market in Europe use the distinction between fixed-term and permanent contract as a criterion,[10] but this criterion is not appropriate for studies of the Japanese labor market. Another characteristic of non-regular workers in Japan is that

The Dual Structure of Japanese Society 27

in many cases their employers do not contribute to social insurance premiums, which I will discuss in more detail later in this chapter.

So, does the increase in the number of non-regular workers imply a change in the Japanese-style employment system? To anticipate my conclusion, it does not. The rise in the number of non-regular workers is a phenomenon taking place *outside* the Japanese-style employment system, and as such does not signal a change in that system.

Let's review the basic trends. Combining several earlier categories, the Japanese government began compiling data for 'non-regular staff' (*hiseiki no syokuin, jūgyō'in*) in the 1982 'Basic Survey on Employment Structure' (*shūgyō kōzō kihon chōsa*, hereinafter 'Employment Status Survey') and in the 1984 'Labor Force Survey' (*rōdōryoku chōsa*).[11] Figure 1.1 uses data from the Labor Force Survey to show the number of workers by employment status since 1984. As the figure shows, the number of non-regular workers has increased rapidly (the decrease seen in 2020 was due to layoffs of non-regular workers in the food service and lodging industries due to COVID-19). The number of regular employees, however, has not decreased significantly. The ratio of non-regular workers to the total number of employed persons has risen because the number of non-regular workers has increased, but this does not mean that the number of regular employees has decreased. The decline, rather, is taking place in the self-employment sector, which consists of self-employed and family workers.[12]

The typical self-employed and family workers in Japan, an Asian country and a latecomer to modernization, were self-employed farmers or merchants and their wives. It was not until 1959 that the number of employees exceeded 50%. As will be discussed later in this chapter, Japan had a large pool of self-employed individuals in agriculture and commerce that provided a supply of employed workers.

The working-age population, as defined by the Japanese government (i.e., the population between the ages of fifteen and sixty-four), was expanding until 1997. Due in part to this effect, the overall number of employed persons was also increasing until this period. Thereafter, however, we can see that the decrease in the self-employment sector was almost entirely accounted for by the number of non-regular workers. This does not necessarily mean that self-employed individuals

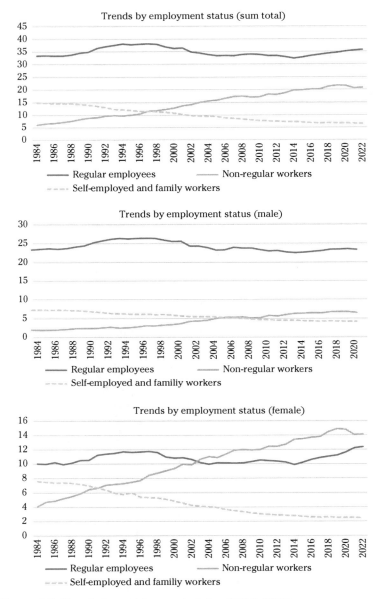

Figure 1.1 Trends by employment status (1984–2022)

Unit: 1 million persons
Source: MIAC (Ministry of Internal Affairs and Communications) Labor Force Survey. The number of employees is from long-term time series data in Table 9(1) of the Survey, averaged for February for 1984–2001 and January-March for 2002–2022. The number of self-employed and family workers are from long-term time-series data in Table 4(1).

The Dual Structure of Japanese Society   29

themselves turned to non-regular employment, but it does mean that we cannot attribute the rise in non-regular workers to a decline in regular employees. It is also worth noting that a consistent trend over the entire period was that the number of female regular employees was about half that of their male counterparts, while the number of female non-regular workers was about twice that of men. Nevertheless, for both men and women, (1) the number of regular employees has remained almost constant, (2) the number of non-regular workers has increased and (3) the number of self-employed and family workers has decreased.

The increase in the number of regular employees since the late 2010s has been fueled by a rise in the number of women employees in the welfare and long-term care sectors in conjunction with Japan's aging society. According to the Labor Force Survey, between 2019 and 2020, while the number of non-regular workers decreased by 970,000 due to COVID-19, the number of regular employees increased by 330,000, with 190,000 of this figure consisting of female regular employees classified as 'health and welfare' employees. However, most care workers in Japan are private-sector employees, and even regular employees have a short average length of service in a specific company and low wages in the Japanese-style seniority-wage system, which will be discussed in Chapter 2.[13]

The three types of working people

Not all of those who are statistically counted as regular employees will be able to realize seniority-based wages or long-term employment. As I discuss in Chapter 2, these advantages, which are considered characteristic of the Japanese-style employment system, are generally only achieved by regular employees at large companies. The prospect of obtaining seniority-based wages in SMEs is bleak for anyone other than core workers, which has a negative impact on worker retention rates in smaller and medium-sized companies.[14]

There is no established method for estimating the coverage of the Japanese-style employment system. Several previous studies have attempted to estimate it based on company size and gender.[15] In the

1993 White Paper on the Labor Economy (*Rōdō Hakusho*), the Ministry of Labour estimated the proportion of employees covered by lifetime employment to be 23.4% in 1985 and 21.6% in 1991 from the Labor Force Survey, by adding the number of (1) male regular employees in the non-agricultural sectors employed in firms with at least 500 regular employees to (2) male regular employees in the public sector, then dividing that total by (3) the total number of employees in the non-agricultural sectors.[16] However, the estimation by the Ministry of Labor has been criticized for excluding women and employed workers in firms with less than 500 employees.[17]

Labor economist Tsuneo Ishikawa employed a more sophisticated estimation method. Based on individual data from the 1990 'Basic Survey on Wage Structure' (*chingin kōzō kihon tōkei chōsa*, hereinafter, 'Wage Census'), Ishikawa and his colleague Takahisa Dejima calculated the relative proportion of a 'primary labor market' in which wages increase with educational background and age, vis-à-vis a 'secondary labor market', wherein they do not.[18] In the Japanese context, the former may be thought of as the proportion of those earning seniority-based wages.[19] They estimated that out of the total number of employees (i.e., workers employed by a company or organization, including those in the public sector), the primary labor market accounted for 32.3% of men and 20.5% of women, and 28.0% of men and women combined. In terms of company size, the primary labor market accounted for approximately half of all employees working in firms with at least 1,000 full-time employees, but only 12% of those working in small firms with between ten and ninety-nine employees. These findings suggest that the proportion of employees in the Japanese primary labor market was about 30%. This was lower than the proportion in the US, which was estimated to be 55% in 1981 in the paper Ishikawa and Dejima referred to.[20] The drawback of Ishikawa's approach is that the Wage Census does not cover workers in firms with fewer than five employees, or self-employed or family workers.

Kazuo Koike, a labor economist, estimated from the 2002 Employment Status Survey that 'roughly one-third' of employees in Japan enjoy seniority-based wages (i.e., wages that increase with age).[21] Koike's estimate was based on the total number of men who were

The Dual Structure of Japanese Society

regular employees at large companies with 500 or more employees, together with the total number of male regular employees in clerical and sales occupations and of male and female regular employees in managerial and professional occupations in all companies, including SMEs. Although this classification was developed by Koike based on his own research experience, the result that about 30% of employees in Japan enjoy seniority wages is also in line with Ishikawa's estimate based on actual wage trends, and may be considered to be a reasonable estimate. Furthermore, labor economist Kyoko Suzuki analyzed individual data from the same 2002 Employment Status Survey that Koike analyzed, using the same method as Ishikawa and Dejima, and estimated the primary labor market to be about 16 million, 29.2% of the total number of employees in that year.[22] The agreement between these estimates indicates that Koike's method and that of Ishikawa and Dejima are almost equally valid for estimating the size of the Japanese primary labor market.

These estimates were static analyses of the size of the Japanese primary labor market in individual years. However, a paper published in 2023 analyzed the Current Population Survey (CPS) data from 1981 to 2021 and confirmed that a stable dual structure exists in the US labor market.[23] According to the paper, the primary sector, which is the group with stable employment, is around 55% of the population, the secondary sector, which experiences steady unemployment, is around 14%, and in the middle of the two groups are people who are not actively participating in the labor market but who also do not experience unemployment very often. Another study analyzing LEHD (the Longitudinal Employer Household Dynamics) data from 1997 to 2014 also confirmed that three groups exist in the US labor market with nearly identical ratios.[24] This ratio was also almost identical to the results of a dual labor market analysis of 1981 CPS data, to which Ishikawa and Dejima referred.[25]

Is there such a stable dual structure in the Japanese labor market? Employing the same method as used for Koike's estimate, I estimated the ratio of employees who enjoyed seniority-based wages to all 'working people', including those in the self-employment sector, based on data from the Employment Status Survey from 1984 to 2022.[26] In my analysis, unlike Koike, the denominator was not the total number of employees, but the total number of working people, including self-employed and family workers. The results are shown in Figure 1.2 and Table 1.1. From the figure, we can surmise the following.

1. The total number of working people rose until 1997, but not thereafter. This is consistent with the fact that the expansion of Japan's working-age population lasted until this period.
2. The number of employees (not including the self-employment sector) has trended consistently upward. The trend since 1997, since which time the total number of working people has remained constant, indicates a shrinking self-employment sector as the relative proportion of employees in the total number of working people has increased.
3. There has been no significant change in the number of regular employees. This indicates that the rise in the number of employees pertains to non-regular workers.
4. The seniority-based wage category accounts for approximately 50% of regular employees and approximately 27% of all working people, and in terms of absolute numbers fluctuates even less than regular employees. This suggests the absence of any significant fluctuations in the group enjoying seniority-based wages and the overall stability of the labor market structure.

Because the total number of employees has been increasing, the relative share occupied by the 'seniority-based wage' group has been trending lower, down from 36.0% in 1982 to 30.5% in 2022. However, as a percentage of the total number of working people, this value has remained largely the same, hovering at around 27%. The overall rise in the number of employees is offset by a corresponding fall in the number of self-employed and family workers, as shown in Figure 1.1.

Synthesizing figures 1.1 and 1.2, we could speculatively divide working people in Japan into the following three groups.

1. Regular employees at large companies and core employees at SMEs whose wages increase with age. This type of employee accounts for about 27% of working people.

The Dual Structure of Japanese Society

Table 1.1 Relative share of the 'seniority-based wage' group (1982–2022)

	1982	1987	1992	1997	2002	2007	2012	2017	2022
Among all working people	26.4%	27.2%	27.8%	28.3%	27.0%	26.6%	26.6%	27.6%	27.7%
Among employees	36.0%	35.7%	34.8%	34.5%	32.1%	30.7%	30.1%	30.9%	30.5%
Among regular employees	46.4%	47.6%	48.1%	49.3%	50.8%	51.2%	50.9%	53.0%	51.4%

Source: MIAC Employment Status Survey.

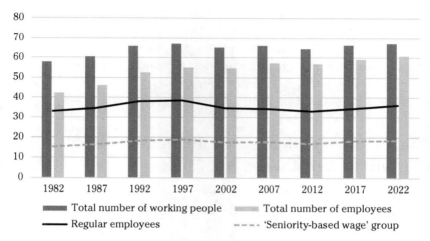

Figure 1.2 Trends in the 'seniority-based wage' group (1982–2022)
Unit: 1 million persons   Source: MIAC Employment Status Survey.

2. Those who are regular employees but whose wages do not necessarily increase with age, such as regular employees at SMEs who are not core employees. This type of employee also accounts for about 27% of working people.
3. Self-employed individuals, family workers and non-regular workers, who together account for the remaining approximately 46% of working people.

Here we see that there are three types of working people in Japan: 27% are 'large company type' employees, 27% are 'SME type' employees,

34   Chapter 1

and 46% are 'informal employment type' workers.[27] As we will see in chapters 2 and 7, legal dismissal restrictions also apply to regular employees of SMEs, but they are highly mobile among firms because of the lack of wage increases. The 27%, those who are able to realize seniority wages, can be considered as the workers who stay in the same company and achieve long-term employment. The relative proportions of these three groups have remained largely unchanged, and their basic structure has remained stable. The consistent changes are the decrease in the number of self-employed and family workers and the increase in the number of non-regular workers. However, this change is occurring *outside* of the Japanese-style employment system, which is known for its long-term employment and seniority wages, and cannot thus be considered a fundamental change to the employment system itself. And the employment regime defined by the Japanese-style employment system is also stable.

'Employment deficit' in the 1990s and the 'Lost Generation'

The existence of such a stable structure has received comparatively little attention. Many researchers focusing on the increase in non-regular employment have attributed this to an upheaval in the Japanese-style employment system. When university graduates faced employment difficulties in the 1990s and early 2000s, after the collapse of Japan's bubble economy, this was also perceived as an upheaval in the Japanese-style employment system. The plight of the young generation that faced difficulties finding employment during this period, commonly referred to as the 'Lost Generation', has itself been the subject of research.[28]

There are also studies supporting the claim that the proportion of regular employees has declined in this generation. The labor economist Ryō Kambayashi analyzed the Employment Status Survey data from 1982 through 2007 and found that the relative proportion of regular employees among men aged twenty-two to twenty-nine declined significantly from the 1990s to the 2000s. Based on this, Kambayashi states that 'the prevailing notion that the increase in the number of non-regular workers correlates with the decrease in the number of regular employees' applies only to men in their twenties during this period.[29]

However, this does not mean that any significant change has occurred in the Japanese-style employment system, or the structures defined thereby. The large number of non-regular workers in this particular generation is mainly due to the large population of this generation, not because of changes in the Japanese-style employment system. The number of new regular employment positions the system supplied each year did not change significantly, but the supply could not keep up with the population of this generation.

As Figure 1.3 shows, the number of university graduates employed in Japan through the 1990s has remained largely unchanged, hovering around 350,000.[30] As I discuss in Chapter 2, the periodical bulk recruitment of new graduates is a common practice among large Japanese companies, which hire extensively among new university graduates every April. As I also discuss in Chapter 2, another common practice on the part of Japanese firms is mandatory retirement, wherein employees who have reached a certain age (stipulated by law as age sixty or older since 1998) are forcibly laid off in March of each year. Thus, each year, Japanese companies lay off a certain number of older employees and hire a certain number of new graduates. According to Tsuguo Ebihara, a consultant specializing in employment and recruitment issues, the total number of career-track employees (*sōgō-shoku*) hired by the 'top 100 most popular companies' according to *Shūshoku shikihō* (Recruitment Quarterly) was estimated to be about 20,000 annually throughout the 2000s. Furthermore, according to the MHLW's 'Survey on Employment Trends' (*koyō dōkō chōsa*), the average number of new university graduates hired during the same period by large companies with 1,000 or more employees was approximately 117,000.[31] Barring exceptions such as the financial crisis of 2009, these numbers show relatively little fluctuation, rising or falling only by 10 to 20% in keeping with economic trends. Furthermore, in Japan, when large firms reduced their hiring of new graduates due to the recession, medium-sized firms increased their hiring and there was a complementary effect as they tried to take advantage of the opportunity to secure new graduates from prestigious universities that such firms would not normally be able to hire.[32]

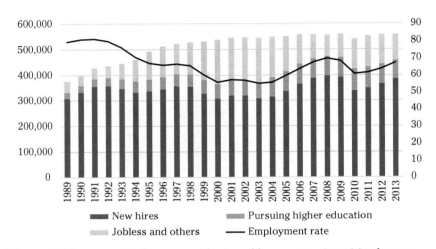

Figure 1.3 Career paths for new graduates of four-year universities by year

Unit: 1 person (left axis), % (right axis)
Notes: 'Others' includes 'dead and unknown', 'temporary job' and 'others'. 'New hires' includes 'clinical residents', whose number has never exceeded 10,000 in the period covered. The employment rate is the ratio of 'new hire' graduates to the number of graduates in a given year.
Source: MEXT Basic School Survey.

In contrast, greater fluctuation was apparent in the proportion of employment for new university graduates (employment rate) at the time of graduation. As will be explained in Chapter 2, opportunities for regular employment by large companies in Japan are limited to those available immediately upon graduation from educational institutions. Empirical studies by Japanese labor economists have shown that individuals belonging to generations less likely to be recruited as regular employees upon graduation from high school or university continue to be affected by this phenomenon as their careers progress.[33] Because of the lifelong impact this has on those who miss this opportunity, the 'Basic School Survey' (*gakkō kihon chōsa*) conducted by Japan's Ministry of Education, Culture, Sports, Science and Technology (MEXT) examines the employment rate at the time of graduation. According to the survey, the employment rate dropped significantly in the 1990s as well as in 2009, when the number of job seekers itself fell due to the global financial crisis. In the 1990s, however, the number of 'new hires' remained relatively unchanged; the falling employment rate occurred in conjunction with an increase in the number of university graduates.

The Dual Structure of Japanese Society

The sharpest decline in the 1990s was in the number of high school graduates going directly into employment, which according to the MEXT 'Basic School Survey' dropped from 607,466 in March 1991 to 208,903 in March 2004 – about one-third of its previous level. Meanwhile, the percentage of high school graduates going on to four-year universities grew from 25.5% in 1991 to 42.4% in 2004. This situation may be attributed to the fact that graduates were no longer able to find jobs with only a high school diploma, leaving them with no choice but to go on to university. As I discuss in Chapter 7, between 1975 and 1986, the number and capacity of universities were deliberately suppressed as a matter of policy. After this was relaxed, the number of four-year universities increased from 450 in 1985 to 772 in 2009. The students now entering these institutions correspond to the same group of people who, prior to 1985, would have found jobs after graduation from high school, or attended special training schools (vocational schools, see Chapter 7) or two-year junior colleges instead of universities.

Moreover, the generation entering university in the 1990s was also larger than the generations that came before or after it. According to Japanese government statistics, the number of babies born during the baby boom period from 1947 to 1949, immediately after Japan's defeat in World War II, was approximately 2.7 million per year, which is why they are known as the 'baby-boom generation' in Japan. While North America and Western Europe experienced a baby boom after World War II and into the 1960s, Japan's baby boom was concentrated in the three years from 1947 to 1949, followed by a sharp decline in birth rates due to the liberalization of abortion.[34] After the defeat of the Japanese Empire, Japan lost 44% of its territory but increased its population by 15%, due to some 6 million people who were repatriated from its sphere of influence in Asia, and due to the postwar baby boom. Facing food shortages, the Japanese government enacted the Eugenic Protection Law in 1949, and it legalized abortion for economic reasons. Thereafter, the number of births declined sharply, but the large number of baby boomers led to a large number of babies being born between 1971 and 1974 (approximately 2.09 million in 1973) who became 'second-generation of baby boomers', or 'baby boomer juniors'. Comparing this with the 1961 figure of approximately 1.59 million and the 1983 figure of approximately 1.51 million, we can see that the number of second-generation baby boomers was approximately 30% larger than the generations immediately before or after them. In the 1990s, when this generation entered university, the number of students swelled even beyond the proportional increase in students pursuing higher education, so that between 1989 and 1997 the number of university students increased by approximately 50%. However, since the number of regular employment positions for new graduates in the labor market remained almost constant, the employment rate for university graduates declined during this period.

In North America and Western Europe, baby boomers born in the 1950s and 1960s faced an increase of unemployment in the late 1970s and 1980s partly because their number exceeded that of new positions in the labor markets of the countries in those regions. Esping-Andersen claims that the 'high fertility in the 1950s and 1960s' and the increase of labor participation of women were major causes of the 'employment deficit' of the 1970s and 1980s in Western countries.[35] Japan's 'baby boomer juniors' experienced a similar situation in the 1990s, but as will be discussed later in this chapter, the Japanese labor market provided a large supply of non-regular employees with low wages and no social security coverage. Therefore, this generation saw an increase in the number of non-regular workers, although the unemployment rate did not increase as much.

The Japanese government of the 1980s anticipated this situation. Owing to the large number of people in this generation, a 1985 report by the Economic Planning Agency forecast that new graduates would have difficulty finding jobs in the 1990s. The report stated as follows. In 1985, 1.08 million new graduates were hired. However, by 1992, when the 'second-generation of baby boomers' begin to seek employment, there would be 1.32 million new graduates looking for work. Moreover, this situation would continue throughout the 1990s.[36] If this proved true, 'then, in order to absorb these new graduates, recruitment would have to increase by 11% annually over the next twelve years relative to the number of new graduates hired in 1984'.[37] However, the number of regular employees in the manufacturing and service industries was

The Dual Structure of Japanese Society

set to decline as the result of industrial restructuring and the shift to microelectronics. Meanwhile, the number of non-regular workers, including part-time housewives, was increasing rapidly. Thus, 'the external labor market [i.e., non-regular workers], which currently represents only one in six [employees], will account for one in three employees by the year 2000'. Were that to happen, 'it would likely be impossible to absorb the vast numbers of high school graduates as regular employees', let alone university graduates.[38] The report made the following assumption.

> Ultimately, a significant portion of the second-generation of baby boomers unable to enter the internal labor market [i.e., regular employees] may be forced to work in the external labor market, for example as part-time workers (*Arubaito*). [...] Young people should have no difficulty making a living on part-time wages, even at their current level. However, once they get married, have children and begin to incur educational expenses or take out a mortgage, it will be impossible for them to live off part-time jobs. But even if one tries to transition from a part-time job to break into the internal labor market around the age of thirty, the barriers to entry are too thick.[39]

This 1985 report proved to be a more or less accurate forecast of the situation as it stood in 2000. The only point where it missed the mark was its estimate of a 4% annual economic growth rate in the 1990s, which actually ended up being between 1% and 2%. So even though the bursting of the Japanese bubble economy of the early 1990s made some things worse than they might have been, the situation itself was foreseen.

As shown in Figure 1.1, the absolute number of regular employees also decreased between the late 1990s and the early 2000s. However, this decrease may be presumed to have taken place among regular employees, who in the past likely would have been male high school graduates, and female regular employees, whose numbers had increased during the Japanese bubble economy period in the early 1990s. From a different vantage point, the employment situation for relatively high-ranking university graduates and in the mid-ranked and higher-tier companies at which they worked did not change significantly. The group most impacted was high school graduates, and those who would traditionally have attended special training schools or women's junior colleges, but who had increasingly pursued university education since the 1990s.

These fluctuations, however, were a temporary phenomenon that took place in that decade. By the 2000s, the annual number of new university graduates had stabilized at about 550,000, the decline in the number of people being hired right out of high school had stopped, and the absolute number of regular employees had stabilized at the level it had been at in the 1980s. This was due in part to the decline in the number of people in the same age group, as the size of later generations declined relative to the 'baby boomer juniors', those born in the mid-1970s. As a result, Japan has not experienced any long-term difficulties in finding positions for new graduates, and the experiences of 'baby boomer juniors' became exceptional.[40]

Of course, those born in the mid-1970s were the hardest hit. As mentioned earlier, in the Japanese-style employment system, opportunities for obtaining a regular employment position at a large company are limited for those who fail to secure a post as a new graduate, and this has a lasting impact on their subsequent working career. As Kambayashi points out, the low ratio of regular employees among men in their twenties in the Employment Status Survey of 2002 and of 2007 may be interpreted as an echo of the decline in the employment rate for new graduates in the 1990s.

However, this does not signal the collapse of the Japanese-style employment system. Kambayashi's analysis of individual Wage Census data from 1991 through 2012 showed a high retention rate for university graduates once they became regular employees for a certain period of time. Although the average length of employment declined, this was due to lower retention rates for women, those with less than five years of service, and those who were mid-career hires. Kambayashi thus concludes that the practice of Japanese-style long-term employment of regular employees has been maintained for male core employees.[41]

The annual number of births in Japan has been declining continuously, from 2.09 million in 1973 to 1.51 million in 1983, 1.19 million in 1993, and 0.76 million in 2023. If job opportunities to become regular employees were fixed at a certain number, choosing to not have more children would be a rational choice. Ironically, then, the Japanese people are acting in a rational manner. If births were to drop to the level of 0.12 million per year, everyone would be able to secure regular employment at a large company upon graduation. Of course, this would only be possible if Japanese society could itself survive such circumstances.

The theory of the dual structure

The existence of a structured employment regime like that described above has not been entirely ignored by Japanese researchers. Up to the 1950s, the existence of a dual structure in Japan was a commonplace view among Japanese economists. It was on this basis that the labor economist Masami Nomura proposed his typology of the Large Company Model, the SME Model and the Self-Employment Model in 1998.[42] According to Nomura, these models related to family formation as follows.

In the Large Company Model, higher income in middle and older age is guaranteed in the form of seniority-based wages. One's middle years are a time when funds are needed for marriage, raising a family, children's education and acquiring a house. In other words, the Large Company Model represents a form of employment that guarantees wages that will be sufficient to support a family on only one person's income. This type of work creates the basis for a type of family in which the man earns the income, the woman becomes a housewife and the children and other members of the household subsist on the man's wages. Nomura refers to this type of family as the 'modern family' (*kindai kazoku*).

In the Self-Employment Model, self-employed and family workers run family enterprises such as farms, shops and small factories. In this case, it is not only men, but also women, children, the aged and anyone else who is able who labor as family workers. They are not employed workers, but rather earn their income by selling their harvest or manufactured goods. Since they are not earning wages by selling their labor by the hour, long hours of unpaid work are taken for granted. Here, no basis has been established for the type of family that subsists off the man's wages. As will be discussed in Chapter 4, in Japan until the 1950s, a developing Asian country, traditional agricultural self-employed households with a cottage manufacturing industry were much more common than in North America or Western Europe.[43] Hence, Nomura defines this as the 'pre-modern family' (*zen-kindaikazoku*).

In contrast, the SME Model is given an intermediate position between the Large Company and Self-Employment models.[44] Although a man will earn a wage working at an SME, this is not sufficient on its own to support his family. Unable to secure seniority-based wages at the SME where he works, he cannot cover the expense of his children's education and other family needs. Therefore, his wife will earn supplemental income by working as a non-regular worker for a relatively meager wage. Neither spouse is self-employed nor a family worker. However, they cannot survive on the man's income alone. Nomura describes this type as the 'pseudo-modern family' (*giji kindai kazoku*). Japanese historians have revealed how Japanese farming families sent out family members to work as migrant seasonal laborers and female laborers, using the wages they earned to subsidize the household budget.[45] In light of this, Nomura's Self-Employment Model and SME Model should be considered as part of a continuum.

In Nomura's typology, it is only in Large Company Model families that women do not need to work, while in the families of Self-Employed and SME models, women work part-time or in other forms to contribute to the household income. According to OECD.Stat, the 2021 female labor participation rate for women aged 15–64 in Japan was 73.3%, while it was 70.0% in France, 68.2% in the US and 59.9% in Korea (Figure 1.4).[46] Indeed, Japan's female labor force participation rate was at its lowest in the 1970s when postwar baby-boomer women gave birth to their first child, but it was higher than the US before the 1960s. The problem with female employment in Japan is not that the

The Dual Structure of Japanese Society 43

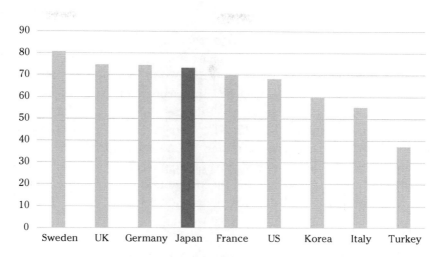

Figure 1.4 Labor participation rate for women 15–64 years old (2021, selected countries)

Unit: %   Source: OECD.Stat, 'Labour force participation rate, by sex and age group', https://stats.oecd.org/index.aspx?queryid=103872# (Accessed on 31 August 2023).

labor participation rate is low, but that many women are in low-wage, non-regular employment.

Nomura's three models are close to how I have classified the types of workers in the employment regime proposed in this book thus far. Even so, he did not go so far as to estimate their relative proportions in terms of the extent to which they actually exist in Japanese society. Nor did he state whether the ratio that these three models hold relative to each other is stable, or whether it fluctuates.

Nomura acknowledges that he referred to the dual structure theory advocated by Japanese economists. From as early as the 1930s, well before Sir William Arthur Lewis published his dual sector model in 1954,[47] Japanese social scientists had advocated the theory that Japan had a dual structure represented by a modern sector consisting of government agencies and large enterprises and a traditional sector of self-employed farmers, microenterprises, unpaid family workers and casual or day laborers.[48] This dual structure theory was adopted in official Japanese government documents as early as the 1950s. The 1957 Economic White Paper prepared by Japan's Economic Planning Agency described this dual structure in the following terms. Japan, it reported, had more self-employed farmers and small enterprises than the US or UK. Japan was characterized by a polarization between 'modern large companies' and 'small enterprises with pre-modern relations between management and labor, as well as family-run microenterprises and farms'. The White Paper described this state of affairs as 'akin to a dual structure in which a developed country and an underdeveloped country coexist within a single nation'.[49] The self-employment sector and SMEs – the 'underdeveloped' part of the dual structure – consisted of people who were excluded from the 'developed' part of the economy. According to the same white paper:

> The labor force that is left out of the modern sector must somehow be absorbed into the capital-poor agriculture and small business sector [...]. Because it takes the form of provisional employment in which people accept any income, no matter how low, in order to survive, there is little manifest unemployment in this sector. This is not full employment [*kanzen koyō*], but rather what might be called total [under]employment [*zenbu koyō*]. With regard to wages, as well, rather than people refusing to work unless they are paid enough to reproduce their labor, they will instead go out to work if they can contribute to their household expenses even a little.[50]

'Total employment' is a concept created by Japanese economist Sei'ichi Tōbata in 1956 to explain Japan's low unemployment rate.[51] This was before the 1957 ninth ICLS (International Conference of Labor Statisticians) adopted the first international statistical definition of underemployment. The self-employed and those employed by SMEs work for little to no wages (self-employment does not offer wages per se) because they have no other option. This situation differs from 'full employment' – that is, those who work for a satisfactory wage except for those who are voluntarily or frictionally unemployed.

The fact that those who work to provide extra support to their household budgets tend to be women, the young and the aged has been recognized since the 1950s. The Japanese economist Mataji Umemura called these people the 'peripheral workforce' in 1957.[52]

The Dual Structure of Japanese Society | 45

They are hired at low wages in boom years and laid off and sent home when recession hits. This results in a constant supply of labor without a rise in unemployment. In this way, they serve as a 'pool of labor'.

The 1957 Economic White Paper was skeptical about the prospect of the elimination of this dual structure, even though Japan had already entered a period of rapid growth. This was because, although the number of active workers in the agricultural sector was rapidly decreasing, it was not the proportion of employees working for large companies that was increasing, but the number of small firm employees and self-employed individuals outside of the agricultural sector. Hence the White Paper's conclusion that, 'To put it bluntly, a shift from agriculture to small business has only taken place on the lower tier of the dual structure, and we see little change at all in the proportionate ratio of the upper and lower tiers'.[53] We have but to replace 'agriculture' with 'self-employment' and 'small business' with 'non-regular employment', and we might say the same thing about the situation in the 1980s and beyond.

This kind of dual structure was said to have been eliminated with the narrowing of the wage gap between different sizes of companies during the period of rapid economic growth that Japan underwent in the 1960s.[54] However, in 1985, just as the number of workers in non-regular employment was beginning to increase, the Economic Planning Agency issued a report pointing to the emergence of a 'new dual structure'. The report described how the dual structure of SMEs and large companies had been transformed into a dual structure of regular employees and non-regular workers.

> The dual structure that characterized Japan's labor market in the early 1950s was between large companies and SMEs. [...] The dual structure of today's labor market consists of an internal labor market, which is highly entrenched, and an external labor market, which is highly liquid but unskilled and low-paid. However, the characteristics of the dual structure, which largely restricts individual movement of workers from the external labor market to the internal labor market, remain fundamentally unchanged. In other words, under Japanese employment practices, people

46 Chapter 1

> typically only have one chance to find a job when they graduate, and those who have [missed the chance and] worked part-time jobs will find it difficult to enter the internal labor market, at least with a large company.[55]

The Japanese employment practice of giving prospective employees only one chance to enter the internal labor market of large companies at the time of their graduation from school is discussed in Chapter 2. The assumption that this characteristic was a root cause of the dual structure of 'a highly entrenched internal labor market and a highly liquid but unskilled, low-wage external labor market' was an underlying premise of the 1985 report.

According to the report, the earlier dual structure of large companies on one tier and SMEs on the other had been at least partially eliminated. This was because, in order to attract young workers after the period of rapid economic growth, SMEs had 'worked to increase employee retention and secure a skilled workforce by increasing starting salaries and adopting employment practices that had once been the exclusive province of large companies such as seniority-based wages, seniority-based promotion and in-house training'.[56] In that sense, although the dual structure based on company size had abated, a new dual structure had appeared. In other words, 'the recent expansion of wage inequality is a phenomenon that emerged in the course of the polarization of Japan's labor market into an internal labor market protected by lifetime employment and seniority-based wages and an external labor market of part-timers and others'.[57] That is, the report predicted that 'the cost of the external labor market is about a quarter of that of the internal labor market, and moreover, its relative proportion is growing rapidly', and that 'the external labor market, which currently [as of 1985] represents only one in six [employees], will account for one in three employees by the year 2000'.[58]

This 1985 report acknowledged that the non-regular workers who comprised the lower tier of the new dual structure consisted largely of women, the aged and the young, just as in the 1950s. However, it did not position this as a particularly serious problem, stating that 'the three main groups of low-wage earners today – women part-timers, the

The Dual Structure of Japanese Society 47

aged and young people who are not regular employees – have core incomes from their husbands, pensions and parents, respectively, and in most cases have no need to work to make ends meet'.[59] Nonetheless, this perception assumes stability on the part of these 'incomes from husbands, pensions and parents'. Perhaps this may have continued to hold true in the households of large-company-type employees, who accounted for 27% of the total. For the other groups, however, the ongoing transition of self-employed husbands and parents into non-regular workers would seem to be the situation that Japan faces in the twenty-first century.

A dual structure in social security

Corresponding to the dual structure of Japanese society, Japan's social security system also exhibits a dual structure. In other words, the upper tier of the dual structure enjoys a more privileged position with respect to the social security system established by the Japanese government.

Esping-Andersen classifies the world's welfare regimes into three categories. In liberal welfare regimes characteristic of countries like the US, people are mainly covered by insurance offered by companies operating in the private sector, while those to whom such relief is unavailable become eligible for tax-based public assistance through means testing. In social democratic welfare regimes such as those found in Scandinavian countries, the state collects taxes and provides welfare services universally without means testing. In conservative welfare regimes like that of Germany, the basis of social security lies with insurance associations that developed out of the mutual aid practiced by guilds (artisans' associations), while the Catholic principle of subsidiarity encourages an emphasis on mutual aid rooted in families and associations.[60]

Esping-Andersen positions Japan's welfare regime as a 'hybrid' of those found in Germany and the US.[61] In Japan, insurance purchased in the market from private companies does not play a very important role. As I discuss in Chapter 5, the universal health insurance system implemented in 1961 by the Japanese government, which is modeled on the German system, consists mainly of a health insurance system run by insurance associations. However, after Japan's wartime defeat, reforms mandated by the US Occupation forces introduced a system of public assistance financed by taxes, and it is this system that subsidizes the social security provided by the insurance associations.

However, and as I also discuss in Chapter 5, Japan's insurance associations started out as associations in which large companies collected premiums from their regular employees, which left self-employed and non-regular workers such as farmers and commercial workers out of the equation. Following the introduction of universal health insurance in 1961, self-employed and non-regular workers were organized into a national health insurance system run by municipalities and a national pension insurance scheme run by the government, but the conditions in these schemes were still poorer than those of the schemes in which regular employees at large companies were enrolled.

Let us take pensions as an example to illustrate this difference in conditions. We will find that the system is designed on the premise that only regular employees at large companies will be able to live on their public pensions, while self-employed and non-regular workers will continue to work even after reaching old age.

Since 1985, Japan's pension system has consisted of a two-tier system somewhat similar to the system in the United Kingdom before 2016: a national basic pension system which covers all citizens including the self-employed, and an employee's pension system which covers employees. Employees at privately incorporated companies are enrolled in their employee's pension (*kōsei nenkin*) system through the company that employs them. Their company collects 18.3% of the monthly standard remuneration paid to the employee as insurance premiums to fund the employee's pension system. The higher the remuneration and the longer the period of participation, the more pension benefits the employee receives. This difference notwithstanding, the average monthly contribution received by the average employee's pension in FY2015 was ¥145,638. Under a system established in 1985, spouses of salaried employees also become eligible for a basic pension upon payment of their husbands' pension premiums. In the model case presented by the MHLW in 2018, the

The Dual Structure of Japanese Society   49

combined monthly benefit for a husband who has worked as a regular employee of a medium-sized or larger company for forty years and a wife who has been a housewife for the same period is estimated to be ¥222,277.[62]

This amount can hardly be said to be sufficient for a couple to be able to live out their retirement on their pensions alone. According to the 2017 'Family Income and Expenditure Survey' (*kakei chōsa*) carried out by the Ministry of Internal Affairs and Communications (MIAC), the total monthly expenditure for a 'no-occupation aged-couple household' is estimated at ¥263,717.[63] In 2019, the director of the MHLW Pension Bureau stated at a meeting of the House of Councilors Health, Labor and Welfare Committee that 'We have never said that [social security income] would be at a level that allows us to live in retirement on our pensions alone'.[64] In other words, unless a man has worked continuously for a major company with high salaries, it will not be feasible for him to cover his post-retirement expenses with his pension income alone.

In contrast, most self-employed and non-regular workers are enrolled in the national pension (*kokumin nenkin*) system and pay about ¥16,000 yen per month out of their own income. At the end of FY 2015, the average monthly old-age pension for national pension recipients was ¥54,464.[65] Even in the model case presented by the MHLW in 2018 (for a pension funded over the span of forty years from age twenty to age sixty), the monthly payout was ¥64,941.[66] Given the ¥263,717 figure noted above for 'no-occupation aged-couple households', a national pension of around ¥50,000 for each is by no means enough to live on.

However, the national pension system was originally designed for self-employed individuals in the agricultural and commercial industries. In the 1950s, when this pension system, introduced in 1961, was planned, only about half of Japan's working people were employees; the rest were self-employed and family workers. It was assumed that householding farmers would be self-sufficient in food from their own fields, and that they would be able to work even in old age. If they cohabited with their eldest son and his wife, who would be the main income earners in the household, there would be no problem, even if their pensions were small. In other words, it could be argued that the system was not originally designed so that people would be able to live on their pensions alone.

Accordingly, many people in Japan worked even at an advanced age. In a 2018 public opinion survey on public pensions (*rōgo no seikatsu sekkei to kōteki nenkin ni kansuru yoron chōsa*) conducted by the Cabinet Office, only 23.0% (23. 8% of those aged sixty to sixty-nine, 45.0% of those aged seventy and over) responded that they 'rely entirely on the public pension system'.[67] This is not due to Japan's economic stagnation since the late 1990s. In a similar government survey, only 18.4% of respondents in 1993 and 21.8% in 1998 said they would 'rely almost entirely on public pensions'.[68] Under this pension system, a decrease in self-employment and increase among non-regular workers would naturally result in an increased number of older non-regular workers.

Figure 1.5 shows an international comparison of trends in the labor force participation rate for the population aged sixty-five and older. In all countries, the number of older workers is increasing as the population ages and inequality widens. Japan and Korea, however, had high labor participation rates among the elderly even in 2002. In fact, Japan's labor participation rate for those aged sixty-five and older was at its lowest in the 2000s (19.8% in 2005), due to the large number of self-employed workers prior to that time and the increase in the number of non-regular workers in recent years.[69] According to the 2022 edition of the Ministry of Internal Affairs and Communications' White Paper on Aging Society (*kōrei shakai hakusyo*), the employment rate for those aged sixty-five to sixty-nine in 2021 was 60.4% for men and 40.9% for women, of which 67.8% for men and 74.7% for women of the employed are non-regular workers.[70] In a nationwide opinion poll conducted by *Asahi Shimbun* from November to December 2018, the proportion of men who felt they would be able to retire by age sixty-five was 35%, and money was the biggest concern in retirement for 48%.[71]

Another characteristic of non-regular employment in Japan was the fact that employers did not contribute to social insurance premiums. In 2018, regular employees paid social insurance premiums equivalent to 31.7% of their wages mainly for pension and health insurance, of which the worker paid 15.3% and the employer 16.4%.[72] However,

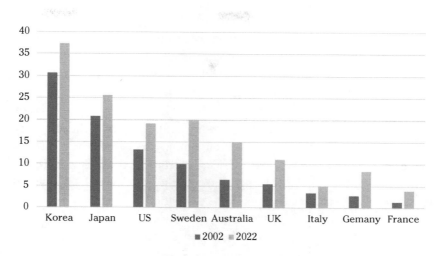

Figure 1.5 Labor force participation rate for 65-year-olds or more (2002, 2022, selected countries)
Unit: % Source: OECD (2023), 'Labour force participation rate (indicator)', doi: 10.1787/8a801325-en (Accessed on 31 August 2023).

most non-regular workers were covered by the same national pension and national health insurance system as self-employed workers, and so paid social insurance premiums from their own wages. In other words, for a regular employee earning ¥200,000 yen in pre-tax wages a Japanese employer would have to spend ¥293,000, as opposed to only ¥200,000 for most non-regular workers, who would pay the full social insurance premiums out of their own wages.

The fact that this type of employment does not exist in other developed countries, with some exceptions such as 'mini-jobs' in Germany, was raised by a study group convened by the MHLW in 2007.[73] Thanks to subsequent reforms, some non-regular workers can now be covered by the same social insurance as regular employees, but eligibility is subject to certain restrictions on factors such as working hours (with and without breaks) and company size. For example, in October 2016, employers were required to contribute to social insurance premiums for part-time workers as well, but only for those who worked at least twenty hours per week and earned a monthly wage of at least ¥88,000, and this requirement only applied to companies with at least 501 employees.[74] From April 2017, it became possible to extend coverage to companies with 500 or fewer employees on a company-by-company basis, subject to agreements between labor and management, and in 2020 the size requirement was scheduled to be lowered in stages to 100 or more employees from 2022, and fifty or more employees from 2024. However, in a survey by JILPT (Japan Institute for Labour Policy and Training), the majority of respondents indicated that if their employers were made eligible for social insurance coverage, they would either dismiss short-time workers or reduce their working hours and wages so that they would not be subject to the requirements for expanded coverage.[75] Moreover, no plan has been developed to apply this model to small enterprises with less than fifty employees, which employ the largest number of female non-regular workers.

A state of disparity

In the US in recent years, it's been said that the gap between the ultra-wealthy top 1% and the remaining 99% has been widening. Although disparity has been increasing in Japan as well, the situation there is different than in the US.

In the US, the share of total income earned by the top 1% of citizens is expanding. According to a study by Chiaki Moriguchi and Emmanuel Saez, however, in Japan, it was not the top 1% that had increased its share from 1997 to 2005, but the top 10%, and especially the bottom half of that group. In 2012, earners in the bottom half of the top decile were earning between 5.8 million and 7.5 million yen per year.[76] Here, the top decile indicates 10% of all Japanese adults, including those with no income. The lower sum of 5.8 million yen represents a typical annual income for regular employees at large companies in Japan. Based on the 2016 National Tax Agency's 'Statistical Survey of Private Sector Wages' (*minkan kyūyo jittai tōkei chōsa*), 18% of 47.94 million salaried workers in 2015 earned annual salaries above 6 million yen, a figure that represents 28% of all male salaried workers. In other words, we may conceive of a widening gap between Japan's top 20% to 30% of salaried workers and the rest of the population. Moriguchi suggests that the increase of the share of the top 10% of citizens may have been

The Dual Structure of Japanese Society

caused by the decline of the remaining 90%, rather than by the growth of the income of the top 10%.[77] This is consistent with my analysis, which suggests that 46% of working people may have become poorer due to an increase in the number of non-regular workers, while the 27% of 'large company type' regular employees has remained stable.

We should confirm the standard of living that can be obtained in Japan with an annual income of 6 million yen. Sociologist Michio Gotō drew on data from the 2012 'Comprehensive Survey of Living Conditions' (*kokumin seikatsu kiso chōsa*) to estimate how much would remain for living expenses after subtracting taxes and public dues such as income taxes and insurance premiums, as well as educational expenses, from annual income. According to his findings, a household with an annual income of four million yen in a small city outside of a metropolitan area with two children in public elementary and junior high school will fall below the poverty line (*seikatsu hogo kijun*, i.e., the level set by the MHLW as a criterion for eligibility for public assistance). He further notes that a household in a big city with two children entering university may fall below the poverty line even with an annual income of 6 million yen.[78] In the background here are rising taxes and public dues and the cost of education. In particular, social insurance premiums have risen due to the aging of society, among other factors. In addition, between 1975 and 2014, tuition fees at private universities increased approximately five-fold, while those at national universities increased approximately fifteen-fold. According to estimates based on data from the MEXT 'Survey of Children's Learning Expenses' (*kodomo no gakushū-hi chōsa*) and 'Survey of Student Lifestyles' (*gakusei seikatsu chōsa*) for 2014, the total household burden of education costs that would be incurred to send a single child to university was found to exceed 10 million yen when all the schools were public, and more than 20 million yen when all of the schools were private.[79]

Economist Aya Abe, in an analysis of data from a nationwide survey she conducted of social life in Japan in 2003, showed there exists a threshold at around 4 to 5 million yen below which the relative deprivation index rises rapidly. The survey examined the index of prevalence of sixteen 'socially perceived necessities' (e.g., microwave ovens, hot water heaters, attendance at relatives' weddings or funerals, visits to the dentist and private family bathrooms) found in more than 90% of households, and the number of items/activities that households do not have/engage in for financial reasons.[80] Basically, Abe claims, an annual household income of 4 to 5 million yen is the minimum level of living what the majority of people in contemporary Japanese society consider a normal life, although this also depends on the number of people in the household. According to the MHLW's 2019 'Comprehensive Survey of Living Conditions' (*kokumin seikatsu kiso chōsa*), the median annual household income in Japan in 2018 was 4.37 million yen, with 45.4% of all households having an annual income of no more than 4 million yen. Although the relative poverty rate was 15.4%, in terms of self-assessed living conditions, a total of 54.4% of households reported experiencing difficulties, with 21.8% of households responding that they found things 'very difficult' and 32.6% finding things 'somewhat difficult'. Among single-mother households, 41.9% found things 'very difficult' and 44.8% 'somewhat difficult', for a total of 86.7%.[81]

The large number of low-income households may be attributed in part to the large number of aged households dependent on pensions and Japan's low minimum wage. According to statistics compiled by the OECD, the ratio of minimum wage to median wage in Japan was 0.45 in 2020, ranking the country twenty-fourth out of the twenty-eight OECD countries.[82] Although minimum wage varies as it is determined at the prefectural level, the national weighted average for FY2021 was 930 yen per hour.[83] Historically, Japan's minimum wage was first legislated in 1959, when wages were rising during the period of rapid economic growth. Even before that, SMEs had coped with rising wages by setting wages via mutual local agreements among businesses so that they would not exceed the solvency of the smallest companies. This was the prototype of the minimum wage system enacted in 1959, which by the 1980s had become the de facto standard for wages for female part-time workers.[84] This is the wage level for women who work to provide auxiliary support for their households while men earn the principal household income, as Nomura envisioned in his SME Model. Although they fall short of the level where one person could survive

The Dual Structure of Japanese Society

on a single wage, it is often the case that wages for non-regular workers are on a par with the minimum wage.

In general, it is the gap between the 20 to 30% of the working people who enjoy seniority-based wages and the rest of Japan's citizens that is widening, rather than a disparity between the top 1% of wealthy citizens and the other 99%. However, even the bottom of the top 20 to 30%, with the approximately 6 million yen annual income found in large company-type employees' households, can hardly be said to support a very affluent life. As I discuss in Chapter 2, in Japan there is relatively little vertical disparity in wages within the same company. Therefore, although extremely high-income earners are few in number, the gap between regular employees at large companies and the rest of the population will tend to widen. According to the 2012 edition of the White Paper on Health, Labor and Welfare, Japan has a high relative poverty rate among OECD countries, and its Gini coefficient – an indicator of inequality – is also slightly higher than that of other countries.[85] Despite the absence of conspicuously high-income earners, many people still live in relative poverty. As a result of the low minimum wage, Japan is thus characterized by a large number of households that are poor even though they are not unemployed. In Japan, based on data from 2015 (or the latest available), the percentage of citizens living in households with a working-age head and at least one worker, with income below the poverty line (here defined as 50% of the national median equivalent disposal income), was 13.3%, which ranked Japan sixth highest among OECD countries.[86]

The locals and declining social capital

Nevertheless, income alone is a poor metric for human happiness. The putative reason that the Japanese government provides only a low level of social security for self-employed individuals in agriculture is that it was assumed that these people own their own houses and enjoy mutual support in their families and local communities. In 1979, the governing Liberal Democratic Party (LDP) published a pamphlet entitled *Nihon-gata fukushi shakai* (Japanese-style welfare society) in which mutual assistance in the spheres of family, community and

56   Chapter 1

Japanese-style company were emphasized in an attempt to reduce the financial burden on the government.[87] In other words, we could say that this was an attempt to leverage the social capital of local communities to make up for the shortcomings of social security in Japan.

There is some truth to the claim that the housing situation in Japan is better outside urban areas. Although the stereotype of Japanese houses being tiny is sometimes discussed, this is a phenomenon that pertains more to big cities like Tokyo. According to the Japanese government's 2009 White Paper on Land, Infrastructure and Transport, the average size of a privately owned house in Japan is slightly smaller than in the US, but about the same as in Germany and larger than in France and the United Kingdom.[88] Where housing in Japan is notably smaller is mainly in large cities, especially the rental housing available in large urban areas. According to the MIAC's 2021 Housing Economy Data (*jūtaku Keizai kanren data*) the average total floor space per dwelling was 145 square meters in Toyama prefecture, sixty-six square meters in Tokyo and seventy-seven square meters in Osaka prefecture, which amounts to a difference of approximately 2.2 times between Toyama and Tokyo.[89]

Also, while there are many people in non-metropolitan areas who have never moved away from the communities in which they were born and raised, these people do have political clout. These are the type of people that local governments think of first as local residents, and those who are settled in their constituencies as voters are the ones most likely to build networks with politicians. In fact, in Japan, the longer people live in the same area, the more likely they are to vote. Those who have lived in the same municipality for fifteen to twenty years have a voter turnout of about 80% in prefectural assembly elections from 1991 to 2011. By contrast, the voter turnout among those who have lived in the same municipality for less than three years is only about 40%.[90]

In addition, many members of local assemblies in Japan come from self-employment backgrounds such as agriculture and commerce, or from organizational backgrounds as staff of agricultural cooperatives or other industrial organizations. In a custom that dates from the nineteenth century, local assemblies in Japan are held during the

The Dual Structure of Japanese Society   57

daytime on weekdays, a practice that makes participation difficult for private-sector employees and civil servants, while favoring self-employed individuals who were the majority of local assemblers at agricultural municipalities. Of the 3,062 candidates standing for election to prefectural assemblies in local elections held in April 2019, less than 10% identified their primary background as working for a company in the private sector. The candidates were fifty-six years old on average, and 12.7% were women. Among the LDP (Liberal Democratic Party, the ruling conservative party in Japan) candidates, only 4% were women.[91]

Salaried workers in Japan's large cities are reputedly more likely to complain about long working hours, daycare shortages and being politically marginalized. By contrast, self-employed individuals born and raised in non-urban areas are much better off in terms of social capital. They enjoy rich local relationships, live close to family and are not alienated from politics. Given this situation, disparities in income and social security may not necessarily become an issue.

Here, we must consider the question of what proportion of the population is well off in terms of local social capital. As mentioned above, Nomura (1998) described the way of life characteristic of large company regular employees who enjoy seniority-based wages and long-term employment, including the type of family this favored, in terms of his Large Company Model. In contrast, let's use the term 'local-type' to describe those who settle with their families in the communities where they were born and raised, pursuing careers in self-employment or as SME employees. How many such people are there? We can estimate the relative proportion of local-type citizens from government statistics by focusing on the relationship between birthplace and area of residence.

According to the 2015 census, 13.8% of Japan's total population has lived in their current place of residence since birth. Those who have lived in the same place for at least twenty years but do not live in their place of birth account for another 31.4%.[92] This latter group, however, also includes large company employees who have lived in suburban residential areas for twenty years or more. If we exclude those living in the three major metropolitan areas of Tokyo, Nagoya and Osaka from those who have lived in the same place for at least twenty years, the total of those who have lived in their current place of residence since birth is 27.8% of the total population.[93]

However, this figure does not include those who, within the last twenty years, have made a so-called 'U-turn' to move back to their hometowns after a period living elsewhere. Conversely, it does include regular employees at large companies and workers at government agencies who have spent their entire lives in Tokyo prefecture. Some may also have moved to other communities from outside the three major metropolitan areas and lived there for more than twenty years. Furthermore, according to a 2015 Ministry of Land, Infrastructure, Transport and Tourism (MLIT) survey, 23.4% of residents outside the three major metropolitan areas are locals who have never lived in a municipality other than the one where they were born, 54.5% are 'U-turners' who lived elsewhere before returning to their home municipality, 14.3% are so-called 'I-turners' or 'J-turners' who now live in a non-metropolitan municipality other than their hometown, and 7.8% were 'residing temporarily in the community due to a job transfer (their own or a family member's), to provide long-term care or nursing care for a family member, to pursue higher education, as the result of an evacuation due to natural/nuclear disasters, or for some other reason'.[94]

With reference to the above, we can estimate the number of locals and 'U-turners' for the entire country as roughly 45.72 million, or 36.1% of the total population.[95] If we trust the MLIT survey, the sum of 'locals' and 'U-turners' outside the three major metropolitan areas is 77.9%, thus constituting an overwhelming majority outside these three areas. These figures may be considered a rough calculation of those who could be classified as 'local-type' citizens as of 2015.

The relative proportion occupied by such local-type citizens in the past is unclear. This is because the census only provides figures for continuous long-term residents since their birth, with no way of identifying U-turners. Another angle on these figures is offered by a survey conducted by the government's Population Research Institute, which found that, in 1966, 90.9% of men and 92.6% of women surveyed were married to people from the same prefecture. By 1972, however, population shifts associated with economic growth had caused intra-prefectural marriages to drop to an average of 59.8% for men and women.[96] Unfortunately, subsequent changes in survey methodology mean that these results cannot be compared with later ones. In a 1955 survey of Kamiina district, Nagano prefecture, 69.6% of marriages were found to have taken place inside the same village (*mura*) and 87.8% inside the same district (*gun*).[97] Presumably, until the 1960s, a significant number of people in Japan got married to partners from the same prefecture, perhaps to the extent that they found partners inside the borders of the old Edo-period domains, and many enjoyed a settled way of life in the community of their birth. In light of this, an estimated value of 36% for 2015 may be considered a remarkable decline.

Another way to measure the historical decline of the local type is to examine changes in the organization rate of the Neighborhood Associations (NHAs, *Jichikai* or *Chōnaikai*). The NHAs are thriving in Japan as local organizations for residents, and they play a role in self-governance, working closely with the municipal government. This has been studied as Japan's social capital, somewhat similar to the parish in the UK.[98]

There are various theories about the organizational rate of the NHAs. The modern NHA has been institutionalized along with zoning by municipal governments and it has become customary for all the households in the area to voluntary/automatically join. As a result, many municipalities are still claiming that the organizational rate of NHAs in the municipality is over 90%. However, a Japanese semi-official organization, the Association for Promoting Fair Elections (APFE, *Akarui Senkyo Suishin Kyōkai*), has conducted sampling surveys of all voters including abstentions at the time of every national election since 1972 asking with which organization have they been affiliating. From this survey, it is possible to interpret the self-recognition of the people with the organizations they are affiliated to, and this can be regarded as a much more realistic reflection of voters' organizational patterns. As Figure 1.6 shows, the organizational rate of NHAs had peaked in 1986 and decreased significantly.[99]

As I discuss in Chapter 2, the practice of relocation assignment among local branches of large Japanese companies (*tenkin*) makes it difficult for workers to maintain continuous residence in a particular community. Accordingly, it is difficult to reconcile being a

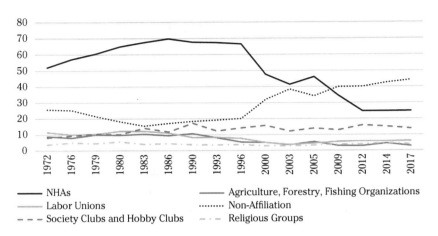

Figure 1.6 Trends by social group organization rates in Japan (1972–2017)
Unit: %   Source: Survey by the APFE (Association for Promoting Fair Elections).
Note: The 2021 survey results are not included due to the difference of wording of the question.

regular employee at a large company and continuing to live in one's hometown. In other words, large company-type employees are less likely to overlap with local-type citizens. The fact suggests that we can estimate the number of people not covered by both. According to the estimates calculated in this book, large company-type employees who enjoy seniority-based wages and long-term employment account for about 27% of all working people. There are no statistics that directly show the percentage of the total population of households formed by these people. However, as we saw earlier, Japan's health insurance system is divided into different systems depending on how people work, and we know who is enrolled in each scheme.[100] The total number of members and dependents covered by large corporate health insurance associations, state and local governments' public servant health insurance associations, and private school health insurance associations in 2015 corresponded to 29.0% of Japan's population in the same year.[101] Of these, municipal officials, excluding those of large cities, are considered to overlap with the 'local-type' citizens, but they and their dependents can be estimated at 1.4% of the total population in 2015.[102]

Although these figures cannot be simply added or subtracted,

The Dual Structure of Japanese Society 61

considering the 'local-type' citizens were found to account for 36.1% of the total population in 2015, and the population of households of 'large company type' excluding municipal officials was 27.6% in the same year, a conservative estimate would be that the leftovers, who have no seniority wage and no social capital, account for 36.3% of the population in 2015. Non-regular workers in urban areas are, in a manner of speaking, a symbol of this type. Their incomes are low, they have no ties with their community, they do not own their homes when they get older and their pensions are low. This type combines the negative aspects of large company-type employees and local-type citizens. The overall decline of self-employed individuals with an increase in non-regular employment has the potential to lead to an increase in these leftover-type citizens.

Trends prior to the 1980s

The phenomenon of a decline in self-employed and family workers as non-regular employment increased was also evident prior to the 1970s. According to Masami Nomura, through the 1970s to 80s, although self-employed and family workers had fallen in number, the number of part-time female employees had risen, with the total remaining stable at around eighteen million.[103] In other words, self-employed and family workers (the latter mostly female) had been replaced by non-regular workers, but the total number of both remained constant.

As mentioned above in this chapter, Japan had a large pool of self-employed individuals in agriculture and commerce that provided a supply of hired workers. In the 1953 Labor Force Survey, only 42.4% of Japan's labor force were employees, with the rest being comprised of self-employed and family workers, mainly farmers. It was not until 1959 that the number of employees exceeded 50%. Based on data from the government's Labor Force Survey, Figure 1.7 shows trends from 1953 to 1983 that were not shown in Figure 1.1. Although no distinction is made between regular employees and non-regular workers prior to 1984, it can be seen that (1) the total number of self-employed workers remained more or less constant, (2) the number of employees increased linearly, and (3) the number of family workers decreased.

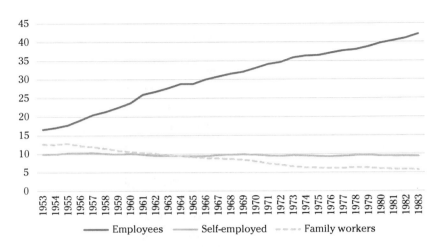

Figure 1.7 Trends by employment status (total for men and women, 1953–1983)
Unit: 1 million persons
Source: MIAC Labor Force Survey, long-term time-series data from Table 4(1).

The increase among employees exceeded the decrease in the number of family workers because the children of self-employed households became employees after graduating from school, so the increase in the working age population was almost entirely due to the increase among employees.

From the late 1950s to 1973, Japan's GDP grew at an average annual rate of 10%, but from 1974, the oil shock plunged the country into recession. Then, what kind of employment was growing during the 1970s? It was not public employment as was seen in Northern and Western European countries. As will be discussed in Chapter 7, the Japanese government enacted the Total Personnel Act (*Sōteiin-hō*) in 1969 to ensure that the number of public employees did not increase. The ratio of public-sector employment to total employment was 4.6% in Japan in 2021, the smallest among OECD countries and one-fourth of the OECD average.[104]

The employment increase in the 1970s was employees in SMEs. One of the definitions that the Japanese government uses for SMEs in the manufacturing industry is that a firm has fewer than 300 employees. On this basis, Figure 1.8 shows the total number of employees since 1956 categorized by company size from the government's Employment

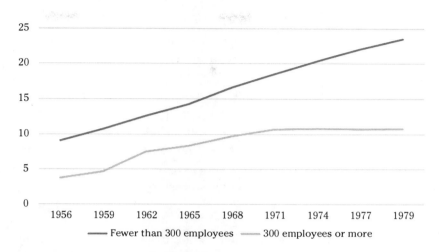

Figure 1.8 Employees in private enterprises by firm size (non-agricultural industries, 1956–1979)
Unit: 1 million persons   Source: MIAC Employment Status Survey.

Status Survey. Between 1956 and 1971, total number of employees rose in both large firms and SMEs, but between 1971 and 1979, employment plateaued in large firms and only continued to rise in SMEs. And Figure 1.1 shows that the increase in employment after the 1980s only happened amongst non-regular workers. To put this another way, the increase in employment in the 1970s was something that took place consistently *outside* of the sphere of 'large company-type' regular employees.

However, even though the total number of the self-employed remained constant through the 1970s, this was the result of a decline in agricultural self-employment offset by an increase in non-agricultural self-employment. Labor economist Kazuo Koike has estimated the fluctuations in the number of hired workers and self-employed individuals in Japan since the 1920s.[105] An increase among hired workers and a decrease among the self-employed appear to be consistent trends, with two exceptions. One was the period immediately after Japan's wartime defeat, when the collapse of urban industries caused by the war forced people to move to rural areas where food was available, which led to a temporary increase in self-employment in the agricultural sector. The other exception was that despite the decline in agricultural self-employment, manufacturing and commerce self-employment continued to rise into the early 1980s. Koike estimates that in the early 1970s, between 30% and 40% of small business employees attempted to start their own business at some point during their working lives.[106] During the high-growth period, the children of self-employed individuals in the agricultural sector moved from rural to urban areas to find work in small businesses immediately upon graduating from junior high school. Numerous testimonials record their dreams of finding independent success by becoming 'master of country and castle' (*ikkoku ichijō no aruji*) by opening and running their own shops and other businesses.[107]

Japan's conservative government of the 1970s and 1980s politically protected self-employment and the SMEs. Political scientist Kent Calder found that the number of retail stores per capita in Japan in the 1980s was about three times that of the UK or West Germany, and twice that of the US, a fact that he attributes to the protections afforded to small retailers by the LDP government, which is closely linked with SME organizations. Calder also points out that the protections on self-employment and SMEs have led to a decline in unemployment, noting that without these effects, Japan's unemployment rate of 2.8% in 1986 would have approached the US rate of 6.9% and the EC rate of 11.7% in the same year.[108] The role of self-employment and small businesses in reducing unemployment in Japan was noted by Japanese economists in the 1950s as mentioned above, and Calder reaffirmed it in relation to politics.

From the 1980s onwards, however, the number of people pursuing non-agricultural self-employment began declining in Japan as well. In the low-growth environment that followed the oil crisis, the benefits of going into business for oneself were no longer as attractive as they had been during the high-growth period. It was also during this period that the shift from self-employment to non-regular work began to occur, initially among female family workers. From the above, we can see that the post-1984 trend identified earlier − i.e., the decline among self-employed and family workers and the proliferation of non-regular workers − seems to have been occurring since the late 1970s. The detailed situation is described in Chapter 7.

The Dual Structure of Japanese Society   65

The period since the early 2000s, contrary to what we saw for the 1970s, has been characterized by declining numbers of employees of small firms with less than thirty employees and an increase in the number of those at large companies with 500 employees or more.[109] However, as I noted earlier, the number of regular employees has remained relatively static. In other words, what has taken place is a shift of workers from the 'pool of labor' represented by self-employment and SMEs into non-regular employment at large companies. As I describe in Chapter 7, the increase in non-regular employment has been taking place in SMEs since the late 1970s. At that time, large companies were beginning to limit the number of regular employees, though their reliance on non-regular employment lagged somewhat behind SMEs. The trend since the 2000s is conceivably the result of a full-fledged adoption of non-regular employment on the part of large companies.

Migration trends

Even so, those who continue to live in their local communities will remain local-type citizens even after switching from self-employment to non-regular employment. As long as their local communities are maintained, with the help of social capital, the low wages of non-regular employment may be less of a problem. However, rural-urban migration remains a constant occurrence.

Immigration overseas has never been at a significant level in post-war Japan, while internal migration was most intense in the 1960s when the baby boomers began entering university and the labor market. The period from 1960 to 1970 saw dramatic increases of more than 20% in the population of the three major metropolitan prefectures and the suburban prefectures around Tokyo (e.g., Chiba and Saitama), while the population decreased in twenty-two other prefectures.[110] However, this population movement decelerated around the time of the oil crisis of 1973. Although the population continued to decline in rural areas supported primarily by farming and fishing, the number of prefectures with declining populations temporarily dropped to zero. As will be discussed in Chapter 7, this was because public works projects and efforts to attract local industry had increased the availability of jobs

66   Chapter 1

in rural areas, causing a lull in outmigration to other prefectures.[111] In 1976, when large companies began to enact belt-tightening measures in the wake of the oil crisis, a phenomenon even occurred in which net migration began to flow *away* from the three major metropolitan areas (see Figure 7.3 in Chapter 7). In 1979, the term 'the era of regionalism' (*chihō no jidai*) entered the popular lexicon. As noted by Calder, this was also the period in which self-employment and SMEs were absorbing the labor force.

Later, another wave of rural-urban migration took place during the bubble economy of the 1980s. However, this ceased with the bursting of the bubble, and by the mid-1990s, the population was flowing back to the countryside once again. Up to this point, population movements had mostly been linked with changes in the economy. From the end of the 1990s, however, rural-urban migration became entrenched, despite not necessarily being accompanied by an economic upturn. Moreover, the population of the Osaka and Nagoya metropolitan areas remained static, with only Tokyo absorbing the arrivals from the countryside. Whereas Tokyo's population surged between 1995 and 2000, twenty-three other prefectures experienced a population decline.[112]

By the numbers, the current wave of migration since late-1990s is not as large as those that took place during the high-growth period, which some went so far as to describe as a 'great migration of the nation'. This, however, was a period when the baby boomers were beginning to flood the universities and job market in large cities. In addition, migration during the high-growth period was closely linked to economic fluctuations. However, since the end of the 1990s, rural-urban migration has become entrenched regardless of economic fluctuations, a phenomenon that is arguably distinct from what occurred in the past.

A research group at Hirosaki University described the migration from the Tohoku (north-eastern) region to Tokyo since the late 1990s as a 'brain drain'.[113] There is a steady stream of people who either enroll in prestigious universities in Tokyo or graduate from universities in the Tohoku region and become regular employees of large companies in Tokyo as new graduates. Unlike in the 1960s, however, it is not possible to become a regular employee of a large company in Tokyo without a

The Dual Structure of Japanese Society

prestigious university degree or higher. Those with low educational backgrounds and middle-aged persons are not actively moving to Tokyo because they would have no choice but to become non-regular workers after migration, which would mean low wages and a high cost of living.

To summarize, the number of regular employees in Japan has not fluctuated much, and the proportion of what I refer to as 'large company-type' employees has remained relatively stable. However, since the 1990s, major changes have taken place in the lower tier of the dual structure, including a shift from the self-employment sector to non-regular employment and the entrenchment of 'brain drain' migration of the young population from regional communities to large cities to be members of the 'large company type'. These factors suggest that the stability of the 'large company type' is accompanied by the increase of non-regular workers and the decline of local communities.

An overview of postwar Japanese history

Based on the above discussion, let's now try to summarize the history of post-World War II Japanese society.

1. From the end of the war to the early 1950s, history flowed backward as the population stayed in the countryside, and the agricultural sector expanded. This was a result of the destruction wrought by the war in urban industries, which forced people to relocate to the countryside.

2. From the late 1950s to 1960s, rapid economic growth began to take place alongside a massive transfer of population from the countryside into the cities. Any decreases in the number of active workers took place mainly among those who family workers in the rural agricultural sector. The postwar baby boomers, who were large in number, came of age around this time, providing a supply of labor that boosted economic growth. For this reason, Japan did not need to invite immigrant workers from outside the country. It was also during this

period that the rate of students pursuing secondary and tertiary education rose sharply due to economic growth.

3. The high growth period ended with the oil crisis of 1973. Rural-urban migration dropped off, due in part to the allocation of public works projects and the dispersion policy of industries, and university enrollment rates were curtailed as a matter of policy. Large companies did not expand regular employment but rather cut the jobs of seasonal and temporary workers, while the excess labor force was absorbed by SMEs and the non-agricultural self-employment sector.

4. From around 1980, however, the increase of the non-agricultural self-employed, which had offset the decrease of the agricultural self-employed, ceased. Around that time, non-regular employment began increasing while the total number of self-employed and family workers declined. Since this period, the number of regular employees has remained more or less constant.

5. In the 1990s, after the bursting of the bubble economy, the labor market for high school graduates shrank sharply, and a higher proportion of students began pursuing a university education. With no corresponding increase in positions for regular employees, however, many members of this 'baby boomer junior' generation, which was also sizeable, found employment as non-regular workers.

6. From around 2000, rural-urban migration as a 'brain drain' became entrenched as the norm, decoupled from economic fluctuations. Self-employment and the number of workers in small businesses declined significantly, and non-regular employment expanded. Nevertheless, the core of the Japanese-style employment system has changed little. A large percentage of non-regular workers come from the 'peripheral workforce' such as women, the aged and young people without a strong educational background.

In the course of the developments described above, the scope of our first two main categories – large company-type employees and local-type citizens – seems to be narrowing. Even so, the number of large company-type employees has been surprisingly stable, whereas it is the decline of the local-type communities and the rise of non-regular employment that seem to be most significant. These changes are likely to lead to a variety of problems. Although the national pension is less of a problem for self-employed individuals who own their own homes and live with their families, it is not sufficient to stop aging workers in non-regular employment who live alone while paying rent, from falling into poverty. While a high employment rate for workers over sixty-five is nothing new in Japan, the fact that this has emerged as a problem in recent years may be attributed in part to the increase in the number of older workers who are not self-employed but work in non-regular employment.

In Japan, the scenery of downtown Tokyo has changed little since the 1990s. The morning commuter rush, the suits in the office districts, and the streetscapes of Roppongi and Kasumigaseki have not changed much. This is partly because the number of regular employees has remained constant. In regional cities, in farming and mountain villages, and even in the suburbs of the Tokyo metropolitan area, however, the landscape has undergone a dramatic transformation. Independent owner-operated shops and farms are on the wane, and the shopping streets outside train stations have been shuttered, even as the roadsides are increasingly dominated by huge nursing care facilities for the elderly and logistics warehouses for Amazon. Many who work in such places are non-regular workers.

The closed nature of the Japanese internal labor market

From the foregoing, the dual structure in Japanese society and its current situation should be evident. So, why did this dual structure emerge? The short answer is that it came about because the labor market of large companies in Japan is closed and difficult to break into except for new graduates. Self-employment in the agricultural sector, once common in Japan, has declined with modernization, while the number of hired workers has increased. Nevertheless, if the large company labor market is closed and admits only a certain number of new graduates each year, the remaining workers will have no choice but to seek employment with SMEs or become non-regular workers.

The 1985 Economic Planning Agency report I cited earlier uses the concept of internal and external labor markets in describing the 'new' dual structure. This distinction is premised on a theory of the dual labor market that has been advanced in the US, notably in a 1971 study by Peter Doeringer and Michael Piore.[114]

According to this theory, the labor market is divided into primary and secondary sectors. In the primary labor market, wages tend to increase with age because education and experience are evaluated and reflected in wages, and workers are able to advance their careers. By contrast, in the secondary labor market, education and experience are not assigned any value, and wages do not increase, since most of the work is simple labor. The former is a labor market with evaluation criteria, and the latter is one without evaluation criteria (this contrast will be discussed in detail in chapters 2 and 8). The 1994 study by Ishikawa mentioned above is an application of this theory to Japan.

These two labor markets are separated from each other. The primary labor market is referred to as an 'internal' labor market because it is closed off to the outside. In contrast, the secondary labor market is referred to as an 'external' labor market, and those who work in this market have difficulty accessing the primary market. In one US study, the primary labor market was regarded as being dominated by white males, while people of color and women predominated in the secondary labor market.[115] In Japan, women, older workers and young people without educational backgrounds are referred to as the peripheral labor force and are well represented in the ranks of non-regular workers, as already noted.

Even in Japan, the labor market for regular employees at large companies and that for non-regular workers and SME workers tend to be separate. In a 1954 paper, the economist Shōjirō Ujihara presented a diagram to schematically illustrate the Japanese labor market based on a survey of workers in the Keihin Industrial Zone (Figure 1.9).

In Ujihara's estimation, Japan had a huge excess labor force due to the number of workers engaged in agricultural and non-agricultural self-employment.[116] With modernization and the penetration of the

The Dual Structure of Japanese Society

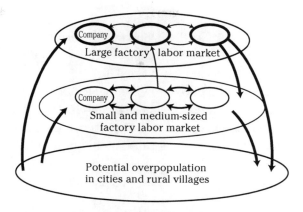

Figure 1.9 The Japanese labor market model (1954)
Notes: 1. The line thickness of the circles indicates the respective degree of labor market insularity. 2. Arrows indicate the direction of labor movement, and their thickness indicates the amount of flow.
Source: Ujihara (1966: 424).

cash economy, the necessity of earning a cash income transformed these workers into an 'unskilled labor force seeking employment opportunities'. Some were 'selected at a very young age, or perhaps slightly older, to begin their professional lives as employees of large companies, and over the years trained to become a skilled labor force that could adapt to the company'. Although some 'worked for the company over the long haul until their retirement', others 'left the company due to the economic recession or personal circumstances'.

However, Japan's large companies are closed to mid-career recruitment. Some of those who leave large companies find management roles in SMEs, but the rest 'either spend their lives as SME workers or end up drifting back into the original pool of excess labor'. SMEs consist of 'a small number of skilled adult workers combined with a large number of workers who are young, female, or older', and are characterized by 'acute labor mobility' and 'low productivity and low wages. [...] Their lives are not as stable as those of large factory workers'. SMEs are subject to ups and downs due to the vicissitudes of the economy, and many workers move from one company to another, though in most cases from SME to SME.

A labor market with these characteristics will be susceptible to two phenomena. The first is a wage differential according to company size.

The second is the viability of SMEs and self-employed individuals with low productivity. In the usual economic scheme of things, workers will gravitate to jobs that offer higher wages. If that is the case, wages will be standardized at the level of large companies, and low-productivity SMEs and self-employed individuals will be eliminated. This is because, to quote Ujihara, 'If wages are standardized, companies with low performance that cannot pay even the minimum wage will be unable to survive'.[117]

However, according to Ujihara, this is not the case in Japan, where the labor market has a dual structure and workers are unable to move to large companies. The upshot of this is that SMEs and the self-employment sector are not in wage competition with large companies and may thus continue to offer low wages. In addition, the self-employment sector and SMEs are supplied with labor in a segregated manner vis-à-vis large companies, and thus will continue to exist. Ujihara states that 'This is one of the reasons for the remarkable disparity between the different sizes of companies'.[118]

So, why is the internal labor market of large companies closed off in this way, giving rise to this dual structure? The reason offered by Ujihara was Japan's belated modernization. That is, he blamed the relative lack of progress in terms of technological modernization and standardization, which he felt impeded the transferability of experience gained at individual companies.[119] Doeringer and Piore, too, made essentially the same observation as to the reason for the existence of the internal labor market.[120] However, if this were the case, then senior positions in large, modernized companies should be highly interchangeable across firms. Yet this is not the case in Japan, where the closed nature of the labor market is strongest among white collar jobs at large companies, which recruit from new university graduates.

Why is this? The conclusion I offer in this book is that it is because Japanese companies must rely on an employment system that is based on in-house rankings, with no cross-firm qualification system. In Chapter 2, after giving an overview of Japan's corporate employment system, I offer a hypothesis to be tested in this book by means of a survey of historical processes based on a comparison with Western Europe and North America.

2 The Japanese-style Employment System and Its Characteristics

In Chapter 1, I described the dual structure of Japanese society, and introduced the theory that this dual structure took shape as a result of the closed nature of internal labor markets in large Japanese companies. In this chapter, I begin by outlining the characteristics of the employment system used by Japan's large companies, the basic feature of which is the absence of any criteria for evaluating employees' qualifications or determining wages apart from an in-house ranking system. All other characteristics, I argue, may be positioned as deriving from this basic feature. Furthermore, after comparing the employment systems of North America and Western Europe, I present two working hypotheses, namely that this feature is the result of (1) a difference in the character of the labor movement in Japan, which had no history of craft unions, and (2) the penetration of bureaucratic influence into the private sector. These working hypotheses will lay the groundwork for my investigation of the historical origins of the Japanese-style employment system in the chapters that follow. Chapter 2 thus serves as a preliminary step toward that end.[1]

Overview of the Japanese-style employment system

Since Abegglen (1958), 'lifetime employment', 'seniority-based wages' and 'enterprise unions' have been regarded to be the three distinctive features of the Japanese-style employment system. Other characteristics often mentioned include long working hours and the bulk recruitment of new graduates. In this section, focusing on an OECD report published in February 2021[2] with supplementary reference to a report published by the Japanese government-affiliated Japan Institute for Labour Policy and Training (JILPT),[3] I offer an overview of the distinctive features of the Japanese-style employment system, from the process by which new graduates are recruited by companies and the in-house treatment and wage structures they experience from their employers, up to and including their mandatory retirement from their firms. Through this, I hope the reader will come to understand how the various features of this employment system stem from the fact that there are no criteria for evaluating employees' qualifications apart from their company's in-house ranking system.

Overview 1: The periodic bulk recruitment of new graduates

Large companies in Japan routinely hire large numbers of university graduates each April. While companies employ a variety of screening methods to select students, as described below, no matter which screening method is used, the trend since the late 1990s has been for selection to begin in the middle of the third year of undergraduate study and finish at the middle of the fourth year. Since 1920, graduation from Japanese universities has taken place in March, allowing students to transition seamlessly to working for companies in April immediately after their graduation.

According to the 2013 'Global Career Survey' conducted by the Recruit Works Research Institute, which surveyed university-educated business professionals between the ages of twenty and thirty-nine, 81.4% of Japanese respondents answered 'yes' to the question 'Was your first job after graduation decided while attending school [university]?' compared to 46.3% of respondents in the US, 42.3% in South Korea, 43.7% in China and 58.5% in Germany.[4] This has prompted some observers to suggest that the hiring practices of Japanese companies have the effect of reducing the youth unemployment rate.

However, this method of recruitment means that companies select students even before they have earned their degree, when they do not yet have any professional experience. Furthermore, for their own part, these students generally have only vague aspirations about the kind of work they would like to do at these companies. Companies do not necessarily recruit by position, but rather hire students on the assumption that the position to which they will be allocated has not yet been determined. Thus, companies screen students for their potential to adapt to in-house training, irrespective of the position

The Japanese-style Employment System and Its Characteristics 75

to which they will be assigned.[5] That is, they are not hired on the basis of their academic majors or work experience, but on their character, motivation, ability to express themselves and history of extracurricular activities.

Since each company conducts its own screening process, these criteria are not clear, but it is an open secret that enrollment at a prestigious university is a strong criterion, since passing the entrance exam at such a university is itself seen as an indicator of one's potential to adapt to any type of in-house company training.[6] School-based athletic clubs and a history of taking part in community activities also tend to be evaluated as indicators of such potential. Conversely, it is also commonly rumored that company recruiters look askance upon any involvement in political activities that are critical of the government. Japan's Labor Standards Act prohibits discrimination in working conditions based on nationality, creed or social status, but a 1973 Supreme Court ruling states that these do not apply at the time of hiring and that refusal to hire someone because of their political beliefs is not illegal.[7]

Aside from university rankings, Japanese companies place an emphasis on graduates' motivation and character. In a 2004 MHLW survey of Japanese companies, the top four points identified as being considered important when hiring new university graduates (respondents were allowed to choose up to three out of multiple responses) were 'enthusiasm, ambition' (64.0%), 'communication skills' (35.1%), 'drive, executive ability' (31.0%) and 'cooperative spirit, sense of balance' (30.9%).[8] Since 1997, the Japan Business Federation, known as Keidanren, has asked its member companies to complete an annual questionnaire concerning the recruitment of new graduates, asking them to choose the top five points considered 'particularly important to them in the selection process'. In 2018, the top five qualities were found to be 'communication skills', 'initiative', 'willingness to take on new challenges', 'cooperative spirit, sense of balance' and 'integrity'. Despite the availability of multiple choices, only 6.2% of companies identified 'language skills' as being particularly important (this quality placed seventeenth), 4.4% chose 'course record, academic performance' (eighteenth), and 0.5% selected 'overseas study experience' (nineteenth).[9] These trends have not changed significantly since the survey began in 1997.

In terms of specific selection methods, there are three main types.[10] The first of these is a referral by a faculty member, which as I discuss in Chapter 4 is a method that has been practiced since the nineteenth century. Companies send information about hiring and recruitment seminars to selected professors at prestigious universities. These professors then recommend to the companies those of their students who have excellent grades and stable character, whereupon the company screens them through a written examination, several rounds of interviews and a medical examination. Although this method, which has been criticized for its bias toward prestigious universities, has not been mainstream since the 1990s, it has continued to be used in the recruitment of science and engineering students even into the twenty-first century.

The second method, which involves company-sponsored seminars, has been the most common method for recruiting graduates in the humanities and social sciences since the 1990s. Students apply to attend information sessions hosted by companies they are interested in working for, and after a formal explanation of the company's business, they are screened by the company in a group interview or meeting, followed by a written test and several rounds of interviews. Many take the view that, by this point, only students enrolled at prestigious universities will have been informally selected. In many cases, the written examination is not relevant to any particular profession but is rather intended to examine general academic prowess. Students' ability to express themselves and their personalities are vetted over the several rounds of interviews.

Since the late-1990s, as the third method, it has also been commonplace for students to apply to companies directly. In this case, students send job applications (commonly referred to as 'entry sheets', *entorī shīto*) directly to firms they are interested in working for. Such applications include a transcript containing the name of the alma mater, an essay indicating the student's motivations for applying to the company and a resume of their involvement in sports and other extracurricular activities. Students who pass the application process are contacted by the company and selected through a written test, several rounds of interviews and a medical examination.[11]

There are thus several types of selection methods, and these have changed over time. Although differences in survey methods make straight comparisons impossible, a 2001 MHWL survey (that allowed multiple responses) found that faculty/school referrals ranked in first place (38.4%), followed by company-sponsored seminars (32.9%).[12] According to the Global Career Survey conducted in 2013 by Recruit Works Research Institute, however, the top-ranking method was individual job searches by means of websites or other publications, while referrals by schools or faculty had fallen to 11.2% of the total responses.[13] In any case, the selection process for each type begins in the middle of the third year of undergraduate study and ends at the middle of the fourth year. So-called 'internships' that involve anything from one to several days of work experience are also becoming more popular and are often offered to first- and second-year university students.[14] With any selection of students that takes place at this stage, it goes without saying that companies can only screen for potential inferred from the name of the university they attend, their personality and their history of extracurricular activity.

Attending seminars, preparing job applications ('entry sheets') and going to interviews are collectively known as 'job hunting activities' (*shūshoku katsudō*), and this process imposes an immense burden on students. Many undergraduates do not even have the time to attend classes from the summer of their third year until June in their fourth year. A June 2022 newspaper article reported that master's students in engineering are also increasingly being hired in a similar format, which is interfering with their research. The article reports the case of a second-year engineering master's student who had been attending internships and company information sessions since the summer of his first master's year who found that he was so busy preparing and submitting job applications and taking online exams that he was only able to visit the laboratory once a week.[15]

Overview 2: Personnel evaluations and transfers

It is only after the student is hired and begins working at the company in April that the job to which they will be assigned within the company becomes clear. In many cases, vocational training, whether on-the-job (OJT) or off-the-job (Off-JT), will take place only after the student is hired by the company.

In the Japanese context, 'regular employees' are hired without a set contract period, but their employment conditions are described only in very vague terms.[16] The company assigns the regular employees that it hires to various roles throughout the company if they are not engineers. When a worker is reassigned from one job to another within the company, this is known as a transfer (*idō*).[17] Although workers' preferences are taken into consideration to some extent, decisions with regard to transfer assignments are decided unilaterally by the human resources (HR) department of the company in question. Japanese companies expand, downsize or reorganize their businesses not through layoffs, but by transfers, i.e., in-house personnel reassignments.[18] This is why the recruitment of new graduates focuses so much on potential and motivation rather than on what they have studied at universities as undergraduates or in graduate school.

In the case of firms that hire new graduates in bulk periodically, these transfers also take place periodically en masse between March and April. A company that hires hundreds of new graduates every April, after all, will need to open up hundreds of positions for them. In order to reassign these hundreds of workers to other positions, the people in those positions will also be transferred between March and April. That the transfer of one person causes several other transfers in a chain reaction is colloquially referred to as 'billiard-ball personnel reassignments' (*tamatsuki jinji*). These large-scale transfers that play out every year are known as 'regular (periodic) personnel transfers' (*teiki jinji idō*).[19]

This is sometimes translated into English as 'job rotation', but it is questionable whether it should be translated as rotation in that the moved employee is not promised a return to their original position and is unlikely to return in reality. And just as new graduates do not know the position to which they will be assigned until they begin work, employees do not usually know the position to which they will next be transferred until the order of management is given in regular personnel transfers. The type of position to which a worker will subsequently be assigned is a matter of great interest to those who work at Japanese companies, since it is impossible for individual workers to predict what they will be doing next.

With the exception of graduates of some technical fields, such as master's level engineers and scientists, the type of position to which a worker is assigned has little to do with their major at university. The knowledge that they learned at university is deemed unnecessary at the company, which provides its own in-house instruction in vocational knowledge. This is one of the reasons why many adults in Japan feel over-educated. In the 'Survey of Adult Skills' 2012 or the 'International Assessment of Adult Competencies' (PIAAC), of the twenty-three participating countries and regions surveyed, Japan had the highest percentage of respondents (31.1%) indicating that their educational qualifications were higher than what their jobs required, compared to the average of 21.4% (Figure 2.1).[20] That does not mean that Japan's graduate school enrollment rate is high. Although Japan's university enrollment rate grew from 36.3% in 1990 to 49.1% in 2000 and 58.5% in 2020, its graduate school enrollment rate dropped from 10.7% in 2000 to 13.4% in 2010 and then to 10.4% in 2020. This decline is conceivably due to the lack of industry demand for graduate-level education. The Wage Census of the Japanese government also did not distinguish between postgraduates and university graduates, placing them in the same category until the 2019 survey.[21]

When a company decides that an employee should be transferred into a managerial position, this is called a promotion.[22] It is relatively rare for someone external to be recruited for a high-level position, especially a managerial post, and in general someone will be selected from among regular employees within the company at the discretion of the company's human resources (HR) department. As I discuss in more detail in Chapter 7, the HR department conducts evaluations for all in-house regular employees, including blue-collar workers, to assess their work performance and character. In the 1960s and 1970s, HR also assessed the ideological tendencies and involvement of activists in the

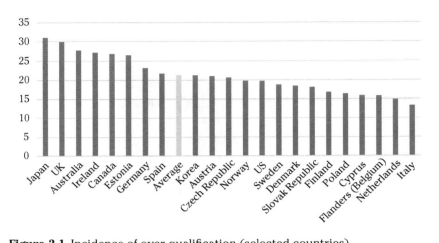

Figure 2.1 Incidence of over-qualification (selected countries)
Unit: % (Percentage of workers whose highest qualification is higher than the qualification they deem necessary to get their job today.)
Note: In terms of the figures for Cyprus, information in this document relates to the area under the effective control of the Government of the Republic of Cyprus.
Source: Survey of Adults Skills (PIAAC) (2012), Table A4.25. http://dx.doi.org/10.1787/888932901733 (Accessed on 30 August 2023).

labor movement, and in many cases, sidelined such individuals in less influential positions in the company.[23]

In large Japanese companies, employees are moved from one position to another every few years through regular (periodic) personnel transfers, thereby raising their salaries by promoting them to higher positions. This results in a kind of position-based pay that corresponds to the difficulty of the position. The employee is not necessarily expected to have the professional skills or educational background appropriate to the new position, but rather to have the potential to fit into any position through in-house training. As discussed below, Japanese companies avoid laying off regular employees and reorganize/expand/downsize their organizations through transfers, sometimes placing existing regular employees in positions that are not related to their previous professional or educational background. They also train personnel by transferring them to positions in which they have no previous experience.[24] Because transfers occur periodically and are linked to salary increases, the result is seniority-based pay based on years of service.

The Japanese-style Employment System and Its Characteristics   81

In large companies, management often orders transfers of workers into positions at company branches throughout Japan and abroad. This is known as *tenkin* (relocation assignment). Married workers are often transferred on their own, leaving their families behind, a practice colloquially known as *tanshin funin* (single-posting transfers). Alternatively, one spouse (which in practice is usually the woman) will quit their job to accompany the other spouse to the transfer location. Many point out that this hinders women's career advancement in companies. Japan's Supreme Court ruled in 1986 that it is not illegal to dismiss an employee who refuses a relocation assignment and ruled in 1989 that the in-house transferal of workers to a different job category is legal.[25]

Overview 3: Mandatory retirement

However, the Tokyo High Court ruled in 1979 that even when closing a department, it is illegal to dismiss the regular employees of that department without making efforts to avoid doing so by transferring them to other positions.[26] Since then in Japan, it has been established by case law that when a company closes a branch office, or when a particular position becomes redundant, the company must endeavor to maintain employment at that company by transferring the workers in question to another position. Empirical studies have shown that even Japanese companies tend not to transfer employees between departments that are overly different.[27] In one rather extreme case from 1992, however, Toyota dispatched 600 surplus university-educated clerical and technical regular employees to work on the factory floor in order to cut labor costs by dismissing seasonal factory workers.[28] The case indicates that maintaining the employment of regular employees and firing non-regular workers are inextricably linked. The practice colloquially known as 'lifetime employment' is thus underpinned by such personnel transfers and barter relationships.

However, employment in Japanese companies is only guaranteed up to a certain age. This is because, given the periodic bulk recruitment of a large number of new graduates as fresh regular employees who will be promoted and have their salaries increased as they are regularly transferred from one position to another, the cost of their salaries will become excessive unless they are collectively dismissed at a certain age. In addition, in order to hire a fresh group of graduates every year, it is necessary to prepare positions for these new graduates by means of personnel transfers and to reduce the number of company regular employees by means of collective dismissals. However, because dismissals are governed by judicial precedents, a system of collective dismissal at a certain age is required. While some cases have been reported of regular employees being encouraged to resign voluntarily through unfavorable transfers or intimidation by superiors (power harassment), such tactics run the risk of drawing public criticism toward the company.[29]

This is why Japanese companies have a system of mandatory retirement (*teinen*). According to a 2018 sampling survey by the Japanese Government's National Personnel Authority, 99.4% of Japanese companies with fifty or more employees have a mandatory retirement system whereby employees are laid off when they reach a certain age (age sixty in 84.9% of instances).[30] The Supreme Court ruled that mandatory retirement is not necessarily illegal in 1968.[31] These dismissals are usually carried out in March, immediately prior to the arrival of new hires each April, for regular employees who reached their mandatory retirement age in the fiscal year. The positions vacated by these collective layoffs are filled by transfers from other departments or by the allocation of freshly hired graduates.

In order to lower the burden on pension financing, the Japanese government obligates companies to continue employing people until they reach a certain age. To this end, mandatory retirement below age sixty was legally proscribed in 1998. In 2013, a law was enacted that will see the mandatory retirement age raised to sixty-five, securing opportunities for people to continue working to that age by 2025. Further, in 2021, this law was amended mandating that employers use their best efforts to retain employees until age seventy, either by raising the mandatory retirement age or securing opportunities for them to continue working after sixty-five. To meet this requirement, many companies now 'rehire' employees as 'entrusted workers (*shokutaku*)'

The Japanese-style Employment System and Its Characteristics 83

after they have reached sixty by signing them to new contracts with significantly reduced wages and working conditions.

The 2018 National Personnel Authority survey mentioned above found that while 97.0% of companies with a mandatory retirement age have a system of continuous employment, 91.0% of these are limited to such 'rehiring' policies.[32] A 2021 survey commissioned by the *Nihon Keizai Shimbun* found that whereas 63.5% of respondents reported that the number of days and hours they worked remained unchanged after being re-hired, and that 47.9% reported that the amount of work remained the same, 53.4% of respondents reported salary decreases of between 40% and 60%, and more than 70% of respondents indicated salary reductions of 30% or less.[33] As I discuss below, this discrepancy – in which wages are reduced even though working hours and workload remain the same – is explained by the fact that wages in Japan are determined not by position, job and professional skill qualification, but by rank within each company.

Another way to maintain this sort of 'indirect employment' is through secondments. Large companies in Japan have many relationships with subsidiaries in which they have made capital investments, as well as with affiliated companies that supply them with parts, services and various other goods. The transfer of employees to such subsidiaries and affiliates is known as a secondment, or an external transfer (*shukkō*). In some cases, this involves the dispatch of personnel to a subsidiary or affiliate as managers or technicians, in which case they may return to their former company for a few years. However, in some cases, middle-aged and older employees who have been working for the company for twenty years or more and who no longer have any prospect of promotion will get a 'permanent external transfer' (where an employee leaves company A and becomes an employee of company B) to a subsidiary or affiliate as a form of indirect job retention.[34] This facilitates staff reductions and lower wage costs for the main company. As I discuss in Chapter 7, the practice of maintaining employment indirectly through means such as external transfers was dubbed 'lifetime employment in the broader sense' by the Federation of Employers' Associations (Nikkeiren) in 1978.

Overview 4: Seniority-based wages

When employees first start working for a Japanese company after graduation, their wages are low. As time goes by, their wages will increase in keeping with their years of service with the company until they are in their mid-fifties. While this practice is known in English-speaking countries as a seniority or seniority-based wage, the relevant criterion is neither one's age nor years of experience in a particular occupation (*keiken nensū* in the Wage Census), but rather an employee's length of service in a company (*kinzoku nensū* in the Wage Census). In Japan, layoffs are uncommon, and it is customary that once a worker leaves a company, they will be considered to have surrendered their status as a regular employee of that company, and their length of service will be reset to zero. This is especially true for white-collar positions in large companies that bring in new personnel chiefly through the recruitment of new graduates. Workers' wages increase with the number of years they are on the company's books, even as they are transferred to various positions within the company.

As I note in Chapter 3 and throughout the book, Japanese companies have in-house rankings similar to those used by the military. If a worker's performance meets a certain standard, their rank is increased according to their educational background and years of service, with a commensurate rise in salary. Although an employee's rank is often linked to their position in the company (e.g., as a manager), the basic salary will rise according to the employee's in-house rank even for those who do not necessarily hold a high managerial position. This is to say that rank and basic salary do not necessarily correspond to the professional position of an employee.

Japanese large companies have a reputation for being slow to promote their workers. New graduates hired in the same year will often not see any marked difference in their promotions or wages until they are in their forties. According to a 1992 survey by JILPT, new graduates hired by large companies in Japan were selected for their first promotion 7.8 years after being hired on average, more than twice as long as the 3.4 years reported in the US or 3.7 years in Germany. Further, the length of service after which more than 50% of those hired in the same year were no longer eligible for promotion averaged 22.3

The Japanese-style Employment System and Its Characteristics 85

years for Japan, once again more than double the reported averages of 9.1 years for the US or 11.5 years for Germany.[35]

In the 1970s, these promotions in large companies were determined almost exclusively by employees' years of service if they had the same educational background. A 1977 report by the All Japan Federation of Management Organizations (Zen-Noh-Ren) summarizing a survey of 216 large companies stated that 'the general course of promotion for an employee hired as a new graduate at age twenty-two [suggesting they were university graduates] is first to become a subsection manager [*kakarichō*] at around age thirty-two, a section manager [*kachō*] five years later at around age thirty-seven, and a director [*buchō*] eight years after that, at around age forty-five'. It also reported that 'differences by industry and by department size are curiously small. This suggests that, as far as the surveyed companies listed on the First Section [of the Tokyo Stock Exchange] are concerned, a kind of social standard has been formed across all companies'.[36]

Even in the twenty-first century, this situation has changed little. According to a survey conducted by the MHLW, whereas it took on average 18.0 years to be promoted to unit chief class (*shunin-kyū*), 21.0 years to be promoted to section manager class (*kachō-kyū*) and 23.3 years to be promoted to director class (*buchō-kyū*) in 1989, promotion to the same classes in 2010 took an average of 19.0 years, 21.5 years and 23.5 years, respectively.[37] In the 1980s, the prevailing theory was that this kind of 'slow promotion' contributed to the productivity of Japanese companies by helping to maintain worker morale and competitiveness.[38]

In large companies in Japan, it is said that around 70% of those hired as new graduates in the same year will have attained management positions by their forties. For the 1976 Labor White Paper, a survey was conducted on promotions among university graduates working at Japanese companies employing at least 1,000 people, based on the 1974 Wage Census. According to the survey, among employees aged forty-five to forty-nine, roughly 30% had become section managers and about 30% had become directors. If we include assistant directors (*jichō*), this means that a total of about 70% had risen to at least the level of section manager.[39] A 2013 study based on the 2010

Wage Census also showed that over 70% of male regular employees in their late forties held managerial positions.[40] However, whereas in 1974 this approximately 70% consisted solely of directors, assistant directors and section managers, this proportion in 2010 also included subsection managers, unit chiefs and low-level supervisors (*shokuchō*), indicating that the level of available managerial positions had fallen. Even so, the customary practice of employees being able to attain managerial positions with continued service remained in place.

How can we explain this? A 1977 report by the All-Japan Federation of Management Organizations stated that promotions based on years of service have been used 'to create expectations of loyalty as well as to maintain a stronger sense of belonging among the more highly educated, who are seen as the backbone of the company'.[41] In Japanese companies, regular employees are transferred among a variety of positions, so there is no incentive for them to develop skills for one particular occupation. That being the case, the only means companies have of incentivizing employees, whether they are in sales or accounting, is to appoint them as directors or section managers. No matter one's particular occupation, an employee can take pride in a promotion to 'section manager class' and will find an incentive to work in the higher wages that go along with it, since the pay scale is nominally based on position. Although 30% may lose out in this competition, if employees can feel that they have 70% odds of securing a promotion, they will be able to maintain their motivation and keep working.

Although many Japanese companies have attempted to abolish such practices to reduce wage costs, their efforts have often been frustrated by the damage they do to employee morale. In a 1986 roundtable discussion among corporate personnel managers organized by a labor industry journal, one participant stated that 'Given fifty people in the same cohort [in the company], if only ten are promoted to section manager class, the morale of the remaining forty will deteriorate. This would also affect those who witness it in the cohort below'.[42] Labor historian Tsutomu Hyōdō likens this to a form of 'karma' that befalls large companies in Japan.[43]

The Japanese-style Employment System and Its Characteristics 87

On the management side, it is becoming increasingly expensive to continue offering seniority-based wages. A 2021 report by the OECD points out that the Japanese-style employment system and seniority-based wages are under pressure to change. It shows how the peak of the wage profiles for male regular employees, which reflects how wages increase with years of service, declined in 2009 and 2019 relative to 2001 from Wage Census data. It also points out that an increasing number of firms have started indicating that they are determining wages by placing more emphasis on job duties than on years of service.[44]

However, the basic shape of the wage profiles shown in the 2021 OECD report, which shows how wages increase with years of service, has remained unchanged from 2001 to 2019, except that the peak has declined. Even if a company indicates on the survey that it determines wages based on job duties, if the position in question is that of a section manager or department director that has been attained via promotion based on years of service, then this is essentially the same as if wages were determined by years of service. As I noted earlier, the practice at large Japanese companies of promoting 70% of university graduate regular employees to managerial positions once they are in their forties has changed little. However, the positions available to employees in their forties or older are at a lower level than they once were. Tying all this together, it seems conceivable that the decline in average peak wage even as the wage curve has retained its shape is due to a decline in the level of positions available to employees in their forties. In other words, while the decline in the wage profile may indicate management's efforts to lower labor costs, it does not indicate that Japanese-style employment has changed.

As a result of this series of customary practices, the ratio of wages to labor productivity in Japan's large companies is low when employees are young but increases in step with their years of service at the same company. Accordingly, for regular employees, continuing to work for the same company over the years is perceived as advantageous.[45] It is also the case that regular employees gain experience in a variety of positions in the company, which helps them to gain a specialized familiarity with the company's internal customs. Moreover, the reason that companies tend to hire mainly new graduates is that hiring

88 Chapter 2

employees with experience and skills in a specific job type is not well suited to the practice of repeatedly transferring employees around the company. Thus, for employees, the option that seems most advantageous is to hire on with a large company that has the most favorable conditions for new graduates, and then to continue working at that company over a number of years. As I mentioned in Chapter 1, although more workers are beginning to switch companies after less than five years of continuous employment with one company, the retention rate after that point has not changed significantly, even in the 2010s.

Overview 5: Open plan office, working hours and the status of women

In Japanese companies, job descriptions are only ever offered in the vaguest of terms. As a result, the position of any one individual on the job and the scope of their responsibilities will also be vague. Furthermore, because transfers are a common occurrence and people learn new jobs through on-the-job training, learning and doing your job requires seeking help from those around you. In Japanese companies, where only department directors and upper management work in private offices, section managers and their staff often work at rows of desks in a large open-plan room. A 2020 online article states as follows.

> For the American coming to work at, or even visiting, a traditional Japanese office, it's a shock. Rather than the individual offices or cubicles that are typical of American offices, in a traditional Japanese office layout there are no walls between desks. Desks are pushed close together, so that each section forms a *shima* (island). The desks are turned to face each other, and the desk of the head of the section is at the end, so that it appears that the whole group is sitting down to a formal dinner party.[46]

Japan's government agencies follow the same format, which the Japanese scholar of public administration Wataru Ōmori has dubbed 'big-roomism'.[47] According to Ōmori, Japanese government agencies,

The Japanese-style Employment System and Its Characteristics   89

after screening potential employees for general abilities using a standardized examination, will then station these new hires in a large room where they learn their jobs under the guidance of their supervisors and colleagues. Because of the collaborative nature of working in large rooms, the specific nature of individuals' positions is unclear, and in most cases will be the scope of their authority and responsibility. Salary assessments thus tend to be based not so much on job performance as on criteria such as 'personality' and 'motivation'. Administrative scholar Muneyuki Shindō found that this way of working obscures the responsibility of individual bureaucrats, while at the same time making it easier for collusion to occur between the department as a group and specific industries.[48]

These work practices and evaluation criteria in turn contribute to longer working hours. Individual workers toil together in a large room to complete a wide range of tasks. The lack of clarity around the scope of individual tasks and responsibilities makes it difficult for workers to feel that they have fulfilled their responsibilities until everyone's work has been completed. Accordingly, individual workers tend to accept longer working hours.[49] The emphasis that Japanese companies place on enthusiasm and cooperativeness when hiring new graduates is well-suited to this way of working.

These practices detract from work-life balance, however, making it difficult for women to advance their careers.[50] Based on her literature survey of empirical research conducted in the US, the Japanese management expert Machiko Ōsawa argues that the wage gap between men and women is smaller where positions are more concretely segmented.[51] Striking a balance with family life is easier if one is able to complete a well-defined job and return home at a set time. Moreover, if a woman's position is one in which knowledge or degrees obtained at school, or technical qualifications accepted as industry standards (i.e., outside the company itself), are highly valued, then the value attached to the worker's skills will not diminish even if she temporarily leaves her job to have a baby or raise young children.

However, there seems little reason to expect such things from the style of working found in Japanese companies, where positions are not clearly defined, people work in large open rooms and enthusiasm

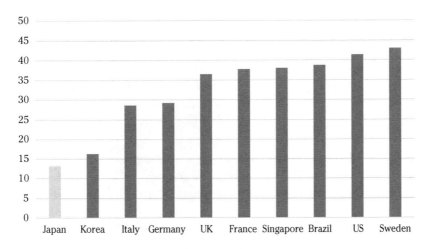

Figure 2.2 Women's share of management positions (selected countries)
Unit: % Note: The term 'management positions' here refers to those corresponding to Category 1 of the major classification according to the International Standard Classification of Occupations (ISCO-08 or ISCO-88). For Japan and the UK, the JILPT calculates the ratio of female workers in Category 1 to the total number of male and female workers in the same category. The Japanese classification is based on Japan's own classification standards and differs from the International Standard Classification of Occupations.
Source: JILPT (2023) Table 3-6. The data were compiled by the JILPT from the sources below.
    Japan: Statistics Bureau (2022.3) Labor Force Survey (Long-term time series)
    United Kingdom: NOMIS (https://www.nomisweb.co.uk/) as of October 2022
    Others: ILOSTAT (https://ilostat.ilo.org/data/) as of October 2022

and cooperativeness are more likely to be valued than specialized knowledge or qualifications. If your spouse is transferred to a remote location, your only recourse is to let them take the posting alone as a single-posting (*tanshin funin*) transferee or else quit your own job and accompany them. Having once quit, however, there is little chance of being hired on again as a regular employee in a large company that primarily recruits new graduates. Estimating from an analysis of individual data from the 14th 'Basic Survey on Fertility Trends' conducted by the National Institute of Population and Social Security Research in 2010, less than 30% of women were able to secure their status as regular employees at private Japanese companies after getting married and having children.[52] According to the JILPT's tabulations, the percentage of women in management positions in 2021 is notably lower in Japan than in comparable countries (Figure 2.2).

The Japanese-style Employment System and Its Characteristics   91

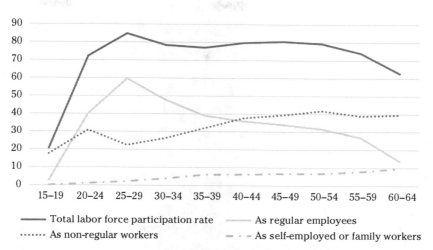

Figure 2.3 Female labor force participation rate by age grade (2022)
Unit: %   Source: 2022 Labor Force Survey (Basic Tabulation, Table 1-2).

Women who have left positions as regular employees often return to work when their children are old enough. However, the Japanese-style employment system makes becoming a regular employee difficult for anyone but new graduates, so women's re-entry into the workforce is often as non-regular workers. The absence of cross-firm social standards for evaluating specialized personnel means that this non-regular employment often ends up being in menial work that pays a minimum wage. The female labor force participation rate by age for 2022 shows a linear decline for regular employees after peaking in the twenty-five to twenty-nine age group. In contrast, the rate of women's employment in non-regular work increases after the twenty-five to twenty-nine age group.

Although the female labor force participation rate for women in Japan is said to trace an 'M-shape' in terms of age grade, this is not quite accurate: the 'M-shape' is merely the product of the total of both regular and non-regular employees.[53] In other words, Japanese women arguably follow a life cycle of being full-time regular employees before marriage and childbirth and non-regular part-time workers after marriage and childbirth. This is different from countries where women's labor participation rates, both full-time and total, do not form

92   Chapter 2

an M-shape (e.g., Sweden, the US and Canada), as well as countries where only full-time rates form an M-shape (e.g., Germany, the UK and Australia). [54]

The basic principle and pros/cons of Japanese-style employment

As I noted at the beginning of this chapter, the distinctive features of the Japanese-style employment system that I have described thus far all stem from this single cause – the absence of any criteria for evaluating employees' qualifications or determining wages apart from an in-house ranking system. The lack of job mobility for personnel outside of their companies, the advantages afforded by long-term service, the fact that the periodical bulk recruitment of new graduates on the basis of their potentiality is the main means of recruiting personnel – all of these stem from the absence of any criteria for evaluating employees apart from in-house ranking systems. Moreover, since wages are determined by rank and not by job type or position, management has free rein to determine transfers and promotions.

Kei'ichirō Hamaguchi, the Research Director General of the JIPLT, categorizes the Japanese-style employment system as a 'membership-type' system, and those found in the US and elsewhere as 'job-type' systems.[55] According to Hamaguchi, in the latter type of system, there is first of all a job, for which someone will be hired based on criteria such as their academic majors, work experience and other qualifications. In Japan, conversely, someone is hired as a member of a company first of all, and only afterward undergoes training while being assigned to a job. Hamaguchi explains this as the difference between 'job-first' and 'person-first' models.

This dichotomy was not invented by Hamaguchi, however, but is one that has been discussed in Japan since the end of World War II. Its origins, as I discuss in Chapter 5, lie in the job-based pay structures promoted by the US occupation forces in the wake of Japan's wartime defeat. In the US, as well, the system of first analyzing an organization's duties to define positions and set corresponding wages, and then hiring people accordingly, was first adopted by the federal government

The Japanese-style Employment System and Its Characteristics   93

in the 1920s before spreading to the private sector.[56] When the occupation forces attempted to introduce this system to Japan, the Japanese viewed the American system as being 'job-first'. Those who argued for the incompatibility of this system for Japan gave rise to a discourse in which Japan was characterized as 'person-first'. In 1948, Yoshio Kaneko, the director of the Japanese government's Bureau of Labor Statistics and Research, was quoted as saying the following to his subordinate, Kyū Kusuda (later a well-known expert on Japanese personnel management):

> [In Japan,] you are hired by a company, and then you are assigned to sales, and then to accounting, and then today to do this or that. In each instance, your job is determined by what the organization needs. If wages were determined by your job, they would go up or down every time you are transferred. It's all well and good if they go up, but what do you do if they go down? Someone in that situation will lose their motivation. Job-based wages won't work in Japan. [Best suited for Japan are] wages that are based on the value of the person.[57]

To this, Kusuda recalls asking, 'So, then how do you determine the value of the person?' to which Kaneko responded by saying 'That's going to be a major challenge for the Ministry of Labor'. Nevertheless, as I discuss in Chapter 3 and the chapters that follow, it was easy to make judgements based on educational background, years of service and 'character'.

Still, the formulation of 'person-first' is not quite appropriate. The specifics of a worker's academic majors or qualifications, or the nature of their career plan, are not seen as relevant. The 'person-first' approach should be interpreted to mean that what is paramount is management's evaluation of the worker, and it is up to management to determine what kind of job to allocate to the worker. The management's decision, moreover, will have nothing to do with what wages the job might command in the open market. Nor does it depend on how the worker may have been evaluated or qualified by any external organization, including their major in university or experience acquired at other companies. The only qualifications that matter inside the company are those determined and assigned by the company's management. Individual management has a monopoly on the authority to evaluate employees, there are no cross-firm criteria, and only one in-house ranking system is used to evaluate personnel and pay wages. This is the basic principle of Japanese-style employment.

The downsides of the Japanese-style employment system are apparent. Workers' own choices and career plans are treated as secondary to the decisions made by management. Workers gain experience in various types of jobs throughout the company and become generalists specialized to that particular company but unsuited to employment at other companies. Promotion within the company is slow, working hours are long, competition for managerial positions continues over more than twenty years, and transfers cannot be refused. A worker transferred to a remote location will have to leave his family to go to the posting alone, or else ask his wife to quit her job to accompany him. Women often end up quitting because they cannot tolerate the long working hours, transfers or relocation assignments out to other branches. One of the reasons why men do not quit their jobs is that once they leave, they have little chance of being hired by a large company on good terms, except as new graduates. Even if they work for many years, at the age of sixty, they will either be laid off through mandatory retirement or resigned to contracts with drastically reduced wages and poorer employment conditions.

In other countries, some workers are willing to work long hours and relocate to remote locations for a chance at promotion. Those hired by a company as executive candidates may also be transferred through many departments within the company. However, Japanese management scholars conducted comparative studies of French and American companies and found that only a small number of people work in this way, and they are promoted quickly.[58] Japanese management scholar Naohiro Yashiro points out that a characteristic of Japanese companies is that they demand all regular employees adopt the working style of Western elites.[59] As will be discussed in Chapter 5, Japanese-style employment was limited to higher staff before World War II, but was extended to lower-level white-collar and blue-collar workers due

The Japanese-style Employment System and Its Characteristics 95

to the postwar labor movement, and this historical background has influenced it to the present day.

In general, the Japanese-style employment system is one with many negative aspects in terms of employees' work-life balance and career plans, particularly for female workers. Nevertheless, it has been maintained because in the past it has proven to be beneficial to both management and workers. From a management perspective, it can eliminate outside intervention in the company's governance. As long as compromises can be reached with the company's internal labor union, then hiring, transfers and wages will not be affected by what the outside market offers for individual positions, nor by any academic majors and certifications that workers may have earned. There is no fear that workers who have been trained internally might end up quitting. The company can control the thoughts and behaviors of its workers, and it can foster loyalty. While competent in-house personnel are available, the company will be able to handle a wide variety of tasks and technological innovations without risking layoffs or labor disputes. These advantages, particularly during the period from the 1960s to the 1980s, helped Japanese companies accumulate skills through the long-term employment of skilled workers in-house, and as such are seen as having supported the rapid growth of Japan's manufacturing industry.[60]

However, this does not mean that the advantages conferred by this employment system are enjoyed by management exclusively. For their part, workers enjoy the guarantees of long-term employment and seniority-based wages. Of course, there is a heavy price to pay, such as significant disadvantages in terms of career planning and gender equality. As I discuss in Chapter 6, however, from the 1960s to the 1980s, this employment system was endorsed by workers, especially by male middle-aged and older factory workers with relatively lower educational background and the labor unions they were a part of. For male workers without degrees or qualifications, the advantages of guaranteed employment and seniority-based wages held much more appeal than the advantage of being able to move between companies. These workers accumulated skills through long-term employment and contributed to Japan's manufacturing industry as versatile workers who could flexibly respond to a variety of on-site labor needs.

To understand this, let's look at Figure 2.4, a comparison formulated in 1980 by Hirohide Tanaka, then a manager of the Labor Economics Section in the Japanese Ministry of Labor. Tanaka formulated this diagram after his visits to North America and Western Europe in the 1970s as a means of emphasizing their contrast with Japan. The diagram shows a strict hierarchical structure in Western companies. Following the dichotomy of this figure, the situation of workers in Europe and North America would be as follows. Shop-floor workers cannot hope to become CEO of their company, let alone a manager or director. They will move to other companies based on their academic degrees and work experience. The lowest level of staff can also move to other companies, but they will stay at the lowest level. Even if a worker stays at the same company for a long time, they may not be promoted, and their wages may not increase.

The dichotomy in this figure may be extreme, and management studies have shown that employment practices in each of the Western countries have their own characteristics.[61] In general, however, North American and Western European companies have a three-tier hierarchy. In the US, for example, there are three types of workers: hourly, salaried nonexempt and salaried exempt, as defined by the Fair Labor Standards Act (FLSA). Hourly workers are often work-site laborers who are paid by the hour in the form of daily or weekly wages, and if they work overtime, they are paid at an overtime hourly rate. Nonexempt workers are typically clerical staff or mid-level technicians who perform the routine jobs they are assigned and are basically paid on a monthly basis with overtime pay, but it would be equally correct to say that they are paid by the hour, and that their hourly wages are paid in bulk on a monthly basis. In contrast, for those working in corporate management and administration, employers are exempted from paying overtime and pay is based on monthly or annual salaries. In a similar three-tier structure, British companies had higher management categories with annual or monthly salaries, weekly paid staff such as clerks, typists and drafting technicians, and hourly-rated laborers such as factory workers.[62] Germany had a three-tiered structure

The Japanese-style Employment System and Its Characteristics

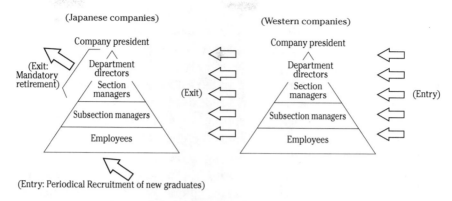

Figure 2.4 A model of the international comparison of differences in hiring practices
Source: Tanaka (1980: 378).

with senior staff (*Beamte*), junior staff (*Angestellte*) and manual laborers (*Arbeiter*).[63] This three-tier structure was widely apparent in Western societies, even if the nomenclature varied from country to country, and was generally linked to educational level (e.g., whether workers had completed higher education, secondary education or compulsory education).

But according to Tanaka's dichotomy, in a Japanese company, although one cannot move to another company, the possibility of upward mobility remains open. That is, if you are hired at the lowest rung of the staff hierarchy, there is still the possibility that you could someday become company president. Even if not, it is still likely that you could be promoted to section manager or department director. Or perhaps, through a secondment, it might be that you become a department director with a corporate affiliate. Of course, competition among those who joined the company in the same year as you, whose promotion is also based on seniority, will be intense, and you will have to endure long working hours, transfers and relocations out to other offices. At the very least, however, if you just keep working at the same company, your wages will steadily increase, and you will be unlikely to be laid off.

To be precise, this is a diagram showing Tanaka's understanding of the situation, not the reality of Western and Japanese companies. In fact, internal promotions are reasonably common in Western firms, and as I discuss later, the Japanese-company system described here actually only applies to large companies. However, for Tanaka, who was well-versed in the Japanese-style employment system, this diagram represents how he understood the contrast between the two.

These contrasts have also been described by contemporary scholars and management consultants who endorse the Japanese-style employment system. One such, Tsuguo Ebihara, has noted that in the American exempted class of employee, selection is mostly over by the early thirties, and that among the executive or 'cadre' class of French employees, 'the final wage differential can be as much as 2.5 times greater, whereas in Japan, the difference when comparing section managers and department directors or section managers and subsection managers between the ages of fifty and fifty-four, when their salaries are highest, is only 20%'.[64] Japanese labor economist Kazuo Koike, noting that blue-collar and white-collar workers receive equal treatment under the Japanese employment system, argues that this boosts morale and nurtures a sense of belonging among blue-collar workers, motivating them to actively accumulate skills and thereby contribute to technological innovation in the Japanese manufacturing industry.[65]

It has also been pointed out that the Japanese-style employment system has the effect of mitigating youth unemployment.[66] Because there is a mandatory retirement age, positions are always available in April for the same number of new graduates as people who have been retired. Moreover, new graduates are employable at large companies even without a master's or doctorate or even any work experience. While it is true that someone who did not attend an elite university is less likely to be hired on by a large company, the question of whether they majored in business or literature is relatively immaterial. What companies screen for is the intelligence, drive and flexibility to be able to handle any job at all.

Also, once a person has joined the company, their hard work on the company's behalf counts more than the name of the university from which they graduated. Sociologist Yō Takeuchi, analyzing the career paths of university graduates who joined a major Japanese financial insurance company in 1966, 1968 and 1985, found that while a university's prestige had a significant effect on graduates' initial placement, any subsequent effect was negligible.[67] Other studies, as well, have found that educational background was either not very important or becoming less important for promotion in Japanese firms.[68] Underlying this, as I will discuss further in chapters 3 and 4, is the fact that the severity of elitist discrimination based on where someone went to university, which was widespread in Japanese companies before World War II, has been ameliorated somewhat thanks to the postwar labor movement.

Of course, even in a Japanese company, whether an employee has graduated from university, as opposed to only having a high school diploma, does have an impact on the speed and range of promotion. Regardless of educational background, however, promotion and salary increases have been almost guaranteed with years of service, albeit at different rates. After conducting a survey of 216 large companies in 1976, the All-Japan Federation of Management Organizations issued a report that stated the following.

> ... in terms of the nature of work, as well, in countries like the US, it is not uncommon for highly educated people to be appointed to management positions at a relatively young age. In Japan, however, it is normal for most highly educated people to work in clerical or sales positions that are essentially the same as those filled by less educated people, and then to gradually rise in status and treatment with age and the accrual of years of service. In other words, seniority-based wages and promotions are available regardless of workers' level of education; it is simply that the rate of advancement varies according to educational background. In this way, the company provides employees in general with stability in their lives and hope for the future to create expectations of loyalty as well as to maintain a stronger sense of belonging among the more highly educated, who are seen as the backbone of the company.[69]

A disparity thus exists between university graduates and those with only high school diplomas. However, even high school graduates can expect their wages to increase with accrued years of service, as well as the possibility of promotion. In addition, while they are still relatively recent hires, there is little difference in the wages that university and high school graduates can expect to receive. In this way, the system was one that proved attractive for the shop-floor workers, primarily male high school graduates, who formed the mainstay of Japan's labor unions.

These benefits of the Japanese-style employment system have also been recognized by workers overseas. In a 2014 report published by the JILPT, a union representative from a major Swedish company, responding to a Japanese survey, was recorded as saying, 'Personally, I think Japan is better [...]. In our country, a fresh university graduate hired as an engineer, even if he has no work experience, can still expect to earn more than a worker who has worked on the line for ten years. I think that is very, very bad. And yet that's the way it is'.[70] This account implies that someone with an engineering degree can secure a high-paying position. It does *not* mean, as we have seen in Japan, that someone who passes the entrance examination of a prestigious university will be afforded preferential treatment no matter what they have studied. Nevertheless, one might be able to argue that in Japan, once someone is in the door at a company, their treatment afterward will be comparatively equal.

In this book, I refer to this as 'equality of company employees'. In fact, as I discuss in Chapter 3, prior to the 1950s, Japan had a three-tier structure similar to Western Europe and the US. As explained in Chapter 5, the term 'company employee' (*shain*) referred to a full membership of the company. Further, as I discuss in Chapter 6, the guarantee of equality for workers, as long as they were regular employees of the same company, was a key demand by workers after World War II. How these factors worked together to shape the characteristics of the Japanese-style employment system will be described in the following chapters.

Small and medium-sized enterprises

The Japanese-style employment system that I have described thus far only applies to regular employees at large companies. The Japanese government's Wage Census defines 'standard workers' (*hyōjun rōdō-sha*) as those who start working for a company immediately after graduation and then continue working for the same company. However, even among university-educated workers at large companies, this definition accounts for only about half, and is even more limited with regard to SMEs and women. According to an estimate from the 1992 Wage Census, among male regular employees aged fifty to fifty-four working for large companies with 1,000 or more employees, the 'standard workers' accounted for 53.2% of university graduates, and 24.3% of high school graduates (at that time, many companies had a mandatory retirement age of fifty-five).[71] In 2016, male standard workers aged fifty to fifty-nine accounted for about 40% of employees in large companies with at least 1,000 employees and only 7% of employees in companies with ten to ninety-nine employees.[72]

Even in Japan, workers in SMEs often move from one company to another. A 2020 MHLW survey revealed that only 4.3% of those who moved to jobs at other companies were from firms with more than 1,000 employees, while 85.6% were from firms with fewer than 300 employees (Figure 2.5). Although there is some data indicating that the number of people switching jobs from large companies has recently been on the rise, according to a 2014 survey by Japan's SME Agency, the most common reason for job changes from companies with 300 or more employees is 'retirement age / expiration of contract period'.[73] In other words, the statistics about job-changers from large companies are likely to have been inflated by job changes on the part of fixed-term non-regular workers and people rehired after mandatory retirement.

So, why is long-term employment so rare in SMEs? First, in SMEs, it is less likely for wages to increase with years of service. In large companies, earnings from various departments are redistributed to ensure stability for wage increases over time. This is not as feasible for SMEs, however. Because wages do not increase automatically with years of service, many employees will move to other firms.[74] Another likely factor is the difficulty of reassigning workers with transfers.

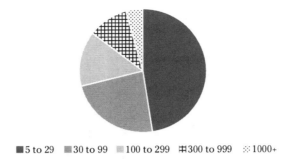

■ 5 to 29   ■ 30 to 99   ■ 100 to 299   ⌗ 300 to 999   ⋰ 1000+

Figure 2.5 Size of previous company of workers who switched companies (2020, no. of employees)

Source: the 2020 MHLW Survey on the Current Situation of Workers Who Switched Companies in Japan (tenshoku-sha jittai chōsa).

As noted earlier, large companies are able to maintain long-term employment in part by transferring and reallocating their workers to various departments. Depending on economic trends and changing demand, workers will be reallocated from unprofitable divisions to those with more prospects for growth. While companies in other countries lay off workers in unprofitable divisions and hire new staff in those that are growing, large companies in Japan avoid layoffs by reallocating workers internally. However, this only feasible for large companies with many divisions.

In fact, as measured by the Employment Protection Legislature Indicator (EPL) set by the OECD, Japan is one of the less strictly regulated countries in the industrialized world.[75] This applies to not only temporary contracts but also regular contracts (Figure 2.6). Japan's Labor Standards Act only requires thirty days' prior notice of termination of contract and prohibits the dismissal of workers who are sick or injured on the job or women who are before or after childbirth. As will be discussed in Chapter 7, Japan's dismissal regulations were established by court precedents in the 1970s, and they only state that dismissal lacking 'objectively reasonable grounds' and not deemed acceptable under 'social norms' is invalid.[76] According to court precedents, employers are required to try to avoid dismissal by transferring within the company as the 'social norm'. However, as for

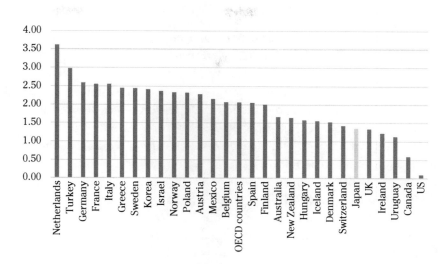

Figure 2.6 Strictness of employment protection in regular contracts (2019, selected countries)
Note: Measured by the Employment Protection Legislature Indicator (EPL).
Source: OECD.Stat, 'Strictness of employment protection – individual and collective dismissals (regular contracts)', https://stats.oecd.org/Index.aspx?DataSetCode=EPL_OV (Accessed on 10 July 2023).

the cases of SMEs that do not have departments into which to transfer, it is easier for dismissals to be legal.

In SMEs, moreover, the bulk recruitment of new graduates is frequently not the primary or only means of recruiting new employees. This is because many workers of SMEs move between companies. In addition, SMEs are less attractive to new graduates, so vacant positions are more likely to be filled by workers moving between SMEs. Labor economist Heikki Räisänen, who conducted a comparative analysis of the job-broking market in Japan and Finland in 2005, observes the following: 'In Japan, the labour market especially in large corporations is still based on life-long employment and therefore, recruitment is much concentrated on new graduates', but 'Small businesses have in one sense represented flexibility in the Japanese labour market as they cannot apply similar recruitment and employment practices as large corporations. In this sense they must operate more like the Finnish or "European type" of labour market in general'. [77]

Recruitment criteria in the labor market that exists for workers moving between companies differ from those used in the bulk recruitment of new graduates, in which potentiality is a standard of evaluation. According to a 2004 survey conducted by the JILPT in which employers were asked to rank multiple responses, the points considered most important in the selection process were job experience (57.7% and 52.7%, respectively, in management and clerical fields), technical knowledge and skills in the case of technical and research fields (68.9%), and enthusiasm and ambition in the case of non-clerical fields (58.9%).[78] As noted by Räisänen, these trends are not unique to Japan, but are similar to those found in Europe and North America.

However, this does not mean that the employment system in Japanese SMEs is entirely identical to is counterparts in the West. The fact that the SME employment system is basically the same as that which prevails in large companies is suggested by the fact that SME wage profiles show that wages increase with age or years of service. Its basic shape is the same, with the difference that the smaller the company size, the lower the upward curve.[79] The difference from large companies lies only in the fact that SMEs cannot fully realize the classic Japanese-style employment system, rather than in the principles by which they operate. In Japan, large companies and SMEs are alike in that the only qualification system that any company has is in-house rank, with no external market price for wages based on degrees or qualifications. This gives rise to wage gaps depending on company size, even when the job is the same. In Japan, the distinction between large companies and SMEs is an important one for workers. A university student hoping to find a position at a large company will talk in terms of the name of the company they want to work for as a regular employee regardless of the occupations that will be assigned to them. The assumption here is that once hired by the company, they will enjoy equal standing with all other regular employees, based on the philosophy of 'equality of company employee'.

There are various lines of argument surrounding whether the firm-size wage gap in Japan is larger than that in Western countries – some studies characterize such differences as larger, while others view them as moderate.[80] What is certain, however, as pointed out by economist

The Japanese-style Employment System and Its Characteristics   105

Toshiaki Tachibanaki, a researcher focusing on size-based wage differentials between Japanese companies, is that whereas this is an important topic in Japan, 'it is not seen as such in Western countries', and studies of this topic are not as popular as in Japan.[81]

One reason for the relative paucity of research is that the firm-size wage gap is a difficult topic to study.[82] Simply comparing wages in firms where engineers make up the majority of employees with those in firms where factory workers make up the majority of employees does not tell us whether firm size is the cause. The wage gap by firm size may just be a pseudo-correlation of other factors with firm size.[83] This makes it a difficult topic for economics, which is related to the paucity of research. Nevertheless, it has remained an important topic for many researchers in Japan. This can be thought of in terms of differences in attitudinal social norms more than whether the firm-size wage gap in Japan is larger than that in the Western countries.

Of course, in both the US and Europe, among those who work for high-performing companies, wages tend to be higher for those in similar positions, so differences based on company size are not unheard of. (As we will see in Chapter 8, they do exist.) However, theoretically speaking, where a large wage gap between different firms exists for the same job, workers will tend to move to the higher-paying firms. Therefore theoretically, where jobs are the same, disparities do not really emerge. Thus, a market value is established for the wages commanded by each position, as well as a qualification system in which wages are determined according to academic degrees and qualifications. In this kind of society, wage differences between different kinds of jobs, or between blue-collar workers and salaried office workers, would be more salient than those due to company size. If a society shared such a mindset, wage gaps based on company size, where they exist at all, would not be seen as an important topic in that context.

Given the assumption, the following dichotomous model might be considered. In the mindset of the West, people tend to be conscious of disparities in terms of what kind of job someone has. In the mindset of Japan, however, people are more conscious of disparities in terms of whether or not someone is a regular employee at a large company.

Whereas Western mindsets pursue 'job-based equality', a philosophy that underlies the objective of equal pay for equal work, the Japanese mindset pursues 'equality of company employee', and in that sense might arguably be characterized as a society in which equal treatment within the same company exists, but equal pay for equal work across companies does not. As I mentioned in Chapter 1, the reason why a significant portion of non-regular workers in Japan work for the minimum wage is partly due to the absence of any society-wide criteria for evaluating the wages of specialized personnel, and partly due to the fact that highly paid part-time workers are unheard of. Although highly paid professional part-time workers might be possible in a society where there are standard evaluation criteria and wage levels for each type of work, this is not the case in Japan, where the primary means for workers to increase their wages is to accrue years of service as regular employees at a single company.

In the 1985 Economic Planning Agency report I referred to in Chapter 1, the gap between large companies and SMEs, which had been prominent up until the 1950s, was positioned as having narrowed after the period of rapid growth that took place in the 1960s. According to the report, this was because SMEs had begun to adopt the same employment system as was used by large companies by giving company employee (*shain*) status to core employees and endeavoring to guarantee them seniority-based wages and long-term employment. Had this not been the case, SMEs would never have been able to recruit new graduates during the rapid growth of the 1960s.

If that were true, however, then SMEs would have had to have had an adjustable element that allowed them to respond to economic trends. This element, I argue, was constituted by workers in non-regular employment. As I discuss in Chapter 7, the rise in non-regular employment first began with SMEs after the oil crisis of 1973. This was conceivably due to the fact that the adoption of the Japanese-style employment system by SMEs meant that they required an element that could adjust to economic downturn trends.

The other factor, also discussed in Chapter 7, is that several court decisions in the 1970s requiring firms to avoid firing regular employees forced SMEs to take this into account with respect to their regular employees. This also contributed to the introduction of non-regular employment, in which it is easier to dismiss employees, in order to allow for employment adjustments in response to economic conditions. As mentioned above, Japanese law is not strict in its restrictions on dismissal; merely court precedents ordered the avoidance of dismissal of regular employees through transfers and other means. It is legal to fire a non-regular worker hired for a specific job when that job is no longer needed, as it does not violate Japanese social norms.

After the 1990s, when the Japanese economy faltered, even large companies increased their non-regular workforce to cope with the economic stagnation. The labor power for this increase among workers in non-regular employment was covered by a contracting self-employment sector. In the 2010s, when the shrunken self-employment sector had finally been depleted as a source of labor, an increase in the number of technical intern trainees arriving from Asia found employment in Japan in SMEs operating in sectors such as agriculture, textiles and services, where the earliest instances of rising non-regular employment had begun to take place in the 1970s.

Hypotheses on the reasons for the emergence of Japanese-style employment

Above, I have described how companies' internal labor markets are closed in the context of the Japanese-style employment system, and how this has led to the emergence of the employment regime and the dual structure outlined in Chapter 1. As I also mentioned in Chapter 1, previous studies have attributed this closedness to a lack of technological modernization and standardization, and to the accumulation of expertise unique to individual companies. None of this, however, can explain the absence of labor mobility between large companies – which are supposed to have modernized – even among university-educated employees in senior positions. The reason for this closed off character, I argue, is the absence of a cross-firm qualification system, so that the only criteria for evaluating personnel that exists in the Japanese-style employment system are those of companies' internal ranking systems.

So, why does such an employment system exist in Japan? As I mentioned in the Introduction, several models have been proposed to account for this problem, namely the Cultural Model which traces the problem to the culture of the Edo period, the Economic Model and the Motivation Model which highlight the system's advantages in terms of employee retention and maintaining motivation, and the Control Model which regards the system as having been introduced to contain the labor movement. However, none of these models seem to provide an adequate response. It is too simplistic to look for origins in Edo-period culture, while the retention of personnel by a company and the maintenance of worker motivation should be attributed to the economic rationality achieved *within* the Japanese-style employment system. They are products of the system, so to speak, and are thus unlikely to be the cause of that system's formation.

What of the Control Model? As I discuss in Chapter 6, it is a fact that middle-aged male blue-collar workers with low levels of educational attainment, who were the mainstay of the Japanese labor movement in the 1960s, were supporters of the Japanese-style employment system. As I discuss in Chapter 5, it is also true that the labor movement, which emerged rapidly after Japan's defeat in World War II, demanded equality of company employees. In this sense, the case can certainly be made that the Japanese-style employment system expanded as a result of opposition between the labor movement and management. However, as I discuss in chapters 3 and 4, the prototype of this system had already been formed among white-collar staff by the 1910s, long before the emergence of the postwar labor movement. By the time that the postwar labor movement began demanding equality of company employees, the prototype of the system was already established among staff employees. Blue-collar workers demanded inclusion in the employment system, and so management attempted to contain the labor movement by extending the existing employment system to shop-floor workers. That is, although the Control Model explains the process by which the Japanese-style employment system expanded, it does not offer any insight into how the prototype was formed.

The Japanese-style Employment System and Its Characteristics 109

To this end, this book proposes two hypotheses, which I will evaluate in the descriptions contained in the rest of the book. The first hypothesis concerns the unique character of Japan's labor movement, and the second concerns the influence of bureaucracy.

First hypothesis: Labor movement differences

The concept of the internal labor market is discussed in Chapter 1. The Japanese-style employment system is an internal labor market characterized by seniority based on years of service within a single company and in-house ranks.

Clerk Kerr, who first proposed the concept of internal labor market in 1954, argued that there is a 'structured' and 'internal' labor market with certain rules for wages and job allocation, and a 'structureless' and 'external' labor market that lacks these rules.[84] In other words, the criterion was not whether the labor market was inside or outside a company, but whether or not there were rules or order. Kerr identified three factors that contributed to the existence of such a rules-based labor market: the labor movement, employers' intentions and government policy. The labor movement demands rules for wages, layoffs and personnel evaluation to counter the arbitrariness of employers. The employers' intention to contain the labor movement and secure superior human resources institutionalizes the rules in the form of a collective agreement between the two parties. The government then supports such agreements and the institutionalization of rules in the hope of social and economic stability.

If we assume Kerr's theory, the character of the internal labor market is influenced by the character of the labor movement in a country. Kerr, with the guilds, which were artisan associations in medieval Europe, and the manors, which were aristocratic families also in medieval Europe, in mind, argued that there were two types of internal labor markets: the 'guild system' and the 'manorial system'. According to Kerr, the guild system became the dominant internal labor market in European countries such as Germany and Denmark, where occupational organizations were strong and workers were organized by occupation. In societies where occupational organizations are weak and the internal labor market is created to secure superior workers at the initiative of company owners, the manorial system is created. In his 1954 paper, Kerr contrasts the movement of workers between firms in these two systems. In the guild system, workers move horizontally between firms, gaining experience and careers in the same occupation. In the manorial system, on the other hand, workers move up the ladder vertically, accumulating seniority within the same company. This contrast is similar to that shown in Figure 2.4, in which Hirohide Tanaka contrasted Western and Japanese firms in 1980. [85]

In the United States, occupational organizations and craft unions were not as powerful as in Europe. And managerial-driven welfare capitalism was established in some major manufacturing firms from the 1930s through the 1970s.[86] But these manorial system firms did not become the majority. One reason is that management had difficulty fostering cooperative unions, since the National Labor Relations Act of 1935 effectively banned company unions in the US.[87] Probably for this reason, major studies conducted in the US in the 1970s and 1980s claimed that internal labor markets are formed by employer's choice within each company, mainly for white-collar workers, and few pointed to the influence of labor unions.[88] As Kerr pointed out, the formation of an internal labor market is influenced not only by trade unions and employers, but also by government policy.

In Japan, however, there were no such legal restrictions on company unions. And in Japan, the seniority wage system has been applied to both blue-collar and white-collar workers. This is because Japan's enterprise unions, and especially the shop-floor workers, who were the mainstay of the labor unions, demanded it. This suggests that the different character of the labor movement influenced the formation of the Japanese-style employment system.

A distinctive element of Japan's labor movement is the enterprise union, which contrasts with the industrial or occupational trade unions characteristic of labor movements in Western Europe. This difference also exerts an effect on worker identities. At the end of the 1960s, British sociologist Ronald Dore undertook a comparative study of English and Japanese factories, focusing on a plant operated in Bradford, UK by English Electric and a factory in the city of Hitachi

The Japanese-style Employment System and Its Characteristics

in Ibaraki prefecture operated by Hitachi, Ltd. In the monograph he based on this study, Dore wrote about the identity of workers living under these different employment systems as follows.

> If you meet a Bradford English Electric foundryman on a train and ask him what he does, the first thing he will probably say is that he is a foundryman, the second thing that he comes from Bradford, and the third that he works for English Electric. His Japanese counterpart would most naturally define himself first as a member of the Hitachi Company, secondly as working at such and such a factory, and thirdly as being a foundryman.[89]

According to Dore, the primary identity in a Japanese worker is that of being an employee of a certain company. In contrast, the British worker will identify primarily in terms of their occupation. This difference seems to derive from differences in the labor movements of the two countries. This is suggested by the following passage from Dore's book.

> The British electrician is assumed to need a strong local and national organization to ensure that the skills of electricians are given their proper price, and that work which should go to electricians is not given to others — and that requires defining both what is electrician's work and who should be entitled to call himself an electrician. He shares his concern for these things equally with other electricians in other firms. An electrician working for Hitachi, on the other hand, probably did not become an electrician until he passed out of the labour market into Hitachi. Once in the firm he is never likely to go into the market again to sell his electrician skills and so he has no particular interest in keeping up their price. Within the firm, given the wage system, his interests coincide rather more with those of non-electricians of the same age as himself [who were hired at the same age as new graduates and have the same length of service] than with those of older or younger fellow electricians. [90]

Chapter 2

As many know, the UK was a country that saw the emergence of occupational or 'craft unions', which the *Encyclopedia Britannica* defines as follows:

> **craft union**, trade union combining workers who are engaged in a particular craft or skill but who may work for various employers and at various locations. Formed to improve wage levels and working conditions, craft unions were established in Britain and the United States in the middle of the 19th century. They derive their power from their control over the supply of skilled labour—a control that is maintained through licensing and apprenticeship arrangements. With such slogans as 'One craft, one union', a local craft union strives to organize all members of its trade (e.g., plumbers, electricians, bricklayers, ironworkers, carpenters, machinists, and printers).[91]

In this system of craft unionism, a sense of identity and camaraderie is formed across companies by workers sharing the same profession, for example as 'electricians'. That is, a sense of camaraderie emerges with electricians in other companies, more so than with other people in other professions within the same company. These things are constructed as units of the solidarity that emerges from their joint participation in the labor movement. Then, as Dore says, '[they must define] both what is electrician's work and who should be entitled to call himself an electrician. [The electrician at English Electric] shares his concern for these things equally with other electricians in other firms'. They are qualified for their proficiency by licenses issued by their union, which allow them to move to other companies and receive wages commensurate with their attested proficiency. However, they cannot move to other professions in the same company.

In contrast, the Japanese system of enterprise unionism leads to the construction of a different sort of identity – one that replaces Dore's 'electrician' with the term 'company employee' (*shain*). It is a system that 'must define both what a company employee is, and who should be entitled to call himself a company employee. The employee of Company A shares his concern for these things equally with other

The Japanese-style Employment System and Its Characteristics 113

employees in the company, regardless of their profession'. They can be moved to other professions and promoted through personnel transfers under a system of seniority-based wages that has been agreed to by management and the union. However, they probably cannot move to a position of the same profession in another company and expect to receive the same wages as they did in their former company. Again, this is due to the absence in Japan of any widely recognized qualification system for the evaluation of workers' skills, for example in the form of union-issued licenses.

Alternatively, one might take the view that the identity of Japanese workers emerges naturally because they are working within a single company. However, this is not accurate. In a large company like Hitachi, which employs tens of thousands of workers, those who have never met each other will by far outnumber those who have. If a sense of camaraderie still arises among 'employees of the same company', then this is simply an imagined community. This fellowship, more so than of direct acquaintance, is rather the historically constructed consciousness of social practices.

The initial conditions for this difference between Japan and the UK, as I discuss in Chapter 3, is the lack of a history of strong occupational organization in Japan. In the UK and Germany, craftsmen's guilds have a long history, so the behavioral pattern of forming unions based on occupation was one that workers took to easily. Japan, by contrast, had no such tradition of broad-based craft unions across different communities. Had occupational organizations enjoyed a historically strong presence in Japanese society, then the phenomenon by which workers' occupations often change as a result of companies' internal personnel transfers, which is a distinctive feature of the Japanese-style employment system, would not have been possible.

In addition, as I touched on in Chapter 1, the origins of social security in Germany were established on the basis of occupational organizations. Though they might have worked for the same company, clerks and shop-floor workers had had different trades and belonged to different unions and insurance societies. In Japan, on the other hand, to work for the same company means to belong to the same labor union and join the same insurance association, even for those engaged in different occupations. The presence or absence of a history of occupational organizations thus also impacts on the state of social security.

Even so, since this book does not touch on Edo-period or earlier historical material, I am only noting the fact that occupational organizations were not historically strong in Japan as a given initial condition. My focus here, rather, is on the question of how these differences in given conditions influenced subsequent differences in the labor movement and the formation of the employment system.

In fact, even in the UK and Germany, craft unions and modern occupational organizations were not actually a simple extension of guilds. The union movement constructs new identities and categories in the process of its development, since it needed to define and organize the new occupations that arose in the course of modernization.

This kind of historical process is well illustrated by the difference between the English engineer, a category that included skilled factory workers, and the German *Ingenieur*, which did not. This development was influenced by the UK labor movement, in which union-certified skilled workers were referred to as 'engineers'.[92] In Germany, however, the classification of *Ingenieur* was created by a coalition of people working in various technical fields such as architecture, civil engineering and electricity that organized a joint movement to improve their status. Until around 1850, the German language lacked a generic term for such occupations.[93] In the course of the movement, however, the concept was developed as a category for people with a theoretical technical education but who did not engage in manual labor. Accordingly, we could say that differences in the type of people who participated, and in the way the movement unfolded, ended up becoming differences in classification and identity.

It does not take much thinking to recognize that architectural engineers and electrical engineers are completely different professions. It is hardly natural for them to have a group consciousness of themselves as *Ingenieur*, or to be socially recognized as such. This type of group consciousness becomes entrenched through a historical process in which people from different occupational groups act together. Is the person on the factory floor an 'engineer'? Is the local technician who fixes broken appliances a licensed electrician? By whom are they certified, and according to what criteria? These were questions that emerged in the process of modernization, and that did not exist in the time of the medieval guilds. The pattern of categorization in a society will change according to the historical processes of modernization that shape it.

Historical processes also shape new occupations. The French term *cadre* is a nomenclature originally derived from France's military officer corps. It only came to refer to senior positions in private sector companies in the mid-twentieth century. Such employees formed organizations across companies, established *cadre* pension insurance and *cadre* unions, and provided job placement services, job search assistance and job market research for *cadre* job seekers. Prior to the 1930s, the term *cadre* had not been used in France to refer to a specific class of people. From the 1930s onward, however, the *cadre* category was constructed as people in various occupations in the technical and managerial fields campaigned for higher status.[94]

Thus, in Germany and France, the categories of *Ingenieur* and *cadre* were constructed through the accretion of people's practices in the form of the worker's movement. Of course, that people took part in such practices en masse is due to the historical existence of occupational organizations. This paved the way for most people in these societies to agree on the creation of a movement for the advancement of individual occupations, and actions to establish trade unions and insurance societies. In saying so, however, I did not intend to imply that these various categories have existed since the Middle Ages, but rather that they have been constructed through practices on the part of a great many people. Once they are established, people construct norms that regard these categories as givens to form the *habitus* of their thoughts and actions. As noted in the Introduction, the French sociologist Pierre Bourdieu proposed the idea of the habitus as a 'structuring structure'. In investigating how such a habitus was constructed, the question of whether its prototype has existed for centuries is not important. What *is* important, however, is determining the historical context in which people have implemented such practices, taking as a starting point the initial conditions that apply to their respective societies, such as for example whether or not occupational organizations were strong since the Middle Ages.

As I discuss in Chapter 5, the identity of Japanese workers as 'company employees (*shain*)' was also constructed by the postwar labor movement. Prior to World War II, the term *shain* referred only to a company's higher staff, rather than ordinary employees. In other words, *shain*, like the French *cadre*, was a category created through the accretion of practices of people in the postwar labor movement. The labor movement in Japan emerged in this form partly as a result of the initial condition of a history in which occupational organizations were not strong. However, the focus of the study undertaken here is not on those initial conditions. Rather, in this book I am concerned with the course taken by such practices in the Japanese context, how they resulted in the construction of the employment system and how this shaped the state of Japan's social security and education, as well as its dual structure.

Second hypothesis: The influence of bureaucracy

What then were the initial conditions that determined the character of the labor movement in the Japanese context, which did not have a history of strong occupational organizations? Labor movements aim to improve the status of workers under given conditions. Of course, such movements themselves play a major role in the formation of employment systems. However, in order for workers to improve their status, some sort of order for determining their status amongst themselves must already have existed as an initial condition.

The second hypothesis of this book concerns the influence of bureaucracy. This is because some of the characteristics of the Japanese-style employment system share certain similarities with European bureaucracies. In fact, the lack of a craft unionism tradition was also pointed out as a formative factor of the Japanese employment system by Japanese labor historian Kazuo Nimura, and by Andrew Gordon who was inspired by him.[95] But they overlooked the influence of the bureaucracy.

The Japanese-style Employment System and Its Characteristics 117

As we will also see in Chapter 3, in his comparative study of factories in Japan and the UK, Ronald Dore observes that 'Hitachi's form of organization is by no means foreign to Britain. It is very much the pattern of the British army or civil service. Japan's peculiarity lies in the fact that a type of organization which in most Western countries is considered suitable only for the army or the civil service is adapted in Japan to private industry'.[96] I should note that Dore did not examine the history of Japanese companies or the Japanese civil service, but merely argued the similarities between the two based on his impressions. However, his observation constitutes the second hypothesis of this book – namely that the Japanese-style employment system may have been influenced by the bureaucracy of the civil service and the army.

Here, Dore had in mind the bureaucracies of the UK and European countries, rather than the federal civil service found in the US government. The OECD categorizes civil service systems around the world into two types, namely career-based systems and position-based systems.[97] In position-based systems, candidates apply directly to a specific post and most posts are open to both internal and external applicants. A typical example of a position-based system is that of the US federal government, which is nearly identical to the system of private-sector employment in the US. Jobs are categorized in advance by job analysis, so that more difficult and challenging roles command commensurately higher wages. A job summary and pay range for a position will be listed in the position description, and when a vacant position becomes available, it will be advertised to the public. Applicants are screened through application documents and interviews to determine whether they have the experience, qualifications and degrees to perform the position, and applications can be submitted from both inside and outside government agencies.

In contrast, a career-based bureaucratic system is characterized by competitive selection by means of a public service qualification examination at an early stage, with higher-level posts open to only those who have passed the examination and have status as public servants. In the OECD classification, this type describes the bureaucracies found in European countries and in Japan. Some researchers refer to the career-based system as a 'closed career system',[98] since in such systems it is not possible to apply for posts from outside the civil service. Dore's description of the employment system found in large Japanese companies as similar to the British army or civil service may partly be due to the closed nature of European bureaucracies. It might be said that Japanese companies regard graduation from prestigious universities as a functional substitute for the 'company service' qualification examination which certifies candidates' general potentiality, rather than job ability or experience.

In fact, it is not uncommon for private companies to be influenced by government or military bureaucracy. For example, as mentioned earlier, the French term *cadre*, which refers to a senior managerial position in the French private sector, is derived from the term for a military officer corps. Moreover, setting salary grades based on job analysis, now a common practice in the US private sector, was first introduced in the US public sector, and was then popularized with government encouragement during the period from World War I through the World War II. The US labor movement also supported job analysis and salary grading to ensure payment of job-based wages and to correct wage inequality among workers, and this also contributed to the spread of this system.[99] If we inquire into its origins, the private-sector employment system that has since become common in the US was originally built through the influence of the public sector. As we will see in Chapter 4, the influence of government bureaucracy on private business was also significant in Germany.

This kind of influence from bureaucracy is more common in latecomers to development whose governments have imported modern institutions and organizations from more developed countries. Japan was one of these latecomers. In sociological studies of colonial areas, it is often pointed out that the bureaucracy and various systems that were implanted from the suzerain state remain as institutions and practices even after independence.[100] In my own research on Korea and Taiwan in the colonial era, I found that there were many institutional implantations from Japan. Not only that, I also described how Koreans and Taiwanese used the institutions and ideas implanted from Japan as tools to improve their own status and to negotiate with the Japanese

The Japanese-style Employment System and Its Characteristics 119

government.[101] In this book, I focus on how bureaucracy was implanted into Japanese private companies from the Japanese government, and how Japanese workers used the implanted bureaucracy as a tool to improve their own status and to negotiate with management. This book also describes how Japanese managers sought to recruit the best and brightest by emulating the government bureaucracy. Many studies have pointed out that scarcity of human resources is a factor that encourages the formation of an internal labor market.[102] In Japan, a latecomer country, there was a scarcity of human resources who could understand modern Western technology and organizational management, but the only model of an internal labor market for private companies to secure them was the government bureaucracy.

As I discuss in this book, however, European bureaucracies do not make a custom of periodical hiring new graduates in bulk or arranging for people to work together in large open-plan rooms. The German and French bureaucracies are restrictive in that applications to executive positions are only open to those who have passed a qualifying examination, and recruitment to these positions occurs when vacancies arise.[103] Thus, the employment system that prevails in Japanese companies and government agencies differs from those characteristic of European bureaucracy.

So how and under what historical circumstances did Japan's bureaucracy influence the employment system now found in private companies? What norms did this create? How did it build the initial conditions for the subsequent labor movement? And how did this result in the establishment of such a peculiar employment system? These questions constitute the second focus of this book's investigation. From Chapter 3 to 7, I will endeavor to provide an outline of Japan's modern history on the basis of these two working hypotheses.

3 Implanted Bureaucracy: The Origins of 'Japanese-style Employment'

In this chapter I begin to describe the historical processes that shaped the Japanese-style employment system. This chapter is an attempt to demonstrate the 'implantation' of bureaucracy in the context of Japanese employment practices.[1] First, I substantiate the claim that Japanese companies in the 1950s had a three-tier structure. However, rather than being based on the job classification of managers, clerks and blue-collar workers seen in other countries, the three-tier structure that emerged in Japan (although it did in the end overlap with job classifications), in fact constituted an order that privileged one's highest level of educational attainment in terms of graduation from university, secondary school or compulsory education.

The origins of this three-tier structure lay in the governmental bureaucratic system. The salaries of bureaucrats and military personnel were determined not by their duties, but by their ranks within civil service. Because ranks were determined actually by their years of service and educational background, their salaries were effectively seniority-based wages that increased with years of service. Their salaries and status were guaranteed in return for an oath of lifetime loyalty and commitment to the government. Bureaucratic and military appointments were also carried out on an 'assignment after appointment' (*ninkan hoshoku*) basis whereby personnel would be appointed to a rank first, and only then assigned to a position. In other words, people were not hired to positions; positions were assigned to people who had been appointed to a rank.

This bureaucratic system spread to Japanese companies during the Meiji period (1868–1912). The origins of modern Japanese industry lay with state-owned enterprises (SOE) founded and operated by the government under the same bureaucratic system as the civil service. Although these SOEs were eventually sold off to the private sector to become the foundation of Japan's large private enterprises, these large companies also inherited the systems of the SOEs. I can confirm that this system shared elements with the competence ranking system (*shokunō shikaku seido*), which was the personnel system employed by Japanese companies in the postwar period.

In addition, with weak tradition of occupational organizations, Japan had a scarcity of personnel able to understand the skills and knowledge being introduced from the West. Because of this, it became possible for those graduating from the Meiji government's newly introduced school system to work in a wide variety of upper-level professional positions, regardless of what they had studied. The fact that large private companies offered this limited number of highly educated graduates' salaries and raises comparable to those in the civil service encouraged this system to spread through the private sector.

However, the prewar employment system differed from its postwar counterpart in that blue-collar workers were subject to harshly discriminatory treatment. They held no rank, and so were not eligible for seniority-based wages or long-term employment. These workers would only attain such eligibility through the struggles of the postwar labor movement.

A three-tier structure observed by Abegglen

To examine the history of the Japanese-style employment system, let us introduce James Abegglen's 1958 book, *The Japanese Factory: Aspects of Its Social Organization*. This book is said to have been the first to suggest the term 'lifetime employment' (*Shūsin koyō*). During his stay in Japan from 1955 to 1956, Abegglen surveyed the factories of nineteen large companies and thirty-four SMEs. He learned Japanese as a Marine during the Pacific War, participated in the battle of Guam and Iwo Jima, and became associated with Japanese studies when he surveyed Hiroshima as a member of the Strategic Bombing Survey. He then studied field research under social anthropologist Lloyd Warner, and conducted participatory research while working as a machinist in an American factory before coming to Japan.[2] As this background shows, Abegglen was a social anthropologist, not an economist, at the time. His research therefore focused on a subject different from that of an economist: the collective norms of Japanese companies.

Implanted Bureaucracy: The Origins of 'Japanese-style Employment'   123

Presenting the results of his study of the relationship between employees' educational background and their position within the organizational hierarchy, based on 'all managers and supervisor and a ten per cent sample of wage and salary workers in a large manufacturing plant', Abegglen found that 'three groups of workers may be broadly identified': university (four-year term) graduates occupying higher-level staff positions, high school (three-year term) graduates occupying lower-level white-collar staff positions, and blue-collar workers who have only completed junior high school (three-year term, 'middle school' in Abegglen's texts), which marks the end of compulsory education in the post-war Japanese education system.[3] Abegglen describes the three groups, including their family backgrounds, in the following terms.

> There is, first of all, a group of workers recruited from the middle schools of Japan. These workers are usually from rural backgrounds and from lower-status families. They are employed in a particular factory and are trained together for work in that factory, and enter a similar status in the factory as apprentices and unskilled laborers.
>
> At the other extreme in the factory status system is that group of employees who are all graduates of universities and of the same or closely related universities. Whatever their place of origin, all of these employees have spent some years in a large urban center, almost always Tokyo. They enter the firm at the same level, and their identifications and loyalties are to the firm rather than to a particular factory. Their family backgrounds are at least middle class, and they are for the most part the sons of professional people, businessmen, or higher status white-collar workers. In nearly all respects – family background, style of life, life chances, experience, and education – there are few points of contact or mutual attitudes, objectives, or experiences between this group and the first group of employees.
>
> Somewhat intermediate to these two groups are those workers [who] graduated from present-day higher schools, who are from a scattering of localities, often urban, sons and daughters of skilled

workers and lower-level white-collar workers, a more heterogeneous group sharing few of the experiences and characteristics of the extremes.[4]

While Japan is not the only country to have such a three-tier structure, Abegglen's observations captured several characteristics of Japanese companies.

First, Japanese companies do not place an emphasis on professional skills that correspond to particular positions. While each of these three groups required prospective employees to sit a written test, these only involve general knowledge questions.[5]

Second, the three-tier structure found in Japanese companies corresponds almost perfectly to educational background. That said, educational background was a category marker that had no bearing at all on aptitude for a position, and while it should not have been too low, it also should not have been too high. Unskilled laborers were limited to junior high school graduates only, and those with a high school education or more were not recruited for such positions. Even so, according to Abegglen, 'the personnel department [of the firm where he conducted his study] believes that some 20 or 30 of the plant's 3,000 laborers have successfully disguised their higher school backgrounds and are now working as laborers'.[6] In other words, plant laborers had to be junior high school graduates, and if there were high school graduates mixed in with them, it was considered out of order.

Third, recruitment involved a rigorous screening of candidates' personality rather than their aptitude for particular positions, and school recommendations were emphasized as a means to this end.[7] Candidates for higher-level white-collar positions were hired only from five designated universities (namely the University of Tokyo, Kyoto University, Hitotsubashi University, Waseda University and Keio University). The company would first of all obtain recommendations from candidates' professors vouching for their character, and then subject prospective employees to a thorough physical examination to eliminate those suffering from any kind of physical disability, as well as investigate their personal and family backgrounds. At the time Abegglen was writing, large companies did not accept any job

Implanted Bureaucracy: The Origins of 'Japanese-style Employment'   125

applications without an academic reference. Candidates for lower-level white-collar positions were selected from among applicants who had graduated from approximately 100 high schools across Japan, once again through academic and physical examinations. For unskilled laborers, the company requested referrals from public employment security offices throughout the country, and only those entering the workforce after graduating from junior high school were hired on the basis of a written test and interview process. In both cases, prospective employees were initially selected through school referrals.

In principle, workers hired in this way would be employed until retirement, while being transferred from one position to another within the company. As Abegglen writes,

> [...] once employed a worker expects to remain indefinitely in the employ of the firm. He has been selected with some care, and once selected he is a permanent member of the firm until the end of his working career. In this system, once the worker has been selected, the company practically speaking forgoes the right to find the worker incompetent. He was not selected for a particular job or because he had acquired a particular set of skills useful in the operation of the plant. He was selected for the qualities of background, personality, and general ability that may not in fact make him a competent employee. However, should the firm find him useless, it cannot dismiss him but may only move him from job to job within the general category of his employment status until he is placed in a harmless and perhaps not useful position.[8]

An employee's position in a Japanese company is not fixed. Once hired, they will not be let go even if found incapable of fulfilling the position. This is why the selection process is so rigorous. Rather than candidates' aptitude for a position, what this process examines is their 'background, personality, and general ability' as observed by their teachers at school. In other words, in this context, educational background is effectively a 'pre-selection' in the sense of being a referral from a designated school. Accordingly, what matters is not that a candidate has a university degree, but rather which school that degree is from.

Through this selection process, the firm establishes a relationship with its employees. Abegglen described this relationship as 'a lifetime commitment', suggesting a lifelong covenant or abiding love between firm and employee. A variant of this term later gained popular currency as the idea of 'lifetime employment' (*shūshin koyō*), although this term did not feature in Abegglen's own 1958 work.[9] As I will discuss later in Chapter 6, a 1969 report by Nikkeiren (the Japan Federation of Employers' Associations) stated that 'the lifetime employment system is a marriage of love between companies and their employees'.[10] This analogy of 'marriage of love' is a better fit with the nuances of Abegglen's 'lifetime commitment' than the idea of 'lifetime employment'.

Nevertheless, Abegglen did acknowledge that SME employees, temporary workers and female employees were highly mobile and that there was no such thing for these workers as lifetime employment. Abegglen was originally trained as a social anthropologist, not an economist. Pledging eternal love at a wedding may be an act that highlights a society's mores, but it does not mean that divorce is unknown in that society. Thus, it would be better to think of Abegglen's 'lifetime commitment' as a discussion of normative consciousness in the social anthropological sense rather than as an economistic form of employment.

Also, he found the status of women in Japanese companies was extremely low. In the 'large manufacturing plant' that Abegglen studied, there were a large number of women working as low-level clerks with high school diplomas and laborers with junior high school diplomas, but women were not recruited into the university-educated ranks of higher-level staff. As Abegglen notes:

> This problem of job status [of women in companies] is not only a matter of performing jobs at the lowest level of competence or responsibility but also involves less formal reinforcements of differential status [such] as the preparing and serving of tea to male visitors to the office, the running of errands at the request of fellow employees, and the performance of other routine or even

menial tasks [...]. A very great increase in the number of women graduates of colleges and universities has been made possible in the postwar period. The proportion of women seeking careers in business, laboratories, and other professional jobs has gone up sharply. In one company, where the problem of the woman's role was looked at rather closely (a company quite westernized in its general approach to personnel problems), a number of women's college graduates have been hired since the war. They appear, to an outsider at least, to be outspokenly unhappy and even bitter at their position in the company. The company's response to the situation has been to curtail entirely the hiring of women college graduates and to confine its recruitment of female employees to high school and middle school graduates.[11]

The Japanese company as Abegglen saw it in 1955 held some things in common with Japanese companies today, though there are also differences. Commonalities with present-day companies include the fact that positions are undefined, and that professional skills and degrees do not come into question. However, Japanese companies in 1955 were characterized by a strict three-tier structure; there was no 'equality of company employees', which became characteristic of the postwar Japanese-style employment system. In the following sections and chapters, I endeavor to examine how these characteristics had been shaped by 1955 and how they were transformed thereafter.

From disorder to a status-based order

Japan did not have its own tradition of craft unions, like those found in Europe. Although occupational organizations (*kabu-nakama*) did exist in the Edo period, these were not national in scope, but rather existed independently in individual feudal domains where they tended to function as organizations that received instructions from the local lord (*daimyō*).[12] These occupational organizations each had their own apprenticeship system during the Edo period (1603–1867), and they also regulated the wages of craftsmen. However, after the 1868 Meiji Restoration, the new government introduced modernization policies

128   Chapter 3

and ordered the dissolution of the occupational organizations, and in 1872 issued an order stating that wages were to be decided by agreement between employer and employee. The abandonment of the apprenticeship system resulted in a shortage of skilled workers and a decline in the quality of exported goods. Because of that, the Ministry of Agriculture and Commerce legalized trade associations in 1884, and former occupational organizations were revived in various regions in the form of trade associations (*dōgyō Kumiai*). However, when Article 22 of the Constitution of the Empire of Japan in 1889 guaranteed freedom of residence and relocation, the trade associations, which had originally been divided by region, lost their power to control apprentices.[13] Wages for traditional craftsmen remained higher than those for unskilled workers until the early twentieth century, but the occupational organizations had lost their power.

To examine the sort of corporate order that came to be established in Japan given these initial conditions, I would like to look at Shinji Sugayama's study of the records of the state-owned Yahata Steel Works from the Meiji and Taishō (1912–1926) periods. When it was initially founded, long-term employment and hiring of new graduates at the Yahata Steel Works were virtually non-existent. Many of those hired as either factory workers or staff employees had previous work experience, and the standard length of service was one to two years. Management frequently reassigned workers, and even among those who had been hired for skilled positions when they joined the company, more than half were moved into new positions. An underlying factor here, as Sugayama points out, was the fact that the state-of-the-art integrated steelmaking facilities introduced from Germany were far removed from Japan's existing technologies.[14] The existing Japanese craftsmen's skills were not fully useful at the Yahata Steel Works, which led to frequent position changes.

This existing technological isolation gave rise to another characteristic, which was that many of the technicians at the Yahata Steel Works were well educated with previous experience working in government posts.[15] For example, consider the case of one engineer from a former samurai family born in 1870 in Ōita prefecture. After graduating from the government service department of a bookkeeping

Implanted Bureaucracy: The Origins of 'Japanese-style Employment'   129

school (the school's name is not recorded) he was employed in the accounting department of the Hiroshima Court of First Instance. After serving for a year and a half, he resigned his post and went to work for the Shigezumi Mine and Refinery operated by the Mitsubishi Joint-Stock Company in Gifu prefecture before enrolling in Tokyo at the Mining and Metallurgy Department of the Assistant Engineer's School (Kōshu Gakkō, forerunner of the current Kōgakuin University of Technology & Engineering). After graduation, he worked for two more mining companies before joining the mining division of the Hōshū Railway in Kyushu and was subsequently hired by the Yahata Steel Works as an engineer in 1900.

Another example is the case of a man born in 1868 who studied the Chinese classics at a private academy, and who after completing his studies at a private secondary school worked as a schoolteacher at an ordinary elementary school (*jinjō shōgakkō*). He then found a management position in civil engineering with the Fukuoka Prefectural Government, and in 1900 became an engineer at the Yahata Steel Works in 1900 after graduating from a civil engineering course at the Kōshu Gakkō. In this way, more than a few such men became engineers from administrative government positions after completing secondary and higher education courses.

It is also worth noting that of the 158 employees hired by the Yahata Steel Works in 1900, seventy-five (47%) were from former samurai families.[16] The ratio of the population of samurai and their families at the end of the Edo period is estimated to be 7%. This suggests that the samurai, who were the intellectuals of the old order, had a head start when it came to securing knowledge-based positions as clerical staff or engineers. Former samurai who had completed secondary and higher education found government positions and other jobs in the intellectual sphere, regardless of the type of work involved. This was a common career path in the Japanese Meiji period. The protagonist in Sōseki Natsume's 1906 novel *Botchan* (Young Master) also graduated from a private academy where he studied physics before becoming a

130   Chapter 3

secondary school teacher in Shikoku, and then later an engineer on one of the Tokyo streetcar lines.

Nevertheless, the position of the samurai class in Japanese society was swiftly waning. The Yahata Steel Works was also seeing a rapid decline in the proportion of staff from samurai backgrounds. Europe's aristocratic families had owned land, and even afterward had maintained their standing in society on that basis. In contrast, Japanese samurai, long severed from the land, were merely stipendiary vassals who had lived in the castle towns of feudal Japan, a fact that has been cited as the reason for their decline after the abolition of hereditary stipends (*chitsuroku shobun*) by the Meiji government in 1876.[17]

In addition, Japan in the Meiji period had not yet seen the growth of any powerful private industry, and occupational organizations and associations had little influence. Thus, not only did the government enjoy a virtual monopoly over modern education, but the first jobs acquired by those who benefitted from this modern education tended to be government positions. Abstaining from any particularity toward types of jobs, Meiji Japan's *modus operandi* was to employ a small number of individuals with a modern education in a variety of knowledge-based occupations regardless of their family backgrounds. Meanwhile, the practices of long-term employment and the bulk recruitment of new graduates, that would become the new order in twentieth century Japan, were as yet undeveloped.

However, in the midst of this upheaval, a certain order emerged at the Yahata Steel Works. Just as Abegglen would later observe at a Japanese company in 1955, the Yahata Steel Works had a three-tier structure consisting of high-level staff, low-level staff and shop floor workers in keeping with their respective educational backgrounds. This was because the Yahata Steel Works was a state-run factory operated on the basis of the government bureaucracy used in government agencies. Staff officials were divided into higher officials (*kōtōkan*) and lower officials (*hanninkan*), below whom were employees such as security guards, caretakers and factotums, and under these were the factory workers who worked on the shop floor. The most important factor in the appointment of staff officials was their educational

Implanted Bureaucracy: The Origins of 'Japanese-style Employment' 131

background, and those who had graduated from a regular secondary school or higher were considered to be 'staff equivalent'.[18]

According to Osamu Nagashima, who analyzed records from the Yahata Steel Works during its founding period, recruitment criteria by educational background had already been established as early as 1901, and a strict disparity and discrimination in terms of educational background, status and salary had been established as early as 1910.[19] Salaries for staff officials were also determined by their official rank (*kantō* 官等).[20] To understand 'official rank' (*kantō*), I need to explain the bureaucratic system of Meiji Japan.

The bureaucratic ranking system

The Japanese bureaucracy's three-tier structure is still in place today. Shō Kawate, a researcher specializing in Japan's civil service institutions, explains it in the following terms.[21] At the top level are the higher officials commonly referred to as 'career' civil servants. These individuals are promoted rapidly, moving from one department to another roughly every two years. Below this group are those referred to as 'non-career' staff. These officials are transferred within a limited scope and become proficient in fulfilling their duties within that scope. Although often more accomplished than career officials in terms of their practical abilities, they still work under the career officials as assistants, and are limited in terms of their eligibility for promotion. Both types of official are recruited by the so-called 'head office' (*honchō*). Both categories include clerical staff with humanities backgrounds and technical staff with scientific backgrounds. Further down the hierarchy are the local officials responsible for on-site labor. This category includes non-regular staff, who are hired by local branch offices rather than the head office. In this way, career officials, non-career officials and local officials constitute a three-tier pyramidal structure.

These days, such a three-tier structure with regard to the handling of personnel is a customary practice without legal basis. However, until the end of the World War II, these statuses were legally determined. The prewar civil service consisted of higher officials (*kōtōkan* 高等官),

Figure 3.1 The three-tier structure of the pre-war civil service

lower officials (*hanninkan* 判任官) and three types of non-officials (*koin* 雇員, *yōnin* 傭人 and *shokutaku* 嘱託). This was the order in accordance with which the state-owned Yahata Steel Works was organized.

The higher class of civil servants was itself made up of two tiers of civil servant, *chokuninkan* (generals in the armed forces) and *sōninkan* (second lieutenants to colonels in the armed forces), which together with the lower class of *hannin* (non-commissioned officers in the armed forces) officials formed a tripartite division that dates back to 1869. In 1871, these categories were divided into fifteen ranks, with the third rank and above corresponding to *chokunin* officials, the seventh rank and above to *sōnin* officials, and those below seventh rank to *hannin* officials. Although there were subsequent changes and reorganizations, the basic form was established in 1911 and continued until it was abolished in 1949 after the war.

The eligibility of the various official ranks (*kantō* 官等) to serve in official positions was prescribed in detail. Table 3.1 shows a schematic diagram of the relationship between rank and position based on a salary schedule for officials from 1886 (although this relationship could vary somewhat depending on the ministry or agency).[22] Thus, we see that despite the different duties carried out by a captain in the army corps, an assistant professor at an imperial university, and a first-

Implanted Bureaucracy: The Origins of 'Japanese-style Employment' 133

Table 3.1 Correspondences between official rank and positions as of 1886

	Corresponding army rank	Corresponding civil service official	Police	Education	Law	Posts and telecommunications
shinninkan	general	cabinet minister	Minister of Home Affairs	Minister of Education	president of the Supreme Court	Minister of Posts and Telecommunications
chokuninkan first rank	lieutenant-general	prefectural governor, minister/vice-minister/director-general of various ministries	police superintendent-general	president of an imperial university	president of the Court of Appeals	vice-minister
chokuninkan second rank	major-general	same as above (depends on the ministry/agency)	same as above	principal of a higher normal school	chief prosecutor of the Supreme Court	director-general of internal affairs and communications bureau
sōninkan first rank	colonel	*shokikan* (equivalent to chief in central bureaucracy)	vice police superintendent-general	president of a branch university of an imperial university (equivalent to a dean)	president of the Court of First Instance	director-general of postal service bureau
sōninkan second rank	lieutenant-colonel	same as above (depends on the ministry/agency)	first-class police superintendent	professor at an imperial university	judge/prosecutor of the Supreme Court	
sōninkan third rank	major		second-class police superintendent / police medical chief	same as above	judge/prosecutor of Court of Appeals	director-general of telecommunications management bureau
sōninkan fourth rank	captain		third-class police superintendent	assistant professor at an imperial university	judge/prosecutor of the Court of First Instance	Master of first-class post office
sōninkan fifth rank	lieutenant		fourth-class police superintendent	principal of secondary school	same as above	
sōninkan sixth rank	second lieutenant		fifth-class police superintendent			
associates *sōnin*		probationer			probationer	
hanninkan first rank	warrant officer		inspector	principal of an elementary school	assistant judge/prosecutor	Master of second or third-class post office
hanninkan second rank	sergeant major					
hanninkan third rank	first sergeant			teacher		
hanninkan fourth rank	second sergeant			assistant teacher	chief prison warden	
non-ranking	private soldier	*koin (yatoi)*	police officer		prison warden	

Note: There was some range in the correspondence between rank and position in practice.
Source: Prepared by the author based on Cabinet Records Bureau ([1894] 1979: 57–64).

class postmaster, they held in common a status and basic salary grade corresponding to a *sōnin* official of the fourth rank.

The highest-ranking higher official was the *shinninkan* (親任官 officials appointed directly by the emperor), a rank appointed in an investiture ceremony conducted by the emperor himself. In the case of military officials, *shinnin* officials corresponded to army generals and navy admirals, and to the prime minister or cabinet ministers in civilian contexts. Below *shinnin* officials were the *chokuninkan* (勅任官), who were appointed by imperial decree. *Chokunin* officials of the first and second rank corresponded respectively to lieutenant-generals (or vice admirals) and major-generals (rear admirals), while civil service officials held positions such as vice-ministers and directors-general of various ministries, presidents of the imperial universities, inspectors-general of police and prefectural governors (prewar Japanese governors were not elected, but were officials dispatched by the Ministry of Home Affairs).

Below these were the *sōninkan* (奏任官 officials appointed by emperor's approval) who were appointed by recommendation with the emperor's approval. For a military officer, being a *sōnin* official of the first rank corresponded to ranking as a colonel in the army (or the captain of a heavy cruiser in the navy), while a civil service official would have held a position equivalent to that of a section chief in today's ministries of central bureaucracy.

Higher officials were an exclusive elite, the equivalent of today's Japanese 'career' officials. In the army or navy, they would have been graduates of the imperial Japanese military or naval academies, while civil service officials were graduates of the imperial university system who had passed the Higher Examination for Civil Officials (*bunkan kōtō shiken*). Higher officials on the elite track (the so-called '*kōbungumi*') who had passed the Higher Examination for Civil Officials, were promoted extremely quickly. After passing the examination and joining a ministry, such individuals would rise through the official ranks while being transferred to different departments every two years or so, and after about ten years of ministry service would have attained the section chief-level position of secretary (*shokikan*, classed as a *sōnin* official of the first rank, equivalent to a colonel's commission in the

Implanted Bureaucracy: The Origins of 'Japanese-style Employment' 135

army).[23] According to a study by political scientist Mitsuhiro Mizutani, in the case of the Ministry of Home Affairs, about half of the elite-track officials who entered the ministry by the 1920s were eventually promoted to the position of *chokunin* officials.[24]

In contrast, the lower class of *hannin* officials, who were subordinate to the higher officials and who would be called 'non-career' officials in today's parlance, were the equivalent of non-commissioned officers in the prewar military. *Hannin* officials in the civil service were those who carried out the practical work of bureaucracy, such as clerical staff and low-level engineers. Although highly qualified and experienced *hannin* officials were sometimes accorded the status of *sōnin* officials of lower rank, they generally remained with the same bureaus or departments in which they had served previously.[25] The non-ranking *koin* and *yōnin* employees were not civil servant (*kanri*), but rather a kind of non-regular official.[26] In some cases, *koin* could be appointed as *hannin* officials after a certain term of service, but their eligibility for advancement to higher ranks was limited.[27]

Whereas *sōnin* officials were promoted rapidly through the official ranks, with commensurate raises in salary, *hannin* officials reached a ceiling after a certain point in terms of both promotion and salary. By promoting according to years of service, the salaries of the *sōnin* officials depicted a seniority-based wage profile with a high peak, while those of the clan appointees depicted one with a low peak.[28] Among *koin* and *yōnin* employees, there were no clear rules for pay increases, and salaries were more or less constant. These three wage profile curves are roughly similar to those of regular employees of large companies, regular employees of SMEs and non-regular workers in today's Japan.

This official system of government organization encompassed the whole of society during the prewar period. It was moreover something that people were well acquainted with, since it was also applied to the state-run sector that included schools, policing, local municipal offices, railroads and state-owned factories. Many men were also enrolled into this system through their military experience as conscripts. As we shall see, this system, in which salaries are determined not by position

136   Chapter 3

but by rank within the organization, represents the origin of Japanese-style employment.

Salary as rank-based pay

Civil servants were conferred with their status by the emperor. Article 10 of the Constitution of the Empire of Japan stipulated that the emperor would appoint civil officials and military officers and set their salaries, which were determined by imperial decrees such as the Imperial Service Regulations (*kanri fukumu kiritsu*), the Edict on Rank and Salaries for Higher Civil Officials (*kōtōkan kantō hōkyū-rei*), the Edict on Rank and Salaries for Lower Civil Officials (*hanninkan kantō hōkyū-rei*) and the Edict on the Appointment of Civil Officials (*bunkan nin'yō-rei*). Higher-ranking civil servants received higher salaries, so there were considerable disparities. According to a salary schedule from 1886, whereas cabinet ministers, army generals and navy admirals received annual salaries of 6,000 yen, the remuneration of *hannin* officials of the tenth rank (e.g., police lieutenants and assistant prison wardens) amounted to only 12 yen per month (Table 3.2).[29]

From the perspective of the private sector, this was an exceptional salary. According to the third edition of the Statistical Yearbook of the Empire of Japan, the average daily wage for male day laborers in 1882 was 0.22 yen, for a total of only 5.9 yen for twenty-seven days of work per month. The daily wage for female spinning hands in textile factories was even lower, at 0.16 yen, or 4.3 yen for twenty-seven days. As described by Hiroaki Inatsugu, in that year *chokunin* officials earned in one month what a day laborer would earn in six years.[30] Even lower civil officials, who earned a monthly salary, also enjoyed the privilege of a more stable income than workers in the private sector who had to earn daily wages. A memoir by Sadakichi Kita, a historian born in 1871, describes his life in the 1880s as follows.

> Monthly salary earners (*gekkyūtori*) in the time of my secondary school days were very prestigious. Even when they were absent due to illness, even on Sundays, and even during the summer vacation, they received a fixed salary. They had incomes that

Implanted Bureaucracy: The Origins of 'Japanese-style Employment'   137

Table 3.2 The Japanese government salary schedule (1886)

		Annual salaries for *kōtōkan*				Monthly salaries for *hanninkan*			Monthly salaries for technical *hanninkan*		
Salary schedule	*chokuninkan*	Prime minister 9,600 yen	Cabinet ministers 6,000 yen		1st rank	higher	lower	1st rank	higher	middle	lower
		1st rank	higher 5,000 yen	lower 4,500 yen		75 yen	60 yen		80 yen	70 yen	60 yen
					2nd rank	50 yen		2nd rank	70 yen	60 yen	50 yen
		2nd rank 4,000 yen	3,500 yen		3rd rank	45 yen		3rd rank	55 yen	50 yen	45 yen
	sōninkan	1st rank	higher 3,000 yen	middle 2,800 yen	lower 2,600 yen	4th rank	40 yen		4th rank	50 yen	45 yen	40 yen
		2nd rank	2,400 yen	2,200 yen	2,000 yen	5th rank	35 yen	5th rank	45 yen	40 yen	35 yen
		3rd rank	1,800 yen	1,600 yen	1,400 yen	6th rank	30 yen	6th rank	40 yen	35 yen	30 yen
		4th rank	1,200 yen	1,100 yen	1,000 yen	7th rank	25 yen	7th rank	35 yen	30 yen	25 yen
		5th rank	900 yen	800 yen	700 yen	8th rank	20 yen	8th rank	30 yen	25 yen	20 yen
		6th rank	600 yen	500 yen	400 yen	9th rank	15 yen	9th rank	25 yen	20 yen	15 yen
						10th rank	12 yen	10th rank	18 yen	15 yen	12 yen

Source: Cabinet Records Bureau ([1894] 1979: 64).

could not be compared to those of daily laborers or farmers, were respected by the public and were the envy of the masses.[31]

Education played an important role in the recruitment of such civil servants. The military had training institutions in the form of the imperial Japanese military and naval academies, but the equivalent for the civil service were educational institutions approved by the Minister of Education. As will be discussed in Chapter 4, the civil service probationary examination (*bunkan shiho shiken*) was introduced in 1887 for the recruitment of higher officials, but graduates of the Imperial University Law School and College of Letters were exempted from sitting it. Although this exemption was abolished in 1893 with the introduction of the Higher Examination for Civil Officials (colloquially referred to as *Kōbun* 高文), those who had completed a course of higher education approved by the Minister of Education were still exempted from the preliminary examination. Lower-ranking *hannin* officials were appointed through the Ordinary Civil Service Examination (*futsū bunkan shiken*), but graduates of secondary education institutions approved by the Minister of Education were exempted from taking it. It thus became customary for graduates of institutes of higher education to become higher officials, and for graduates of secondary educational

138   Chapter 3

institutions to become *hannin* officials. As a result, differences in education translated into difference in rank, which in turn were expressed as differences in salary. Sadakichi Kita recalls his secondary school days in the 1880s as follows.

> At the lowest grade, I must first count elementary school teachers. In those days, the starting salary for a normal school graduate in Tokushima prefecture was 6 yen per month.... For secondary school teachers, this was usually 15 to 30 yen per month. There, a certain graduate of Imperial University's Faculty of Law was paid 60 yen a month as principal, and a certain teacher who had been to a higher normal school was paid 40 yen a month as vice principal. In those days, one could live on a monthly stipend of 1 yen and 50 *sen*, which meant that the former could have supported 40 people and the latter 36 or 37. The salary for a prefectural governor was even more impressive at 250 yen a month! [...] The respect accorded to high earners by the public was also remarkable, and their power and influence were likewise considerable.[32]

Comparing the salaries cited by Kita with the 1886 salary schedule, it seems that the vice principal of a secondary school who had graduated from a higher normal school was a *sōnin* official of the sixth rank (equivalent to a second lieutenant in the army), that a university-educated principal was a *sōnin* official of the fifth rank (equivalent to a lieutenant) and that a prefectural governor was a *chokunin* official of the second rank (equivalent to a major general). Supposing that the 6 yen earned each month by an elementary school teacher who graduated from a normal school would be the equivalent of a monthly salary of 5,000 USD today, the monthly salary of a school principal would be the equivalent of 50,000 USD while that of a prefectural governor would be 200,000 USD.

According to the recollections of Nobuaki Makino, a politician who became governor of Fukui prefecture in 1892, local citizens would drop to their knees to greet the governor. He recalled, 'when I walked through the residential areas of Yamanote in Tokyo, most of the prominent residences belonged to government officials'.[33] Although this

Implanted Bureaucracy: The Origins of 'Japanese-style Employment'

situation would change during and after World War I with the rise of private industry, civil servants in the Meiji period still enjoyed considerable prestige.

In this context, then, salaries in the public service sector, where the emphasis was on academic credentials, exerted a strong influence on society.

The principle of 'assignment after appointment'

This circumstance stoked fierce academic competition, which I will not go into here. What is important is that the salaries of civil servants were determined by rank, rather than being wages determined by a particular position. Civil servants were characterized by the lifetime security they enjoyed in return for their limitless loyalty to the emperor and government. In other words, civil servants had a 'duty of faithful and limitless service to the emperor and his government in accordance with their status', and their 'salaries were regarded as appropriate to maintain their status and appearance as civil servants'.[34] In other words, these men were promised lifetime security in exchange for their 'lifetime commitment' to the state.

Government officials did not have set working hours, as work with no fixed hours was the general rule. In the early Meiji period, the bureaucracy's working hours were extremely short. Although regulations concerning office hours existed for government ministries and agencies, the actual working day stipulated in regulations from 1869 was only three hours long, with arrival at the office at 10:00 a.m., departure at 2:00 p.m., and a one-hour lunch break.[35] This changed to 9:00 a.m. to 3:00 p.m. in 1871 and 9:00 a.m. to 5:00 p.m. in 1886. Nevertheless, the practice of working only during the morning in the summer persisted until the 1930s. In addition, in reality, while the *hannin* officials who dealt with practical tasks arrived at the office on time, it was customary for higher officials to arrive at the office at 10:00 a.m. Since they were unable to work until the higher officials to whom they reported arrived at the office, the *hannin* officials who arrived on time often 'passed the time reading the newspapers and chatting'.[36]

After their retirement, civil servants were also awarded a pension from the state budget as lifetime security. Since this pension benefit was linked to the official rank they had attained, high-ranking military officers and civil servants were able to maintain a dignified lifestyle even in retirement. The higher one's official rank, the shorter the hours one had to work, the higher the salary and the bigger the pension. In a certain sense, this runs counter to the principles of economics.

Civil servants and military officers were not, however, engaged in economic activities. Their salaries were determined not on the basis of how much economic profit they generated, but on the basis of their ability to maintain a status and appearance commensurate with their status. Because this was the case, their salaries were not compensation for the position they held but were rather basically determined by their official rank. As we have already seen, salaries were determined by the official rank on the civil servants' salary schedule. What was important was their official rank; position was secondary.

Thus, an army lieutenant-general, a prefectural governor, the police superintendent-general and an imperial university president all basically received the salary of a *chokunin* official of the first rank, despite their respectively differing positions. The military offers a classic example of this principle. A rear admiral in the navy might plan a strategy at fleet command or serve as the captain of a battleship. They might have their own area of specialty, but they can assume a variety of positions at the discretion of the top brass. Nevertheless, their basic salary will be determined by their rank as a rear admiral.[37] This principle is known as 'assignment after appointment' (*ninkan hoshoku*).[38] In other words, officials were first of all appointed (*ninkan* 任官), and only then assigned to a position (*hoshoku* 補職).

Even today, salaries for Japanese public servants are determined by a combination of official rank (salary class) and position (level). Of these, salary classes (*gōhō*) represent competence ranks determined by years of service, among other factors, while level (*kyū*) refers to official position such as section manager, subsection manager or head clerk. In the military, the former could be said to correspond to an officer's rank (e.g., major general) and the latter to their duties (e.g.,

Implanted Bureaucracy: The Origins of 'Japanese-style Employment'   **141**

being captain of a ship). A public servant's remuneration is the total of this salary and various other allowances.

This principle itself, however, is typical of military organizations in any country. The continental career-based bureaucracies of Germany and France, on which that of Japan was modeled, also use a two-tier system of pay grades and positions.[39] In this sense, then, this system is not all that unusual in a military or bureaucratic context.

If we were to single out one component that was unique Japan, it would be the fact that this system was positioned as an extension of ranks that could be traced back to the Ritsuryō system of the eighth century.[40] The Grand Council of State (Dajōkan) system of the early Meiji period made use of ranks derived from those of the Ritsuryō system, such as *shō ni-i* (正二位 senior second rank) and *ju san-mi* (従三位 junior third rank).[41] Although these were abolished in 1871, they were reorganized as ranks of decoration in the Regulations for Investiture (*joi jōrei*) in 1877, after which it became customary to confer decorations in conjunction with official ranks attained through promotions. Official ranks were thus more than just a salary grade; they also had the sense of conferring status.

Another characteristic of the Japanese bureaucracy is that officials do not move across ministries. In the French bureaucracy, officials belong to professional groups called *corps* and they each have a rank (*classe*) within their *corps* and receive salary according to their rank, and move across ministries in the same *corps*. They are selected through an examination for each *corps* and are then hired by a government ministry, and they retain their rank even if they lose their ministry positions.[42] This form of mobility and career development is similar to Kerr's 'guild system' discussed in Chapter 2. In the German bureaucracy, too, there are career tracks called *Laufbahn* based on professional categories.[43] In the Japanese bureaucracy, however, officials are selected through a national standardized examination and then hired by a ministry, and they lose their rank if they lose their ministry position.[44] They rotate among various professional positions within the particular ministry where they were hired, but they do not move across ministries like Kerr's 'manorial system.' This is prob-

142   Chapter 3

ably due to the lack of a tradition of occupational organizations in modern Japan.

One further characteristic of Japan is the influence of this military and bureaucratic system on the private sector. As I will discuss later, in Japanese companies, just as in the bureaucracy, a qualification scheme developed in which salaries were determined by rank.

A pyramidal structure

The government's organizational structure was a pyramid, with only a few individuals at its summit. According to the fifty-fourth Statistical Yearbook of the Empire of Japan, the civil service in 1935 consisted of 1,609 *chokunin* officials, 13,985 *sōnin* officials and 120,098 *hannin* officials. In contrast, the government employed 358,880 *koin* as non-regular workers, who made up 73.6% of all civil officials. Although higher officials (*chokunin* and *sōnin* officials) made up only 3.1% of the total number of government employees, they accounted for 12.7% of the total payroll.[45]

The prewar *koin*, *yōnin* and *shokutaku* employees were non-regular workers hired directly by local government agencies.[46] Generally speaking, *koin* were clerical workers who assisted civil servants, *yōnin* were manual laborers who performed tasks on site as required by the public service, and *shokutaku* were hired to compensate for temporary capacity shortages on the part of the full-time civil servants.[47] While the status of higher officials and *hannin* officials was stipulated in the Edict on the Appointment of Civil Officials, employees classed as *koin, yōnin* and *shokutaku* were simply employed to government agencies under private legal contracts, and were hired and fired as dictated by increases or decreases in the bureaucratic workload. There was no uniform standard for salaries, with each ministry or agency paying wages according to its own internal regulations as its budget permitted.[48] As clerical employees, *koin* and *shokutaku* often served in positions that resembled those fulfilled by the lower-ranking *hannin* officials or younger higher officials. However, the discriminatory treatment that prevailed in the bureaucracy at that time was blatant: cafeterias and wastebaskets were labeled 'For use by higher officials

Implanted Bureaucracy: The Origins of 'Japanese-style Employment' 143

only', and the desks of higher officials were covered with green fabric. Although restrooms still only had a single entrance, they were divided beyond that into compartments for the exclusive use of higher officials on one side, and everyone else on the other, so that bathrooms were colloquially referred to as '*zubon*' (trousers).[49]

In the context of this book, the important thing here is that this order of official rank spilled over into the private economic sphere. This spillover first began at state-owned factories. At the Yokosuka Shipyard, which was under the jurisdiction of the Naval Department, the Dajōkan (Grand Council of State) issued an ordinance in 1877 classifying *sōnin* officials of the fourth to sixth rank and *hannin* officials of the first to seventeenth rank as technical officers (*gikan*), and everyone else as assistant engineers (*kōshu*).[50] As we have already seen, the government-run Yahata Steel Works had a hierarchical structure based on official ranks from its earliest establishment. In 1921, the workforce at the Yahata Steel Works consisted of 1,745 staff officials (*shokuin*) and 18,249 factory workers (*shokkō*). The former group was characterized by a hierarchy of 101 higher officials and 303 *hannin* officials, as well as 1,341 *koin* and *yōnin*. Below these, factory workers were either main workers, who were employed on a long-term basis, or temporary and probationary workers, who were hired on a short-term or trial basis. The most important factor in the appointment of staff was their educational background, and those who had graduated from a regular secondary school or higher were considered to be 'staff equivalents'.[51]

This system was similar at other SOEs. For example, even with the state-owned railways (Japanese Government Railways, the predecessor of Japanese National Railways), an order based on official ranks was introduced in 1885 with the adoption of a bureaucratic system for the Railway Bureau (*tetsudō-kyoku*). A local stationmaster was deemed to be a position for *hannin* officials, on the same level as an elementary school principal or a second- or third-class post office-master.[52] This rank-based hierarchy was also incorporated into state-owned factories in terms of working hours. In shipyards and ordnance factories operated under the Ministry of the Navy, bureau officers (*kan'in*) worked a four-hour shift from 8:00 a.m. to 12:00 p.m., while the shopworkers on the

144   Chapter 3

factory floor (*shokunin*) worked a ten-hour shift from 6:00 a.m. to 4:00 p.m.[53]

In the Meiji period, companies and factories were still experimenting with the development of a modern order that had yet to be firmly established. This confused situation would be given structure by the adoption of the bureaucratic system, like a catalyst bringing instant solidity to a pharmaceutical compound.

The implanting of the bureaucratic system into private industry

By the late Meiji period, the three-tier structure consisting of higher officials, lower officials and shop-floor workers had begun to appear not only in SOEs but in private industry, where these three tiers of status were sometimes collectively referred to as company employees (*shain* 社員), associate company employees (*jun-shain* 准社員) and factory workers (*shokkō* 職工).[54]

For example, from March 1919, the Mitsubishi industrial conglomerate (*zaibatsu*) divided its staff employees into regular company employees (*seiin*) and associates (*jun'in*). Regular company employees corresponded to those who had completed higher education and were employed at the head office of the Mitsubishi Joint-Stock Company. Prior to 1919, they had been referred to simply as head office employees (*honsha shiyōnin*).[55] On the other hand, 'associate' was a qualification corresponding to those who had completed secondary education, and referred to lower-ranking staffs such as draftsmen, electricians, accountants and general clerks, who prior to 1919 had been called site-limited employees (*bashogen yōnin*) because they were hired locally at each worksite.[56] Needless to say, there would also have been on-site manual factory workers working under these staff employees.

Salaries at Mitsubishi were determined in accordance with titles (*yakumei*) and ranks (*tōkyū*) that bore no relation to specific positions. Table 3.3 reproduces the rank schedule in Mitsubishi's 'In-House Rules for Employee Promotion' (*shiyōnin shinkyū naiki*), which went into effect in January 1917. As will be immediately obvious, this is very similar to the bureaucratic salary schedule seen earlier. Titles are

Implanted Bureaucracy: The Origins of 'Japanese-style Employment'   145

Table 3.3 Mitsubishi salary schedule (1917)

Ranks / Titles	Kanji	Riji	Sanji	Shuji	Jimu/Gishi	Jimu ho/Gishi ho
1st	800	600	500	400	300	150
2nd	700	500	450	360	280	140
3rd	600	400	400	330	260	130
4th	500		350	300	240	120
5th			300	275	220	110
6th			260	250	200	100
7th			230	225	190	90
8th			200	220	180	85
9th				175	170	80
10th				150	160	75
11th				135	150	70
12th				120	140	65
13th					130	60
14th					120	55
15th					110	50
16th					100	45
17th					90	40
18th					85	36
19th					80	32
20th					75	28
21st					70	25
22nd					65	22
23rd					60	20
24th					55	
25th					50	

Source: Mitsubishi Company History Publication Society (ed.) (1979–1982: vol. 23, 3189).

equivalent to the classification of *chokunin*, *sōnin* and *hannin* officials in government offices, which were divided into the categories of administrator (*kanji*), director (*riji*), councilor (*sanji*), manager (*shuji*), clerk/technician (*jimu/gishi*) and clerical/technical assistant (*jimu ho/gishi ho*), each of which is assigned a series of ranks.[57]

As history was to show, this system would also be inherited by Japan's large corporations after World War II. Table 3.4, which shows the qualification scheme introduced in a 1978 report by a personnel management employee of Konishiroku Photo Industry (later Konica), has an almost identical format. We can clearly see the adoption of

Table 3.4 Konishiroku (Konica) qualification scheme

Specific ranks	Official positions	Qualification ranks		
		Range of ranks by official position	Rank	Starting rank
	Director (*buchō*)	Advisor (*sanyo*)	Advisor	
	Deputy director (Equivalent position)	Deputy councilor (*fuku sanji*)	councilor	
			Deputy councilor	
	Section manager	Councilor (*sanji*)	Manager	
Rank	Deputy section manager (Equivalent position)	Assistant manager (*shuji ho*)	Assistant manager	
11	Subsection manager (Equivalent position)	Deputy councilor	Supervisor	
10		Assistant supervisor (*shukan ho*)	Assistant supervisor	
9	Group leader	Manager (*shuji*)	Competent (*shumu*)	
8	Acting group leader (Equivalent position)	1st class company employee		
7			1st class company employee	University graduate class A or above
6	General staff	Assistant manager .	2nd class company employee	University graduate B Junior college graduate A
5		4th class company employee	3rd class company employee	Junior college graduate B high school graduate
4			4th class company employee	Junior high school graduate

Source: Imazawa (1978: 101).

the principle of assignment after appointment, in which positions exist separately from titles and ranks. Starting rank upon entering the company differs depending on whether the employee is a university, high school or junior high school graduate, as well as according to the status of the university attended.

In the postwar period, as will be discussed in Chapter 6, this practice was referred to as a competence ranking system (*shokunō shikaku seido*). The heading 'Range of Ranks by Official Position' on the Konishiroku schedule refers to the range of ranks appropriate to each official position, in the same way that the commander of a regiment corresponds to a colonel, the commander of a company to a captain, and so on. Postwar businessmen themselves understood such a ranking system in terms of the military metaphor. For example,

Implanted Bureaucracy: The Origins of 'Japanese-style Employment'   147

as Takeo Naruse (born 1933), the executive director of Nikkeiren (the Japan Federation of Employers' Associations) since 1988, stated in 2010:

> A soldier's pay is determined by his rank, not by the operation to which he is currently assigned. That's what competence rank (*shokunō shikaku*) is, and that [rank] is what determines pay. [...] Though they are both warship captains, the captain of a destroyer and the captain of a battleship or aircraft carrier have different competence ranks. On a submarine or destroyer, you could be a sub-lieutenant 1st or even 2nd class, but on the Yamato [a large battleship in commission during the Pacific War], you had to be an admiral or the Admiral of the Fleet.[58]

In the context of private industry, societies in which separate in-house ranks exist broadly independently of positions or industry level professional qualifications are unknown. Ronald Dore, who studied English Electric in the UK and Hitachi in Japan, stated as follows:

> English Electric does not have a distinction between ranks (e.g., 'captain') and functions (e.g., 'company commander'). All titles [such as section manager or foreman] refer to functions. Hitachi does make such a distinction. It is possible, therefore, for promotion systems to provide for a regular progression through ranks without necessarily involving a succession of functions. [59]

Dore also discusses the psychological effects of this Japanese-style system. Even in the UK, soldiers undergo intelligence tests and a physical examination to enter the military, and receive training in their unit after enlistment. It is not the case that they learn military skills through training in civilian jobs and are then recruited by the military. Thus, the soldier's 'primary identification [is] with the corps rather than the trade'. In the UK, as well, there was a sense of camaraderie and familism in the military, and there was a tendency to accord greater respect to those with a greater length of service. In Dore's view,

148   Chapter 3

it is a mistake to say that Japanese-style management is a product of Japanese culture.

> Hitachi's form of organization is by no means foreign to Britain. It is very much the pattern of the British army or civil service. Japan's peculiarity lies in the fact that a type of organization which in most Western countries is considered suitable only for the army or the bureaucracy is adapted in Japan to industry.[60]

Although Dore did not delve into the history of Japanese companies and the bureaucracy, but merely noted the similarities between the two as a matter of impression, his intuition seems to have been correct.

An order based on seniority and educational background

So how were promotions determined in this type of ranking system? As an example, let us look at the Promotion Selection Criteria Table (*shōkaku senkō kijun-hyō*) used in the prewar period by Ishikawajima Heavy Industries (Ishikawajima Dockyard until 1945, Ishikawajima-Harima Heavy Industries after 1960). This chart was published in a Nikkeiren publication in 1960 by the then deputy director of the Ishikawajima Labor Department (*kinrō-bu*) (Table 3.5-7). As explained by the Labor Department's deputy director, these 'old rules' were applied until they were revised in 1948 as a result of the postwar labor movement's demands to eliminate discrimination. In other words, although this table is from the 1940s, it represents a good source for assessing the situation in the prewar period. From this, we can see that promotion was closely regulated according to educational background and years of service.

To understand Ishikawajima's tables, let me explain the prewar Japanese education system. Although details of the system had changed over time, it can generally be understood as follows. First there was a compulsory six-year elementary school (four years until 1906), and then a two-year higher elementary school. After graduation from elementary school, those who wished to go on to higher education

Table 3.5 Ishikawajima Heavy Industries Promotion Selection Criteria Table (1)

Rank/title applied for	Length of service	Age of applicant	Education level	Calculated from 1 December 1948	Length of service	Age of applicant	Education level	Calculated from 1948 (proposal)
yōkoin		16	Higher elementary school	prior to 1947		16	Higher elementary school	prior to 1947
		16	Elementary school	prior to 1945		16	Postwar junior high school	prior to 1948
Associate company employee (*jun-shain*)	2 years or more	25	Semi-professional school or higher	prior to 1945	2 years or more	25	Officials' vocational school or higher	prior to 1945
	3 years or more	25	Class A vocational school	prior to 1942	3 years or more	25	Class A vocational school	prior to 1942
	4 years or more	27	Class B vocational school		4 years or more	27	Class B vocational school	
	5 years or more	30	Higher elementary school		5 years or more	30	Higher elementary school	
Company employee (*shain*)	2 years or more as *jun-shain*	26	Private professional school or higher	prior to 1943	2 years or more as *jun-shain*	25	Vocational school	prior to 1946
		28	Semi-professional school/Night professional school	prior to 1942		28	Officials' vocational school	prior to 1942
	3 years or more as *jun-shain*	29	Class A vocational school	prior to 1937	3 years or more as *jun-shain*	29	Class A vocational school	prior to 1937
		31	Class B vocational school			31	Class B vocational school	
	5 years or more as *jun-shain*	35	Higher elementary school		5 years or more as *jun-shain*	35	Higher elementary school	
Assistant manager (*Shuji ho*)	3 years or more	32	Imperial university	prior to 1941	3 years or more	33	University	prior to 1940
		33	Class A private university	prior to 1940				
		34	Class B private university	prior to 1939				
	4 years or more	35	Imperial professional school	prior to 1937				
	5 years or more	37	Private professional school	prior to 1935	5 years or more	36	Vocational school	prior to 1936
		37	Semi-professional school	prior to 1932		37	Officials' vocational school	prior to 1932
	6 years or more	38	Class A vocational school	prior to 1929	6 years or more	38	Class A vocational school	prior to 1929
		41	Class B vocational school			41	Class B vocational school	
	7 years or more	45	Higher elementary school		7 years or more	45	Higher elementary school	

Source: Ōbori (1960: 121).

entered a five-year secondary school through an entrance examination, then a three-year high school through a further entrance examination, and finally a three-year university. As will be described in Chapter 5, imperial universities were established first and had a higher prestige than private universities.

However, in 1940, the percentage of students who went on to secondary school for elementary school graduates was only 7%. Others, if they sought education beyond compulsory education, went on to vocational schools. These were divided into Class A and B according to the length of study, with the A type being three or four years and the B type being within three years. Furthermore, those who did not go on to a high school and university after graduating from secondary school went on to a three-year professional school (single-department college) or a two-year semi-professional school. Since men and women were separated in secondary school and above, higher schools for girls were provided for women. Those who went on to all these institutions beyond compulsory education accounted for 25% of all elementary school graduates in 1940.[61] Post-World War II educational reforms abolished these systems, making six-year elementary schools and three-year junior high schools compulsory, with three-year high schools responsible for secondary education and four-year universities for higher education.

At Ishikawajima Heavy Industries, the lowest in-house rank was 'hired hand' (*yōkoin*, which was a combined term from *yōnin* and *koin*), a rating that was open to anyone who had completed elementary or higher elementary schooling and was at least sixteen years of age. If we calculate from 1 December 1948, which was the date this system was abolished, then anyone who graduated from elementary school prior to 1945 or from a higher elementary school prior to 1947 was eligible to apply.

The next rank was associate company employee (*jun-shain*). Those with only an elementary school education would not advance to this level. Those who had graduated from a higher elementary school and had at least five years of service as a hired hand could apply for promotion, but only from the age of thirty. However, those with a semi-professional school education or higher were eligible for promotion

Implanted Bureaucracy: The Origins of 'Japanese-style Employment'   151

after only two years. Having graduated from a Class A vocational school meant that one could apply after three years of service, and from a Class B vocational school after four years of service. Furthermore, those with a university education were eligible to become company employees (*shain*) after one year of apprenticeship without having to serve any length of time as an associate. From there, promotion was differentiated by type of post-secondary education (e.g., imperial university, Class A private university, Class B private university, or imperial professional school) (Table 3.6).

At Ishikawajima Heavy Industries, education and length of service cast their shadow even in the world of the non-elite. To be promoted to the rank of 'female associate company employee' (*joshi jun-shain*), a woman who had graduated from a five-year higher school for girls (the equivalent of a secondary school for boys) had to have accrued seven years of service as a hired hand, while a graduate of a higher elementary school had to have ten years of service. In domains where educational background was not at issue, eight years of service as a patrolman was required to become a guard, and three years of service as an assistant foreman was required to become a foreman (Table 3.7). The rank of 'foreman' (*shokuchō*) was for the supervisor of factory workers on the worksite. The chart makes no mention of the factory workers who were at an even lower level. According to the Labor Department's deputy director of Ishikawajima, the distinction between 'first-class workman' and 'second-class workman' (likely modeled on 'first-class soldier' and 'second-class soldier' in the imperial army) was made only for convenience.[62]

One line of thinking holds that the reason private universities were ranked lower than imperial universities (e.g., in terms of starting salaries) was that prior to the Universities Edict of 1918, the length of a course of study at the former was shorter than at the latter.[63] Some studies also point out that large manufacturers tended to place more weight on academic background than other enterprises, such as department stores and wholesalers.[64] Seen in this light, the case of Ishikawajima Heavy Industries cannot be used as a wholly representative example. Nor, of course, can it be used to discuss Japanese companies in the postwar era.

Table 3.6 Ishikawajima Heavy Industries Promotion Selection Criteria Table (2)

Rank/title applied for	Length of service	Age of applicant	Education level	Calculated from 1 December 1948	Length of service	Age of applicant	Education level	Calculated from 1948 (proposal)
Manager (*shuji*)		35	Imperial university	prior to 1938	3 years or more as assistant *shuji*			prior to 1937
	3 years or more as assistant *shuji*	36	Class A private university	prior to 1937		36	University	
		38	Class B private university	prior to 1936				
	4 years or more as assistant *shuji*	37	Imperial professional school	prior to 1933	4 years or more as assistant shuji	40	Professional school	prior to 1932
	5 years or more as assistant *shuji*	40	Private professional school	prior to 1930	5 years or more as assistant *shuji*			
	6 years or more as assistant *shuji*	44	Semi-professional school			44	Semi-professional school	
		44	Class A vocational school	prior to 1922	6 years or more as assistant *shuji*	44	Class A vocational school	
	7 years or more as assistant *shuji*	48	Class B vocational school		7 years or more as assistant *shuji*	48	Class B vocational school	
Councilor (*sanji*)		41	Imperial university	prior to 1932		42	University	prior to 1931
	6 years or more as *shuji*	42	Class A private university	prior to 1931	6 years or more as *shuji*			
		43	Class B private university	prior to 1930				
		43	Imperial professional school	prior to 1927				
		47	Private professional school	prior to 1923		47	Professional school	prior to 1925
		52	Semi-professional school			52	Semi-professional school	
	7 years or more as *shuji*	52	Class A vocational school	prior to 1924	7 years or more as *shuji*	52	Class A vocational school	prior to 1924
		56	Class B vocational school or lower			56	Class B vocational school or lower	
Director (*riji*)		47	Imperial university	prior to 1926	6 years or more as *shuji*	50	University	prior to 1923
	5 years or more as *shuji*	50	Class A private university	prior to 1923				
		51	Class B private university	prior to 1922				
		51	Imperial professional school	prior to 1919				
	7 years or more as *shuji*	56	Private professional school	prior to 1914	6 years or more as *shuji*	55	Professional school	prior to 1915
	9 years or more as *sanji*	60	Semi-professional or lower	same as above	9 years or more as *shuji*	60	Semi-professional school or lower	

Source: Ōbori (1960: 122).

Implanted Bureaucracy: The Origins of 'Japanese-style Employment'   153

Table 3.7 Ishikawajima Heavy Industries Promotion Selection Criteria Table (3)

Rank/title applied for	Length of service	Education level	Calculated from 1 December 1948	Length of service	Education level	Calculated from 1948 (proposal)
Guard	8 years or more as patrolman			8 years or more as patrolman		
Female associate	7 years or more	5-year higher school for girls	prior to 1939	7 years or more	5-year higher school for girls	prior to 1939
company employee	10 years or more	Higher elementary school	prior to 1935	10 years or more	Higher elementary school	prior to 1935
Technical staff or *shokuchō* (foreman)	3 years or more as assistant technical staff or assistant *shokuchō*			3 years or more as assistant technical staff or assistant *shokuchō*		
Qualification for regular recruitment		University Imperial professional school Private professional school Secondary school	*Shain* after 1 year of apprenticeship *Jun-shain* after 1 year of apprenticeship *Yōkoin*		University Professional school Secondary school Postwar junior high school	*Shain* after 1 year of apprenticeship *Jun-shain* after 1 year of apprenticeship *Yōkoin* *Yōkoin* apprenticeship for 1 year

Source: Ōbori (1960: 123).

However, as we will see in Chapter 5, Ishikawajima Heavy Industries used promotion criteria that differed little from that in place before the war in the postwar 1950s. And as quoted in Chapter 2, a 1977 report by Zen-Noh-Ren (the All Japan Federation of Management Organizations) stated that 'the general course of promotion [in 216 large Japanese companies surveyed by the organization] for an employee hired as a new graduate at age twenty-two is first to become a subsection manager at around age thirty-two, a section manager five years later at around age thirty-seven, and a director eight years after that, at around age forty-five'. It further stated that 'differences by industry and by department size are curiously small. This suggests that, as far as companies surveyed listed on the First Section [of the Tokyo Stock Exchange] are concerned, a kind of social market has been formed across all companies'. This correspondence between age and official position does resemble the in-house regulations in place at Ishikawajima Heavy Industries. Based on the above, it can be inferred that Ishikawajima Heavy Industries' prewar promotion criteria was not very different from those adopted by large Japanese companies in the latter half of the twentieth century. Also, such ranking systems were introduced by various different companies without any inter-firm compatibility. Someone could work for one company for many years and rise to, for example, the second grade of councilor, and yet not be worth a cent at any other firm. If that were so, then there would have been no reason to seek out jobs at other companies.

Bureaucracy as a model for the private sector

As for the origins of the Japanese-style employment system, some researchers have suggested that Japanese large corporations of the Meiji period may have taken their cue from the central bureaucracy.[65] Yet, these suggestions have been no more than piecemeal hints, and there have been no systematic studies on the relationship of influence between the bureaucracy and private firms.[66]

The arguments made in this book are as follows. Japan lacked a tradition of occupational organizations. Modern industry was introduced in the society, mainly through government state-owned enterprises (SOEs), which were organized in a bureaucratic system. These SOEs were sold off to the private sector, which became the origin of Japan's private heavy industry. In other words, the government bureaucracy was implanted in a society where no other ways for organizing modern organizations could be found.

In addition to the selling off of SOEs to the private sector, there were other reasons for the implantation of government bureaucracy to the private sector. First, since there were few modern clerical and technical posts in government-related organizations in the early Meiji period, the highly educated class first worked in government organizations and then in the private sector, thus propagating the organizational principles of government organizations to the private sector. Second, since private firms competed with government agencies for highly educated personnel, it was necessary to emulate the qualification and salary schemes of government agencies. And third, the conscription system meant that many men had experienced life in military organizations, and they conceptualized it as the normative model of the modern organization.

Firstly, let us look at the impact of the selling off of SOEs. Ishikawa-jima Heavy Industries was established in 1876 when the state-owned Ishikawajima Shipyard, which had been under the jurisdiction of the Ministry of the Navy, was sold off to private capital. Mitsubishi also grew out of the divestment of the state-owned Nagasaki Shipbuilding Bureau run by the Ministry of Industry. Ishikawajima and Mitsubishi are only two examples of the many other SOEs whose divestment by the government laid the foundation for Japan's mining and manufacturing industries.

The SOEs had adopted a bureaucratic three-tier structure and official rank system even before they were sold off to the private sector. It seems likely that the private companies that took over the SOEs would have inherited this bureaucratic organizational structure while arranging it to suit their own purposes. For example, Nippon Cement, founded in 1883, grew out of the divestment of a state-owned cement works built in 1872 by the Construction Bureau of the Department of Civil Engineering, which was part of the Ministry of Finance. Although the company revised its corporate regulations in June 1913, a three-tier structure of permanent salaried staff, monthly waged employees and day laborers was already in place.[67]

The fact that educated personnel in the early Meiji era first worked for government agencies and then for private companies is evident from the aforementioned job histories of the Yahata Steel Works employees. A 1960 report organized by the Director of the Research Bureau of the Economic Planning Agency introduced the 1882 salary rank schedule of 'a bank' established in the early Meiji era and pointed out that it was 'based on the salary rank schedule of government officials'. The report stated that the reason for this was that personnel were invited from government offices at the time of the bank's establishment. According to the report, the bank's president and vice president at the time of its founding were the current vice minister and secretary (*syoki-kan*) of the Ministry of Finance, and major positions of the bank were occupied by former officials of the same ministry.[68]

As this was also an era when people tended to respect bureaucrats and look down on the citizenry, the bureaucracy and SOEs were highly esteemed. As later recalled by Seihin (Shigeaki) Ikeda, who joined Mitsui Bank in 1895, even the industrialist Eiichi Shibusawa (adopted as the portrait on the 10,000-yen bill from 2024), who even then was considered to be one of the 'giants of the business world', was 'so hard-wired with respect for the government and disdain for the people that he would bow with his hands down below his knees when a government official came, even when he was the one hosting officials at a banquet in his bank's meeting hall'.[69]

Beyond this, there were also salary differences between the public and private sectors. As recalled by Masatsune Ogura, who became the president of the Sumitomo *zaibatsu* (conglomerate) after graduating from Tokyo Imperial University's Faculty of Law and becoming a civil servant at the Ministry of Home Affairs, he left to join Sumitomo in 1899 at the age of twenty-four, at which point his salary was reduced from 1,200 yen per year to 35 yen per month.[70] The main character in the aforementioned 1906 novel *Botchan* was a secondary school teacher in Matsuyama who was paid 40 yen per month, and after resigning from his post, he became an engineer on one of the Tokyo streetcar lines, where his monthly salary dropped to 25 yen.

Moreover, at this time, these reductions meant more than simply pay cuts. In term of the 1886 salary schedule shown earlier in Table 3.2, for Ogura this would have been the equivalent of being demoted from a *sōnin* official of the fourth rank to one of the sixth rank, and for the teacher in *Botchan* being reduced from a *hannin* official of the fourth rank to one of the seventh. In military terms, Ogura's jump to a position with Sumitomo was akin to being demoted from the rank of an army captain to a second lieutenant. In addition, according to Ogura's recollection, Sumitomo Bank employees at that time wore aprons over traditional Japanese dress, just like those in stores of the Edo Period, and almost no one wore Western style clothing.

Implanted Bureaucracy: The Origins of 'Japanese-style Employment'   157

Given these circumstances, private industry was competing with the bureaucracy for the talents of Imperial University graduates. As recalled by Seihin Ikeda, Hikojirō Nakamigawa, the head of Mitsui, was of the belief that 'bankers should enjoy an elevated social status, on a level with civil servants [...] and sought to undermine the view that lauded bureaucrats over the general populace by extensively recruiting school graduates and hiking their monthly salaries'.[71] This statement by Nakamigawa is arguably a direct application of the concept of status pay, in which the maintenance of status and appearance serves as the basis for determining the amount, to bank employees. This underlines how, in competing with the bureaucracy for talent, private companies came to adopt the principle of status pay of the governmental office.

Nakamigawa became a director of Mitsui Bank in 1891. According to Ikeda, salaries at Mitsui Bank at that time were unheard of for a private enterprise: 'Executives were paid 300 to 350 yen, managers below them 150 yen, and branch managers in smaller areas about 40 yen'.[72] Comparing this with the 1886 salary schedule for government officials, an executive with Mitsui Bank was equivalent to a *chokunin* official of the second rank (a major general in the army), a manager to a *sōnin* official of the second rank (lieutenant colonel), and a local branch manager to a *sōnin* official of the sixth rank (second lieutenant). Presumably, salaries would have been determined by referring to those of civil servants of similar ages and educational background.

Nor was this practice limited to Mitsui. It appears that many industrial conglomerates and affiliated companies were offering starting salaries to university graduates almost on a par with what they might expect working for a government office. In 1931, the economic journal *Jitsugyō no Nihon* (Business Japan) conducted a survey on the educational backgrounds and starting salaries of business leaders who had entered the workforce in the late Meiji period. According to the survey, those who graduated from the law faculty of an imperial university or the Tokyo Higher Commercial School (later Hitotsubashi University) around 1907 were paid 40 yen as a starting salary irrespective of whether they joined the Ministry of Finance, Mitsui Bank or Mitsubishi Corporation.[73] Most likely this was because Mitsui and Mitsubishi based their starting salaries on what was being offered to those who passed the higher civil service examinations and were hired as civil servants.[74] According to a survey following up on Tokyo Imperial University graduates at the end of 1902, 25.6% of law graduates had become administrative civil servants, 20.6% judicial civil servants, 11.9% graduate students, 7.7% lawyers and 12.3% 'bank and company employees'.[75] These ratios indicate that the bureaucracy was a significant presence in the job market for higher education graduates. Amidst this competition over the acquisition of new talent, the major private companies seem to have put in place salaries and organizational structures that were akin to those of the bureaucracy.

This also signified the formation of a structure in which the remuneration of corporate officers was determined independently of their positions and the market economy. The salaries of Japanese civil servants and military personnel were determined in large part by their educational background and length of service, regardless of what position they held or how much economic profit they generated. Thus, even as the private-sector firms competed with the bureaucracy over the acquisition of human resources, they had no choice but to be subject to its influence.

Influence of a military-type worldview

Furthermore, Japanese people at that time tended to understand business organizations by comparing them to the military. A prerequisite for this was the existing culture of understanding high salary as an indicator of in-house rank in Japanese companies. Yukio Wakabayashi, who has studied Mitsui & Co., has revealed the existence of a staff register from 1903 that listed employees in descending order according to their salaries.[76] A characteristic feature of this staff register is that employees were listed in descending order of salary amount, regardless of their position in the company. This seems likely to have been due to the fact that Japan did not have a tradition of occupational organization and so placed less emphasis on professions. Another background factor may have been that salary amounts were perceived as an indicator of management's evaluation.

Implanted Bureaucracy: The Origins of 'Japanese-style Employment' 159

At the time, corporate organization was still flexible. Japanese occupational organizations did not have the power to control wage standards, and the Japanese-style seniority wage system had not yet been established. The reality was that raises and promotions for employees were determined at the discretion of those in charge.[77] As a result, in more than a few instances, selections were made without regard to length of service. Indeed, on the 1903 staff register of Mitsui & Co., employees were listed in descending order of salary without any regard to their length of service. In the context of such an order, salary amounts were direct reflections of the evaluation of employees by their superiors and constituted a ranking within the organization. In 1976, Yosaburō Itō, who joined Mitsui & Co. in 1905 (and who would later become the company's managing director), offered the following recollection of his time with the company:

> With as many employees as we have today, it would hardly be feasible, but in my day, many promotions were made by selecting the most suitable personnel [*batteki jinji*]. And if someone's monthly salary was even one yen higher, then that would change the pecking order. So, you would ask for an extra 1 or 2 yen raise in your monthly salary, not for the money itself, but because you wanted to be higher up the ladder. There was a special staff register – only the executives and department and branch managers had copies of this – that listed employees in order of salary [...]. Not in alphabetical order or [the traditional Japanese] *iroha* order. The fellow with the highest monthly salary was listed at the top.[78]

This suggests a pre-existing awareness on the part of companies that they were creating a pecking order with salaries that bore no relationship to specific positions or professions. The introduction of bureaucratic-style ranks would thus have been implemented with little sense that such a thing was out of place in the private sector; it would simply have been a matter of annotating the 'special staff register' that listed employees by salary with corresponding ranks.

Moreover, when discussing corporate organization and education, people of that era tended to understand things in reference to military analogies. Thus, those with a higher education were likened to commissioned officers, those with a secondary education to non-commissioned officers and those with only a primary education to rank and file soldiers. For example, in 1889, then Minister of Education Takeaki Enomoto delivered an address at a graduation ceremony held at the Tokyo Technical School (*Tokyo shokkō gakkō*, the forerunner of the current Tokyo Institute of Technology). In his lecture, Enomoto stated that factory organizations 'should be divided into three ranks, namely master craftsmen, foremen and factory workers, just as soldiers are divided into generals, officers and the rank and file'. He positioned the training of the 'master builders' who corresponded to officers as 'the province of the technical colleges', while the training of the 'foremen' who corresponded to the non-commissioned officers was 'the main duty of this Technical School'.[79]

Similar metaphors could also be found in the corporate world. At a meeting of Mitsui & Co. branch managers in 1916, the manager of the personnel section of the head office compared 'those with higher education' to the company's 'high-ranking commissioned officers' and said that 'Commercial warfare is still military warfare, and lower-ranking and non-commissioned officers are also required to yield to high-ranking officers'. In 1914, the managing director of Mitsui & Co. described the personnel assignments of school graduates in terms of 'actual warfare' and 'combatants'.[80] Those who worked at Mitsui & Co. in the 1930s recollect his days equating a commercial school graduate with an aspiring drill sergeant or a veteran, and a university graduate with a second-class private that might hatch to become a trainee officer.[81] Yukio Wakabayashi holds that this conception of order was very likely to have been a very common feeling.[82]

In other words, members of the business community of that era shared two types of hierarchical consciousness. One regarded salaries as an in-house company hierarchy that bore no relation to actual professional positions. The other was a mindset that ranked people as 'commissioned officers', 'non-commissioned officers' and 'rank and file soldiers' according to their educational backgrounds. In this context, we can see how the existence of this twin hierarchical mindset laid

Implanted Bureaucracy: The Origins of 'Japanese-style Employment'   161

the groundwork for the easy penetration of bureaucratic/military-type ranking systems into private industry.

A 'status'-discriminatory order

A three-tier structure of company employees (*shain*), associate company employees (*jun-shain*) and shop-floor workers (*shokkō*) based on education history was becoming increasingly widespread, particularly in large manufacturing companies. At Hitachi Works (the original manufacturing arm of Hitachi Ltd.) in the 1930s, the entire workforce was divided into white-collar staff employees and blue-collar factory workers. The former group was further differentiated into a higher tier of salaried employees (*shokuin*), who comprised the senior-ranked clerks and engineers, and a lower tier of clerical and technical assistants (*koin*). Also, 98% of *shokuin* hired between 1932 and 1938 were graduates of higher educational institutions, while 85% of *koin* and *koin* apprentices had graduated from vocational schools.[83]

By contrast, the factory workers who worked on the shop floor were not regarded as company employees (*shain*) of Hitachi. Until the 1910s, even in Japan, companies tended not to employ factory workers directly, but rather used a subcontracting system in which foremen assembled their own teams of independent workers. Even after the introduction of direct employment, factory workers were initially hired as day laborers, and if they performed well, would later be hired on as regular-basis workers.[84]

The lack of a tradition of professional organization, a characteristic of Japan, also affected the way workers were organized. Just as at the Yahata Steel Works in the late nineteenth century, reassignments were a frequent occurrence at Hitachi Works in the 1920s and 30s. Between 1920 and 1933, every worker on Hitachi's books experienced reassignment after around seven years in a job. There is no trace of the existence of a concept of standardized wage rates by job type that held across companies.[85]

Like higher civil servants, salaried office staff were paid on an annual or monthly basis, with no specified working hours. By contrast, factory workers were paid daily, but had no explicitly stated rules

162   Chapter 3

regarding wage increases. Factory workers at Hitachi would carry out their assignments in groups of five or six; the foremen (group leaders) were paid a fixed daily wage, while others were allocated among the groups according to their performance and the number of hours worked. Raises were given twice per year, but these were subject to the whims of the foremen and staff employees.[86] Such arrangements were typical at that time, and by no means unique to Hitachi Works. One man who had worked as a labor relations manager for Oji Paper recalls that factory workers' wages were affected by 'whether or not they went to their boss's house to chop wood or help sweep the chimneys, and it was not uncommon for there to be a difference in pay raises between those who were liked by their bosses and those who were not'.[87] A trade unionist at Oji Paper, recalling his experiences during the prewar period, stated in 1957 as follows:

> Back in those days, the salaried staff employees were treated like gods. Since they didn't have to clock in, young factory workers like us had no idea when they would come to work or go home. We didn't even know their faces. Sometimes, the duty foreman would tell me to go over to so-and-so's house to help out, and I'd grudgingly be sent over to chop wood, sweep the chimney or clear snow. It was taken for granted that we were available to be used like servants in the private lives of staff employees. I got completely fed up with being used as an errand boy after working a twelve-hour night shift [...]. If we ever tried to talk back to staff, we'd be shouted at angrily and told that we didn't have to come in to work the next day.[88]

Even at Oji Paper, we see a clear correspondence between educational background and status, a trend that became even more pronounced after World War I, when the various types of school systems spread throughout society. According to figures calculated by management scholar Hiroshi Hazama based on a 1930 survey by the Vocational Education Affairs Bureau of the Ministry of Education, 92% of graduates from universities and professional schools (single-department

Implanted Bureaucracy: The Origins of 'Japanese-style Employment'   163

colleges) became salaried office staff, while only 0.5% of ordinary elementary school graduates were employed at the same level.[89]

There was a considerable income disparity among three status levels of those employed at Hitachi Works. While the wages of higher-level staff employees rose rapidly with years of service, and those of lower-level staff employees rose moderately, the wages of factory workers hardly rose at all. Shinji Sugayama's analysis of salaried staff employee remuneration as of 1936 shows that salaried staff employees were paid a seniority-based wage, with those who had accrued between twenty and twenty-four years of service being paid three times more than those with four years of service or less. Nevertheless, there was a difference between higher-level staff employees who graduated from imperial universities and lower-level staff employees who had graduated from vocational schools. Based on what was earned by factory workers in each age group, the average annual income (including bonuses and housing allowances) was 3.5 times higher among higher-level staff with degrees from imperial universities in the twenty-five to twenty-nine age bracket and 6.15 times higher for those in the forty to forty-four age bracket. Similarly, compensation for lower-level staff who had graduated from vocational schools was 1.7 times higher than what factory workers of the same age earned in the twenty-five to twenty-nine age bracket, and 4.41 times among the forty to forty-four age bracket. The difference of these two seniority wage profiles was very similar to that of the *sōnin* officials and *hannin* officials.[90]

In Hitachi city, company housing rented to staff employees was known as 'officer's housing' (*yakutaku*), while factory workers' accommodations, located a considerable distance away, were known as 'factory workers' tenements' (*shokkō nagaya*).[91] Of course, salaried staff employees were a very exclusive and privileged class. At Oji Paper in 1935, salaried staff employees at the associate level or above accounted for 12.5% of the total workforce, while the percentage of company employees (*sei-shain*, higher staff employees) was 5.5%. While some factory workers were occasionally promoted to associate or even higher, such cases accounted for only 6% of factory workers.[92] The gates, cafeterias, bathrooms and other facilities were also separate for salaried staff employees and factory workers. In January 1946, after the end of the war, the labor union at Hitachi Works submitted a list of demands 'for the elimination of discriminatory treatment' that included the following: that staff company employees (*shain*) should no longer be permitted to arrive late or leave early, that the library should be open to factory workers and that factory workers should not be the only ones subjected to physical searches when entering or leaving the plant premises.[93]

People were moreover aware that their place in the prevailing order was determined by their educational background. As one Hitachi worker recalled from his younger days before the war:

> Seeing a balding factory worker being dressed down by a young associate staff apprentice, it was like watching myself. Realizing how differently graduates were treated, I felt not so much wretched as frustrated beyond measure.[94]

For the Japanese people of that time, this was perceived as a status-based order. People were also aware that this was a bureaucratic type of order. The 1 June 1926 issue of *Kurokane* (black iron), the official newspaper of the Yahata Steel Works, carried the following statement by the factory's works section manager:

> The idea that the status of a factory worker is inferior to that of one of the staff employees is a prejudice rooted in the idea that government bureaucrats should be lauded over the regular populace and a contempt for labor. However, such ideas and notions are not unique to steel mills but reflect a general tendency that has prevailed widely and for a long time in our country.[95]

However, a kind of pecking order also existed among factory workers. There was no orderly system for pay raises, no qualification ranks as in the case of staff employees, and daily wages were subject to the whims of superiors. That said, since a worker could receive raises in pay if they were diligent and enjoyed the favor of their superiors, the level of their daily wage came to represent the employer's cumulative

Implanted Bureaucracy: The Origins of 'Japanese-style Employment' 165

evaluation of them. Therefore, as was the case with Mitsui & Co. in 1903, the amount of daily wages that workers received came to be associated with their ranking inside the company.

According to Tateshi Mori, who has studied the prewar records of the Yahata Steel Works, factory workers' daily wages did not change unless they received a pay raise, but their job types and placements were changed frequently. Whereas the type of job they held did not become their identity, their daily wage 'came to represent a marker for the factory workers, like a number on their backs. It might be said that the steel works managed the factory workers by assigning them a specific daily wage amount, as though they had assigned them all with a number on the back of their uniforms'.[96]

Economist Jong-won Woo also points to three tiers of factory workers that he refers to as leader-grade, regulars (*jōyatoi*) and temps (*rinjiyatoi*). In SOEs such as Yahata Steel Works and Japanese National Railways, the leader-grade workers were treated similar to staff civil servants, while there was an apparent tendency among the regulars to exclude temps in order to heighten their own status.[97] Although it was out of the question for them to equate themselves with civil servants in terms of status, positioning themselves in a higher grade would have allowed them to liken themselves to *koin*, who were clerks in the governmental organization in line with *hannin* officials, albeit outside the ranks. These factors would lay the groundwork for the spread of the doctrine of the 'equality of company employees (*shain*)' in postwar Japan, with its attendant competence ranks, even among factory workers, and the associated relegation of non-regular workers and women to an 'outsider' status.

Differences from the UK and US

Although discrimination against factory workers in prewar Japan could be severe, as discussed in Chapter 2, the existence of three-tier structures in companies is not unique to Japan. According to Sanford Jacoby, a scholar of American labor history, prior to World War I, the white-collar employee, who was paid on an annual or monthly basis, 'was treated like a gentleman'. Their status was guaranteed, and 'until

166   Chapter 3

the 1910s, American courts interpreted payment of a monthly or yearly salary as evidence that the employer had made an implicit employment commitment for the period of compensation, meaning that the salaried employee could not be dismissed at will'. In contrast to manual laborers, who were easily dismissed, white-collar employees, even in the event of failure, would often only be reassigned to unimportant sinecure posts.[98]

Labor historian Kazuo Nimura points out that status-based discrimination within companies was also severe in the UK, and notes that its existence in prewar Japanese companies was 'likely a practice transplanted [from the West] along with the factory system'.[99] Mikio Sumiya has pointed out that factory workers did not enjoy long-term employment or seniority-based wages, and that the labor market and labor-management relations in prewar Japan were 'extremely similar to those found in Western societies'.[100]

However, Japan's corporate order also incorporated elements that were distinct from those in the UK and US, namely in-house ranks that were not linked with positions or skill qualification and an emphasis on academic background. Ronald Dore, in his comparative study of Japanese and British companies, noted that while UK companies also had a three-tier structure, Japanese companies were much more educationally oriented.[101] Even in 1969, when Dore conducted his survey, UK companies still placed more emphasis on professional qualifications than education. Of the 167 managers and high-level technicians he surveyed at English Electric, only 24% were university graduates and only 10% had graduated from full-time technical colleges. The rest had attended vocational evening courses or obtained credentials from professional associations in fields such as accounting or engineering.

Also, according to Dore, the more important element for promotion to executive positions in the UK companies of the day was how managers were seen 'in terms of class status, rather than of education'. That is, the graceful and dignified airs and manner of speaking of the upper class were more important indicators than education. Dore cites the results of a 1958 sample survey of UK firms, which showed that university graduates represented only 21% of British managers, and only 24% of the 200 top managers in top-tier firms, which he

Implanted Bureaucracy: The Origins of 'Japanese-style Employment' 167

describes as being 'in contrast with Japan, where nearly all managers are university graduates'.[102]

Moreover, the US since the end of World War I has seen the introduction of position analysis and subsequent changes in employment practices. As I discuss in Chapter 4, position analysis and position-based pay were introduced in the US federal civil service in 1923, along with measures to prevent the appointment of individuals who lacked the necessary competence for a given position.[103] These changes signaled the beginning of a shift in the standards required of employees in the federal government and private companies from having the status of 'gentlemen' to possessing job-based competence and academic degrees.

In modern Japan, by contrast, the introduction of position analysis never took off. Neither the technical credentials issued by professional associations, nor the elegant mannerisms of the upper classes carried much weight. In this context, educational background proved to be the sole indicator of suitability. However, the educational background was based on whether or not they had graduated from a government-approved institution of higher or secondary education, not on what they had studied there. One's educational background in Japan did not necessarily signify the possession of a degree that substantiated professional competence. This practice of placing emphasis on academic credentials began with the bureaucracy, and job-based training and promotions were based on educational background and length of service at individual companies.

In this context, having graduated from a given university was not seen as an indicator of competence in any particular position but was simply perceived as the 'status' of having graduated from that institution. This is illustrated by the account of an upper-level staff employee formerly in charge of labor affairs at Hitachi Works, who recalled conversing with some young factory workers who had joined the socialist labor movement in 1933. The reference in the passage to 'Nissenkō' is to the Hitachi Industrial Skills Academy (*Hitachi kōgyō senshū gakkō*), a training center for factory workers employed at Hitachi Works. The factory workers in question were Nissenkō graduates.

> ... As we talked, I gradually began to understand their point of view. For example, in the crew assigned to the design department right after graduating, the Nissenkō graduates were better at their jobs in the beginning than those who had been to university or professional school, who they were working with side by side at the desks. Some of them were old classmates from elementary school, and a few said that back then, their own grades had been higher than these other fellows'. Anyway, those who graduated from a professional school or above were treated as staff from the start, but the Nissenkō graduates were destined to be treated as shop-floor workers. Because of the status-based discrimination in the way company workers were treated, they started thinking about how they'd have gone to university, too, if they'd had the money [to accommodate tuitions]. They started reading books like [Japanese socialist] Hajime Kawakami's *Binbō Monogatari* [Tales of Poverty] and became acutely aware of the contradictions in the world. They told me that when they became interested in the leftist movement, they plunged right in [...].[104]

In the Japanese way of doing things, positions were not linked with academic degrees. Therefore, these workers had the opportunity to work in the same positions as university graduates in the same open plan office, only to realize that they had superior capabilities. Thus, the difference in their circumstances was perceived only as 'status-based discrimination' due to their educational backgrounds.

This function of a person's academic background differed some-what from the role it played in other societies. In the case of the UK and elsewhere, a meritocratic principle based on the certification of degrees rendered obsolete the practice of assigning positions of responsibility to individuals from the upper classes who did not have diplomas. Here, academic background and status were opposed to each other. In the case of Japan, however, as discussed above, the samurai class ended up experiencing a rapid decline. In other words, in Japan, the upper class fell before educational background and status became opposites.[105] This fact may be behind the somewhat contradictory phenomenon of the transformation of educational background into a kind of status marker.

Implanted Bureaucracy: The Origins of 'Japanese-style Employment' 169

As noted in Chapter 1, labor economist Shōjirō Ujihara noted in 1954 that the Japanese labor market was characterized by a dual structure. In 1959, noting that large Japanese companies had a three-tier 'management status order' (*keiei mibun chitsujo*) of company employees, associate company employees and shop-floor workers, Ujihara observed the following:

> Japan's labor market was formed, first and foremost, as a labor market organized by employee groups and by educational background. [...] Of course, level of education would be a major factor in determining one's competence and training in any country, so a labor market will always be of this nature, more or less. However, what may be said to be a peculiarity of its Japanese expression is that it took an especially prominent form, one that gave shape to a status-based hierarchy, particularly as a norm but also as an institution.[106]

Ujihara said nothing about the origins of this order, nor did he compare it to the corporate order in other countries. Nevertheless, we should note that Ujihara was not at all mistaken when he identified the extreme connection with educational background as 'a peculiarity of its Japanese expression'.

We should also note, however, that long-term employment and seniority-based wages did not apply to factory workers. Although bureaucracy-style seniority-based promotions were widespread, in the prewar period they remained limited to salaried staffs. In other words, there was no such thing as an 'equality of company employees' which has become characteristic in Japanese-style employment since the 1960s. Even in the 1950s, when Abegglen and Ujihara pointed out the existence of a three-tier structure, the corporate order that had existed before the war was still very much in place. How was this order subsequently transformed to give shape to equality of company employee? How did the series of practices that include the bulk recruitment of new graduates and regular personnel transfers (rotation) come into being? These questions require further investigation, a task for the following chapters.

4 The Formation of Norms

This chapter describes the formation of the 'collective norms' that emerged in the civil service and in large companies in prewar Japan and were carried over into the postwar era.[1] These include the periodical bulk recruitment of new graduates, regular personnel transfers, a system of mandatory retirement, large open-plan offices and personnel evaluations that emphasize character and potentiality, all of which were discussed in Chapter 2.

Although the Japanese civil service emulated Germany's bureaucratic institutions, Japan lacked a ready supply of highly educated personnel. In Japan, there was no tension between the government and the civil service, unlike the situation in Germany. This chapter describes how those differences fostered the norms of the Japanese-style employment system, such as the bulk recruitment of new graduates, regular (periodic) personnel transfers and large open plan offices. Further, the age-based compulsory retirement of the Japanese military spread to the private sector as the institutionalized norm of mandatory retirement. In the system of collective norms thus formed, Japan's schools served the role of introducing quality-assured talent to companies. In the beginning, letters of recommendation from university faculty served this function, but before long graduation from a particular university came to have a signaling effect, regardless of one's specific course of study. However, the Japanese system applied only to salaried staff, and did not extend to laborers or women.

The historical spread of civil service institutions to the private sector also took place in Germany. However, in that country, the duties of individual bureaucrats were clearly defined, and the impact of the bureaucracy on the private sector took the form of the clarification of the duties attached to specific positions. Here, what was important was an occupational identity that transcended individual companies. Moreover, the movement to improve the status of lower-level clerical staff encouraged the development of the formation of cross-firm cleri-

172   Chapter 4

cal identities. While a salaried staff movement did exist in Japan in the 1920s, it was organizationally weak, and it did not lead to the formation of cross-firm occupational identities among clerical workers.

The custom of referring to white-collar salaried staff as 'company employees' (*shain*) in the sense that they were regular members of the company had emerged in the Meiji period (1868–1912). However, in the prewar period of intense discrimination against blue-collar workers, this identity did not extend to include common laborers. Company-wide employee identities that included bule-collar workers only began to take shape with the rapid postwar emergence of the enterprise union movement, which is described in Chapter 5.

Origins of the bulk recruitment of new graduates

The existence of pay grades separate from positions in the military and government offices is not unique to Japan. Nevertheless, the bureaucracies of Germany and France are not characterized by bulk recruitment of new graduates or regular personnel transfers. These Japanese characteristics were involved in the social conditions of Japan's modernization. This section describes how the scarcity of modern higher-educated human resources provided the background for the origin of the bulk recruitment of new graduates.

Japan's system of examinations and appointments for civil servants began with the Regulations Concerning Examination, Probation and Training of Civil Officials (*Bunkan shiken shiho oyobi minarai kisoku*), promulgated in 1887, which were formulated with reference to the Prussian system. Civil service examinations were divided into higher examinations (for the recruitment of higher officials) and ordinary examinations (for the recruitment of *hannin* officials). Those who passed the higher examinations were certified as trainee (*shiho*) candidates and those who passed the ordinary examinations as apprenticeship (*minarai*) candidates, and each ministry hired them as trainees or apprentices as required. After three years of administrative training, trainees would be formally appointed as *sōnin* officials and apprentices as *hannin* officials.[2] This system was intended to pre-

The Formation of Norms

173

vent appointments based on nepotism and to establish competence-based recruitment.

Certainly, Japan's bureaucracy resembles that of Germany in many respects. For example, even in Germany, civil servants (*Beamte*) receive their salary not under the terms of a private law labor contract but for their status guaranteed under public law (*Öffentliches Recht*) and their loyalty to the state. This is why their salaries are not remuneration for their labor, but rather a status-based salary to ensure livelihood and economic independence to guarantee their dedication to public duties. They also receive a pension that is paid after retirement. Further, Germany's bureaucracy has pay grades that are independent of specific job positions and is characterized by a hierarchical order.[3]

However, even if its institutions are used as a reference, social conditions in Germany were nonetheless quite different from the situation in Japan in the late nineteenth century. Perhaps the most significant difference lay in the number of people who pursued higher education. By the first half of the nineteenth century, Prussia already had a surplus of university graduates. In 1820, the total number of high-ranking civil service posts was 598, whereas the total number of university students was 3,144 (including 938 in law). What is more, by 1831, the number of high-ranking posts had been reduced to 476, while the number of university students in the previous year had increased to 6,160 (including 1,628 in law).[4]

Obtaining the stipend of a high-ranking administrative civil servant in the German system took a considerable amount of time. The institutions of the Prussian system established in 1846 may be characterized as follows. First, after pursuing a minimum of three years of university education, the candidate had to apprentice at the court and had to pass a jurisprudence exam and an oral exam to attain the administrative trainee rank of *Referendar*. After further and varied practical training in prefectural administrations, and after sitting the major state examination (*große Staatsexamen*), which consisted of both written and oral components, the candidate would receive the administrative probationary rank of *Assessor*. However, in principle, the rank of *Assessor* was unpaid. In the 1901 to 1903 fiscal years, the average age of the typical Prussian administrative civil servants who attained the rank of *Assessors* was 29.5 years old, and the average age of those promoted to become salaried counsellors was 40.2 years old.[5] In other words, becoming a high-ranking official entailed earning a living by some other means until the age of around forty. This was unfeasible unless one had wealthy or aristocratic parents, or had married into a wealthy family. Of the high-ranking officials in Westphalia from 1876 to 1900, 29% had fathers who were major landowners, 30% who were high-ranking officials, 12% who were business owners and 6% who were military officers, and only 10% had fathers who were only middle class or below, such as mid-ranking civil servants or teachers.[6] Given the circumstances described in this section, recruiting for posts as they became vacant seems to be the only form that could have developed.

As compared to Germany, however, Meiji Japan was experiencing a shortage of personnel with higher education. In 1886, the year prior to the establishment of the civil service probationary examination, the total number of graduates from Tokyo Imperial University was forty-six, of whom only eleven came out of the Faculty of Law. Even in 1894, when the First Sino-Japanese War broke out, the law faculty still produced only seventy-seven graduates.[7] Meanwhile, government ministries and agencies were demanding an immediate supply of talent to meet an increasing administrative demand. For this reason, university graduates were given preferential treatment. Graduates of the Tokyo Imperial University Faculty of Law and Faculty of Letters were deemed to have studied the specialized fields of knowledge required of administrative officials. As such, they enjoyed the privilege of being hired as trainee (*shiho*, probationary officers) without taking an examination. Those appointed through examinations consisted of the graduates of private academies.[8]

Moreover, ministries and agencies that wanted to fill personnel shortages soon preferred to hire probationary officers from among Tokyo Imperial University graduates who had not sat the higher examinations over those who had passed them. This was because while those who had sat and passed the examinations could be hired only once a year, Imperial University graduates, who were exempt from the examinations anyway, could be hired at any time. Thus, as these graduates began to be given priority in recruitment, the demand

The Formation of Norms 175

for those who had passed the probationary examinations fell off. In 1891, when ministries and agencies were able to fill their available positions entirely with Imperial University graduates, demand for probationary administrative officers fell to zero, and the examinations themselves were cancelled.[9] In effect, it could now be said that one had only to graduate from the Imperial University to be appointed as a new graduate without taking an examination. It was also the case that probationers were treated as *sōnin* officials and were guaranteed a salary as such regardless of the fact that they were still in a trial period. Thus, some Imperial University graduates entered government service with the aim of earning an income as quickly as possible.[10] This situation may be said to represent another difference from that of Germany during the same period.

Because the probationary examination was no longer fulfilling its intended function, the system was revised in 1893 with the Edict on the Appointment of Civil Officials (*bunkan nin'yō rei*). The intent was to abolish the prerogative of Imperial University graduates to be appointed without an examination and to require everyone to take the higher civil service examinations. At the same time, however, those who passed the higher civil service examinations were able to serve as *sōnin* officials without going through a probationary period. For the government ministries and agencies suffering personnel shortages, the three-year probationary period was seen as too long, and it was hoped that this measure would allow them to recruit officials to permanent office more quickly.[11] Furthermore, individual ministries and agencies continued recruiting Imperial University graduates, allowing them to take the examinations after they were hired. The best students were hired upon graduation in July and given a de facto leave of absence to prepare for the examinations in November.[12] This was the effective start of the bulk recruitment of new graduates, which came about due to a scarcity of university graduates relative to the expansion of administrative tasks.

Owing to this situation, in modern Japan, one need not have come from a wealthy or aristocratic background to become a high-ranking official. In the sense that it was possible to become an Imperial University student regardless of one's origins, Meiji Japan was more

176   Chapter 4

equal than the Germany of the day.[13] On the other hand, however, those who graduated from Imperial University to become civil servants became members of an exclusive and privileged class. This reinforced the tendency of educational background in Japan to serve in lieu of status in the European context as discussed in Chapter 3.

The origin of seniority-based promotion and regular personnel transfers

The civil service in modern Japan also gave birth to other norms, namely seniority-based promotion and regular (periodic) personnel transfers.

Administrative scholar Shō Kawate identifies the 1886 Edict on Rank and Salaries for Higher Civil Officials as the juncture at which promotions based on years of service became customary.[14] This salary edict stipulated that an individual could not be promoted to the higher civil service unless they had served at an official rank for at least five years. In 1885, the previous year, the number of officials had been approaching 100,000, and their salaries then accounted for 28% of the national budget. Because of this, 1886 saw the implementation of a large-scale administrative reorganization that reduced the number of officials to about 55,000. Even so, the most drastic reduction took place among non-regular civil servants such as *koin*, while the number of *hannin* and higher officials continued to increase.[15] Reducing salary expenditures was a government priority at the time, and the restrictions on the promotion of higher officials were part of this effort.

Kawate does not mention this, but Article 4 of the 1874 Ordinance on the Promotion of Army Officers included a provision for 'years-in-rank on active duty' (*jitsueki teinen*), specifying the number of years an officer had to serve at a given military rank before becoming eligible for promotion (Table 4.1).[16] This ordinance stipulated that promotion to a higher rank was contingent on service for a certain minimum number of years at the current rank, for example, two years for a second lieutenant or three years for a major in peace time. The navy had a similar system. It seems likely that the existence of such a provision for military officers provided a model for civilian officers to emulate.

The Formation of Norms

Table 4.1 Rules for years-in-rank on active duty in the Ordinance on the Promotion of Army Officers (1874)

Ranking	Years-in-rank on active duty	Minimum timeframe
	Peace time	War time
General		
Lieutenant-general	Battle experience	
Major-general	3 years	1.5 years
Colonel	2 years	1 year
Lieutenant-colonel	2 years	1 year
Major	3 years	1.5 years
Captain	4 years	2 years
Lieutenant	2 years	1 year
Second lieutenant	2 years	1 year
Chief warrant officer	2 years	1 year
Sergeant	1 year	6 months
Corporal	1 year	6 months
Private soldier of the first rank	1 year	6 months
Private soldier of the second rank	1 year	6 months

Source: Cabinet Official Gazette Bureau (ed.) (1874: 1006).

This provision under the Edict on Rank and Salaries for Higher Civil Officials underwent several amendments, including a relaxation to three years, and was again amended in September 1895 to two years. This period saw the number of government officials begin to increase as the territory to be administered expanded in accordance with the establishment of colonies following Japan's victory in the Sino-Japanese War in April of that same year. The previous year, 1894, had also been the first year in which Imperial University graduates were to take the higher civil service examinations, but the graduates had boycotted the examinations, demanding restoration of their special exemption privileges. Getting them to take the November examinations made it necessary to negotiate an improvement in their conditions, and it was around this time that stays of promotion were relaxed to two years.[17]

This, however, had an unforeseen consequence. Namely, it encouraged a norm whereby those who passed the higher civil service examinations (the so-called '*kōbun-gumi*') would be promoted every two years after joining a ministry as they were transferred from one

178　　　　　　　　　　　　　　　　　　　　　　　　Chapter 4

department to another within the ministry. The provision in question had not stipulated that officials would be promoted every two years, but had only set a minimum timeframe for promotion. Afterward, however, a pattern of promotions emerged whereby a member of the *kōbun-gumi* would be transferred from one position to another every two years, climbing the ranks each time, so that within ten years of ministerial service, he would have been promoted to become a *sōnin* official of the first rank (the civilian equivalent of an army colonel) to assume office at the section manager (*kachō*) level. Thus, Kawate tells us, did the 'career path of the *kōbun-gumi*, with repeated promotions after every two years of service at a position', come to be firmly established.[18]

In effect, we can regard this as the origin of regular personnel transfers and seniority-based salary increases. In the case of civil servants, salary increases occur automatically as they rise through the ranks. If a person's rank is promoted for years of service at two-year intervals, their salary will follow a seniority curve. This pattern of promotions may also have reinforced the tendency for officials to take on a number of different positions in order to rise through the ranks with each move.

Moreover, with these restrictions on promotion, in order to advance in one's career as a civil servant, it became advantageous to secure an appointment as an official immediately upon graduating and then be promoted internally. If one took a lower-ranking position at an older age, there would be an age-based limit on promotion. In addition, in 1899, the principle was established that even imperially appointed *chokunin* officials had to pass the higher civil service examinations,[19] effectively closing off the possibility of mid-career hires to executive ranks from outside the service.

Further, as discussed in Chapter 2, the bulk recruitment of new graduates facilitates regular personnel transfers. Assigning new hires to positions every academic year-end makes it necessary to free up those positions via large-scale personnel transfers. If we add to this the norm whereby all of these workers are promoted every two years, then large-scale personnel transfers will become even more likely to take place.

The Formation of Norms 179

Although a relationship between the bulk recruitment of new graduates and regular personnel transfers has been suggested, empirical studies on the topic are few. One of the handful of studies available, analyzing the Toyota Motor Corporation, found that there was a gap of about twenty years between the entrenchment of regular bulk recruitment and the regularization of personnel transfers.[20] Presumably, after twenty years of regular mass recruitment drives, an organization will have no choice but to make regular personnel transfers. Such regular transfers in the central bureaucracy are believed to have begun occurring around 1900. This was about twenty years after the institution of the civil service probationary examination, when the bureaucrats hired as new graduates from Tokyo Imperial University were being promoted to the upper echelons of power.[21] By the time these bureaucrats had reached the top ranks of the various ministries and agencies in the 1910s, this norm was more or less firmly entrenched.

These norms may have spread to the private sector as well. As we saw in Chapter 3, Ishikawajima Heavy Industries stipulated a certain number of years of service for promotion of rank, and as we will see in chapters 5 and 6, more than a few companies introduced a system to promote employees to a higher grade every two to three years of service.

It is worth noting that while the Edict on Rank and Salaries for Higher Civil Officials was abolished after World War II, the norm of career bureaucrats being transferred and promoted every two years survived. Until 1920, the old university system observed September enrollment and July graduation, and new graduates joined the ministries in July. Accordingly, in the prewar period civil service personnel were mostly transferred from June to July. After 1920, university graduation shifted to March, and eventually massive regular personnel transfers in Japanese private companies came to take place in that month. However, many Japanese civil service personnel continue to be transferred in July, even though more than 100 years have passed since 1920. Once norms are formed within an organization, they will have continuity even if their original basis is no longer in place.

The historical background of defined duties in the US and Prussia

These developments differed from the characteristics of officialdom in other countries. The US federal government was plagued by office-seekers who sought to use their connections to secure patronage appointments in what was known as the spoils system. In the early period, 65% of federal government employees came from wealthy backgrounds, such as those whose families had significant interests in land or large businesses.[22] As public criticism of this system grew, measures were taken to introduce job analysis to try to block the patronage appointment of individuals who were not qualified for the jobs they were hired to do. This principle began to be adopted in the 1880s and was formalized with the Classification Act of 1923. Under this system, as openings came up for each classified position, applicants were invited to apply from inside or outside the department, with appointment based on open competition through examinations and past career performance. The percentage of public employment under the merit system was just over 10% of the total in 1884, but by the end of World War I it had exceeded 70%.[23]

On the other hand, Germany and France, which Japan sought to emulate, had adopted a system whereby qualified high-level bureaucrats were screened through examinations for promotion within the bureaucracy. Even today, the movement of personnel between the civil service and the private sector is not as active in Europe as it is in the US. However, promotions and appointments after passing an examination are based on vacancies and open recruitment, so that regular personnel transfers and bulk recruitment of new graduates are unheard of.[24] As mentioned earlier, in Prussia during the same period, the number of university graduates and successful examinees exceeded the number of empty posts in the civil service, so that there were enough personnel to fill any vacancies.

The Prussian monarch also insisted that bureaucrats should be professionals in the fulfilment of their duties, a requirement that stemmed from a history of rivalry between the monarch and the bureaucracy. The Prussian bureaucracy had long been occupied by members of the aristocracy, who were constantly taking advantage

The Formation of Norms   181

of the perquisites of their official positions. *'Je mehr Diener, je mehr Diebe* (the more bureaucrats, the more thieves), was practically a Hohenzollern family motto. The eighteenth-century Prussian monarchy did not trust bureaucrats, and ordered them to deliver service reports to the king. The matters discussed in these reports included civil servants' performance, their contribution to the treasury, their professional abilities and the speed with which they performed their duties. Moreover, to prevent collusion and arbitrariness on the part of bureaucrats, all administrative activities were documented. In Prussia, the introduction in the eighteenth century of an examination system for the appointment of officials, as in Japan, was intended to eliminate personnel practices based on personal sentiments. However, a consequence of the tension between the bureaucracy and the monarchy was the encouragement of the professionalization of bureaucrats and the clarification and documentation of their duties and authority. A Japanese scholar of German history identifies the existence of such tensions as the underlying cause of differences between the bureaucracies of Prussia and Japan.[25] The government and bureaucracy of Meiji Japan did not have rivalries, and bureaucrats were not required to limit or clarify their individual duties.

By the end of the nineteenth century, German officialdom had acquired a reputation for meticulous record-keeping and professionalism. Max Weber described the bureaucrats as consummate 'professionals', and even while lamenting their obsession with record-keeping, observed that, 'Officialdom has passed every test brilliantly wherever it was required to demonstrate its sense of duty, its objectivity and its ability to master organisational problems in relation to strictly circumscribed, official tasks of a *specialised* nature'.[26] Article 33(2) of the current Basic Law for the Federal Republic of Germany also stipulates that eligibility of individuals for public office (including appointment and promotion) shall be in accordance with their professional ability (*fachlichen Leistung*).[27] The Joint Rules of Procedure of the Federal Ministries (*Gemeinsame Geschäftsordnung der Bundesministerien*; GGO) also stipulate that the duties and remit of each salaried staff member must be clearly defined, and that the staff member must sign any correspondence they prepare themselves.[28] Nevertheless, these are probably better understood as historical norms than as mere legal provisions.[29]

Nation states, including Japan, have universally introduced examination systems for government official positions in order to eliminate recruitment/promotion based on nepotism. However, in each case, the resulting form of bureaucracy has been different, reflecting the historical particularities of each country's development.

The origin of the 'large open plan office'

The fact that Japan had followed a different path than the US or Germany, whereby the scope of staff duties was not clearly defined, opened the possibility for Japanese civil servants to work together in large open-plan offices. Private offices had never been available in the early years of Japanese bureaucracy. Korekiyo Takahashi (later prime minister from 1920 to 1923), who had worked as a translator at the Ministry of Finance Post Office (*ekiteiryō*) in 1872, recalls that 'at that time, the director general, section managers, and section staff all worked together in a large office'.[30]

More noteworthy than this spatial organization, however, is the fact that no division of duties was deemed necessary below the section level. Meiji Japan was a rather hastily organized administrative system. Accordingly, a variety of government offices were quickly established, and only later were the administrative affairs under their respective jurisdictions codified into law. Further, the establishment directives (*secchi tsūsatsu*) issued by the ministries and agencies were extremely vague, containing definitions such as 'Banking Section: to administer affairs concerning banks' and 'Translation Section: to administer all documents concerning foreign countries' (from an 1879 Ministry of Finance directive).[31] Unlike the US, which introduced job analysis, and Prussia, where the monarch required a clear definition of duties, these regulations were open to broad-based interpretation by civil servants in the field. In addition, the ministry and agency establishment directives

The Formation of Norms

183

only determined sectional jurisdictions, and did not go so far as to stipulate the duties or remit of individual salaried officials.

This situation remains basically unchanged today. Wataru Ōmori, a scholar of public administration, notes that in Japan's bureaucracy, 'jurisdictional affairs under the government's jurisdiction are defined only up to the sectional level', and that 'in the usual case the arrangement is one room per section'.[32] In other words, office rooms were separated as far as the sectional level, the level to which jurisdictions were stipulated, after which point each section was laid out as a large open-plan office. Buildings are tangible expressions of the mindsets of those who use them. Even if the buildings built in the early Meiji period lacked private offices, buildings with private offices would surely have been constructed if the duties of each official were clearly defined and if the mindset ever arose that each person needed a private room. That buildings with large open plan rooms arranged in units known as sections remain in use today is merely a reflection of a mindset that holds that it is not necessary to define duties at a more granular level.

This also meant that sections were separated from their directors and acquired private rooms of their own, so to speak. As recalled by Korekiyo Takahashi, cited earlier, 'the director general, section managers and section staff all worked together in a large office'. In the subsequent civil service, however, although the section manager and members of staff worked in the same large rooms, directors were set apart in private offices. Ōmori observes that the section, i.e., the unit comprised by those in the large office, represents a kind of independent kingdom, in which 'the section manager (kachō) is like the lord of the realm'. Each section has its own laws under its jurisdiction and industries to oversee. Accordingly, 'in terms of matters under their jurisdiction, it is fair to say that each section of the ministry is, in effect, the government of Japan itself [...]. The sections are the units of administrative activity, and the intermediate bureaus and departments are their coordinating units'. According to Ōmori, each ministry or agency is a federated assemblage of sections with their own independent rooms, and 'the Government of Japan is not a monolith, but a "confederation"'.[33]

184   Chapter 4

In other words, the large-room principle of dividing the workforce up into units composed of sections is an expression of the lack of clearly defined duties for individual legislators and, simultaneously, of the idea that these sections claimed the right to a sovereign authority independent of their surroundings. Underlying this development was the absence of any countervailing power, as with the Prussian monarch or public opinion in the US, to monitor the civil service. If there is an origin of Japan's large-room principle, it would have to be the presence or absence of such tensions beyond merely the physical layout of early Meiji architecture.

An emphasis on examination performance

Incidentally, if the duties of individual staff members are not clear, then what are the criteria for promotion? As it turns out, in the prewar civil service, these criteria consisted of years of service and test score. As mentioned earlier, the *kōbun-gumi* (those who passed the higher civil service examinations) were transferred to new positions every two years as they climbed the official rank ladder. How high a rank they could attain was determined by their standing in the higher civil service examinations and their grades during their years at university.

According to political scientist Mitsuhiro Mizutani, this emphasis on test scores was compatible with the personnel practices of the Japanese bureaucracy. Bureaucrats in the Meiji period were under pressure to learn and catch up quickly with advanced Western knowledge. In addition, because there was a shortage of personnel with modern education, it was necessary to transfer these few personnel to many different departments and assign them to a variety of duties. Therefore, rather than those who had acquired expertise in a particular field, the government needed people who could quickly learn many different fields of knowledge and adapt to new environments. As an example of the adaptability of Japanese bureaucrats, Mizutani refers to the case of a bureaucrat in charge of revising inheritance laws in the Taxation Bureau of the Ministry of Finance, who learned this area within five days of his transfer.[34] In order to measure the potential to meet these demands, those who had demonstrated high, unbiased

The Formation of Norms

performance in a number of subjects in university examinations and civil service examinations were suitable.

In his 1999 monograph, Mizutani offered the following remarks from his interview of a former prewar bureaucrat on the topic of career advancement; 'Well, you know, it's your grades – your grades in school and your marks in the civil service examinations'.[35] To validate this account, Mizutani traced the career trajectories of the top seventy and bottom seventy higher civil service examinees between 1912 and 1918. Based on his findings, the percentage of those who attained positions at the *chokunin* level (e.g., director or director-general of the central civil service or governor of the interior) was about 60% for the top seventy and about 20% for the bottom seventy.[36] Although the results of the higher civil service examinations would not have been the whole story, there was arguably a strong correlation.

This norm of emphasizing grades cast a shadow not just over hiring and promotion, but over daily life as well. According to political scientist Jirō Kamishima, at Tokyo Imperial University during the prewar period, where Kamishima himself graduated from, 'everyone's grades were remembered for life, no matter who, and it is perhaps for this reason that alumni lists were often arranged according to [grade] order, providing a means to confirm this'.[37]

However, this emphasis on grades had its origins in a mid-Meiji regulation, namely an 1889 Cabinet Instruction that had set salary amounts for probationary officers based on their score in their university's graduation examination.[38] For Imperial University graduates appointed as probationary officers, this amounted to an annual salary of 600 yen if their average score was eighty-five or higher, 550 yen for scores between eighty and eighty-four, 500 yen for scores between seventy-one and seventy-nine, and 450 yen for a score of seventy or less. Since Imperial University graduates were exempted from the probationary examination at the time, this may have been a measure imposed in its stead. While this measure was soon abolished, it may still have set the precedent that linked promotion to examination standing.

Incidentally, this salary range of 500 to 600 yen seems to have originated from an incident that took place in 1878. In that year, a graduate of the University of Tokyo appointed as an assistant judge was paid a starting salary of 25 yen per month. Students who had not yet completed their studies were incensed by this low salary and resolved that they would take up civilian work the following year if that was all they could expect. In response, the government promised to appoint them at a starting salary of 45 yen.[39] In the salary schedule of the time, this was equivalent to being appointed as a *hannin* official of the first rank, rather than of the third rank.[40] As mentioned in Chapter 3, starting salaries in the private sector at the end of the Meiji period were also linked with those of the civil service, with a monthly salary of 40 yen as the baseline. Ironically, the amount decided in the 1878 case involving students of the University of Tokyo was arguably the event that priced the market for university graduates' starting salaries.

Military 'performance evaluation sheets'

The same tendency to emphasize grades also applied to military officers. In the context of advancement in the army, what was first important was an officer's class standing when he graduated from the Military Academy (*rikugun shikangakkō*), and second, whether he had graduated from (the main course of) the Army War College (*rikugun daigakkō*). Officers could sit the entrance examination for enrollment at the Army War College after receiving a recommendation from their superior during their time as a first or second lieutenant, and one's completion of the college program and grades were important requirements for promotion to the rank of major. So, a student's standing among his military academy peers at the time of his promotion to the rank of major represented the order in which he would be promoted to the rank of general. According to one empirical study, more than 70% of those who graduated from the Army War College were promoted to the general staff.[41]

Thus, even in the military, grades were always taken into consideration. Jirō Kamishima, the political scientist introduced earlier, served on the Philippine front in the Pacific War as an army second lieutenant. In his recollection, 'the sense of hierarchy in the military academies was even more pronounced [than at Tokyo Imperial University]. The

The Formation of Norms

187

pecking order was always accompanied by discriminatory treatment, and not just among those who earned the Imperial Sword [*onshi-gumi*, i.e., the top graduates of the Army War College]. It pervaded the order of command, the order of seating at meetings, the order of declaration, and so on, which made the impression it gave all the more serious'.[42]

However, in addition to their examination scores, military officers were also subjected to overall performance evaluations, known as *kōka*, to review military personnel for promotion. The army used the performance evaluation sheet (*kōka-hyō*) stipulated in the 1874 Army Officer Evaluation Sheet and Its Purpose (*rikugun bukan kōka-hyō narabi sono shushi*), while the navy used that stipulated in the 1890 Regulations for the Evaluation of Military Officers (*bukan kōka-hyō kisoku*). These performance evaluation sheets took the form of an overall assessment of the character (*jinbutsu*) of the candidate for promotion scored on a five-point scale, to which the comments of the relevant superior officer were appended.[43] The components of performance evaluation sheets according to regulations for the handling of naval personnel are listed below.[44] It is evident that potentiality to handle any job assignment was more important than skills for specific positions. As we will see in Chapter 5 and after, private companies in postwar Japan used similar evaluation forms to evaluate employee promotions.

(2) Character Evaluation
5. Personnel shall be evaluated on the four elements of character and conduct, ability, work and constitution, with the greatest emphasis placed on character and moral fiber, and the greatest importance on those with integrity and loyalty.
6. The following points shall be examined in the evaluation of character and conduct:
   a. Personality (evaluation based on the degree of mastery of the martial spirit)
   b. Character (evaluation of qualities necessary for military personnel, such as fortitude, perseverance, decisiveness and alacrity)
   c. Ideology, faith
   d. Obedience, harmony

188 Chapter 4

    e. Language, attitude

    f. Interests, tastes.

7. The following points shall be assessed in the evaluation of ability:

    a. Intelligence (comprehension, perception, judgment and degree of imagination)

    b. Discernment

    c. Skill

    d. Academic knowledge

    e. Experience

    f. Execution.

8. Evaluation of practical performance shall be based on (a) attendance at work, and (b) excellence in performance.

9. Evaluation of stamina shall be based on the following points:

    a. Health and physical fitness

    b. Visual and auditory acuity

    c. Aptitude.

The spread of similar performance evaluation sheets in the private sector in postwar Japan, and the involvement of businessmen who had served in the Japanese military in the spread, will be discussed later in chapters 5 through 7. According to economist Kōshi Endō, the terms *kōka* and *kōka-hyō* for performance evaluation and performance evaluation sheet began to appear in the writings of people like the executive director of the Japan Efficiency Federation (*Nihon nōritsu rengōkai*), who was discussing methods of personnel evaluation in private companies, around October 1937, just after the outbreak of the Second Sino-Japanese War.[45]

Even earlier, the In-House Rules for Employee Promotion set out by the Mitsubishi Joint-Stock Company in October 1916 included a provision for 'considered investigation' (*kōkaku*) by superiors. As mentioned in Chapter 3, Mitsubishi had established in-house qualification ranks to determine salaries. The rules stipulated that 'section chiefs and site supervisors shall carry out a considered investigation of the personalities, ability, attendance and other qualities of the employees in their charge, and shall submit their applications for

The Formation of Norms

189

promotion to the managing director of their department by the date indicated on the left'. Submission of the results of the review were required by the end of March for those who were to be promoted in June and by the end of September for those who were to be promoted in December.[46] The evaluation criteria set out in Mitsubishi's internal rules (i.e., personality, ability and attendance) were identical to those set out for the character evaluation mandated by the navy's regulations for the handling of personnel. As a company, Mitsubishi had grown out of the navy's Nagasaki Shipyard, and it is possible that the influence of the navy's performance evaluations may have been felt from around this period.

Thus, a series of norms had taken shape in the civil service and military by the middle of the Meiji period. Although these norms reflected the particulars of Japan's experience of modernization, many began contingently as measures that were initially temporary or as the result of unforeseen incidents. Yet, just as rails once laid determine a future trajectory, these norms would come to exert their influence on society as a whole.

Military provisions on mandatory retirement

Another example of the influence of the civil service and the military on private firms is the concept of a mandatory retirement age (*teinen*). This word was denoted with Chinese character meaning literally 'stopping year' (停年) during the prewar period, while the current notation meaning 'fixed year' (定年) is believed to have first been used by the National Personnel Authority (*Jinji-in*) of the Japanese government (equivalent to the Civil Service Commission in the US) in the postwar period.[47]

The earliest appearance of the word in a legal context dates to the 1874 Ordinance on the Promotion of Army Officers (*Rikugun shinkyū jōrei*).[48] As mentioned above, this ordinance included a provision for 'years-in-rank on active duty' (*jitsueki teinen*), stipulating that promotion to a higher rank was contingent on service for a certain minimum number of years at the current rank. The number of years for which promotion was 'stayed' at each rank was referred to as *teinen*

(停年). In parallel, the military also saw the establishment of a system of mandatory retirement from service at a certain age. The 1875 Edict on the Retirement of Naval Officers (*kaigun tai'in rei*) stipulated that 'naval officers and civil service mariners' who had passed the 'fixed years of service and age' would be pensioned out, and set mandatory retirement ages for each rank (sixty-five years old for generals, sixty for lieutenant generals, fifty-five for major generals, fifty for colonels and forty-five for lieutenant colonels and below). In the following year, 1876, 'age limits' (*nenrei teigen*) for release from military service at each rank were likewise stipulated in the Edict on Army Officer Pensions (*rikugun onkyū rei*).[49]

Furthermore, in 1884, the Edict on Pensions for Civil Officials (*Kanri onkyū rei*) was enacted and it was succeeded to the Act on Pensions for Civil Officials (*Kanri onkyū hō*) in 1890. This law stipulated that civil servants who had been in office for fifteen years or more who were injured, ill or retired after the age of sixty, would be entitled to a lifetime pension based on their years in office and salary at the time of their retirement. That same year, it was also stipulated that salaried staff at public schools and schoolteachers at municipal elementary schools would be entitled to lifetime retirement benefits, again based on fifteen years of service by age sixty.[50]

However, the provision regarding civil officials stipulated only the right to receive benefits, not their compulsory dismissal at that age. First and foremost, career civil servants – 'the emperor's officials' – held office for life, and until the postwar revision of the National Public Service Act in 1981, there was no mandatory retirement age. Instead, it was customary for officials to resign voluntarily upon recommendation that they do so.[51] While judicial officials were subject to age-based tenure restrictions, and the Imperial University's bylaws also included a provision on retirement age for professors, there was no mandatory retirement age for civil officials. Although a movement to establish a retirement age for civil officials emerged in the early 1930s as part of bureaucracy reform, this never came to fruition.[52]

Military regulations, however, required those who reached a certain age in each rank to retire from service, which was not the case for civilian officials. The specified ages were lower than current

The Formation of Norms 191

mandatory retirement ages in Japanese private companies for some ranks. The 1876 Edict on Army Officer Pensions set the age-in-grade (*teigen nenrei*) limit at age forty-five for first and second lieutenants and at thirty-five for privates and non-commissioned officers. Conceivably, this was because military personnel, unlike civilian officers, are required to meet a certain standard of physical fitness.

This regulation spread to the military's government-run factories in a different form with the introduction of a system that mandated factory workers' compulsory dismissal upon reaching a certain age. According to Masaru Ogihara, who has researched the history of Japan's mandatory retirement system, the origin of *teinen* in a corporate context can be traced to 1887 regulations for workers at the Naval Ammunitions Arsenal, which stipulated that 'the retirement age [*teinen*] for factory workers shall be set at fifty-five years, and those who have reached that age shall be released from service'. Here, the term *teinen*, which had previously been used to refer to a restriction on advancement, had changed to mean age-in-grade for retirement from service. In 1889, the Yokosuka Naval Arsenal also issued Rules for the Dismissal of Hired Workers, which stipulated that workers who had reached the age of fifty 'shall be dismissed'.[53] However, these regulations also provided for the possibility of extending the term of service for those who were highly skilled or physically capable. This seems to have been based on the Edict on the Retirement of Naval Officers and the Edict on Army Officer Pensions, which had almost identical provisions.

The Naval Regular Workers' Ordinance (*kaigun teiki shokkō jōrei*) of 1896 extended these regulations for individual factories to naval manufactories as a whole. The ordinance stipulated that 'those eligible for employment as regular laborers shall be between the ages of twenty-one and forty-five years old, and their working age shall be up to age fifty-five. However, those with special skills may be allowed to work up to age sixty'. Similar provisions were carried over into the Naval Factory Workers' Regulations (*Kaigun shokkō kisoku*) of 1904 and the Naval Construction Regulations (*Kaigun kōmu kisoku*) of 1911.[54]

The spread of mandatory retirement to the private sector

Similar regulations soon spread to other state-owned factories and private companies. Matsuyama Bōseki, a private textile company, and the state-owned Yahata Steel Works respectively issued regulations for factory workers in 1894 and 1907. In both cases, the regulations included the provision that workers would be dismissed upon reaching age fifty or fifty-five, and that they would be allowed to extend their employment for several years if they were highly skilled or in other similarly exceptional circumstances.[55]

Japan was not fully involved in World War I, and the size of large corporations expanded due to the export boom. In addition, the war caused inflation, which led to a series of wage hikes. From that time, such compulsory dismissal provisions broadened their scope to include not only factory workers but also salaried staff. In 1916, the corporate by-laws of the Yokohama Specie Bank stipulated that 'when a secretary reaches the age of sixty, he shall retire unless he is specifically ordered to remain in office'. In 1917, the Mitsubishi Joint-Stock Company stipulated that 'the age-in-grade limit for the company's regular company employees (*sei-in*) shall be fifty-five years of age [...]. However, if the company has reason to deem it necessary, a special order may be issued to allow an employee to remain in his position'. The Mitsui Bank's Regulations on Age-in-Grade Limits of Service, issued in 1926, contained more or less identical provisions.[56]

As is clear from these texts, despite minor differences in detail, the common pattern was compulsory dismissal based on age and the extension of employment only for those who were specifically selected. While these were the in-house regulations issued by individual companies, it seems likely that the Naval Regular Workers' Ordinance was the prototype that came to be emulated throughout the country.

It should be noted that Japanese people at that time did not have the custom of counting their age on their individual birthdays, and instead collectively aged on January 1. For this reason, bulk dismissals due to mandatory retirement should also have been carried out collectively at the end of each fiscal year. This was conducive to preparing positions for the bulk recruitment of new graduates in each April. It is also worth

The Formation of Norms

noting that the 1897 Worker's Relief Program (*Shokkō kyūgo hō*) at Mitsubishi's Nagasaki Shipyard provided for the payment of 'retirement benefits' (*tai'in teate*) by assigning ranks according to workers' titles (e.g., section leader [*kogashira*] or group leader [*kumigashira*]) and by setting different retirement ages according to each rank.[57] This provision was modeled after those of the Servicemen's Pension Law (*Gunjin onkyū hō*), which stipulated different retirement ages for different ranks. This could be considered, in effect, to be the origin of the retirement allowance, a lump-sum payment that is paid to an employee by an employer when 'lifetime employment' is terminated, which is common among Japanese companies.

The Yokohama Specie Bank, in 1916, and Yasuda Mutual Life Insurance Company, in 1922, also introduced systems of retirement allowances and bonuses in recognition of services rendered (*irōkin*) along with age-based dismissal rules. Further, just as in the military, there were also cases of provisions that changed the age-in-grade limit depending on the competence rank in the company, such as the Inabata Dyestuffs Factory, a joint-stock company, which stipulated that the retirement age for 'fifth grade and above shall be sixty years old and for sixth grade and below shall be fifty-five years old'.[58]

The reason that companies introduced mandatory retirement policies was to shed the aging part of their workforces. Initially, organizations would have grown in a rambling fashion and allowed older employees to retire individually, but as they expanded, it became necessary to have clear-cut provisions for retirement. For example, in the corporate history of the Sumitomo Bank, we find that the reason for imposing a mandatory retirement age rule in 1914 was that 'the organization had grown so large that a mandatory retirement age policy became a natural condition of its operation'. A seventy-year retrospective on Tokyo Gas also states that the company used the financial crisis of 1927 'to implement an employee retirement policy'.[59] As described in Chapter 3, when Mitsubishi set its own retirement age in 1917, it introduced a civil service-style ranking scheme the same year. Thus, from World War I to the 1920s, a series of collective norms was formed.

However, as pointed out by Katsunori Miyachi, a historian of social security, the introduction of a retirement age during this period was also intended as a kind of social security policy. Takashi Katsura, who spearheaded the introduction of a mandatory retirement age policy at Tokyo Gas in 1931, stated that his objectives in doing so were twofold: 'to maintain corporate efficiency' and 'to fulfill part of the company's social responsibilities'. According to Katsura, a mandatory age policy, 'in conjunction with a retirement allowance system that might be called uniquely Japanese', was 'an important measure for the development of an industrial society'. It also placed the onus for amassing employees' retirement benefits on the company. In fact, the retirement allowance offered by Tokyo Gas, which Katsura played a key role in introducing, was an extraordinary amount for a private company at the time. Notably, Katsura also served as a member of the government's Advisory Council on Social Security (*shakai hoshō seido shingikai*) after World War II.[60]

Basically, the mandatory retirement policy, at the same time as being a way to maintain corporate efficiency by eliminating aging workers, was also a form of corporate social responsibility in the sense that it provided security in old age in the form of retirement benefits. Considering that the mandatory retirement system had its origins in the edict of servicemen's pension and was imposed together with the provision of retirement benefits, the combination of the two likely seemed a natural idea at the time.

The mandatory retirement system was gaining traction due to the twin aspects of maintaining corporate efficiency and contributing to companies' fulfilment of their social responsibilities. During the Great Depression after 1929, the Bank of Japan and firms like Shibaura Seisakusho (later Toshiba) and Fukushima Bōseki lowered their mandatory retirement age by five years, forcing the dismissal of older workers. The Great Depression resulted in widespread layoffs and labor disputes, which in 1936 prompted the government's enactment of the Severance and Retirement Allowance Reserve Law (*Taishoku tsumitatekin oyobi taishoku teate hō*), which mandated that plants and mines with fifty or more employees pay and fund severance pay, thereby contributing to the further diffusion of mandatory retirement

The Formation of Norms   195

age policies. According to a 1932 survey by Zensanren, the All-Japan Federation of Industrial Organizations (*zenkoku sangyō dantai rengō-kai*), seventy-one out of 162 companies had introduced mandatory retirement age policies, as had 140 out of 336 factories surveyed by the Social Affairs Bureau of the Ministry of the Interior that same year.[61]

In the US, discrimination based on gender and age is prohibited, and dismissal based on age is against the law. However, even in that country, age restrictions and mandatory retirement ages are still permitted among certain professions, including police officers, fire-fighters, air traffic controllers and military personnel.[62] For people in prewar Japan, conscription was a commonplace experience. In this sense, Dore's point that Japanese companies resemble the army, mentioned in Chapter 3, also applies to the prevalence of the mandatory retirement age system.

The term '*shain*' (company employee)

Another influence of the civil service on private companies is the norm of referring to staff employees as '社員 *shain*'. The term *shain* has been a part of the Japanese lexicon since the 1880s. At that time, however, it referred not to employees, but to investors. Even today, in the legal parlance of the Companies Act, *shain* refers to an investor. More precisely, an investor in a general partnership company, limited partnership company or limited liability company is called '*shain*' (member), while an investor in a joint-stock company is called '*kabunushi*' (shareholder).[63]

The change resulted from an imperial ordinance issued by the government in 1890, entitled 'On the Matter of the Payment of Personal Bonds for Officials in Charge of the Receipt and Disbursement of Funds', that required civil servants who handled more than a certain amount of cash or goods to deposit a personal bond in order to prevent them from spending it themselves.[64] The government of the day held civil servants personally liable for compensation to the state in the event of accidents such as the loss of specie by the civil servant handling it. The origins of this system can be traced to the accounting laws of imperial France, and it was incorporated into Japanese accounting laws formulated under the guidance of French advisors to the Meiji government. The system was extended first to include compensation for goods, and then to the payment of personal bonds.[65]

The personal bond system spread first to state-owned enterprises (SOEs). In 1893, the Ministry of Posts and Telecommunications established regulations for handling the personal bonds of civil servants tasked with handling funds, which were then applied to the Japanese Government Railways.[66] In the 1890s, regulations obliging high-level staff to provide their employer with a personal bond of up to twice their annual income also spread to private companies. Labor historian Ryōji Kaneko has suggested that these norms may have been the origin of the use of the term *shain* to refer to salaried staff employees.[67] Although stock companies were still in their infancy at the time, many companies required in their articles of incorporation that their managers held a certain number of shares in order to mitigate risk for investors. Also, the personal bonds collected from salaried staff were invested by the company.[68] This was originally why salaried staff depositing a bond with a company came to be identified as an investor (*shain*) in the management of the business.

The convention of securing personal assurances also existed among the merchant houses of the Edo period. Western companies today have a stock option system whereby executive staff make an investment in a company, for which they receive a dividend. Nevertheless, it is notable that Japan's modern system of personal bonds originated with practices in the civil service and SOEs.

Universities as a conduit for introducing new graduates

The recruitment of new graduates, which began with the civil service, spread to the private sector around the turn of the twentieth century, beginning with Nippon Yūsen and Mitsui, who first incorporated this practice in 1895.[69] The Yahata Steel Works also began hiring engineering graduates from Tokyo Imperial University in 1897, the year that the construction of the facility started, and began hiring new graduates as clerical staff the following year, also from Imperial University.[70] The

The Formation of Norms

practice became commonplace in the 1900s, especially among the large industrial conglomerates and their affiliates, and spread to medium-sized firms during the economic boom that coincided with World War I.

Nevertheless, it is difficult to imagine that companies expected the knowledge that graduates had learned in university to be useful on the job. As discussed in Chapter 3, the training of apprentices by occupational organizations was declining in Japan. Until the early Meiji period, it had been typical for companies to train and raise those who had acquired basic reading and writing skills by the age of fourteen or so (a practice known as *kogai yōsei*). At the time, most private Japanese companies were not in the business of taking advantage of the advanced modern education at the Imperial University. While it was sometimes the case that vocational school graduates were hired as lower-level salaried staff to handle matters like accounting and other 'skilled clerical work', employees likely found few opportunities to make use of knowledge acquired at the Tokyo Imperial University Faculty of Law or Faculty of Letters.[71]

Besides Tokyo Imperial University, Kyoto Imperial University was founded in 1897 (another five imperial universities were founded by 1939). By the 1890s, Tokyo Higher Commercial School (which later became Hitotsubashi University), and other prestigious private universities such as Waseda and Keio had also been founded. As seen in Chapter 3, these five universities (Tokyo, Kyoto, Hitotsubashi, Waseda, Keio) were designated by the large manufacturing company surveyed by Abegglen in 1955 as graduation universities for its higher-level staff employees. By the early twentieth century, Japan's large corporations had come to pay graduates of imperial universities and prestigious colleges salaries as high as those in government offices, as also mentioned in Chapter 3. However, the modernization of Japanese industry had not progressed far enough to take advantage of the modern education learned at these universities and colleges. The 1905 booklet 'Contemporary Guide to Employment for Students' offered the following observation.

> As for which parts of your schooling [at the Faculty of Law] you will find most helpful after joining a bank or company, you will

find things that received little emphasis in school to be of most use, and public international law, contract law and other subjects you wrestled with to be of no use at all. So, you ask, what does a company employee need to do each day? Firstly, traditional Japanese arithmetic. Second, you must write neatly and quickly Chinese characters and be clever in your correspondence. Then there is bookkeeping. [...] If that is the case, it might seem better simply to learn bookkeeping [at vocational school] instead of finishing your higher education. But while bookkeeping alone might be enough to get you a spot at a merchant house for 15 yen or so, it will not get you into a company or bank of the middling or higher rank.[72]

So, what exactly did companies expect from the universities and colleges? Most likely, they expected them to screen for general intellectual ability and information about their graduates' 'character'.

As is still the case today, there are limits to the amount of personal information a company can obtain at the time of recruitment, and screening all applicants through independent tests and interviews would be too labor intensive and costly. What is used, therefore, is pre-screening information, such as applicants' background, degrees, grades and recommendations from people who know them well. Contemporary European and American companies, for example, make use of postgraduate degrees, language examination rankings, work experience in other companies, certificates from public vocational training institutions and technical qualifications. In the early half and middle of twentieth-century Britain, a similar role was also played by accountancy licenses issued by private associations and trade union-recognized skilled trade certificates.

In a society like that of Meiji Japan, however, where institutional credentials were as yet poorly established, introductions by those familiar with applicants played a major role. Such referrals and social connections, or the involvement of a guarantor, were commonplace elements of corporate recruitment in the mid-Meiji period.[73] The role of universities, as well, began in part through personal connections. While many university graduates in the Meiji period also found

The Formation of Norms

199

employment through referrals by their acquaintances and influential connections, their university professors were also a part of these networks of introduction. According to a 1904 book that surveyed the in-house rules of forty-three large companies at that time, eighteen of these companies required prospective graduate hires to be introduced by an 'influential person of great reputation', or a person connected with the company.[74]

Accordingly, university students at that time made use of networks such as prefectural residents' associations (*kenjinkai*) and alumni associations to find referrals. Universities represented one such network, and introductions by professors were a powerful resource. According to Yasutaka Fukui, who has studied the history of the labor market for university graduates, until the mid-Meiji period, more than a few graduates of Keio University (founded in 1858 as a private school, established as a university in 1890, and approved as a private university by the government in 1920) obtained jobs through introductions by the founder Yukichi Fukuzawa, whose portrait was on the 10,000-yen bill from 1984 to 2024.[75]

Personal introductions by professors, the credibility of a school's name, the estimation of those who had completed higher education – all these elements were interconnected. The 1904 book that surveyed the in-house rules mentioned above, in a discussion of the Meiji Life and Fire Insurance Company, notes that 'there are so many Keio University graduates at the company by virtue of the fact that [the company's] President Abe [Motozō] is an alumnus of the same school'. The same book describes how Mitsui & Co. 'hires graduates from the imperial universities, the Tokyo Higher Commercial School, and the departments of Keio University who have been introduced by influential people with good reputations, depending on the availability of open positions'.[76] This could be described as an intermediate state between trust in the good name of a school and personal ties. Also, as the latter statement suggests, in 1904, even though the company was hiring new graduates, it appears to have been doing so to fill vacant positions.

From personnel scarcity to the bulk recruitment of new graduates

At the time, however, like the Japanese government, the large Japanese companies of the time were looking for people with a broad understanding of various Western technologies and institutions. To this end, it was more effective to hire people with intellectual potential who could understand diverse fields and train them within the company rather than hiring those with specialized professional knowledge and skill. The number of those graduating from institutes of higher education was still small, and competition for talent was intense. Only about 2,000 students were graduating from five imperial universities each year, until eight private schools were approved by the government as universities in 1920 under the 1918 University Edict (*Daigaku rei*).[77] Moreover, in the wake of World War I, Japan's economy surged, and the number of companies expanded rapidly, resulting in even fiercer competition for higher education graduates. This set the scene for the establishment of the norm of hiring new graduates in bulk right after they graduate.

In 1918, the personnel section at Mitsui & Co. explained that when hiring graduates of the Tokyo Higher Commercial School (later Hitotsubashi University), 'although the graduation period may not be until April or June, graduates are usually selected at the start of the year, if not the end of the previous year'. Even then, it explained, 'as it is not possible to hire them at such short notice when they graduate, we have started offering advance engagements to those who will be graduating in the next year'. Requests would then be made to the company's various departments to submit their staffing needs for the upcoming year to the personnel section as soon as possible.[78]

By the end of the Meiji period, some Imperial University students were even passing the higher civil service examinations in November and receiving offers of employment from government ministries and agencies while they were still enrolled as students. Yoshinari Kawai (later Vice Minister of Agriculture and Forestry and Minister of Health and Welfare), after passing the exam while still a student in 1910, saw this as sufficient reason to turn down a job offer from Sumitomo through one of his professors.[79] As noted earlier, it was also

The Formation of Norms

becoming common practice for government ministries and agencies to hire Imperial University students as new graduates and then have them take the higher civil service examinations afterward. These circumstances likely also influenced the situation facing Mitsui & Co., which found itself unable to hire new graduates without offering 'advance engagements' in the year prior to graduation.

According to a study by management historian Yukio Wakabayashi, until 1916, Mitsui & Co. arranged a one-year apprenticeship period for new hires, and individual letters of employment were issued to graduate recruits randomly throughout the year. In 1917, however, this apprenticeship period was reduced to only three months, and the issuance of letters of employment was concentrated in July and August. This signified that a norm had emerged whereby the start of three-month apprenticeships was concentrated in April, suggesting that this period marked a shift from filling vacancies as they arose to the bulk recruitment of new graduates.[80]

Around the time the University Edict was issued in 1918, graduation dates for institutes of higher education were also standardized to fall in March. This process was completed in 1920, when Imperial University, the final holdout, changed its graduation date from July to March. This period may be considered to have marked the emergence of the pattern of 1 April as the date of the arrival of higher education graduates as new employees, which is the dominant norm in today's Japan. As mentioned above, this was also the time when the civil service-type ranking schemes and the mandatory retirement system began to spread to companies in the private sector as a series of collective norms.

From grades to 'character'

Initially, the information that companies wanted most from institutes of higher education was students' grades at the time of graduation. As noted earlier, this seems to have been an echo of the importance placed on graduation examination marks in the civil service. Seiji Noma (who would go on to found the Kodansha publishing house), who moved to Tokyo in 1907 to work as a clerk at Imperial University, later recalled the following.

> In those days, depending on your score on the graduation examination, you could go to the Ministry of Finance or the Ministry of Home Affairs, but you absolutely had to score at least seventy-five to be hired by any government office. Even in the business world, again, there was a tendency to determine acceptance or rejection based on your score. When a student visited a kind and obliging professor to ask for a job, he would write his score on a name card for the sake of convenience. Back then, there were even rumors that a certain professor would not meet with those who scored less than seventy, since nothing could come of it.[81]

As mentioned earlier, at one point, an official's starting salary in the civil service depended on his university test score. This practice may also have carried over into the private sector, as evidenced by the case of one employee who started with Mitsui & Co. in 1900 who proudly recalled how, by virtue of his good test scores, his starting salary was 5 yen higher than that of a classmate, even though both had joined the company as freshly minted graduates of Tokyo Imperial University's Faculty of Law.[82] This difference in pay indicated that he had been appointed one rank higher in terms of the civil service hierarchy.

A 1908 case from the Yahata Steel Works has also been identified in which the company only checked resumes and transcripts sent from the Nagasaki Higher Commercial School and made hiring decisions without contacting new graduates at all.[83] This case exemplifies how companies at the time relied heavily on screening information from schools.

One reason for the emphasis on school performance was the lack of screening capabilities in the private sector at the time. In 1912, Mitsui & Co., then in the midst of ramping up its recruitment of new graduates, established a personnel section that would be independent of the firm's general affairs section, which had dealt with personnel matters up to that point. For the total workforce of more than 1,000 employees, however, the personnel section initially consisted of only

The Formation of Norms   203

six people, all of whom held concurrent positions.[84] Considering the effort required to screen applicants with so few people, referrals and grades from schools they had hired from in the past would likely have constituted important information.

From around the 1920s, however, companies began placing less emphasis in their selections on grades and referrals, and more on 'character' (*jinbutsu*). Although applicants were required to have at least moderate grades at the time of their graduation, recruits were selected from the pool of applicants via a face-to-face interview. Yasutaka Fukui lists several reasons for this development.[85] First, thanks to educational reforms accomplished from the 1910s, performance evaluations were no longer based on quantitative test scores, but rather on a method using grades such as 'excellent', 'good', 'acceptable' and 'unacceptable'. This ruled out the possibility of fine-grained evaluations that could be differentiated by a single point. Moreover, companies realized from their experience of using new graduates that high achievers were not necessarily savvy in terms of business matters. The most significant factor, however, was the rapid increase in the number of university graduates entering the job market as private vocational schools became recognized as 'universities' under the 1918 University Edict. The number of university graduates, which had been less than 2,000 until 1919, surpassed 6,000 in 1924, 8,000 in 1927, and 10,000 in 1930.

With this development, the utility of the screening function played by university grades and referrals deteriorated. This marked a qualitative change away from the period when the number of students was limited, and when they had kept to social circles that were limited to people of the same competence level. Companies therefore began to place more emphasis on selection through in-house interviews and other means that would allow them to take the measure of applicants' 'character'.

Institutionalized school referrals

With the increase in university graduates in the 1920s, it was no longer a seller's labor market as it had been in the Meiji period. The ranks

204   Chapter 4

of staff employees earning monthly salaries also swelled, and lightly pejorative epithets such as *koshiben* (literally 'lunchbox hanging from the waist', a reference to low-paid office workers) and *sararīman* (salaryman) entered the popular lexicon.[86]

Nevertheless, schools continued to refer new graduates to the workforce. In fact, schools began to institutionalize these introductions by creating specialized job placement departments. Companies established relationships with specific schools and asked the schools to recommend students. For their part, schools would then select students for recommendation based on grades and other criteria. Even in the Meiji period, companies had looked to schools not so much to issue degrees guaranteeing professional competence as to provide an advance screening function to vet students' character. The institutionalization of school referrals in the form of enhancing this screening function could be characterized as the schools' attempt to deal with the situation that began to develop from the 1920s.

Particularly for the newly emerging private universities, job placements were an important challenge since the performance of their graduates on the job would affect the management of the school. Waseda University established a provisional 'personnel desk' in 1921, which was made permanent and upgraded to a 'personnel section' in 1925. Meiji University also established a personnel section in 1924 and organized an employment committee made up of leading professors and board members. As graduates found it increasingly difficult to secure employment in the Great Depression after 1929, universities began to focus more and more on their job placement services, with Tokyo Imperial University establishing an employment research committee in 1931 and Keio University establishing an employment section in 1939.[87]

This trend spread not only among universities, but also among secondary schools and vocational schools whose graduates became lower-level technical workers and salaried staff. According to a 1927 survey by the Central Employment Bureau of the Ministry of Home Affairs (whose function was later taken up by the Social Affairs Division of the Ministry of Home Affairs, the Social Affairs Bureau of the Ministry of Health and Welfare, and the Occupational Division of the

The Formation of Norms

Ministry of Health and Welfare), 44% of the 109 companies nationwide with capital of at least 10 million yen that responded to the survey hired new graduates on a regular basis. Among banks, trust companies and insurance companies in particular, this proportion rose to 77%. That year, only 23% of the companies in the mining and manufacturing industries were regularly hiring new graduates, but by the time of the 1935 survey, that figure had risen to 63%. Companies arranged for the top-performing students from designated schools to be referred to them, and selected employees through face-to-face interviews based on their 'character, intellect and constitution'.[88] Drawing on a survey conducted by the Central Employment Placement Office of the Ministry of Home Affairs and its successor organizations, Yasutaka Fukui has calculated the ratio of employment decisions accounted for by school referral. He finds that in 1934, this ratio was 74.8% for university graduates, 78.5% for professional school graduates and 85.9% for graduates of Class A vocational schools, and that this ratio continued to rise steadily until 1939.[89]

In view of this background, we find that the role consistently fulfilled by Japan's schools was that of providing quality assurance for prospective staff employees. If schools would recommend individuals who were deemed trustworthy after being observed over a long period, then firms could reduce their screening costs. Thus, we can say that what initially began as referrals through social or personal connections was eventually institutionalized in the form of organizational recommendations by schools. This also came to constitute a referential criterion for in-house promotions.

Even if the impact of higher education on productivity remains unclear, its function as an index of ability represents what is known as 'signaling' in the field of economics. To that extent, this is a constant across all countries. Nevertheless, as we have seen, in all likelihood the main reasons for school referrals to have developed as they did in Japan were firstly that companies focused on the potentiality of new graduates rather than degrees that corresponded to specific professional positions, and secondly the absence of the certification of qualifications by occupational organizations in comparison to European countries.

Yet, in comparison to the US, another factor at play was the fact that the Japanese government had now standardized school curricula. Labor historian Sanford Jacoby has noted that for US employers in the first half of the twentieth century, it would have been out of the question to hire new graduates to long-term positions without reliable personal information. One reason for this was that the US education system differed between states and school districts, making a uniform comparison of skills impossible. Jacoby tells us that, among US employers, the long-term employment of laborers was only feasible after they had undergone a set probationary period, and after a careful and lengthy selection by the employers and foremen.[90] And in Japan after the 1960s, the university's referrals would become less important, and only the name of the graduating university would serve as a signal of a new graduate's potential to respond to in-house job training.

Limits of the higher education market

Thus, while the hiring of new graduates has increased, the quality of jobs available to those who have completed higher education has declined. In the late 1920s and early 1930s, the employment rate for university graduates declined, a situation that found cinematic expression in Yasujirō Ozu's 1929 film production of *Daigaku wa detakeredo* (I Graduated, But...).

While this was partly due to the economic recession of the time, it was also true that demand could no longer keep pace with the rapid increase in the supply of university graduates.[91] The trends in the number of university graduates and the number of job seekers at the time show that rather than stemming from a decrease in the number of hires (i.e., the number of spots available at companies), this difficulty in finding employment resulted from an oversupply of graduates.[92] This situation was similar to the experience of the 'Lost Generation' of the 1990s and early 2000s, as seen in Chapter 1. In the 1930s, the overall number of students enrolled in higher education, including professional schools, plateaued until the wartime economy that emerged with the outbreak of the Second Sino-Japanese War in 1937 brought increased demand.[93] This could be characterized as the

The Formation of Norms

207

prewar social structure having reached saturation, unable to absorb any further increase in the number of higher education graduates.

Of course, this was hardly surprising given the three-tier structure of the civil service and of private companies. As mentioned in Chapter 3, in 1921, the workforce at the Yahata Steel Works consisted of 101 higher officials, 303 *hannin* officials, 1,341 *yatoi* and *yōnin*, and 18,249 factory workers. Given the maintenance of a three-tier structure organized along the lines of educational background and assuming that university graduates would have become higher officials, we can calculate that for each additional university graduate, there would have had to have been sixteen more people who had completed their secondary education and 182 more who had completed their primary education. In other words, while this structure remained the underlying premise, the top tier of the pyramid would have been unable to expand beyond a certain point.

It is difficult to estimate the exact number and percentage of salaried workers at that time. In 1929, labor activist Shirō Koike, later a parliamentary member of the Socialist Masses Party (*Shakai taishūtō*), estimated that the number of people earning salaries in the public and private sectors, even with the addition of doctors and other professionals, was 1.7 million from the 1921 Statistical Yearbook of the Empire of Japan.[94] According to the 1920 census, the number of persons whose 'main occupation' was 'staff employee' was 1.51 million, which was 5.5% of the total number of persons with a 'main occupation'.[95] Incidentally, in the breakdown described above for the Yahata Steel Works, higher officials and *hannin* officials account for only 2.0% of the total workforce, and even with the inclusion of *yatoi* and *yōnin*, the relative proportion of all salaried staff was 8.8%. Considering that agriculture, which was mostly self-employed, accounted for more than 50% of the workforce in the 1920s, one could assume that the figure of 8.8% divided by half was close to the percentage of salaried staff employees in society as a whole.

Labor economist Shōjirō Ujihara, who as we saw in Chapter 3 outlined the peculiarity of the particular expression in the Japanese case of the three-tier structure of companies by educational background, describes the situation as follows in 1959. Based on data from the

Social Affairs Bureau of the Ministry of Home Affairs, it is estimated that in 1931, the percentage of students who went on to secondary education was about 31%. University and professional school graduates accounted for only about 3% of the total number of elementary school graduates, which falls to 0.8% if we limit this to only university graduates. In other words, at that time, 'one candidate for middle management-level positions appeared in the labor market each year for every three to four elementary school graduates, and one candidate for leadership-level positions for every 300 to 1,000 elementary school graduates'. Yet, 'even then, people were decrying the surplus of highly educated workers'.[96]

In fact, the view that higher education was producing too many graduates had appeared much earlier. At a meeting of Mitsui & Co.'s branch managers in 1916, the manager of the head office, after stating that 'those with higher education [are] high-ranking officers', went on to argue the following.

> Our firm could be said to have a lot of officers, but only a few enlisted men, so the upper and lower ranks are somewhat out of balance. In view of this, in future, we need to keep in mind that we must strive for harmony by avoiding the error of employing a relatively large number of business graduates and becoming too big-headed.[97]

With a surplus of 'high-ranking officers', the organization had become 'too big-headed', and there were too few 'enlisted men'. This means that in order to maintain the organization's balance, they sought to increase the number of recruits with only a secondary education or lower. In fact, in the late 1920s, as the number of university graduates burgeoned, a trend emerged whereby companies' recruitment rate (i.e., employees hired as a proportion of all applicants) was inversely proportional to the level of education. According to a tabulation prepared by Yasutaka Fukui based on data from the Central Employment Placement Office of the Ministry of Home Affairs and its successor organizations, the employment rate was lowest for university graduates and highest for secondary school graduates.[98]

The Formation of Norms

Moreover, even after 1937, when the employment situation improved due to the economic boom that accompanied Japan's war footing, the increase in the employment rate for secondary school graduates was greater than for university graduates. The declining employment rate among the educated population was recognized as a social problem in the 1920s and 1930s. One 1930s employment guide offered the following description:

> Perhaps the most alarming thing is that the highly educated are now joining the ranks of the free laborers because of the difficulty of finding work, now reportedly as many as 300 people with a secondary level of schooling or higher are working among the free laborers in Tokyo alone. The danger is that these intellectuals-turned-free-laborers lean ideologically to the extreme left and curse society, inciting the unschooled free laborers by instilling them with socialist ideas. The vigilance and prevention of this issue is the most urgently to be studied as a countermeasure to the unemployment problem.[99]

However, the guide did not refer to any factual evidence of a connection between the difficulty that highly educated individuals faced finding employment and the rise of socialism. The text only cites vague figures when it states the existence of those with a secondary level of schooling or higher working among laborers. Moreover, the number was only 300. Such examples are more appropriately regarded as expressions of anxiety about upheavals in the existing order rather than indications of empirical fact. Shōjirō Ujihara describes the tone of this period as follows.

> One important reason why the problem of unemployment among the highly educated, who were so small in number as to be inconsequential, had to be taken up as a special social problem apart from unemployment in general, is precisely that the surplus in this class was related to the very existence of the order itself.[100]

Japanese society had developed a hierarchical structure based on educational background that was disconnected from professional position. However, under this structure, the employment rate of new graduates from universities declines as more people complete higher education. This dilemma, as Ujihara notes, was an issue related to 'the existence of order itself'. Then, in the 1960s high-growth period, when the rate of higher education took a quantum leap from prewar levels, the three-tier structure of prewar companies was also forced to undergo a transformation. This will be discussed in Chapter 6.

Utilization of female office staff

In the clerical domain, to maintain this structure, female office staff were considered 'enlisted men'. The popularization of typewriters and adding machines in the 1920s contributed to an increase in the number of women handling clerical work. Management historian Yukio Wakabayashi highlights the following conversation at a Mitsui & Co. branch managers' meeting in 1921.

A: Trialing the use of female clerks for mechanical work is one method.

B: In the Lumber Division, we've hired only local employees and have been slow to raise wages, but even so expenses have been mounting. If business volume were to increase as it has in the past, this would have been fine, but when the time comes when it is necessary to save money, we need to develop personnel who will be satisfied with a fixed income throughout their lives.

C: For example, it is sometimes the case that someone who needn't be paid more than 100 yen in our company must be given a raise along with other employees.

B: However, that's precisely why our company attracts so many talented people.

D: Even if the likes of women should be content with a set income, it must be difficult for men with aspirations, and truly difficult to the extent that they can work according to their own wish.[101]

The Formation of Norms

The reason why Mitsui & Co. attracted talent was that it offered uniform salary increases, even for employees whose job performance did not necessarily merit a higher salary. Even locally hired lower-level salaried staff expected raises. Accordingly, there was no question of abandoning the civil officials-type seniority-based wage system. However, continuing to increase wages would mean being unable to withstand rising costs during periods of economic stagnation. Therefore, they would have to hire people who would 'be satisfied with a fixed income throughout their lives'. A concrete example given was female office workers. This was the gist of the above conversation.

However, Japanese companies did not actually have a system for hiring salaried staffs at fixed job-based wages. As a result, the method taken involved making these female office workers retire before they were due for a seniority-wage increase. According to its 1934 regulations, when Mitsui Bank first began hiring female employees on a temporary basis, temporary workers engaged in miscellaneous work had to retire upon reaching their twentieth birthday. Later, even in 1938, when the bank began hiring female office staff as temporary workers who were treated like regular salaried staff, they had to retire upon reaching their twenty-second birthday.[102] In reality, however, only a few companies explicitly introduced young mandatory retirement age provisions for female staff, and most retired in line with customary practice or by informal recommendation.

Note that although they were also women, we do not see any provisions for younger retirement ages for female factory workers, who did not receive seniority-based wage increases like salaried staff did.[103] The mandatory retirement at a young age for women was introduced to resolve the contradiction between the civil officials-type seniority wage system and the market principle in the private sector, and was not necessary for female factory workers who were not paid by seniority.

Female office workers were non-career lower-level clerks with secondary educations, the equivalent of companies' 'non-commissioned officers'. According to a 1937 survey on professional women conducted by the Osaka Prefectural Social Affairs Department, 76.7% of female office workers were graduates of girls' high school (*kōtō jogakkō*, equivalent of a boys' secondary school in the prewar education system) or other secondary education institutions. In terms of seniority, 81.8% had been with the company for five years or less, and 53% for three years or less.[104] Compared with male salaried staff, whose salaries continued to increase until middle age, female office workers were far less costly. As a result, lower-level male clerks – especially typists – were rapidly replaced by women.

Women, however, could not be promoted to the upper echelons of the Japanese corporate order. Especially before World War II, secondary education was offered on a single-sex basis, while higher education was available only to men, in principle. Although some universities accepted female students and auditors, companies were not willing to accept women with university degrees at that time. A 1936 survey by the Social Affairs Bureau of the Ministry of Home Affairs asked large companies with capital assets of at least 10 million yen about new hires they had made that year. The survey found that of the 2,292 workers who were university graduates, only two were women, and of the 2,097 who were professional school graduates, only sixteen were women.[105]

The hiring of women as typists and for other lower-level clerical positions in the 1910s and 1920s, with women's comparatively low wages as the rationale, also occurred in the US and other countries. So, Japan was not unique in this respect. What could be characterized as the Japanese variation of this system was the fact that these practices were based on the seniority-based wage system for men in combination with the institutionalized mandatory retirement of women at a young age.

What happened to the women who were laid off due to the mandatory retirement system is unknown. However, it is likely that many of them worked in other ways after marriage. This is because men's wages were not so high at that time.

Historian Akiko Senmoto analyzed the household income and expenditure structure of factory workers, government officials, company employees and teachers from the Cabinet Statistics Bureau's 'Household Accounting Survey Report' from fiscal 1926 to 1941.[106] According to her analysis, in all categories, the incomes of the men

The Formation of Norms

213

of the households were consistently in the 80–90% range of total household income, which was supplemented by the income of the spouse and family members, loans and other sources. The sources of income for spouses were diverse, but the most common among households headed by government officials and company employees was domestic work in sewing, which was compatible with household chores.

There is some debate among scholars regarding the female labor participation rate in prewar Japan, as informal or side jobs may not have been reflected in government statistics. In Japan at that time, women were often engaged in contract work in the cottage industry, including wage weaving. In Western countries, cottage handicrafts declined due to competition from factory production. In Japan, however, a collaboration was established whereby large factories produced the yarn and women wove for wages at home.[107] One reason was the spread of small, inexpensive machines that could be installed in the home, such as small looms, sewing machines and electric motors.[108] Thus, unlike in Western countries, where large factories emerged in the age of the steam engine, mechanization was possible even in home handicrafts. This phenomenon shows that technological advances made it possible to work at home, and concentration on large factories was not an inevitable part of modernization.

According to Senmoto's analysis, in 1926, households with a monthly income of 200 yen or more had household expenditures that were less than the mean of household income. In 1921, economist Atsukichi Morimoto estimated that the annual income required for a standard household of the time, a married couple and three children, to maintain a middle-class lifestyle by Western standards in urban areas was 3,000 yen, a monthly income of 250 yen. However, Morimoto estimated from a 1919 tax survey that 0.72% of households had an annual income in excess of 3,000 yen, and 1.38% had an income of 2,000 yen or more.[109] A monthly income of 200 yen or more was equivalent to the salary of a middle or higher level government official. For this class, the 'male breadwinner' ideology could have been realized. For other households, however, women often worked in some capacity as well. As we saw in Chapter 1, the female labor participation rate in

214   Chapter 4

Japan is high because of the limited number of high-income men, and has historically not ever declined as much as in Western Europe and North America.

Differences vis-à-vis Germany

The influence of civil service and military norms on the private sector is also not a phenomenon unique to Japan. For example, the French term *cadre*, which originally referred to officers who had graduated from military academies, was co-opted as a term for executives in private companies.[110] Also, a rating scale developed in 1916 by the Carnegie Institute of Technology in the US for evaluating aspects of people's character was employed by the US Army during World War I to select officers for rapid training. Later, a simplified version of this scale was introduced into performance evaluations by private companies and for federal government public servants.[111] As discussed in Chapter 2, during and after World War I, the US federal government introduced job analysis in military industries, and eventually US labor unions demanded equal pay for jobs that job analysis deemed to be equivalent.[112]

The influence of civil service and military institutions on the private sector during the process of modernization was a general phenomenon, hardly something unique to Japan. In their subsequent history, however, employment practices in the private sector became distinguished from one another depending on the difference of social norms that ran counter to the public sector, as well as on differences in the nature of the civil service institutions themselves. An interesting comparison with Japan is the case of Germany.

Government bureaucracy also spilled over into industry in Germany, which like Japan was a latecomer to the world stage. The historian Jürgen Kocka tells us that in Germany, 'bureaucratization preceded industrialization, and bureaucratic structures, processes, and values therefore profoundly shaped the process and character of industrialization in Germany, in contrast to Great Britain and the United States'.[113]

The Formation of Norms

215

German bureaucracy demanded unstintingly loyal service to the state, in return for which civil servants were rewarded with high salaries and benefits. Even the occupations of lower-ranking officials such as post-office clerk or police officer enjoyed high esteem and popularity. Moreover, in Germany, the government also operated enterprises such as mining and road construction. Kocka estimates that the proportion of salaried positions in government offices in Germany in 1890 was about twice that of Great Britain.[114]

The boards of directors at large German companies also included retired military officers and state bureaucrats. The founder of Siemens, Kocka tells us, was a retired technical officer who had 'received part of his training in a technical military school in Berlin and had spent 15 years in a military career before starting his own business'. Kocka notes that Siemens' written factory rules and hierarchical chain of command were strongly influenced by the bureaucracy, which 'resulted from the acceptance of traditional organizational models developed outside industry'.[115]

The same terminology used in the civil service and military also spilled over into German private industry, just as in the Japanese case for terms for 'mandatory retirement age' (*teinen*) and 'section manager' (*kachō*). Large German companies from the end of the nineteenth into the twentieth century were characterized by a three-tier structure of manager and higher salaried staff (*Beamte*), lower-level technicians and white-collar workers (*Angestellte*) and laborers (*Arbeiter*). The German term '*Beamte*' had originally signified civil servants appointed by the state, and the salaried staff of private firms were called *Privatbeamte* ('private civil servants'). Kocka points out that this self-image on the part of clerical and technical staff of themselves as 'private civil servants' was not present in either the US or Britain.[116]

According to Kocka, in terms of their status, salaried employees at Siemens 'were comparable to civil servants' in many respects, including the emphasis on seniority. For the company, to the extent that it emphasized loyalty, 'the civil servant ethos of employees was in the interest of management'. The firm was also similar to the civil service in that there were many management and staff positions that only university graduates could reach, and in that there were general rules for hiring, compensation and promotion. Even the German word *Ingenieur* (engineer) had been used until the mid-nineteenth century only in the military sense of referring to a member of 'the specific military formation responsible for the construction of roads, bridges, and war machines'.[117]

However, this is where the similarities between Germany and Japan end. While both countries shared the points that bureaucratization had preceded industrialization and that bureaucracy had influenced the business world, they differed in terms of the nature of the bureaucracy.

In his definition of bureaucracy, Kocka draws on Max Weber's definition of bureaucratic organizations as being 'characterized by formal employment, salary, pension, promotion, specialized training and functional division of labor, well-defined areas of jurisdiction, documentary procedures, and hierarchical sub- and super-ordination'.[118] Of these, although 'specialized training and functional division of labor, well-defined areas of jurisdiction, [and] documentary procedures' were prominent in German bureaucracy, they were not necessarily key elements of its Japanese counterpart.

Accordingly, Kocka highlights the effect of these characteristics in the bureaucracy's influence on German industry. The salaried staff at Siemens were hired on the basis of their professional educational qualifications in industry or commerce to perform 'highly specialized and routinized' activities. Factory production followed documented and standardized processes, and the sales departments and field offices 'worked according to most detailed, centrally issued regulations'. The influence of this bureaucracy in Germany had started to progress toward the subdivision and clarification of duties at the turn of the twentieth century. While this resulted in processes resembling those of Taylorism, this development took place well before its importation to Germany from the US. Furthermore, the evolution of technical universities and industrial institutes in Germany proceeded in parallel with this specialization.[119]

These processes were unlike those that unfolded in Japan. While there are many practices that may be considered bureaucratic influences on Japanese business, the key elements here were the bulk recruitment of new graduates, large open plan offices and regular

The Formation of Norms

personnel transfers. Thus, even if a bureaucratic influence was similarly present, we could say that the nature of that bureaucracy was different in Japan and Germany.

The impact of occupational oraganizations in Germany

What was even more distinct from Japan's experience were the deeply entrenched position of technical credentials in German society and the professional awareness of its engineers and salaried staff employees.

Large modern manufacturing firms like Krupp used technologies that were unsuited to conventional apprenticeship schemes. Krupp had put in place a factory-based apprenticeship scheme that allowed laborers to learn modern technologies, and it accredited the most accomplished workers with in-house certifications.[120] In Germany, however, a cross-firm system of occupational apprenticeships was deeply entrenched. For firms as well, rather than training complete novices, it was preferable to hire apprentices and repurpose them, for example, from locksmiths to finishers. Even when companies established proprietary training programs, this was only due to a shortage of apprentices, or a result of the high turnover rate among experienced apprentices who were confident in their abilities. Social qualifications also enjoyed more public recognition than corporate qualifications. In this context, companies began making efforts to have their in-house technical accreditations recognized by society as being equivalent to conventional professional qualifications.

From the 1900s through the 1920s a widespread effort emerged to systematize the certifications offered by individual companies as well as to standardize occupational regulations and training periods. As a result, in 1938, a ministerial decree by the Reich Education Ministry granted such certifications the same formal recognition as the more traditional artisan trade examinations. This process paralleled with the modernization and unification of traditional artisan apprenticeship and *Meister* credentials throughout the country. Within this process, the *Handwerkskammer* – the regional chambers of handicrafts or artisan organizations – were not necessarily at odds with companies, and indeed, sometimes collaborated to organize examination committees.

These two sides of the movement developed into the official industrial *Meister* system and Germany's dual system of vocational training.[121]

The unification of vocational training and accreditations was also promoted by a movement organized by engineers to raise the social standing of industrial technologies.[122] German engineers formed assorted associations and conducted various campaigns to raise their status, one of which involved enhancing professional educational institutions associated with industrial technologies and having their diplomas recognized as accreditations of professional competence. These workers were competing against lower-level salaried staff who had only received in-house training at their companies to become technicians or draftsmen. In contrast, engineers sought to differentiate themselves from their companies' skilled workers and elevate their social standing by furthering the specialization of technical universities and industrial technical colleges.

The Deutsche Techniker-Verband (German Federation of Engineers and Technicians), founded in 1884, considered the completion of professional school education in a technical specialty as a prerequisite for membership. During this movement, the German term *Ingenieur* was coined to refer to technicians who had a theory-based vocational education rather than simply on-the-job training. Thus, the German term '*Ingenieure*' was established as a generic concept for people in various technical occupations who had a specialized technical education and did not engage in manual labor. Hence, unlike the British term 'engineer', the German term '*Ingenieure*' does not include skilled factory workers. A similar movement also emerged among clerical employees, who formed their own professional body to differentiate themselves from and compete with accountants and orderlies who had received only in-house training.[123]

Germany's vocational education and technical accreditations were not a direct continuation of the guild tradition. Rather, they were the result of a movement by handicraft artisans and engineers that led to the establishment of a modern and unified institution that, by way of a different process than in the US, led to the creation of clearly defined and specialized positions and a cross-firm labor market. This is why cross-firm job training and hierarchies had such a significant impact,

The Formation of Norms   219

even in companies that, like Krupp, emphasized in-house training. In the late nineteenth century, many of Krupp's senior technicians were people who were already of high status who, after pursuing higher education in the field of engineering, were singled out for promotion to factory superintendent or laboratory director before the age of thirty. Many lower-level salaried staff, such as draftsmen, clerks and technicians, had already worked as salaried staff outside of Krupp or had been hired after completing an apprenticeship, and suffered no apparent disadvantage in terms of salary, even when they were hired mid-career.[124]

Differences of the workers' movement

The movement by German engineers and salaried staff to improve their social standing, in addition to being motivated by competition from skilled workers and lower-level salaried staff that had been trained in-house, also emphasized the uniqueness of the salaried staff in opposition to the manual workers' labor movement.

Like the *Ingenieur*, the *Angestellte* (mid- and lower-level white-collar employee) was another generic concept for employees in various clerical occupations formed in the midst of a movement. Originally, *Angestellte* referred to employees, and in the context of the government, has been used to refer to clerks hired by the government under private legal contracts, as opposed the *Beamte*, the civil servants who were appointed by the state under public law.[125] Unlike the *Arbeiter*, or manual workers, who were paid a daily rate, the *Angestellte* were mostly paid by the month, which is why the term was sometimes glossed as *sararīman* (salaryman) in Japanese translations.[126]

The lower-level salaried staff, who had their own positions in individual firms, did not act in solidarity or join common-interest organizations until the 1880s. Even at Krupp at the end of the nineteenth century, positions such as secretary, draftsman, foreman and storekeeper were classified neither as *Beamte* nor as *Arbeiter*.[127] As the labor movement lead by the working class coalesced, however, lower-level salaried staff from various occupations began to act in solidarity so as to distinguish themselves from laborers. That is, the salaried staff began to campaign to be treated more in accordance with civil servants than laborers.

Symbolic of this campaign was the establishment in 1881 of the *Deutscher Privatbeamten-Verein* (German Private Officials Association).[128] This association, which included membership from various types of salaried staff, including engineers, bookkeepers, office workers and bank employees, among others, sought to provide an insurance scheme that would approximate as closely as possible the pension benefits enjoyed by retired civil servants. With the introduction of Bismarck's social insurance schemes, lower-level salaried staff with annual incomes below a certain threshold were enrolled in the same old-age pension system as laborers. Deeming this to be unbecoming of their status, they demanded their own pension insurance. The result of this movement was the 1911 *Versicherungsgesetz für Angestellte* (Law Relating to Insurance of Salaried Employees). The passage of the insurance law was supported by government and political parties, who were concerned about the burgeoning labor movement and sought to win the support of lower-level salaried staff. It was in the course of this movement that the *Angestellte* identity was brought into being among lower-level salaried workers across companies.

The same was true of the French *cadres*. Although the origin of the term *cadre* lay with the military, the social category of *cadre* was constructed from the 1930s as the result of a joint movement by salaried staff and technicians across a variety of fields. They, too, have pension insurance and a confederation of unions as *cadres*.[129]

In the US, as mentioned earlier, job analysis began in the military industry under government guidance during World War I, and the rating scale spread from the military to the private sector. However, the former was used by the labor movement as a tool to demand equal pay for equal work as discussed in Chapter 2, and the latter disappeared after the 1970s. In the wake of the civil rights movement of the 1960s, anti-discrimination regulations took effect and arbitrary assessments were no longer an option. As a result, character assessment methods, which had spread from the US Army to the private sector, fell into disuse after the 1970s. In studies of lawsuits from the late 1970s onward, it was concluded that companies were more likely to lose cases when they

The Formation of Norms

conducted assessments that emphasized 'traits' of the workers rather than work-related 'behavior', and when the assessment system was not based on a job analysis.[130] The evaluation of personnel without regard to race or gender and the clear presentation of contractual terms in job descriptions are practices that have taken root in the US through the labor movement and anti-discrimination movement.

In Great Britain, as well, managers sometimes conceived of companies in military terms. James Nasmyth, Scottish engineer and philosopher, who opened a foundry near Manchester in 1836, referred to his favorite foremen as his 'workshop lieutenants'. He was in favor of the in-house training of workers hired by the company, ignoring skill accreditation issued by the unions. Naturally, there are those in any society who dream of a militaristic corporate order that operates under their command. In Britain, however, such attempts failed to gain traction owing to the strength of the craft unions that existed at the cross-firm level.[131]

In the course of modernization, the influence of military and civil service institutions on private companies has been a universal phenomenon. However, in Germany, France, the US and Great Britain, this influence may be said to have developed along different lines than it did in Japan owing to the impact of factors beyond the level of individual companies, particularly social movements in the interests of labor, salaried staff and civil rights.

This does not mean that Japan was not without its own movements similar to those of salaried staff in France and Germany. In June 1919, the Salarymen's Union (*Hōkyū seikatsusha kumiai*, or SMU), was founded, and by 1927 was working alongside the Socialist Masses Party (*Shakai taishūtō*) to enact a law to protect the interests of salaried staff.[132] This was because, as discussed earlier, by the 1920s, the status of salaried staff with higher and secondary education was declining, and lower-level salaried staff were now finding it difficult to make a living due to inflation caused by the First World War.

Women also joined the SMU, and in March 1920, a typists' union was organized under the SMU, with a founding convention held at the Ōtemachi Central Sanitary Hall. An article in the Tokyo *Asahi Shimbun* newspaper reported that about 1,000 people (80% of them women) participated in the convention, which raised two demands: (1) a monthly wage of 50 yen for an eight-hour workday, and (2) that 'government offices should promptly make us regular officials (*hon-kan*) and commercial companies should promptly make us regular company employees (*sei-shain*)' and called for the 'elimination of discrimination'. As far as I can confirm, this was the first time the term 'regular company employee' (*sei-shain*) was used in a Japanese newspaper to refer to an employment issue.[133] The demand that they be made the government's regular officials is probably because many of these women were non-regular *koin* clerks, employed by the Ministry of Telecommunications and other agencies.

Even so, as of 1926, the SMU is estimated to have enrolled only about 1% of salaried employees in the workforce.[134] The union was also advocating an alliance with the labor movement, rather than seeking to differentiate themselves from it. For its part, the Japanese government suppressed the activities of the SMU in parallel with its suppression of the socialist labor movement. This development contrasts with the trajectory of the salaried staff movement in Germany. A possible reason for this was that unlike Germany, the Japanese labor movement at that time was relatively week. Because the labor movement did not take off, the salaried staff movement was not motivated to differentiate itself from it, and nor did the government have any motivation to enlist the salaried staff movement as an ally against the labor movement.

The failure of the salaried staff movement to gain momentum provided the groundwork for the rise of enterprise unions in postwar Japan, which included both salaried staff and factory workers as members. These enterprise unions called for the elimination of discrimination between salaried staff and factory workers, as will be discussed in Chapter 5. This paved the way for a development that would prove distinct from the experience of other countries, in that norms formed within the limited domain of civil servants and salaried staff expanded to encompass all 'company employees' (*shain*), including shop-floor workers. In other words, in contrast to the labor (and salaried staff) movements of other Western countries, which formed a class consciousness that cut across companies, the Japanese labor movement formed a 'company employee' (*shain*) consciousness that cut across classes.

5 | Democratization and Equality of '*Shain*' (Company Employee)

This chapter explains the pursuit of equal status for 'company employees' (*shain*) in the wake of Japan's defeat in World War II and through the subsequent labor movement.[1]

The labor shortage caused by the war improved the status of laborers. A critical awareness of the military and the upper echelons of the corporate world found expression in the form of the democratization and labor movements after Japan's wartime defeat. Moreover, the rapid inflation and hardships in the aftermath of the war prompted salaried white-collar staff employees to join the labor movement alongside laborers. In Japan, the fact that occupational and industry-based labor movements had not been well developed before the war allowed the rapid emergence of a company-based union movement. These enterprise unions advocated the elimination of discrimination against laborers and demanded that all company employees should be referred to as such, using the term '*shain*'. Further, to cope with inflation, they demanded a 'livelihood' wage, the Japanese version of the living wage, that would allow laborers to support their families, which was achieved in the form of wages based on age and family size. These resulted in the extension of the seniority wage scheme, which had been the privilege of employees before the war, to shop-floor workers.

However, owing to push-back on the part of management, the three-tier structure that had prevailed before the war was not so easily dismantled. Management was critical of the livelihood wage policy, and mass layoffs and numerous major disputes resulted in the late 1940s and early 1950s. As a compromise between management and labor, a wage structure was established that emphasized years of service as a regular employee in a specific company, which was easily linked to age from the view of labor unions, as well as to the level of skill within the company from the view of management. In addition, the corporate and

223

civil service ranking schemes that prior to the war had been applied only to staff employees were now applied to laborers as well.

Once the equality of company employees and an improvement of the situation of laborers had been to some extent achieved in large firms, a dual structure composed of large enterprises on one end and small and medium-sized enterprises (SMEs) on the other formed and came into view in the mid-1950s. In the prewar period, the disparity between salaried staffs and shop-floor workers was greater, but after the disparity in large companies with labor unions improved, then the disparity due to firm-size became more significant. In the late 1950s, the social insurance system was also institutionalized in accordance with this dual structure.

Meanwhile, the American-led Allied Occupation attempted to introduce a US-style employment system and job-based wages into Japan's civil service and private sector. Although the Occupation's civil service reforms were frustrated by resistance on the Japanese side, by the early 1960s, the government and some in the business world envisioned reforms that combined job-based wages, social security and a corporate cross-firm labor market, based on the model of Western Europe. Nevertheless, neither Japanese laborers nor company managers proved willing to embrace such reforms.

Patriotism and the elimination of discrimination

The war had two major effects on the state of employment in Japan. The first was the elimination of workplace disparities as a result of a labor shortage as well as the practices of the wartime regime. The second was the criticism of status discrimination that was linked with the rise of nationalism. Both of these factors provided the groundwork for achieving employee equality in the postwar period. In this section, I first explain the impact of the labor shortage and the wartime regime.

The wartime munitions boom led to a labor shortage that increased workers' wages and contributed to a tendency for them to leave firms where they were poorly treated. As a result, companies had no choice but to improve the way that they treated factory workers. When Oji Paper improved conditions for its factory workers in April 1943, one

Democratization and Equality of '*Shain*' (Company Employee) 225

of the reasons given in explanation was that 'with the labor force so strained and the number of people leaving their jobs on the rise since the outbreak of the Second Sino-Japanese War [in 1937], we have had difficulties replacing them'.[2]

At the same time, there were increasing calls for staff employees and shop-floor laborers to cooperate to increase production. In the Draft Outline for the Establishment of a New Labor Regime (*Kinrō shintaisei kakuritsu yōkō gen'an*) prepared in October 1940 by the government's Planning Agency, it was argued that companies should become 'production and management entities' (*seisan keiei-tai*) in which management, staff employees and laborers comprised an integrated body, and that they should exercise their abilities 'regardless of status or category'.[3] In November 1941, the Greater Japan Industrial Patriotic Service Association (*Dai Nippon sangyō hōkokai*) published a pamphlet featuring companies that had adopted a monthly wage system for their factory workers (*shokkō*), who had generally been paid on a daily basis.[4]

In the midst of these circumstances, in January 1939, Hitachi revised the nomenclature used for factory workers at its Hitachi Works plant, replacing the term *shokkō* with the more neutral *kōin* ('*in*' connotes 'member' which was used in the term '*shain*').[5] Oji Paper adopted the same change in April 1943, also arranging for higher-ranking factory workers to be paid monthly and institutionalizing a career path that enabled their promotion to salaried staff employee positions.[6]

Nevertheless, the direct impact of Japan's total war footing was limited. The renaming of *shokkō* as *kōin* made little actual difference on the shop floor. Moreover, the monthly wage scheme for factory workers that was endorsed by the Greater Japan Industrial Patriotic Service Association was only actually introduced in a limited number of firms.[7]

An even more significant impact of the war was likely the leveling effect caused by economic inflation and the sense of common destiny that had arisen out of a burgeoning nationalist sentiment. This led to a critique of status discrimination in companies, which represented the second impact of the war.

The wage increases due to the war and the decline in financial assets caused by inflation prompted a relative rise in the status of laborers. Critiques of Western liberalism in the form of slogans decrying luxury as 'the enemy' were rife, and a climate that featured criticism of Western capitalism and the former privileged classes was on the rise. The social critic Kiyoshi Kiyosawa, who earned his living from real estate and stocks, recorded this situation in his wartime diary. Lamenting the rise in wages for laborers, he wrote, 'Our [i.e., the intelligentsia's] income is ever decreasing, while laborers' income is rising to the rafters'. He was also concerned about the wartime criticism that 'using a maid is extravagant', and he came to the conclusion that 'as a result of this war, the deformation of capitalism will be inevitable'.[8] The upsurge of nationalism and criticism of the privileged classes, in combination with wartime mobilization, created a climate that was oriented toward the elimination of discrimination. Oji Paper's labor relations manager recalled the lead-up to the improvement of factory workers' treatment in April 1943 as follows.

> After the outbreak of the Second Sino-Japanese War [in 1937], the Military Service Law [*Heieki-hō*] had been expanded to impose obligatory military service on both staff employees (*syoku-in*) and factory workers (*kōin*) without prejudice. Moreover, the implementation of a rationing system of daily commodities forced the citizenry to live in equal poverty. Switching to a new industrial labor regime based on the Imperial-Japanese view of work (*kōkoku kinrō kan*) [that was critical of Western capitalism] stirred an egalitarian sentiment, and status discrimination against laborers came to be seen as old-fashioned and out of step with the times.[9]

The experience of the war also impacted labor disputes in the wake of Japan's defeat. In the *Yomiuri Shinbun* dispute that broke out in September 1945, highly educated executives and staff employees took the lead in calling for the abolition of the company's 'status system' (*mibun-sei*). One of these, a chief political and economics editor, recalled his wartime experience as 'the starting point for my participation in the Yomiuri Dispute'. In particular, he recalled visiting a Kamikaze

Democratization and Equality of '*Shain*' (Company Employee)   227

special-attack unit base in Kyushu, where he found that young suicide pilots (the so-called 'kamikaze' pilots) were stationed in farm hovels while officers were 'encamped in well-appointed barracks'.[10]

One non-commissioned pilot in the Naval Air Corps offered the following recollection after the war.

> At the front, in the most egregious cases, the NCO quarters and officers' quarters were situated about four or five kilometers apart [...]. Not a single officer deigned to come see the kind of life his men were leading, what kind of food they ate, or what kind of fighting they would do [...]. Sometimes, some errand or other would take me to the officers' quarters, four clicks away, where I'd see a bunch of greenhorn lieutenants, still just two or three days out of their extended training, each of them drinking their own bottle of Johnny Walker Black (looted from enemy territory), while we didn't even get beer with any preservatives.[11]

More than a few such accounts recall how their narrators' experiences during the war caused them to question the existing system, which in turn led to their postwar orientation toward democratization.[12]

The war also fostered a critical view of management and administrative roles. At the time, munitions factories were allocated supplies on a preferential basis, putting managers and administrators in a position to make exorbitant profits by diverting those supplies. As recalled by one woman who was mobilized to work at 'H Works' manufacturing plant:

> Even though the coverage in the daily papers kept trying to impress people with Japan's victories in the war, workers on the factory floor were always talking among themselves about how "It would be a miracle if we're able to win with this sort of thing". Whatever our molding foundry, which made the bones of Japan's aircraft, was reporting about our output, the workers on the shop floor knew best just how many defective products there were in those factories. They also knew that the cause of such defective products was not only due to Japan's straitened circumstances at

228   Chapter 5

the time, but also due to the various lies and diversions of materials by the bosses.[13]

This relationship between wartime experience and postwar democratization had rarely been explicitly expressed by the people at that time.[14] However, as we shall see below, the elimination of the status system, the pursuit of war responsibility on the part of company executives and 'industrial reconstruction' were often key issues in postwar labor disputes. These demands indirectly speak to how laborers were angry that company executives had hampered production efficiency through fraud, and so led the country to ruin. It was against this backdrop that the postwar labor movement unfolded.

The rise of enterprise unions

Japan suffered 3.1 million deaths in the war, or 4% of its population in 1940. The number of refugees who returned to Japan after the war was 6.25 million, or 9% of the population in 1940. The war caused the loss of about a quarter of Japan's national wealth, including 80% of its ships, 25% of its buildings and 34% of its factory machinery and equipment. As of August 1945, industrial production was one-tenth of the prewar level, and black-market rice prices were forty-nine times the official government ration price in October 1945.

In October 1945, after Japan's surrender in August, the Occupation authorities issued a series of directives encouraging the formation of labor unions. This led to the rapid formation of labor unions across the country, and by June 1949, the number of such unions in Japan had increased from only two with a combined membership of 1,077 in September 1945 to 34,688 with a total of 665,483 members in June 1949, equaling an estimated union density of 55.8% of the total employment.[15]

In August 1947, the Institute of Social Science at the University of Tokyo (ISS) undertook a large-scale survey of labor unions, which found that most of the unions surveyed were plant-based or enterprise-based, and that 80.7% were 'mixed unions' (*kongō kumiai*) consisting of both bule-collar laborers and white-collar staff employees.[16] At the time, the Japanese Communist Party (*Nihon kyōsantō*, JCP) and the Japan

Confederation of Labor (*Nihon rōdō kumiai sōdōmei*, abbreviated as Sōdōmei) found this development puzzling. In Europe and the United States, trade unions were generally made up of blue-collar laborers, and it was common knowledge that their membership did not extend to include staff employees. Although the prewar labor movement in Japan could not have been described as very active, with union density having peaked at 7.9% in 1931, the aim, at least, had been to establish industry- or occupation-based labor unions.[17] This was why, in January 1946, the Central Preparatory Committee for the Expansion of Sōdōmei criticized the creation of mixed unions at the enterprise level as a 'delusion'.[18] However, the trend of the labor movement did not shift.

Why did Japan's postwar labor unions evolve in this way? It has been pointed out that the wartime Industrial Patriotic Service Associations (*sangyō hōkokukai*, or Sampō), which were official organizations formed by order of the government to control workers, were enterprise-based employee organizations, and that this experience may have had some impact. However, there are no known cases of such an organization evolving directly into a labor union.[19] Andrew Gordon's 1979 interviews with heavy industry factory workers also testify that Sampō was a formal and nominal organization that did not improve the situation of workers, and that there was a significant gap between staff employees and blue-collar workers even during the war.[20]

Then, why did they form as mixed unions at the enterprise level? Labor historians Tsutomu Hyōdō and Kazuo Nimura have suggested that the reason lies with the fact that Japan did not have a tradition of craft unions like those of Europe.[21] It has also been pointed out that few laborers would have had experience in the prewar labor union movement, so there was no widespread norm of creating unions that distinguished between staff employees and laborers.[22] In a survey conducted by the University of Tokyo's ISS, only 9.9% of union organizers had any experience in the labor movement.[23]

An additional background factor cited by Nimura is that during the period between the outbreak of war and Japan's defeat, businesses became an important part of people's lives. As a result of wartime rationing, businesses became important channels for the distribution of goods and food. Rationing continued after the war due to a shortage of supplies, and people were not officially allowed to purchase goods privately from the market. Nimura cites the following account from May 1946, included in a history of the union at the NKK (Nippon Kōkan, Japan Steel Pipe) Kawasaki Steel Works.

> On 17 May, a union meeting was called to establish a Food Crisis Breakthrough Committee to mobilize all of the organizations and functions of Kawasaki Steel to try to secure food supplies for the employees [...]. The committee's purpose was to do everything in its power to overcome hunger for all employees, which it would accomplish by working with the Health and Welfare Section to manage the purchase and distribution of all foodstuffs, and then asking the manager of the Health and Welfare Section to store the purchased goods and then distribute them in consultation with the committee [...]. As a first step, they asked the plant manager for permission to produce salt, and then began salt production in each branch. Since the company had stopped its functions after the defeat in the war, people formed up into groups to pump seawater to make salt using the company's fuel, which was then exchanged for food. In order to incentivize production, branches that produced a lot of salt were given increased dividends in proportion to the amount produced.[24]

Here, the company was indeed acting as a commune. According to this account, the NKK Kawasaki Steel Works also made company-owned land available to employees for the production of vegetables and potatoes, and also provided them with company-owned supplies such as coke for fuel. At the time of the defeat, the city's industries were destroyed, and citizens had fled to farming villages where food was available, hoping to rely on their relatives. As Nimura explains, 'those who remained in the blasted cities were those who had no countryside home to return to. For them, the companies were the last bastion of support'. He points out that this was the primary reason behind the creation of mixed employee enterprise-based unions.[25]

Elimination of discrimination and the 'company employee' (*shain*)

Elements that had an even greater impact were a heightened desire to eliminate discrimination, nationalism and the hardships of postwar life. In a 1947 survey by the University of Tokyo's ISS, labor unions that took part in the survey offered several reasons for having decided to become mixed unions of staff employees and factory workers. The most common responses were as follows: 'staff employee (*syokuin*) or factory worker (*kōin*), we're all employees (*jūgyōin*)' and 'in their essential identity as workers, there is no difference between staff employees and laborers'.[26]

After Japan's wartime defeat, in addition to their economic demands, labor unions also pressed for the elimination of discrimination. Examples of such demands included unifying the service gates by which employees entered the workplace, opening facilities previously reserved for staff employees to all employees, requiring staff employees to observe the same arrival and departure times as other workers and making salary and holiday regulations that applied to staff employees standard for all.[27] This led to the idea that staff employees and factory workers should form a single union. Economist Kazuo Ōkōchi, summarizing a survey by the University of Tokyo's ISS, described the idea of such 'mixed unions' (*kongō kumiai*) as 'a product of the egalitarian idea of eliminating status systems'.[28]

From the late stages of the war, many Japanese people believed that inadequate production planning and the hierarchical injustices such as executive diversions were the causes they were losing, but they could not speak out about it because of suppression of speech. This patriotic sentiment was expressed in the postwar period in the insistence that scientific rationalization of production, freedom of speech, elimination of 'status discrimination' and democratization were necessary for the postwar reconstruction of their country.[29] In the ISS survey summarized by Ōkōchi, many labor unions cited industrial reconstruction as the reason for their decision to adopt mixed unions. One union's response likened staff employees and factory workers to 'brains and brawn', arguing that 'both must be integrated to achieve efficiency'.[30] This orientation toward industrial reconstruction was also linked to patriotism. In October 1946, members of the Japan Electric Power Industry Labor Union, the federation of enterprise unions of electric power companies known as Densan or Densankyō, demanded a wage that would enable them to maintain their livelihood, addressing the following arguments to management:

> Can you really revive the industry by beggaring your workers? We truly love our country. We want to rebuild our beloved Japan. But in order to do so, we must first of all eat and reproduce [our labor power]. How else can we help our country? What we are saying is that we must cultivate that power [...]. Could we rebuild Japan if we were dead? You must think about this clearly. If you are truly patriots, you should be able to make the right decision.[31]

Here we see that the maintenance of livelihoods, industrial reconstruction and patriotic spirit were all interconnected.

Fumihiko Takaragi, who would become the chairman of Zentei (*Zenteishin rōdō kumiai*, the Japan Postal Workers' Union), recalls the hardships of life at that time as follows. Born in 1920, Takaragi was demobilized from the army in January 1946, at which time he resumed his old job at the post office. However, whereas his monthly salary at the time was 75 yen, a single *shō* of rice (1.8 liters, equivalent to the daily consumption of two or three people at that time) cost 65 yen on the black market. 'I can't support my mother and sister with this', he recalled. Therefore, he rode his bicycle to Chiba to buy peanuts to sell on the black market in Tokyo himself. Thus, while working at the post office, he also worked as a black-market trader until March 1946.[32] Under such circumstances, management had little choice but to sympathize with laborers' demands. Hyūga Orii, who was in charge of labor affairs at NKK (and was later to become a company director), recalled the situation immediately after Japan's defeat in the war as follows.

> [...] At the collective bargaining table, we were getting bawled out, with the workers saying things like, "Look at the factory worker's cafeteria! We go days on end without seeing a scrap of rice. How

Democratization and Equality of '*Shain*' (Company Employee) 233

can we do the hard work of rebuilding the industry with only four or five dumplings in a broth so thin you can't even taste the miso? Prices are going up. Even the rationed food prices have openly doubled and even tripled. We want a cup of rice a day. We want the money to buy it". We, too, had likewise not been eating well, and could understand the hardship of living on the bare minimum, so management was forced to take a passive line in its attitude.[33]

Here we see that the managers and staff employees shared the same hardships as the factory workers, and that this fostered a sense of solidarity. This also encouraged the formation of mixed unions. Reasons for forming mixed unions cited in responses to the ISS survey included the fact that 'staff employees and factory workers are treated equally poorly' and that 'staff employees have fallen to the level of laborers'.[34] Before the war, staff employees had been a privileged group and discrimination against factory workers (then called *shokkō*) had been severe. Given this situation, the fact that mixed unions had not been able to make any inroads at the time was only natural. Mixed unions at the enterprise level were not a cultural tradition in Japan, but rather a phenomenon that emerged against the backdrop of the reduced circumstances of staff employees due to the war and defeat.

In addition, many staff employees, concerned about the future of their companies, were critical of management's inability to set policies in the turmoil that followed Japan's defeat. Such criticisms were often combined with demands for democratization, a voice in management and acknowledgement of war responsibility for Japan's defeat and devastation.

The Chiyoda Life Insurance Company Employees' Union (*Chiyoda seimei jūgyōin kumiai*), for example, set the following conditions for the appointment of company officers: 'An individual who is proactive in management regardless of educational background or age', and 'An individual of high character and integrity who understands the union movement'. The Japanese Government Railways Employees' Union Preparatory Association (*Kokutetsu jūgyōin kumiai junbi-kai*) demanded 'the dismissal of incompetent or anti-democracy executives', 'opposition to the old-boy network's monopoly on promotions',

234   Chapter 5

and 'purging the University of Tokyo's Faculty of Law graduates' clique'.[35] The prewar corporate order, in which even incompetent staff employees were eligible to be promoted to senior management based on their academic background and seniority, came under criticism from younger staff employees.

In the confusion of the war's aftermath, such criticisms were becoming imbricated into the demands of daily life. At Hitachi Works, following the defeat, there was 'roaring condemnation' of executive diversions and fraud during the war, supply rationing that favored particular staff employees, 'assessments of salary increases based on personal sentiment' and the 'militaristic direction of factory workers' by executives. In January 1946, the union submitted a list of demands that included 'the elimination of discriminatory treatment', 'the purging of executives', 'the doubling of wages' and 'the establishment of an eight-hour workday'.[36]

Symbolic of the demand for the elimination of discriminatory treatment was the adoption of the designation 'company employee' (*shain*). The Proposal for the Elimination of the Status System (*Mibun seido teppai-an*) submitted by Oji Paper's union federation to the Central Executive Council in April 1947 read as follows.

1. The designations "staff employees" [*shokuin*] and "factory workers" [*kōin*] and discrimination on that basis should be abolished, and they should be uniformly referred to as "company employees" [*shain*].
2. The [former hierarchical] system of company employees [*shain*], associate employees [*jun-shain*], assistants [*koin*], senior factory workers, and first-, second- and third-class factory workers should be abolished.
3. No status system should be established at all.[37]

Before the war, *shain* had referred exclusively to salaried higher-staff employees as a privileged class, like the German *Beamte*. The postwar labor movement thus started with the demand for all employees within the same company to be referred to as *shain*.

Such a demand was sometimes expressed as a demand that the enterprise be a community shared by company employees. The labor

Democratization and Equality of '*Shain*' (Company Employee)   235

movement immediately after the defeat in the war was characterized by a thriving union-management movement, in which production continued under the management of the unions, rather than by strikes. This was in line with the workers' ideology of rebuilding Japanese industry and was also a countermeasure to the situation in which survival was not possible without production. In the *Yomiuri Shimbun* dispute, workers held the president responsible for war propaganda, while the newspaper was published under the workers' self-management. In the 2 November 1945 issue of the Yomiuri Dispute Daily Bulletin, a demand was made that 'every company employee (*shain*) who has reached a certain number of years of service should be given shares', and in the 7 November 1945 issue, another demand was made that 'discriminatory treatment in terms of status be abolished and that all workers be made company employees (*shain*)'.[38] The union wanted to oust the president, who was responsible for the war propaganda, and continue publishing the newspaper with the company as the common property of all employees. As we saw in Chapter 4, '*shain*' legally means investors.

There was also an attempt to create a new designation, different from the traditional *shain*, as a generic term for employees after the elimination of discrimination. For example, at Hitachi Works, a collective agreement was reached in January 1947 'to abolish the status of company employee (*shain*) and factory workers (*kōin*), and to begin referring to both of them as site employee (*shoin*)'.[39] However, this term did not spread very far, and the widely used *shain* became common as a new generic term. This is likely because such demands were often made alongside the enrollment of factory workers, who had generally been paid on a daily basis, into a monthly salary scheme that was the privilege of staff employees.

Flexible working hours for salaried employees, with daily wages for factory workers and monthly wages for salaried higher-staff employees, are not unique to prewar Japan. However, for Japanese laborers, the fact that salaried employees were paid on a monthly basis and were free to come and go at any time was seen as discriminatory practice. This discrimination appears not to have been seen any differently than more irrational forms of discrimination such as having different service entrances.

The economist Kōshi Endō tells us that 'postwar democracy as it was understood by Japanese workers was equal treatment within a company, irrespective of position or educational background'.[40] That is, for Japanese laborers, we could say that 'postwar democracy' was expressed as a demand that everyone be treated as a company employee (*shain*), i.e., on equal terms with the university-educated salaried staff employees.

A living wage determined by age and family size

Even so, if the distinction between salaried employees and factory workers were eliminated, what then would be the basis for determining wages? After the war, the labor movement demanded that wages be determined by age and the number of dependents, on the grounds that wages should be sufficient to maintain a livelihood. This was known as the 'livelihood wage' (*seikatsu-kyū*) in Japanese labor history.

As a concept, the livelihood wage was proposed by technical rear admiral Takuo Godō of the Kure Naval Arsenal in 1922 to calm the labor movement, but it spread only through the postwar labor movement. As Chapter 3 of this book describes, seniority salary was common in civil officials and staff employees in large firms and was also gradually applied to factory workers in the large heavy industry companies of the 1920s. However, labor historian Tsutomu Hyōdō concludes that in the case of factory workers in the 1920s, it was not wages based on age or years of service in a company, but wages based on workers' skills, which were pseudo-proportional to their age.[41]

The concept of the livelihood wage had also been advocated by the government during wartime. In order to cope with the difficult living conditions brought on by inflation during the war, the Outline of Wage Measures (*chingin taisaku yōkō*) authorized by the Cabinet in March 1943 called for the establishment of a 'system of basic wages according to age and length of service [...] to ensure constancy in the lives of working people'.[42] Despite wage controls at the time, family allowances had been permitted from 1940 and were moreover justified by the familistic ideology of wartime Japan. Nevertheless, it would be difficult to argue that the idea of a livelihood wage found any purchase

Democratization and Equality of 'Shain' (Company Employee)

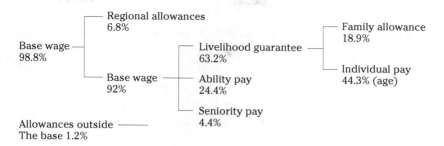

Figure 5.1 The average Densan 'livelihood' wage, January 1947
Note: All percentages are proportions of total income.
Source: Gordon (1985: 353), based on Keieishi hensyūshitsu (ed.) (1965: 223–225).

during the war. Although family allowances became widespread during the war, these remained at the level of around 10% of real wages and only rarely exceeded 20%.[43] It was only through the postwar labor movement that a livelihood wage became widely realized in practice.

In October 1946, the Densan the Japan Electric Power Industry Labor Union demanded 'the elimination of wage inequalities based on ranking systems, as well as on educational background and gender'.[44] Further, based on the caloric intake required for adults, the union developed a wage system that came to be known as the Densan Wage Model. The most distinctive feature of the Densan Wage Model was that 63.2% of wages were a 'livelihood guarantee' that was determined by a laborer's age and number of family dependents. The concept, in other words, was that middle-aged and older workers with families should be paid higher wages. As shown in Figure 5.1, while the wage structure demanded by Densan did include ability pay (24.4%), seniority pay (4.4%) and other allowances (8.0% in total), the relative proportion of these components was small, and the bulk of the wage was the livelihood guarantee combining individual pay (44.3%) and family allowance (18.9%) determined by the employee's age and the number of family members.[45]

The Densan Wage Model was widely emulated as a demand by labor unions across Japan in the aftermath of the defeat and against the backdrop of rampant inflation and the hardships of life after the war. During the food shortages immediately after the defeat, it was considered natural for Japan to set wages on the basis of workers' ability to buy food for their families. In the period between the war and the aftermath of defeat, wages were controlled by the government under the command economy, despite rapid inflation. Therefore, both the government and private companies responded to labor union demands by increasing various allowances.[46] Substantially, the Densan Wage Model was the institutionalization of these allowances by integrating them into the basic wage.

One labor relations manager who joined Shikoku Machinery Industries (later Sumitomo Heavy Industries, Ltd.) in 1949 recalled the impact of the spread of this wage model in the following terms.

> The president was only forty-seven or forty-eight years old, but his driver was about sixty, well past the age of retirement. And his salary was higher than the president's. Everything was based on age. There were no job-based differences in wages.[47]

During this period, the Occupation authorities ordered a purge of war collaborators and older executives were expelled, so the management teams of Japan's major corporations were younger. In terms of the calories needed for biological survival, there is no fundamental difference between the requirements of the family of the president or the family of the driver. In the aftermath of war, when simply getting enough to eat was of paramount importance, it was felt that wage differences should be determined on the basis of securing survival, rather than on the basis of ability or the nature of the job.

That said, the recollections of this labor relations manager need to be taken with a grain of salt. Wage disparities did not in fact disappear. For example, at Japanese Government Railways (JGR, reorganized as Japanese National Railways in 1949), even immediately after the defeat, the most senior employees were still making six times the wages of the lowest ranking employees.[48] However, even at JGR, it was true that the wage gap between staff employees and shop-floor laborers had narrowed compared to the prewar period, and the trend toward livelihood wages was getting stronger.

This kind of wage system reflected what might be called 'age-based equality'. In one respect, however, it also brought the wages of shop-

Democratization and Equality of '*Shain*' (Company Employee)   239

floor laborers a step closer to the seniority-based wages of salaried staff employees.

The Densan union leaders who created the Densan Wage Model were actually salaried staff employees and technicians who had graduated from higher educational institutes such as Kyoto University Faculty of Law and Tohoku Imperial University Faculty of Engineering before the war. For these highly educated salaried workers, seniority-based salaries that enabled them to support their families once they reached their middle years had been increasingly prevalent since before the war. The prewar laborer's wage and lower staff employee's salary, however, as Chapter 4 describes, had not necessarily been sufficient for a man to be able to support his household as a sole breadwinner. Economist Masami Nomura has suggested that the notion that a family should be supported solely by a man's wages may have been popularized by these highly educated union leaders in the form of the Densan Wage Model.[49] Several studies have pointed out that many of the leaders of the postwar labor movement, including those who were influenced by Marxism as students before the war, were staff employees with higher education.[50]

This phenomenon was made possible by the fact that postwar Japan's labor unions were mixed unions of staff employees and factory workers. In Germany and France, salaried staff employees formed their own unions and demanded more preferential treatment than laborers. In Japan, however, staff employees' unions had remained only poorly developed, and after Japan's defeat in the war, both staff employees and factory workers suffered equal hardships. Under these conditions, mixed unions and livelihood wages took hold, so that the treatment of laborers came to approach that enjoyed by salaried staff employees.

The effects of military experience

Another factor that must be considered when it comes to the postwar labor movement is the effects of military experience. Many of those who took part in the postwar labor movement were demobilized soldiers and young officers who had served in the Japanese military. Fumihiko Takaragi, himself a demobilized soldier, offers the following recollection of his participation in the founding of Zentei (the Japan Postal Workers' Union) at the Imperial Theater in May 1946.

> Going in [to the Imperial Theater], I was taken aback. To describe the attire of the people gathered there, I'd say that most were wearing military field caps, some were carrying duffel bags, and some had soldier's canteens on their waist. They had army boots on their feet, and were dressed in regimental uniforms or seaman's outfits from the navy. Even better, some were dressed in the flying corps's choicest flight uniforms.[51]

People wore military uniforms not only because of supply shortages, but also because they were considered a kind of formal attire. According to Takaragi, some of the workers from the postal administration who owned suits 'were nattily dressed in their suits and neckties, since this was the inaugural convention ... [but] young people like us, who had come out of the military, didn't have suits and so we came wearing our regimental uniforms'.[52]

At the time, laborers like these harbored ambivalent feelings toward patriotism and the military. As noted earlier, a member of the Densan union committee had couched the union's demands for a livelihood wage in the language of patriotism and industrial reconstruction. At the same time, however, that same committee member asked 'Who made us pay lip service to the empty prayer of patriotism during the war? Was it not you that pushed the people to their deaths with your patriotism?'[53] Wartime slogans and behaviors were deeply ingrained in these men as objects of both love and scorn.

Therefore, the labor movement of the time often acted in a curiously militaristic manner even as it advocated pacifism and opposition to war. Kanson Arahata, a prewar Marxist who became the first chairman of the Kantō Metal Workers' Union (*Kantō kinzoku rōdō kumiai*) immediately after the war, recalled an experience at that time in his autobiography as follows: 'At one of the large factories I visited in Shinagawa, the employees formed up in ranks and formed a line. The leader barked out the order, "Salute the chairman!" at which point they all bowed in unison'.[54]

Democratization and Equality of '*Shain*' (Company Employee)   241

Another such military custom that had taken root among laborers also influenced the negotiation of the Densan Wage Model – that is, the criteria used on personnel evaluations.

As mentioned earlier, the Densan Wage Model was centered on an age-based individual pay and a family allowance determined by the number of family members. However, the model also included 'ability-pay' (*nōryoku-kyū*), albeit in a relatively smaller proportion. According to an October 1946 demand by the union, ability pay was to be assessed on a 'comprehensive consideration of each person's skills, abilities, experience and academic knowledge'.[55] These four items were very similar to the evaluation criteria on the navy's performance evaluation sheet, which was introduced in Chapter 4. In the navy's performance evaluation, 'ability' was to be assessed by synthesizing '(a) intelligence, (b) discernment, (c) skill, (d) academic knowledge, (e) experience and (f) execution'.

It remains unclear why the union at the time demanded that 'ability' (*nōryoku*) be measured by these assessment criteria. In later years, a former union leader stated that, at the time, they had had 'only conceptual ideas, without any specific methods of assessment'.[56] Kōshi Endō, who has researched this process, also stated that 'neither the definitions nor the methods of measurement were specified' in the available extant documents.[57] Nevertheless, if the individuals involved at that time had been in positions of authority in the army or navy, then they would have had experience with writing evaluation sheets in accordance with such regulations. Those with higher education, in particular, were often appointed as reserve officers due to the shortage of officers during the war. After demobilization, such individuals would have joined labor unions or become labor relations officers in companies.

Endō does not suggest any potential influence by Japan's military. However, he does cite the influence of the US Army's personnel rating system.[58] As we saw in Chapter 4, a rating method for evaluating aspects of people's character was adopted by the US Army during World War I for use in selecting officers. In 1920, a Japanese psychologist introduced this rating method to Japan as the US Army Officer Rating Method (*Beigun shōkō hyōtei-hō*), which eventually spread to researchers at the Institute of Industrial Efficiency (*Sangyō nōritsu kenkyūjo*) and elsewhere. In October 1946, the executive director of the Japan Efficiency Federation (*Nihon nōritsu rengōkai*), which had introduced the American personnel rating system before the war, published a booklet titled *Beikoku bunkan nōritsu hyōtei-hō* (The US Civil Service Efficiency Rating System). At the time, this newly published book served as a reference for those involved in the negotiation of the Densan Wage Model in March and April 1947.

Even so, that did not take place until the spring of 1947, so the source of the initial request in October 1946 for the 'comprehensive consideration of each person's skills, abilities, experience and academic knowledge' remains unclear. At the time, Japanese companies had not yet developed any systematic methods of personnel evaluation or assessment; everyone was still seeking their own solutions. It seems likely that, under the combined influence of a variety of factors, the performance evaluation methods of the Japanese and US militaries came to be reflected in the assessment criteria adopted by postwar Japanese companies. At first, the proportion of ability-based pay subject to assessment was relatively small. As we shall see, however, once companies' management began to roll back their concessions to labor, this initially small proportion would begin to increase.

In any case, through war and democratization, a series of collective norms came into being. It was a system in which all company employees received equal treatment, and in which wages were determined by age and family size. While wages did include an ability-based element, this was still proportionately small. Thus, a model of Japanese-style employment in which all company employees receive seniority-based wages was being formulated in the context of war and democratization.

Japanese-style 'clarification of rules'

Nevertheless, the system that coalesced immediately after the war was also distinct from the Japanese-style employment that would follow.

One of the differences was the value assigned to years of service in a particular company. In fact, although the Densan Wage Model system emphasized employees' age and number of family members,

Democratization and Equality of 'Shain' (Company Employee)

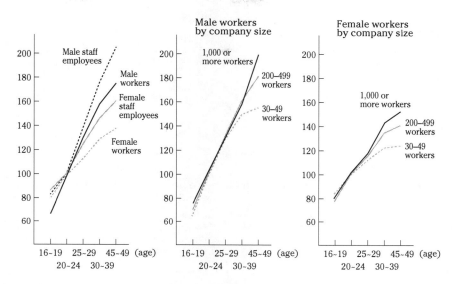

Figure 5.2 Wages by age category and company size (1946)
Note: Wages for twenty- to twenty-four-years olds are indexed to 100. Survey of 233,971 industrial workers; people aged fifty and older were excluded from consideration.
Source: Reproduced from Nishinarita (1995: 18), based on data from Labor Policy Bureau, Ministry of Welfare (1947).

years of service were not given much weight. Economic historian Yutaka Nishinarita points out that in 1946, wages for both men and women rose with age rather than with years of service regardless of company size (Figure 5.2).[59] For a time after the end of the war, when larger factories were still reeling from the shock of Japan's defeat, small and medium-sized factories, which were more flexible, tended to be faster to pivot to civilian demand and resume operations. With higher operating rates, they could offer higher wages, and the wage gap between companies virtually disappeared.[60] At a time when everyone was struggling to survive, there would have been a strong trend in favor of livelihood wages where compensation was determined by age, regardless of years of service and company size.

These circumstances also affected the government's method of statistical data collection. The report of a wage survey conducted by the Labor Policy Bureau, Ministry of Welfare in June 1946 only examined correlations between age and wages and did not collect data on

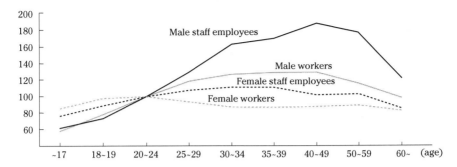

Figure 5.3 Correlation between age and wage of workers with 0 years of service (1965, manufacturing industry)

Note: Wages for twenty- to twenty-four-year-olds are indexed to 100.
Source: Data from Labor Statistics and Research Division, Ministry of Labor (Rōdō daijin kanbō rōdō tōkei chōsa-bu), *Chingin kōzō kihon tōkei chōsa hōkoku* (Report on the Basic Survey on Wage Structure, the Wage Census), 1965, vol. 1, compiled by Nishinarita (1995: 17).

years of service. According to Nishinarita, it was not until the 1950s that government wage surveys began to place any emphasis on years of service.[61]

This trend lasted until as late as 1965. Figure 5.3 below, which Nishinarita prepared based on that year's Wage Census, shows that wages increased with age for male staff employees, even when their years of service in a specific company were nil. Female workers, however, were already outside of the livelihood wage structure, and even with salaried men a 30% wage gap existed between those with zero years of service and those with between twenty and twenty-nine years of service.[62] Nevertheless, this graph, which shows that wages for male salaried staff trended upward with age even among those who had not yet accumulated any years of service, could be said to reflect the character of the postwar livelihood wage system.

This is distinct from the later form taken by Japanese-style employment in that no weight is given to years of service in a particular company. This also had something to do with the relationship between unions and management.

Wages are determined through negotiations between laborers and management. Management scholar David Marsden states that the rules agreed to by laborers and management are entrenched in each society

Democratization and Equality of '*Shain*' (Company Employee)   245

because increased unpredictability in labor-management transactions increases transaction costs. The rules must ensure not only economic efficiency, but also enforceability to ensure that the rules are followed. To ensure enforceability, the rules must be clear and simple. This is because if the rules are complex and ambiguous, they are more likely to lead to different interpretations and disputes between laborers and management, increasing unpredictability and transaction costs. Marsden refers to the clarification of positions and wages based on job descriptions in the US and the clarification of worker treatment and wages based on skill qualifications and industrial collective agreements in Germany as examples of the ways of rule clarification in each society.[63]

In general, management will try to increase the scope of its own interpretation and discretion. In some cases, management may try to extend more favorable treatment to laborers whom they like. For their part, laborers try to limit management's discretion as much as possible. An effective strategy in this regard is the clarification of rules. For example, as discussed in Chapter 4, requiring clear job descriptions and assessment criteria, which has been an achievement of the labor movement and lawsuits in the US, can help prevent racial and gender discrimination.

Labor unions in postwar Japan did not demand explicit job descriptions. They also did not seek to establish cross-firm skill qualifications or industrial level collective agreements. Even so, age and number of family members were objective indicators that could not be changed at the discretion of management. They were unrelated to length of service, and even served as cross-firm indicators that would not put mid-career hires at a disadvantage. An emphasis on age was something that labor unions in Europe and the US also demanded of management, for example in the form of seniority rights. In other words, one could argue that the Japanese labor movement of the time was also trying to curtail the discretion of management by introducing explicit rules.

More than this, the Japanese labor movement was strongly oriented toward narrowing management's discretionary latitude. Many collective labor agreements concluded between enterprise unions and management in each company immediately after the war mandated union consent on a wide range of matters, including hiring, dismissal, transfers and promotions, as well as rewards and punishments. Unions had strong control over the workplace; for example, at Nissan Motor Co. prior to the major strike of 1953, the Nissan Workers' Union (the Nissan chapter of Zenji, the All-Japan Automobile Workers' Union) had 'controlled not only wage decisions but also promotions, work pace, and job assignments'.[64]

They should also be seen as a reaction to the prewar order, in which management and supervisors had effectively held dictatorial authority over the workplace. In prewar coal mines, for example, wages were often paid on a piece-rate basis by volume. However, higher volumes were more likely for miners assigned to a vein where extraction was easy while lower volumes were the norm for those assigned to a vein where extraction was dangerous. In the prewar period, management held the authority to determine who was assigned to which vein of ore. This was a source of power for salaried employees and foremen, as well as a target for laborers' animosity. In contrast, the postwar labor unions sought to establish workplace rules. The workplace committee of the Mitsui Miike Coal Mine Workers' Union ensured that they had a say in job assignments, the regulation of piece-rate wages and mine safety.[65] The union's goal was to end 'long-despised practices of favoritism and arbitrary authority'. Its representatives explained that 'the appropriate supply of labor (to management) is natural, and our goal is not to refuse work orders or loaf'.[66] Such control over the workplace on the part of laborers was also apparent in other countries.

Japan's postwar labor movement was oriented toward the establishment of such rules in personnel affairs, promotion, safety administration and wages, among other domains. The clarification of assessment criteria and achieving a livelihood wage determined by age and family structure are both examples of such. While the livelihood wage was also a function of 'equality of company employees (*shain*)' in that it narrowed the gap between staff employees and laborers in individual companies, it also had an aspect of age equality that transcended individual companies.

A persistent three-tier structure

Nevertheless, the old three-tier structure did not fade away so easily. Even though workers were now uniformly referred to as 'company employees' (*shain*) and their wages tended to be more akin to a livelihood wage, the order itself survived.

For example, the executive management at Hitachi Works declared in January 1947 that they were 'abolishing the status of company employee and factory worker'. However, the new order subsequently proposed by management attempted to segment the company by job function (*shokunō*). Specifically, this new order would bifurcate the company into 'intellectual labor' and 'manual labor', with the former subdivided further into 'planning' (*kikaku*) and 'administration' (*shitsumu*). Since this was tantamount to maintaining the old three-tier structure, the union protested, saying that the proposal 'reeked so much of status that it was impossible to accept'.[67]

A similar move was made at Oji Paper. In April 1947, the union federation demanded that all workers be treated as company employees (*shain*), but the company insisted on a system based on job functions (*shokunō*). This system was first of all divided into two categories, namely 'business workers' (*gyōmu-in*) and 'production workers' (*seisan-in*) with the former subdivided further into 'office workers' (*jimu-in*) and 'front-line workers' (*genmu-in*). In the end, this proposal was actually implemented, but during the negotiations, the union 'stressed the prevention of a reversion back to or revival of the status system'.[68]

The rollbacks by management became even more pronounced in 1949. At the recommendation of Joseph Dodge, who arrived in Japan in February 1949 as an advisor to the General Headquarters, Supreme Commander for the Allied Powers (GHQ–SCAP, hereinafter GHQ), various government subsidies to key industries were abolished. Although this policy stemmed inflation, a deflationary depression soon set in, triggering personnel restructuring at large companies. As a proportion of the existing workforce, layoffs between 1949 and 1950 accounted for 21% of the workers at Toshiba, 35% at NEC, 17% at Hitachi, 23% at Nissan and 21% at Toyota.[69]

In June 1949, moreover, the Labor Union Act was amended, nullifying many collective labor agreements that had been in force since the end of the war. Management called for the restoration of 'management prerogatives' and sought to regain the right to make decisions on personnel matters, including promotions and dismissals. From the late 1940s through the 1950s, these developments painted the backdrop for a series of large-scale disputes and strikes. Fuyuko Kamisaka, who joined Toyota Motor Corporation in April 1949, offers the following recollection of the 1950 dispute:

> In those days [of Economic Crisis and Food Shortages], company employees would each be served only three steamed sweet potatoes [as a worker's lunch due to lack of rice rationing] in the company cafeteria, so the prospect of losing your job was that much more of a cause for concern. As soon as the "rationalization plan" was announced, folks dressed in thousand-miler shirts [factory worker uniform] from the forging and foundry plants literally surged toward the two-story office like an angry wave. They climbed up the pine trees planted at the front entrance, waving red flags and singing "The Internationale" in support of the negotiations between the union and management that were being held on the second floor of the office. At the time, when negotiations came to a head, the union side would press forward, saying "All I want to hear from you is yes or no", and then suddenly toss an ashtray on the table in front of management. Needless to say, this was a misappropriation of General Tomoyuki Yamashita's ultimatum on his successful invasion of Singapore [when he urged the British general to surrender in February 1942].[70]

Nevertheless, this series of disputes followed a pattern in which staff employees, foremen and other defectors established a second union, after which the first union was isolated and defeated.[71] The solidarity between staff employees and factory workers that had arisen out of their shared experience of the hardships of life immediately after the war had crumbled with the end of inflation, which could be said to have exposed the inherent weakness of mixed unions.

Democratization and Equality of 'Shain' (Company Employee)   249

In this way, management regained its authority over personnel and other matters, bringing about a return to the old order. For example, at Hitachi, a job-functional group system was introduced in November 1950. This system divided all employees into three main categories: planning, administrative and direct shop-floor jobs, to which were added indirect shop-floor jobs such as driving and packing, and special jobs such as medical work and catering. In 1958, the director of Hitachi's Labor Relations Division confided that, 'everyone has the impression that the planning positions are for the old company employees (*shain*), the administrative positions are for the old associate company employees (*jun-shain*), and then there are the shop-floor positions.'[72] In April 1953, as well, Yahata Steel introduced a job classification system that consisted of clerical, technical and operational positions. Although this system allowed for the possibility of promotion based on length of service and job performance, the path for factory workers to become staff employees was effectively closed.[73] Approached with the company's proposal, union members were taken aback, crying 'the status system is back!'[74]

This revival of the old order was accompanied by the restoration of the ranking scheme. A 1958 Nikkeiren (Japan Federation of Employers' Associations) survey of 1,053 companies nationwide found that 47% of all companies, and more than 60% of large companies with 3,000 or more employees, had adopted a ranking scheme.[75] Also, a 1955 survey by the Kansai Employers' Association found that thirty-four of sixty-one member firms had a ranking scheme, nineteen of which observed a distinction between staff employees and factory workers.[76] Many of the ranking schemes that were revived during this period seem to be somewhat modified versions of those that existed before the war. For example, despite the postwar labor movement having succeeded in getting Ishikawajima Heavy Industries to abolish its status system in 1948, the company insisted that it could not disregard the 'ground-level norms that had been established over the years', and adopted a new ranking scheme in December 1949. In the revised 1953 ranking scheme, eligibility for promotion was determined by educational background and length of service, and the basic pattern of the scheme was more or less unchanged from the prewar system except for minor changes of ranks' names.[77]

Nevertheless, even while demanding the elimination of discrimination, the laborers would still naturally have wanted to improve their credentials, something that might be likened to criticizing discrimination in education while yearning for a degree from a prestigious university. For example, although the Densan union temporarily succeeded in abolishing the ranking system in electric power companies, it was soon reinstated. What is more, according to Yoshitarō Fujikawa, a Densan union activist, the reinstatement of the 'rank and ranking system' took place at the request of the union membership. According to Fujikawa's testimony,

> In those days, we had the statuses and ranks of engineer / assistant engineer and technician / assistant technician on the technical side, and chief / assistant chief and clerk / assistant clerk on the clerical side. We got rid of all those. We had the attendance books and other records that were ordered by title rearranged in Japanese aiueo alphabetical order, but this only lasted about a year before they were put back the way they were. The thing was that the laborers still wanted to have ranks [...]. One laborer, a fellow who was purely self-taught, told me, "After all, we've all been working to better ourselves to some degree, and if we're stripped of our 'ranks', it will feel like losing what we've been working toward just when it was within our grasp".[78]

A similar sentiment can be seen in the following testimony by a director of the labor relations division at Hitachi: 'There's a sense, you know, that an administrative job is better than a job on the shop floor, and if you are in an administrative job, then it is not enough if you are not to be promoted to a planning job, and that if you get a planning job, then it's time to cook up the *sekihan* to celebrate'.[79] We see here that there was an intuitive sense of the old order that was deeply ingrained in the company's laborers. In fact, at Ishikawajima Heavy Industries, as well, the union had proposed in 1949 'to abolish the status system and adopt a rank system'.[80] Not only did the laborers place value on levelling up their ranks, but it may not have been unnatural for the mixed enterprise union, which included staff employees who were

Democratization and Equality of 'Shain' (Company Employee) 251

university graduates, to propose a ranking scheme that emphasized academic background and seniority.

This swing of the pendulum back to the old order shows that the workforce was still strongly influenced by norms that had existed since the prewar period. According to a 'Special Survey of Salary Schemes' conducted by the Ministry of Labor in September 1957, 24.9% of the 1,570 companies surveyed paid both laborers and staff employees on a monthly basis, while the form of payment for the two groups differed in more than 50% of companies.[81] The three-tier structure was not so easily broken, it seems, even after the experience of war and defeat.

Public sector reforms

The postwar changes also extended to the civil service, but here too, the three-tier structure proved resilient. However, the changes to the prevailing order that took place in the civil service after Japan's defeat paralleled the postwar changes that took place in the private sector.

As noted in Chapter 3, Japan's prewar bureaucracy was modeled on German institutions. There was a three-tier structure in which higher officials (*kōtōkan*) who had received higher education and lower officials (*hanninkan*) who had received only secondary education were considered civil servants (*kanri*), with all others regarded as being outside of officialdom. These non-officials were mainly the *koin* (*yatoi*), who were clerical employees, and *yōnin*, who were manual laborers.

A similar system existed in Germany. In addition to the *Beamte*, or civil officials, who were appointed by the state under public law (*Öffentliches Recht*), German government agencies also employed *Angestellte* (salaried employees, mainly clerical workers) and *Arbeiter* (workers, mainly manual laborers) who were employed by the state under private law (*Privatrecht*).[82] As civil servants, the *Beamte* were loyal to the state, and while they received salaries and benefits commensurate with their status in exchange for this loyalty, their right to engage in labor disputes and collective bargaining was curtailed. *Angestellte* and *Arbeiter*, however, who were employed under private law, were not denied the right to dispute and collective bargaining, since they were employees who receive payment in exchange for their labor. As we saw in Chapter 4, the fact that salaried employees in the German private sector claimed themselves *Privatbeamte* ('private officials') was due to the influence of the German bureaucracy.

In the US, however, no distinction is made between public and private law, and the typical salaried government employee is basically employed under the same laws that prevail in the private sector. On the other hand, unlike in Germany, federal government employees in the United States are uniformly restricted in their right to dispute. And until 1978, the US Civil Service Commission, an arm of the federal government, conducted job classifications to hire the best people for particular positions.[83] After Japan's defeat in World War II, it was this system that served as the basis for the US Occupation's attempts to reform the Japanese bureaucracy.

In November 1946, Occupation officials enlisted the aid of a team of advisors headed by Blaine Hoover, an expert on civil service institutions. Under their guidance, the Japanese government's National Personnel Authority (*Jinji-in*; hereinafter NPA) was established in December 1948. By April 1949, the NPA had prepared a draft proposal that classified national public service jobs into 519 categories. In January 1950, the S-1 Examination was administered to national public servants then in office, which served as a written test to determine whether they had the appropriate expertise for their positions.

However, Japanese bureaucrats in the various ministries resisted these reforms by delaying the submission of results for the job surveys requested by the NPA.[84] For the Japanese officials, who had been promoted through personnel transfers from one position to another, the US-style job classifications proved unacceptable. What's more, 25.6% of senior national public servants at the time were removed from their posts after failing the S-1 Examination, which only reinforced the bureaucrats' opposition.[85] The NPA Secretary General who administered the exam later recalled a disgruntled ministry official telling him, 'You will go to hell'.[86] When the Occupation ended in April 1952, the NPA lost its backing, and although the organization itself remained, its reforms came to a halt.

However, Japanese interests brought different agendas to these reforms, and the Japanese bureaucracy was also transformed. The

Democratization and Equality of '*Shain*' (Company Employee)   253

postwar labor movement among Japanese public sectors used the Occupation's attempt to eliminate the distinction between prewar civil servants (*kanri*) and non-regular officials to achieve equality among all public servants (*kōmuin*). Higher-level bureaucrats, on the other hand, took advantage of the Occupation's policy of paying higher wages for more responsible and difficult jobs, and tried to raise their own salaries. Conservative politicians then tried to use this reform to deprive public servants of their right to dispute. The combined result of these endeavors was that Japan's public service system was transformed into something similar to the Japanese-style employment system that would later emerge.

As in the private sector, this series of changes took place against the backdrop of postwar inflation. Non-regular officials (*koin* and *yōnin*) and lower-level *hannin* officials joined the labor movement and asserted their entitlement to a livelihood wage. Government ministries and agencies responded to this pressure with the generous issue of emoluments that had been introduced during the war, such as temporary family allowances, long-service allowances and temporary bonuses.[87] Among lower-ranking civil servants, these disbursements favored middle-aged and older staff with dependents, and the gap between the highest and lowest salaries, which had been a factor of fifteen in April 1946, was reduced to a factor of 4.3 in February 1947.[88]

The labor movement in the public sector also constituted a power base for the Socialist Party and the Communist Party and caused a constant headache for conservative politicians and higher-level bureaucrats. Shigeru Yoshida, the conservative prime minister and former ambassador to the United Kingdom, sought to use the Occupation's reforms to rein in labor activists in the civil service. On 6 February 1947, Yoshida invited Hoover's advisory team to a dinner party and explained that members of the government's employees were spending their working hours on strike. Hoover expressed surprise at this news and explained to his host that in the US, strikes by government employees were restricted.[89] The prewar Japanese interpretation of the law was based on the situation in Germany, where the employment of non-regular officials (*koin* and *yōnin*) was interpreted as being governed by private law, which granted them the right to strike.[90] In the US public service, however, where there was no such distinction, disputes by public servants were uniformly limited. Yoshida decided that he would try to take advantage of this point.

The government agency that sought to make another use of the US-led reforms was the Ministry of Finance's Remuneration Bureau, which was in charge of the public service payroll. At the time, through the efforts of the labor movement, public servants' salaries tended for the most part to be a livelihood wage based on their age and number of dependents. Insisting that this situation be reviewed 'in the spirit of [the US model of] job classification', the Remuneration Bureau prepared a draft proposal for determining salaries that it put forward in April 1947. This proposal was based on a vertical hierarchy of individual jobs ranked according to their difficulty, with a ranking scheme by which high-level bureaucrats who had graduated from former imperial universities would receive higher salaries. However, despite the emphasis on the vertical hierarchy of difficulty, there was in fact no classification of professions and job types. At a 1956 retrospective remark, Kazuo Imai, the director of the Remuneration Bureau, who prepared the guidelines, characterized the scheme as a 'phony (*inchiki*) job classification system'.[91]

It was around this time that Hoover's advisory team hosted a lecture on the US model of job classification for Japanese officials who would later become the staff of the NPA. The Japanese staff, however, had difficulty wrapping their heads around the US system.[92] An exasperated Hoover drafted a US-style National Civil Service Bill on his own, which he hand-delivered to Prime Minister Tetsu Katayama in June 1947. Instructing the Prime Minister to get the bill passed into law within a few weeks, he promptly returned to the US.[93] Katayama was the leader of the Socialist Party, which had just wrested power from the conservative faction led by Shigeru Yoshida in that year's April election.

Hoover's bill, however, found no support from anyone on the Japanese side. The socialist government, who drew their base of support from the public service unions, had no desire to deprive public servants of their right to dispute as advocated by Hoover's bill. High-ranking bureaucrats in the various government ministries protested

Democratization and Equality of 'Shain' (Company Employee)   255

the newly established NPA's loss of authority over personnel, as well as the categorical inclusion of non-regular officials like *koin* and *yōnin* as public servants. In October 1947, the Japanese government passed the National Public Service Act (*Kokka kōmuin-hō*), which revised these parts of Hoover's proposal.[94] Further, in May 1948, the New Salary Implementation Act (*Shin kyūyo jisshi-hō*), which was based on the Ministry of Finance's original proposal, came into force, replacing the prewar government ranks with fifteen salary grades putatively based on the degree of job responsibility and difficulty, but without any actual job classifications.[95]

When he returned to Japan in January 1948, Hoover was incensed at this development, and arranged for the National Public Service Act to be amended in October 1948 to be more in keeping with his original intention. Due to push back from GHQ's Labor Division, which supported the Japanese labor movement, Japanese Government Railways and other monopolies were divested from the government to become public corporations, but public servants, including those in the postal sector, were stripped of their right to dispute. The prime minister who saw this amendment to the National Public Service Act through was the conservative Shigeru Yoshida, who was returned to power that October.[96] In December 1948, the National Personnel Authority was established with Hoover's support, but as noted earlier, subsequent reforms were hampered by resistance on the part of bureaucrats and then the end of the Occupation in April 1952.

Ultimately, the reforms sought by Hoover were used to strip workers in the public sector of their right to dispute, and bureaucratic norms in Japan remained largely unchanged. From 1949, the prewar higher and ordinary civil service examinations were replaced with new recruitment examinations for entry into the upper and middle ranks of the fifteen grades (these were renamed Advanced and Intermediate in 1957 and then again as Type I and Type II in 1985). The official position of the NPA as of 1949 was that the only difference was the level of entrance, and that subsequent promotion depended entirely on performance, but few placed any stock in such assurances.[97] Finally, with the 2007 revision of the National Public Service Act, the remaining legislation concerning job classifications that had been brought in by the Occupation was repealed.

A byproduct of the Occupation's reforms, however, was the elimination of the old distinction between civil servants and non-regular officials. As a result, *koin* and *yōnin* employees, who had accounted for almost 80% of the prewar Japanese bureaucracy, were now recognized as 'public servants' (*kōmuin*), and eligible for the same employment protections and pension system as staff officials.[98] Lower-level clerks and manual laborers were also assigned ranks with salaries that increased with accumulated years of service. Around 1955, a plan to create a category of national labor service employees that would be employed under private law by the Japanese government, in imitation of the German system, came under consideration but was ultimately abandoned.[99]

Japan's prewar governmental bureaucracy system had a division between appointed regular officials and employed non-regular officials somewhat similar to that in Germany. The US Occupation authorities attempted to reform it and make all public servants government employees as in the US, but the result was that all public servants became more like German *Beatme* who were guaranteed appointed status but no right to dispute. However, lower-level clerks and manual laborers were recruited through the elementary-level public servant examination (renamed Type III in 1985), and the three-tier structure among public servants in Japan has continued to persist informally.[100]

In this way, the postwar Japanese bureaucracy underwent certain changes. There was continuity in that professions and jobs were not classified but rather ranked according to 'pay grade', and a three-tier structure was retained. However, there was also change in that all staff were now public servants, laborers were also graded, and their salaries increased with years of service. In other words, an equality among public servants was achieved by extending the old system enjoyed by the upper echelon to the lower ranks. Similar changes would be seen in the private sector in the form of the rise of 'equality as company employees' (*shain*). And still, as in the private sector, outside of the 'equality of public servants' (*kōmuin*) achieved in the postwar period,

Democratization and Equality of '*Shain*' (Company Employee) 257

'non-regular public servants' (*hiseiki- kōmuin*) would arise, but this would come later as we shall see in Chapter 7.

Ranking schemes extended to laborers

Similar trends to the postwar changes in the public sector were also apparent in the private sector. These included the fact that lower-level clerks and shop-floor laborers, who had come to be acknowledged as 'company employees' (*shain*), were also assigned ranks, which suggested the possibility of promotion based on years of service. Here, too, war and democratization led to greater equalization even as the three-tier structure was maintained.

One such example is JGR (Japan Government Railways), which adopted an organization modeled on the civil service. In 1941, the staff of JGR was made up of 0.4% *sōnin* officials, 15% *hannin* officials (including train drivers who were treated as such), 44% *koin* (*yatoi*) and 41% *yōnin*. In 1946, after the war, these proportions were 0.6% for second-class officials (the revised term for *sōnin* officials), 31% for third-class officials (*hannin* officials), 64% for *koin* and 3% for apprentices (*yōnin*).[101] In other words, despite the persistence of a three-tier structure, each level of the whole had been promoted, so that the overall trend was toward equalization. Even if the structure itself had not changed, this was nevertheless a big change for individual laborers.

In a series of major disputes in the late 1940s and 1950s, management was able to reassert the control it had lost immediately after the war. Even so, the longer disputes often resulted in shutdowns lasting between several months and nearly a year, which caused significant losses for companies. In many cases, hostility persisted in the workplace and personnel in charge of labor relations regularly experienced harsh treatment. In the aftermath of these developments, Nikkeiren announced the following at its sixteenth regular general meeting in 1963.

> Over the course of the eighteen years since the end of the war both labor and management have gained precious experiences that have brought them to where they are today. We have seen firsthand

how a sense of class antagonism between labor and management, a bias toward political strife and anti-union prejudice have led to many disruptions in relations between labor and management, as well as in the social order.[102]

After this series of major disputes, a chastened management elected to seek compromise with the labor unions. What found purchase was an attitude of caution with regard to layoffs and the provision of regular pay raises. In practice, this was accomplished with the extension of long-term employment and seniority wages based on years of service, which had been limited to staff employees before the war, to the level of laborers on the shop floor.

The ranking schemes introduced in the 1950s also differed from those of the prewar period in that it was not uncommon for shop floor laborers to be assigned ranks as well. Before the war, salaried 'company employees' (*shain*) were assigned ranks, but factory workers were not. In addition, according to Mitsubishi's 1919 in-house bylaws for employee promotion, whereas 'regular company employees' (*sei'in*) were assigned status titles (such as 'administrator' [*kanji*] or 'manager' [*shuji*]), 'associate employees' (*jun'in*) had only salary amounts and grades, with no titles.[103]

As mentioned in Chapter 3, prewar factory workers also followed the custom of considering their wage amount as their effective rank. Hence, even before the war, companies graded factory workers by the amount of their wages, resulting in the norm of their classification as 'first-class factory workers', 'second-class factory workers', and so on.[104] Nevertheless, in most prewar companies, there was no route for promotion from the level of factory worker to that of staff employee. This was one of the reasons why the postwar labor movement originally demanded the elimination of ranking schemes.

However, the ranking schemes that began to be introduced from the 1950s were different in character than their earlier counterparts. Some of the ranking schemes of this period, like the 'job classifications system' introduced at Yahata Steel in 1953, that might have been inspired by the 'phony job classification system' in the public sector, did not even assign a rank to blue-collar laborers (*sagyō-in*).[105] On the

Democratization and Equality of 'Shain' (Company Employee)

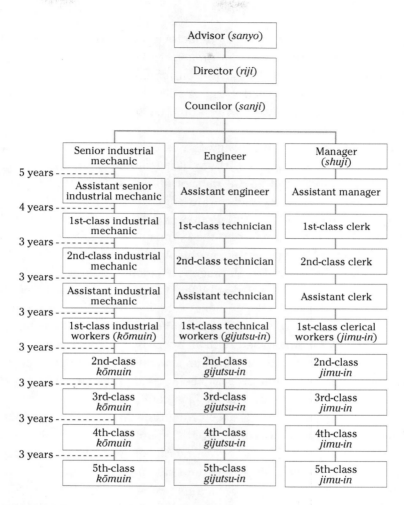

Figure 5.4 A ranking scheme introduced by Nippon Light Metal (1953)
Source: Makiuchi (1960: 274).

other hand, there were also many schemes that recognized factory workers and staff employees as having equal status, even if only formally, and which suggested that even factory workers could be promoted to senior management positions.

For example, the ranking scheme introduced by Nippon Light Metal in 1953 (Figure 5.4) assigned ranks to industrial workers (*kōmuin*, who corresponded to the old category of factory worker [*shokkō*]) as well as clerical and technical workers (*jimu-in* and *gijutsu-in*, respectively, both of whom corresponded to the old category of staff employee [*shokuin*]) in parallel. This scheme institutionalized the possibility for even industrial workers to be promoted to the staff position of councilor (*sanji*).

That being said, when we tally the years of service required for such a promotion as indicated by this chart, it would take at least thirty years for a person hired at the rank of fifth-class industrial worker to be promoted to the councilor. Moreover, the firm's employment regulations also stated that 'initial ranks' were to 'respect educational background', with those entering the company at age fifteen (i.e., as junior high school graduates) being eligible for an initial rank as fifth-class workers, those hired at eighteen (i.e., as high school graduates) as fourth-class, and those hired at twenty-two (i.e., as university graduates) as second-class.[106] Given these facts, it would have been quite unlikely for factory workers to be promoted to executive positions, since university graduates had such an overwhelming advantage.

Even so, compared to the prewar system, the fact that factory workers and salaried staffs were ranked as though they were on equal terms, even if only formally, was a significant change. What is more, this also meant that seniority-based promotions and pay raises, which had been the exclusive privilege of staff employees before the war, were now also extended to factory workers. Furthermore, the ranking scheme at Nippon Light Metal was amended in September 1960 with the revision of the collective labor agreement, resulting in the creation of the two groups of 'clerical workers' and 'technical workers'. In an agreement with the labor union driven primarily by factory workers, the category of 'industrial worker' was abolished and merged into 'technical worker'.

In that sense, despite the introduction of ranking schemes – or rather despite the forms that this process took – the 'equality of company employees (*shain*)' was steadily becoming more firmly established. A labor relations manager at Nippon Light Metal stated in 1960 that 'We'd like to unify these two categories into a single scheme, if only someone could point to a suitable rank nomenclature that synthesizes the

Democratization and Equality of 'Shain' (Company Employee)

two'.[107] Just such a system – one that ranked everyone as a 'company employee' (*shain*) – would be realized in the late 1960s, as we shall see in Chapter 6.

Years of service as an indicator of 'ability'

One trend that became entrenched through this process was the tendency to place emphasis on years of service.

For its part, management sought to revisit the livelihood wage that was developed after Japan's defeat, with the aim of determining wages based on personnel assessments. Labor activists, however, remained averse to the arbitrary assessments and disadvantageous treatment based on educational background that had prevailed before the war.

The compromise that eventually emerged was years of service. For management, years of service bore a relation to workers' proficiency in the company and was thus preferable to age or number of family members. For labor, years of service was simultaneously an objective measure that could not be changed at the whim of management as well as a means of achieving the seniority-based wages that staff employees had enjoyed before the war.

An illustration of the process by which years of service emerged as a compromise in the struggle between management and labor can be seen in the way that wages were determined at JGR. In April 1947, a wage structure for public-sector laborers like those employed by JGR and Japan Post was agreed upon as a result of negotiations between labor and management. The basic wage consisted of three parts: an individual pay determined by age, the family allowance determined by the number of family members and an ability pay determined by a performance evaluation.[108] This structure was nearly identical to that of the Densan Wage Model, but with a heavier weighting assigned to the ability-based element.

The discussion then turned to the question of whether 'ability' should be evaluated in terms of education, experience or skill. In August 1947, the JGR leadership, at a meeting of representative officers for various positions tasked with job evaluations, proposed emphasizing '1) education, 2) experience and 3) creativity and ingenuity'.[109] The high value attached to education and creativity can only have amounted to paying higher wages to staff employees with higher educational backgrounds.

The counter proposal offered by labor, however, went as follows: '1) experience, 2) training and 3) effort' or '1) how much proficiency is required, 2) how long does it take to become a fully trained worker, and 3) what is the maximum amount of effort required'.[110] In other words, the labor side was insisting that evaluation of experience and effort should tend to favor middle-aged and older laborers on the shop floor.

Negotiations between labor and management proceeded with difficulty, and the wage structure itself was changed, but somewhere in the process, the negotiators on the labor side began to insist that evaluations should include years of service. Like 'experience', years of service was an indicator that tended to favor middle-aged and older shop-floor laborers. Then, in November 1948, the JGR labor union adopted the view that 'ability is proportional to years of service'. They reasoned that if proficiency was interpreted as ability, then this could be equated with years of service. Jong-won Woo, who has studied these negotiations, comments that 'the reason they reinterpreted years of service as ability was that they had determined that this was the only way could they enjoy a seniority wage similar to that of white-collar workers'.[111]

The original intention behind the livelihood wage had been to help employees cope with the hardships of postwar life while simultaneously extending seniority-based pay, once the exclusive privilege of staff employees, to laborers. When management began to try to roll back concessions, laborers attempted to maintain their hold on the livelihood wage by claiming that length of service was an indicator of ability.

At the same time, this was consistent with the swing of the pendulum back to ranking systems. According to Jong-won Woo, JGR's inclusion of years of service into evaluations at that time was also a practical solution that applied the fact that the prewar qualifications for non-regular *koin* officials to be appointed as *hannin* officials had basically taken the form of 'education plus years of service'.[112] In other words, this new emphasis on years of service was acceptable to

Democratization and Equality of '*Shain*' (Company Employee)   263

both labor and management, since they were both accustomed to the prewar civil service-type order.

'Equal pay for equal work' and 'years of experience'

Against this backdrop, in 1952, the principle of 'equal pay for equal work' and the demand that years of experience be recognized was added to the mix by the Nissan Motor Workers Union. The story of how this came to be is worth mentioning. This is because the principal and the demand are contradictory when workers with different years of experience do the same job, and it is necessary to examine how Japanese labor unions have considered this contradiction.

In the summer of 1952, the All-Japan Automobile Workers' Union (known as Zenji), an industrial union representing workers in the automobile industry, formulated three wage principles. Of these, the second, which demanded 'equal pay for equal work', insisted that 'wages should not be kept low because a worker is young or has a small family', and that 'there should be no wage discrimination on the basis of sex, nationality or any other factor'. The third principle stated that the first two principles 'should be regarded as a common principle throughout the automotive industry, one that prevails beyond the frame of any one company'.[113] As I note later in this chapter, the Occupation authorities encouraged job-based wages after the end of the war, which to a certain extent had led to a popular awareness of the principle of equal pay for equal work, as well as a trend among Japanese labor unions to take a page out of the same book.

Nevertheless, in the September 1952 wage dispute at the Nissan Motor Company, the union demanded that wages be determined by the level of proficiency as measured by years of experience. Here, moreover, the 'years of experience' in the union's context was implicitly meant to account for employee age and number of family members. What the union had envisioned was that 'unskilled labor' with zero years of experience would merit 'a wage sufficient to guarantee the livelihood of a single person', and that 'intermediate proficiency' with eight years of experience would merit 'a wage that guarantees the minimum cost of living to support the worker, his wife and one child'.[114] In other words, the Nissan Workers' Union (the Nissan chapter of Zenji) had issued a demand that, while upholding the principle of equal pay for equal work, positioned years of experience in such a way that wages would increase with age and number of family members. Why had they come up with such seemingly contradictory demands?

In fact, the first of the three principles of Zenji's wage policy had advocated 'ensuring that all employees, no matter their level of skill, what kind of company they work for, or what kind of work they do, as long as they work in the workplace, are paid enough to live in a way that respects their humanity, supports their families, and allows them to continue to work, all within a seven-hour workday'. In other words, the second and third principles called for equal pay for equal work across the industry, while the first principle demanded a livelihood wage.

In 1952, even after the postwar inflationary period had ended, the quality of life was still poor. While people were well aware that the labor movement in the US was championing the idea of equal pay for equal work, there was also the possibility that, if this principle were simply applied by rote in Japan, everyone would end up with low wages. Therefore, as its first principle, Zenji had no choice but to establish a demand for wages that would be sufficient to maintain workers' household economies.

The 'years of experience' in the demand emerged as a compromise between the two principles of equal pay for equal work and the livelihood wage. Zenji's second principle also eliminated discrimination based on gender, nationality and age, but recognized wage differences based on the intensity and difficulty of the work, and the level of proficiency required for the jobs that its laborers were doing. Thus, years of experience was now considered as a reflection of an employee's degree of proficiency.[115] This incorporation of years of experience also reflected the demands of blue-collar shop-floor workers. The November 1952 issue of the union's newsletter *Zenjidōsha* (All-automobiles) featured the following dialogue between a white-collar worker (A) and a blue-collar worker (B) engaging in a workplace debate.

Democratization and Equality of '*Shain*' (Company Employee)   265

A: I guess I just find it disheartening that the pay differential in our next wage increase request is based solely on years of experience. There are differences in skill, and then there's demonstrated ability. These should be factored in […].

B: You went to school, so you probably don't know how it is! Experience is knowing that the sun rises in the morning and sets in the evening. That's in one day. There are 365 days in a year. But it's not that simple. There are cold days, hot days, air raids and sometimes your hands are so greasy you're liable to slice yourself. Sometimes, someone will say something obnoxious to you, and you'll clench your teeth. It's like that. That's experience. Skills and demonstrated ability are both in there too. […] But if you don't know that much about experience, how about I tattoo it onto your flesh?[116]

Of course, at that time, Japanese companies were not as uniform as they would come to be in later years. The Nissan Workers' Union used the phrase 'years of experience' rather than 'years of service', apparently because many workers entered Nissan after working for other companies, and because the union took into consideration those whose years of employment had been shortened due to military service. Economist Makoto Yoshida has studied the process of the negotiations that took place at Nissan in 1952 and introduces a position paper drafted by seventeen workers that had been kept by a member of the cast mold cleaning team's workplace committee. According to the paper, eleven of the seventeen signatories had previous experience working outside the company. In addition, a laborer in the paper observed that 'because of the delays with demobilization, there are considerable pay disadvantages [due to shortened years of service] as compared to people who did not serve in the military, or who had been demobilized earlier'.[117]

According to Yoshida, the question of how to count time spent in military service, at school and at other companies toward 'years of experience' was one for which there was no consensus, even within the Nissan Workers' Union.[118] Zenji's third principle, as noted earlier, was that the first and second principles should be applied 'beyond the frame of any one company', but this may have reflected the fact that automobile industry workers at the time experienced more mobility between companies than they do today.

Even amidst these fluctuations, the postwar livelihood wage, with its emphasis on age, was continuing to move closer to a seniority-based wage that emphasized years of service. As we shall see in Chapter 7, we could say that the basic salary system for regular employees in Japan has remained constant since the 1950s, even into the twenty-first century. It was a mixture of the ability pay, which management assessed, and the livelihood wage based on age and family size, which management could not change. The unions then tried to negotiate so that the ability pay was determined as much as possible by years of service, thus bringing it closer to the livelihood wage. As time passed, however, more and more emphasis was being placed on ability pay, and the relative importance of 'performance', which management could discretionally assess, gained ground on years of service. Even so, the prototypical expression of the system itself could be said to have become more or less fully established in the 1950s.

In other words, the seniority-based wages of postwar Japan were the product of a confluence of several factors. First, the seniority-based wages of the prewar category of staff employees existed as a goal to be attained. Second, the livelihood wage won by the postwar labor movement achieved a wage that was based on age. Finally, a compromise between management rollbacks and opposition by labor was realized in the form of seniority-based wages, in which years of service were taken into consideration in the evaluation of ability.

The inside and outside of seniority-based pay

However, unlike the livelihood wage, which was determined by age, length of service is dependent on an employee's tenure at a particular company. Also, since the 1950s, women, especially, have been positioned outside of this wage structure.

Labor historian Yutaka Nishinarita demonstrates this through statistics. In 1946, wages increased with age for both men and women. By 1954, however, whereas men's wages were increasing with both age

Democratization and Equality of 'Shain' (Company Employee) 267

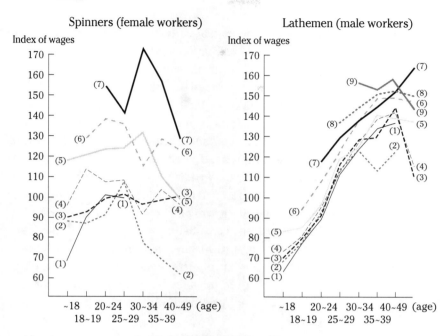

Figure 5.5 Wages by age and years of service (1954)

Notes: Years of service or years of experience: (1) less than six months; (2) six months to less than one year; (3) one year to less than two years; (4) two years to less than three years; (5) three years to less than five years; (6) five years to less than ten years; (7) ten years to less than fifteen years; (8) fifteen years to less than twenty years; (9) twenty years to less than thirty years. Wages for twenty- to twenty-four-year-olds with between one year and less than two years of service are indexed to 100.
Source: Data is based on volumes 2 and 4 of Ministry of Labor (1954), *Shokushu-betsu-tō chingin jittai chōsa kojin betsu chingin chōsa kekka hōkoku-sho* (Report on the Results of the Occupation Wage Survey and the Individual Wage Survey), Tokyo: Rōdōshō Rōdō Tōkei Chōsa-Bu (Ministry of Labor Statistical Research Division), compiled by Nishinarita (1995: 20).

and length of service in a particular company, women's wages were no longer increasing with age. Perhaps reflecting this situation, government wage surveys in the 1950s began to place more importance on length of service in a particular company. Based on the Ministry of Labor's 1954 report on the results of its 'Occupational Wage Survey' (*shokushu-betsu-tō chingin jittai chōsa*) and 'Individual Wage Survey' (*kojin-betsu chingin chōsa*), Nishinarita plotted wages for lathemen (male workers) and spinners (female workers).[119] Looking at the resulting graphs (Figure 5.5), we see that whereas men's wages increased with both age and years of service, women's wages did not increase with age, indicating that only years of service had any effect.

In other words, even as the earnings of lathemen retained the character of a livelihood wage determined by age, they were increasingly subject to the influence of years of service. Female spinners, however, were already no longer eligible for a livelihood wage, as their wages no longer increased with age. However, since they were often paid on a piece-rate basis, their wages increased as a function of their in-house proficiency, which was determined by their years of service.

As discussed earlier, in 1946, Densan had insisted on the elimination of gender-based wage inequality. However, the reality at the time was that labor unions had themselves established a gender-based pay gap in wages for union secretaries, and in one case even a union leader had gone so far as to argue that 'surely the idea that women are paid less than men is a socially accepted norm in Japan'.[120] As noted earlier, the Densan Wage Model was itself premised on the male breadwinner model of family structure.

Here, we may recall Abegglen's study, which featured in the discussion in Chapter 3. At the large firm that Abegglen surveyed in 1955, a three-tier structure was still in place. At the same time, however, long-term employment and seniority-based wages had been extended to factory workers, and wages increased in conjunction with years of service. Moreover, women had been excluded from consideration for such a 'lifetime commitment'.

Before the war, factory workers had not been eligible for long-term employment or seniority-based wages. In this respect, the corporate order that Abegglen studied was considerably different from the order that prevailed before the war. However, in that the three-tier structure remained so clearly apparent, it also differed from the model of Japanese employment that would appear after the 1960s. Moreover, the increased importance that length of service had in determining wages differed from the emphasis that had been given to the livelihood wage immediately after the end of World War II. In other words, what Abegglen observed was a snapshot of the Japanese company circa 1955. It was a transitional state in which 'equality of company employees'

Democratization and Equality of '*Shain*' (Company Employee)

was making significant inroads, even as the three-tier structure of the prewar system was preserved.

Emergence of the dual structure paradigm

We should remember, however, that the achievement of the 'equality of company employees' (*shain*) during this period was largely confined to large companies. As noted earlier, for some time after the end of the war, SMEs tended to have higher operating rates and offer higher wages than even the large manufacturers. By the 1950s, when this was no longer the case, the wage gap between different sizes of companies had widened.

Wage disparities based on company size in heavy industry is considered to date from the 1920s.[121] Even so, it was not until the late 1950s that it was to attract attention and enter the public discourse as a social issue. Conceivably, this is partly due to the fact that although wage disparities existed between large and small companies even before the war, the more obvious disparities were those that existed between staff employees and shop-floor laborers. In postwar Japan, staff employees and shop-floor laborers both joined mixed unions, and in firms where such unions existed they worked together to achieve some degree of equality. However, enterprise unions had no bargaining power over disparities between companies. This background explains the emergence of the wage gap between large and small companies as an issue beginning in the mid-1950s.

The academic expression of this idea was the 'dual structure' paradigm (*nijūkōzō-ron*). As mentioned in Chapter 1, this term entered popular usage after its appearance in the 1957 Economic White Paper. It positioned the relationship between 'modern large companies' and 'small enterprises with pre-modern relations between management and labor, as well as family-run microenterprises and farms' as being 'akin to a dual structure in which a developed country and an underdeveloped country coexist within a single nation'. As also mentioned in Chapter 1, the Economic White Paper in question claimed that dual structure-style barriers to labor mobility existed between large firms and SMEs in the labor market, as well.

This application of the dual structure paradigm to the labor market, again, as noted in Chapter 1, was a doctrine advocated by the economist Shōjirō Ujihara. Ujihara, however, relied on the same ideas as the other dual structure theorists of his day. He believed that this dual structure had been engendered by Japan's failure to modernize. The salient points of his theory in 1954 may be summarized as follows.

According to Ujihara, large companies have a seniority-based workplace order, wherein wages increase with years of service. Since to quit one's position at a company would be tantamount to 'abandoning the vested rights one has acquired over the years', the labor market in large companies takes on a closed-off character.[122] So why, then, do wages increase with years of service?

In Ujihara's view, Japan's manufacturing industry had yet to achieve any operational standardization, and its laborers were poorly educated. This meant that complete novices who had grown up on farms or in shops had no choice but to learn methods of working and ways of operating machinery that were different in each company. The intuitive and embodied knowledge that this approach produced was not standardized; it might be proportional to the number of years of service at any given company, but it was useless anywhere else. Thus, a seniority-based order came into being in which wages increased with years of service.[123]

Hence, Ujihara believed that these norms would change as laborers became better educated and manufacturing processes became more streamlined. In his view, 'this late start with industrial technology has not resulted in skills that are more objective or teachable [...] it has produced skills that are only ever applicable to the company in question'. Even so, he expressed his hopes for modernization by observing that 'nevertheless, this special character of skill is being transformed with technological advancement and the streamlining of work processes'.[124] Ujihara also felt that these problems stemmed from the fact that the self-employment and agricultural sectors comprised a high proportion of the labor market, as well as the ongoing supply of a surplus labor force with little education and no skills. Proponents of the dual structure paradigm at the time typically saw these as problems that would be resolved naturally with the advance of modernization.[125]

Democratization and Equality of 'Shain' (Company Employee)

Seen in hindsight, the dual structure paradigm of this period not only expected too much from modernization, but also failed to capture the realities of the Japanese situation. Ujihara's ideas applied only in the case of female spinners, whose wages were based solely on years of service. Seniority-based wages, where wages increase with both age and length of service, were indecipherable to an economic analysis such as Ujihara's. Only later would it become clear that Ujihara's analysis was somewhat simplistic.

The formation of a dual structure in social security

In reality, modernization and institutionalization proceeded in ways that actually confirmed and even reinforced this dual structure. One example of this is social security institutions. As it turns out, social security in Japan was initially established for the benefit of the employees of large corporations, while institutions that covered the rest of the population emerged only later. This only reinforced the division between regular employees at large corporations, on one hand, and everyone else, on the other.

Arguably, the origins of social security in Japan can be traced to civil service pensions. More often, however, its origins tend to be attributed to the Kanebō Mutual Aid Association, established in 1905 by workers at the Kanegafuchi Cotton Spinning Company (*Kanegafuchi Bōseki-gaisha*, or Kanebō for short).[126] The association, which counted all employees as members, used contributions from association members, subsidies from the company and donations from related parties to cover medical treatment for injuries and illnesses, including work-related accidents, and provide pensions after retirement.

In 1907, the Imperial Railways Relief Association was established for employees of the state-run JGR. The association made membership compulsory for all active employees, from whom it collected insurance premiums, with the government subsidizing two-thirds of the total amount. Since JGR's staff employees were also civil servants, they were entitled to pensions, and one of the purposes of the association was to bridge the gap that existed between them and the blue-collar employees.

With the proliferation of such mutual aid associations in the Taishō period (1912–1926), this trend was confirmed with the promulgation of the Health Insurance Act (*Kenkō hoken-hō*) in 1922. This law covered both regular-basis laborers and staff employees earning less than 1,200 yen per annum at establishments subject to the Factory Act (*Kōjō-hō*) and the Mining Act (*Kōgyō-hō*) and required that enterprises employing more than 300 people form health insurance associations, with health insurance for smaller establishments to be administered by the government. Small enterprises not subject to either the Factory or Mining Act were not covered by either of these provisions. In effect, this meant that large companies were forced to create associations, medium-sized firms were administered by the government and small enterprises were exempt. The agricultural and other self-employed workers were never even considered. In 1930, those who qualified for health insurance amounted to about 6% of the working population.[127]

This system is often explained as being inspired by German practices.[128] The Kanebō Mutual Insurance Union, for instance, was modeled on the mutual support fund in place at Krupp, a German heavy industry firm.[129] Social security in Germany, however, was built around the *Krankenkasse*, or health insurance funds, which had traditionally served specific trades. In Germany, mutual aid organizations based on occupational categories have been popular since the Middle Ages. When the government established a medical insurance system in the 1880s, mutual aid associations based on specific trades and industries were given corporate status and recognized as *Krankenkasse*.[130] While there were *Krankenkasse* for specific companies, these were far from the mainstream. Also, as noted in Chapter 4, toward the end of the nineteenth century, people from various occupations such as clerks, office workers and draftsmen came together to identify collectively as *Angestellte*, or lower-level salaried employees, which led to the passage of the *Versicherungsgesetz für Angestellte* (Law Relating to Insurance of Salaried Employees) of 1911.

In Japan, the basic unit of mutual aid in the health insurance system was not the occupational category, but the firm. Large companies had their own insurance associations, medium-sized firms were administered by the government, and small enterprises, the

Democratization and Equality of 'Shain' (Company Employee)

self-employed and farmers were left over as the system's residual elements. This leftover part of the system could thus be said to have been formed institutionally. After World War II, the Allied Occupation created a tax-financed public assistance system, but this was never fully applied. Essentially, it was this leftover element that was likened to an 'underdeveloped country' in the 1957 Economic White Paper. It included both self-employed individuals and employed workers in a variety of industries and was of a character that could only be described as what was left over by the modern large company model.

Japan's National Health Insurance was created as a system to provide coverage for this leftover element. Originally introduced in 1938 as a form of universal health insurance (*kokumin kai hoken*, a play on the term *kokumin kaihei*, or 'universal conscription'), it was designed to create insurance associations with local communities as the basic unit. Hidefumi Kawamura, the Home Affairs bureaucrat who drafted the original 1938 National Health Insurance system, claimed that 'the idea of a National Health Insurance system was unprecedented in any country'. He recounted that he had surveyed the systems of other countries, but could find nothing that would serve as a reference. He wrote that 'Local solidarity, a product of family and feudal institutions, remains powerfully present in Japan's rural villages, which have inherited the beautiful legacy of neighborliness and mutual support'. His idea was 'to demarcate specific areas based on the presence of such local solidarity where local health insurance funds could be created under the guidance and supervision of the national and local governments'.[131]

To summarize, in Japan, health insurance associations were created first for large corporations and only after that for local communities. A Japanese scholar specializing in the study of social security systems explained that 'Japan's system was built on the basis of identity groups that constitute the basic units of Japanese society, namely, the *kaisha* [company] and the *mura* [local community]'.[132] Be that as it may, these identity groups were not pre-existing traditional entities, but were in fact the products of modern policies. The community (*mura*) was not a real entity, but rather a miscellaneous jumble of people left out of the large companies (*kaisha*). It would thus be even more accurate to say that it was the social security system that institutionalized norms that regarded company and local community as the basic units of Japanese society.

The case of the National Pension is remarkably similar. In 1944, the Welfare Pension Act (*Kōsei nenkin-hō*) was passed to cover employed workers except for those in small enterprises, self-employed, and family workers. Then the National Pension System, which provided coverage for workers not eligible under the act, was established in 1959. According to the recollections of a Welfare Ministry bureaucrat at the time, the original draft of the National Pension System had been based on the principle that it should cover the entire population. However, after strenuous opposition from the Ministry of Finance, this guiding principle was changed to the existing system's goal of providing coverage 'for the majority of the population who are still uncovered'.[133] Although the National Pension System did eventually become a basic pension in 1985, the gap between regular employee pensioners and self-employed (and non-regular workers) remains considerable even today, as Chapter 1 describes.

Even though the 1938 National Health Insurance program effectively collapsed after Japan's defeat in World War II, the scheme's financial resources were stabilized in 1951 with the creation of a National Health Insurance Tax that could be collected by municipalities, and the program was relaunched in 1958 under a municipal management model (implemented in all municipalities in 1961). Since associations that had been created by local residents would not be able to keep up with premium payments, municipal governments began operating the program and collecting premiums as a tax. One Welfare Ministry bureaucrat involved in the establishment of the National Health Insurance Tax recalls, 'As far as insurance premiums go, Japanese people have a strong bias toward considering them as voluntary, so it was common knowledge that referring to them as taxes would improve collection results'.[134] Even if bureaucrats thought that the leftovers of the employees of large and medium-sized companies would mutually support each other simply by virtue of being from the same area, it would be fair to say that the community (*mura*) was not as substantial as the bureaucrats had expected.

Democratization and Equality of '*Shain*' (Company Employee)

Further, since the National Health Insurance program was premised on the propensity for mutual aid that existed in rural areas, it was believed from the outset that it would be 'quite difficult to apply to large cities'.[135] Thus, those who were neither employed by large companies nor lived in a rural area amounted to 'left over leftovers', so to speak. To provide coverage for these people, a special occupation-based national insurance program was created in 1938, but its coverage could hardly be described as extensive. Even after National Health Insurance became a municipal program, it was rarely implemented in cities with populations of more than 500,000 citizens. It was only after 1959, when Tokyo's special wards began to implement the system, that other cities started to follow suit.[136]

Thus, the dual structure was institutionalized by the social security system of the late 1950s. One might say that the dual structure was an unexpected side effect of postwar democratization, the labor movement and the development of social security.

The Allied Occupation and job-based wages

Nevertheless, for management, the spread of long-term employment and seniority-based wages proved to be a heavy financial burden. Before the advent of full-scale rapid growth in the 1960s, even companies had little capacity to pay seniority wages. To address this, through the 1950s and early 1960s, Nikkeiren advocated the adoption of the principles of equal pay for equal work and job-based wages to change employment norms at Japanese companies. The government of the day also issued reports in support of these ideas and investigated prospects for reforming the social security system. These debates suggested the possibility that Japanese society could have followed a different trajectory. I will use the remaining sections of this chapter to examine this argument.

The popular spread of job classification in the US largely failed to reach Japan during the prewar period.[137] The introduction of job classification and job-based wages to Japan is generally attributed to the Allied Occupation in the wake of World War II. In July 1946, a US Advisory Committee on Labor arrived in Japan at the invitation of GHQ

276 Chapter 5

to review the labor situation in Japan. The resulting report criticized a wage and salary system based on differences in age, sex and marital status as being economically unsound and unfair to the employees concerned, and recommended the adoption of a system based on the duties and responsibilities necessary for work modeled on the sound principle of job classification.[138] The report issued by the April 1947 Japan mission of the World Federation of Trade Unions (WFTU) took a more or less identical view.[139]

An orientation toward job-based wages also made inroads in Japan, following the trend set by the American model. In November 1946, the Japanese government's Headquarters for Economic Stabilization (*Keizai antei honbu*) published a 'Draft Basic Policy on Wage Payment Methods' (*Chingin shiharai hōhō ni kan suru kihon hōshin-an*) advocating the basic principle that wages should be paid for the performance of duties and work.[140] That same month, as part of the Occupation-led reforms, the introduction of job-based wages and job classifications were mandated for public servants, and when the National Public Service Act came into force in October of the following year, a stipulation was included for the implementation of a job classification system.

The business world welcomed these developments. In part, this was due to the US-influenced climate, but another reason was that job-based wages would also have the effect of suppressing wages for middle-aged and older workers. Under a job-based approach to payment, wages do not increase with length of service or age. At a time when labor unions were demanding a livelihood wage that increased with age, job-based wages were seen as a logical counter to this demand.

In June 1947, during a wage increase dispute at the Tokyo Express Electric Railway (Tōkyū) Corporation, management proposed job-based wages, which was introduced the following month. The 1949 Nikkeiren White Paper on Wages criticized the livelihood wage as being 'unscientific' and argued that it should be replaced by a job-based wage determined by 'the objective value of the work based on scientific job classification and a proper evaluation of laborers' ability'. That same year, job-based wages were introduced at several companies, including Jūjō (former Oji) Paper, Toho Gas, Nippon Light Metal and Kawasaki

Electric.[141] In 1955, Nikkeiren prepared a report entitled *Shokumu-kyū no kenkyū* (A Study of Job-Based Wages) in which it claimed that 'the essence of the job-based wage is the modern wage principle of equal pay for work of equal value'.[142]

The labor unions, however, argued against job-based wages, feeling that such an approach would not only lower the wages of middle-aged and older workers, but also widen the gap between staff employees, who would be more highly valued as intellectual workers, and the laborers on the shop floors. In fact, at JGR, which introduced job-based wages in April 1948, it became clear that following management's proposal would mean that the wage gap between the most and least well-paid employees, which had narrowed to about a factor of six after the war, would widen to a factor of around ten.[143] A pamphlet that had been distributed in December 1952 by the General Council of Trade Unions of Japan (Sōhyō) argued that 'Nikkeiren [...] disingenuously advocates the principle of equal pay for equal work, which it promptly substitutes for their way of job classification, and then seeks to use job-based pay, with its extreme wage disparities, to eliminate laborers' livelihood wage'.[144]

Moreover, labor unions in Japan were mixed unions organized at the enterprise level. To introduce job-based wages would necessitate determining which jobs deserved higher wages and which deserved lower. This might not have been problematic for occupation-based trade unions, but for Japanese enterprise unions, which included both staff employees and shop-floor laborers in various occupations, such an approach entailed the risk of schism.

In 1952, union leaders at Nissan Motor Co. attempted to introduce the principle of equal pay for equal work, but when the union was unable to reach a consensus on the disparity between different types of jobs, they demanded that wages instead be determined on the basis of years of experience.[145] In a book entitled *Danjo dōitsu rōdō dōitsu chingin ni tsuite* (Equal Pay for Equal Work for Men and Women Alike) published in 1951 by the Women and Youth Bureau of the Ministry of Labor, economist Takeshi Fujimoto stated, 'I'm no stranger to unions myself, but when it comes to this job classification issue, there are internal disputes that never reach consensus', adding that 'fights break out among workers' over this question.[146]

Partly due to the Japanese context, the principle of equal pay for equal work did not necessarily enjoy workers' full support. Some years later, in 1969, a survey by Ronald Dore asked workers 'Do you think that a man with longer service should receive higher wages than a man with shorter service, even if they are doing the same work?' According to the results, this question elicited a 'no' response from 67% of UK respondents, but only 18% of Japanese respondents.[147]

Japanese management in the 1950s had advocated job-based wages, however, this form of wages did not prove to be very popular. According to a 1951 'Salary Composition Survey' (*kyūyo kōsei chōsa*) conducted by the Ministry of Labor, only 9.4% of establishments in all industries and 7.2% in the manufacturing industry adopted job-based wages.[148] In addition to opposition from the labor unions, the inherent difficulty of job classification proved to be another contributing factor. As is still the case even in today's Japan, breaking down the work performed in a hazily defined collaborative relationship in open plan offices into definite duties is no easy matter. After analyzing each job in terms of its content, difficulty, responsibility and the knowledge and skills it requires, each job needs to be rated according to which job deserves which wage. This is a labor-intensive and costly process, as well as a likely source of friction within a company.

In the US, where job classification had been conducted by the government since the 1920s, published reference materials such as job dictionaries were readily available in the 1940s. At the suggestion of GHQ, the Japanese government also studied data supplied by the US Department of Labor to undertake its own job classifications on an industry-by-industry basis in 1948. The results were compiled in 1953 as the *Shokugyō jiten* (Dictionary of Occupations), which contained job classification tables and entries with the names of approximately 34,000 occupations.[149]

Even so, the job-based wages introduced by Japanese companies in the postwar period were based on different standards in different companies, and job classification was itself often conducted in an ad hoc manner. Nikkeiren's 1955 report also acknowledged that with

Democratization and Equality of '*Shain*' (Company Employee)

regard to the job-based wages that had been introduced in Japanese companies up to that point, 'these were only arbitrarily linked to wages based on completely inadequate job classifications, evaluations and ratings'.[150] It is hardly surprising that the labor unions protested.

Actually, the job-based wages introduced by the US steel industry in the 1930s had been introduced on a firm-by-firm basis. The fact that there was no correspondence across companies as well as the lack of transparency around what criteria were used to determine wages elicited strong dissatisfaction from laborers. The protest movement by the steel industry unions in the US led to a review of these companies' arbitrary job analyses and the fairness of the job-based wage market.[151] The job-based wage approach in Japan had never reached this stage.

A government that aspired to a Western-style society

This is not to say that Nikkeiren did not understand these issues. The authors of the 1955 report on job-based wages stated that 'democratic discussions between labor and management' were essential in setting job-based wages, and that 'social security systems', 'cross-firm labor markets' and 'vocational and technical education' had to be developed as parallel infrastructure.[152] Job-based wages might suppress wages for middle-aged and older workers. Effective compensation for this would be to provide child allowances and public housing for middle-aged and older workers with dependents, as has indeed been done in Western and Northern European countries. Furthermore, it would be desirable to create a cross-firm labor market through the provision of job training, skills accreditation and wages based on collective agreement for each industry and occupational category as has also been done in Western and Northern European countries. Any attempt to introduce job-based pay without such measures would be resisted by middle-aged and older workers who would try to maintain seniority-based wages to cover the costs of educating their children and acquiring housing. Nikkeiren was well aware of this issue at the time.

The Japanese government was also investigating such policy packages. Two notable examples were the 1960 National Income Doubling Plan formulated by the government's Economic Deliberation Council (EDC), and the same body's 1963 report titled *Keizai hatten ni okeru jinteki nōryoku kaihatsu no kadai to taisaku* (Problems and Strategies in Labor Capacity Development in the Context of Economic Growth).

The 1960 National Income Doubling Plan argued that labor management in companies should be urged 'to move beyond the corporate silos of employment to promote the diffusion of the principle of equal pay for equal work, to facilitate labor mobility and to encourage labor unions to organize on an industrial or regional basis rather than a company basis. Other proposals advanced in conjunction with 'the correction of the seniority-based wage system' included the more systematic development of a public national pension and the introduction of a 'system to provide a universal family child allowance'. The plan also advocated 'the shortening of working hours', 'the establishment of a vocational training system', the raising of welfare standards, the revision of 'medical assistance, housing assistance and educational assistance', and the construction of public rental housing.[153]

The 1963 EDC report on labor capacity development was a proposal that extended this line of thinking even further. At the time, the EDC included several economists who advocated the elimination of the dual structure, such as Hiromi Arisawa, Sei'ichi Tōbata and Shōjirō Ujihara. Another committee member was Hiroko Kageyama, later a well-known pioneer of the study of female managers and at that time a thirty-one-year-old student of labor relations at Cornell University.[154]

The report also advocated the formation of a cross-firm labor market, enhancement of vocational education and skill credential schemes, the unification of employee pensions and the National Pension System, improvements to public housing, and higher standards of public assistance. In particular, the Child Allowance System was clearly positioned as a system that would 'contribute to labor mobility across companies for middle-aged and older workers' by 'turning their salary into a form of job-based wage and covering the necessary expenses for

Democratization and Equality of 'Shain' (Company Employee)   281

raising families (children) with a system kept separate from wages'. It also included a section on the 'utilization of the female workforce' and advocated 'a personnel policy of recruitment, assignment, training and promotion according to the ability and aptitude of individuals regardless of gender'.[155]

In addition, instead of the piecemeal introduction of job-based wages by individual companies, the report called for the standardization of job classification by 'a third-party organization outside the corporate sector, such as the national government'. This was because labor mobility across companies would continue to be hindered until job classification and evaluation standards could be standardized across companies. As stated in the report:

> In future, the job-based wage system is expected to replace the seniority-based wage system, which has until now hindered the mobility of the labor force and created problems in terms of the utilization of personnel capacity within companies. However, this will require standardization and objectification of job types and skills. Although some of these wage systems have already been partially implemented, the further standardization and objectification of job types and skills will be necessary. Job classification is an effective way to standardize and objectify job types and skills, and to this end it will be necessary to establish a third-party organization outside the corporate sector, such as the national government, to create job classifications for key jobs.[156]

As noted earlier, it was Shōjirō Ujihara's view that the existence of seniority systems in large companies was a consequence of the lack of skills standardization across companies. The EDC report could be said to have represented the culmination of these economists' views.

The report also expressed high regard for the US labor movement, citing its approval of how American unions 'have eliminated nepotism and personal connections as factors in recruitment and dismissal [...] and have established the principle of equal pay for equal work through many years of dedicated struggle', and noting its appreciation of the fact that the 'development of job classification in the US was made possible by the development of a collective bargaining system with strong labor unions'.[157]

Nevertheless, the authors of the report understood that the enterprise unions of the Japanese labor movement had taken a different path than the US labor movement. In light of this, it concluded that 'standing apart from the position of individual companies, the government is likely in the best position to formulate such uniform job classifications, and, in some cases, it would be necessary to express its views on uniform standards'. In the future, it would aim for the 'standardization of wages at the industry level' based on job-based wages and 'the principle of equal pay for equal work', and 'would be required to develop norms for unions and managements for collective bargaining at the industry level'.[158]

In parallel with these initiatives on the part of the government, in 1964 Nikkeiren established a Job Classification Center inside its secretariat and dispatched a research team to the US. In a 1962 report, Nikkeiren had advocated the initial introduction of job-based wages in large companies, followed by 'efforts to align wage rates horizontally' for 'standard jobs that are common to all firms', and then ultimately to 'national standardization'.[159]

In this way, the Japanese government of the day and Nikkeiren were advocating for a policy package that sought to expand social security and cross-firm labor mobility. Had this been realized, Japanese society might have followed a trajectory that would have brought its employment situation closer to that of Western and Northern Europe. This would have changed the nature of the Japanese-style employment system, social security and education, and may have led to the emergence of social democratic political parties based on industrial trade unions that would have changed the political landscape. However, Japan's business leaders and its citizens proved unwilling to accept such a trajectory.

Corporate opposition to cross-firm standards

The EDC's 1963 Labor Capacity Development Report drew fierce criticism from labor unions and teachers' unions. This was because the report advocated the 'modernization of the managerial order' by such means as the introduction of job-based wages and because they were full of what was then still unfamiliar jargon, including terms such as 'high-talent manpower' and 'investments in education'. These gave rise to criticisms that the program was intended to devalue the wages of middle-aged and older workers and train personnel that would conform better to the needs of capitalism.

It would be difficult to frame these criticisms as having been based on any nuanced understanding of the policy package that was proposed. However, understanding a policy framework that integrated various components including employment, education and social security was not easy for people at the time. Hence, it seems that there was something of a kneejerk reaction to keywords like 'investment in education' without first having a good understanding of the report's overall aims.

For their own part, even Japanese bureaucrats themselves were not inclined to accept job classification or job-based wages. As described earlier, the Occupation's reforms of the public service were brought to a standstill by bureaucratic opposition. In addition, the Ministry of Finance, under the pretext of 'the spirit of job classification', had in fact widened the gap between the highest and lowest salaries in the public service, and the impression proliferated in the Japanese labor movement that job-based wages and job classification had been pretexts for intentionally increasing the gap.

Moreover, the policy package advocated in the Labor Capacity Development Report drew opposition from both the Ministry of Finance and the business community.[160] Following on from a series of reports from the EDC, in 1964 the Central Child Welfare Council proposed a child allowance for families. This allowance would provide benefits beginning with a family's first child and would not be subjected to any means test. For employees, funding for the program was to be borne by employers, and by the government for the self-employed. Because this also entailed an increased burden on the government and businesses, however, the Ministry of Finance and the business community were critical of the program. While a child allowance program was finally enacted in 1971, its benefits ended up being subject to means testing

284   Chapter 5

and were only issued from a family's third child. There was no chance
that such a system could compensate for the wage drop that job-based
wages would have caused among middle-aged and older workers.

Nor did the government adopt any policy emphasis on public
housing provision. Instead, it chose to encourage home ownership
in the hope of stimulating the economy during the period of rapid
economic growth, as signaled by the enactment of the 1966 Housing Construction Planning Act (*Jūtaku kensetsu keikaku-hō*) and
the 1966 Japan Workers' Housing Association Act (*Nihon kinrō-sha
jūtaku kyōkai-hō*).

Many business leaders were also of the opinion that the introduction of job-based wages would be technically difficult and would
prevent the free transfer of personnel between positions in a particular
company. In 1963, the vice president of Nippon Express criticized the
introduction of job-based wages, stating that 'It's hardly feasible to
determine units of responsibility for each employee [...]. And even if it
were possible, it would be of only limited utility in terms of the needs
of management'. Also, he remarked, 'depending on the company, there
can be a need for operational flexibility that allows for diversion to
different work areas as the workload increases or decreases'.[161]

Another reason why management was loath to accept job-based
wages was that it was thought that the creation of a cross-firm
standard would constrain the rights of management. Yoshitaka Fujita,
who served as the manager of Nikkeiren's First Labor Administration
Section, gave the following explanation for why job-based wages failed
to take root:

> [Job-based wages] were also recommended by GHQ, [Nikkeiren]
> set up a Job Classification Center, and many companies conducted
> job classifications and evaluations, but job-based wages did not
> take hold in Japan. I suspect that a reason for this may have been
> companies' awareness that this would give rise to cross-firm wage
> standards. This is because it would mean the socialization of wages,
> the socialization of labor-management relations and externalization
> from a company – in other words, a move away from the company-
> specific, in-house and company-based wage system that serves as

the basis of Japanese-style labor-management relations and the starting point of Japanese-style wage determination.[162]

The EDC report had argued that job classification should be carried out by the government and that wages should be standardized and labor-management negotiations should be conducted at the industry level. This would have meant strengthening the power of the government and labor unions even as the hands and feet of management were tied. It is true that there was a time when Japanese managers had praised job-based wages and cross-firm labor markets. Their motivation for doing so, however, had been lowering wages and facilitating layoffs for middle-aged and older workers. If a cross-firm labor market had have been truly established, however, it would no longer have been possible to determine jobs and wages solely in-house. Once managers realized this fact, they suddenly became wary of job-based wages.

Better, in that case, to compromise with the enterprise unions in exchange for long-term employment and seniority-based wages, which would allow management to keep a grip on its right to make decisions in-house. In the US, company unions were effectively banned by the National Labor Relations Act of 1935, but in Japan, such a compromise between enterprise unions and management was possible. In the US during World War I, managers had resisted job classification and job-based wages promoted by the government and the unions in the name of 'managerial freedom'.[163] A similar reaction was also observed on the part of management in Japan in the 1960s.

So it was that the introduction of job-based wages and the associated policy package faded into obscurity. In its place, a Japanese-style relationship between labor and management took root that reached a compromise with enterprise unions in exchange for long-term employment and seniority-based wages. In the next chapter, I will examine how the old in-house three-tier structure was transformed during Japan's period of rapid economic growth and how Japanese-style employment completed its development.

6 | High Growth and the Completion of the Japanese-style Employment System

In this chapter, I describe how the Japanese-style employment system was brought to completion during Japan's period of rapid economic growth, which lasted through the 1960s until 1973.[1]

In the 1950s, the old three-tier structure still persisted and 'equality of company employees' had not been fully realized. It was in the 1960s that this situation started to change. A factor in this development was the change in the educational system due to the Occupation reforms. The prewar Japanese education system, which had emulated the German model, limited enrollment in secondary and higher educational institutions. With the Occupation's postwar reforms to the system, however, a US-style system was introduced that promoted universal access to secondary and higher education. From the late 1950s to 1973, Japan's GDP grew at an average annual rate of nearly 10%, while the rate of enrollment in secondary and higher education institutions also experienced a steep rise. Due to the increase in the rate of students choosing to pursue higher education, it became more difficult for Japanese companies to maintain the traditional three-tier structure.

As a result, high school graduates with secondary education, who enjoyed lower staff employee positions in the traditional structure, were assigned to work on the shop floors, while even university graduates began working in sales positions. This in turn led to higher turnover rates and student unrest. In the end, Japanese companies dissolved the three-tier structure and introduced a new corporate order to adapt themselves to the new environment. Management implemented an accreditation system in which all company employees (*shain*), both white-collar staff employees and blue-collar workers, were assessed according to their respective abilities and promoted according to their company rank. This system was an extension of the prewar civil service and military-type system, a fact well known to corporate personnel managers.

In addition, because the postwar labor movement had made it difficult for companies to fire workers, they became more cautious about hiring at the level of individual laborers and began to extend the practice of hiring new graduates in bulk based on the information that was available from schools to blue-collar workers. In this way, the Japanese-style employment system characterized by its ranking scheme and the bulk recruitment of new graduates, which were limited to staff employees in the prewar era, extended to all company employees (*shain*), and achieved its complete form in the 1960s.

However, in order to maintain employee morale and find a middle ground with the labor unions, the system also had to guarantee long-term employment and seniority-based wages for all company employees. With the stagnation of Japan's economic growth following the 1973 oil crisis, the expense the system entailed became too costly for companies, which led to an increase in the number of non-regular workers.

The shock of education reforms

Why did the popularization of educational attainment result in the dissolution of the three-tier structure? The short answer is that, in Japan's corporate order, jobs were not linked to degrees.

Many companies in other countries observe a three-tier structure consisting of higher-level salaried staffs, lower-level salaried staffs and shop-floor workers. This structure comprises decision-makers, clerical staff and manual laborers, with each category requiring qualifications, degrees and professional competencies corresponding to their jobs. In this case, a three-tier structure would be unlikely to collapse, even if a society were to see the rise of the higher-education enrollment rate. This is simply because lower-level staff employees' positions that had previously required a two-year college degree would now require a four-year bachelor's degree, and higher-level staff employees' positions that previously required an undergraduate degree would now require a graduate degree. In fact, in the US in the early 1970s, an increasing number of university graduates found employment in non-exempt lower-level salaried positions that had previously been considered

High Growth and the Completion of the Japanese-style Employment System 289

suitable only for high school graduates.[2] With job-based pay, even if someone hired for a given job has a more advanced degree, this is not in itself a reason for their being paid a higher wage.

In Japan, however, there was no such link between degrees and jobs. Rather, it was customary for higher-level staff employees to have a higher education degree, lower-level staff employees to have a secondary diploma, and shop-floor laborers to have completed compulsory education (i.e., elementary school in the prewar era and junior high school in the post-war era). Moreover, Japanese companies determined wages based on ranks reflecting educational background and age, regardless of their actual job.

Under this kind of order, hiring workers with more advanced educational backgrounds would increase wage costs, even if their jobs were identical. If the percentage of people pursuing higher education in society as a whole were to rise, then the pyramidal three-tier structure would no longer be sustainable. As we saw in Chapter 4, this problem has been discussed since the prewar period in terms of a surplus of 'high-ranking officers' and a shortage of 'enlisted'. In the case of Japan, postwar educational reforms have also had an impact in this context. Japan's prewar education system had been influenced by Western Europe, whose nations were generally class-based societies that tended to limit access to higher education. In prewar Japan, as well, only elementary (four-year term, extended to six years from 1907) school was compulsory, and enrollment at secondary school (five-year term) was open only to those who were selected through examinations. Also, only a very small number of people were admitted to the higher professional schools (single-department colleges) and universities.

Abegglen points out that, in 1958, 'the fit of the older system of education to the factory system of recruitment was a good one'.[3] This was because the prewar three-tier structure according to educational background had only been established due to the enrollment limitations of the prewar secondary and higher education systems.

The postwar reforms, however, were carried out on the basis of the US education system. Unlike Western Europe, with its deeply rooted class system, education in the US was oriented toward raising the educational level of citizens universally. Thus, in postwar Japan,

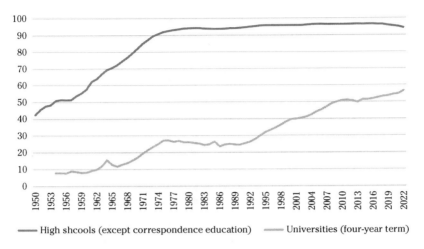

— High shcools (except correspondence education)　— Universities (four-year term)

Figure 6.1 High school and university enrolment rates (1950–2022)
Unit: %　Source: MEXT '2023 Basic Survey of Schools' (Gakkō kihon chōsa).

junior high school (three-year term) became compulsory, and high schools (three-year term) became secondary education institutions where students could enroll without having to take an examination until the early 1950s. Furthermore, the number of prewar professional schools accredited as universities (four-year term) greatly increased, and emphasis was placed on the popularization of higher education.

Meanwhile, the people, even as they rebelled against a status order that was determined by educational background, nevertheless wanted to ensure that their children received advanced educations. The high school enrollment rate, which was 42.5% in 1950, rose to 51.5% in 1955, 70.7% in 1965, and 91.9% in 1975 (Figure 6.1). While high schools, where enrollment had been open to all immediately after the end of the war, now began to impose entrance examinations, this still did not stem the increasing rate of educational advancement.

The rising rate of educational attainment also upset Japan's corporate order. In 1964, the head of the personnel department at NKK (Nippon Kōkan, Japan Steel Pipe) stated that, as a result of this shift, 'the way educational backgrounds are managed in companies has been critically jeopardized at its most fundamental level'.[4] So, what was this crisis?

The educational background-limiting effect

When Abegglen was conducting his survey of Japanese companies in 1955, he observed a clear three-tier structure determined by educational background. In the company he studied, he wrote that 'only graduates of middle [junior high] school are considered as candidates' for employment as factory workers, and that their education 'must not exceed the present middle school level'.[5]

A rapid increase in high school enrollment triggered a crisis in this order. Companies' first reaction was to stick to hiring junior high school graduates, although these were now fewer in number. In 1962 and 1963, a pedagogical researcher Shirō Kurauchi led a team that conducted surveys on the recruitment of shop-floor workers at leading manufacturing companies and establishments. Based on their results, they found that compared to the rapid increase in high school enrollment, there was very little corresponding rise in the recruitment of high school graduates specifically, only an expansion of the general recruitment of 'junior high school and high school graduates'. Moreover, there was a pronounced tendency among large firms to recruit *only* junior high school graduates.[6] In other words, large firms continued hiring these graduates exclusively, while small and medium-sized enterprises (SMEs) had little choice but to start hiring more high school graduates.

Kurauchi wrote that 'for companies, the recruitment of junior high school graduates [i.e., those who have only completed their compulsory education] as shop-floor workers was already part of their corporate disposition in terms of its being a system that they had maintained for a long time'. However, he stated that due to the rapid rise of the high school enrollment rate resulting in a decline in the number of new junior high school graduates entering the workforce, 'it has become "inevitable" that they [the SMEs] must now employ high school graduates as shop-floor workers, as well'.[7]

A similar trend has also been pointed out by labor historian Shinji Sugayama. According to a 1961 report by the Economic Planning Agency entitled *Shinki koyō ni kan suru chōsa hōkoku* (Report of the Survey on New Employment), no male high school graduates had been hired in the regular factory worker recruitment drive in large manufacturing firms employing 5,000 people or more in the three major industrial regions surrounding Tokyo, Osaka and Nagoya. By contrast, manufacturing companies with between 1,000 and 4,999 employees had had to rely on high school graduates to fill 23.3% of the positions opened for regular factory worker recruitment, while those employing 999 or less did so for 32.6% of their regular recruitment.[8]

The large manufacturing industry firm that Abegglen studied in 1955 was also already feeling the pinch from the decline in the number of junior high school graduates. One of the measures taken by this company was to dispatch staff employees to local public employment security offices in 'a particular agricultural area' in Kyushu, where the percentage of students going on to higher education was still low, to recruit new junior high school graduates from rural areas. Even when recruiting high school graduates as lower-level staff employees, the company chose to hire from rural high schools, since the best high school students in large cities would be more likely to go on to university.[9]

For larger firms such as the one surveyed by Abegglen, it was still possible to hire new junior high school graduates who fitted into the firm's three-tier structure, even considering the time and expense this entailed. The consequence of this, presumably, found expression in the fact that large firms were more likely to adhere to a hiring norm that targeted junior high school graduates exclusively to fill factory worker positions.

From the conventional standpoint of economics and pedagogy, it is odd to see people with higher levels of education being shunned by the corporate sector. In particular, the period in question was one in which technological innovation was being advanced at the sites of production, when the intuitive and embodied knowledge of 'gut feelings' and 'knacks' based on experience were losing their significance, and it was alleged that high school graduates who could read and digest machine manuals would be placed at an advantage. As pointed out by sociologist of education Yuki Honda, for companies, 'to be able to hire large numbers of new graduates with higher levels of knowledge, ability and maturity than new junior high school graduates

High Growth and the Completion of the Japanese-style Employment System **293**

should have been a godsend', yet this did not prove to be the reality for Japan.[10]

With job-based pay, wages will remain the same for the same position, even if a worker is older or has a more advanced educational background. In a society where this is the norm, a higher standard of education among workers would be a welcome development. Also, in prewar Japan, wages for shop-floor workers were essentially determined on a piece-rate basis.

In postwar Japan, however, thanks to the labor movement and democratization, wages for company employees (*shain*), a category that now included shop-floor workers, increased according to their educational background and length of service, with the only exception being temporary workers. Therefore, hiring older workers with more advanced educational backgrounds as shop-floor workers would increase wage costs, even if the positions they held were the same. Under these conditions, an educational background-limiting effect was put into play, so that firms preferred hiring fifteen-year-old junior high school graduates over eighteen-year-old high school graduates.

In any society, companies will pursue profit and act rationally under given conditions. Even so, these 'given conditions', such as how wages are determined, will be subject to the norms of that society. As such, what constitutes 'rational' behavior will differ from society to society.

Government measures to curb the pursuit of higher education

A second response by private companies to this situation was to call on the government to curb the pursuit of higher education. In the context of high growth, large manufacturers wanted to hire middle- and lower-level engineers who had graduated with a vocational education, and did not need more than a certain number of graduates from ordinary high schools.

In 1940, before Japan's entry into World War II, only 7% of students pursued secondary education in the old secondary school system. If we include girls' high schools, vocational schools, and the various other types of secondary educational institutions, the total is still only 25%.[11] In 1955, the percentage of students entering the new high school system exceeded 50%. To maintain the corporate order that had existed since the prewar period, it was necessary to either curb the number of students pursuing higher education or to channel them toward vocational education.

In 1956 and 1957, Nikkeiren issued various position papers, including 'Views on Technical Education to Meet the Demands of the New Era' (*Shin jidai no yōsei ni taiō suru gijutsu kyōiku ni kan suru iken*) and 'Views on the Promotion of Science and Technology Education' (*Kagaku gijutsu kyōiku no Shintō ni kan suru iken*). These papers dealt variously with the enhancement of technical high schools to train lower-level engineers and site supervisors, the promotion of scientific and vocational education at the compulsory education level, and the streaming of secondary education (i.e., the establishment of vocational high schools).[12]

The government also responded in kind. In the official Ministry of Education guidelines for 1958 on courses of study for elementary schools and junior high schools, 'trades and home economics' (*shokugyō / katei-ka*, the former is for boys and the latter for girls) was rebranded as 'technology and home economics' (*gijutsu / katei-ka*). Then, 1960's National Income Doubling Plan stipulated that secondary education 'should be improved so that the current ratio of 6:4 students in the general course versus vocational courses will be 5:5 by 1970'.[13] The 'general course' was designed for students who wanted to pursue university education, while the 'vocational courses' were designed to prepare high school graduates to find various types of jobs.

In response to this, in 1960, the Ministry of Education established a basic policy stating that about 60% of new public high schools and 35% of new private high schools should have industrial courses, and that classes with agricultural and commercial course components should also be expanded.[14] In 1962, a new five-year technical high school system was implemented, and in many areas new vocational high-schools were established one after the other. Toyama prefecture declared that it would follow the so-called '3:7 system', which aimed for a ratio of seven vocational high schools for every three general high schools.[15]

High Growth and the Completion of the Japanese-style Employment System   295

As we saw in Chapter 5, the 1963 report by the Economic Deliberation Council of the government proposed the introduction of job-based pay and the transformation to a cross-firm labor market as part of a policy package that also included improvements to social security alongside enhancements to vocational training and education, which was modeled on Western European countries. In societies like Germany, vocational education and social security were well established. At the same time, however, eligibility for higher education was limited to those who had passed standard examinations such as the *Abitur* in Germany or the *baccalauréat* in France. In the early 1960s, these people were a relatively small elite group provided with education at national universities free of charge. Meanwhile, the majority of citizens were expected to enter the workforce through vocational education and training.

If we keep in mind this kind of Western-style policy package, a report by the Economic Deliberation Council of the day took what we might call a systematic approach. In some ways, however, one cannot avoid interpreting this as an attempt to return to the streamed educational system that prevailed in prewar Japan. This was all the more obvious in consideration of the fact that conservative politicians of the time were making disparaging remarks about the general public and advocating measures to curb the pursuit of higher education.

Popular reactions to the education policy

These moves on the part of the business community and government were subjected to fierce criticism. For the people of the time, securing a better education for their children was a cherished dream, and any attempt to interfere with this was seen as unpardonable. Children, too, reflecting their parents' hopes, harbored a burning enthusiasm of their own to pursue higher education. An education-journalism book published in 1965 quoted the following passage, written by a girl attending junior high school in Kumamoto prefecture.

> I said I wanted to take an elective English class, but my teacher wouldn't let me. He said that elective English classes were only

for students who would be going on to high school. I begged him to let me listen in from the hallway, but it was no use. I was so disappointed and frustrated that I wanted to be reborn so that I could go to high school, too. If I couldn't be reborn, I thought, then I didn't want to let my children at least feel this way.[16]

For this student, the purpose of learning English would not have been to find a job that would give her an opportunity to use it. In prewar Japanese society, educational background had nothing to do with one's ability to perform a job but served rather as an indicator for determining status.[17] Learning English and going to high school would have been symbolic acts that were seen as a way of escaping discriminatory pigeonholing.

Educators and parents at the time were strongly opposed to the government's education policies and demanded the establishment of more general high schools. This sentiment found symbolic expression in the Movement for Universal High School Enrollment (*kōkō zen'nyū undō*) and its slogan 'We won't make them cry in the spring of their fifteenth year' (*Jūgo no haru wa nakasenai*; spring at age fifteen in Japan is when students graduate from compulsory junior high school education). In response to agitation by organizations that included the Japan Teachers' Union, the Japan Mothers' Congress, and the General Council of Trade Unions of Japan (Sōhyō), the National Council on Universal High School Enrollment was convened in April 1962, garnering broad support. To borrow the words of Kōshi Endō, as quoted in Chapter 5, this could also be described as 'postwar democracy as it was understood by Japanese workers'.

Against this backdrop, a 1963 report by the Economic Deliberation Council, which advocated the enhancement of vocational education, drew strong criticism. The fact that the report was actually a comprehensive policy package that included a cross-firm labor market and social security reforms was not well understood, and it was instead perceived as a way to curb the expansion of general high schools and intensify competitive entrance examinations.[18]

With an increased public appetite for furthering education, it became more difficult to attract the brightest students to industrial and technical high schools. Even in Toyama prefecture, with its vaunted '3:7 system', companies appraised graduates of general courses as 'good' and those from technical and commercial courses as 'bad'.[19] As a result, even major companies gradually had no choice but to start hiring new high school graduates as factory workers. In 1964, the head of the personnel review subsection in NKK's personnel division opined that 'The reality is not so much that the factory workers we get out of high school graduates are the result of technological innovation, but rather that our only supply of factory workers is from the high schools'.[20]

Nevertheless, there was still a popular expectation that simply getting a high school education would be enough to find a staff employee's position, just like before the war. Education scholar Takashi Ōta points out that 'for many people at the time, the image they held of the postwar new high school system was analogous to the prewar old system [...]. In some cases, the new high schools even instituted the white-striped student cap, which had been a symbol of the old higher school system'.[21] One nineteen-year-old woman who had become a product inspector after graduating from high school offered the following statement in an entry submitted in 1969 to an essay contest featuring 'Writings on the Lives of Working Youth' organized by the Ministry of Labor's Women and Youth Bureau.[22]

> In a society where it's taken for granted that girls who graduate from high school will be clerks or office workers, I wonder if it was my own vanity that made me feel uncomfortable about working on the actual production line.
> "Where do you work?"
> "Matsushita Electric".
> "A clerk! That's great!"
> "No, I'm, uh…"
> This was a conversation I had with a neighbor, but I just couldn't continue. I just couldn't say the simple phrase, "No, I'm on the production line".

For those who graduated with a secondary education in the prewar system, it was a matter of course that they would become lower-level staff employees, who were considered to enjoy a different status than factory workers, regardless of sex. This was something that was taken for granted by the parents of the generation who came of age during Japan's high growth period. Even so, the younger generation also found it difficult to break away from this norm.

School as employment agency for bulk recruitment of new graduates

This situation was not helped by the response on the part of companies. As is still the case today, Japanese companies were strongly disinclined to prepare job descriptions and to explain the sorts of positions for which they were hiring. It is a matter of management discretion as to which positions newly hired graduates are assigned. The nineteen-year-old inspector mentioned above was shocked when she was told after being hired that she would be assigned to a shop-floor position, 'to the extent that I have no recollection of what was said in the rest of the meeting'.

In February 1964, the Hyōgo prefecture SME Labor Management Center conducted a survey of graduating junior high school students and high school students scheduled to begin jobs from April in western Japan. Asked what type of job they had been offered, the survey found that 56.1% of junior high school boys and 62.0% of junior high school girls responded, 'I don't know'. Among prospective high school graduates, these percentages were 52.9% for boys and 32.2% for girls. Beyond this, even at the time of the survey, conducted shortly before their graduation in March, even when they knew the name and location of the company where they would be employed, close to 40% of respondents admitted to not knowing the company's size or the type of industry it was in.[23] In other words, though assured of having found a job, they had no idea of the nature of their employers or the kind of work they would be doing.

Underlying this was the fact that the hiring process was conducted through their schools. By the early 1960s, Japanese schools, in cooperation with public employment security offices, were functioning to supply students as workers to employers throughout Japan. In the

High Growth and the Completion of the Japanese-style Employment System   299

Hyōgo survey, only 19.8% of junior high school students and 29.1% of high school students 'decided for themselves' where they would seek employment. The most common answer, for 34.3% of junior high school students and 43.4% of high school students, was their 'teacher's recommendation'. Other responses included referrals by 'members of the household', 'relatives and acquaintances', and 'friends and senior peers'.[24]

As we saw in Chapter 4, school referrals have served a qualification function for workers in Japan since the prewar period. The lack of technical qualifications and occupational organizations meant that information obtained through long-term observation by teachers at schools was vital.

Before the war, however, this type of school referral was primarily used only for those who would take positions as staff employees. Although some prewar factory workers were young trainees, it was more typical for such laborers to be recruited by contractors through personal connections or from among those who had already worked at a factory for a certain period of time without any problems. In other words, the recruitment of factory workers was not as selective as the hiring of staff employees. One reason for this was the relative ease in the prewar period with which laborers could be dismissed. For companies, it seems that while dismissal was easy, then there was little need to bother with a rigorous screening process, which would be costly and time consuming.

After the war, however, things changed. In the aftermath of the postwar democratization and union movement, factory workers could no longer be so easily dismissed. As a result, companies were forced to be more selective when hiring.

This change was clearly evident in the Japanese company that Abegglen observed in 1955. The firm did not dismiss factory workers, who had only a junior high school education, choosing instead to reassign them. Because of this, even factory workers with only a compulsory education were rigorously screened at the time of recruitment. At the company that Abegglen observed, school referrals were essential for higher-level staff employees with university education and lower-level staff employees who had graduated from high school;

individual applications that were made without such introductions were rejected outright. For factory workers, the company requested referrals from public employment security offices nationwide and went to 'considerable' lengths to recruit junior high school graduates of 'stable natures' from rural areas.[25] In fact, postwar public employment security offices partnered with junior high school teachers to provide companies with information on their applicants. This recruitment system was premised on a 1949 revision to the Employment Security Act (*Shokugyō antei-hō*).[26]

Public employment agencies had their origins in the enactment of the Employment Placement Act (*Shokugyō shōkai-hō*) in 1921 and were nationalized in 1938 in order to reallocate labor to military industries. Following Japan's postwar democratization, the 1947 Employment Security Act stipulated freedom of choice in employment and in principle prohibited worker supply services other than public employment security offices. Underlying this prohibition were the many private employment agencies that exploited workers before the war, when human rights violations had continued unabated. Moreover, in order to correct practices such as the focus in the prewar textile industry on recruiting women workers from poorer areas, public employment security offices were prohibited from providing job placement services over a wide area.

However, universities and high schools (the former secondary schools) protested these provisions. These schools had been the ones that had introduced students to companies nationwide before the war. Since school-based employment referrals were now regarded as a 'worker supply service', students could not be placed in jobs without permission from the Minister of Labor.

In 1949, the act was amended to allow schools to provide job placement services, provided that they notified the Minister of Labor. In conjunction with this, schools were also allowed to provide job placements on a nationwide basis. Further, schools that did not have the practical knowledge to provide job placement services now had the option of cooperating with or sharing responsibility with employment security offices to do so. The stipulation that schools had to cooperate with employment security offices provided an opportunity to spread

High Growth and the Completion of the Japanese-style Employment System   301

this norm to the new junior high schools, which still lacked the know-how necessary to provide job placement services. According to a 1952 Ministry of Education report entitled 'Industrial Education Survey Report' (*Sangyō kyōiku chōsa hōkoku*), nearly 70% of the new junior high schools elected to cooperate with the employment security offices, while almost 30% chose to share this responsibility.[27]

After this, the practice of bulk recruitment new junior high school graduates spread rapidly. Before the war, most compulsory education graduates had been employed through personal connections. In March 1933, for example, 60.6% of boys graduating from Tokyo's higher elementary schools (attended by students who completed elementary school but who would not go on to secondary school, two years at that time) found jobs through acquaintances or family members, while only 26.5% did so through school referrals and only 12.9% via employment agencies.[28] After the war, however, the alliance between employment security offices and the new junior high schools all but wiped out employment through personal connections.

This meant that the bulk recruitment of new graduates, which before the war had been focused primarily on the level of staff employees, was now expanded to the level of workers on the shop floors. This was due to the fact that postwar democratization had led to the extension of long-term employment to the entire workforce, thereby increasing the need for selective hiring. Thus, a series of norms that had been limited in the scope of their application before the war was extended across the board with reciprocal effect.

Meanwhile, most high schools either offered job placement services in their own schools or limited their relationship with public job security offices to one of shared responsibility. This was because, with either of these two options, schools were able to receive job offers directly from individual companies with whom they could build direct relationships. As of 1970, 38.1% of high schools were opting to make referrals themselves, while 58.8% chose to share this responsibility with job security services.[29]

Abegglen notes that the large manufacturing firm he studied in 1955 had designated about 100 high schools across the country as being 'of a level adequate to provide company employees'. High school principals and teachers also believed that 'the placement of good students in good positions is seen as one of their responsibilities', to which end they 'usually [took] some part of their summer vacation' to approach the company, 'asking that their student or students be considered as applicants'.[30]

Nevertheless, the spread of the practice of hiring new graduates in bulk at the laborer level did not come all at once. In 1959, Shōjirō Ujihara and colleagues surveyed nine large companies that had established operations in the coastal area of Chiba prefecture. They found that 418 workers had been hired in the middle of their careers, as compared to eighty-eight who were hired as new graduates. Ujihara and his colleagues summarized policy by observing that 'with the staff employees, university and high school graduates are hired at the time of their graduation. With middle-ranking and core factory workers, junior high school graduates are hired as trainees upon graduation, or else graduates of [high school] industrial courses are hired upon graduation. With general factory workers, hiring takes place regardless of the time of year or educational background'.[31]

In general, we can say that, in 1959, companies were ramping up the hiring of new junior high school graduates as factory workers while continuing to maintain the prewar three-tier structure. From the mid-1960s onward, however, the hiring of new graduates in bulk became the norm in large companies. Labor historians often argue that periodical bulk recruitment of new graduates and so-called lifetime employment took root in Japan in the 1960s.[32] It is certainly true that it was not until the 1960s that this practice spread to the shop-floor workers, who comprise the majority of society.

Nevertheless, the Japanese people were well aware that the bulk recruitment of new graduates, seniority wages and long-term employment had been enjoyed by civil officials and staff employees of large firms in the prewar period. With their universal pursuit of secondary education and extension of the nomenclature of 'company employee' to all workers, the applicability of these norms was expanded on a huge scale. We might even be able to say that this, too, was 'postwar democracy as it was understood by Japanese workers'.

A surge of university graduates

The increased rate of students pursuing higher education occurred not only in high schools, but also at the university level. Along with the transition to the new postwar university system, many normal schools and professional schools were upgraded and accredited as universities. As a result, the number of recognized universities in Japan jumped to 226 schools in 1953. The total number of undergraduates also ballooned six-fold, from 71,737 at the old universities in 1943 to 420,528 at the four-year universities in 1952.[33]

This state of affairs upset the corporate order, which had long regarded university graduates as prospective candidates for higher-level staff employees. Abegglen, conducting his survey in 1955, wrote of this new reality that 'They are not employable at the higher white-collar level owing to sheer numbers, and yet the attitude and expectations of both students and employers remain as before'.[34]

At this point, however, there were still not many problems. This was because the large firms had put in place a system of designated schools and were hiring only those students who were referred by a few highly ranked universities. Abegglen notes that, because of this, 'a furious competition [has developed] for entrance to the few highly ranked universities'.[35]

Also, while universities had increased in number, they had not yet undergone a qualitative change. This is because many of the new universities were newly accredited educational universities that had been normal schools in the prewar period.[36] Until the 1950s, the percentage of students enrolling in four-year universities and two-year junior colleges was around 10%, and only 8% for four-year universities alone, so higher education was still limited to a small percentage of the population.[37]

However, this situation was to change radically in the 1960s. The four-year university enrollment rate, which had been less than 8% until 1956, reached 10.0% in 1962, then soared rapidly to 17.1% in 1970 and 27.2% by 1975. Among males in particular, enrollment exceeded 20% in 1967 and had reached 41.0% by 1975. On top of this, due to the large number of baby boomers who were born from 1947 to 1949

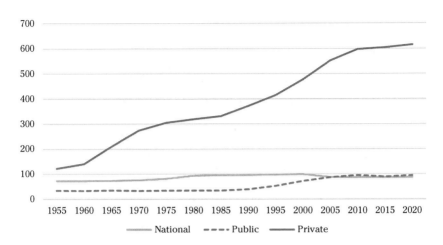

Figure 6.2 Trends in the number of Japanese universities (1955–2020)
Unit: 1 school   Source: MEXT 'Statistical abstract (Table 113, Universities & Junior Colleges)' (2022)

(see Chapter 1) entering higher education, the number of students increased at an even faster rate than enrollment.

This change was significant in terms of quality as well as quantity. Whereas the number of universities increased from 228 in 1955 to 317 in 1965, 382 in 1970, and 420 in 1975, the number of national and public (prefectural and municipal) universities increased by only nine over the same period. Most of this growth took place among newly established private universities (Figure 6.2). For its part, the government not only checked the increase of national and public universities, but it also placed an emphasis on training personnel in the science and engineering fields that were being sought by the business community. In 1970, 77% of the graduates of national universities were from the faculties of science, engineering, medicine, agriculture or pedagogical training, while only 23% were graduates of law, economics, commerce or literature.[38]

Many of the newly established private universities, however, were not equipped with science and engineering departments, which required costly equipment. Private universities that had existed since the prewar period also greatly increased their enrollment to meet the popular demand for higher education, leading to the emergence

High Growth and the Completion of the Japanese-style Employment System   305

in some cases of 'mammoth universities' with enrollments in the tens of thousands of students. In marked contrast to the national universities, 68% of private university students in 1970 graduated with undergraduate degrees in law, economics, commerce or literature.[39] Under Japanese employment norms, higher education in fields other than science, engineering and pedagogical training normally had little to do with professional competencies used in the workplace. The rapid increase in the number of university graduates after 1955 was concentrated in these areas.

Naturally, companies regarded the quality of the university graduates who comprised this sudden surge of prospective employees to be somewhat 'uneven'. However, under Japanese employment norms, recruitment was conducted not by professional diploma, but according to the status of the graduated university candidates. And with the democratization of the postwar period and the rise in the percentage of students going on to higher education, the populace no longer tolerated discrimination based on school status as it had before the war. Hence, if all university graduates were not treated in a uniform manner, this might be seen as grounds for the criticism of school-based discrimination.

In a 1957 Ministry of Labor report on its 'Special Survey on Pay Systems' (*Kyūyo seido tokubetsu chōsa*), only one of the 129 firms surveyed employing at least 5,000 workers differentiated starting salaries for university graduates by the type of school they attended (i.e., national, public or private). In addition, only four companies differentiated starting salaries based on the faculty that the graduates had attended.[40]

Before the war, starting salaries for science and engineering graduates had been higher than those for law and literature graduates (see note 74 of Chapter 3). In addition, as mentioned in Chapter 3, before the Universities Edict of 1918, the length of study at imperial universities and private universities differed, with commensurate differences in starting salaries that remained in place until years afterward.[41] Such differences between schools and faculties, however, had already received criticism for being discriminatory even before the war.[42] The Corporate Accounting Control Ordinance (*Kaisha keiri tōsei-rei*) of 1940 unified starting salaries according to educational background (e.g., junior high school graduate, university graduate), finally eliminating this difference between schools.

Nevertheless, as Chapter 3 describes, companies like Ishikawajima Heavy Industries still differentiated between public and private universities in their in-house regulations regarding promotion. Also, as Abegglen saw, large companies in the 1950s adopted a system of designated schools in which they hired recommended applicants from a very small number of universities and did not accept applications from anywhere else. However, as the competition for higher education heated up, large companies' designated school systems came under increasingly strict scrutiny.

Under pressure from public opinion, in 1970 the Ministry of Education inaugurated its 'Survey on the Recruitment and Employment of New Graduates' (*Shinki gakusotsu-sha no saiyō oyobi shūgyō jōkyō-tō ni kan suru chōsa*). This survey was conducted 'for the purpose of understanding the facts concerning the way that companies evaluate educational backgrounds, with a focus on the actual situation regarding exclusive designated school systems in the employment of new university graduates, in order to redress a social tendency toward placing undue emphasis on educational background'.[43] Accordingly, it became difficult for companies to openly maintain their designated school systems. Even so, it proved impossible to continue placing all of the rapidly increasing number of university graduates in positions that they would once have been entitled to expect.

Transformation of the university graduate labor market

Companies responded to this situation by assigning university graduates to positions that had once been filled by junior high school and high school graduates. According to the Ministry of Education's 'Basic School Survey' (*Gakkō kihon chōsa*), among new male graduates assigned to 'sales' positions in 1955, 58% were junior high school graduates, 38% were high school graduates, and 4% were university graduates. By 1970, however, the number of university graduates

High Growth and the Completion of the Japanese-style Employment System **307**

employed in sales positions had increased to 40%. Conversely, whereas in 1955, 79.8% of university graduates with undergraduate degrees in law, politics, commerce or economics had been employed in 'administrative' positions, by 1970, this percentage had dropped to 53.1%.[44]

This development impacted the mentality of university students in various ways. One such reaction was the university student protests of 1968.[45] One of the largest student protests at the time took place at Nihon University, a private institution that had rapidly increased its enrollment during the high growth period, from around 30,000 students in 1955 to about 85,000 in 1968. The following excerpt is taken from a published statement by a professor at Nihon University in August 1968.

> Even if we include those who have become employees at top-tier companies, national public servants, and others, I'd guess only around 20,000 university graduates have positions they can be proud of. And more than half of them are from the five or six top universities.
>
> [...] Even among the students I have personally encountered in the classroom, young men who would surely have excelled in the advertising departments of large corporations have become office managers at the riverbank quarries where dump trucks pick up gravel, or else salesmen of ready-to-wear clothing, traveling from one retail store to another. If they were going to do these jobs, surely, they did not need to go to university. High school would have sufficed.
>
> [...] Moreover, their parents aspire for their sons to have the status befitting a [traditional] university graduate – that of a high-level public servant or a staff employee of a prestigious company. Caught between their parents' expectations and their own uncertain future, these students see themselves as pebbles on a conveyor belt. Hysterically, they scream, "This is happening because this profit-oriented university has brought in so many students. Even the teachers take as much notice of me as they would a pebble. Let's smash this university to pieces!"[46]

Although this statement may speculate somewhat more than is justified about the students' psychology, it is representative of many observations that were offered at the time. For example, political scientist Michitoshi Takabatake, who participated in the movement against the Vietnam War at that time and was closely involved with his students, published an article in 1969 where he observed the following: 'It may be that the hostility of today's student movement toward capitalist society and, to a greater extent, toward the "administrated society" [*kanri shakai*] has been kindled [...] by class resentment at having been denied their path to status-based prestige and success.' 'This often finds expression in students' leaflets and speeches in phrases such as "We can no longer hope to be anything more than run-of-the-mill salarymen or non-commissioned officers for the rest of our lives"'.[47]

In 1968, the then chairman of a new left group faction of Zengakuren (*Zen Nihon gakusei jichikai sō rengō*, the All-Japan Federation of Student Self-Government Associations) published a manifesto, *What Zengakuren Thinks*, that included the following passages.

'We all had high hopes when we entered university.' 'But what the university offers to students, who have opened their eyes to the modern world with a new hope, is too meager.' 'The overwhelming increase in the number of students has greatly diminished the social status of university graduates, and graduating from university can no longer be said to guarantee employment at a large company.' 'The student movement of today, amidst changes in social status such as I have already mentioned, a decisive gap between [unchanged] elite consciousness [of students] and their reality, and schools that are shifting toward a mass production model, has been built on the basis of the popular spread of a constant desire to recover the truth of what it means to be human.' 'Against this backdrop, students' frustrations and anxieties are building up to the point that, no matter what spark touches off the struggle at one school, it will develop into a similar struggle at all universities.'[48]

High Growth and the Completion of the Japanese-style Employment System   309

Nevertheless, the analysis of the student protests is not the central theme of this book. What is important for the argument here is the fact that this social unrest occurred when university graduates began to be employed in positions that were once held by high school graduates, when cracks began to emerge between expectations about educational backgrounds and social reality.

Avoidance of educated workers and increased turnover

In economics and education, the phenomenon of highly educated individuals filling jobs once done by people with less education has been referred to as 'overeducation' or 'degree inflation'. This is a phenomenon that occurs universally as societies become more highly educated. This is because in any society, the proportion of highly specialized occupations and managerial duties will be limited. In 1951, American sociologist C. Wright Mills quoted one author's observation on behalf of an office management association as follows: 'as there are not enough stimulating jobs for the hordes of college graduates we see descending upon us in the years to come like swarms of hungry locusts, they will have to take jobs that satisfy, or perhaps even now do not satisfy, the high school graduate'.[49]

However, this phenomenon has usually been discussed in terms of the problem of those with lower levels of education losing their jobs to more highly educated individuals. According to the 'job-competition' model proposed in 1975 by economist Lester Thurow, companies prefer to hire workers who are less expensive to train. Accordingly, if they are hiring for the same job, they will welcome workers with a higher level of education, while those with less education will be pushed out. On the other hand, since wage disparities are determined not by educational background but by jobs, they will not change even if society as a whole becomes more educated.[50] Because of this, in the US, since the 1950s, people have been increasingly unable to enter professional or managerial positions simply by attending a two-year college or a four-year university. Even so, the fact that such jobs could still be attained after completing higher degrees led to an increase in graduate school enrollment.

What unfolded in Japan in the 1960s, however, was a different phenomenon than in the case of the US. In Japan between 1966 and 1974, lifetime wage disparities by educational background narrowed, while those in the US remained essentially unchanged between 1946 and 1972.[51] And in Japan in the same period, despite the rapid shift to higher education, there was no rise in the rate of postgraduate enrollment. Rather, the hierarchical ranking of universities became increasingly pronounced.

Also, large companies, which had the advantage in terms of recruitment, tended to avoid workers with high educational backgrounds. In 1975, the Japan Recruitment Center surveyed the opinions of a total of 3,507 exchange-listed and leading non-listed companies with regard to educational background. According to the survey, 7.7% of large companies employing 5,000 people or more were staffed by at least 50% university graduates, compared with 29.2% of companies with ninety-nine or fewer employees. Among companies employing less than 10% university graduates, 35.9% had 5,000 employees or more, 22.2% had ninety-nine employees or fewer, and 12.7% had between 100 and 499 employees.[52] In other words, on a per capita basis, the larger firms had more employees with lower educational backgrounds.

Of course, the major manufacturers would have had many shop-floor workers with only junior high and high school educations, and so would naturally have tended to have a lower proportion of university graduates. However, a 1977 report by Zen-Noh-Ren (the All Japan Federation of Management Organizations) described the results of this survey in the following terms.

> [During the period of high growth], there was an extreme shortage of young graduates, and it was basically impossible for small and medium-sized firms to hire those available. Even so, there were also situations in which companies had no choice but to hire highly educated people, whether they liked it or not, because they were a relatively plentiful source of labor.[53]

High Growth and the Completion of the Japanese-style Employment System　311

As the number of university graduates increased rapidly, large Japanese companies secretly hired only new graduates of prestigious universities for their staff at the time of selection, and continued to hire non-university graduates as shop-floor workers. Graduates from less prestigious universities found jobs in traditional high school occupations or in SMEs. In Japanese companies, starting salaries, at least, are determined by education and age, not by jobs. Statistically, this resulted in a narrowing of the wage gap by educational background. On the other hand, Japanese companies did not need postgraduates, because companies expected universities to screen students' potential and trained workers within the company once they hired them. Therefore, the graduate school enrollment rate remained static.

These conditions have disappointed young people who went to high school and universities with high expectations. In addition, as noted earlier, Japanese companies would often hire employees without informing them of the positions that they would be filling, and then assign them to positions that were at odds with their expectations. This tactic resulted in lowered worker morale and increased turnover. The nineteen-year-old high school graduate working as an inspector, quoted earlier, described her response after her neighbor mistakenly assumed that she worked as a clerk.

> I just couldn't say the simple phrase, "No, I'm on the production line". Just thinking about on how many times I've had this conversation makes my heart sink as I realize how uninspired I am to work. About a hundred girls from my old high school got jobs working for various companies, but only three of us, including me, work in manufacturing. And one of them quit early.[54]

According to a survey published by the Ministry of Labor in 1969, among new graduates who graduated in March 1966, as many as 51.9% of men and 54.1% of women had left their jobs within three years of graduation. Nikkeiren was also concerned around this time about the possibility of the Communist Party's youth wing infiltrating the ranks of disaffected young workers.[55]

312   Chapter 6

Certainly, both membership in the Communist Party and its share of the popular vote were on the rise at the time, as was the frequency of student protests. It is hard to say that it was a major social disorder, but it was a psychological threat to business executives. The apprehension of the social order is often described as a 'socialist threat' that only exists on an imaginary level, however, one unrelated to the actual situation. In the 1920s, the surplus of secondary and higher education graduates became problematic, and as we saw in Chapter 4, a discourse emerged that superimposed this issue onto the threat of the socialist movement.

Another issue for Japanese companies at the time was that some employees became staff employees and others became shop-floor workers, even though both had the same educational background. Such treatment tended to create resentment toward the company and breed conflict in the workforce. A personnel manager at the clock manufacturer Seikosha (now Seiko) said in 1965 that 'The issue of how to treat high school students (both male and female) hired at the same time and assigned variously to staff and production divisions is not limited to our company, [and] is likely to become a labor management challenge that each company must seriously engage with as a future social problem'.[56] For a society accustomed to a series of norms based on educational background, having different 'statuses' in a company order for people with the same educational background, or having people with the same 'status' but different educational backgrounds, was considered a serious social problem.

Delayed promotions and a shortage of posts

The rapid shift to higher educational backgrounds gave rise to another phenomenon, namely a delay in promotions.

Abegglen also identified this problem at the major manufacturing firm he surveyed in 1955. In Japanese companies, frequent personnel transfers were carried out on the assumption that all university-educated staff employees would be promoted to senior management positions. However, in addition to the increase in the number of university graduates, more staff employees had also been hired as a

High Growth and the Completion of the Japanese-style Employment System   313

result of the production increases during the war. Abegglen pointed out that a 'result of these factors is the presence in most Japanese firms of a very large number of management and staff personnel proportionate to those in laboring and clerical positions'. Although Japanese companies were creating a large number of unnecessary positions, such as 'deputy and assistant managers of sections', Abegglen saw that 'the net effect has been to retard sharply career progress among company executives'.[57]

In fact, this problem had also arisen in the postwar civil service. Kazuo Imai, president of the Federation of National Public Service Mutual Aid Associations, made the following statement in 1969. He was the director of the Remuneration Bureau of the Ministry of Finance in 1946, who characterized the post-war civil servant salary scheme as a 'phony job classification system' (see Chapter 5).

> On the assumption that there would be considerable attrition in the war, after 1940, all of the ministries started hiring on twice as many new graduates as before as civil service cadets. These gentlemen were conscripted and went to the front a fair bit, but even so, most of them did not end up dying in the war. It's a bit odd. You could say that during the war, they were given comparatively safe assignments or placed in safe areas [...] we only lost about 10% of these cadets. So, we were stuck with this dilemma. All we could do was to create unconventional posts and statuses like directors (buchō), deputy directors (jichō), attachés (sanjikan), councilors (shingikan) – all of these were made up for that reason. But they kept pushing out the top people [in order to get promoted]. That's why the top guys couldn't stay in their posts very long, and it got to the point where they had to create public corporations or public companies [to employ them]. These numbers were researched by authoritative experts and are hidden statistics.[58]

During the war, the Japanese military had a system whereby university graduates could become reserve officers, so the more highly educated had a lower death rate in the war.[59] The generation that was massively recruited as new graduates during this period suffered few deaths

314   Chapter 6

in the war and were promoted through regular personnel transfers. In order to give them posts, Imai says, postwar government offices created new posts that did not exist before the war. Moreover, in the postwar period, the pension benefits system for civil officials that had been in place before the war was abolished and national and local public servants had to join their Mutual Aid Associations and pay premiums for social security.[60] As mentioned in Chapter 4, prior to the revision of the National Public Service Act in 1981, there was no mandatory retirement age; it was simply customary for officials to resign voluntarily. While this presumably would have strengthened the tendency for civil service officials to stay in office longer, in cases where this was deemed adverse to the organization, the only option was to parachute senior public servants into senior roles in public corporations or public companies, a practice known as *amakudari* (descent from heaven). We can presume that this was the situation that prevailed.

In fact, delays in the promotion of civil officials had been happening since before the war. From a survey based on the history of the Ministry of Home Affairs, Mitsuhiro Mizutani, a political scientist specializing in public administration, has demonstrated a year-on-year decline in the relative proportion of those entering the Ministry of Home Affairs after passing the higher civil service examinations who were promoted to receive imperial appointments as *chokunin* officials.[61] When the higher civil service examinations had only been in existence for not so many years, those who had graduated imperial universities and had passed the Higher Examination for Civil Officials (the so-called '*kōbun-gumi*') constituted a minority within the organization, and the majority of them were able to be promoted to *chokunin* rank. However, such a situation would be unsustainable if the relative proportion of the '*kōbun-gumi*' officials in the organization were increased. Unless the organization itself were expanded or these officials were assigned to *chokunin*-level posts in other ministries and agencies, it would no longer be possible to maintain the old rate of promotion.

In prewar Japan, only a small percentage of people attained higher education. This was why higher civil officials and higher-level staff employees were promoted so much more quickly as compared to our

High Growth and the Completion of the Japanese-style Employment System   315

current experience. Economist Kazuo Koike, comparing promotions among university-educated staff employees in the postwar period with those in other Western countries as well as those in prewar Japan, states that 'It is apparently only the large postwar Japanese firms that are slow in promoting their employees'.[62] Koike credited this 'slow selection' and long-term assessment with motivating employees' appetite for competition, and giving rise to the strength of Japan's corporate sector.[63] However, it remains unclear whether large Japanese companies in the postwar period intentionally slowed promotions to achieve such an effect, or whether they did so simply because of the rising numbers of salaried employees with university educations.

Either way, this constituted a structural weakness within Japanese-style employment. The only way to keep promoting university-educated staff employees is to keep adding superfluous positions or else make the organization bigger, and the only way to make the organization bigger is to hire a large number of new graduates. When an economic downturn hits, however, the number of new hires will have to be curtailed. When this happens, more executives without subordinates have to be created as superfluous positions. This vicious cycle would seem to have become the fate of Japanese companies.

'Equal treatment for workers with the same educational background'

In this way, the increased pursuit of higher education made the old order untenable in a number of respects. Tadashi Nishikawa, who managed the personnel evaluation subsection at NKK, argued in 1964 that 'our only supply of factory workers is high school graduates. [...] And consequently, one could say that the way we manage educational background in the company is fundamentally at risk of collapse'.[64]

One potential option would have been to maintain the three-tier structure and shift to higher educational backgrounds across the board. This would have necessarily entailed adopting a policy of concluding employment contracts tailored to specific jobs. If this option were to have been adopted, companies would have had to put in place job-specific criteria such as skill qualifications, skilled worker certifications and professional degrees, which would then have constituted the basis for determining wages and promotions. Working in NKK's personnel department, Nishikawa would also have been cognizant of this. As he put it:

> For example, with the US model of job-based pay, the job is first, and then qualification requirements are set based on that job. When looking for someone who best meets these job qualification requirements, you establish what grade of ability is needed for what job, which is to say, is it a job for a skilled worker or can it be done by an unskilled worker?[65]
> [...] In Europe and the US [...] there are socially established grades of ability, such as skilled, semi-skilled and unskilled workers. And skilled workers are paid a minimum wage as skilled workers, no matter where they go.[66]

What Nishikawa proposed, however, was a completely different approach. 'Regrettably', he observed, 'nothing like these grades of ability have been established in Japan, save perhaps for educational background'. What he means here by educational background is not specialized degrees, but merely a classification of the highest level of educational attainment in terms of whether someone is a junior high school graduate, high school graduate or university graduate.

Yet, as we saw in Chapter 2, Japanese personnel managers still regard those who pass high-level entrance examinations as having great potential. They are expected to have general abilities such as intelligence, to make steady effort, and to be generally good at dealing with what comes their way. While these attributes are not directly related to the execution of any specific job, they can be expected to serve as potentials that can be adapted to any post and any in-house training.

It is in this sense that Nishikawa talks about how there is no 'grade of ability' in Japan 'save perhaps for educational background'. He goes on to propose that the distinction between staff employees and shop-floor workers should be abolished based on the principle of 'equal treatment for workers with the same educational background'.

High Growth and the Completion of the Japanese-style Employment System   317

> Such being the case, I believe that we need to recognize educational background as a grade of ability, and to consider equal treatment for workers with the same educational background to be applied to both blue- and white-collar workers. In this regard, the European and American approach is that there should be a distinction between white-collar and blue-collar workers, but in Japan we believe that there should be no discrimination in the way the two are treated. The reasons for this are as I have already stated. That is, to regard educational background as a grade of ability necessarily entails to a certain extent the systematic equalization of the relationship between staff employees and factory workers so that those with the same education are treated and promoted in the same way, whether they joined the company on the shop floor or in the ranks of the office staff [...].[67]

The problem in Japanese corporate order at the time was that some workers became factory workers and others became staff employees, even though they had also graduated from high school. Nishikawa said that the only way to resolve this problem was to abolish the distinction between factory workers and staff employees and treat them as high school graduates in terms of treatment and promotion. If this were possible, there would be no problem if some university graduates became staff employees while others became salesmen. Of course, high school graduates and university graduates would be promoted at different rates regardless of their duties, but this was consistent with the norms of Japanese society.

Unlike the West, Nishikawa's view was that there was no measure of ability grade in Japan other than educational background. Therefore, if all factory workers were to become more highly educated, then the only way to transform the system was to treat them the same as staff employees and to abandon the three-tier structure. This was Nishikawa's principle of 'equal treatment for workers with the same educational background'. In other words, the three-tier structure should be abandoned not because of a disregard for educational credentials, but *because of the emphasis on them*. Although Japanese firms originally observed a three-tier structure similar to that of Western companies, this was not an order based on professional position but rather a three-tier order based on educational background. When this three-tier structure became incompatible with an order determined by educational background, we could say that the former was abandoned in favor of the latter.

Nishikawa's proposal was in line with a policy shift at NKK. As we saw in Chapter 5, even after Japan's wartime defeat, NKK had refused to eliminate the status distinction between staff (*shokuin*) and factory workers (*kōin*) on the grounds that doing so 'would risk disrupting the labor order'. However, in January 1964, when Nishikawa's paper was published, the company clarified its policy of 'referring to all workers as "company employees" [*shain*]' as a means of responding to the reality of 'the improvement of the composition of educational background among workers on the factory floor'.[68] This policy also reflected the wishes of factory workers. According to an employee survey conducted by NKK in 1963, 73% of factory workers desired the 'abolition of the "staff employee" and "factory worker" designations', which was far higher than the corresponding rate of around 30% among staff employees.[69]

Similar reforms aimed at the 'equality of company employees (*shain*)' took place in parallel at other firms, as well. In 1966, the Yahata Steelworkers' Union called for 'the abolition of all status-based discriminatory treatment and the unification of the company employee (*shain*) system', demanding that 'basic salaries should be standardized for all company employees (*shain*) [...]. In the meantime, starting wages should be set according to educational background, and the application of regular salary increases should be revised so that the same table is used for all company employees (*shain*)'.[70] This demand for 'the unification of the company employee system' was to be realized when Yahata Steel and Fuji Steel merged in 1970 to form the Nippon Steel Corporation.[71]

Underlying the demand that 'starting wages should be set according to educational background' was the increasing number of factory workers with high school educations, which meant that disparities with staff employees with the same level of education was becoming an issue. In other words, also in Yahata Steel Works, the principle of

High Growth and the Completion of the Japanese-style Employment System   319

'equal treatment for workers with the same educational background' advocated by Nishikawa had destroyed the distinction between staff employees and factory workers.

This demonstrates that the labor union also regarded the basic order to be constituted by educational background rather than by jobs. If starting wages were to be set according to educational background, then the starting wages of staff employees with a high school diploma and factory workers with a high school diploma would be equal, but there would be a difference between factory workers with a junior high school diploma and factory workers with a high school diploma, even though the two groups held identical positions.

Nevertheless, the Yahata Steelworkers' Union chose to demand equal treatment for workers with the same educational background rather than equal treatment for workers with identical jobs. This was likely the 'less objectionable' choice for the families of young workers who had sent their children to high school. This, too, may have been 'postwar democracy as it was understood by Japanese workers'.

Military-style ranking systems

In parallel with this unification of workers' status as company employees, companies each introduced their own competence ranking systems (*shokunō shikaku seido*).[72] Such systems became the new order for Japanese companies following the breakdown of the three-tier structure.

To explain this, I should first review what was the Japanese ranking system. As we saw in Chapter 3, Japanese companies characteristically had ranks (*shikaku*) and titles such as councilor (*sanji*) and manager (*shuji*) that existed separately from positions such as accounting section manager or sales director. In military terms, these would be ranks such as colonel or second lieutenant, while position would correspond to duty posts such as the commanding officer of an air force squadron or infantry platoon leader. Although positions change occasionally at the discretion of one's superiors, if an employee is recognized as competent in the assigned position, they may be promoted to a higher level of rank and given a position commensurate with this new rank;

and their salary is determined by their rank, not by their position. This is the ranking system, briefly put.

So, what did 'competence (*shokunō*)' mean in the context of the Japanese post-war business world? In the 1950s, the introduction of job-based pay meant that job classifications had to be carried out by each firm. In this context, the Japanese term *shokunō* seems to have originated as an abbreviation of *shokumu suikō nōryoku* ('the ability to carry out one's job' or 'functional competency'). In 1960, Nikkeiren's educational director stated that amidst the difficulties with the introduction of job-based pay, 'attempts began to be made around 1951 to support the managerial hierarchy by focusing on functional competency (*shokumu suikō nōryoku*), which could be called a middle ground between the professional and personal aspects of a job'.[73] In parallel, as we saw in Chapter 5, by around 1950, the term *shokunō* was often being used in the meaning of 'job function' to guarantee the status of highly educated staff employees. By the 1960s, however, the term's sense as a general ability that encompassed not only educational background but also qualities such as adaptability and cooperativeness appeared to have become entrenched.

As we saw in Chapter 4, prewar Japanese companies focused on elements of 'character' and 'personality' in interviews when hiring university graduates. This term was used to describe job competency that cannot be measured solely by educational background in Japanese society, which lacks a tradition of occupational qualification. Prewar army and navy performance evaluations also emphasized individuals' potential to adapt to any assignment. The term functional competency (*shokunō*), which became current during Japan's high growth period, can be said to have had much the same nuance.

In other words, the competence ranking system was one that assigned an in-house rank based on an employee's potential for adapting to any position. It was also an extension of the 'assignment after appointment' that had been in place since the Meiji period (see Chapter 3). However, the business community of the day preferred to call it a 'person'-centric hierarchical order, in the sense that workers' personalities and characters were evaluated in the selection process, and wages were paid to the persons rather than positions.[74]

High Growth and the Completion of the Japanese-style Employment System 321

Since NKK is well known as a company that introduced a competence ranking system in the 1960s, I will review the characteristics of this example.

As mentioned earlier, since 1964, NKK had adopted a policy of referring to all of its workers as 'company employees (*shain*)'. At that time, however, the former factory workers were still being referred to as Class A company employees, while the old staff employees were being called Class B company employees. However, this distinction was abolished under the 'new ability-based (*nōryoku shugi*) company employee (*shain*) system' rolled out in April 1966, which institutionalized a path for promotion from factory worker to staff employee.[75] Figure 6.3 shows the competence ranking system introduced under this new ability-based company employee system.

In this system, where one started differed according to one's educational background. Specifically, university graduates joined the company as Class 1 or Class 2 company employees (*shain*), junior college graduates as Class 3, high school graduates as Class 5, and those with less education Class 6 or 7. University graduates were promoted to Class 2 managers (*shuji*) as soon as they completed their apprenticeship and were selected for promotion every two years. However, those with only a high school education or less who started as Class 5 company employees or below would probably only attain Class 2 manager rank (likely regarded as equivalent to a warrant officer's commission in the old Imperial Navy) by the time they reached mandatory retirement age.

Even though all employees are considered company employees, there are also categories such as management-level company employees (*kanri-shoku shain*), key company employees (*shuyō-shoku shain*), supervisory company employees (*kantoku-shoku shain*) and general company employees (*ippan-shoku shain*). Management-level company employees are 'those who possess the ability to serve in the position of subsection chief or higher', key company employees are 'those who possess the ability to serve in administrative and technical positions to do with planning, decision-making and general oversight', supervisory company employees are 'those who possess the ability to serve in the position of site manager or foreman', and general company employees

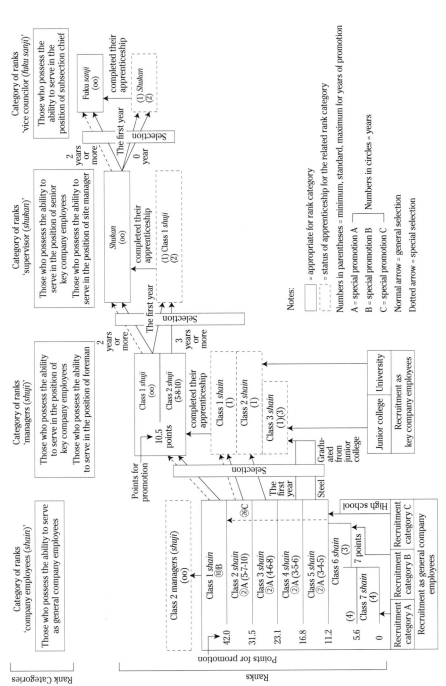

Figure 6.3 Competence ranking system at Nippon Kōkan (1966)   Source: Orii (1973: 45).

High Growth and the Completion of the Japanese-style Employment System   323

Management-level company employees	
Key company employees (Clerical workers) (Technical workers)	Supervisory company employees
General company employees (Clerical workers) (Technical workers) (Operator)	

( ) = occupational categories

Figure 6.4 Employee categories and occupational categories at Nippon Kōkan (1966)
Source: Orii (1973: 41).

are 'those who possess the ability to perform the work that needs to be done in accordance with a certain standard' (Figure 6.4).

This seems hardly any different from the prewar three-tier structure. However, according to management's explanation, these categories were 'regarded not as position-based classifications, but rather as classifications based on functional competence'.[76] In line with the principle of equal treatment for workers with the same educational background proposed by Tadashi Nishikawa, the personnel manager quoted above, high school graduates would have started out as Class 5 company employees, regardless of whether they were office workers or factory workers. Furthermore, under the terms of this system, junior high school graduates, high school graduates, university graduates, office workers and factory workers alike were all eligible for promotion if their 'ability' was recognized in the positions to which they were assigned.

Before the war, ranking systems had been applied only to staff employees. After postwar democratization, ranking systems were extended to shop-floor workers through the 1950s, but there were still many cases in which staff employees and laborers were subject to separate ranking schemes. With the shift to higher education in the 1960s, however, all employees were now subject to a unified ranking scheme of graded ranks as company employees.[77] In that sense, it also marked the elimination of discrimination. As a former personnel manager at NKK remarked in 2004:

> Before the war, there was only a ranking system for the white-collar employees. There was nothing like a ranking scheme for the workers on the shop floor, but then a unified ranking system along the same lines was established that included both shop-floor and white-collar workers, and many efforts were made to eliminate status differences in various ways.[78]

Thus, the 'equality of company employees' was achieved, at least in principle. Regardless of the position to which they were initially assigned, employees who met management's expectations in the jobs they were given were selected for promotion. In other words, company employees became equal in the sense that management's assessment was applied without discrimination based on status. Hyūga Orii, who was in charge of labor affairs at NKK and later became a company director, has characterized this as 'blue-sky labor management'.[79] This phrase was also a slogan used at the Yahata Steel Works around the same time. It presumably referred to a system in which even recruits who had only completed their compulsory education could become officers if they were evaluated solely in terms of their ability to perform their assigned tasks.

Labor researchers are divided in their evaluation of these competence ranking systems. Positive evaluations see them as egalitarian systems that opened the door to promotion for shop-floor workers, thereby increasing their motivation to work. More critical assessments see them as systems that transformed workers into 'corporate drones' who are devotedly loyal to their companies by forcing them to work excessively and compete for promotion.[80] It seems likely that these are simply two aspects of the same reality.

Regardless of how they are seen, such ranking systems were introduced at different companies in a piecemeal manner that meant they were mutually incompatible. For example, if a factory worker who has become a Class 2 company employee after a long period of continuous service were to leave a company, then all of that accumulated experience would be lost. The extension of such ranking systems to the level of shop-floor workers can thus be regarded as a

High Growth and the Completion of the Japanese-style Employment System   325

factor contributing to the decline in the rate at which such workers switched between companies.

Regular personnel transfers and mandatory retirement for women

Yet another change took place, although at a somewhat later period than the introduction of these systems; namely, the practice of regular personnel transfers at a company-wide level.

In 1976, when competence ranking systems had become widespread in large companies, Zen-Noh-Ren conducted a survey of 213 companies which found that 70% of these companies had placed university graduates in sales and production positions when they joined the company. However, because morale would suffer if university graduates were kept on the shop floor, many companies adopted a transfer and rotation system that saw such workers moved to other departments within a few years.[81] As a result, regular personnel transfers became necessary between the production and administrative divisions, which had not previously shared mutual reassignments.[82] According to Katsuji Tsuji's research on the Toyota Motor Corporation, regular personnel transfers were initially limited to staff employees in clerical and technical fields, and did not become company-wide until the 1980s, when the production divisions also became involved.[83]

Prewar civil officials and staff employees at large companies were regularly promoted and transferred. Most factory workers, however, were hired on an as-needed basis; long-term employment was not guaranteed, nor were regular promotions. Moreover, there was little in the way of personnel interactions between staff employees and factory workers. In light of this, company-wide periodic personnel transfers were a sign of the achievement of the 'equality of company employees'. Tsuji commented on the fact that regular company-wide personnel transfers became entrenched about twenty years later than practices like the bulk recruitment of new graduates in the 1960s. He writes that 'this was likely because the phenomenon of regular personnel transfers represented the comprehensive and overall culmination of the various systems and norms related to Japanese-style employment'.[84]

Supporting this system from behind the scenes, as well, were staff clerical employees with high school diplomas or junior college degrees, most of whom were women. After the late 1950s, when long-term employment and seniority-based wages became relatively widespread, an increasing number of companies began to explicitly stipulate a system that mandated women's retirement at marriage, or else a gender-based retirement age limit that allowed women to be laid off before their wages increased.

In cases that have come to light in lawsuits filed by such women, we see that in 1958, Sumitomo Cement stipulated mandatory retirement for women upon marriage or at age thirty-five, and in 1966, Tōkyū Kikan Kōgyō (Tokyu Engine Industry, later Nissan Engine Industry) reached an agreement with its labor union to introduce mandatory retirement ages of fifty-five for men and thirty for women.[85] Both cases involved the companies' institutionalization of early retirement for women as a way of avoiding the burden of regular salary increases. Both lawsuits were won by the plaintiffs; however, mandatory retirement age was not the only area in which staff female employees faced discrimination. The verdict in the 1966 lawsuit against Sumitomo Cement revealed that the company had the following in-house regulations:

[In connection with the recruitment of staff employees, the company shall] carry out recruitment procedures for young men only for university or high school graduates, and for young women, as a general rule, only for high school graduates. Young men shall be hired by the head office, and women shall be hired whenever a vacancy arises at a workplace. With regard to their status after employment, young men shall initially be employed as assistants [koin] at the lowest level, but may be successively promoted to become core employees and be reassigned to other workplaces. The difference between male and female staff employees was clarified, for example, by stipulating that since female employees were hired on a temporary basis until marriage, they would not be promoted beyond the rank of assistant and would not be reassigned to other workplaces.[86]

High Growth and the Completion of the Japanese-style Employment System   327

This account suggests that the old Meiji period distinction between head office employees and site-limited employees, as well as the distinction between civil officials employed at the main office and assistants (*koin*) and manual workers (*yōnin*) employed by local branches (see Chapter 3), was being applied mutatis mutandis to staff female employees.

Furthermore, major electronics manufacturers began hiring middle-aged and older women as *paat* (part-time workers) from the mid-1960s. It was from this period that the labor force participation rate for women by age grade began to show an M-shaped curve, declining temporarily during the period corresponding to marriage, childbirth and raising young children, and then rising again during middle age and later life.[87]

Part-time employment was increasing in Japan from the early 1960s. According to a 1965 Ministry of Labor survey, 97% of female part-time workers were married, and 82% were over the age of thirty. More than 80% of the companies employing part-time workers were in the service, wholesale/retail and manufacturing business including electronics, textile and food processing. In the annual survey conducted by the General Council from 1966 to 1972, about 50% of the female part-time worker respondents each year answered they had previously engaged in contract work in the cottage industry at their home.[88] As we saw in Chapter 4, many Japanese married women had been working at home to supplement their family budget before the war, but in the 1960s they had become part-time workers. As described in Chapter 1, in Japan, the decline in the number of family workers and the increase in non-regular employment have been complementary, and this is particularly true for women.

Management's control over the evaluation of 'ability'

Competence ranking systems proliferated rapidly. After NKK in 1966, Yahata Steel and Fuji Steel introduced new ranking systems in 1967, followed by Mitsubishi Electric in 1968, Matsushita Electric (later Panasonic), the Toyota Motor Company, Mitsubishi Heavy Industries and Mitsui Engineering & Shipbuilding in 1969, and Nissan Motor in 1970.[89]

The labor union at the Yahata Steel Works commended the new personnel system introduced in 1967 for 'reforming the status-based system and establishing an order for company employees centered on work'. Labor historian Jong-won Woo suggests that this appreciation was based on the fact that the system granted ranks to shop-floor workers, as well, and 'brought blue-collar workers' base salary increases to a level on par with those of white-collar workers'.[90] For shop-floor workers, this meant that treatment that had only been shown to salaried employees before the war was now being extended to them, signaling the achievement of the principle of 'equality of company employees'.

Management emphasized that this new system differed from the prewar order in that it was an order based on ability (*nōryoku*). According to Nikkeiren, 'the difference is that whereas prewar qualifications were determined by educational background and continuous service, the new postwar qualifications are determined primarily by ability'.[91] Indeed, the competence ranking systems of the 1960s institutionalized promotions and salary increases based on the evaluation of ability. This was paralleled by an increase in the relative proportion of ability pay, which was a relatively smaller part of the 1946 Densan Wage Model (see Chapter 5), in overall wages.

A 1954 policy document from the Kantō Employers' Association asserted that 'functional competency (*shokumu suikō nōryoku*)' was to be understood as 'merit in value-producing activities in the context of management'.[92] This was also supposed to correspond to ability pay, which was determined based on personnel evaluations within the framework of management rights. In other words, 'ability' represented not a degree or skill qualification accepted across companies, but rather merit in the context of a specific company's management.

At a roundtable discussion included in a 1969 Nikkeiren report, it was stated that under these new 'ability-based (*nōryoku-shugi*)' ranking systems, 'though they might have the right educational background and a track record of continuous service, those who lack ability will be passed over for promotion'. For example, for those who 'lack the academic prowess of a university graduate despite having a university

High Growth and the Completion of the Japanese-style Employment System   329

degree, and who are always eager to go on strike', educational background was not seen as a marker of ability.[93]

Age, family composition, educational background and length of service are all elements that cannot be changed at a manager's discretion. Determination of 'ability', however, is subject to that discretion. This model was thus even more advantageous to management than job-based pay or skill qualifications, both of which had the potential to constrain management. One of the goals of the business community in originally championing the introduction of job-based pay was to cut livelihood wages for middle-aged and older workers. However, this objective could also have been achieved by limiting promotions and wages linked to ability-based performance evaluations. Had this been the case, there would have been no need to insist on the introduction of job-based pay.

Also, the new competence ranking systems were only measures of in-house qualifications and did not comprise a cross-firm model. Even if a person was deemed qualified in one company, this qualification was not applicable in other companies. For managers, this had the advantage of stemming the outflow of human resources that had been developed through in-house training. Until the early 1960s, both government and industry had advocated the development of industrial schools and vocational training programs. However, as economic growth kicked into high gear, companies increasingly tended to focus on developing their personnel through in-house training. Given these circumstances, the government introduced a technical skills certification system, but the response from the corporate side was less than enthusiastic. Ronald Dore, who studied employment practices at Hitachi, suggests that Hitachi was wary of the possibility of losing human resources if its employees were to obtain 'nationally valid qualifications', and was accordingly hesitant towards this proficiency examination.[94]

As a result, even as technological innovation progressed, work processes were standardized and workers became better educated, the tendency of the labor market in large companies to become more insular did not change. The situation was not developing in accordance with Shōjirō Ujihara's predictions in the 1950s, which we examined in Chapter 5.

The competence ranking systems also had another advantage in that they addressed the problem of delayed promotions. A personnel manager at the Yahata Steel Works described one of the reasons for introducing the new ranking system in 1967 as follows: 'now, in cases where there aren't any posts for people who should be promoted to section manager [based on the year they joined the company], we can just assign them a [same grade of section manager] councilor rank'.[95] In naval terms, ship postings may be limited, but an officer can still be promoted to the rank of captain.

Furthermore, positions were not limited under the competence ranking system, which made it easier for employees to be reassigned to different duties. This had a positive impact on technological innovation during the high-growth period. As the high-growth period kicked into high gear, large companies built new plants and rationalized their older factories. Nevertheless, they had learned their lesson from the mass layoffs of the 1950s, which had led to large-scale labor disputes, and now sought to respond by reassigning workers rather than laying them off.

For example, the reassignments and relocations that took place when Yahata Steel built the new Kimitsu Steel Works, located approximately 500 km (310 miles) from the original Yahata Steel Works, were on such a large scale that some observers characterized them as a 'great migration'. Such reassignments would have been almost impossible if the workers had been employed in fixed positions. The Yahata Steelworkers' Union agreed, stating in the agenda for its 1966 annual meeting that 'in the event of a surplus of necessary personnel, support and reassignment will continue to be permitted under certain criteria from the standpoint of the lifetime employment system'.[96]

In this way, long-term employment and reassignments came to have a kind of barter relationship, so to speak. This was made institutionally possible thanks to the competence ranking system. In a 1960 report by Nikkeiren, as well, we find an argument that a ranking system was necessary 'in cases like Japan, where there is an implicit expectation of job transfers, given the practice of lifelong employment'.[97]

The flexibility afforded by reassignments was also well regarded in the service industry, which is characterized by fluctuating demand.

High Growth and the Completion of the Japanese-style Employment System   331

In 1963, the vice president of Nippon Express stated that job-based pay did not allow for 'nimble management that diverts [personnel] to different fields of work in response to fluctuating workload' and advocated a 'gradual reorganization of the wage system with functional competency as the main component'.[98]

Reassignments were first identified as a means of avoiding layoffs in 1955 with the establishment of the Japan Productivity Center (Nihon Seisansei Honbu), which stated in one of its three founding principles that 'to the greatest extent possible, appropriate measures should be taken in cooperation with the public and private sectors to prevent unemployment through reassignment and other means'.[99] Until around 1960, however, there were still many disputes over the dismissal of designated workers such as the Mitsui Mike dispute in 1960. According to labor historian Tsutomu Hyōdō, 'It is only from the 1960s that lifetime employment has actually become entrenched as a norm'.[100]

Unions unable to set policy

In terms of how competence ranking systems were received by workers, the diversity of voices on the side of labor makes it difficult to generalize. Nevertheless, labor historians generally agree that Japanese workers were not necessarily against the idea of being evaluated on the basis of ability. Although they were vehemently opposed to being differentiated according to their educational background, they were rather positive about being evaluated on their ability and competence as workers. In 1966, a seventeen-year-old sheet metal worker (indicating that he started to work immediately after graduating from junior high school) offered the following account of his feelings of rivalry with fellow factory workers who had graduated from high school:

> I have the skills and confidence to stand shoulder to shoulder with them, but I have one weak point. Namely, my educational background. [...] No matter how competent you are, a junior high school graduate is always going to be seen as a junior high school graduate.[101]

In the Japanese corporate order, there were sometimes even situations where university graduates, high school graduates and junior high school graduates held the same positions at the same open plan office. As one evening high school student who worked at a newspaper company wrote in 1969, 'I may have been cocky, but I was doing the same job as high school and university graduates, and there was no way I was going to let them beat me'.[102] There was a delicate overlap between these workers' voices and the arguments being made by management. Nikkeiren's 1969 report stated that under the new 'ability-based' (nōryoku-shugi) ranking systems, 'neither educational background, age, nor length of service are in themselves regarded as ability'.[103]

Labor historian Kazuo Nimura tells us that 'the real demand that Japanese workers were making was "treat me like a person". That is to say, they sought to be recognized as full members of the company, and for their abilities and efforts be duly evaluated as such'.[104] The 1947 demand by Japanese Government Railways workers that their 'efforts' (doryoku) be evaluated was discussed in Chapter 5.

Further, younger workers during the high growth period were becoming increasingly dissatisfied with age-based livelihood wages. For example, at the Tobata new plant set up by Yahata Steel Works in 1958, a young worker voiced his frustration, asking 'Why is it that our [wages] are only a fraction of those of the older workers at Yahata plant, even though we're putting out the same product as they are at Yahata plant but faster?'[105] If voices like these were to be taken into consideration, the labor unions would not have been allowed simply to insist on an age-based livelihood wage.

Japanese labor unions encompassed younger, middle-aged and older workers, unskilled laborers and skilled workers, shop-floor laborers and staff employees in a company, all within the same organization. Their different positions made it difficult to achieve consensus in their demands without dividing the union.

Labor unions such as Tekkōrōren (the Japan Federation of Steel Workers' Unions), from a relatively early stage, displayed a cooperative stance vis-à-vis management in exchange for guarantees of long-term job security. Left-leaning unions such as Sōhyō (the General Council of

High Growth and the Completion of the Japanese-style Employment System   333

Trade Unions of Japan), however, were opposed to job-based pay, but also argued the need to set wages by industry at a cross-firm level.[106] This was because they, too, had learned from the kinds of movements that the American and German labor unions had been involved in.

However, according to union activists of the time, even if they were to 'directly import a foreign method of paying wages' in the form of cross-firm occupation-based wages, the 'conditions for the general public to understand their broader significance' were lacking. Reading economist Mitsuo Ishida's summary of the discussions on the part of the trade unions at the time, we can see that although a 'wage system that would not drive a wedge between workers' was called for, views were expressed that this would require 'a long and careful process' and 'democratic debate from the bottom up', suggesting that the ultimate priority was 'unity and solidarity toward a substantial wage increase'.[107]

By contrast, a competence ranking system, wherein wages were determined by ability, was more easily supported by workers, since 'ability' was a word that could be interpreted in a multiplicity of ways.

In September 1963, NKK conducted a company-wide opinion survey with the cooperation of the University of Tokyo's Department of Sociology. To the question of what should be emphasized in the evaluation of wages, the survey recorded the following responses. 'Seniority' was the least popular answer, selected by 3.9% of respondents of all ages, 'job and ability' by 8.2% (mainly relatively new employees) and 'primarily seniority, but with job and ability taken into account' by 34.9% (mainly veteran employees), while 'primarily job and ability, but with seniority also taken into account' was the most popular overall, selected by 52.6% of respondents.[108]

It seems likely that younger factory workers and staff employees, considering flexibility in adapting to new technology to be an 'ability', therefore chose 'job and ability'. Middle-aged and older factory workers considered experience to be 'ability', and so chose 'primarily seniority, but with job and ability taken into account'. The majority, however, chose 'primarily job and ability, but with seniority also taken into account'. Staff employees with university degrees would likely have agreed, considering their knowledge and educational background in terms of 'ability'. Presumably, this support for the ability-based ranking system was due to the fact that it was open to such diverse interpretations. Thus, the 'equality of company employees', which emphasized 'effort within the company' over educational background, became the new order for corporate Japan.

This also resulted in the creation of a situation in which Hitachi foundry workers could self-identify as members of the Hitachi Company, as Dore described in contrast to the situation in British foundrymen, as we saw in Chapter 2.[109] Prewar Japanese factory workers were not *shain* and would have been unable to self-identify as such. It was only with the postwar enterprise union movement's realization of the principle of equality of company employees that the tens of thousands of employees who had never met each other were able to form a shared identity as '*shain* of the company'. This phenomenon was similar to that which led to the creation of identity by the staff employee movements in Germany we saw in chapters 2 and 4.

In the 1960s, many popular films that featured the 'salaryman' as the main character were released. Ueki Hitoshi, a comedian who often acted in those films, had the character name of 'Mr. Average' (*Taira Hitoshi*) in one film.[110] In reality, American researcher Ezra F. Vogel estimated only 18.1% of males fifteen years of age and older could be classified as 'salarymen' from the 1960 census 'if one considers professional and technical workers, managers and officials, clerical workers, and protective-service workers as salary men'.[111] However, sociologist Katō Hidetoshi pointed out even salaried factory workers or shop staffs began to have self-consciousness as 'salarymen'.[112] The rapid decrease in the self-employed farming population, the radical increase of salaried employees, and the massive migration to big cities in the 1960s created the impression that 'salarymen' were the typical Japanese workers.

Thus, through the 1960s, a series of norms of Japanese employment took root. This was the result of the expansion of norms that had existed since the Meiji period beyond the three-tier structure, a development that was brought about by the effects of total war, democratization, the labor union movement and the shift to a more highly educated workforce.

Effect of military experience

In 1969, Nikkeiren published a report entitled *Nōryoku-shugi kanri: Sono riron to jissen* (Ability-Based Management: Theory and Practice). The report, written by the Ability-Based Management Study Group, a group of personnel managers from large companies, abandoned the argument in favor of introducing job-based pay that Nikkeiren had once advocated, reevaluated norms such as long-term employment and seniority-based pay, and praised the competence ranking system.

The report stated that 'the lifetime employment system is a marriage of love between companies and their employees'. Lifetime employment and seniority-based pay had the advantages of 'instilling loyalty to the company', 'retaining and securing a talented workforce' and 'carrying out long-term staffing and professional development plans'. On the other hand, the report also advocated corporate management by a 'capable few', stating that 'respect for ability should replace respect for seniority' and that promotions should be based solely on ability.[113] The means of achieving these objectives was a competence ranking system in which employees were assessed based on their ability.

As we have seen thus far, the competence ranking systems were similar to military institutions, and the personnel managers at large firms who wrote this report were not unaware of this. An anonymous roundtable discussion of personnel managers that was held in October 1968 and appended to the end of the report featured the following discussion.

> C: I think that the rank system of the old army and navy was exactly like our competence ranking system. The ranks of second lieutenant, first lieutenant and captain were based on functional competence.
>
> D: This was truly output-based – performance-based. And then pay raises were determined by their prospect. Even among those who graduated from the Imperial Military or Naval Academies in the same year, ten years later one might be a first lieutenant, while another might already be a major. There were lots who had graduated more recently and were younger but had a higher rank.

E: What's more, even among second lieutenants, one might command a company, while another could command a battalion. It was a complete two-ladder system [of ranks and positions], wasn't it. Moreover, the rank of second lieutenant and the position of company commander were both assigned on the basis of ability. And the way in which ranks and positions are tied together was also the same kind of range we emphasize [i.e., a wide range of reassignments to various positions].

G: That is exactly the same as what we are trying to accomplish.

D: Well, you know, that's probably because this study group includes many Naval Academy alumni.[114]

In postwar Japan, the military was temporarily abolished, even though it was rebuilt as the Self-Defense Forces in the 1950s, and those who attended army or navy academies during the war had to become businessmen. Not only them, men in their forties and fifties in the late 1960s would have had military and wartime experience and would have been familiar with military institutions. The rapid spread of the competence ranking system during this period may have been due in part to the fact that middle-ranking executives at various companies were all familiar with this system as a result of their experience in Japan's total war.

However, these men overlooked an important point. During their time in the army and navy, the military organization was expanding rapidly due to the war, not to mention the fact that officers and commissioned officers were dying in large numbers. As a result, there were always many openings for posts, and those who were deemed competent were promoted rapidly through the ranks. Situations such as they describe, in which 'ten years later one might be a first lieutenant, while another might already be a major', or 'even among second lieutenants, one might command a company, while another could command a battalion', were merely exceptional phenomena of the wartime period.

Also, 1969, when this report was issued, was during the period when Japan's GNP was growing rapidly at an annual rate of around 10%. During this era, the rising wage costs that would be brought on by

High Growth and the Completion of the Japanese-style Employment System 337

extending the principle of 'equality of company employees' to the level of shop-floor laborers could still be accommodated.

However, the oil crisis of 1973 marked the end of this period. Yet once extended, the 'equality of company employees' could no longer be withdrawn. In the period that followed, a new dual structure would manifest that was to limit the principle of 'equality of company employees' so that it only applied to *seishain*, the 'regular employees'.

7 A New Dual Structure

In this chapter, I describe how the Japanese-style employment system created a new dual structure following the end of Japan's period of rapid economic growth.[1] The quantitative expansion of the number of regular employees (*seishain*) in large companies came to a virtual halt in the 1970s. Enrollment in higher education also began to be capped from this point onward. The scramble for slices of a pie that was no longer growing found expression in the intensifying competition around university entrance examinations.

Nevertheless, the late 1970s was a period when inequality in Japan was at its lowest point. This was not because the Japanese-style employment system covered all workers, but because the lower tier of the dual structure was bolstered by other factors. With the introduction of infrastructure construction projects and efforts to attract industry by conservative governments, an increasing number of people in regional districts found jobs to supplement self-employment in the agricultural sectors, and the number of self-employed people engaged in commerce and other non-agricultural sectors also increased, which had the effect of stemming population migration to the Tokyo metropolitan area. In fact, this state of affairs reinforced the popular notion that Japan had achieved an 'all-middle-class society' (*sōchūryū shakai*).

In the wake of the 1973 oil crisis, large companies maintained employment by capping wages and transferring workers out of unprofitable divisions. SMEs that could not afford to take such steps were laying off workers, prompting lawsuits that led to the establishment of dismissal regulations that set a legal precedent in the 1970s. Thus, the existing norm of long-term employment became institutionalized as a legal system, with effects that, to some degree, now extend even to non-unionized SMEs.

However, this 'all-middle-class' situation was unsustainable over the longer term. In the 1980s, observers' attention began to shift from the traditional dual structure of large companies and SMEs to a new dual structure characterized by the distinction between regular employees and non-regular workers. Even in SMEs, the institutionalization of dismissal regulations for regular workers had led to the progressive introduction of non-regular workers. Large companies were also struggling with long-term employment and the rising cost of seniority-based wages, and were now moving forward with the introduction of non-regular workers. Since many of these non-regular workers were women, the Japanese employment system also manifested itself as a gendered dual structure. Meanwhile, regular employees, in exchange for retaining seniority-based wages and long-term employment, had their work-life balance compromised by longer working hours, frequent job transfers and stricter personnel evaluations.

Although calls to reform the Japanese-style employment system have been being advanced since the 1990s, Japanese industry has yet to introduce cross-firm standards for personnel evaluation, and the norms of long-term employment and seniority-based wages have remained unchanged. Since the main objective on the part of management has been to hold down wages, the various reforms that have been attempted have been hampered by worker resistance and declining morale. As a result, the core Japanese-style employment norms have been maintained even as the scope of their application has been restricted.

'Japan as Number One'

The experience of rapid economic growth profoundly changed the consciousness of the Japanese people. According to public opinion surveys conducted by the NHK Broadcasting Culture Research Institute, when asked about the 'relative superiority' of Japanese vis-à-vis Westerners, in 1951, 28% of respondents had viewed the Japanese as superior, while 47% felt that the Japanese were inferior. By 1963, however, the balance had tipped in favor of the Japanese, and by 1968, 47% of respondents viewed the Japanese as superior.[2]

Western evaluations of Japan had also changed. In 1972, the administrative undersecretary of the Ministry of Labor proclaimed the following.

A New Dual Structure

An interest in Japanese-style employment and wage practices has been common among Westerners who have been paying attention to Japan in recent years. For example, in his book *The Age of Discontinuity*, Peter Drucker points out that British and American craft unions are no longer sufficiently responsive to technological and skilled innovations based on new knowledge, and suggests that we should learn from the fact that lifelong employment in Japan facilitates job changes within companies while allowing for continuous training. Similarly, although they differ in their perspectives, authors such as Herman Kahn, James Abegglen and Robert Guillain, among others, have all demonstrated extra-ordinary interest in this issue in their discussions of Japan.[3]

These words were part of the foreword to the advance Japanese translation of the OECD's labor report on Japan.[4] The OECD report assessed Japan's employment norms as follows.

[...] It also means that workers are interested in the productivity of their firms and that they adapt to new occupations and methods of work without the difficulties experienced in countries with rigid barriers between craft occupations, and without the fear of redundancy, otherwise a cause for resistance to technical progress [...]. Another advantage of the Japanese employment system is the fact that income developments through each individual's life parallel the development of family expenditure needs relatively well, rising with the number and age of children.[5]

Even so, the report was not unreserved in its praise of Japan, noting not only the closed nature of the labor market on the part of large corporations and the lack of public vocational training, but also that employment norms in the large corporations are 'neither universal in the economy nor applicable to all employees in the firms where [they exist]'.[6] Nevertheless, such international commendations inspired confidence in Japan's political and business circles.

The attitude of the Japanese government also changed. The first Basic Plan on Employment Measures (*Koyō taisaku kihon keikaku*), approved by the Cabinet in 1967, still advocated 'the formation of a modern labor market centered on vocational skills and job categories'. However, the second plan, approved by Cabinet resolution in January 1973, stated that 'Japan's employment wage norm, which is characterized by lifetime employment, a seniority-based wage system and enterprise-based labor unions, should be highly commended for having facilitated the training of engineers and skilled workers in line with corporate progress, and for bringing stability to employment and to the lives of workers'.[7]

Nor did this confidence waver, even after the end of the high-growth period, which followed the oil crisis of October 1973. In fact, this high regard for Japanese employment norms actually grew.

When the oil crisis seemed to be resulting in an unemployment crisis, the government helped Japanese companies to avoid layoffs by putting these employment norms to work. One specific example of a measure taken by the government was its enactment of the Employment Insurance Act (*Koyō hoken-hō*), which subsidized leave allowances with employment adjustment benefits and supported the secondment of employees to affiliated firms.[8]

Labor unions also prioritized the maintenance of employment by exercising restraint over demands for wage increases and tolerating even more reassignments. In his New Year's address for 1979, Nikkeiren's then chairman, Bunpei Ōtsuki, stated that Japanese companies had been able to weather the oil crisis by dint of their efforts to streamline management, improve productivity and keep wages low. 'Underlying these efforts', he continued, 'were Japan's labor-management norms, particularly the existence of enterprise unions with a sense of the unity between labor and management and the idea of their shared destiny'.[9]

The 1970s was also an era that saw the proliferation of discourses about the Japanese identity that are collectively known as Nihonjinron. These Nihonjinron analyses often adopted the cultural logic that Japanese corporate management and the relationship between labor and capital in Japan followed the logic of '*ie* society' (that is, they were based on the symbolic structures of the traditional Japanese family), or else had their origins in the collectivism of rural villages. Most such analyses, however, were little more than projections of employment

A New Dual Structure

343

norms that had become prevalent in large companies after the 1960s onto the canvas of Japanese history.

The end of the quantitative expansion of Japanese-style employment

Nevertheless, the period of quantitative expansion of Japanese-style employment was gradually coming to an end. This was reflected in the leveling off of the number of regular employees in large companies in the 1970s as we saw in Chapter 1. In the wake of the oil crisis at the end of 1973, employment adjustments began to be carried out among the major manufacturers and other large employers. The number of people employed in large companies with 500 employees or more peaked at 9.26 million in 1974, and had fallen to 8.72 million by 1978. Thereafter, the number of employees rebounded somewhat as the economy recovered, but as a share of the total number of employed persons, it remained in the higher 20% range after peaking in 1974 at 30.6%.[10] As noted in Chapter 1, labor economist Kazuo Koike has estimated the proportion of workers for whom wages rise with age. As also shown in Chapter 1, using the same sample calculations as Koike's, we find that the ratio he calculated has remained stable at about 27% of the working people since 1982. While Koike notes that changes prior to 1982 are unclear, he positions the proportion of workers whose wages rise with age as having experienced 'only a slight downward trend if we consider the period since 1968'.[11]

As mentioned in Chapter 1, government statistics before 1982 do not distinguish between regular employees and non-regular workers, so it is difficult to trace trends before that time. Here, for reference, let's look at hiring trends at Toyota Motor Company from 1962 to 1980. After weathering a major labor dispute in 1950, Toyota resumed hiring new graduates in 1953. In 1962, the company switched to hiring new high school graduates to work on the factory floor (as *ginōin*, or 'skilled workers'), and began hiring seasonal workers during the agricultural off-season from 1963. In addition, the category of 'associate employees' (*jun-shain*) corresponded to conventional temporary workers. Looking

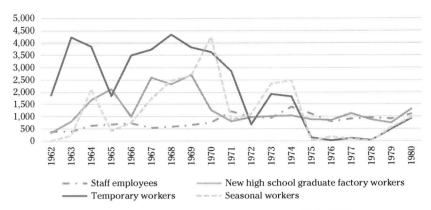

Figure 7.1 Hiring trends at Toyota Motor Company (1962–1980)
Unit: 1 person   Source: Based on the table in Yamamoto and Tanaka (1982: 67).

at the number of such hires over time, we can identify three distinct trends (Figure 7.1).[12]

First, the number of workers hired as 'clerical and technical workers, etc.', who would correspond to the traditional category of staff employees and 'staff employees' in Figure 7.1, has fluctuated less with economic trends than the numbers of other types of employees. Nevertheless, we see a gradual increase during the high-growth period until 1974, after which the number of new hires reached a plateau. Organizations with long-term employment and seniority-based promotion need to hire new graduates on a regular basis. This is because if the number of new hires falls off, then middle-aged and older staff employees will no longer have any subordinates, even if they would have been regularly transferred with expectations to be promoted to managerial positions. Conversely, if the number of new hires rises too much, then wage costs will eventually become a burden. Presumably, this is why the number of new hires tended to remain constant after the organizational expansion of the high-growth period had come to an end.

Second, there is a trend among 'skilled workers' – factory workers who were hired as new graduates with a high school education. Although the number of such hires fluctuated wildly in step with economic trends up to the 1960s, this number became more or less constant from about 1970 onward. It seems likely that by this period,

A New Dual Structure 345

the principle of 'equality of company employees' was now being extended to the 'skilled workers'.

And third, we can see that seasonal workers and temporary workers were now acting as a buffer against economic trends. Looking at man-hour periods including adjustments among non-regular employees, Japanese labor researchers have concluded that the speed of employment adjustment in Japan after the oil crisis was not significantly slower than in Europe and the US, where unemployment was high.[13]

Of course, it's impossible to generalize from a single company's trends. Nevertheless, it may be that, with the end of high growth, the relative increase in the proportion of regular employees whose wages tended to rise with age had essentially leveled off. And there were considerable numbers of non-regular workers who were acting as a buffer against the economic trend and who were excluded from Japanese-style employment.

Emergence of a school hierarchy

The recession triggered by the oil crisis took hold in 1974, marking a period that also saw the halt of increasing enrollment in higher education.

In 1974, high school enrollment exceeded 90%, and enrollment at universities and junior colleges reached 37.8% in 1975 (27.2% at four-year universities). However, under the Act on Subsidies for Private Schools (*Shiritsu gakkō shinkō josei-hō*), promulgated in 1975, in exchange for receiving government subsidies, private schools were now subject to supervision by the Ministry of Education. Beginning in 1976, the enrollment capacity of private universities was changed when admissions were switched from a notification system to an approval system, which limited the establishment of private universities and junior colleges as well as their admissions capacity. As a consequence, the enrollment rate at universities and junior colleges was constrained so that it remained flat until around 1990.[14] The government and the business community had both long been aware of the excessive number of graduates from higher education, especially private humanities-

346   Chapter 7

oriented universities. The 1975 Act on Subsidies for Private Schools was highly effective at moderating this part of the problem.

However, this did little to stem the popular enthusiasm for pursuing higher education. One underlying factor was that high school graduates could no longer find jobs as they had done during the period of rapid economic growth. As a result of the recession after the oil crisis, the number of job openings for new graduates in March 1976 was down 40% compared to the previous year. In particular, the new employment rate for high school graduates dropped from 48.0% to 42.2% between 1974 and 1976. With fewer prospects for employment, the proportion of high school graduates hoping to pursue higher education rose from 44.2% to 47.7% over the same period.[15]

However, this was precisely the period when the admission capacity of universities and junior colleges was being capped. The consequence of this was an overheated competition to secure the limited number of places available through university entrance examinations.

Educational researcher Akio Inui, surveying the index of magazine articles in the Sōichi Ōya Collection, observed a sharp increase in exam-related articles in general weekly magazines beginning in 1974.[16] In particular, he observed an increase in the number of articles in magazines for young people and women with titles such as 'Emergency research for entrance exams, here are the universities you can get into!' (*Pureibōi*, 27 November 1975) and 'The frenzied boom in exam preparation schools: One mother's theory on how "Investment in education comes first"' (*Josei sebum*, 12 March 1975).

Furthermore, newspaper-affiliated publications such as *The Yomiuri Weekly* and *The Sankei Weekly* began to publish high school rankings for successful applicants to individual universities. *Sunday Mainichi* was the first to publish this type of feature, beginning in 1973 with its 'Comprehensive survey of higher education acceptance by university for 1,000 high schools across Japan'. Other articles that appeared included 'List of the best cram schools in Japan' and 'How to tell a good cram school from a bad one' (both from the 25 October 1975 issue of *The Yomiuri Weekly*) and 'Information on university selection: Here are the universities and faculties that will definitely be advantageous on the job-hunting front five years from now' (in the 15 and 22 January

A New Dual Structure   347

1976 issues of *The Gendai Weekly*). According to Inui, until that point, the rankings of successful applicants had only ever been published for select universities such as the University of Tokyo. However, rankings beyond that scope began to appear from this point onward. In this way, the tendency to rank not only certain high-prestige schools but also high schools and universities at the nationwide level grew increasingly stronger. Labor economist Makoto Kumazawa stated in 1992:

> What management demands of elite salarymen, especially the white-collar workers, who support Japanese companies is, above all, a flexible approach to work. They do not want their employees to stick to specific skills or scope of work. This being the case, the best candidates are naturally those who have high achievements in multiple subjects and who are highly adaptable in terms of personality.[17]

However, this academic orientation only went as far as the undergraduate level. After the 1950s, Japan's high school and undergraduate university enrollment rates rose extremely rapidly, and eventually surpassed those of Western European countries in the 1970s. However, the ratio of graduate students to undergraduates in 1978 was 3%, which was significantly lower than corresponding ratios in other countries, such as the 1975 levels of 15% in the US, 24% in the UK and 19% in France.[18]

Japanese companies emphasized graduation from a university with difficult entry requirements as an indicator of a new graduate's potential for in-house training, but considered graduate education unnecessary. In 1980, economist Naohiro Yashiro pointed out that the form taken by 'credentialism' in Japanese society exhibits rather different aspects than it does in other countries. In Japan, such aspects included a low rate of students pursuing graduate-level education and a large number of so-called *rōnin* (students enrolled in examination prep-cram schools after graduation from high schools) aspiring to get into a university with difficult entry requirements. Yashiro attributes these phenomena to the strong demand for 'horizontal educational backgrounds', such as attendance at first- and second-rate schools,

348   Chapter 7

rather than 'vertical educational backgrounds', that include master's and doctoral degrees.[19]

'A struggle for exclusive survival'

As the admissions capacity of the private universities and junior colleges was curbed, a new category of special training schools (*senshū gakkō*) was established in 1976. Although postwar reforms abolished the prewar system of vocational schools, many of which were elevated to high schools, a number of private schools for vocational training emerged, and these training schools were institutionalized.

Akio Inui points out that the decline in the job placement ratio for high school graduates in the late 1970s and 1980s was almost matched by a corresponding increase in the number of students enrolled in special training schools and miscellaneous schools (*kakushu gakkō*, schools that are not subsidized by the government as approved training schools). According to Inui, many of the 'high schools where the majority of students are those who will go on to special training schools and miscellaneous schools' are 'the so-called "bottom schools" in the general course', which 'are often in a much worse position than the vocational course with respect to the job market'. In Inui's estimation, the 'special training schools and miscellaneous schools' attended by students from the '"bottom schools" of the general course' who have been shut out of both higher education and the labor market 'function in large part as a pool for semi-unemployed youth'. Inui describes the situation taking place in the education system as 'a struggle for exclusive survival'.[20]

The popularization of such selection through schooling, which was not linked to occupational choice, was corelated to the decline of self-employment. In the past, it was possible for students with poor grades in school to find a variety of occupations through self-employment, but the decline of self-employment has made this difficult. As noted by labor economist Makoto Kumazawa in 1992:

> This is a far cry from the situation in the 1950s, for example. In those days, parents took a certain amount of pride in the various

A New Dual Structure 349

common professions, even if they might have had certain hang-ups about them, as well. That's why there were many parents who opposed their children's teachers, insisting that children who were expected to take over their parents' professions "not be made to study too much". In some cases, the parents who were self-employed farmers, artisans, shopkeepers and others would even become furiously angry with the teachers, saying that their children were "studying too much and not helping out at home" or accusing them of stirring up their children with all this talk of study to the point that they had expressed a desire to go to university. "What about the family business?" Now this is unthinkable. Instead, parents encourage their children not to think about taking over the family business, but rather to get into a good university and get a job at a large company.[21]

In this way, society became polarized into two groups, with regular employees at large companies at one end and everyone else at the other. This also led to the decline of the self-employed who were the core supporters of local communities. Sociologist Kazushi Tamano, who conducted a survey in a local community in Tokyo from the 1980s into the 1990s, observed in 2005 that 'the neighborhood's core supporters did not really have any idea of having their children follow in their self-employed footsteps. They led lives of extreme frugality in an attempt to provide their children with the high level of education that they never had the opportunity to obtain'. As Tamano observes, 'This, in turn', would reduce the number of people who support the community'.[22] As we saw in Chapter 1, the organization rate of the Neighborhood Associations peaked in 1986 and rapidly decreased thereafter.

However, this phenomenon was also a consequence of Japan's postwar democratization and the economic levelling brought on by rapid economic growth. Competition grew more intense because long-term employment and seniority-based wages, which had been the privilege of civil officials and staff employees during the prewar period, now seemed to be within reach, if their children only studied hard enough in schools.

350   Chapter 7

Sociologist Kenji Hashimoto, who has analyzed disparities over the period from 1955 to 2005 based on the Social Stratification and Social Mobility (SSM) Survey, points out that the gap in starting salaries by educational background was smallest in 1975, when the gap between university graduates and high school graduates had narrowed to a factor of only 1.19. Despite this, Hashimoto argues that one of the reasons why the 'credentialist society' (*gakureki shakai*) became a problem during this period was that the increase in university enrollment made even those who had little to do with higher education before aware of the economic benefits that a university education could bring.[23]

In a 1984 article entitled '"Futsū" no tame no "moretsu"' (Working like mad to become standard), Kumazawa wrote that 'a defining feature of the postwar democracy chosen by the Japanese people is the absence of clear-cut distinctions in the lifestyles of different social classes'.[24] People disliked occupational and class distinctions, and everyone wanted their children to go to prestigious universities and become regular employees of large companies. As noted in Chapter 2, the Japanese government's Wage Census defines 'standard workers' as those who start working for a company immediately after graduation and then continue working for the same company. For Japanese bureaucrats, this was the standard way of life, but it was not attainable for many Japanese. In this context, the atmosphere of 'a struggle for exclusive survival' and 'working like mad to become standard' was becoming ever more intense.

An all-middle-class society of 100 million people

Meanwhile, until the 1970s, agriculture and other self-employment had declined comparatively moderately. Certainly, the ratio of workers in the agricultural, forestry and fisheries sectors to the total labor force declined from 30.6% in 1960 to 18.1% in 1970. However, the number of farming households did not decrease as much as did the number of workers, which can mainly be attributed to a shift toward side jobs of family workers of faming households.

A New Dual Structure   351

This decline in the self-employed agricultural sector is something that has taken place in all countries around the world. What was characteristic about the Japanese case, however, was that although the number of farming households did not decrease to any great extent, they increasingly shifted to dual income livelihoods. This has been attributed to the efforts of Liberal Democratic Party (LDP) politicians to maintain the rural vote with public works projects and incentives to attract businesses to rural areas, as well as the promotion of agricultural policies that allowed farmers to stay in their communities while earning a dual income as part-time farmers working other jobs. In 2010, political scientist Jun Saitō summarized the LDP's agricultural policy as 'frankly nothing more than a cartel policy for maintaining dual-income rice farmers'.[25]

During the 1950s and 1960s, the absolute percentage of votes of Japan's conservative parties (mainly the LDP) declined constantly, while that of progressive opposition parties such as the Japan Socialist Party (JSP), as well as abstentions, consistently increased. In the 1970s, however, the conservative parties' vote grew (Figure 7.2). On this issue, the journalist Masumi Ishikawa proposed his own theory.[26] According to Ishikawa, the LDP was actually an aggregation of local conservative politicians from various regions who organized voters through their own regional networks, and it became difficult for the LDP to keep voters on track as migration to urban areas increased. Those who migrated to the big cities would most probably either abstain from voting or join a labor union, which rendered them JSP supporters rather than voters for conservative parties. But the outflow of population from provincial areas to the three major metropolitan areas decreased sharply in the 1970s, halting the further shrinkage of the LDP voter base.

I conducted research that corroborated Ishikawa's theory.[27] The LDP government banned the building of new factories in large cities in the 1960s and dispersed industry to rural areas. Furthermore, by building railroads and highway networks, they made it possible to transport semi-finished products from coastal industrial areas to inland rural areas. In the inland rural areas, micro-factories using the cheap labor of female family workers of farming households increased,

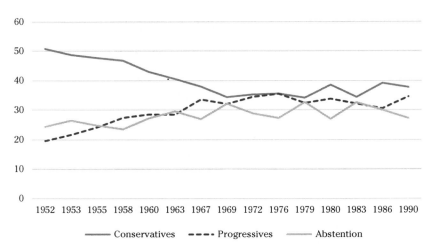

Figure 7.2 Absolute percentage of votes* in general elections (1952–1990)
Unit: %   Notes: The classification of parties as 'Conservatives' and 'Progressives' follows Ishikawa (1995).
*The concept of the absolute percentage of votes (the portion of votes as a percentage of the total number of eligible voters, including abstentions), which is distinguished from the relative percentage of votes (the portion of votes garnered by a party as a percentage of actual votes cast), has been popular in Japanese media and political science.
Source: The House of Representatives' general election results, published by the Ministry of Internal Affairs and Communications.

assembling electrical products and automobile parts. The tradition of Japanese cottage industry that was discussed in Chapter 4 contributed to this development. This led to side-job employment for those women and economic growth in rural areas, which in turn led to an increase in financial, construction, real estate and commercial self-employment in those rural areas. Thus, the wage gap between rural and urban areas was narrowed and the migration to urban areas was halted (Figure 7.3). In parallel, the then Ministry of Home Affairs (*Jichisyō*) implemented a model community policy that assisted in organizing neighborhood associations in local communities, which led to the organization of residents and an increase in the conservative vote.

These factors led to the increase in SMEs, non-agricultural self-employment, and the growth in the organization rate of neighborhood associations from the 1970s to the early 1980s that we saw in Chapter 1. Economist Masami Nomura points out that despite the decline in

A New Dual Structure

Figure 7.3 Net migration to the three major metropolitan areas and regional income gap ratio in the years 1955–1997

Notes: The unit of net migration is 1,000 persons (left axis). 'Regional income gap ratio' is the division of average income per capita of the best five prefectures by that of the worst five prefectures (right axis).
Source: Statistics Bureau, 'Annual report on internal migration' in Japan derived from the basic resident registration (for net migration) and NLBP 2006 (for the regional income gap ratio).

self-employment in the agricultural sector, the absolute number of self-employed workers remained stable until around 1980.[28] This happened because the increase in the manufacturing, commerce and other sectors offset the decrease among self-employed farmers. It was only from the 1980s that the number of farm households, including dual-income farmers, began to decline significantly, and that the self-employment sector began to shrink as a whole.

As we also saw in Chapter 1, among the self-employed as a whole, the number of family workers also shows a consistent decline while the number of the self-employed remained constant until the early 1980s. On the other hand, the number of employed workers continued to increase. In other words, until the 1970s, farm households and self-employed manufacturing and commerce households seem to have worked as 'whole-family' enterprises that provided workers by having children serve as employed workers, women as side-job part-time workers and heads of households as seasonal workers in large factories or construction sites who also held down jobs outside the home. As we saw in Chapter 1, Japanese government statistics have set the category of 'non-regular workers' since 1982, but even before that there were many part-time and seasonal workers.

However, the presence of these non-regular workers was not a major problem as long as the mutual support of self-employed households was maintained. Rather, the increase in dual employment increased the income of farm households. As a result of 'whole-family' labor patterns and the shift to dual employment, non-agricultural income had started to exceed farming income as a share of farm household income by 1964, and by the mid-1960s, farm household income began to exceed the household incomes of non-agricultural employed workers.[29] Per capita household expenses for farming households also began to exceed those of employed households in 1972.[30]

Meanwhile, the momentum of population movement to the three major metropolitan areas came to a halt in the early 1970s. By 1976, after significant layoffs of temporary workers and others in the wake of the oil crisis, the net population flow was actually moving from the three major metropolitan areas to the countryside. We saw earlier that Toyota used seasonal and temporary workers as a buffer against economic trends, but even if they were laid off, they had jobs if they returned to their hometowns in the 1970s. As discussed in Chapter 1, the reason Japan's unemployment rate did not rise after the oil shocks of the 1970s was not so much because of Japanese-style employment as because of the large supply of jobs *outside* the Japanese-style employment system. The rapid depopulation that had characterized the high-growth period was no longer apparent, and in 1979 the term '*chihō no jidai*' ('an era of regionalism') became a popular catchphrase.

Another reason why self-employed and SMEs were responsible for job growth in the 1970s was that public employment did not increase. Postwar reforms to Japan's public service sector turned prewar non-regular officials such as *koin* and *yonin* into regular public servants, and everyone was now appointed and paid based on years of service. However, that resulted in the increase of public sector salary costs, just like in the case of the regular employees at large companies. To address this, the Japanese government enacted the Total Personnel Act (*Sōteiin-hō*) in 1969 to ensure that the number of public servants did not

A New Dual Structure   355

increase.[31] As we saw in Chapter 1, the ratio of public-sector employment to total employment was 4.6% in Japan in 2021, the smallest among OECD countries and one-fourth of the OECD average. However, the local self-employed maintained neighborhood associations, organizing residents and cooperating with the local government to maintain social order, so there were few problems even given the small number of public servants.[32]

Owing to these developments, Japanese society entered a kind of homeostasis in the late 1970s. Although competition to secure places at good universities continued to intensify, the relative proportions of self-employed and large company employees appeared to have reached an equilibrium. Wage disparities between communities and annual income disparities between social classes were at their lowest around 1975, and the overall poverty rate was also falling.[33] It was during this era that phrases such as 'an all-middle-class society of a hundred million people' (*ichioku sōchūryū*) and the 'new middle class' (*shin chūkan taishū*) became popular, and Ezra Vogel summarized Japan's success during this period in his 1979 publication *Japan as Number One*.[34] In the Japan that Vogel portrayed, public investment had created stunning highways and modern factories, and the society enjoyed low unemployment rates, well-ordered schools, a small but highly efficient public sector, and the maintenance of local communities and social order.

However, this equilibrium was to be only temporary. After the 1980s, the number of self-employed people and the organization rate of the neighborhood associations began to decline, and the increase of non-regular workers who were not secured by the mutual support of households and local communities began to be problematic.

'Overeducation' and 'aging' of the workforce

Moreover, Japan's large companies had begun to feel the burden of the now expanded scope of Japanese-style employment. A particular problem in this regard was the wage costs incurred as a result of the number of university graduates being hired in companies and the increasing number of middle-aged and older workers. In December

1977, Nikkeiren established a subcommittee to examine the issue of the shift toward higher education and then in April of the following year another subcommittee to tackle the issue of the 'aging' labor force.[35] The 'aging' here referred only to the increase in the number of middle-aged staff employees who bring seniority-wage costs to large firms. This period saw the publication of several reports and books concerned with what they framed as the problem of an increasingly 'overeducated' and 'aging' workforce.

As mentioned in Chapter 2, according to the 1976 Labor White Paper, about 30% of university graduates working for large Japanese companies employing at least 1,000 people were promoted to section managers between the ages of forty-five and forty-nine, about 30% to the director level. If we also include deputy directors, this means that a total of about 70% had risen to at least the level of section manager or higher. The speed of promotion was also determined by the 'social norm rate' at large companies. This indicates that the prewar norms of promotion based on educational background and seniority remained strong.

Reflecting this, young employees with university degrees at the time entertained similar expectations. In a 1978 survey of young single university graduates, when asked to offer their predictions for the year 2000, when they would be in their forties, the majority replied that 40% of them would be section managers and just under 30% would be directors.[36]

Companies, however, were finding it difficult to increase the number of managers. At NKK, for example, between 1957 and 1977, the number of directors (*buchō*) had been increased by a factor of 5.3, the number of deputy directors (*jichō*) by a factor of 6.4 and the number of section managers (*kachō*) by a factor of 4.7. The proportion of male staff employees accounted for by managerial roles at the level of subsection chief (*kakarichō*) and above ballooned to 41.6% (Table 7.1).[37] One business text published in 1979 compared this situation to the game of *shōgi* (Japanese chess) under the title 'An Economy Without "Pawns"'.[38]

This increase in the number of management positions was supposedly controllable by selecting candidates on the basis of 'ability'

A New Dual Structure

Table 7.1 Increasing trends in management positions at Nippon Kōkan (1957–1977)

Year	1957		1965		1975		1977	
	Number of workers	%	Number of workers	%	Number of workers	%	Number of workers	%
Director	28	0.7	54	0.9	162	2.1	147	1.8
Deputy director	63	1.7	125	2.1	349	4.4	400	4.9
Section manager	250	6.7	524	8.8	936	11.9	1,181	14.4
Subsection chief	544	14.6	1,064	18.0	1,650	21.1	1,679	20.5
Total of managerial roles (increase rate)	885 (100)	23.7	1,767 (200)	29.8	3,097 (350)	39.5	3,407 (385)	41.6
Male staff employee	2,837	76.3	4,180	70.2	4,735	60.5	4,780	58.4
Total	3,722	100.0	5,947	100.0	7,832	100.0	8,187	100.0
Female staff employee	414		1,452		2,251		2,342	

Source: Kizaki (1978: 56).

through a competence ranking system. However, in a 1976 report of a survey of 213 companies, Zen-Noh-Ren's Center for Human Resource Development found that 'the prevailing trend in the management of labor is toward modification so as to take ability into account, but this has yet to fundamentally threaten the situation in which in-house hierarchies are still dominated by educational background and seniority'.[39]

Most commonly cited by companies as a reason for this was the difficulty of gauging employees' 'potential' to handle any job assignment, and 'the absence of any clear barometer of this other than educational background'.[40] According to a 1986 roundtable discussion of corporate personnel managers, the reality of the situation was that not promoting people according to their educational background and length of service risked compromising morale. As one participant remarked, 'although we call it ability, we create so many requirements around it that I think it is really only a pretext'.[41]

Situations like this have ironically led to responses that have increasingly reinforced Japanese-style employment. In a 1976 survey by Zen-Noh-Ren, when companies were asked how they would respond to a shortage of posts (with multiple answers allowed), 39.2% answered 'position rotation' such as regular personnel transfers, and 63.9% answered 'adopt a ranking system' whereby promotions would be by rank, rather than position.[42] Looking at the spread of competence

358   Chapter 7

Table 7.2 Cumulative timeline of the introduction of competence ranking systems

Year	Prior to 1954	1955–64	1965–69	1970–74	1975–79	After 1980
5,000 or more workers	17.3	40.8	58.1	75.2	95.0	97.5
Manufacturing among them	17.6	49.0	60.8	74.5	96.1	96.1
1,000–4,999 workers	10.5	27.6	48.9	69.3	87.9	98.7
300–900 workers	4.2	13.6	28.9	52.9	78.6	98.7

Source: Data from General Research Institute for Employment and Trades, Employment Promotion Projects Corporation (Koyō Sokushin Jigyō-Dan Koyō Shokugyō Sōgō Kenkyūjo) (1984) Survey Report on Ranking Systems (Shikaku seido ni kan suru chōsa hōkokusho), January 1984, compiled by Kagiyama (1989: 111).

ranking systems, we can see that they began to be more prevalent from the 1970s, when university graduates hired during the high-growth period would have reached their thirties (Table 7.2). Nevertheless, this never became a fundamental solution for companies. Functional ranking systems, in which promotions are given by rank (e.g., a naval rank of captain) rather than position (e.g., captain of a warship), do indeed reduce the number of managers, at least nominally. However, if wages are based on ranks, this will only increase the number of highly paid people without positions, and will do nothing to rein in wage costs.

A stronger role for personnel evaluations

As a counter to this trend, companies began placing a stronger emphasis on personnel evaluations. That is, they sought to rigorously select and limit the number of people eligible for promotions and seniority-based wages.

The Japanese personnel evaluation system was characterized by the fact that it covered all employees, including shop-floor workers and lower-level clerical staff, and by its emphasis on personality evaluation. In Japanese-style employment, all employees have opportunities for promotion and salary increases, so all employees must be assessed in order to reduce wage costs. In addition, in Japanese-style employment, where personnel transfers occur frequently, personality evaluation is emphasized.

A New Dual Structure

According to a 1979 survey by the Japan Recruit Center, personnel evaluations were being conducted at 93% of firms surveyed to assess eligibility for salary increases, promotions and bonuses. Ninety-two percent of the companies evaluated individual performance, 80% evaluated functional competence (*shokumu suikō nōryoku*) and 76% evaluated the attitudes and character of their employees.[43]

The actual facts with regard to personnel evaluations are difficult to investigate, in part because few companies make such information public. In 1989, labor economist Makoto Kumazawa conducted a survey of the actual situation with regard to personnel evaluation in so far as it could be assessed based on various media reports, public documents and evaluation sheets collected with the cooperation of workers. Taking an example from the 1986 *Jinjikōka jirei-shū* (Personnel Evaluation Casebook) edited by the Industrial Labor Survey Institute, Kumazawa described the following evaluation criteria used by Renown, a clothing manufacturer.

- Conformity: (a) Frequency of instances of tardiness, leaving early and absenteeism; (b) Violation of company rules or refusal to obey orders without justifiable reason; (c) Neat and proper attire and grooming; (d) Wearing uniforms and name tags; (e) Idle talk or unauthorized absences from the office during office hours; (f) Responding with alacrity and using appropriate language as a working professional; (g) Politeness in the workplace; (h) Ability to distinguish between public and private matters on the job; (i) Behavior in private life that may reflect badly on the company; (j) Careful attention to health and safety and disaster prevention in the workplace; (k) Respect for voluntary rules in the workplace.
- Responsibility: (a) Makes efforts to confirm uncertainties about work through study or asking questions; (b) Keeps promises to concerned parties inside and outside the company; (c) Makes efforts to complete assigned tasks by the deadline; (d) Takes early action when timely completion seems unlikely; (e) Conceals any personal inconveniences.

- Proactivity: (a) Offers opinions and ideas on work procedure and methods; (b) Makes efforts to expand scope of expertise in terms of both quantity and quality, as and when the situation allows; (c) Studies to improve one's abilities at work.
- Cooperativity: (a) Assists superiors and subordinates with their work needs; (b) Participates in work as a member of the team; (c) Shows consideration for the convenience of co-workers engaged in related tasks; (d) Makes effort to cooperate with team members to create a cheerful and comfortable work environment without emotional tension, even with people of different personalities and ways of thinking.[44]

Based on these desiderata, employees' direct supervisors grade each individual and assign them an overall rating of A to E and also write down their own observations (Figure 7.4). According to the aforementioned 1979 survey by the Japan Recruitment Center, with respect to the basis for the five-point evaluation, 30% of large companies assigned an absolute rating, 20% a relative rating and 45% a combination of the two. Nevertheless, in terms of salary increases and bonuses, it was reported that many companies had a fixed system, such as, for example, 'A and E are 5% each for individuals holding the same qualifications, B and D are 15% each [...] C is 60%', and that 'A's bonus payment is twice that of E'.[45]

In Japan, it is customary for all regular employees to receive bonuses equivalent to one to three months of salary in June and December, i.e., 10 to 30% of their annual wage, and the size of this ratio determined by management's discretion facilitated wage adjustments. The bonus was a privilege mostly reserved for staff employees before the war, but after the war the privilege was extended to all 'company employees' and has not been available to non-regular workers. In the 1970s, large Japanese firms came to avoid laying off regular employees even in a recession, but they lowered wages by assessing each individual and reducing bonuses and ability pay for each, even while base pay based on years of service and educational background were fixed.[46] Japanese labor unions also accepted these wage decreases in favor of maintaining employment.

A New Dual Structure

Figure 7.4 Personnel evaluation form for a worker at Misawa Homes Co., Ltd. (1987)

Attitudes	Responsibility	4
	Cooperativity	3
	Conformity	4
	Proactivity	3
Abilities	Expertise	4
	Planning ability	3
	Judgement	3
	Leadership	3
	Public relations	3
	Management ability	3
Performances	Goal achievement level	6
	Efficiency	6
	Project management	6
	Difficulty level	8
	Originality and ingenuity	6
	Total	65
	Overall rating	C

Findings by primary evaluator: The worker has a strong sense of responsibility and is well disciplined. I hope that the worker will also develop their own skills in planning and public relations.

Findings by secondary evaluator: I like the fact that the worker is shedding the professional idiocy that is often seen in technicians. I also like the positive attitude. I have high expectations for future growth.

Transfer: I'd like to transfer the employee over the next year or so.

Note: Evaluations are on a five-point scale each for attitude and ability and a ten-point scale for performance. The overall rating is indicated as A = outstanding, B = excellent, C = satisfactory, D = somewhat lacking, and E = insufficient.
Source: *Asahi Shinbun*, Tokyo version, evening edition, 6 December 1987, p. 13.

Thus, employees were subject to observation over the long term, with evaluations being conducted not only with respect to their performance, but their personalities as well. Furthermore, many companies had their rank-and-file employees set self-reported goals during meetings with their supervisors at the beginning of each fiscal period, such as for example 'increasing sales by 7% to 8% over the past year', or 'developing ten new customers'. In the majority of cases, employees were not able to access their evaluations. A 1986 survey by the Japan Industry and Labor Research Institute (*Sangyō rōdō chōsasho*) found that only 32% of large companies had adopted systems where the results of evaluations were made available to the employees themselves.[47]

Employees were assessed according to such performance evaluation sheets and then promoted with ranks such as '2nd-class company employee' (*shain-2-kyū*) or '3rd-class manager' (*shuji-3-kyū*). As a part of this, the relative proportion of 'ability pay', which had been minor during the period that followed immediately after Japan's wartime defeat, now increased significantly. In 1988, Nippon Steel increased the ratio of broadly defined ability pay to 60%.[48]

In the US and Western Europe, laborers and lower-level salaried employees, especially unionized workers, were generally not evaluated, and goal-based management was likewise generally only applied to high-level salaried employees. Also, as discussed in Chapter 4, assessments that emphasized the workers' 'traits' were disregarded through the efforts of the anti-discrimination movement.

Then, the norm among Japanese companies of assessing even shop-floor workers meant that all employees were treated like high-level staff employees. As mentioned in Chapter 2, Japanese management scholar Naohiro Yashiro points out that a characteristic of Japanese companies is that they demand all regular employees adopt the working style of Western elites. Kumazawa characterizes this as 'class-blind ability-based egalitarianism'.[49] In other words, as discussed in Chapter 6, company employees became equal in the sense that management's assessment was applied without discrimination. As I noted in Chapter 2, since the end of the 1960s, there has been an increasing tendency in Japanese companies for promotions to be determined more by hard work on the company's behalf than by educational background.

At the same time, however, many offered the criticism that such personnel evaluations negatively impacted union activism and employees' activities outside the company, and were used to bust unions. In addition, 'ability-based egalitarianism' gave rise to intense competition, a phenomenon comparable to that seen in education. Kumazawa points out the similarity between personnel evaluations and school applications in Japan, writing that, 'school transcripts include not only students' grades in various subjects, but also a record and evaluation of their conduct. I would be curious to know whether companies look closely at transcripts when hiring [new graduates]'.[50]

Educational sociologist Takehiko Kariya has actually conducted such a survey. Based on data from various surveys, including a 1983 school survey of school officials charged with facilitating graduating students' transition to the workplace at 2,345 schools nationwide and

A New Dual Structure   363

student surveys conducted in 1983 and 1984 that focused on the career choices of 2,899 high school students in the Kantō region, Kariya found that the job placement of high school graduates who find employment through school referrals is influenced by school grades, attendance and participation in school activities. In particular, students with grades in the top five of their class had a significantly higher chance of getting a salaried staff job at a large company.[51] No such trends were evident in the employment of high school graduates in the UK or US, which Kariya used as cases for comparison.

Companies' creation of 'external' categories

As well as rigorous selections through personnel evaluations, another response for companies was to create employment categories that lay 'outside' the scope of 'equality of company employees'. Specifically, these included secondment (external transfer, *shukkō*), non-regular workers and women. Let's discuss each of these in turn.

In the 1977 Zen-Noh-Ren survey mentioned earlier, 36.1% of all companies and 38.7% of manufacturing companies in particular cited 'external transfer to affiliates' as a suitable response to the shortage of posts.[52] As mentioned in Chapter 2, since it was not possible to find positions for all university graduate hires, it was necessary to transfer middle-aged and older employees who had been working for the company for twenty years or more and who no longer had any prospect of promotion to a subsidiary or affiliate as a form of indirect job retention. In the case of 'permanent external transfer', the employee leaves large company A and becomes an employee of affiliated small- and medium sized company B. This is similar to the way government agencies used public corporations and public foundations as postings for senior bureaucrats, a practice known as *amakudari* (descent from heaven) as we saw in Chapter 6.

Secondments and 'permanent external transfers' to affiliates were used not only to address the shortage of positions for middle-aged and older university-educated workers, but also to maintain employment for shop-floor workers. In 1978, Nikkeiren proposed 'lifetime employment in the broader sense' that included selective mandatory retirement and inter-company transfers. Likewise, in 1979, the Kansai Association of Corporate Executives (*Kansai Keizai Dōyūkai*) also advocated 'a system of lifetime employment in the broader area' that included transfers outside the company.[53]

From the 1970s onward, major companies began to actively pursue diversification strategies through the creation of spin-offs and subsidiary firms. According to surveys conducted in 1987 and 1988 by the General Research Institute for Employment and Trades (*Shokugyō Sōgō Kenkyūjo*), 60% of exchange listed companies had increased their number of affiliates over the previous five years. In addition, more than 90% of 'parent' companies employing 1,000 people or more indicated that they had seconded their employees to their affiliates.[54]

Labor unions were willing to accept such secondments and external transferss in the interests of maintaining employment. The labor union at Hitachi had demanded a system of prior consultation with regard to transfers and secondments in the 1960s, but by the time its collective agreement was revised in 1982, this issue had been struck from the list of demands for revision in the union's official newsletter.[55]

The increase in secondments and transfers led to an increase in relocation assignments (*tenkin*) and single-posting (*tanshin funin*) transfers away from home. The Employment Status Survey for 1987 indicated the presence of approximately 420,000 *tanshin funin* employees, nearly two-thirds of whom were middle-aged or older male workers between the ages of thirty-five and fifty-four. According to a survey conducted by the Ministry of Labor in 1990 (which allowed for multiple responses), the most common reason of workers for choosing *tanshin funin* was 'children's education and entrance exams' (85.1%), and the burden of the increase in household budgets incurred to support the *tanshin funin* member was estimated at about 100,000 yen per month, while the minimum wage per hour in Tokyo was 548 yen.[56]

The second response was a reliance on non-regular employment. Steps in this direction had already been taken in the 1960s with the introduction of 'outside workers' (*shagai-kō*) from affiliated SMEs contracted on a temporary basis, seasonal workers from rural villages and middle-aged women working in part-time roles.[57] In 1976, the Kantō Employers' Association announced a series of employment

A New Dual Structure 365

adjustments based on a policy of the successive liquidation of workers with weak ties to the company. First, part-time and temporary workers and seasonal laborers were to be eliminated, followed by a hiring freeze and suspension of filling any vacancies, then the reassignment, secondment, permanent external transfer and furlough of current employees, and finally, if further measures were necessary, the solicitation of volunteers for early retirement.[58]

Dispatch workers also joined the mix. In October 1984, the Japan Association of Corporate Executives (Keizai Dōyūkai) proposed the idea of an 'intermediate labor market', which it described as 'an intermediate cushion in both the market and the firm', and advocated 'the new business of temporary staffing' in certain specialist job categories (e.g., microelectronics engineer) as well as the utilization of 'the older workers and female labor force (especially housewives)' as non-regular workers. In July 1986, the Act for Securing the Proper Operation of Worker Dispatching Undertakings and Improved Working Conditions for Dispatched Workers (*Rōdōsha haken hō*, generally called the Worker Dispatch Act in English) was enacted for a limited number of thirteen job categories, which was expanded to sixteen three months later.[59]

The third response was the 'utilization' of women. As noted in the previous chapter, the introduction of gender-based retirement schemes became prevalent during the high-growth period. Successful lawsuits by women against such schemes, and losses on the part of companies, made overt gender-based retirement systems illegal, but the practice remained customary, nevertheless. As mentioned above, in 1977, a personnel manager at NKK prepared a chart showing the increase in management positions (Table 7.1). The chart, however, only calculated the percentage of management positions held by male company employees; women were excluded from the outset.

After the ratification of the Convention on Elimination of All forms of Discrimination Against Women and the enactment of the Equal Employment Opportunity Law in May 1985, an increasing number of companies introduced the 'course' classification of career-track (*sōgō-shoku*) and general office positions (*ippan-shoku*) in hiring new graduates. According to a survey conducted by the Ministry of Labor

366   Chapter 7

in October 1992, 49.3% of companies with 5,000 or more employees had introduced course-based management, which differentiated employee management based on their presumed career path.[60] Women employed in general office positions were expected to retire upon marriage. Then, in the 1990s, these positions were filled by dispatched workers. As stated by the manager of a financial institution in 1985, 'The essence of competence ranking systems is that total upward mobility [by educational background and seniority] is their sole philosophy [...]. The reason they have not collapsed thus far is that women have generally left at the age of twenty-five or twenty-six'.[61]

Seniority-based promotions and pay raises were originally the norm for civil officials, basically independent of their economic cost, and in the prewar private sector were the exclusive privilege of a small minority of staff employees. It was not feasible to apply these norms to all employees, save in exceptional periods such as the period of rapid economic growth. Even so, if long-term employment and seniority-based wages were to continue, the only way to proceed would be to limit those who were eligible to core workers. The way that this would be achieved was via the careful selection of employees through personnel evaluations, and the creation of an 'external' category of secondment, non-regular employment and women.

Simultaneous emergence of dismissal regulations and non-regular workers

It is worth remembering that until the 1970s, there was no generic term for these various forms of employment. I conducted a keyword search of journal articles at the National Diet Library, and found that the term 'non-regular' (*hi-seiki*) was mainly used in the context of statistical terms such as 'non-regular distribution' until the 1970s. The term 'non-regular workers' first appeared in journals in 1981.[62] As mentioned in Chapter 1, Japanese government statistics established the category of 'non-regular workers' in 1982.

Originally, factory workers in the prewar period were not eligible for long-term employment or seniority-based wages. Then, during Japan's period of rapid economic growth, the scope of long-term

A New Dual Structure

employment expanded to encompass shop-floor workers as well. The fact that 'non-regular' became the umbrella term for the leftover of the workforce indicates that long-term employment and seniority-based wages, which had been the preserve of the privileged few before the war, came to be regarded as the 'regular' norm by the 1970s, by which point quantitative expansion had already ceased.

The term 'non-regular workers' appeared around 1980, about the same time that the 1979 Tokyo High Court decision legislated restrictions on layoffs in Japan.[63] As we saw in Chapter 2, Japanese dismissal regulations are not explicitly stated in law, but are institutionalized by precedents that emphasize 'social norms'. This situation was shaped by the postwar labor union and litigation movements.

The Japanese Civil Code enacted in 1896 placed no restrictions on dismissing workers on employment contracts with no fixed term, aside from giving two weeks' notice. After the World War II, the Labor Union Act (*Rōdō kumiai-hō*) was enacted in 1945 followed by the Labor Standards Act (*Rōdō kijun-hō*) in 1947, which excluded reasons such as membership or activities in labor unions as grounds for dismissal, as well as reasons such as nationality, creed or social status, but the principle of free dismissal remained unchanged.[64] Therefore, as mentioned in Chapter 5, large companies' experience of mass layoffs and major disputes in the 1950s led to the entrenchment of long-term employment as a norm.

This was only a norm, however, with no basis in law, and nor did it extend to SMEs without unions. In SMEs that had no labor unions, however, arbitrary dismissals by management were rife. Since labor unions in Japan are enterprise unions, there is a large difference in the union density depending on the size of the company. According to a 1992 government survey, the union density was 57.2% for companies with 1,000 employees or more, while the rate for companies with fewer than 100 employees was only 1.8%.[65] After workers laid off by SMEs responded by bringing lawsuits against their former employees, several court decisions from 1975 to 1979 imposed limits to restrict employers' abuse of their right to dismiss. The upshot of these decisions was that efforts such as reassignments and the suspension of new hires must be made prior to any employee reductions, that the selection of those to be laid off must be fair, and that any measures must be subject to negotiations and consultations between labor and management.[66]

As we saw in Chapter 2, although in practice it remained difficult to realize long-term employment and seniority-based wages in SMEs, for regular employees, these precedents put a stop to employers' abuse of their right to dismiss. The term 'non-regular workers' appeared in the media and government statistics as the umbrella term covering temporary workers, part-timers and others shortly after a series of such rulings established restrictions on the dismissal of regular employees.

The establishment of the dismissal restrictions was not only the establishment of non-regular workers, but also the legalization of personnel transfers and the relocation assignment of regular employees. In a series of dismissal regulations, the Supreme Court granted companies extensive freedom in connection with hiring new employees and transferring personnel. As described in Chapter 2, the Supreme Court ruled in favor of companies in several lawsuits, including a company's refusal to hire on the basis of political beliefs (1973), the dismissal of a worker who refused to comply with a relocation (1986) and the transferring of workers to a different job category (1989). In essence, the Supreme Court established regulations for the dismissal of workers once they were hired as regular employees, but left companies free to decide whether or not to hire them as regular employees in the first place, as well as how they would be transferred or relocated within the company.

As we saw in the last section, in 1976, the Kantō Employers' Association announced a policy of employment adjustments. First, part-time and temporary workers and seasonal laborers were to be eliminated, followed by a hiring freeze of new graduates, then the reassignment and transfer of current regular employees and the solicitation of volunteers for early retirement. The dismissal of regular employees was to be a last measure. A series of court decisions were consistent with this policy, and regular employees were forced to accept transfers and relocations. Non-regular workers were those who did not have to accept transfers or relocations, but who could not help

A New Dual Structure

but be laid off. Regular employees and non-regular workers in Japan were established as such around 1980.

Debate over a new dual structure

Since the legal precedent restricting the dismissal of regular employees, companies and local governments have increasingly relied on non-regular workers. This trend started with SMEs, which had less leeway in adjusting to economic shifts than Japan's large companies.

Then, in the 1980s, debate arose over the idea of a new dual structure paradigm. The dual structure of the 1950s was characterized by a division between large companies and SMEs. In the 1980s, however, the debate concerned the emergence of a new dual structure comprised of regular employees on one tier, and non-regular workers on the other.

The old dual structure was said to have been ameliorated during the period of rapid growth. One reason for this was that the bulk recruitment of high school and junior high school graduates by large companies forced SMEs to raise starting salaries for new graduates, narrowing the gap between large companies and SMEs in this respect. Another reason was that the number of SMEs that received stable subcontracting orders from large companies was also on the rise. The 1970 edition of the White Paper on Small and Medium Enterprises in Japan (hereinafter, 'SME White Paper') positioned the situation of SMEs as having 'greatly improved on the whole'.[67]

After the period of rapid growth had drawn to a close, however, the wage gap between companies of different sizes began to widen once more. The gaps between large companies and SMEs for value added per employee and for annual labor costs in the Corporate Statistics Yearbook (*Hōjin kigyō tōkei nenkan*) reached a minimum in 1975, since which time they have continued to widen.[68] Nevertheless, the 1980 edition of the SME White Paper did not change its view that the 'former dual structure' had been 'relatively weakened by the transition to a labor shortage economy after 1960'.[69]

The position taken by the SME White Paper and the Labor White Paper of this era was that wage disparities based on company size were merely superficial.[70] On average, large companies and SMEs have different labor force compositions in terms of variables such as age, level of education, gender and length of service. Level of education and length of service are reflections of workers' productivity and skill levels. Accordingly, this meant that SMEs had lower apparent average wages. A 1985 report by the Economic Planning Agency expressed this more directly, explaining as follows:

> Small enterprises have more workers with fewer years of service and less education, as well as more female workers than large companies, which increases the apparent wage gap [...]. The wage gap between large firms and SMEs has been significantly reduced by bringing worker composition into line, with its size peaking at 16.3% between large companies and small firms in 1983.[71]

In other words, if we compare only men with the same education and the same length of service, differences in terms of company size are minor.

In contrast, some economists argued that this was indeed a new dual structure. A debate among economists over the existence of a dual structure took place in the pages of the popular economics press in 1982.[72] Economist Ryōji Takata argued that the relative strength of the presence of middle-aged and older women and older workers in the labor force composition of SMEs indicated that those who had been positioned as the peripheral labor force in the 1950s dual structure paradigm (see Chapter 1) had flowed over into SMEs as low-wage workers. Furthermore, Takata noted that only 12.4% of those who changed jobs during the one-year period from October 1981 moved from companies with less than 300 employees to companies with 300 or more employees. Takata's argument was that with the labor market in large firms thus closed and in the absence of perfect competition, it would be a mistake to explain the wage gap by differences in labor force compositions.[73]

According to Takata's analysis, large companies responded to the recession after the oil crisis with employment adjustments such as the dismissal of temporary workers, the implementation of hiring freezes and the secondment and transfer of regular employees. However,

A New Dual Structure

measures like this were not available to SMEs, whose efforts to rein in labor costs led to an increase in the number of part-time workers.[74] When a series of court decisions in the 1970s made it more difficult for SMEs to lay off regular employees, the use of part-time workers by SMEs went even further. In fact, of the 3.06 million women in short-term employment in 1985, 56.5% worked for companies with fewer than thirty employees, and only 16.7% at companies with 500 or more employees.[75] During this period, large companies had not yet begun to take advantage of non-regular employment on a large scale, but non-regular workers were increasingly common in SMEs where total labor costs were limited.

This fact was also recognized in the 1985 Economic Planning Agency report, though its evaluation of the situation was quite different, as follows.

> While large companies were hesitant to introduce low-priced labor such as female and student part-timers [*paat* and *arubaito*], SMEs, which have more flexibility, moved ahead with the introduction of low-priced labor. The result of this, as it happens, has been reflected in the wages of SMEs, thereby widening the wage gap between large companies and SMEs; it does not follow that there has been any re-division of the labor market between large and small enterprises.[76]

Even so, as cited in Chapter 1, despite the report's insistence that the dual structure of large companies and SMEs had disappeared, it did acknowledge that 'the dual structure of today's labor market consists of an internal labor market, which is highly entrenched, and an external labor market, which is highly liquid but unskilled and low-paid'. At the same time, however, it was also informed by a basic awareness that 'the three main groups of low-wage earners today – women part-timers, the aged and young people who are not regular employees – have core incomes from their husbands, pensions and parents, respectively, and in most cases have no need to work to make ends meet'.[77]

Thus, despite these differing evaluations, it was recognized that a 'new dual structure' of regular employees and non-regular workers had emerged in the 1980s. This, as the Economic Planning Agency report stated, was distinct from the former dual structure that had existed between large companies and SMEs. It came into being as the principle of 'equality of company employees' expanded into medium-sized firms.

From self-employment to the non-regular workforce

The low cost of SMEs was also supporting the competitiveness of large firms, particularly in the manufacturing sector of the 1980s. The shift to affiliated SMEs accelerated during the period of rapid growth. By 1981, 65.5% of manufacturing SMEs with fewer than 300 employees had begun subcontracting from larger firms.[78]

Many factories that were dispersed to rural areas in the 1960s and 1970s were labor-intensive subcontracting companies that supplied parts to the metropolitan industrialized areas. According to a 1984 survey by the Institute for Economic Research of Chūō University (IERC) on Aoki village in Nagano prefecture, there were twenty-nine subcontracting manufacturing companies in Aoki. The breakdown was thirteen for automobile parts, eight for electric appliances, four for general equipment, two for communications equipment and two others. Among the twenty-nine companies, the largest had seventy employees, sixteen had five to fifty, twelve had fewer than five and many workers in those with less than five were family members. Of the employed workers of all companies, 69.5% were females and most of them were women aged thirty-five and above from farming households.[79] The IERC also estimated the wage gap of Hitachi and its subcontracting companies in 1975. Whereas the 'minute-unit' price of a processing wage at the Hitachi parent plant was 45 yen, the unit price received by primary subcontractors was between 18 and 20 yen, then 10 yen for secondary subcontractors, and 7 yen for tertiary subcontractors. Even further down the chain, the rate for pieceworkers at home was 2 to 3 yen.[80]

In the late 1980s, General Motors in the US had about 800,000 employees and produced about five million passenger automobiles per year. By contrast, Toyota had about 70,000 employees and produced

A New Dual Structure

about four million a year. Whereas GM produced about 70% of its automobile parts in-house, Toyota produced most of its parts through a group of about 270 subcontractors. At the time, Toyota had an in-house parts production rate of 20–30%, as did other Japanese automakers through the 1980s.[81] Circumstances might have been different if the parts had been produced by workers earning the wages being paid at Toyota proper, or if Toyota and its subcontractors had been organized into industry-wide labor unions and paid equal wages for equal work. At that time, however, regular employees at large companies were, in a manner of speaking, poised at the pinnacle of the Japanese-style order.

The heyday of Japanese manufacturing did not last long, however, as the Plaza Accord of 1985 doubled the value of the yen against the US dollar, and China's entry into the global market began to gain momentum in the 1990s. The number of workers in the manufacturing sector, as shown in the Labor Force Survey, peaked at 16.0 million in October 1992, then dropped to 10.6 million in October 2009. It has remained virtually unchanged since then, standing at 10.6 million in June 2023. This is the same as the 10.6 million recorded in August 1961, meaning that the number of manufacturing workers in Japan has declined by about two-thirds from its peak to the level of the early 1960s.

However, this decrease was greater on the outside of the Japanese-style employment system. According to the Japanese government's Survey of Establishments and Enterprises and Economic Census, the number of privately owned manufacturing establishments declined from 1986, the year after the Plaza Accord. The rate of decline was greater for smaller establishments, such as those found in Aoki village, with those with one to nine employees decreasing to 55.5% of the 1986 level in 2014. A 1994 hearing survey by the Small and Medium Enterprise Research Institute records such testimonies from owners of subcontracting SMEs. 'The parent company is demanding price reductions of 10% to a maximum of 30%, citing the strong yen and the difference between domestic and foreign [Chinese] prices, and we are not sure what to do' and 'We are now receiving only 60% of the unit sales price compared to before. We are compared to overseas unit prices, and it has become a matter of course to downgrade the quotations we provide to our customers by 30% or 40% compared to before'.[82]

The decline in the number of small manufacturing firms was also facilitated by technological advances. The development of digital technology led to the extensive use of high-precision machine tools, which increased the initial investment costs required to start a small-scale manufacturing firm. According to a field survey of SMEs, until the 1980s, Japanese die and mold manufacturers were said to be able to start a business with a single skilled worker using a second-hand milling machine, but by the 2010s, the initial investment was said to be 'at least 100 million yen'.[83] The decline in the number of small businesses without investment capacity was also evident in commerce. The number of retail stores peaked in 1982 and declined to 57.5% of its 1982 numbers in 2016, and 30.9% for stores with two or fewer workers.[84] It is estimated that self-employed or micro-manufacturing and commercial households became non-regular workers, first for the women in the household and then for the men who headed the household.[85]

The impact of the decline in manufacturing employment was greater for women than for men. In the case of Aoki village in 1984, 69.5% of the employed workers of all surveyed manufacturing SMEs were females and most of them were women aged thirty-five and above. According to the National Census, manufacturing employment declined from 8.4 million men and 4.7 million women in 1995 to 6.6 million men and 2.9 million women in 2015. The decline was 21.3% for men and 38.8% for women.[86] The share of the manufacturing sector among all employed persons decreased slightly from 21.8% to 20.0% for men, but the decrease was greater for women, from 18.5% to 11.4%. In terms of the share of health and welfare (the sector where labor demand is increasing with the aging of the population) among all employed persons, the increase for men was from 2.3% to 5.1%, while the increase for women was from 10.6% to 20.6%. The shift from manufacturing to elder care was much larger for women.

On the other hand, non-regular employment in the service industry has increased since the 1980s in a different context. According to the 2020 Small Enterprises White Paper by the SME Agency of the Japanese government, there is a large disparity in labor productivity and wages

A New Dual Structure 375

between the size of companies in the manufacturing and construction industries, while the disparity between the size of companies in the retail industry and the service industry such as food services and accommodation is small.[87] The manufacturing and construction industries are known for their multiple subcontracting structure. On the other hand, according to the Cabinet Office's Annual Economic and Fiscal Report 2006, the ratio of non-regular employment to the regular workforce is low in the former and high in the latter.[88] In other words, as a way of procuring low-wage labor, from the 1980s the former has adopted a strategy of utilizing workers from SMEs as subcontractors, while the latter adopted a strategy of utilizing non-regular workers.[89]

Also, as noted in Chapter 1, the number of self-employed and family workers declined while the number of non-regular workers increased. As the number of regular employees at large companies stopped expanding, a shift in the labor force seems to have been taking place from the self-employment sector to non-regular employment. This reality was obfuscated by the economic climate of the 1980s, however. It was only after the bubble economy ended in 1991 that the growth of non-regular employment began to attract attention.

Rising university enrollment and non-regular employment

The 1990s also saw renewed growth in university enrollment. Unlike the situation in the 1960s, however, this increase was not accompanied by a corresponding rise in regular employment.

The increase in enrollment began in 1986, when the government eased the cap on the number of students at private universities and junior colleges in anticipation of the large number of 'baby boomer juniors' who were expected to pursue to higher education (see Chapter 1). The number of university graduates increased as new universities were established, more faculties were added to existing universities and junior colleges and other institutions were converted to four-year universities.[90]

Since the 1970s, there have always been lots of people aspiring to pursue higher education, even though university capacities have been controlled. Moreover, as discussed in Chapter 1, between March 1992 and March 2003, the number of jobs available for high school graduates plummeted to almost one-third of their former levels. As a result, what took place in the 1990s was a simultaneous increase in non-regular employment among young people and a rise in the university enrollment rate. Also, as noted in Chapter 1, a 1985 report by the Economic Planning Agency predicted that a significant portion of the 'second-generation baby boomers' unable to enter the internal labor market may be forced to work in the external labor market.

As had been the case in the 1970s, those most disadvantaged by this steep decline in high school graduate employment were the graduates of low-ranking general high schools. According to Mary Brinton's study of twenty public low-ranking schools in Kanagawa and Miyagi prefectures in the mid-1990s, although school-based employment referrals were still practiced at vocational high schools, at the general high schools, as many as 30 or 40 % of graduating seniors neither went into jobs nor higher education.[91]

Pursuing a university education no longer had the same significance that it once did. Educational sociologist Hirokazu Ōuchi relates a story he heard from 'a counselor at a certain public university' about a student who enrolled in the school even though he could not afford the tuition or living expenses. When the counselor asked the student why, then, had he enrolled at the school, the student replied, 'Because I was the seventh highest student in my class'. At the high school from which this student had graduated, only the top five students would receive employment referrals, and thus, with no job, he had had no choice but to pursue higher education.[92]

Educational researcher Akio Inui, describing the situation in the late 1970s and 80s, stated in 1991 that 'special training schools and miscellaneous schools function in large part as a pool for semi-unemployed youth' and that 'a certain portion of graduates from special training schools, miscellaneous schools, and vocational high school graduates are being recruited into the "flow-type" labor market that includes temporary dispatch workers'.[93] In the 1990s and 2000s, graduates of non-prestigious universities found themselves in the same situation. Even though university capacity restrictions had been

A New Dual Structure 377

relaxed and more people were pursuing higher education, Japanese society was still not in a position to absorb them.

The number of non-regular workers increased not only in the private sector but also in the public sector. The 1969 Total Personnel Act limited the number of regular national public servants with guaranteed seniority salaries and long-term appointment, and further limited the number of regular local government public servants under the guidance of the central government. Although the increase in the number of non-regular public servants in local governments had been pointed out in a survey by the All-Japan Prefectural and Municipal Workers Union (*Jichirō*), it was not until 2005 that the Ministry of Internal Affairs and Communications conducted its first survey. In the 2005 survey, non-regular public servants accounted for 13.0% of all public servants in local governments. In the 2012 survey, the percentage increased to 17.9%, and 74.2% of non-regular public servants were women. In the survey, temporary public servants differed from the regulars by only thirty minutes per week on average in working hours, but their annual income was 23 to 27% of the regulars'. One of the reasons for the salary disparity was that bonuses, which are a privilege of regulars and account for 26.0% of their annual income, are not given to non-regulars.[94] According to a 2020 Ministry of Internal Affairs and Communications survey, the rate of non-regular public servants in local governments accounted for 20.1%, while in towns and villages it was 37.0%, and 32.1% in cities and wards.[95]

Japanese-style management remains unchanged

On the other hand, the series of Japanese employment norms has not fundamentally changed since this point. What has changed since the 1990s is that the scope of those to whom the principle of 'equality of company employees' does not apply has widened, in addition to a strengthening of the restrictions on eligibility for seniority-based wages through more rigorous selection criteria.

In 1995, Nikkeiren published a report entitled '"Japanese-style Management" for a New Era' (*Shin jidai no 'Nihon-teki keiei'*). This report is widely known among Japanese researchers on account of its advocacy of an 'employment portfolio' that divides employees into three groups: those making use of skills accumulated over the long term, those making use of highly specialized skills and those characterized by flexible employment. In the 2000s, it was said that this report's introduction of the 'flexible employment type' marked the beginning of the rise of non-regular employment.

For all that, as we have already seen, the increase in the number of non-regular workers had been a major trend among SMEs since the 1980s and had been advocated by the business world as well. In a seminar held in Karuizawa in August 1992, Nikkeiren had already proposed two types of workers: 'stock-type' employees who were premised on long-term employment, and 'flow-type' employees who consisted largely of housewives and older people.[96] In addition, the 1995 report did not advocate any reform to Japanese-style employment. Rather, it contrasted the Japanese model with Western companies in the following manner.

> Western companies have at their base a functional organization, wherein people are assigned to organizations and posts. In Japan, people are not assigned to organizations; rather, these organizations are run to maximize the abilities of each individual member. We should focus on the concept based on a person-centered (i.e., respectful) philosophy based on stability of employment, job satisfaction, improvement of ability and in-house promotion – one that leads to good labor-management relations and supports "management from a long-term perspective".[97]

As we saw in Chapter 6, Japanese management has preferred the description 'person-centric hierarchical order' when they contrast the Japanese-style employment system to those of Western countries. The central argument of the report concerned control over the overall cost of personnel. As a means of achieving this, it advocated not only the use of 'flexible employment', but also the introduction of a small number of elite workers of the first type (who made use of skills accumulated over the long term) through competence ranking systems and goal-oriented management systems, and of the second type (who made use

A New Dual Structure 379

of highly specialized skills) through dispatch placement contracts of about three years in length.[98] As we have already seen, these were all policies implemented or at least advocated by the business community through the 1970s and 1980s. Arguably, the gist of the intention behind this report was to limit the portion of employees eligible for Japanese-style employment without changing it, and to systematize policies that had already been established.

In subsequent years, the business world increasingly emphasized the downsides of seniority-based wages and lifetime employment, in large part because regular employees at large companies who were hired as new graduates during the high-growth period in the 1960s and the bubble era in the late 1980s had reached middle age in the late 1990s and wage costs had become so burdensome. However, the basic policy of limiting these elements to core employees without modifying Japanese-style employment remained unchanged.

Certainly, the business community proposed various reforms. In December 2000, for example, Nikkeiren's Special International Committee issued a report entitled 'Innovation of Japanese-style Personnel Systems in Response to the Globalization of Management: On the White-Collar Personnel System' (*Keiei no gurōbaru-ka ni taiō shita Nihon-gata jinji shisutemu no kakushin: Howaitokarā no jinji shisutemu o megutte*), in which it argued in favor of 'a shift from a system of seniority-based pay and ability-based pay to a one of role-based pay and job-based pay, and in terms of evaluations a shift from an emphasis on the organization to an emphasis on individual performance'. In May 2002, Nikkeiren's Special Committee on Labor-Management Relations issued a report entitled 'Toward the Construction of a Multi-Tier Wage System: Wage Systems in the Performance-Based Era' (*Taritsu-gata chingin taikei no kōchiku e: Seika-shugi jidai no chingin shisutemu no arikata*) that advocated the introduction of job-based and performance-based pay, as well as multi-stream personnel management.[99]

However, the 2002 Nikkeiren report in question also stated that 'job groups whose job descriptions change from time to time in response to their level of competence, such as those concerned with planning, research and assorted types of negotiation and coordination' would be compensated with traditional ability-based pay (*shokunō-kyū*). Job-based pay would be applied to technical, general clerical and sales positions, while performance-based pay would be applied to sales and R&D divisions. In other words, this proposal could be seen as an attempt to further limit the portion of regular employees eligible for Japanese-style employment, and to apply job-based and performance-based wages to the remainder. Meanwhile, none of the systematic policy proposals that were advanced included social security, as had been included in such proposals up until the early 1960s.

Persistence of the collective norms

Since the 1990s, 'performance-based' approaches and goal-oriented management systems had also been touted in Japanese companies. However, without changing the existing series of norms, introducing any system based solely on performance would have been unfeasible. Moreover, even if only one company were to introduce job-based pay, it could not help but be incomplete given the absence of social security or a well-developed cross-firm labor market.

In 1999, labor economist Takeo Kinoshita carried out a study of reforms implemented by Japanese companies. Many such 'reforms', however, consisted of the replacement of the names of older competence rankings with 'job grades' or 'bands', and the reduction of the number of ranks to allow for a wider range of assessments. Although some companies did create job descriptions and introduce job-based pay, a seniority curve was still added to job-based pay schemes in order to cushion the resulting decline in wages for middle-aged and older workers.[100]

In 2013, labor law researcher Kei'ichirō Hamaguchi pointed out that performance-based pay is ill-suited to Japanese employment norms. With performance-based pay, Hamaguchi noted, 'individual wages are determined by assessing the degree to which the expected results of each job are achieved'. However, 'since Japanese personnel management is not job-based, a so-called performance-based approach will just be a system of [traditional] ability pay without the seniority component'.[101]

A New Dual Structure   381

Moreover, even if a company were to implement job-based personnel management, without being based on a unified standard across companies, it still would not be able to create a cross-firm labor market. Without such a unified standard, each company would end up defining its own jobs, leading to each company's creation of a large number of incommensurable positions, so that neither an industry-wide job-based wage rate nor a cross-firm labor market could emerge.

The fundamental dilemma facing Japanese companies is that even if each company were to assign values to its own jobs internally, these would only ever form a single-company in-house hierarchy, which as a result would be transformed into internal ranking schemes without seniority wage. In the absence of a cross-firm labor market, then, it would be almost impossible to fundamentally change Japanese-style employment without provoking worker resistance and demoralization. In 2009, after evaluating experimental initiatives by Japanese companies, economist Mitsuo Ishida described an attempt to shift from ability pay, in which employees are graded according to functional competence, to role-based pay, in which employees are graded according to their roles such as section mangers. However, this ended as a 'bitter experiment', due to 'the absence of any [cross-firm] market wage for regular employees in long-term employment in Japan'.[102]

The trend away from the Densan-type wage model toward the reduction of age- and seniority-based wages and the expansion of ability wages, which are determined by assessment, had been ongoing since the 1950s. However, in order not to cause a decline in worker morale, the reality was that 'ability' was in effect determined by length of service and educational background, even though it was called ability pay. If 'performance-based' approaches in Japan simply result in a system of 'ability pay without the seniority component', and if 'performance' in this case refers simply to sales performance, then it might even be seen as a return to the prewar system of piece-rate pay for factory workers and miners.

Tateshi Mori, who studied the evolution of wage systems at the Yahata Steel Works, summarized how the company's basic wage system had a 'two-tier structure' consisting of a seniority-based portion and a performance-based portion, and how 'frequent changes to the system retained the two-tier structure while adjusting the relative weight of the first and second tiers, or by changing the content of the second [performance-based]' tier.[103] What Japanese management has tried to do since the 1990s is to increase the portion of the second that can be reduced in response to economic fluctuations. By doing so, they have been able to respond to the recession by lowering wages while maintaining long-term regular employment, i.e., Japanese-style employment. Economist Hiroshi Yoshikawa attributes Japan's long-term deflation since the 1990s to the country's wage-determining system, which maintained employment by depressing wages.[104]

The introduction of performance-based approaches fraught with such contradictions often resulted in confusion in companies.

According to Shigeyuki Jō, who worked in Fujitsu's human resource department, the company introduced a performance-based policy and goal-oriented management in the 1990s without clarifying the job description and duties of individual employees. What's more, the company's internal ranking scheme, which was based on functional competence, remained unchanged. As a result, the structure of high salaries for managers was maintained, whereas mid- and lower-level employees were forced to work longer hours under nominal discretionary and set targets even though their duties remained unclear.[105]

Nevertheless, the company introduced this performance-based policy in an effort to cap the salaries of mid-level employees who had joined the company in large numbers during the bubble period. This proved to be detrimental to the morale of junior and mid-career employees, resulting in higher turnover rates. In addition, to compensate for capped wages, a growing number of company employees stayed at work longer to receive overtime pay, resulting in a nearly 20% increase in labor costs.[106]

Middle-aged and older managers, who were supposed to evaluate the performance of their subordinates, proved incapable of adopting a new mindset. According to Jō, 'In interviews we conducted in 2000, when we asked business managers about "the qualities they were looking for in the young people of the twenty-first century", more than a few managers responded with "stamina and perseverance"'.[107]

A New Dual Structure 383

As noted in Chapter 2, in a 2018 survey, the top five abilities that Keidanren member firms placed importance on during the selection of new graduates were communication skills, initiative, a willingness to take on new challenges, a cooperative spirit and integrity. In conducting these experiments, Japanese firms are gradually losing their room to maneuver their in-house trainings. According to an estimate by economist Tsutomu Miyazawa, total corporate spending on education and training in 2015 had fallen to about one-sixth of what it was in 1991.[108]

Although many reforms have been introduced, Japanese companies are still sticking to a ranking scheme. A March 2019 article in an economics journal equated the career paths of university-educated company employees at Toyota Motor Company with *the Game of Life* board game:

> According to a source, company employees who joined Toyota as new graduates are promoted to "3rd-Class Manager" (*kikanshoku-3-kyū*) in their late thirties, earning approximately 15 million yen a year. They then move up the ladder to 2nd-Class and then to 1st-Class, with each step taking four to five years. Only about 10% of the same cohort make it to 1st-Class, with an annual salary of approximately 20 million yen. For the lucky 1% of the cohort who manage to enter the elite ranks of the senior executives, their annual income jumps to more than 30 million yen.[109]

A series of reforms since the 1990s has gradually limited eligibility for promotions and salary increases to a carefully selected core of employees. Nevertheless, the basic pattern of the collective norms that have defined Japanese society does not seem to have changed significantly since the Meiji period.

8 | Japan's Employment System and Dual Structure

My research objectives in writing this book were to consider the Japanese-style employment system as a system of collective norms that defines the structure of Japanese society, and to clarify the processes of this system's historical construction. These processes were elucidated in chapters 3 through 7. In this final chapter, I situate the Japanese-style employment system based on the concept of the internal labor market to analyze how the dual structure of Japanese society was formed under the influence of this employment system. Then, after highlighting the contribution this book makes to the academic literature, I endeavor to provide some suggestions for readers in other countries.

The Japanese-style employment system as internal labor market

In the previous chapters, I have confirmed that the Japanese-style employment system was something more than a legal system; it was, in fact, a historically constructed system of collective norms. In the field of labor economics, this kind of employment system has been conceptualized as an 'internal labor market'.

Labor markets are defined by various extra-market factors such as legal regulations, social security systems and collective bargaining agreements. According to Gøsta Esping-Andersen, 'the labor market as autonomous from politics is a myth, sustained by ideology and defended by antiquated theory'.[1] A company can choose not to sell a washing machine below cost, but workers in the absence of an adequate social welfare system must sell their labor or else they will starve to death. Many societies have therefore institutionalized not only a social welfare system, but also minimum wages and layoff regulations to ensure that the price of labor does not fall below the cost of survival. Because these extra-market factors and the extent to

385

which they apply vary from country to country, different countries end up with different employment regimes.

Extra-market factors need not be institutionalized in national laws and are often found in practices that have been constructed through historical processes such as collective bargaining between management and labor. As mentioned in Chapter 2, in 1954, Clark Kerr distinguished between a structured, internal labor market with institutionalized rules and an unstructured, external labor market. In 1971, with references to Kerr, Peter Doeringer and Michael Piore proposed a division of the labor market into two domains, the internal labor market and the external labor market.[2] In the latter, wages and working conditions are determined by supply and demand because the influence of the market economy is unconstrained. If market conditions deteriorate, workers will be laid off, wages will fall and education and training will not be provided. In the former, however, the influence of the market economy is constrained, and certain rules are in place governing practices such as wage payments, salary increases, education and training, personnel evaluations, placement and dismissals.

As also mentioned in Chapter 2, Kerr divided the internal labor market into two types: the guild system and the manorial system. Doeringer and Piore also divide internal labor markets into two types: craft markets and enterprise markets.[3] Enterprise markets institutionalize rules for wages, layoffs, personnel evaluations and promotions within specific firms in order to exert control over market influences. Examples of such markets developed in the mid-twentieth century in large, well-managed manufacturing firms.[4] In contrast, craft markets controlled market influences by having occupational organizations or craft unions provide vocational training and certification and by demanding set wages for qualified craftsmen.

The first type had characterized the European labor market. In Western Europe and Scandinavia, industrial trade unions bargain collectively with industrial employers' organizations, and the collective agreements on wages and working conditions reached therein are applied or extended to employers and workers throughout the country.[5] The details vary from country to country, but in much of

Europe, minimum standards for wages based on job type and skill level, ranging from clerks to cashiers to janitors, are determined through centralized bargaining at the national and subnational level. The origins of the collective wage agreements based on these job classifications can be traced back to nineteenth-century labor agreements in France and Germany.[6] In other words, the history of occupational organizations and craft labor markets to some extent informs the employment norms of contemporary European countries.

In the United States, craft unions declined in the early twentieth century as the industrial unions of unskilled workers became dominant. However, the tendency to demand constant wages regardless of market trends and to require consistent evaluation of personnel with professional qualifications persisted, albeit in a different form. The government introduced job analysis in military industries during World War I and II, and US labor unions demanded equal pay for jobs that job analysis deemed to be equivalent.[7] Teachers and other professional organizations also became involved in vocational graduate education programs. This history led to the widespread use of job analysis and job descriptions, as well as to the evaluation of human resources beyond the level of individual companies.

In contrast, in Japan, which has no history of nationwide occupational organizations and craft unionism, internal qualification schemes modeled on that of the civil service became widespread. As a result, Japan's internal labor markets developed only as enterprise markets developed, and long-term employment in specific companies became the most advantageous option. This led to the entrenchment of the bulk recruitment of new graduates, seniority-based wages and long-term employment, which are now seen as characteristic Japanese practices.

This can also be said of the Japanese bureaucracy, which also shows no evidence of having been influenced by occupational organizations. This has led to the practice of transferring highly educated personnel to various professional positions. Furthermore, the scarcity of modern, higher-educated personnel led to the bureaucracy's practice of bulk recruitment of new university graduates. As a result, the Japanese bureaucracy has a strong tendency to train personnel within the organization. The custom of training inexperienced people within an organization is strongest in the military of any country. The fact that Japanese private-sector executives often spoke of business organizations in terms of the military is a reflection of the characteristics of the bureaucracy that influenced Japan's private-sector companies. The influence of the bureaucracy on the private sector employment system is not limited to Japan. However, as discussed in Chapter 3, the characteristics of Japanese bureaucracy differed from those of Western European countries due to the lack of an occupational organization tradition.

Although enterprise markets also exist in Europe, the influence of craft markets means that personnel evaluation and wage standards exist beyond the individual enterprise level. To some extent, the US also shares the fact that craft markets were weaker than in Europe, which led to the development of company-specific internal labor markets. However, since the National Labor Relations Act of 1935 effectively banned company unions, the enterprise market, also called 'modern manors', did not develop to the same extent as in Japan.[8] The US federal government also introduced a system of human resource promotion based on the position-based system described in Chapter 2. This system was based on job analysis to determine job duties and wages, and to hire people for those positions. This system spread to the private sector with a push for the formation of rules that guaranteed equal pay for equal jobs, and thus became the basis for the existence of personnel evaluation and wage standards that transcended the boundaries of the companies. In other words, the bureaucracy was different in Japan and the US, and this influenced employers' intentions and labor union movements, resulting in differences in the nature of the internal labor market.[9]

As noted in the Introduction, David Marsden classified the employment systems of the US, Japan, the UK and Germany into four types based on a combination of two axes and positioned Japan as the 'competence-rank' rule.'[10] I basically agree with Japan's position in this classification. Marsden explains the factors that led to the different employment systems in the UK and Germany, in particular, by referring to historical background studies.[11] He does not, however, offer such an explanation for Japan. In contrast, this book points out that Japan lacked a history of occupational organizations and that the nature of

Japan's Employment System and Dual Structure 389

its bureaucracy differed from that of the US and Germany. Bureaucracy provides a model for private sector rules in many countries, thereby influencing the mode of activity of trade unions and employers in setting the rules. The book shows that because of these differences, a unique employment system took hold in Japan.

Factors behind the formation of the Japanese-style employment system

In Chapter 2, I presented two hypotheses as to why the Japanese-style employment system was established: labor movement differences due to the lack of a tradition of strong occupational organizations and the significant influence of the bureaucracy. These hypotheses were confirmed in Chapter 3 through 7. As we saw in Chapter 4, the influence of the bureaucracy was also present in the German private sector, but Germany's experience differed from that of Japan owing to the greater influence of occupational organizations.

That said, the absence of a tradition of strong occupational organizations and the 'implantation' of the bureaucracy are hardly unique to Japan, and are typical of many Asian and African countries. Why, then, did the Japanese-style employment system evolve as an archetype unique to Japan?

Sociologist Ronald Dore, who is referred to in the Introduction and Chapter 2, emphasized not only cultural antecedents but also the late development effect as factors in the establishment of the Japanese-style employment system. Dore argued that because Japan imported modern technology and modern organizations from the West, skills learned in schooling became more dominant than private-sector job training, and the organizational forms of private industry became more susceptible to bureaucratic influence.[12] Dore, however, limited himself to offering these claims as speculation based on existing research.

The history of the formation of the Japanese-style employment system revealed in this book partially supports Dore's assertions. In Meiji Japan, the few people who had learned modern knowledge in school were able to work in a variety of advanced positions, and norms such as the bulk recruitment of new graduates and personnel evaluation came into being that emphasized schooling. Given the limited number of industrial organizations that existed that could provide modern vocational training, the emphasis on seniority within an organization also made sense, and it was this rationale that led to the implantation of the bureaucratic system to the private sector through the privatization of state-owned enterprises. It is certainly reasonable to point to the late development effect as having contributed to the development of the prototype of the Japanese-style employment system in the Meiji period.

On its own, however, the late development effect offers only a partial explanation of the Japanese-style employment system. This was the conclusion Dore came to on the basis of his joint study of labor-management relations in twenty firms in Senegal, Sri Lanka and Mexico. In these three countries, too, a dual structure was found in working conditions and employment security in companies in the manufacturing sector. In the researched companies, the percentage of regular employees changing companies was also low, and enterprise labor unions were also dominant. However, in these countries there was also a significant gap between white-collar and blue-collar workers, which differed from the Japanese case. Moreover, blue-collar workers were generally paid a job-based wage, and only state-owned enterprises in Sri Lanka had adopted a system whereby these workers received wage increases with years of continuous service. Reflecting on the results of this later research, Dore admits that he should have paid more attention to cultural factors in Japan.[13]

In contrast, Chapter 5 through 7 of this book shows that the differences between Japan and other late developing countries are post-World War II historical differences. Unlike the other late developers Dore studied, Japan experienced a surge of nationalism as a result of the total war and inflation following its defeat. This led to a sharp reduction in the income gap as well as the psychological distance between staff employees and factory workers, and a sense of solidarity that prompted them to join the same enterprise labor union. In Japan, too, discrimination between staff employees and laborers was strong before the war, and white-collar unions such as the Salarymen's Union (SMU) were separated from blue-collar labor

Japan's Employment System and Dual Structure

unions. The reason that enterprise mixed unions of staff employees and factory workers became dominant in postwar Japan is related to Japan's historical experience of total war and defeat, and in this respect, it differs from the other late-developing countries that Dore studied.

Postwar Japan's enterprise unions demanded 'equality of company employees', as well as long-term employment and a livelihood wage determined by age and family size. In this way, the employment system that had previously developed under the influence of the bureaucracy and which applied only to staff employees was now extended to laborers, as well. The Control Model mentioned in the Introduction explained that the Japanese-style employment system came into being as a compromise between management and the labor movement. Although this explanation is not sufficient to account for how the prototype of the employment system emerged by the 1910s, it does explain how this system was extended to blue-collar workers.

It was not until the 1960s, however, that the broad expansion of this employment system actually became possible. Until then, the wage costs of Japanese-style employment had been too high for firms to consider extending it to shop-floor workers. The extension was made possible by the corporate margins afforded by rapid growth in the 1960s. Another factor was, as discussed in Chapter 6, the increasing rate of higher education that broke the three-tier structure of corporate order, but it also became possible due to the rapid growth. Japan's experience of rapid growth was also a historical development that did not exist in the other late-developed countries Dore studied.

The expanded employment system thus contributed to the competitiveness of Japanese firms by raising worker morale, retention and skill levels. Although this is pointed out in the Economic Model mentioned in the Introduction, it merely amounts to an after-the-fact explanation of the positive effects of the employment system on Japanese business management and fails to account for how the system came to be. The Japanese-style employment system is not always rational for company management. As noted in Chapter 6, Abegglen described the system as inefficient in 1958, when he pointed out that Japanese companies had a surplus of unnecessary managers.

Also, as I mentioned in Chapter 7, legal precedents in the 1970s led to the institutionalization of long-term employment in Japanese companies when even non-unionized SMEs became subject to restrictions on dismissal. In addition, as discussed in Chapter 6, the establishment in 1958 of a social insurance system that also conformed to the dual structure, and the expansion of this system in the 1970s, also contributed to this institutionalization. Thus, Japan's employment system and the dual structure established as a result were transformed into an institution with legal backing. The system thus institutionalized proved resistant to change even after the economic rationality claimed by the Economic Model had disappeared; there was no longer any need to suppress the labor movement, as advocated by the Control Model. As discussed in Chapter 7, even when individual companies tried to change the system, it was not easy for them to do so because there were no criteria for evaluating personnel beyond the level of individual firms.

Thus, the Japanese-style employment system differs not only from those in the US and Europe, but also from the other late-developed countries that Dore studied. The Japanese-style employment system was established through a historical process wherein a prototype was formed by the absence of strong occupational organizations and the implantation of the bureaucracy. The resulting system was then extended to blue-collar workers through Japan's wartime defeat and subsequent high growth, before finally being institutionalized in the 1970s.

A Japanese-style dual structure

I explained how the Japanese-style employment system was formed and why it has not been easily changed. Next, let us move to the other objective of this book, an analysis of how the dual structure of society and the employment regime took shape under the influence of the employment system.

As I showed in Chapter 1, Japan's labor market exhibits a remarkable dual structure. In simple terms, this dual structure is the division between Japanese-style internal labor markets and the external labor

Japan's Employment System and Dual Structure

393

market. A dual structure will emerge in a society characterized by a large gap between internal labor markets, which impose rules on wages and working conditions, and the external labor market, which directly reflects market supply and demand. The nature of a country's dual structure is determined by the nature of its internal labor markets and their share of the total labor market.

Japan is not the only country with a labor market informed by a dual structure. Reviewing the labor market in industrialized countries, Gøsta Esping-Andersen observes that 'where trade unionism was less centralized and coverage [of collective agreements] limited, as in the United States, the result was more segmentation, dualism and, hence, inequality'.[14] Collective agreements define wages and working conditions independently of market trends. In other words, the coverage of a collective agreement is close to, if not exactly equal to, the coverage of the society's internal labor market. In countries with low coverage of collective agreements, a dual structure is likely to arise: workers protected by collective agreements and workers who are not protected by them. The latter is susceptible to the influences of the market economy trend.

As noted above, in continental Europe and Scandinavia, industrial trade unions and industrial employers' organizations bargain collectively at the national or state levels, and the collective agreements on wages and working conditions reached in these negotiations are then generally applied or extended to workers at the respective industrial level. The system of extension differs from country to country, but the coverage of collective agreements is higher than the union density, because of the high rate of organization of employer associations or the extension of industrial collective agreements by law or court order.[15] As Figure 8.1 shows, countries with high collective agreement coverage are either those with a higher density of employers' organizations than union organizations or those with legal extension systems, such as France and southern Europe. The US and Japan, however, have no such system of collective agreement extension, and agreements reached by individual unions apply only to workers who belong to those unions.[16] Thus, the coverage of collective agreements in those countries is little different to the union densities. According to the

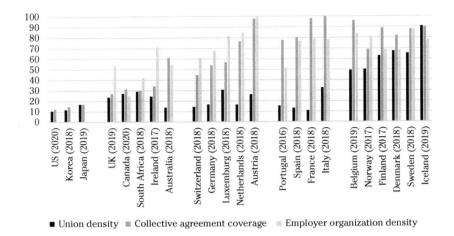

Figure 8.1 Collective agreement coverage of selected countries
Unit: % Note: Employer organization densities are for the latest year available.
Source: OECD/AIAS ICTWSS database data version 1.1 https://www.oecd.org/employment/ictwss-database.htm (Accessed on 1 October 2023).

most recent figures available in the OECD/AIAS ICTWSS database, the percentage of workers covered by collective agreements was 96% in Belgium, 88% in Sweden, 80% in Spain, and 54% in Germany, but only 12.1% in the US.[17]

If workers are covered by a collective agreement at the industrial level, the agreement determines their wages to some extent, regardless of the company they work for. As we saw in Chapter 2, the firm-size wage gap is difficult to study since there are many related factors. However, according to estimates by the JILPT, the wage gap by company size tends to be smaller in countries with higher collective agreement coverage (Figure 8.2). Although Japan is not included in the figure due to the different classification of company size in Japanese statistics, the firm-size wage gap is almost the same as in the US.[18]

The problem with societies with a high rate of collective agreement coverage is that unemployment tends to remain high. Theoretically, in a society where wages are easily determined by market adjustments, wages fall when demand for labor declines, stimulating demand for labor. However, in a society where wages are determined by collective agreements, wages do not fall even if labor demand declines, and

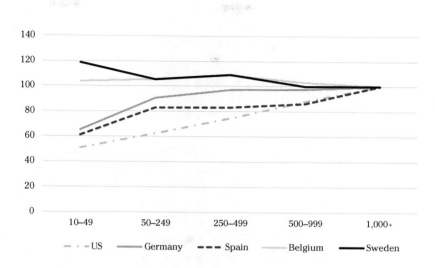

Figure 8.2 Wage gap by establishment size, selected countries

Notes: Percentage of wages of employees in companies with more than 1,000 employees as 100. The JILPT compiled data from the following sources using the following method.

The US: Bureau of Labor Statistics (BLS) (2022.12) Quarterly Census of Employment and Wages. The data for the first quarter of 2021 and for privately-owned establishments of non-agricultural industries. Calculated from average weekly wages.

European countries: Eurostat (2021.8) Structure of Earnings Survey 2018. Data for firms with ten or more employees and for non-agricultural industries excluding public administration, defence and mandatory social security. Calculated from total average monthly wages.

Source: JILPT (2023), table 5-13.

unemployment rates tend to remain high, especially among young people with no work experience.[19] As discussed in the Introduction, Sweden reduced its unemployment rate by increasing employment in the public sector, especially female care workers in the 1970s. In 2021, general government employment accounted for 29.3% of total employment in Sweden, compared to 15.0% in the US, 11.1% in Germany and 4.6% in Japan.[20] Germany implemented labor reforms in the 1990s and 2000s to reduce its unemployment rate, including the introduction of atypical employment, but this resulted in a dual structure of the labor market.[21]

Since the 1990s, the coverage of collective agreements has also declined in continental European countries due to increased bargaining at the enterprise level, where employers withdrew from employer's organizations that bargain collectively, and the rise of atypical employment. In Germany, collective agreement coverage was close to 90% in the 1980s but fell below the 60% mark in the 2010s.[22] British sociologist Duncan Gallie characterizes the state of affairs in which a large gap exists between a core workforce of unionized male workers and the rest of the workforce as a 'dualist employment regime', and points to Germany as an example.[23]

As I've noted, Japan is not the only country with a labor market with a dual structure. A characteristic feature of its expression in Japan, however, is that the salient division is determined not by the worker's level of skill or education, but rather by whether the worker is a regular employee of a large company. This is because the coverage of Japanese collective agreements is effectively limited to regular employees of large companies with unionized employees. Japanese labor unions are enterprise unions, and management/worker negotiations are conducted at the enterprise level. In other words, this means that whether workers are covered by a collective agreement most likely depends on whether a labor union exists in that enterprise. While Japan's Labor Union Act provides for the extension of collective agreements by geographical region, there are few examples of its functional application. In addition, the Act does not have any provision for extension to the industry level.

According to the latest figures from the OECD/AIAS ICTWSS database, the collective agreement coverage rate in Japan is 16.8% (figures for 2019), which is roughly the same as its labor union density. Also, according to the government's 'Basic Survey of Labor Unions' (*Rōdō kumiai kiso chōsa*), the estimated unionization rate in 2021 was 16.9%, but it was 39.2% for large private companies with more than 1,000 employees, 11.1% for those with 100 to 999 employees, and 0.8% for those with ninety-nine or fewer employees. In 1992, these figures were 57.2% for companies with more than 1,000 employees, but only 1.8% for those with fewer than 100 employees.

The government's 'Basic Survey of Labor Unions' shows that Japan's union density initially declined from 55.8% in 1949 to 32.1% in 1959, then rose slightly to 35.4% in 1970, since which time it has fallen off. However, as Figure 8.3 shows, the total number of unionized workers has not declined much since the 1970s. Thus, the decline in

Japan's Employment System and Dual Structure

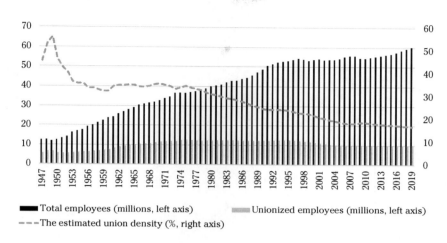

Figure 8.3 Unionization trends in Japan (1947–2019)   Source: MHLW (2019b: 8).

the unionization rate is largely due to the increase in the number of employed workers in the denominator.

There are various theories on the causes of the decline in the labor union organization rate, including globalization and the decline of the manufacturing industry, generational turnover, the increase in white-collar workers due to higher education, and the increase in non-regular employment, and the situation in each country is considered to be significant.[24] Japanese labor unions are based on the union shop system, which means that workers hired as regular employees by a unionized company will semi-automatically become unionized workers. In other words, if a large company with an enterprise union were to recruit additional regular employees, the total number of unionized workers would also increase semi-automatically. However, as discussed in chapters 1 and 7, large companies stopped hiring more regular employees in the 1970s, and numbers only continued to increase among workers in SMEs and among non-regular workers. Hence, even if regular employees of large firms continued to be unionized workers, the overall unionization rate would conceivably still have declined.

One of the definitions that the Japanese government uses for SMEs in the manufacturing industry is that a firm has fewer than 300 employees. On this basis, Figure 8.4 shows the total number of

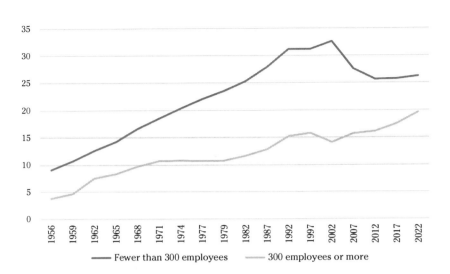

Figure 8.4 Employees in private enterprises by firm size (1956–2022, non-agricultural industries)

Unit: 1 million persons   Source: The MIAC, Employment Status Survey.

workers employed since 1956 categorized by company size from the government's 'Employment Status Survey'. Between 1956 and 1971, employment levels rose in both large firms and SMEs, but between 1971 and 1979, as discussed in Chapter 1, employment levels plateaued in large firms and only continued to rise in SMEs. As also noted in Chapter 1, both large firms and SMEs increased employment after 1982, but the fact that the total number of regular employees has remained more or less static since then would suggest that this increase occurred only among non-regular employees. With the exception of a decrease in 2002, employment levels in large companies have continued to grow, while employment in SMEs has decreased since reaching a peak in 2002, with a particularly large drop owing to the closure of micro-enterprises with fewer than thirty employees, as we saw in Chapter 7.[25]

The cessation of employment growth in large companies in the 1970s can be attributed to the end of Japan's period of rapid growth and corporate belt-tightening in the aftermath of the 1973 oil crisis. However, in terms of the review undertaken in this book, in the context of large enterprises at the end of the 1960s, the establishment of internal

Japan's Employment System and Dual Structure

399

labor markets based on long-term employment and a seniority-based wage appears to have been an equally important factor. As discussed in chapters 2 and 5, few restrictions on dismissals were codified in Japanese law, and even large Japanese companies engaged in mass layoffs until the 1950s. Also, while seniority-based wages had spilled over to large private-sector companies through the influence of the civil service, these mostly tended to be limited to staff employees. After the major disputes of the 1950s, however, layoffs were no longer so easily accomplished, and by the late 1960s, seniority-based wages, previously an exclusive privilege of staff employees, had been extended to shop-floor workers, as well. Thus, with the establishment of a typically Japanese-style internal labor market, large Japanese companies were no longer able to easily increase the number of shop-floor workers. As shown in Chapter 7, it was not until the 1970s that the number of high school graduates factory workers hired by Toyota Motor Corporation was no longer being determined by market supply and demand.

However, the 1970s was a transitional period. The typically Japanese-style internal labor market had been established as a norm for large companies in the late 1960s, but as we saw in Chapter 7, it was not until 1979 that layoff restrictions were extended to SMEs through court precedents. As discussed in Chapter 2, even after the 1979 decision, legal dismissals are easier than in larger firms in SMEs that do not have departments into which to transfer employees, but even so, the restrictions on dismissals have become stricter. In other words, until 1979, workers in SMEs could easily be laid off, and large companies were able to respond to market supply and demand by adjusting the volume of work they outsourced to SMEs. Throughout the 1970s, employment grew only in SMEs, which were not yet subject to layoff restrictions.

With the 1979 court decision, even SMEs were no longer able to easily add to their regular workforce, and the number of regular employees stopped growing across the entire workforce, including in SMEs. Meanwhile, non-unionized medium-size enterprises that had the economic means to do so began to form internal labor markets for their regular employees, emulating the norms prevailing in larger firms.[26] However, as shown in Chapter 1, the estimated proportion of workers eligible for long-term employment and seniority-based wages is about 27% of the total workforce (working people) and 50% of regular employees, and this state of affairs has changed little since 1982. The only subsequent increase has been among non-regular workers, who are more easily dismissed.

This stability of the employment regime is not unique to Japan. As we saw in Chapter 1, the dual structure is also stable in the US labor market. A study of the labor market in South Africa between 1985 and 2003 indicated that the total number of jobs in the formal sector remained almost constant and that the increase of jobs was mainly in the informal sector.[27] A 2011 study of France also noted that while various types of non-regular employment accounted for a high share of new employment growth, there was no significant trend toward a decline in regular employment.[28] In EU countries, however, the 1997 and 1999 EU Directives prohibit in principle discrimination between comparable full-time and part-time workers, and between permanent and fixed-term employment. Japan has no such provisions, and the large disparities in wages and social security benefits were discussed in Chapter 1.

To put this another way, in Japan, this increase in employment was something that took place consistently in the *external* labor market. Before the establishment of an internal labor market model in large firms at the end of the 1960s, both large firms and SMEs were adding to employment. In the 1970s, after this model had been established in large firms, only SMEs continued to add to employment. After the 1980s, when it had become difficult to lay off regular employees and the internal labor market model had been adopted by medium-sized firms as well, only the number of non-regular workers continued to increase. As we saw in chapters 1 and 2, the Japanese-style employment system (i.e. the Japanese-style internal labor market) is typically found only in regular employees of large companies; regular employees of SMEs are only partially covered by it, and non-regular workers are outside this employment system. The disparities between regular employees of large firms, regular employees of SMEs and non-regular workers in Japan are largely due to differences in their respective degrees of market influence restriction by the Japanese-style

Japan's Employment System and Dual Structure

401

internal labor market, which is consistent with the historical process described above.

Although Japan's unemployment rate was consistently low, this was not so much because large Japanese firms limited the layoffs of regular employees as because the external labor market provided employment with lower wages and easy dismissal. In large companies where the Japanese-style employment system exists, dismissals are not easy to implement. As discussed in Chapter 7, Japanese companies respond to recessions by first reducing bonuses and the performance-based portion of salaries, thereby lowering wages. They also lower wages by rigorously assessing middle-aged regular employees with high seniority. In addition, they transfer regular employees from unprofitable to profitable sections. At the same time, the company will lay off non-regular workers. As we saw in Chapter 1, the wages of non-regular workers were consistently low, and companies did not have to pay a social security premium for the most of them. Therefore, labor demand for non-regular workers was high and unemployment was consistent low. Studies of informal employment in the Asia-Pacific region have argued that social security systems applied to the formal employment sector often serve as a discriminating feature, rather than as a mechanism for social cohesion.[29] In addition, as we saw in Chapter 7, wage cuts in large corporations and low wages for non-regular workers contributed to Japan's persisting deflation since the 2000s.

The reason that non-regular workers were able to survive despite low wages was because mutual assistance existed within households and local communities in Japan, at least in the past. However, in Japan, where there was no culture of mutual assistance based on religious group or occupational organizations, mutual assistance within local communities was based on the assumption that many households were agricultural self-employed. The increase in the number of employees was also accompanied by a commensurate decline in the number in the self-employed sector as shown in Chapter 1. In 1953, only 42.4% of Japan's labor force were employees, with the rest being comprised of self-employed and family workers, mainly farmers. It was not until 1959 that the number of employed workers exceeded 50%. As mentioned earlier, Japan's history after World War II was different from that of other developing countries, though it was still influenced by its history as a late developer in that it experienced a mass internal migration of workers from the self-employed sector to become company employees.

Self-employed households sent their young people to the cities to find work as employees, while women found low-wage manufacturing and service-industry jobs in nearby SMEs. This shift manifested itself in the mass migration of new graduates to metropolitan areas and in the increase in the number of dual-income farm families described in chapters 1 and 7. Self-employed men also became seasonal workers in the off-season. As discussed in Chapter 1, Japanese non-regular workers were covered by the same social insurance system as the self-employed and were considered distinct from regular employees. This was because the origin of Japan's non-regular workforce was the part-time or seasonal work of self-employed farmers' households.

Until around the early 1980s, however, the total number of self-employed remained stable, even including new businesses such as self-employment in the manufacturing and commercial sector. Moreover, the increase in total household income due to farmers' dual employment statistically manifested itself in the form of rural economic growth. This led to a narrowing of the gap between urban and rural areas and increased the export competitiveness of Japan's manufacturing sector by providing a supply of low-wage labor. Thus, as discussed in Chapter 7, Japan in the 1970s and 1980s achieved what was characterized as an 'all middle-class society'.

As we saw in Chapter 1, however, not only the number of family workers, but also the number of self-employed workers has been in decline since 1984. It was around this time that self-employed households in the agricultural and non-agricultural sectors were no longer able to establish themselves as such, even if some of the household members were able to subsidize the household income as non-regular workers. While agricultural households continued to farm, housing and food self-sufficiency were ensured, and the cost of living was kept low through mutual assistance networks within families and the local community. However, when even self-employed workers have no choice but to become non-regular workers, the cost of living rises and poverty, which is more likely to occur when people work as non-

Japan's Employment System and Dual Structure

regular workers away from their home communities, becomes more of an issue. As we saw in Chapter 1, the share of the total population that continued to live in their home municipality in 2015 was estimated to be only 36% and the organization rate of neighborhood associations has declined since the mid-1980s.

In general, two parallel processes took place in twentieth-century Japan: the shift from self-employed households to employed workers, and the limited establishment of an internal labor market. Among those who made the transition from self-employed households to employed workers, new graduates with a certain level of education were able to enter this internal labor market, but the rest had no choice but to work in the external labor market. When the size of the internal labor market reached equilibrium around 1980 at 27% of the working people, the employment regime identified in Chapter 1, in which another 27% of regular employees were unable to secure long-term employment or seniority-based wages and the remaining 46% of workers were shifting from the self-employment sector into the non-regular workforce, became more or less fixed. The structure of this employment regime has defined the dual structure of society as a whole, a system that also defines social security and population mobility. This is the system of Japanese society, defined by the Japanese-style employment system.

What is a fair society?

I now present a summary of what this book reveals and clarify its contribution to the academic literature.

The Japanese-style employment system is most notable for its lack of any criteria for personnel evaluation beyond the level of individual companies. This is due to the fact that Japan had no tradition of occupational organizations, and that the prototype of the employment system was created under the influence of bureaucracy implanted from the civil service. This employment system became a Japanese-style internal labor market through Japan's postwar labor movement and experience of economic growth, and eventually shaped the dual structure that characterizes Japanese society today. The prototype of this employment system emerged at the beginning of the twentieth century in Japan, a late-comer country with a scarcity of modern-educated human resources, due to the intention of management to retain them. The system was only applied to highly educated white-collar workers until the 1930s, but expanded during the period of postwar democratization in the late 1940s and rapid economic growth in the 1960s, and was institutionalized by law and in the social security system in the 1960s and 1970s. The employment system created a dual structure in Japanese society, but in the 1970s it maintained a certain societal equilibrium, including the self-employed and SME employees. This equilibrium has since been lost, but once institutionalized, the employment system is difficult for individual companies to change. Moreover, changes in the employment system must be accompanied by a reorganization of the entire society, including laws and the social security system, and this is not an easy task. In contributing to the academic discourse, this book has defined the character of the Japanese-style employment system, analyzed its character and the factors that led to its establishment by describing its historical emergence, shown how the employment system engendered the employment regime and the dual structure of Japanese society, and clarified the current state of Japan's dual structure in numerical terms.

Having reviewed these contributions, I would like to further consider the following questions. First, is Japanese society a fair society? And second, are the Japanese satisfied with this society?

In every society, workers want fair rules and resent employers who arbitrarily set wages and working conditions, but the nature of fairness varies from society to society. The US labor movement first demanded equal pay for equal work, and later criticized discrimination based on sex and race. Germany's lower-level salaried employees and engineers created their own craft labor market to pursue their own empowerment and social security. In Japan, the labor movement expanded access to long-term employment and seniority-based wages, formerly the exclusive privilege of white-collar staff employees, to blue-collar workers, and created enterprise markets based on length of service.[30]

Japan's Employment System and Dual Structure 405

A system created by its own particular sense of fairness will also have its own inherent drawbacks. US workers accepted disparities between salaried staff and shop-floor laborers due to differences in their respective jobs, and accepted disparities in eligibility for those jobs based on whether workers had a college degree. German workers accepted disparities by profession and between skilled and unskilled workers. Japanese workers accepted that jobs could be transferred at management's discretion and took disparities between companies for granted. The Japanese labor movement, which sought to achieve 'equality of company employees', led to the creation of an internal labor market with an advanced work ethic and accumulation of skills, which in turn led to the emergence of the Japanese-style dual structure.

Perhaps the group most disadvantaged in Japan's employment system is highly educated women. As discussed in Chapter 5, after Japan's defeat in World War II, workers employed at Japanese Government Railways demanded that 'effort' and 'experience' should be valued more than educational background, and this demand was met in the form of an internal labor market that emphasized length of service. Although this was a victory for Japan's postwar labor movement, it arguably also entrenched norms that were disadvantageous to women. Even if a woman has specialized skills and a university degree, once she leaves the workforce to give birth or raise children, she will no longer be valued in Japan's internal labor market and has no choice but to work as a low-wage worker in the external labor market. According to the World Economic Forum (WEF), Japan's Gender Gap Index ranked 116th out of 146 countries in 2022, and according to OECD statistics, Japan's gender wage gap ranked forty-first out of forty-four member countries.

Nevertheless, until the 1980s, Japan's employment system was accepted by the Japanese people. This was because the skills of Japanese workers, developed through long-term employment and in-house training, had brought Japanese manufacturing to global dominance. Moreover, those who were unable to become regular employees of large corporations tended to be members of self-employed households that were rich in local social capital, and thus enjoyed a certain degree of stability. As we saw in Chapter 2, even in the 2010s, a Swedish union activist said, 'I think Japan is better' in comparison with the situation in his country.

When it becomes possible to manufacture products according to blueprints sent digitally to countries where wages are lower than in Japan, however, workers' skills no longer matter. As manufacturing centers shifted to other parts of Asia and as growth industries in developed countries shifted to sectors requiring advanced expertise such as finance and IT, Japan's employment system, which does not place a premium on expertise, began to work to its disadvantage. Meanwhile, on the lower tier of the dual structure, the hollowing out of local communities due to declining levels of self-employment and the poverty faced by non-regular workers have emerged as pressing issues.

Nevertheless, any given social system is the product of historically generated collective norms. Researchers can examine the facts and the history behind them, present possible options and raise arguments for or against them. However, a government or researcher may advocate reforms based on examples from another country, but these ideas can only find purchase in the wider society if the people of that society agree. The onus is on Japanese society to recognize its current situation and the history behind it, and then build a consensus to realize a new kind of fairness. This book is preparation to this end. I would encourage readers from other countries to think about the kind of fairness that would be desirable in their own societies, based on their knowledge of Japanese history. In my view, this is the true significance of studying the history of other countries.

NOTES

Introduction

1. ILO (2016: 284).
2. Saijō Ikuo, 'Keidanren, kono osorubeki dōshitsu shūdan' (The Japan Business Federation, that terrible, homogeneous group), *Nihon Keizai Shimbun*, 21 June 2018. Digital edition, https://www.nikkei.com/article/DGXMZO31995500Q8A620C1X12000/ (accessed on 30 July 2018). This article was written by a senior writer (*hensyū iin*) of the *Nihon Keizai Shimbun* and also appeared in the *Nikkei Sangyō Shimbun*, 22 June 2018, p. 2.
3. As for the 'working people', see note 21.
4. Sullivan and Peterson (1991: 82–85). Although this typology is a classification from the standpoint of business administration, I introduced it because it is useful for this literature review. Labor historians would claim that the 'Control Model' is a categorization from the management perspective.
5. E.g., Abegglen (1958, 1973); Dore (1973); Cole (1979); Clark (1979); Hazama (1979); Gordon (1985).
6. E.g., Abegglen (1958); Levine (1958); Hazama (1964); Dore (1973); Karsh (1984).
7. E.g., Hofstede (1980, 1984); Lebra (1976); Baba et al. (1983); Tanaka (1988).
8. E.g., Gordon (1985); Moore (1983); Taira (1970); Tanaka (1981); Shirai (1983).
9. E.g., Aoki (1984); Koike (1988); Koshiro (1984).
10. E.g., Price and Mueller (1986); Campbell and Pritchard (1976); Ilgen, Fisher and Taylor (1979); Locke and Latham (1984).
11. Koike (1981) is a representative example of the Economic Model, whereas Hyōdō (1971) and Sumiya (1976) are examples of the Control Model.
12. According to labor dispute statistics published by the Japanese government's Ministry of Health, Labour and Welfare (MHLW 2020a), although the total number of annual disputes was 7,477 in 1982, this number had fallen to 1,839 by 1987 and remained in the range of 1,100 to 1,300 through the 1990s. Since 2000, the annual number of disputes has stayed consistently under 1,000.
13. E.g., Rebick (2005); Imai (2011); Yamaguchi (2019).
14. Nomura (2007) reviews the development of labor history research after the 1980s. As for works of management historians such as Sugayama (2011), see note 1 of Chapter 3 of this book.
15. E.g., Houseman and Osawa (2003); Rebick (2005); Cooke and Jiang (2017).
16. E.g., Brinton (2010); Fu (2012).
17. E.g., Kawanishi (2005); Aoyagi and Ganelli (2013).
18. Nitta (2009); Kambayashi (2017); Gordon (2017). Of these, Gordon (2017) provides the most comprehensive analysis, but fails to point out that the stability of regular employment is the root of the problem. This is probably due to his evaluation of the Japanese-style employment system established in the twentieth century as a major achievement of the labor movement. See also note 30 of Chapter 8 of this book.
19. Gordon (1985: 46, 423).
20. E.g., Inatsugu (2005); Shimizu (2007).
21. The 'working people' in this book are the 'Persons engaged in work' in the Employment Status Survey of the Japanese government. In the survey, 'Persons

408 The System of Japanese Society

engaged in work' (*yūgyōsha*) are those who usually work for income and will continue to do so at and after the survey date, and those who have a job but are currently absent from it among the population aged fifteen years or more. Family workers are also considered as 'Persons engaged in work' even if they do not earn an income, as long as they are working as their usual status. In the Labor Force Survey, 'Employed persons' (*syūgyōsha*) are basically the same category as 'Persons engaged in work' in the Employment Status Survey but the survey method is different in that it ascertains the status of employment and non-employment during the last week of the month from the survey date. In the Labor Force Survey, the 'labor force' (*rōdōryoku jinkō*) is the sum of the 'employed persons' and unemployed persons, and the sum of the 'labor force' and 'not in the labor force' (*hi-rōdōryoku jinkō*) such as students and housewives is equal to the population aged fifteen years and more. As for the English translation of these terms, see Statistics Bureau of the Japanese government, 'English Translation of the Table Stubs of the Labor Force Survey', https://www.stat.go.jp/english/data/roudou/report/2020/pdf/ap06e.pdf and '2017 Employment Status Survey, Summary of the Results', https://www.stat.go.jp/english/data/shugyou/pdf/sum2017.pdf (accessed on 24 August 2022). This book principally uses these English translations by the Japanese government, but to avoid complications here, 'persons engaged in work' (*yūgyōsha*) is translated as 'working people'.

The most problematic is the English translation of the term for 'non-regular workers'. The translation by the Japanese government of '*hiseiki no syokuin, jūgyō'in*' is 'Non-regular staff' in the Labor Force Survey and 'Irregular staff' in the Employment Status Survey (the translation of '*seiki no syokuin, jūgyō'in*' is 'Regular staff' in both surveys). However, these translations are not considered appropriate because many non-regular workers (and regular employees) in Japan are not staff but shop-floor workers. The Labor Force Survey divides 'employees excluding executives of companies and corporations' into 'Regular staff' and 'Non-regular staff', and the latter includes sub-categories of '*Paat*' and '*Arubaito*' (Part-time workers, see Chapter 1), 'Dispatched workers from temporary agencies', 'Contract employees', 'Entrusted employees' and 'Other'. Although some researchers use the term 'non-regular employees' as the English translation and some others use 'non-regular workers', I use 'non-regular workers' in this book. The reason for this is that workers without employment contracts are included in this category, as evidenced by the inclusion of 'Other' in the Labor Force Survey's subcategory of 'Non-regular staff'. As will be seen in Chapter 1 and note 75 in Chapter 2, the boundary between employment contract workers and non-employment contract workers is blurred because employment contracts in Japan can be concluded orally rather than in writing.

22. The concept of informal employment is becoming considered relevant not only for developing countries, but also for developed countries. See OECD/ILO (2019).

Criteria for measuring informal employment in international comparisons include whether the employment contract is clear, whether the employed enterprise is micro or small, and whether the employee is excluded from the social security system (Koettl-Brodmann et al. 2012: 24; ILO 2013: 6). In EU member countries, the European Social Survey asks about employment status and the existence of employment contracts, but in countries where such surveys are not conducted, the employment contracts cannot be used as a criterion. The indicators used by the ILO for international comparisons

Notes

are based primarily on firm size and exclusion from social security as follows. First, employment in the form of non-firm premises (e.g., self-employment) that is not a formal enterprise, the family members, and employment in an enterprise with less than five employees that is not covered by social security or tax are considered informal employment. Furthermore, even if the size of the enterprise is large, employment that is not covered by employment related social security or does not allow paid vacation or paid sick leave is classified as informal employment. In other words, self-employed, family workers and hired workers who are not covered by employment-related social security are considered workers in informal employment (ILO 2018: 7–12). Using this methodology, the ILO calculated that informal employment in Japan in 2016 was 18.7% of all employed persons. This is lower than South Korea's 31.5%, but comparable to Italy's 19.0% and the United States' 18.0%, and higher than France's 9.4% and Germany's 10.2% in the same year (ILO 2018: 31).

This ILO estimate does not specify how it measured employment without social security coverage in Japan. The Japanese Ministry of Health, Labour and Welfare's 'Survey on Employment Structure' (*Koyō ni kansuru jittai chōsa*) includes social insurance coverage rates for non-regular workers, which the ILO appears to have based its data on. However, the survey design significantly biases the responses toward fixed-term workers ('Dispatched workers' and 'Contract employees') in large companies that have a high percentage of workers covered by social insurance. I therefore believe that the ILO's estimate of informal employment in Japan is too low. As discussed in Chapter 1, most non-regular workers in Japan pay their own premiums to join the national social insurance system and are not covered by employment-related social security (see note 74, 75, and 100 in Chapter 1). Also discussed in Chapter 1, the Japanese government has been enrolling part-time workers employed by large companies in employment-related social security since 2016, but as of March 2021, 235,562 part-time workers were covered by association administered health insurance schemes, a small number compared to the 20.7 million non-regular workers in the same year (National Federation of Health Insurance Societies 2022: 12). In this book, I refer to the type consisting of non-regular workers, self-employed workers, and family workers as the 'informal employment' type workers, referring to the ILO's definition of informal employment as workers who are excluded from employment-related social security, as well as self-employed workers and their family workers. Also in this book, when self-employed and family workers are lumped together, they are referred to as the self-employment sector.

23. I excluded Ken'ichi Tominaga's works such as Tominaga (1991) that discusses the modernization of Japanese society based on Talcott Parsons' structural functionalism and social systems theory, because they do not consider the employment system as a determining factor.

24. Labor economist Mikio Sumiya and economic historian Keiji Ushiyama proposed the concept of 'urban miscellaneous business class' (*toshi zatsugyō sō*) and 'rural miscellaneous business class' (nōson zatsugyō sō) respectively, which were almost identical to the concept of 'informal sector' proposed by Keith Hart, an anthropologist who surveyed Kenya in 1971. See Sumiya (1960); Ushiyama (1975); Hart (1973); and Bangasser (2000).

25. Ujihara ([1954b] 1966).

26. Nomura (1998) and Ishikawa and Dejima (1994), as well as Hashimoto (2009), mentioned in chapters 1 and 7, are exceptions in that they refer to the dual structure theory of the 1950s.
27. Esping-Andersen (1990).
28. Esping-Andersen (1999).
29. Miyamoto (2008: 90–93).
30. Esping-Andersen (1990).
31. Estevez-Abe (2008); Miura (2012); Osawa (2011).
32. The management or sociological studies that survey and analyze the current state of Japanese-style employment systems and compare them to systems in different countries are not reviewed in this book for two reasons. First, they study the function of the employment system in management, but not the history of its formation. Second, they study the employment system as itself, not the social structure formed by its effects.
33. Marsden (1999). As for the details of Marsden's classification, see note 10 in Chapter 8 of this book.
34. Marsden (1999) explains why these divergences arose from the history of the UK and Germany (see note 11 in Chapter 8). But as for Japan, he does not provide such a historical explanation since his information on the Japanese-style employment system mainly comes from the works of economists such as Kazuo Koike who does not conduct historical studies of the Japanese-style employment system.
35. Jacoby (2004: 7).
36. Weber ([1905] 1930).
37. Gibbs (1965: 589; emphasis added).
38. Bourdieu ([1973] 1979).
39. Berger and Luckmann (1966).
40. Foucault ([1966] 1970).
41. Oguma (2002a); Oguma (2014); Oguma (2017).
42. Skocpol (1984: 356–391).
43. Nakane (1970).
44. Nakane (1967: 187–188).
45. A classic example is Murakami, Kumon and Satō (1979).
46. Examples of such critical studies include Mouer and Sugimoto (1986) and Yoshino (1997).

Chapter 1

1. There are multiple streams of existing research that relate to the analysis I conduct in this chapter. One is the estimation of employment statuses using government statistical data, which includes Ishikawa and Dejima (1994), Koike (2005) and Kambayashi (2017), which are referred to in this chapter. The other is the dual structure theory advocated by Japanese economists in the 1950s, to which this chapter also refers, and Nomura (1998) is its successor. I referred to these studies and improved on the method they took, quantitatively estimating and modeling the employment regime and dual structure in Japan. I also referred to the studies on neighborhood associations (*Jichikai* and *Chōnaikai*) such as Pekkanen (2006) and Tsujinaka et al. (2014), and added the perspective of decline in social capital to my analysis of the dual structure. Further, I

Notes

411

investigated the dual structure in relation to the social security system from the perspective of the welfare regime theory I referred to in the Introduction. To my knowledge, this is the first attempt to present a model and estimates on the dual structure of Japanese society from these multiple perspectives. Also, this is the first attempt to estimate the number of residents who settled in the specific municipality where they were born. Since Japanese government statistics do not include any ethnic breakdowns, I did not analyze the dual structure from this perspective.

2. As for the definition of 'working people' in the Japanese statistics, see note 21 of the Introduction.

3. As discussed in Chapter 8, sociologist Duncan Gallie proposed three types of employment regimes that differ from Espin-Andersen's. One of them is the 'dualist employment regime' in which there is a large disparity between male workers in the core workforce and other workers. My use of the term 'employment regime' is based on this concept. However, Gallie only used European countries for his comparison, and no research has been conducted applying this concept to Japan. See Gallie (2007) and note 23 in Chapter 8.

4. Although 'regular staff' is a term used by the Japanese government in its statistics, it is not a legal term, and it is not illegal for an employer to refer to an employee as 'regular staff' even if they have a fixed-term contract. Because of the existence of the exceptional case of regular employment, some reports by the government and research such as Kambayashi (2017) use the category of 'permanent regular employees'. This chapter ignores such exceptional case in the use of the term 'regular employees'. As for the English translation of terms in Japanese statistics, see note 21 in the Introduction.

5. ILO (2016: 27, 66). The Part-Time Labor Law enacted in 1993 defines a 'part-time worker' as one whose prescribed weekly working hours are shorter than those of regular employees at the same establishment without providing a standard for working hours.

6. 'Irregular' in the Employment Status Survey contains other related categories such as 'Temporary Employees' (in a different definition from the Labor Force Survey) and 'Daily Employees'.

7. Asao (2011: 1).

8. Comparing wage censuses in Japan, Germany, the US, and the UK, Marsden (1999) points out that German wage statistics are rich in data on the relationship between wage and skill qualifications, while Japanese wage censuses lack such data and are rich in data on firm size and length of service.

9. Calculated from data in Chart 1.3.24 of the White Paper (MHLW 2020b: 41).

10. E.g., Bentolia et al. (2019).

11. As for the English translation of terms in Japanese statistics, see note 21 in the Introduction.

12. A handful of researchers have drawn attention to the fact that although the number of non-regular workers is increasing, the corresponding decrease is not occurring among regular employees, but rather in the self-employment sector. The earliest example of such an observation is by the economist Michio Nitta (2009, 2011). Andrew Gordon, citing Nitta, makes a similar point (2012: 4766; 2017: 18). Kambayashi (2017) positions what this book calls the 'self-employment sector' as the 'informal sector'.

13. The average number of years of service in a company at ages fifty-five to fifty-nine is twenty years for all industries, but six years for long-term care workers. See MHLW (2022a: 26).

412 The System of Japanese Society

14. The fact that the majority of workers who switch jobs between firms are SME workers will be discussed in Chapter 2.

15. Taira (1962: 167) suggests that the system applies to permanent regular employees in the firms employing 500 or more regular workers who were no more than a fifth of all wage-earners in Japanese manufacturing. Dore (1973: 304–305) adds to Taira's definition by including government sector employees and unionized employees of the firms with 100 to 500 in white-collar industries, and using 1970 Japanese statistical data, estimated the coverage to be half of all employees, or about one-third of the labor force. Cole (1979: 61) explains that women are rarely covered by lifetime employment, and revises Dore's estimates downward to 32% of all employees, or 20% of all gainfully employed.

16. Ministry of Labor (1993), Section 3 of Chapter 3. Hereafter, the 'agricultural sector' in this chapter refers to the 'agriculture, forestry, and fisheries industries' in Japanese government statistics.

17. Ono (2006) criticized the estimation by the Ministry of Labor and claimed that the proportion of 'lifetime workers' remaining in the labor force at age fifty to fifty-four was 23% for men and 4% for women in 2000. His estimation is based on a category in the Wage Census called 'standard workers' (hyōoujun rōdōsha) which refers to those who were employed immediately after school graduation and have been continuously employed by the same employer. Ono (2006) also estimated the proportion of workers who survived thirty years of employment with the same employer was 20% using cross-sectional microdata from the 1995 Social Stratification and Mobility Survey. The drawback of Ono's methods is that they only account for the coverage of the system in a specific cohort, not the coverage in the entire workforce at that point.

18. See Ishikawa and Dejima (1994). Owing to limitations with the Wage Census, which does not include workers in small firms, these authors take the liberty of assuming that all part-time workers and workers employed by firms with less than ten 'regular-basis employees' (jōyō rōdōsha) are in the secondary labor market and all public sector workers are in the primary labor market. The term 'regular-basis employees' (jōyō rōdōsha) in this survey means workers who are employed on a regular basis, not temporary or seasonal, and includes non-regular workers who are employed on a regular basis. They took the denominator, the total number of employees, from the 1987 Employment Status Survey.

19. The distinction Ishikawa and Dejima (1994) employed is a standard classification in the study of dual labor markets in economics such as Dickinson and Lang (1985). Namely, the primary labor market is one where wages increase with experience and education, and where workers are not easily laid off. In the secondary labor market, wages do not increase and there are no rules regarding dismissal, etc., for simple jobs that require no experience. The fact that wages increase with education and age signifies the existence of a labor market in which workers' education and work experience are given recognition in the form of higher wages. However, the government Wage Census data that Ishikawa and Dejima (1994) used for their analysis only allowed them to look for relationships between educational background (i.e., whether the worker graduated from high school or university), age and wages. Thus, in the context of the Japanese employment system, the primary labor market ratio that they calculated is effectively identical to that for individuals in regular employment at large companies with wages that increase with years of service. This is

Notes

413

consistent with the assertion I make in Chapter 2 that the only criteria that exist for valuing a company's personnel are in-house ranking systems, and that only employees of large companies and some core workers of SMEs are able to realize this recognition in the form of higher wages.

20. Dickens and Lang (1987). Ishikawa and Dejima (1994) analyzed the Japanese data using the method used by Dickens and Lang (1985) and Dickens and Lang (1987).

21. Koike (2005: 7). Koike arrived at his estimate as follows. Taking regular employees from the Employment Status Survey, he selected (1) men and women in professional and technical occupations, (2) men and women in managerial occupations, (3) men in clerical occupations, (4) men in sales occupations, and (5) 21.9% of other male regular employees as employees whose wages increased with age. This 21.9% figure represents the percentage of all employees in companies with 500 or more employees in the 2002 Employment Status Survey. Also worth noting is that the occupational classification used in the Employment Status Survey includes government and municipal offices. The denominator, the total number of employees, includes executives in the statistics.

22. Suzuki (2020).

23. Ahn et al. (2023).

24. Gregory et al. (2021).

25. Dickens and Lang (1987). However, the categorization of this study is based on wage structure, and the criteria for group categorization differ from those used in Ahn et al. (2023) and Gregory et al. (2021) examining unemployment risk. It is interesting to note, however, that the resulting ratios were consistent despite the different criteria.

26. As for the definition of terms and its English translation of the Employment Status Survey, see note 21 in the Introduction. From 2017 to 2022, the number of 'professional and technical occupations' increased significantly by 15.8% (1.19 million). Although I employed the same method as used for Koike's estimates shown in note 21, in the tabulation of the 2022 data, I excluded regular employees categorized in 'social welfare professional occupations' (916,400, of which 700,300 were women) from the 'professional and technical occupations'. Such adjustment is not possible for data prior to 2022 because the breakdown of 'professional and technical occupations' has not been published.

27. As for the reason why the type in the text is referred to as the 'informal employment type', see note 22 in the Introduction.

28. E.g., Brinton (2010).

29. Kambayashi (2017: 173). According to Kambayashi, 76% of the male population aged twenty to twenty-nine were permanent regular employees (*muki seishain*) in 1982, but since increasing slightly to 77% in 1992, this proportion has continued to decline, reaching 64% in 2002. The percentage of women of the same age group in permanent regular employment also increased from 40% in 1982 to 50% in 1992, but had dropped to 43% by 2007. Nevertheless, these fluctuations may be described as the loss of gains made during the bubble period and a return to levels seen in the early 1980s. Also, during this period, women who had been out of work began returning to work, many becoming non-regular workers. In other words, Kambayashi paints the general picture of a situation in which the number of regular employees has not decreased, but the number of non-regular workers has increased.

30. Since the 1990s, the number of applicants for two-year junior colleges has declined in Japan, while the percentage of students entering four-year universities has increased, making two-year junior colleges less common. From the 1960s through the 1980s, a substantial gender order existed, with women tending to enroll in two-year junior colleges and men in four-year universities. In this book, four-year universities and colleges are referred to as universities unless otherwise noted.
31. Ebihara (2012: 44–48).
32. Nomura (1998: 104–105).
33. Genda (2010: Chapter 2).
34. Norgren (2001).
35. Esping-Andersen (1999: 28).
36. Although Japanese baby boomers are limited to those born between 1947 and 1949, their childbearing years are widely spread throughout the 1970s, and moreover, their children are dispersed into high school and university graduates, resulting in a twelve-year period of high new-graduate job seekers.
37. Economic Planning Agency Planning Bureau (ed.) (1985: 110). This publication by the Economic Planning Agency's Planning Bureau was originally entitled *2000-nen ni mukete gekidō suru rōdō shijō: Aratana nijūkōzō o shuppatsu-ten to shite* (Labor market in upheaval toward the year 2000: A new dual structure as a starting point), but the title was changed at the time of publication.
38. Economic Planning Agency Planning Bureau (ed.) (1985: 52, 110).
39. Economic Planning Agency Planning Bureau (ed.) (1985: 111–112).
40. After the number of students graduating from four-year universities reached over 550,000, and stopped rising, the number of 'new hires' in the School Basic Survey increased in the 2010s more than before the early 2000s. This can be attributed to the effect of the lower tier of university graduates taking the traditional jobs of high school and junior-college graduates. According to the Basic School Survey, the ratio of those employed in the position of 'sales occupations' and 'professional and technical occupations' which includes female care workers increased in the 2010s among 'new hires' after university graduation.
41. Kambayashi (2017: Chapter 3); Kambayashi and Katō (2016).
42. Nomura (1998).
43. Tanimoto (2013).
44. Nomura (1998: 90).
45. E.g., Sawai and Tanimoto (2016).
46. OECD.Stat, 'Labour force participation rate, by sex and age group', https://stats.oecd.org/index.aspx?queryid=103872# (accessed on 31 August 2023). Japan's female labor force participation rate has been on a remarkable rise especially since 2010, at 63.2% that year, partly due to the aging of the population and the lack of labor force.
47. Lewis (1954).
48. Yamada (1934); Arisawa (1956).
49. Economic Planning Agency (ed.) (1957).
50. Economic Planning Agency (ed.) (1957).
51. Tōbata (1956).
52. Umemura (1957).

Notes   415

53. Economic Planning Agency (ed.) (1957).
54. Minami (2002).
55. Economic Planning Agency Planning Bureau (ed.) (1985: 112).
56. Economic Planning Agency Planning Bureau (ed.) (1985: 17–18).
57. The original sentence of the 'part-timers and others' is '*paat taimā, arubaito tō*'.
58. Economic Planning Agency Planning Bureau (ed.) (1985: 17, 52, 70).
59. Economic Planning Agency Planning Bureau (ed.) (1985: 3).
60. Esping-Andersen (1990).
61. Esping-Andersen (1999: 90–92). Takegawa (2007) criticizes this view as 'welfare Orientalism'.
62. MHLW (2018). To be precise, this model case is the 'standard pension amount for a married couple, including the basic old-age pension' when calculated based on the 'initial benefit level for a household in which the husband worked for forty years at an average monthly income (monthly equivalent including bonuses) of ¥428,000 and the wife was a full-time housewife for the entire period'.
63. On 3 June 2019, the Financial Services Agency issue a report entitled 'Asset Formation and Management in an Aging Society' (*Kōrei shakai ni okeru shisan keisei kanri*, https://www.fsa.go.jp/singi/singi_kinyu/tosin/20190603/01.pdf; accessed on 30 August 2022) which estimated the monthly income of a model aged-couple household, including social security benefits, at ¥209,198. Pointing out that this was approximately ¥55,000 less than the monthly expenditure shown in the 2017 'Family Income and Expenditure Survey', the report also called for asset building through investment.
64. Minutes of 198th Diet Session, House of Councillors, Committee on Health, Labor and Welfare, No. 17, June 13, 2019, https://kokkai.ndl.go.jp/#/detail?minId=119814260X01720190613&current=1 (accessed on 27 August 2022).
65. MHLW Pension Bureau (2017: 17).
66. MHLW (2018).
67. Cabinet Office Public Relations Department (2019: 45).
68. Figure 2 of Cabinet Office Public Relations Department (2003).
69. The rate was 19.7% in 2011 which was lower than that of 2005, but it was due to the temporary effect of the Great Eastern Japan Earthquake and the Fukushima nuclear disaster.
70. MHLW (2022b: 23–24).
71. 'Nan-sai made hatarakimasu ka? Risō wa 65-sai genjitsu wa 70-sai?' (How long will you keep working? The ideal is to 65, the reality is to 70), *Asahi Shimbun*, 4 January 2019, morning edition.
72. Cases for employed workers over forty years of age. Premium rates include unemployment, workers' compensation and long-term care insurance premiums.
73. MHLW (2007). The study group also noted that part-time workers in the UK with an annual income of less than £4,368 (as of 2007) were also not obligated to contribute to their pension premiums.
74. Even before that, from 1980, part-time workers were made eligible for the same social insurance system as regular employees as long as they worked at least three-quarters of the regular working hours and days of regular employees (30 hours or more per week for an 8-hour day/5-day week). However, its coverage is very limited (see note 22 in the Introduction).

75. JILPT (2013). Among non-regular workers, 'dispatched workers from temporary agencies' and 'contract employees' are said to have higher coverage of employee's pension insurance, but they only accounted for 25% of non-regular workers in 2021. Although the actual situation is unknown, the majority of part-time workers ('*paat*' and '*arubaito*'), who accounted for 70% of non-regular workers in 2021, are likely covered by the National Pension System and National Health Insurance System prepared for the self-employed. Also see note 22 in the Introduction.
76. Moriguchi and Saez (2008) made this estimate from tax statistics of Japan and the US. Moriguchi updated the data analysis to 2012 and the results are published in Ōtake and Moriguchi (2015).
77. Moriguchi, however, states that tax statistics do not adequately capture the lower income groups and therefore her suggestion remains speculative. See Ōtake and Moriguchi (2015: 35–36).
78. Gotō (2016: 40–41).
79. Watanabe (2016: 99).
80. Abe (2006a, 2006b).
81. MHLW (2019a: 10, 16, 14).
82. OECD, 'Minimum Wages Relatives to Median Wages', https://doi.org/10.1787/data-00313-en (accessed on 30 June 2022).
83. MHLW, 'Chiiki betsu saitei chingin kaitei jōkyō' (Minimum wage revisions by region), https://www.mhlw.go.jp/stf/seisakunitsuite/bunya/koyou_roudou/roudoukijun/minimumichiran/ (accessed on 30 June 2022).
84. Ogoshi (1987).
85. MHLW (2012: 104–108).
86. The top five are Turkey (15.5%), Mexico (15.3%), Spain (14.8%), Israel (14.2%) and Chile (13.8%). The OECD average is 8.2%, and the US is 11.0%. OECD (2018a: 2).
87. LDP (1979).
88. MLIT (2009). According this report, the average size of privately owned house is 124 square meters in Japan (2003), 157 in the US (2005), 95 in the U.K. (2001), 127 in Germany (2002), and 114 in France (2002).
89. MIC (2021).
90. Sugawara (2015: 85).
91. 'Josei kōho 13-pāsento tomari' (Only 13% female candidates), *Asahi Shimbun*, 30 March 2019, morning edition, p. 4.
92. '2015 Census, Tabulation of Results of Population Movement by Sex, Age, and Other Factors: Summary of Results' (Heisei 27-nen kokusei chōsa, idō jinkō no danjo nenrei-tō shūkei kekka: Kekka no gaiyō), p. 12, http://www.stat.go.jp/data/kokusei/2015/kekka/idou1/pdf/gaiyou.pdf (accessed on June 1, 2019). Note that the percentage of residents living in the same community where they were born for Tokyo was 9.8%.
93. The 'three major metropolitan areas' encompass the prefectures of Tokyo, Chiba, Saitama, Kanagawa, Aichi, Gifu, Mie, Osaka, Kyoto, Nara and Hyogo.
94. MLIT (2015: 30).
95. My calculations were as follows. By the 2015 census, Japan's total population, excluding the three major metropolitan areas, was 61,285,000. From this, based on the 2015 MLIT survey, I calculated the number of U-turners (54.5%) to be

Notes 417

33,400,325. To this number, out of those whose place of residence as indicated in the census had not changed since birth, I added the 9,015,000 individuals living outside the three major metropolitan areas, and half of the 6,971,000 who did live in the three metropolitan areas, bringing the total to 45,715,500, including U-turners. This number, divided by the total census population, is 36.1%.

The inclusion of 50% of the 'locals' (i.e., those who have not changed their place of residence from their place of birth according to the census) living in the three major metropolitan areas is a measure I have taken in consideration of the fact that a significant number of these long-term residents fall into the category of large company-type employees and their families. Although a variety of potential ratios might be suggested based on various lines of approach (e.g., the university enrollment rate in Tokyo prefecture or the inclusion of permanent residents in Saitama and Gifu prefectures), no definitive figures are available. Accordingly, I have tentatively adopted a value of 50%.

Nevertheless, even if this ratio were to be increased or decreased by 20%, the final estimate of the nationwide percentage of local-type citizens would only rise or fall by around a single percentage point. This is because the relative proportion of those who lived in their current place of residence since birth in the three major metropolitan areas is itself only 5.5% of the total national population. The MLIT survey was an Internet-based sampling survey, which may have biased the responses. Also, the MLIT survey defines 'locals' (*chihō teijūsha*) as 'individuals whose current place of residence is outside the three metropolitan areas, whose current place of residence coincides with their home prefecture, and who have never lived in another municipality', which differs slightly from the Census definition of 'individuals who have lived in their current place since birth'. Although the MLIT survey indicates that 23.4% of respondents are 'locals', using the Census figures to calculate the proportion of 'those who have lived in their current place since birth' among those living outside the three largest metropolitan areas reveals that the ratio of those people is 14.7%. There is no frame of reference that would allow us to determine whether this discrepancy is due to survey bias or differences in definitions. The possibility that the MLIT survey is also biased with respect to the percentage of U-turners cannot be ignored, but there were no other reliable surveys.

96. See Shinozaki 1967); Shinozaki (1974).

97. Fukuda and Sekiguchi (1955).

98. Pekkanen (2006); Tsujinaka et al. (2014).

99. Tsujinaka and his colleagues also included a figure from the same APFE data in their Japanese publication in 2009 but it was deleted in the English translated version (Tsujinaka et al. 2014). I published the figure in Oguma (2021).

100. There are five major schemes. The first is the association administered health insurance (*kumiai kenkō hoken*) scheme, in which large corporations form associations and enroll their employees and their dependents. The second is the National Public Service Mutual Aid Associations (*kokka kōmuin kyōsai kumiai*) and Local Public Service Mutual Aid Associations (*chihō kōmuin kyōsai kumiai*) scheme, in which national and local government public servants and their dependents are enrolled. The third is the Japan Health Insurance Association administered health insurance (*kyō kai kenpo*, the successor of the government administered health insurance scheme until 2008) scheme in which SME workers and their dependents enroll. The fourth is the National Health

418   The System of Japanese Society

Insurance (*kokumin kenkō hoken*) scheme, which was privately subscribed to by self-employed, family and non-regular workers. The fifth is Private School Mutual Aid Associations (*shigaku kyōsai kumiai*) scheme, in which teachers and staffs of universities and schools and their dependents enroll. In the case of the association administered health insurance, associations have discretion in setting the premium, but it must have at least 700 insured persons at any given time if a company establishes an association. If the association establishes a partnership jointly, the total number of insured persons must be at least 3,000 at any given time.

101. The numbers of members and dependents of each health insurance association since 1970 were taken from Table 9 of the 'Annual Report of Social Insurance Statistics' database of the National Institute for Population and Social Security Research: https://www.ipss.go.jp/ssj-db/ssj-db-top.asp (accessed on 28 August 2022). Since the 1990s, the number of associations has remained stable at about 15 million for the association administered health insurance scheme (for employees of large companies) and 4 million for Public Service Mutual Aid Associations. This is roughly consistent with the fact the number of large company-type employees has been stable at approximately 18 million.

102. The number of regular public servants in Japan's municipalities excluding the twenty largest cities (government-ordinance designated cities) was 1,054,423 in 2017. The number of their dependents was calculated assuming the same ratio of members and dependents in the local government public servant health insurance association.

103. Nomura (1998: 116).

104. OECD (2023). In the OECD Government at a Glance 2021, the 2019 figure for Japan was 5.89%, but in Government at a Glance 2023, the 2019 figure was revised to 4.43%. The reason is not stated. The change in the figure is thought to be due to the exclusion of non-regular public servants, as the Japanese government has made all non-regular public servants in local governments single-year appointees (*kaikeinendo Nin'yō syokuin*) since April 2020. See Chapter 7 for more information on non-regular public servants.

105. Koike (2005: 5). The 'agricultural self-employment' in the text refers to the 'agriculture, forestry, and fisheries self-employment' in the Japanese government statistics.

106. Koike (2005: 179).

107. See, e.g., Kase (1997: Chapter 3).

108. Calder (1988: 313–316).

109. SMEA (Small and Medium Enterprise Agency) (2016: 45), Figure 1.2.19.l.

110. Shindō (2004: 269).

111. Oguma (2021).

112. Shindō (2004: 269).

113. Ishiguro et al. (2011). The English translation of the title of their book printed on the front cover is 'The Brain Drain: Why Japanese Youth Move to Tokyo'.

114. Doeringer and Piore (1971).

115. Dickens and Lang (1985).

116. The quotes that follow are found in Ujihara's chapter on labor market models (1966: 424–425, 454). For Ujihara's assumption of excess labor as a precondition for the decline of mutual assistance inside villages, see his discussion of 'workers and poverty' (*rōdōsha to hinkon*) (1968: 45).

Notes 419

117. Ujihara (1966: 454).
118. Ujihara (1966: 454).
119. See Ujihara's discussion on 'characteristics of workers in large factories' (*Dai kōjō rōdō-sha no seikaku*) (1966: 367–369).
120. Doeringer and Piore (1971).

Chapter 2

1. This chapter describes the characteristics of the Japanese-style employment system from a perspective different from that of management studies. Please note that the characteristics of the Japanese-style employment system described in this chapter are based on the facts and data referenced, but they are sociological ideal types, and do not necessarily point to the full realization of these characteristics in actual individual Japanese companies. As mentioned in note 32 of the Introduction, I do not review existing management studies that survey and analyze the current state of Japanese-style employment systems (e.g. Jacoby 2005), but I learned a lot from management studies and used them as secondary sources for this chapter.
2. OECD (2021).
3. JILPT (2012).
4. Recruit Works Research Institute (2013: 53).
5. JILPT (2012: 68).
6. Ebihara (2015).
7. The Supreme Court's ruling of 12 December 1973, in the Mitsubishi Plastics case. On rulings related to discrimination in hiring, see Mizumachi (2019: 77–79).
8. JILPT (2012: 73).
9. Keidanren (2018: 6).
10. JILPT (2012: 72).
11. The latest information can be found in popular online articles, e.g., Mynavi (2022).
12. JILPT (2012: 71).
13. Recruit Works Research Institute (2013: 56).
14. Internships of less than one week are almost always unpaid. That said, the number of startups offering paid internships for six months or more also increased in the 2010s.
15. 'Haru no daigaku: Ashi tōnoku shūshi gakusei' (Spring university: Master's students increasingly absent), *Asahi Shimbun*, 11 June 2022, evening edition, p. 7.
16. OECD (2021: 41). In Japan, most working conditions are stated in the 'company work rules' (*shūgyō kisoku*) set by the company, which apply to all workers in it. Japan's Labor Standards Act requires companies that employ ten or more workers on a regular basis to prepare work rules describing working conditions, obtain the opinion of a representative of the majority of their employees, and submit the regulations to the Labor Standards Inspection Office. The employment contract between employer and employee defines the contractual relationship with the employer, and with the contract the worker agrees to abide by the work rules. The articles on transfers, relocation assignments and mandatory retirement are often included in the work rules, but they often

stipulate only general working conditions and do not describe the duties or job descriptions of individual workers. See Mizumachi (2019: 45–58).

The origin of the 'work rules' was the enforcement ordinance of the revised Factory Act of 1926 that required companies to submit work rules to the local government. In Japan, where it was not customary for individual workers to sign employment contracts, the system was introduced to allow companies to determine working conditions and for the government to supervise them. See Hamada (1994).

17. In management terminology, it is difficult to distinguish between transfers and job rotations. Generally speaking, rotations are done to accumulate skills for a variety of jobs within a company, but workers retain their original positions and expect them to be temporary transfers. Transfers, on the other hand, are considered permanent in that the worker does not return to their original position. Japanese *idō* has been often explained by management as being for the accumulation of skills, but workers do not expect to keep their original positions, so I adopted 'transfer' as the English translation.

18. JILPT (2012: 75).

19. For a discussion of the connection between the bulk recruitment of new graduates and periodic personnel transfers, see, e.g., Tanaka (1980: 377–381).

20. The tabulation was published in Figure 4.25a of OECD (2013: 171).

21. The post-2020 wage census shows higher wages for postgraduates across all ages, but this is due to the fact that until the 1990s there were few non-engineering master's degree holders, and the small number of engineering master's degree holders went into higher-technical positions in large firms.

22. JILPT (2012: 76).

23. Kumazawa (1996).

24. JILPT (2012: 75–76).

25. The Supreme Court's ruling of 14 July 1986 in the Tōa Paint case; the Supreme Court's ruling of 7 December 1989 in the Nissan Automobile Murayama Factory case. As for precedents related to personnel transfers, see Hamaguchi (2011: 84–89).

26. The Tokyo High Court's ruling of 29 October 1979 in the Tōyō Oxygen Corporation case has referred embodying 'the four requirements for dismissals' as a precedent. See Mizumachi (2019: 65–66) and note 76 of this chapter.

27. In a case study of university-graduate white-collar workers at one major heavy industry employer circa 1987, it was found that with the exception of general affairs positions, about 50% of transfers placed workers in jobs functionally similar to their previous postings (e.g., in sales, purchasing and HR management). See Hisamoto (2008: 136). As for trials seeking to improve the training schemes of Japanese companies, see Satō (2016).

28. 'Toyota, kōjōj ni jimu, gijutsu syoku 600 nin wo haken' (Toyota transferred 600 office workers and engineers to its factory floor), *Nihon Keizai Shimbun*, 1 December 1992, morning edition, p. 11.

29. Shōhei Sakakura, director and editor of the youth labor advocacy group and magazine *Posse*, describes many examples of such power harassment (Sakakura 2021). Power harassment is illegal under Japanese law, but the number of lawsuits is generally low in Japan, partly due to the small number of legal professionals and the encouragement of settlement. In 2018, there were 7,126 labor-related lawsuits in Japan, about 1/21 of those in

Notes

421

2015 in France and 1/51 of those in 2016 in Germany. See Mizumachi (2019: 224–225).

30. Staff Welfare Division, Staff Welfare Bureau, National Personnel Authority (Jinji-in Shokuin Fukushi-kyoku Shokuin Fukushi-ka) (2019: 34).
31. The Supreme Court's ruling of 15 December 1968 in the Akikita Bus case. See Mizumachi (2019: 75–76).
32. Staff Welfare Division, Staff Welfare Bureau, National Personnel Authority (Jinji-in Shokuin Fukushi-kyoku Shokuin Fukushi-ka) (2019: 34).
33. 'Kyūryō 4 ~ 6 warigen ga kahan, teinen-go saikoyō no kibishii genjitsu' (Majority report salary reductions of 40% to 60%: The harsh reality of rehiring after mandatory retirement age), *Nihon Keizai Shimbun*, 25 February 2021, https://www.nikkei.com/article/DGXZQOFK222QX0S1A220C2000000/ (accessed on 30 August 2022).
34. JILPT (2012: 75). The 'external transfer' is the translation of the '*shukkō*' the JILPT uses in the reference.
35. JILPT (2012: 76).
36. Labor Capacity Development Center (1977: 13).
37. JILPT (2012: 77).
38. Koike (1981).
39. 1976 Labor White Paper (*Rōdō hakusho*), p. 120.
40. Ebihara (2013).
41. Labor Capacity Development Center (1977: 11).
42. Institute of Labor Administration (ed.) (1986).
43. Hyōdō (1997, vol 2: 405).
44. OECD (2021: 47). Figure 2.6 of this report shows wage profiles of 'standard male employees' by age of workers. However, it notes that 'standard employees denote those regular workers who are employed by enterprises immediately after graduating schools and have been working for the same firms' which is the 'standard workers' in the Wage Census of Japan. Since this is so, the wage curve with worker age in this figure is effectively the same as years of service.
45. OECD (2021: 40, 42).
46. R. Kopp 'Why Do Japanese Like Open Plan Offices?', *Manabink*, 26 December 2020, https://manabink.com/en/2020/12/26/why-do-japanese-like-open-plan-offices/ (accessed on 31 August 2022).
47. Ōmori (2006: 61–62).
48. Shindō (1992: 101–104).
49. OECD (2021: 41).
50. Yamaguchi (2019).
51. Ōsawa (1993: 101).
52. Shintani (2015: 339). According to Shintani's analysis, 33.7% of female regular employees left their job upon marriage in private companies with 300 or more employees and 33.0% in those with less than 300 employees, while 59.2% and 56.7% retired at childbirth, respectively. Multiplying the rates at marriage and at childbirth yields a retention rate of about 28% after marriage and childbirth in private companies of both categories.
53. There are a very small number of statistical 'executives' but they are omitted from Figure 2.3.

54. See Figure 6.2 of OECD (2018c: 219–220). This figure displays female labor participation rates by age group for thirty-two countries by type of employment in 2015 or latest year available. According to this figure, South Korea also shows a sharp decline in full-time employment for women starting in their thirties, followed by an increase in self-employment and forming an M-shape in total. Women are more likely to participate in informal employment-type labor in both countries: non-regular employment in Japan and self-employed in Korea.
55. Hamaguchi (2013a: 31).
56. Jacoby (1985); Naff et al. (2014).
57. Kusuda (2004: 51).
58. Koike (1993); Hayama (2008).
59. Yashiro (1997: 75).
60. Koike (1981).
61. E.g., Marsden (1999).
62. Dore (1973: 74–77).
63. Kocka (1981a).
64. Ebihara (2013).
65. Koike (1988).
66. OECD (2021: 39).
67. Takeuchi (1995: 178). Takeuchi also draws attention to the 'World Youth Survey' (*Sekai seinen ishiki chōsa*, 1977–1993), in which 'individual effort' and 'individual talent' were the top two responses among Japanese youth to the question 'What do you think is important for success in society?' (1995: 88). Moreover, he points out that whereas respondents in most countries ranked 'academic background' as the next-most important factor, the proportion of Japanese respondents who did so was comparatively much lower, ranging from 7.8% (in 1983) to 14.1% (in 1977).
68. E.g., Koike and Watanabe (1979); Tachibanaki and Yagi (2009). As we will see in Chapter 7, Japanese management felt the burden of seniority-based wages determined by educational background and length of service since the 1970s, and they have begun to assess all regular employees more rigorously. This was the background of the diminishment of the relationship between academic background and promotion during the period studied by Takeuchi, Koike, Tachibanaki and Yagi. Nevertheless, the characteristics of the Japanese-style employment system, in which management has strong discretion and professional education is not emphasized, can be seen here as well.

Moreover, even if the difference between graduates of prestigious universities and those of unknown universities decreases after recruitment into the company, the difference between university graduates and high school graduates will remain, as is clear from the figures of competence ranking systems of Japanese companies in Chapter 3 or 6. In the descriptions of Japanese companies that follow, it may seem contradictory that, on the one hand, educational background tends to be less important than effort within the company, and, on the other hand, there are no evaluation criteria other than educational background. However, this is not a contradiction if one understands that the former is the difference in the rank of universities within university graduates and the latter is the difference between university and high school graduates. Still, however, it is true that the postwar democratization and the competence ranking system, in which management examines the abilities of

Notes

423

workers regardless of their educational background, have narrowed the gap between high school and university graduates.

69. Labor Capacity Development Center (1977: 11).
70. Nishimura (2014a).
71. Nomura (1994: 39).
72. OECD (2021: 41). The Japanese government's wage censuses do not survey firms with less than five employees.
73. SMEA (2017: 85), Figure 1-3-14.
74. Nomura (1994: 36).
75. The OECD has evaluated employment protections in Japan as follows. First, termination notice procedures can be established orally and are put in writing only when requested. The advance notice period is only stipulated as thirty days prior, regardless of length of service. There is no provision for severance pay. There is also no provision for compensation for unfair dismissal or reinstatement, which can only be obtained if the worker files a lawsuit and wins the case, and the details of the lawsuit vary depending on the judgment. There are also no legal provisions on the period of time required for an unfair dismissal lawsuit or a finding of unfair dismissal. Regarding the definition of unfair dismissal, there is no clear-cut provision, except for dismissal for reasons such as work-related injury, although there is an established precedent that the court determines whether there is 'objectively reasonable grounds' and whether the employer made efforts to avoid dismissal. While there are criticisms of the OECD's EPL for being different from the actual situation of dismissal regulations, the fact that Japan's regulations are customary and there are few clear regulations in the legal text is underrated. See OECD, 'Japan: Regulation in force on 1 January 2019', https://www.oecd.org/els/emp/Japan-EPL.pdf (accessed on 30 July 2023).
76. The 'objectively reasonable grounds' (*kyakkanteki ni gōriteki na riyū*) and 'social norms' (*shakai tsūnen*) first became fixed wording in the ruling of the Supreme Court on 24 April 1975 in the Nihon Syokuen Seizō (Japan Salt Processing) case. They were made into law in 2008 with Article 16 of the Labor Contracts Act. The specific contents of 'reasonable' and 'social norms' were written in rules in the 1970s and 1980s and the summary of those contents are well known as the 'Four Requirements for Dismissal', as follows: (1) the need to reduce the workforce must be recognized; (2) efforts must have been made prior to the reduction in the workforce to avoid dismissal, such as by reducing overtime, suspending new hiring, reassignments and transfers, furloughs, soliciting voluntary retirement, and the reduction of executive compensation; (3) the selection of employees to be dismissed must have been fairly conducted based on objective criteria; and (4) reasonable procedures, including negotiations and consultations between labor and management, must have been followed when conducting a dismissal for reorganization purposes. The Tokyo High Court's 29 October 1979 ruling in the Tōyō Oxygen Corporation case has referred embodying these four requirements as a precedent. These points were codified in the 2003 amendment to the Labor Standards Act and transposed into the Labor Contracts Act (*Rōdō keiyaku-hō*) enacted in 2007. However, as discussed in chapters 7 and 8, most Japanese SMEs do not have labor unions, which should be the counterpart in labor-management negotiations and consultations. According to a 2012 JILPT survey, only 19.9% of companies without labor unions held consultations with employee representatives when dismissing employees. See Sugeno and Araki (eds.) (2017).

77. Räisänen (2005: 13).
78. JILPT (2012: 74).
79. The 'Summary Report of Wage Census Results' by the Japanese government describes wage profiles by firm size.
80. Tachibanaki (1996) takes the former view, while Koike (1981, Chapter 2, Section 1) is well known as an example of the latter.
81. Tachibanaki (2015: 96).
82. Lester (1967); Brown and Medoff (1989); Idson and Feaster (1990); Green et al. (1996); and Troske (1999) are often cited in studies of the topic.
83. See Idson and Oi (1999) for considerable variables on this topic.
84. Kerr (1954).
85. See Fig. 1 of Kerr (1954). Figure 17-1 of Marsden (1990) is also similar to Tanaka's contrast.
86. Jacoby (1997).
87. Jacoby (1997) describes how attempts by welfare capitalist firms to foster cooperative unions have had to contend with the intervention of the US judicial authorities.
88. Creedy and Whitfield (1988) and Althauser (1989) provide comprehensive reviews of research studies of internal labor markets prior to the 1980s.
89. Dore (1973: 115).
90. Dore (1973: 114).
91. *Encyclopedia Britannica*, s.v. 'Craft Union', https://www.britannica.com/topic/craft-union (accessed on 9 May 2022).
92. Onozuka (2001: 201–202).
93. Kocka (1981a).
94. Boltanski (1987).
95. Nimura (1987); Gordon (1985). Gordon (1985: 449) states as follows: 'Nimura Kazuo first suggested to me that a very different tradition of craft organization pointed Japanese labor history in a direction distant from that in Europe'.
96. Dore (1973: 275).
97. OECD, 'Public Employment and Management, Acquiring Capacity', https://www.oecd.org/gov/pem/acquiringcapacity.htm (accessed on 19 March 2020).
98. E.g., Bhatta (2005: 98).
99. Jacoby (1985).
100. E.g., Lange et al. (2006).
101. Oguma (2017).
102. See Althauser (1989).
103. Muramatsu (ed.) (2018). This book is a survey of the bureaucracies of the US, the UK, Germany and France by Japanese administrative scholars from a comparative perspective with Japan. As such, the authors study practices of bureaucracies in those countries such as absence of regular personnel transfers or bulk recruitment of new graduates that have not been described by researchers in their respective countries or in comparative research from the Western perspective.

Notes

425

Chapter 3

1. The influence of the bureaucracy on employment practices in Japan has been touched upon in piecemeal fashion as shown in notes 65 and 66, but no study has yet addressed this topic head-on. As discussed in the Introduction, Japanese employment practices have been studied in labor history and business history, but labor historians have not paid attention to the practices applied to white-collar workers, although they have clarified how practices that already existed among the white-collar employees were extended to blue-collar workers. Also, business historians, especially those who studied state-owned enterprises (SOEs), such as Shinji Sugayama (2011), described the existence of the bureaucracy in the SOEs, but did not examine the government bureaucracy. Most researchers on administrative history mainly looked at the relationship between politics and the bureaucracy, and only a few such as Hiroaki Inatsugu (2005) paid attention to the personnel practices of bureaucratic organizations, and they have not examined the influence of the bureaucracy on private companies. Labor historian Yutaka Nishinarita (1995a) suggested that the government's introduction of heavy industry, such as railroads and shipbuilding, was the origin of the wage grade system for Japanese workers, but did not explore this further or investigate its connection to the government bureaucracy. This chapter addresses the lacuna across several academic disciplines by synthesizing the research conducted separately in each discipline. In the following chapter notes, I introduce references to this topic in studies from those disciplines and others.

2. Abegglen (2004: 6, 195–197). For the 2004 new Japanese translation and publication of his 1958 *The Japanese Factory*, Abegglen contributed a preface and a separate section on his background.

3. Abegglen (1958: 29).

4. Abegglen (1958: 44–45).

5. Abegglen (1958: 34–43).

6. Abegglen (1958: 36).

7. Abegglen (1958: 31–35).

8. Abegglen (1958: 43–44). Note also that whereas university graduates are hired on a company-wide basis and move from one position to another within the company, junior high school graduates are hired locally at an office or factory and only move within that particular job site. So, while some difference does exist in this sense, the observation that the dismissal of junior high school graduates is also avoided through transfers intriguingly indicates a difference from the prewar period.

9. Kuniyoshi Urabe, who first translated Abegglen's book into Japanese in 1958, glossed 'a lifetime commitment' as *shūshin kankei* (lifelong relationship), and '"permanent" or "eternal" employees' as *'shūshin-teki' naishi 'kōkyū-teki' jūgyōin* ('lifetime' or 'perpetual' employees) (Abegglen 1958: 17, 19 in Urabe's translation). It seems likely that some mixture of these terms gave rise to 'lifetime employment' (*shūshin koyō*), a term that Abegglen did not in fact use. Unlike 'permanent employment', a 'lifetime commitment' is hardly economic terminology for an employment relationship. As noted in this chapter, Abegglen, who had trained in social anthropology, likely used this term to denote a normative consciousness in an organization.

426 The System of Japanese Society

10. Japan Employers' Federation Merit-Based Management Study Group ([1969] 2001: 84).
11. Abegglen (1958: 103–104).
12. Miyamoto (1938); Nimura (1987: 82–86).
13. Fujita (1995).
14. Sugayama (2011: 38, 54, 55, 89).
15. For the following examples, see Sugayama (2011: 74, 75).
16. Sugayama (2011: 70).
17. Ueyama (1964: 6–12).
18. Sugayama (2011: 65, 95).
19. Nagashima (2008: 206, 207).
20. Mori (2005: 23–26).
21. Kawate (2005: 1–4).
22. For details on official posts and salaries, see Cabinet Records Bureau (ed.) ([1894] 1979). In the case of military officers, official rank corresponds to grade, while titles such as 'ship's captain' or 'staff officer' correspond to positions. While there are some predetermined equivalencies, such as how the captain of a heavy cruiser in the navy corresponds to the army rank of colonel and the captain of a destroyer to the rank of major, the position of 'ship's captain' does not always correspond one-to-one with a particular grade (i.e., official rank). The same goes for civil service officials. The titles of 'bureau chief' and 'professor' shown in the table are positions akin to 'ship's captain', and thus, even on the Official Ranks Table, we see that some positions are open to a certain range of ranks, such as *sōnin* officials of the first or second rank (although a professor at an imperial university would never be classed as a *sōnin* official of the fifth rank). Even on the Official Ranks Table for 1886, we find a difference between positions with only one corresponding rank (e.g., cabinet ministers) and positions with a wide range of potential corresponding ranks (e.g., governors or university professors). While there are other differences from the table reproduced here, such as how the title of *shinninkan* was not yet listed in 1886, and how the ranks of *hannin* officials are listed up to the tenth rank, I have simplified things for the sake of clarity.
23. Kawate (2005: 11).
24. See Mizutani ([1999] 2013: 137, Figure 5).
25. Such individuals were given the special title of 'chief' (*rijikan*) within the ministry, which could be equivalent to warrant officer in the military. See Kawate (2005: 13).
26. Hamaguchi (2013b) considers *koin* and *yōnin* employees as the origins of non-regular public servants in postwar Japan.
27. *Koin* 雇員 were called *yatoi* 雇 in the early Meiji period, referring to apprentices of *hannin* officials, but the term was defined as non-regular clerk officials in 1886. However, due to their history as apprentices of officials, there was a provision (Article 5 of the 1893 Civil Service Appointment Decree) that allowed them to be appointed as a *hannin* official after five years of service as *koin*, and this was applied to some *koin*. *Yōnin* 傭人 was introduced in 1889 as a generic term for those who served in the navy doing chores and manual labor, and this term spread to other government agencies. See Ishii (2016) and note 112 in Chapter 5.
28. Inatsugu (2005: 189).

Notes

427

29. Cabinet Records Bureau (ed.) ([1894] 1979: 64–78). Official Rank Salary Table from 31 December 1886. In a chapter dealing with military salaries in prewar Japan, Kazuo Koike looks at army salaries based on the Edict on Army Salaries (*rikugun kyūyo-rei*) of 1890 which is almost the same as in the 1886 version (Koike 2009: 118–123). In general, the salaries of *hannin*-class military officers were lower than those of civilian officials, conceivably to account for the fact that non-commissioned officers in the military lived in barracks where they were provided with board and lodging.
30. Inatsugu (2005: 10).
31. Kita (1933: 51).
32. Kita (1933: 51–52).
33. Makino (1948, vol. 1: 170, 181).
34. National Personnel Authority (ed.) (2008, Book 1, Part 2, Section 1.1). This explanation, essentially identical to that advanced by Minobe (1936: 683), was the standard legal interpretation prior to World War II.
35. Suzuki (2002: 91–95).
36. Suzuki (2002: 93–94); Mizutani ([1999] 2013: 66, 68).
37. According to the salary table for official ranks enacted on 31 December 1887, which appears in Cabinet Records Bureau (ed.) ([1894] 1979: 54–78), there are no position-based differences in salaries for general officers. Slight differences in salaries can be seen for field officers depending on specialty, such as whether one is an infantry colonel, military police colonel or a colonel with the corps of engineers, while in the case of junior officers there is a difference between first- and second-class officers.
38. National Personnel Authority (ed.) (2007, Book 1, Part 1, Section 1).
39. Muramatsu (ed.) (2018: 157, 213).
40. In Japan, the tendency to accord high priority to ranks is reputed to have dated from the introduction of the Ritsuryō system with the Taihō and Yōrō codes and the establishment of a bureaucratic system in the eighth century. Japan at that time modeled itself on the Ritsuryō system of Tang Dynasty China, which also observed a dual system of position and rank. In China, however, it was position that determined the hierarchy of bureaucrats, while rank (*pin jie*, Jp. *honkai*) was merely an indicator of the grade of a government position. In Japan, however, the active principle was that rank (*ikai*) determined the hierarchy, and that officials were assigned to the government positions that corresponded to those ranks.

    This Japanese system has been called the 'official rank equivalent system' (*kan'i sōtōsei*) by Japanese historians (Ōsumi 1993). In China, the court had the effective power to confer government positions, but in Japan, real power lay with the powerful regional clans. Accordingly, this method is regarded as having been adopted as a result of the emperor's establishment of a hierarchy by conferring ranks on the samurai families. Even in the Edo period, when the emperor no longer exercised real authority, the custom of formally conferring ranks remained, and this practice seems also to have been applied to the bureaucracy following the Meiji Restoration.

    Even so, as discussed in this chapter, the dual system of pay grades and positions is not unique to the Japanese bureaucracy. Even if there were differences between the eighth-century Japanese bureaucracy and the Chinese bureaucracy, there is no evidence that these differences survived to become characteristics of the Japanese bureaucracy in the nineteenth century and

428   The System of Japanese Society

after. Such discussions require substantiation, and we should be cautious about making any frivolous claims to Japanese exceptionalism.

41. Cabinet Records Bureau (ed.) ([1894] 1979: 6).

42. Rouban (1999); Gottschall (2015). In France, the right to retain rank after losing one's position had been guaranteed by law since 1834 for military personnel, and the right was extended to civilian officials in 1946.

43. Goetz (1999); Reichard and Schröter (2021).

44. Shimoi (2017). Japanese bureaucracies also have a system of secondment to other agencies, but their group of belonging is the ministry where they were initially hired, and there is no equivalent of the French bureaucratic *corps*.

45. Bureau of Statistics, Cabinet Office (ed.) (1935: 408). In the Japanese Imperial Statistical Yearbook, *koin* 雇員 were tabulated in the categorical name of *yatoi* 雇 even after their official name was revised in 1886. As for the statistical analysis of prewar payment hierarchy, see Hayakawa and Matsui (1979).

46. As for the legal status of *yatoinin* and *yōnin*, see Hamaguchi (2013b).

47. See note 27 and Ishii (2016).

48. Ishii (2016).

49. Kawate (2005: 11).

50. Nishinarita (2004: 181–182). In the Yahata Steel Works, *koin* 雇員 were tabulated in the categorical name of *yatoi* 雇 as in the Japanese Imperial Statistical Yearbook.

51. Sugayama (2011: 95–96).

52. For a discussion of the rank system of the government railways, see Woo (2003: Chapter 1.1).

53. Suzuki (2002: 91–92). These were the summer working hours.

54. See Shōjirō Ujihara ([1959] 1968). However, this view of a three-tier structure could be arguably somewhat simplistic. In government offices, clerical *yatoi* held a higher status than *yōnin*, who performed manual labor. In the context of private industry, clerical assistants (*koin*) and foremen (*shokuchō*) were considered higher than factory workers. Were we to consider these workers as an independent tier, then we would have a hierarchy of four tiers, not three. It is also difficult to judge whether associate employees (*jun-shain*) in private industry correspond to *hannin* officials or to *koin* in the context of the bureaucracy. I should also note that while Ujihara offers a four-tier hierarchy of staff employees, associate employees, factory workers (*kōin*) and dispatched workers employed by subcontractors (*kumifu*), I have simplified this here to only three tiers.

55. Yoshida and Okamuro (2016: 8). That said, Ichihara (2012) reveals that not a few regular employees (*sei-in*), mainly engineers, were promoted from associates (*jun-in*).

56. See the figure in Nakanishi (2003: 463).

57. In addition, on the revision of September 1919, it was noted that this grade list and titles applied to 'regular employees' and that 'the title of clerical assistant / technical assistant shall be assigned to newly hired employees'. See Mitsubishi Company History Publication Society (ed.) (1979–1982, vol. 30: 4917).

58. Yashiro et al. (2015: 85).

59. Dore (1973: 67). German workers are classified into grades according to their professional qualifications, but these are cross-firm grades in the industrial level and the wages for each grade are determined by a cross-firm collective agreement negotiated in the industrial collective bargaining. The grades differ

Notes 429

from the in-house ranks of Japanese companies, which are grades within individual firms.

60. Dore (1973: 275–276).

61. Ministry of Education (1999). Professional school in the text is a translation of prewar *Senmon Gakkō*, Class A vocational school is a transōlation of *Kōsyu Jitsugyō gakkō*, and Class B vocational school is a translation of *Otsushu Jitugyō Gakkō*. However, the Japanese government abolished the classification of vocational schools as Class A and Class B in 1921, and semi-professional schools did not exist as an official government classification. The Ishikawajima Heavy Industries' academic classification, including the division of private universities into A and B, reflects the common norm of Japanese society at that time rather than the official classifications.

62. Ōbori (1960: 98).

63. Wakabayashi (2014). Even so, it is reported that the disparity in starting salary tended to persist at the Yahata Steel Works and some of the other former SOEs after 1918.

64. See Fujimura (2014).

65. E.g., Koike (2009: 106).

66. Nomura (2007: 73) states that, based on the government's divestment of business enterprises, 'there is a strong possibility that the state bureaucratic system defined the managerial order of private companies after privatization'. Beyond this, however, he does not offer any concrete examination of similarities with the bureaucratic system.

67. Usami (1960: 66).

68. Shōwa Comrades' Association (ed.) (1960: 337–338). The first author of this report is Yoshio Kaneko, who was the first director general of the Bureau of Labor Statistics and Research of the Ministry of Labor, created after World War II, and became the director of the Research Bureau of the Economic Planning Agency in 1957. This 'bank' could be the Bank of Japan, but even in that case it is likely that the Bank of Japan formed the standard for private banks.

69. Ikeda (1951: 47).

70. Mizutani ([1999] 2013: 83).

71. Ikeda (1949: 47).

72. Ikeda (1949: 47).

73. 'Yo ga hajimete syūsyoku sita toki no kinmusaki to hōkyū' (The firm and salary when I first started working) *Jitsugyō no Nihon* 34(4), 15 February 1931 edition, pp. 48–51. Among those whose starting salary was 40 yen were Kōzō Matsumoto, who graduated from the law department of Tokyo Imperial University and entered the Ministry of Finance's Monopoly Bureau in 1908, Yoshihisa Shikamura, who graduated from the Tokyo Higher Commercial School and joined Mitsubishi Bank in the same year; and Kyōhei Katō, who graduated from the law department of Tokyo Imperial University and joined the Mitsubishi Joint Stock Company in 1905.

74. The salary schedule for officials (Figure 3.3) shows that the stipulated monthly salary of a technical *hannin* official was set at 5 to 10 yen higher than that of a clerical *hannin* official, even for officials of the same rank. This trend seems likely to have been the basis for the fact that starting salaries at industrial conglomerates and their affiliates were also higher for graduates of the faculty of science and engineering of universities than for graduates of the faculty of liberal arts, and for graduates of industrial business schools than for graduates

430   The System of Japanese Society

of commercial business schools. See Nomura (2007: 24, 25). Regarding bureaucratic influence on the distinction between the arts and sciences in the Japanese education system, see Oki (2018: 100–102).

75. The tabulated results of the follow-up study may be found in Fukui (2016: 16).

76. Wakabayashi (2007: 162). This kind of register system of Mitsui was introduced in 1873 (Senmoto 1989). Its origins are unknown, but a mixing with a military-type worldview occurred afterwards, as described in the text.

77. Nomura (2007: 248).

78. Japan Business History Institute (ed.) (1976: 153).

79. Tokyo Institute of Technology (ed.) (1940: 67).

80. As cited in Wakabayashi (2007: 169, 178).

81. Yano (1982: 11).

82. Wakabayashi (2007: 170).

83. Sugayama (2011: 176). The higher educational institutions include universities and professional schools (single-department colleges).

84. Gordon (1985); Nishinarita (1988); Sugayama (2011).

85. Sugayama (2011: 52, 178).

86. Sugayama (2011: 179).

87. Hirohide Tanaka (1983: 43).

88. Ōji Seishi Rōdō Kumiai (Oji Paper Labor Union) (1957), *Ōji seishi rōdō kumiai undō-shi* (A History of the Labor Union Movement at Oji Paper), Tokyo: Ōji seishi rōdō kumiai, p. 73; as cited in Nomura (2007: 188–189).

89. Hazama (1964).

90. As for the wage profiles of the *sōnin* officials and *hannin* officials, see Inatsugu (2005: 189).

91. Sugayama (2011: 177, 180, 181).

92. Calculations based on the table in Ishida (1992, Part 1: 46). The figures are for factory managers and those under them, excluding company executives (*yakuin*).

93. Nomura (2007: 34, 35).

94. Midori Suzuki, 'Kako 12 nenkan wo jijo den fu ni kataru' (Autobiographical account of the past 12 years), *Kaihō* (Bulletin of the Nikkō Alumni Group), March 1930; as cited in Sugayama (2011: 180).

95. As cited in Nomura (2007: 6).

96. Mori (2006: 24–26). Mori also tell us that when the state-owned Yahata Steel Works were drafting the Factory Workers' Regulations of 1900, which would set the amounts for factory workers' daily wages, factory workers were classified into thirty ranks, with daily wages to be paid according to rank. In the final draft of the regulations, however, factory worker ranks were eliminated, and only a wage schedule by grade was established.

It is also worth noting that, according to Ishida (1992, Part 1: 39), prior to the scheme's revision in 1943, factory workers at Oji Paper had ranks ranging fourth- up to first-class. In this case, however, 'ranks were not categories for determining daily wages, but were on the contrary determined by daily wages'. This seems to be an intermediate form between the two types of hierarchies, namely, the staff hierarchy at Mitsui & Co. that was determined by salaries and the bureaucratic qualification scheme in which salaries were determined by rank. In the 1943 revision of the scheme, factory worker ranks were renamed

Notes   431

as 'third class, second class, first class and senior class' (i.e., the equivalent of the ranking scheme for staff employees) as a part of efforts to eliminate discrimination against factory workers.

Kinoshita (1999: 67) notes that monthly-paid factory workers at the Yokosuka Shipyard in 1873 were paid according to ranks that were similar to those used for plasterers and suggests that this may have been a cross-firm position-based wage. Indeed, given the mobility of factory workers at that time, it is possible that the in-house wage ranks mentioned above were based on ranks in the cross-firm craftsman wage market. Nevertheless, as noted in this chapter, Shinji Sugayama takes the position that there were no such standard wage rates by job type. If he is right, it is possible that the aforementioned wage ranks for factory workers were simply an in-house system. It is difficult here to determine which explanation is accurate.

97. Woo (2009), as reprinted in Enoki and Onozuka (eds.) (2014: 323–324, 337–338).
98. Jacoby (1985: 279).
99. Nimura (1994: 59).
100. Sumiya (1967: 54).
101. Dore (1973: 42, 43).
102. Dore (1976: 43–44; 1973: 43).
103. Naff et al. (2014).
104. *Manda-san 80 sai wo iwau* (Celebrating 80 years of Manda-san), privately published, 1986. As cited in Sugayama (2011: 200). Recollections of Goro Manda who joined Hitachi Works after graduating from Tokyo Imperial University Faculty of Law in 1929.
105. The early Meiji era saw a rivalry between 'Restoration bureaucrats' appointed from the ranks of the samurai retainers who had administered the feudal domains and 'scholar bureaucrats' who had passed examinations, but the history of the opposition between status and academic background was minor and short-lived. For a more detailed account, see Shimizu (2013).
106. Ujihara ([1959] 1968: 75).

Chapter 4

1. This chapter synthesizes the facts mentioned in the individual studies introduced in the text to highlight the 'transplantation' of the bureaucracy, and additionally compares these with the case of Germany and the US. No previous study has integrated individual facts in this manner to present an overview of the formation of the practices that they entail.
2. Shimizu (2007: 26).
3. Gottschall (2015); Muramatsu (ed.) (2018: 154–159); Reichard and Schröter (2021).
4. Nomura (1995: 44).
5. Nomura (1995: 21–24, 34).
6. Nomura (1995: 34, 28).
7. Mizutani ([1999] 2013: 111).
8. Shimizu (2007: 27).
9. Shimizu (2009: 199–200).
10. Shimizu (2007: 37, 58).
11. Shimizu (2007: 46, 42).

12. Shimizu (2009: 210–214). By the 1910s, however, two unofficial classes of recruits had emerged: a 'first class', who were hired at graduation and who sat their examination after taking a leave of absence, and a 'second class', who were hired only after passing their examination.

13. According to Yō Takeuchi, who has analyzed the family background of students at the First High School (at that time the preparatory school for Tokyo Imperial University), although 60.9% of the students in 1886 were from samurai families, this percentage declined rapidly to 27.1% in 1910. The occupations of students' parents in 1910–1913 were as follows: government official 8.9%, company or bank staff employee 8.1%, professional 18.6%, self-employed in commerce and the manufacturing industry 19.2%, self-employed in agriculture, forestry and fisheries 16.7%, military 2.0%, landowner and assemblyman 1.3%, blue-collar worker and clerk 0.4%, unemployed 6.1%, deceased 3.4%, and unknown or unclassifiable 15.3% (Takeuchi 1999: 173, 177).

14. Kawate (2005: 11, 12).

15. Shimizu (2007: 52, 53).

16. 'Rikugunbukan shinkyū jōrei' (Army Military Officer Promotion Ordinance), 18 November 1874, Rikugun-shō tappu (Army Ministry Notification) No. 448; included in the Cabinet Official Gazette Bureau (Naikaku Kanpō-kyoku) (ed.) Hōrei zensho (Complete Book of Laws), 1874 edition.

17. I am indebted to Yuichirō Shimizu for suggesting the background of this period. For details on the expansion of the number of government officials, see Shimizu (2007: 52).

18. Kawate (2005: 12). However, while Kawate notes that the amendment to a two-year period was made with the revision of the Edict on Rank and Salaries for Higher Civil Officials in Edict No. 123 of 1894, the correct version is Edict No. 123 of 1895 (promulgated on 21 September of that year). I thank Yuichirō Shimizu for pointing this out to me.

19. The principal was introduced to block patronage appointment by political parties. The parliamentary system was introduced in Japan and the Imperial Diet was first convened in 1890, and the government was afraid that opposition parties would appoint higher officials to government offices.

20. Tsuji (2011: 73, 74).

21. I thank Yuichirō Shimizu for pointing this out to me.

22. Henry (1999: 282).

23. Naff et al. (2014: 8).

24. Muramatsu (ed.) (2018: 161, 164, 221).

25. Ueyama (1964: 18–24, 237–240). This book is an attempt by Japanese historians of German history to identify the historical origins of the characteristics of the Japanese bureaucracy in comparison with the German bureaucracy.

26. Weber ([1918] 1994: 177, original emphasis).

27. Grundgesetz für die Bundesrepublik Deutschland (Basic Law for the Federal Republic of Germany), Article 33(2), http://www.fitweb.or.jp/~nkgw/dgg/ (accessed on 4 June 2019).

28. Sections 11 and 17. English translation available online: https://www.bmi.bund.de/SharedDocs/downloads/EN/themen/moderne-verwaltung/ggo_en.pdf (accessed on 4 December 2022).

29. Legal tradition is another norm in society, and with it comes different bureaucracies. See Tepe (2015).

Notes

433

30. Mizutani ([1999] 2013: 70).
31. As cited on p. 21 of *Ōkurashō-tatsu* (Ministry of Finance Directive) (sent to all administrative divisions, 16 December 1879); included in Akagi (1991).
32. Ōmori (2006: 139, 142).
33. Ōmori (2006: 139, 142).
34. Mizutani ([1999] 2013: 391–392). Mizutani also points out, however, that it is questionable whether the knowledge acquired in just five days was a sufficient level of professional knowledge, even if the bureaucrat was smart.
35. Mizutani ([1999] 2013: 138).
36. Mizutani ([1999] 2013: 143).
37. Kamishima (1962: 104).
38. 'Teikoku daigaku sotsugyōsha o shiho ni saiyō no sai hōkyū-gaku no ken' (The matter of salary when hiring Imperial University graduates as probationers), July 1889, Cabinet Instruction No. 23; in Navy Minister's Secretariat (Kaigun daijin kanbō) (1939: 901).
39. Takeuchi (1999: 64). Takeuchi also attaches a table of monthly wages for government officials as of 1877.
40. On the 1886 salary schedule, the salary range for a *sōnin* official of the sixth rank was between 400 to 600 yen per annum, and the difference in salary based on performance in 1889 fell within this range. Accordingly, we cannot necessarily conclude that this salary difference was immediately linked to a difference in rank. If it were, however, the salary difference would be equivalent to the monthly salary of a *hannin* official of the second to fifth rank plus benefits.
41. Ishida and Hamada (2006: 58).
42. Kamishima (1962: 104).
43. The Chinese characters used to write *kōka* differed between the army and navy, with the former using 考科 and the latter 考課. For details on the regulations and operation of the evaluation system, see Ishida and Hamada (2006) and Navy Minister's Secretariat (Kaigun daijin kanbō) (1939: Part 6, Chapter 2, Section 1).
44. As cited in Ishida and Hamada (2006, *Shiryō* 1 [Document 1]: 76–77). Regulations applicable to the evaluation of lieutenant-commanders and lieutenants in the navy, and of majors and captains in the army.
45. Endō (1999: 124). Endō, however, overlooks the fact that the military had been producing such evaluation sheets since the early Meiji period. Although Endō notes that the term *kōka* was used in classical Chinese texts in reference to judgements of the performance of officials, and that the term was also used in the Ritsuryō system of ancient Japan, he locates the origins of Japan's modern personnel assessment system in American methods of the 1920s (see Chapter 5). In his view, 'there is a disconnect between the *kōka* system for civil servants in ancient China and ancient Japan and personnel evaluation systems in modern Japan, which originated with personnel evaluation systems in the United States' (1991: 125). Nevertheless, since the Imperial Japanese military used the term *kōka* from the Meiji period, it may be necessary to reexamine the possibility of earlier influence.
46. Mitsubishi Company History Publication Society (Mitsubishi Shashi Kankōkai) (1979–1982, vol. 23: 3190).
47. Nomura (2007: 110).
48. Amanuma (1982: 73).

49. Ogihara (1984: 2–6); Rohl (2005: 163–165).

50. Ogihara (1984: 6–8).

51. Jinji-in (National Personnel Authority), 'Kokka kōmuin ni okeru teinen seido no ikisatsu-tō' (Chronicle of the National Public Service Retirement System), https://www.jinji.go.jp/kenkyukai/koureikikenkyukai/h19_01/shiryou/h19_01_shiryou10.pdf (accessed on 4 June 2019).

52. Kawate (2015: 98–102). However, the 1933 *Heibonsha Encyclopedia*, cited in Amanuma (1982: 78), in its entry for *teigen nenrei* (age-in-grade), states in its description of the Edict on Army Officer Service (*rikugun bukan fukueki rei*) that the term is 'synonymous with *teinen* [retirement age], in other words, the age at which a civil servant is normally required to retire when he or she reaches a certain age'. Presumably, it was customary for officials to retire at the age at which they became entitled to receive benefits.

53. Ogihara (1984: 1–2). Although I am heavily indebted to Ogihara's work in this section, his is a purely factual account that does not enter into a discussion of mutual influence or the similarity of the employment systems of companies. While the prewar mandatory retirement system has been discussed elsewhere by scholars including Masami Nomura (2007: Chapter 2) and Mikio Sumiya (1980), for some reason they do not discuss the aspect of the military's influence. This was presumably because, as economists, they were trying to analyze employment practices from an economic perspective and not from the sociological perspective of norm propagation from the public sector. Regarding retirement benefits, Kiyoshi Yamazaki (1988: Chapter 1) and Nomura (2007: 269–270) describe the facts of the prewar period, but again do not discuss the influence of the military.

54. Ogihara (1984: 8–11).

55. Ogihara (1984: 11–13).

56. Ogihara (1984: 41–45).

57. Ogihara (1984: 12).

58. Ogihara (1984: 42, 55).

59. Ogihara (1984: 44, 94).

60. Miyachi (2015); Katsura (1930: 66).

61. Ogihara (1984: 94, 102–103, 107). As for the history of severance and retirement allowance, see Nishinarita (2009).

62. Player (1992: 128, 130).

63. See the English translation of the Companies Act: https://www.japaneselawtranslation.go.jp/en/laws/view/2035#je_pt1ch3 (accessed on 30 August 2023).

64. *Suitō kanri mimoto hoshōkin nōfu no ken*, 20 January 1890, Imperial Ordinance No. 4; included in the Cabinet Official Gazette Bureau (Naikaku Kanpō-kyoku) (ed.), *Hōrei zensho* (Complete Book of Laws), 1890 edition.

65. Kai (1994).

66. See the chronological table in Nihon Kokuyū Tetsudō (Japan National Railroad) (1997).

67. Kaneko (2013: 40). However, during the Meiji period, owing to the high rate of theft of materials and other items by its workers, the Yahata Steel Works required that a security deposit be deducted from wages (to be returned at the time of their retirement). In this sense, then, a personal bond was not something that was only applied to high-level salaried staff employees (Nagashima 2009: 172).

Notes

68. For a more detailed account of the personal bond system and its operation at Mitsui & Co., see Yamafuji (2018: 184–186).
69. Takeuchi (1995: 162).
70. Sugayama (2011: 98, 99).
71. Amano (1992: 260).
72. Seikō Editorial Team (ed.) (1905: 20–21).
73. Amano (1992: 260).
74. Iwasaki (1904). Also worthy of note, according to Shimizu (2009: 213), is the fact that by the end of the Meiji period, the recruitment of Imperial University students to positions in the civil service through their professors, even prior to their taking the civil service examinations, had also become a regular occurrence.
75. Fukui (2016: 18–19).
76. Iwasaki (1904: 47, 262).
77. The five imperial universities were Tokyo, Kyoto, Tōhoku, Kyūsyū and Hokkaidō. The eight private schools approved as universities in 1920 were Keio, Waseda, Meiji, Hōsei, Chūō, Nihon, Kokugakuin and Dōshisha.
78. As cited in Wakabayashi (2007: 154, 155).
79. Shimizu (2009: 213).
80. Wakabayashi (2007: 155).
81. Noma (1936: 241).
82. Iwase ([2006] 2017: 182). Recollection of Seisha Makiyama, managing director of Imperial Sugar Co..
83. Sugayama (2011: 109).
84. Wakabayashi (2014: 124).
85. Fukui (2016: 36, 38, 45).
86. As for the latest development in the cultural history of the 'salaryman', see Suzuki (2023).
87. Fukui (2016: 68).
88. Sugayama (2011: 127, 128).
89. Fukui (2016: 75).
90. Jacoby (1985).
91. Fujii (1991: 109).
92. Fukui (2016: 45). Fukui confirmed the fact from his analysis of data from the Research Division, Research Bureau, Ministry of Education (1957).
93. Ministry of Education (1962), *Nihon no seichō to kyōiku* (Growth and Education in Japan), Chapter 2, Section 2.5, 'Kōtō kyōiku no kakudai' (The expansion of higher education), http://www.mext.go.jp/b_menu/hakusho/html/hpad196201/hpad196201_2_014.html (accessed on 4 June 2019).
94. Koike (1929: 49).
95. The 1920 census was the first nationwide census of Japan. In the 1920 census, the major categories of occupation were 'main occupation', 'side occupation' and 'domestic servant', and the major categories of occupational status were 'business owner', 'staff employee' and 'laborer'. The 'business owner' includes the self-employed. The breakdown of 'main occupation' was 9.71 million as 'business owner', 1.51 million as 'staff employee' and 16.1 million as 'laborer', 27.4 million in total.

96. Ujihara ([1959] 1968: 79).
97. As cited in Wakabayashi (2007: 169–170).
98. Fukui (2016: 77).
99. Inoue (1930: 82).
100. Ujihara ([1959] 1968: 77).
101. As cited in Wakabayashi (2007: 200).
102. Wakabayashi (2007: 201).
103. Katsunori Miyachi (2015: 285) cites a 1932 report edited by the Zenkoku sangyō dantai rengō-kai jimukyoku (All Japan Federation of Industrial Organizations Secretariat) entitled *Wagakuni ni okeru rōmusha taishoku teate seido no genjō* (The Current State of the Workers' Retirement Allowance System in Japan), which indicates that 71 of the 162 large companies surveyed had set a mandatory age of retirement for their workers, and that in most companies this was 55 or 50 for men and 50 for women.
104. Nomura (2007: 31).
105. Nomura (2007: 26). Hokkaido University began accepting women as elective students in 1918, and after that, other universities including Kyoto Imperial University, Tokyo Imperial University and Waseda University accepted women as auditors. Universities that began accepting women as full-time students from 1923 included Dōshisha University, Kyushu Imperial University, Tokyo University of Literature and Science and Hiroshima University of Literature and Science. See Nomura (2007: 83, 84).
106. Senmoto (1990).
107. Tanimoto (2013).
108. Saitō (1984); Hareven (2003); Gordon (2011).
109. Morimoto (1921). Morimoto suggests, however, that tax statistics may not reflect the reality of self-employed households because self-employment income was not sufficiently supplemented by the tax office at that time.
110. Boltanski (1987).
111. Schinagl (1966: 46–59). In South Korea, as well, a management system developed in the US that was introduced via military channels in the 1960s is believed to have influenced training in private firms. See Ahn (2015: 2).
112. Jacoby (1985).
113. Kocka (1981a: 456).
114. Kocka (1981a: 455).
115. Kocka (1981a: 458).
116. Kocka (1981a: 462). Tanaka (2001: 166–168). However, it was not until the twentieth century that the various ranks of non-senior salaried staff began being collectively referred to as *Angestellte*.
117. Kocka (1981a: 458, 463–464).
118. Kocka (1981a: 453); cf. Weber ([1918] 1994: 145–146).
119. Kocka (1981a: 459, 460, 462–463).
120. The following history of the formation of in-company and occupational qualifications in Germany is based on Tanaka (2003).
121. Greinert (1994).
122. Kocka ([1981b] 1992: 82–89).
123. Kocka ([1981b] 1992: 79–89); Kocka (1981a: 462–463).
124. Tanaka (2001: 181–190).

Notes

437

125. Gottschall (2015).
126. The 1979 Japanese translation of Siegfried Kracauer's 1930 monograph on *Die Angestellten*, for example, was entitled *Sararīman*. Cf. Kracauer (1998).
127. Tanaka (2001: 168).
128. The following discussion of the formation of a movement by lower-level salaried staff draws on Kocka (1981a: 465–66).
129. Boltanski (1987). The French Confederation of Management–General Confederation of Executives (*Confédération française de l'encadrement-Confédération générale des cadres*, CFE-CGC) is one of the five major French confederations of trade unions.
130. Schneier (1978); Werner and Bolino (1997).
131. Onozuka (2001: 184, 185).
132. For a detailed account of the SMU, see Takahashi (2001).
133. 'Kanchō mo kaisha mo tomoni honkan ka sei-shain ni' (Both government offices and private companies should make us regular officials or regular company employees), Tokyo *Asahi Shimbun*, 28 March 1920, Morning Edition, p. 9. In the databases of the *Asahi Shimbun*, the *Yomiuri Shimbun* and the *Mainichi Shimbun* prior to this case, I could only find articles that used the term '*sei-shain*' to refer to members (investors) of the Japanese Red Cross Society.
134. Takahashi (2001: 22).

Chapter 5

1. This chapter draws on existing research to describe the processes leading to the emergence of characteristic elements of the Japanese-style employment system, including the equality of company employees (*shain*), seniority-based wages and personnel assessments. This chapter also describes the extension of the rank system in the 1950s and the trials of the reform of the Japanese-style employment system by Nikkeiren and the Economic Deliberation Council in the 1960s. I have been unable to find an attempt to provide a comprehensive description of these issues. I should also note that while the series of reports by the Economic Deliberation Council have been discussed firstly from an educational viewpoint by Akio Inui (1990), from the perspective of social security by Michio Gotō (2004), and from the perspective of the legal system by Hamaguchi (2011), the fact that business managers opposed these reforms as an infringement of their management rights has not received their attention.

   That seniority wages and long-term employment, which had been the privilege of higher-staff employees before the war, were extended to factory workers has been shown by Gordon (1985) and Japanese labor historians such as Nimura (1994) and Sugayama (2011). Gordon (1985) credits this as a movement in which the Japanese labor movement sought and achieved 'fuller membership' of their companies. I do not dispute this point, but Gordon (1985) does not emphasize the impact of the following two factors. The first is the rise of nationalism caused by the war and the second is the economic downfall of staff employees due to postwar inflation. Those factors led to the participation of staff employees in the labor movement, which created a situation where the staff employees and shop-floor workers were organized in the same company union. This chapter emphasizes that those were factors of the extension of the system of Japanese-style employment, which had applied only to staff employees, to include shop-floor workers.

438   The System of Japanese Society

2.   Tanaka (1984: 461). From an internal memorandum circulated for executive approval at the time.
3.   For the draft of this outline, see Okazaki (1991: 386–391), from which I have also drawn the quote reproduced here.
4.   Hyōdō (1997, vol. 1: 25).
5.   Sugayama (2011: 182).
6.   Tanaka (1984: 461–464). However, this monthly wage scheme was in fact a 'daily wage / monthly pay scheme' in which accumulated daily wages were paid on a monthly basis.
      The core of the 1943 reform of the Oji Paper ranking system was the introduction of ranks and a mandatory retirement age system for factory workers. This established the ranks of senior, first-, second- and third-class factory workers, and specified minimum and maximum years for promotion. Senior factory workers were to receive 'treatment equivalent to that accorded a staff member (*syokuin*)', which in military terms corresponded to the status of a corporal. In addition, mandatory retirement for factory workers at age 60 was introduced, with the idea that compulsory retirement for lead workers (*kōtō*) would open up the possibility of promotion for younger workers. These policies could be said to have been at the vanguard of the postwar ranking schemes introduced for factory workers.
7.   Hyōdō (1997, vol. 1: 28).
8.   Kiyosawa (1960: 44, 135, 318–319).
9.   Tanaka (1984: 463).
10.   Miyamoto (1994: 82, 84).
11.   Katō ([1991] 1995: 320, 321). Recollections of Saburō Sakai.
12.   See Oguma (2002b: Chapter 1).
13.   Takeda (1953: 40).
14.   Oguma (2002b) is the attempt to prove the relationship between the wartime experience, the rise of nationalism and postwar democratization.
15.   Nimura (1994: 41, 67).
16.   Ōkōchi (1956: 92). Gordon (1985: 342) states a 'feature of workers in early postwar unions at the factory level was their tendency to form separate blue- and white-collar unions'. That might be true in the very early stage, but as the 1947 ISS survey shows, the majority were mixed unions. Nimura (1994: 55) points out that industries such as mining and shipbuilding, where discrimination against manual laborers was intense and prewar union activists were suppressed by staff employees, were the exceptions, with blue-collar workers forming unions without white-collar workers joining them. Gordon's assertion could have been made about the five heavy industrial companies in the Keihin industrial area (three of which were shipbuilders) that were his main research subjects. Even among the five companies, Gordon (1985: 342) wrote that 'all employees below the extremely high post' formed a single union in Toshiba, and in the other four companies, white-collar staff joined the unions formed by blue-collar workers several months later.
17.   The prevailing theory is that the prewar Japanese labor movement was dominated by industrial unions. However, labor historian Ryuji Komatsu argues that this is because the movement was unable to organize workers (especially white-collar employees) within companies due to repression, and individual workers joined unions outside their companies, resulting in the formation of

Notes 439

industrial unions. According to Komatsu, the leading heavy industry labor unions in prewar times were company- or plant-based. See Komatsu (1971).

18. Hyōdō (1997, vol. 1: 42).
19. Nishinarita (1995b: 19).
20. Gordon (1985: 312).
21. Hyōdō (1997, vol. 1: 43); Nimura (1994: 51–52).
22. Nimura (1994: 56).
23. Ōkōchi (1956: 26).
24. As quoted in Nimura (1994: 57).
25. Nimura (1994: 57).
26. Ōkōchi (1956: 93).
27. Nimura (1994: 59).
28. Ōkōchi (1956: 13).
29. See Oguma (2002b: Chapters 1 and 2).
30. Ōkōchi (1956: 93, 95).
31. Minutes of the negotiations; as cited in Kawanishi (1999: 230).
32. Takaragi (2003: 6, 7).
33. Orii (1973: 5).
34. Ōkōchi (1956: 94).
35. As cited in Nimura (1994: 64).
36. As cited in Sugayama (2011: 193, 194).
37. Jūjō seishi rōdō kumiai (Jūjō Paper Labor Union) (1961), *Shi* (History), pp. 149–150; as cited in Ishida (1992, part 1: 63).
38. Institute of Social Science, the University of Tokyo (ed.) (1973: 102, 105).
39. As cited in Sugayama (2011: 196).
40. Endō (1999: 275).
41. Hyōdō (1971: 454–470). According to Hyōdō, in the large heavy industry companies of the time, wages for skilled workers were correlated to their age, even for mid-career employees, and thus wages based on skills appeared to be pseudo seniority-based wages. Gordon (1985) also describes that even though corporate familism was preached as an ideology in the 1920s and 1930s, neither seniority wage systems nor long-term employment were established for factory workers at that time.
42. As cited in Hyōdō (1997, vol. 1: 26).
43. Sasajima (2012: 37).
44. Institute of Social Science, the University of Tokyo (ed.) (1979: 255).
45. The English translation of the individual names of pays and allowances follows Gordon (1985: 353).
46. Gordon (1985: 350).
47. Seisaku kenkyū daigakuin daigaku COE Ōraru seisaku kenkyū (National Graduate Institute for Policy Studies COE Project for Oral History and Policy Enrichment) (2003), 'Hyōdō Tsutae (Kabushikigaisha Ōshima Zōsensho sōdan'yaku) ōraru hisutorī' (Oral history interview with Tsutae Hyōdō [Senior Advisor, Ōshima Shipbuilding Co., Ltd.]), National Graduate Institute for Policy Studies; as cited in Hisamoto (2007: 59).
48. Woo (2003: 146).
49. Nomura (1998: 79).

440   The System of Japanese Society

50. Nimura (1994: 46–48); Ōkōchi (1956: 69).
51. Takaragi (2003: 13–14).
52. Takaragi (2003: 14).
53. As cited in Kawanishi (1999: 230).
54. Arahata ([1960] 1975, vol. 2: 345)
55. Endō (1999: 239). At the stage of reviewing the model inside the Densan, 'academic background' (*gakureki*) was used as the criterion rather than 'academic knowledge' (*gakushiki*), so this change was made by the time the model was submitted to management as Densan's demand.
56. Kawanishi (1999: 132). Recollection of Masao Tanaka.
57. Endō (1999: 233).
58. The following discussion draws on Endō (1999: 119–123, 129, 262). Densan activist Masao Tanaka vouched for having referred to 'the US Civil Service Efficiency Rating System'. However, he also testified that he may have used 'the efficiency rating method used by the US Air Force in Japan' as a reference. The simplified version of Endō (1999) has been published in English as Endo (1998).
59. Nishinarita (1995: 17–18).
60. According to data from a survey conducted by the Osaka Chamber of Commerce and Industry in November 1946, the wage level of SMEs employing 30 to 99 workers was 1.51 times higher than that of large factories employing 200 or more workers (Hashimoto 2009: 74–75).
61. Central Labor College (1946); Nishinarita (1995: 17, 18).
62. Nishinarita (1995b: 23).
63. Marsden (1999: 31–56).
64. Gordon (1993: 381).
65. For a detailed account of efforts by the Miike Coal Mine Workers' Union to create order in the workplace, see Hirai (2000: Chapters 2 and 4). See Thomann ([2016] 2023) for the working and living conditions of Japanese coal miners from the 1920s to the 1960s and their improvement.
66. 1957 clarification. Uchiyama (1980: 89), as cited in Gordon (1993: 382).
67. Sugayama (2011: 196, 197). 'Manual labor' was also subdivided into 'direct work' and 'indirect work', which corresponded to the categories of factory workers and foremen.
68. Ishida (1992, vol. 1: 63–64).
69. Nomura (2007: 102–103).
70. Kamisaka ([1959] 1981: 209), from the 'Afterword to the paperback edition'.
71. This is how the situation was summarized by Nimura (1994: 71).
72. Nomura (2007: 190–191). The quote is from 'Toppu manejimento no kataru shōshin seido no mondaiten' (Problems with the promotion system as described by top management), *Rōmu kenkyū* (Personnel Management Studies), October 1958 issue, p. 19; as cited in Nomura (2007: 191).
73. Hyōdō (1997, vol. 1: 159); Watanabe (2004: 55).
74. Yahata seitetsu rōdō kumiai (Yahata Steel Labor Union) (1959), *Yahata seitetsu rōdō undo-shi* (History of the Labor Movement at the Yahata Steel Works); as cited in Woo (2016: 17).
75. Japan Employers' Federation Public Relations Department (ed.) (1960: 4).
76. Hisamoto (1998: 61).

Notes 441

77. Ōbori (1960: 100).
78. Kawanishi (1992: 227).
79. 'Toppu manejimento no kataru shōshin seido no mondaiten' (Problems with the promotion system as described by top management), *Rōmu kenkyū* (Personnel Management Studies), October 1958 issue, p. 19; as cited in Nomura (2007: 191).
80. Ōbori (1960: 100). Even so, the union's proposal stated explicitly that 'salaries shall not be affected by ranks'.
81. Hisamoto (1998: 62, 63).
82. The distinction between *Angestellte* and *Arbeiter* was abolished in 2005 (2006 for the *Länder*) and unified as *Tarifbeschäftigte*, but their dual structure in relation to the *Beamte* remains essentially unchanged (Gottschall 2015; Reichard and Schröter 2021).
83. From 1979, the Civil Service Commission was divided into the Office of Personnel Management and the Merit Systems Protection Board, but the overall system remains essentially the same.
84. Okada (2003: 99–100).
85. Kawate (2005: 154–159).
86. National Personnel Authority (ed.) (1968: 18–19). Memoir of Asao Sato.
87. Inatsugu (2005: 39–55).
88. Hayakawa and Matsui (1979: 61). The 'civil servants' in the text dose not include non-regular officials.
89. Okada (1994: 68).
90. Hamaguchi (2008).
91. As cited in Kawate (2005: 93).
92. Okada (2003: 92).
93. Okada (1994: 78).
94. Okada (1994: 79–99).
95. Kawate (2005: 108–121).
96. Okada (1994: 99–106).
97. Kawate (2005: 143–153, 160–169).
98. More precisely, the prewar system of benefits for officials and military personnel, which was financed by taxes, was abolished by order of the occupying authorities, and instead all public servants were integrated into the Public Service Mutual Aid Association's (*kōmuin kyōsai kumiai*) pension system based on reserve funds.
99. Hamaguchi (2008).
100. The Type I, II and III examinations for national public servants were abolished in 2011, since which time a Type I-equivalent has been offered as the Comprehensive (*sōgō*) Service Examination (two versions depending on whether examinees have completed graduate school or have only an undergraduate degree), a Type II-equivalent as the General (*ippan*) Service Examination (for university graduates), and a Type III-equivalent as the General Service Examination (for high school graduates). This change, which is based on the Basic Act on the Reform of the National Public Service (*Kokka kōmuin seido kaikaku kihon-hō*) enacted in 2008, brings the examination nomenclature closer to the norms of the Japanese-style employment system that prevails in the private sector.
101. Woo (2003: 145, 146).
102. As cited in Kinoshita (2004a: 131).

442 The System of Japanese Society

103. Mitsubishi Company History Publication Society (ed.) (1979–1982, vol. 26: 4919).
104. According to Ishida (1992, Part 1: 39), prior to the scheme's revision in 1943, factory workers at Oji Paper had ranks ranging from fourth- up to first-class. In this case, however, 'ranks were not categories for determining daily wages, but were on the contrary determined by daily wages'. This seems to be an intermediate form between the two types of hierarchies, namely, the staff hierarchy at Mitsui & Co. that was determined by salaries and the civil service ranking scheme in which salaries were determined by rank. In the 1943 revision of the scheme, factory worker ranks were renamed as 'third class, second class, first class and senior class' (i.e., the equivalent of the ranking scheme for salaried employees) as a part of efforts to eliminate discrimination against factory workers.
105. Woo (2016: 18).
106. Makiuchi, (1960: 145).
107. Makiuchi (1960: 144). The background of the restructuring of the three-category system into a two-category system is also described on the same page.
108. More accurately, in the proposal submitted in January 1947 by the Joint Struggle Committee of the All-Japan Council of Government and Public Workers' Unions (Zenkankō), the portion of wages comprising ability-based pay included both ability-based and experience-based components. In other words, the union was demanding a Densan-type wage structure, which included both an ability-based element determined by taught skills and a length-of-service element determined by tenure at the company. This demand was agreed at the Committee for the Improvement of Treatment of Government and Public Employees (*Kankō shokuin taigū kaizen iinkai*), where the negotiations were held in April that year (Woo 2003: 142–144).
109. Woo (2003: 152). More precisely, these were not criteria for the evaluation of ability, but rather a negotiation over the criteria for job evaluations in conjunction with the introduction of job-based remuneration. Nevertheless, I have simplified the flow of the negotiations in order to illustrate how the years of service came to be read as an indicator of 'ability'.
110. Woo (2003: 152).
111. Woo (2003: 166).
112. Woo (2003: 159). As note 27 in Chapter 3 describes, since '*koin* (*yatoi*)' originally meant an apprentice to an official, Article 5 of the 1893 Civil Service Appointment Decree stipulated that if a person has been a *koin* and served in the same government office for more than five full years, there was a possibility of being promoted to a *hannin* official after a thorough examination. See Ishii (2016).
113. For the full text of the three principles, see Yoshida (2007: 10–11). Kinoshita assesses Zenji's three principles as being 'far more ambitious than the Densan Wage Model' (Kinoshita 1999: 147).
114. As cited in Yoshida (2007: 72).
115. Yoshida (2007: Chapter 3).
116. 'Shokuba tōron no naka kara (Shizuoka shibu)' (Overheard in the workplace [Shizuoka chapter]), *Zenjidōsha* (All-Japan Autoworkers' Newsletter), no. 147, 5 November 1952; as cited in Yoshida (2007: 70–71).
117. As cited in Yoshida (2007: 46).

Notes

118. Yoshida (2007: 72).
119. Nishinarita (1995b: 20).
120. Shiozawa (1980: 166).
121. See Hyōdō (1971); Odaka (1984).
122. Ujihara ([1954b] 1966: 419)
123. Ujihara ([1953] 1966: 367–369). This theory of firm-specific skills is almost identical to that advanced by Doeringer and Piore (1971), who popularized the theory of the internal labor market.
124. Ujihara ([1953] 1966: 368). Ujihara also refers to the fact that Japan had no tradition of craft unions (p. 405). His point, however, was the absence of occupation-based gatekeeping in the Japanese labor market, and to position this as a precondition for there being an unlimited supply of surplus labor from agriculture and self-employment.
125. In general, Ujihara tended to regard the Japanese-style employment system as a relic of a still mostly premodern status system. For example, he considered the existence of ranks such as common laborer and first-, second- and third-class laborers in large factories to be a relic of the premodern status system ([1953] 1966: 378). However, as I have already mentioned, Oji Paper did not introduce such ranks for its factory workers until 1943, and its motivation at the time had been to institutionalize a path to promotion for factory workers as well. What Ujihara saw as a relic of the premodern status system was in fact new at the time of his study. Ujihara also considered the fact that male workers were paid a livelihood wage to support their families while female workers were not was 'a principle of patriarchal labor management, which reproduces the rural family system' ([1954a] 1966: 451). However, the idea of supporting a family on the wages of one man is qualitatively different from the rural family system, in which the entire family contributes. Ujihara did not consider the patriarchy as a form of modernization. In general, one can say that Ujihara believed strongly that long-term employment and the seniority wage system were older norms that had not yet been modernized ([1954a] 1966: 434).
126. The following description of the prewar social security system summarizes Ikeda (1994: 155–161).
127. Ikeda (1994: 157).
128. E.g., Hiroi (1999: 39).
129. McCreary (1968).
130. Tsuchida (1997).
131. Kawamura (1974: 238, 239). To characterize Japan's National Health System as 'unprecedented in any country' is something of an exaggeration, however. Even in Germany under Otto von Bismarck, local municipalities (*Gemeinde*) established medical insurance for the compulsorily insured who were not covered by any *Krankenkasse*. However, as a result of the development of other *Krankenkasse*, the rollout was limited, and the system was ultimately abolished in 1911. See Tsuchida (1997: 223). Because of this, in the end, Japan's National Health Insurance system can be said to have been an example of something rarely seen in other countries.
132. Hiroi (1999: 59).
133. Koyama (1980: 49). Tomitarō Hirata, a member of the Social Security System Council (*Shakai hoshō seido shingikai*), expressed indignation about these new systems, which he said were being 'established helter-skelter' (Campbell 1992: 73).

134. Yamamoto (1974: 270).
135. Kawamura (1974: 239).
136. Tsuchida (2011: 10).
137. Endō (1999: 126–127).
138. Supreme Commander for the Allied Powers, Advisory Committee on Labor (1946).
139. Kōda (2002: 81).
140. Nakayama (ed.) (1956: 546).
141. Kōda (2002: 82–84).
142. Nikkeiren (1955: 7).
143. Woo (2003: 146–147).
144. Sōhyō (General Council of Trade Unions of Japan) (ed.) (1952), 'Saitei chingin-sei kakutoku tōsō taishū tōgi shiryō' (Materials for mass discussion on the struggle for a minimum wage system), 26 December; as cited in Nikkeiren (1955: Materials Appendix, p. 66).
145. Yoshida (2007: 78).
146. Women and Youth Bureau, Ministry of Labor (ed.) (1951: 82).
147. Dore (1973: 316).
148. Nikkeiren (1955: 44).
149. Nakajima (1988: Chapter 5).
150. Nikkeiren (1955: 39).
151. Jacoby (1985).
152. Nikkeiren (1955: 75–79). 'Reasonable labor norms' such as seniority rights systems and temporary layoffs were also listed as requirements.
153. Economic Deliberation Council (ed.) (1960: 33, 37, 62). In the list of various committee members on p. 321, the names of Sei'ichi Tōbata and Hiromi Arisawa are listed among the members of the Econometric Analysis Section.
154. A list of committee members can be found in Economic Deliberation Council (ed.) (1963: 345–347). The name 'Shōjirō Ujiie, Associate Professor, the University of Tokyo' appears on p. 345, and is likely a misprint for Ujihara. The characterization of labor mobility across companies in the report mirrors that found in Ujihara's argument, including the closed nature of the large company labor market. For more information on Hiroko Kageyama, see Oguma (2009, vol. 2: 959).
155. Economic Deliberation Council (ed.) (1963: 132, 263, 320, 321).
156. Economic Deliberation Council (ed.) (1963: 50).
157. Economic Deliberation Council (ed.) (1963: 122).
158. Economic Deliberation Council (ed.) (1963: 125, 127).
159. Wage Committee of Manager's Association in the Kanto Area (ed.) (1962: 36–37).
160. On the child allowance and housing policy, see Gotō (2004a: 199–203).
161. Irie (1963: 25–27).
162. Fujita (2010: 36).
163. Jacoby (1985).

Chapter 6

1. This chapter demonstrates how, in prioritizing an order determined by educational background and management rights amidst the trend toward higher education that emerged with Japan's rapid economic growth, Japanese companies achieved 'equality of company employees' by abandoning the old three-tier structure. In writing this chapter, I was most inspired by Chapter 2 of Honda (2005), in which Honda makes the excellent observation that internal friction in companies caused by greater numbers of high school graduates in blue-collar positions was an underlying factor in the spread of competence ranking systems. Honda, however, does not attend to the estrangement of positions and professional educations in the context of Japanese firms or its relationship to the prewar corporate order. She also overlooks the relationship whereby Japanese firms abandoned the three-tier structure due to their new emphasis on educational background.
2. Shaeffer (1983).
3. Abegglen (1958: 42).
4. Nishikawa (1964: 14).
5. Abegglen (1958: 36–38). Also, a policy was in place whereby both apprentice and temporary laborers were only hired from among junior high school graduates.
6. Kurauchi (1963: 15), based on a sampling survey of 200 companies in 1962 and 247 companies in 1963. In 1962, the percentage of firms hiring junior high school graduates exclusively was 53% for firms with less than 1,000 employees versus 66% for firms with 1,000 employees or more (25% versus 38% in 1963).
7. Kurauchi (1963: 15–16).
8. These figures were calculated from a table prepared by Sugayama (2011: 429). Although he takes the view that medium-sized enterprises were 'relatively free' of such 'demarcation by educational background' (2011: 430), I suspect it is highly likely that this choice was 'inevitable' for SMEs as well.
9. Abegglen (1958: 36).
10. Honda (2005: 54).
11. Ministry of Education (1999).
12. Shiomi (1994: 295).
13. Economic Deliberation Council (ed.) (1960: 138).
14. Iida (1992: 38–39).
15. Nishimoto (2004: 167).
16. Muramatsu (1965: 115).
17. Honda takes the view that 'the correspondence between educational background and one's job was more clearly established' in the corporate order that characterized prewar Japan (2009: 80). As a corollary, she points out that in a joint Ministry of Education-Nikkeiren survey conducted in August 1953, only 11.6% of all employees with a higher education degree said that they 'did not make use of their major' (2009: 82).

    Even so, as I have already mentioned in this book, aside from in fields related to science and engineering, it is difficult to say that any relationship existed between the majors in higher education and jobs, even in prewar Japan. As Honda also notes, the survey in question was conducted by categorizing 'those engaged in an apprenticeship in anticipation of becoming future executives at their company or business entity' and 'those who have passed

446 The System of Japanese Society

the civil service examination and have been hired at government or public agencies, and those in similar positions' as 'making use of their major' and having such respondents answer 'company / business entities' or 'government agencies / public corporations' (Ministry of Education 1961: 154). Although this shows that those who completed their higher education in 1953, when the prewar order was still largely in place, were treated as executive cadets (i.e., candidates for senior management roles), it would be a stretch to say that it indicates that their majors were linked to their jobs. We should also keep in mind that until 1953, the bulk of higher education was provided by national universities, primarily in the fields of science and education, and by the prewar professional schools, which focused on engineering or accountings.

18. Commenting on the report, education scholar Akio Inui (1990: 38) notes that 'it has come to be seen as the starting point for the competitive "deviation-value-oriented education" education system [i.e., a "cramming" model that stresses studying and passing exams to raise one's relative ranking] that has dominated Japanese society since the late 1960s'.   .

19. Nishimoto (2004: 174).

20. Nishikawa (1964: 14).

21. Ōta (1978: 144).

22. Women and Youth Bureau, Ministry of Labor (ed.) (1969: 217–218).

23. Wakisaka (2004: 73, 76). However, citing the example of the Yahata Steel Works, Inui (1990: 158) writes that 'until the early 1960s, the recruitment and hiring of high school graduates was conducted by job category. It was not until the latter half of the 1960s that the company established the method of hiring new graduates as unallocated resources whose workplace assignments and job categories would be determined later'. It is not clear whether Yahata Steel Works (which was known for its relatively early and systematic recruitment of high school graduates as factory workers) was atypical in this regard. It seems likely that in the 1950s when fewer students were pursuing secondary education in high school, high school graduates with technical skills would have been treated along the same lines as technical workers who graduated from secondary education before the war, and that such treatment was gradually eliminated as more high school graduates were employed in factory worker positions.

24. Wakisaka (2004: 76).

25. Abegglen (1958: 36).

26. A detailed background account of the revision of the Employment Security Act can be found in Inui (1990: 149–152) and Sugayama (2011: Chapter 5).

27. Sugayama (2011: 355, 356).

28. Inui (1990: 150).

29. Inui (1990: 152).

30. Abegglen (1958: 34).

31. Ujihara and Takanashi (1971, vol. 1: 409).

32. E.g., Sugayama (2011).

33. Ministry of Education (1981).

34. Abegglen (1958: 42).

35. Abegglen (1958: 43).

36. Ministry of Education (1981). Since the number of normal school students had been 276,422 in 1943, this reclassification alone was equivalent to approximately

Notes

80% of the increase in the number of university students in 1953. The Ministry of Education (1981), noting also that citizens repatriated from overseas after the war, the natural increase in population, the postwar acceptance of newly eligible female students, and evening classes all contributed to the increase in student numbers, explained that the 'numbers of universities and students are not necessarily larger than before the war, and it may be said that the relative proportion of male students in particular is in fact decreasing'.

37. Ministry of Education (1999).
38. Amano (1986: 162).
39. Amano (1986: 162).
40. Nomura (2007: 39).
41. Wakabayashi (2014).
42. Takeuchi (1995: 86–88).
43. Research and Statistics Division, Minister's Secretariat, Ministry of Education (1978: 83).
44. Amano (1986: 162–163).
45. Oguma (2015).
46. Miura (1968: 293–294).
47. Takabatake (1969: 245).
48. Akiyama and Aoki (1968: 122, 125–126, 137–138). The faction he joined was *Chūkakuha*.
49. H. K. Tootle, quoted in Mills (1951: 247).
50. Thurow (1975).
51. Asō and Ushiogi (eds.) (1977: 138–142).
52. Labor Capacity Development Center (1977: 5).
53. Labor Capacity Development Center (1977: 8).
54. Women and Youth Bureau, Ministry of Labor (ed.) (1969: 218).
55. Honda (2005: 71–72).
56. Labor Law Association (ed.) (1965: 84).
57. Abegglen (1958: 87–88).
58. 'Hageshii kabu no atsuryoku: Kono hito to kanryō-ron, Kyōsai kumiai renmei kaichō, Imai Kazuo-shi rensai taidan Matsuoka Hideo (6)' (The strong power from the bottom: Interviews with bureaucrats: Kazuo Imai, Chairman of the Federation of National Public Service Mutual Aid Associations; Interview Series with Hideo Matsuoka [6]), *Mainichi Shinbun*, 27 May 1969, Tokyo version morning edition, p. 5.
59. Hashimoto (2009: 63–64).
60. As for Public Servant Mutual Aid Associations, see note 100 in Chapter 1.
61. Mizutani ([1999] 2013: 137).
62. Koike (1993: 169). However, Koike is only speculating with regard to firms other than the large postwar Japanese firms. There is still relatively little empirical analysis on whether the promotion of staff employees on the management track was faster in the case of Japan's large corporations before the war. Yoshida and Okamuro (2016), analyzing the careers of regular company employees (*sei'in*) at Mitsubishi Shipbuilding, found some cases of extremely early promotion, along with others that were not so early. While the career tree included in their article (2016: 14–15) suggests that regular employees who joined in 1918 were promoted earlier than those who joined in 1921, it is nevertheless difficult to draw any immediate conclusions.

63. Koike (1981, 1993, 2005).
64. Nishikawa (1964: 14).
65. Nishikawa (1964: 17).
66. Nishikawa (1964: 16).
67. Nishikawa (1964: 16). Nishikawa's article is also cited by Honda (2005: 75–76), who positions it as corroborating evidence that 'the gap between high school education and university education' persisted because 'the competence ranking system, which was based on workers' "potential", ironically had to refer to educational background as a rough classificatory criterion for that "potential"'. In my view, however, Honda's understanding seems backwards. That is, what Nishikawa suggested was that the three-tier structure should be abandoned because of its emphasis on educational background, and that doing so would open the way for a competence ranking system. As noted in the text, Nishikawa claimed abandonment of the discriminative three-tier structure not because of a disregard for educational credentials, but *because of the emphasis on them*.
68. Orii (1973: 40). Note that the policy of referring to all employees as *shain* (company employees) was adopted in January 1964, and that Nishikawa's article appeared in the 1 February issue of *Rōmu kenkyū* (Personnel Management Studies) the same year.
69. Orii (1973: 41, 88).
70. Tekkōrōren Yahata seitetsu rōdō kumiai (Japan Federation of Steel Workers' Unions Yahata Steel Works Labor Union), 'Dai 43-kai rinji taikai gian-sho' (Agenda for the 43rd Extraordinary Congress), 28 May 1967; as cited in Woo (2016: 18).
71. Hyōdō (1997, vol. 1: 187).
72. There is no established English translation of the *shokunō shikaku*. Here I followed the English translation, 'competence rank', that is used in Marsden (1999: 44–45).
73. Nakayama (1960: 3).
74. Irie (1957: 2).
75. Orii (1973: 40).
76. Orii (1973: 41).
77. Such trends did not proceed in a straight line, however. In 1958, Nihon Cement introduced a unified competence ranking system by abolishing 'the distinction between company employees (*shain*) and factory workers (*kōin*)' as a result of the increased number of factory workers with high school degrees brought on by the social shift to higher education (Usami 1960: 69–70). Under this system, however, 'the ranking scheme itself is determined by the job in which someone is engaged. Therefore, because it is not attributed to the person, if the same person's job changes, then the applicable ranking scheme will also change' (Usami 1960: 77). This is interesting as a transitional period between the job-based pay and job classification introduced after the end of the war and the competence ranking systems introduced in the late 1960s. It is also worth noting that in this ranking system of Nihon Cement, job classes (Classes 1 through 7) were unified along job lines, while rankings were divided into a dualistic scheme, as for example with Class 6 clerk and Class 6 specialist worker (cf. the figure on p. 90 of Usami [1960])

Notes 449

78. Seisaku kenkyū daigakuin daigaku COE Ōraru seisaku kenkyū purojekuto (National Graduate Institute for Policy Studies COE Project for Oral History and Policy Enrichment) (2004), 'Okuda Kenji (moto Nippon Kōkan rōmu-bu shokuin, moto Jōchi daigaku kyōju) ōraru hisutorī' (Oral history interview with Kenji Okuda (Former salaried employee with the NKK Labor Division, former professor at Sophia University), National Graduate Institute for Policy Studies; as cited in Hisamoto (2007: 60).

79. Orii (1973: 40).

80. Positive assessments include those by Kazuo Koike and Mitsuo Ishida, while more critical evaluations include those by Makoto Kumazawa, Kimitsugu Endō and Masami Nomura. Also see Gordon (1998: 202–206).

81. Calculated based on the chart in Labor Capacity Development Center (1977: 44). According to the same publication (p. 56), 42.9% of the firms surveyed listed 'job reassignment and rotation systems' as a measure to counter the shortage of shop-floor workers and the increased overall level of education in the labor force.

82. Labor Capacity Development Center (1977: 57). The same publication states that if highly educated employees are to be assigned to the shop floor, then 'at the very least, the white-collar / blue-collar management categories must be abolished'.

83. Tsuji (2011).

84. Tsuji (2011: 74).

85. Hamaguchi (2014: 214, 219).

86. Text of the Tokyo District Court Ruling, 20 December 1966, in the Sumitomo Cement case.

87. Hyōdō (1997, vol. 1: 194).

88. Takano (2018: 35–36).

89. Hyōdō (1997, vol. 1: 184).

90. Woo (2016: 23–24).

91. Nakayama (1960: 3).

92. Kantō Employers' Association (1954).

93. Joint Committee of the Japan Employers' Federation Labor Management Committee and Merit-Based Management Study Group (1969 [2010]: 375). For a transcript of the roundtable discussion, on 14 October 1968, see Japan Employers' Federation Merit-Based Management Study Group ([1969] 2001).

94. Explaining Hitachi's reasoning for allowing its workers to take the government's proficiency examinations despite its reluctance, Dore writes that 'They decided that to *seem* to be afraid of possibly losing skilled men who got a nationally valid qualification would be bad for morale' (1973: 48, original emphasis).

95. Satō (1970).

96. Yahata Seitetsu Rōso (Yahata Steelworkers' Union) (1966), *Dai 42-kai teirei taikai gian-sho* (Proposed Agenda for the 42nd Regular Assembly); as cited in Hyōdō (1997, vol. 1: 172).

97. 'Tōron shikaku seido no un'yō o megutte' (Discussion: On the operation of ranking systems), in Japan Employers' Federation Public Relations Department (ed.) (1960: 161–198). The citation is from p. 191.

98. Irie (1957).

450 The System of Japanese Society

99. Nihon Seisansei Honbu 'Seissansei undo ni kansuru san gensoku' (The three principals of the movement for productivity), 20 May 1955, https://www.jpc-net.jp/movement/assets/pdf/domestic_19550520.pdf (accessed on 20 August 2023).
100. Hyōdō (1997, vol. 1: 171).
101. Ministry of Labor Women and Youth Bureau (ed.) (1966: 185).
102. Ministry of Labor Women and Youth Bureau (ed.) (1969: 274).
103. Joint Committee of the Japan Employers' Federation Labor Management Committee and Merit-Based Management Study Group (1969 [2010]: 375).
104. Nimura (1994: 60).
105. Institute of Labor Administration (ed.) (1963).
106. Ishida (1990: 56–57).
107. As cited in Ishida (1990: 56, 58, 61).
108. See Table 5–9 in Orii (1973: 90).
109. Dore (1973: 115).
110. The film *Nippon Musekinin Jidai* (The Irresponsible Time of Japan) was made in 1962 and distributed by Toho Co., Ltd.
111. Vogel (1963: 6).
112. Katō (1957).
113. Japan Employers' Federation Merit-Based Management Study Group ([1969] 2001: 84–85, 95).
114. Joint Committee of the Japan Employers' Federation Labor Management Committee and Merit-Based Management Study Group (1969: 375).

Chapter 7

1. This chapter attempts to describe the emergence of a new dual structure in Japanese society, including the public service sector and the situation of local communities. In this regard, I used the works of Japanese labor researchers such as Makoto Kumazawa and educational researchers such as Akio Inui. Gordon (1998) also describes changes in labor-management relations in large Japanese manufacturing firms up to the 1990s. I learned a lot from those works, but they do not situate their research in the context of changes in society as a whole.
2. NHK Broadcasting Culture Research Institute (ed.) (1975: Chapter IX).
3. From the Foreword to OECD and Ministry of Labor (1972), the advance Japanese translation of OECD Manpower and Social Affairs Directorate (1973).
4. OECD Manpower and Social Affairs Directorate (1973).
5. OECD Manpower and Social Affairs Directorate (1973: 11).
6. OECD Manpower and Social Affairs Directorate (1973: 11, 99).
7. As cited in Gotō (2004a: 209–210).
8. Hyōdō (1997, vol. 2: 353–355).
9. As cited in Kinoshita (2004b: 151).
10. See table 6 included in Nishinarita (1995b: 30).
11. Koike (2005: 8). For the period prior to 1982, i.e., before the Employment Status Survey started to classify workers as regular employees and non-regular workers, Koike states that 'using a loose classification of employees, the percentage [of the seniority wage group accounted for the total number of employees] has dropped only slightly from 45% in 1968 to 43% in 2002'. It is also

Notes

451

worth noting that Kambayashi (2017: Chapter 4), considering the possibility of using working hours and length of labor contracts, attempts to estimate the number of non-regular workers prior to 1982, although as he acknowledges, it is difficult to arrive at a complete picture.

12. See the table showing the number of hires by type in Yamamoto and Tanaka (1982: 67). The number of 'clerical and technical workers, etc.' ('staff employees' in Figure 7.1) represents the sum total of 'clerks', 'technicians', 'young women' (*joshi*) and 'medical personnel' in the table. The 'young women' category included several university graduates each year in the 1960s and around twenty through the 1970s, so it is unclear whether these could be uniformly classified as auxiliary personnel. Also, in the 'skilled worker' ('new high school graduate factory workers' in Figure 7.1) category, as many as 300 people were accepted from the self-defense forces each year in the 1960s, but this number declined sharply in the 1970s.

13. Hyōdō (1997, vol. 2: 333).

14. Nishimoto (2004: 181); Statistics Bureau, Ministry of Internal Affairs and Communications (Sōmushō tōkeikyoku), 'School enrollment rate and ratio of students who pursue higher education' (Shūgaku-ritsu oyobi shingaku-ritsu).

15. Inui (1990: 236, 250).

16. Inui (1990: 220–222). The following articles are mentioned: 'Daigaku juken kinkyū risāchi, kimi ga zubari gōkaku dekiru daigaku wa koreda' (Emergency research for entrance exams, here are the universities you can get into!), *Pureibōi* (Playboy), 27 November 1975; 'Kyōran no shingaku juku būmu, aru haha no "kyōiku koso tōshi"-ron' (The frenzied boom in exam preparation schools: One mother's theory on how 'Investment in education comes first'), *Josei sebun* (Women 7), 12 March 1975; 'Zenkoku sen hyaku kōkō no daigaku betsu shinro zen chōsa' (Comprehensive Survey of Higher Education Acceptance by University for 1,000 High Schools Across Japan), *Sandē Mainichi* (Sunday Mainichi), 1 July 1975 ; 'Zenkoku yūryō juku ichiran' (List of the best cram schools in Japan), *Shūkan Yomiuri* (Weekly Yomiuri), 25 October 1975; 'Yoi juku, warui juku no miwake-kata' (How to tell a good cram school from a bad one), *Shūkan Yomiuri* (Weekly Yomiuri), 25 October 1975; 'Daigaku sentaku jōhō, 5-nen-saki no shūshoku sensen ni zettai yūrina daigaku gakubu wa koko da' (Information on university selection: Here are the universities and faculties that will definitely be advantageous on the job-hunting front five years from now), *Shūkan Gendai* (Contemporary Weekly), 15 and 22 January 1976.

17. Kumazawa (1993: 116–117).

18. Yashiro (1980: 17).

19. Yashiro (1980: 18). Yashiro further notes the existence of a large difference in the enrollment rates of men and women at four-year universities, and the fact that women tended to attend junior colleges.

20. Inui (1990: 239–241).

21. Kumazawa (1993: 106).

22. Tamano (2005: 272).

23. Hashimoto (2009: 150). However, Hashimoto also suggests that another reason is that it was during this period that 'a relationship between educational background and the class or social stratum to which one belongs' was established, whereby high school graduates were equated with the working class, and university graduates with the new middle class. Even so, the establishment

of such equivalencies does not mean that the relationship between educational background and class affiliation did not exist before that time. It would be more appropriate to think of this as a change in the way high school graduates, who had been a source of lower-level staff employees in the 1950s, had now become a source of manual labor as the percentage of students pursuing secondary education increased.

24. Kumazawa (1996: 250); a revised and updated version of the 1984 article, translated in Kumazawa (1996) under the title 'Working like mad to stay in place'.
25. Saitō (2010: 59).
26. Ishikawa (1978: 73–81); Ishikawa (1995: 206–210).
27. As for the discussion in this paragraph, see Oguma (2021).
28. Nomura (1998: 62–64).
29. Watanabe (2004: 65, 106).
30. Hashimoto (2009: 146).
31. Maeda (2014) analyzed the political process of the Total Personnel Act but did not discuss the employment practices of the Japanese civil service, which is discussed in this book.
32. Oguma (2021).
33. Hashimoto (2009: 142–143).
34. Vogel (1979).
35. Hyōdō (1997, vol. 2: 361).
36. Honda (1978: 66).
37. Kizaki (1978: 54).
38. Kamijō (1979).
39. Labor Capacity Development Center (1977: 19).
40. Labor Capacity Development Center (1977: 20).
41. Institute of Labor Administration (ed.) (1986).
42. Labor Capacity Development Center (1977: 41).
43. Kumazawa ([1989] 1998: 56).
44. Kumazawa ([1989] 1998: 72–73). Kumazawa notes that he 'introduces the expressions used in an abridged format', and that he has added quotation marks to item (d) under the heading 'Cooperativity'.
45. 'Kodomo yorimo kibishii! Papa no tūchihyō: bōnasu morauno kowai!' (More demanding than school kids! Dad's report card: Afraid to know how much my bonus is! Salarymens' 'report cards': Including A to E ratings in Misawa Homes and others), *Asahi Shinbun*, Tokyo version, evening edition, 6 December 1987, p. 13.
46. Kambayashi (2017) demonstrates in a comparative study of wage censuses that Japan experiences greater wage declines and fewer layoffs during recessions than other Western countries.
47. Kumazawa ([1989] 1998: 58, 62).
48. Kumazawa ([1989] 1998: 91). This is Kumazawa's characterization, but a more accurate breakdown would be 40% base salary, 30% job-related pay, 20% job evaluation pay and 10% performance pay. See Mori (2007: 72).
49. Kumazawa ([1989] 1998: 67).
50. Kumazawa (1993: 117).
51. Kariya (1991: 188, 201). Also see Brinton and Kariya (1998).

Notes

52. Labor Capacity Development Center (1977: 41).
53. As cited in Hyōdō (1997, vol. 2: 333, 361).
54. Hyōdō (1997, vol. 2: 381).
55. Gotō (1994: 280–281).
56. Policy Research Department, Labor Minister's Secretariat (ed.) (1991: 15, 28, 40).
57. Hyōdō (1997, vol. 1: 194–195).
58. Kantō Employers' Association (Kantō Keieisha Kyōkai) (1976).
59. Hyōdō (1997, vol. 2: 391–393).
60. Hyōdō (1997, vol. 2: 386).
61. Sakurai (1985: 19).
62. The first article using 'non-regular workers' is Ogata (1981).
63. See Chapter 2.
64. Sugeno and Araki (eds.) (2017: 17).
65. Policy Research Department, Labor Minister's Secretariat (ed.) (1992).
66. As for the so-called 'Four Requirements for Dismissal' (*Kaiko shi yōken*), see note 76 of Chapter 2.
67. As cited in Ueda (2004: 33). For a more detailed discussion of the changing tone of the SME White Paper, see Chapter 2 of the same book.
68. Takata (1989: 24, 25).
69. As cited in Ueda (2004: 34).
70. On the claims made in the 1980 SME White Paper and the 1984 Labor White Paper, see Takata (1989: 69–70).
71. Economic Planning Agency Planning Bureau (ed.) (1985: 10).
72. See, for example, Takahashi (1982) and Sasaki (1982).
73. Takata (1989: 71, 89, 90).
74. Takata (1989: 25, 26).
75. Takata (1989: 47).
76. Economic Planning Agency Planning Bureau (ed.) (1985: 18).
77. Economic Planning Agency Planning Bureau (ed.) (1985: 112, 113).
78. Takata (1989: 93).
79. IERC (ed.) (1985).
80. IERC (ed.) (1976: 8).
81. Yonekura (1995: 213, 214) and Watanabe et al. (2022: 134).
82. Kurose (2018: 402, 378).
83. Seki (2017: 25).
84. Watanabe et al. (2022: 237–239).
85. Nomura (1998: 116–118).
86. The census is conducted every five years, but prior to 1990, the method of industry classification was different. In addition, the statistical treatment of non-respondents in 2020 is different from that before. For this reason, they are not included in the comparison.
87. SMEA (2020), Section 2 of Chapter 2, Part 1.
88. Cabinet Office (2006), Appendix, figure 3-1.
89. Gordon (2017) also argues that the pattern of increase of non-regular workers by industry was different.

90. MEXT Kōtō Kyōiku-Kyoku (MEXT Higher Education Bureau) (ed.) (2009), 'Daigaku no ryōteki kibo-tō ni kan suru shiryō' (Materials concerning the quantitative scale of universities), 23 April 2009, p. 5, http://www.mext.go.jp/b_menu/shingi/chukyo/chukyo4/028/siryo/__icsFiles/afieldfile/2009/05/08/1262971_6_1.pdf (accessed on 5 June 2019); see also Nishii (2016).
91. Brinton (2010: xiv).
92. Ōuchi and Komikawa (2012: 72).
93. Inui (1990: 241–242).
94. Kanbayashi (2015).
95. Kanbayashi (2021). All percentages in the text are percentages of non-regular public servants who meet the requirements of a term of office of at least six months and a workweek of at least 19 hours and 25 minutes per week. If those who do not meet these conditions are added, the total percentage in the 2020 survey increases to 29.0% in all local governments, 47.1% in towns and villages and 43.5% in cities and wards.
96. 'Nihonteki keiei minaoshi ha huyō? Nikkeiren seminar: cyōsyo wo saininshiki, yōgoron ga zokusyutsu' (No need for revision of Japanese style management? Nikkeiren seminar: Recognizing advantages, a number of defensive augments), *Nihon Keizai Shinbun*, 21 August 1992, morning edition, p. 5.
97. Japan Employers' Federation Research Project on the New Japanese-Style Management Systems (ed.) (1995: 23–24).
98. Japan Employers' Federation Research Project on the New Japanese-Style Management Systems (ed.) (1995: 8–9). According to an oral history of this report (Yashiro et al., 2015: 306–307) in the section 'Koyō pōtoforio to wa nani datta no ka' (What was the employment portfolio?), Takeo Naruse, the report's principal author, anticipated that the second type of worker, who made use of highly specialized skills, would consist of 'experts with marketable skills' on 'contracts of about three years'.
99. Nikkeiren Kokusai Tokubetsu Iinkai (2000) and Nikkeiren Rōshi Kankei Tokubetsu Iinkai (2002), as cited in Kinoshita (2004b: 147–148).
100. Kinoshita (1999: 95–115). The survey covered cases from Kanematsu Corporation, NCR Japan, Dentsu, Hewlett-Packard Japan and Takeda Pharmaceutical Company.
101. Hamaguchi (2013a: 228).
102. Ishida and Higuchi (2009: 22, 23, 43).
103. Mori (2007: 72). In addition, in note 14 of his paper, Mori remarks that 'As to the extent to which the case of Yahata Steel Works can be generalized, we can only wait for further case studies to accumulate'.
104. Yoshikawa (2013).
105. Jō (2004: 74, 134–136).
106. Jō (2004: 70–72, 191).
107. Jō (2004: 165).
108. 'Hito e no tōshi oshimu kigyō' (Companies skimping on investments in persons), *Tōkyō Shinbun*, 27 March 2019, morning edition.
109. 'Shokku ryōhō de kiki-kan o aoru: Toyota no gōhō' (Toyota's no. 1 issue, 'stirring up a sense of crisis with shock therapy'), *Shūkan tōyō keizai* (Weekly Toyo Keizai), 16 March 2019, pp. 32–33. This article reports on a January 2019 personnel reform at Toyota that saw the across-the-board reclassification of 460 1st-class managers and 1,729 2nd-class managers (*kikan-shoku 1-kyū* and

Notes

kikan-shoku 2-kyū, respectively, renamed from *buchō-kyū* and *jichō-kyū* under a 1996 reform), 163 grand experts positions (*gihan-kyū*; the titles of technical officer, engineer and master engineer [*gihan, kōhan* and *kōshi*] were established in 1943), and twenty-six senior general director (*jōmu riji*) positions as 'senior professional/senior management' (*kanbushoku*) roles in 'a wide range of posts'. This 'reform' consolidated the gradations of Toyota's various competence ranking systems and assigned people to vacant posts at the bottom, effectively reducing the salaries of employees with the highest ranks while subjecting them to assessment. This type of reform has been a standard practice in Japanese companies since the 1980s. See Kumazawa ([1989] 1998: 91).

Chapter 8

1. Esping-Andersen (1990: 146).
2. Doeringer and Piore (1971).
3. Doeringer and Piore (1971: 1–4).
4. Jacoby (1997).
5. Müller et al. (ed.) (2019).
6. See, e.g., Saglio (2000).
7. Jacoby (1985).
8. Jacoby (1997).
9. Japanese labor economists such as Kazuo Koike and Mikio Sumiya claimed that the Japanese-style employment system is an internal labor market which is common in industrialized countries. However, they did not pay attention to the concept of craft markets proposed by Doeringer and Piore and did not analyze the Japanese-style employment system in comparison with it. This indicates that they were still constrained by the mindset of the Japanese-style employment system even while analyzing it. See Nomura (2003).
10. Marsden (1999). The two axes are whether the society's job demand is the production approach or the training approach, and whether the focus of enforcement criteria is task-centered or function/procedure-centered. The US and France are classified as the 'work-post' rule, having a combination of the production approach and being task-centered, Japan as the 'competence-rank' rule, having a combination of the production approach and being function/ procedure-centered, the UK as the 'job territory/tools of trade' rule, having a combination of the training approach and being task-centered, and Germany as the 'qualification' rule, having a combination of the training approach and being function/procedure-centered. As I understand it, the division between the industrial and training approaches could correspond to whether human resource development takes place in the enterprise market or the craft market, and the division between task-centered and job/procedure-centered could correspond to the division between position-based and career-based (see Chapter 2).
11. According to Marsden, in the Anglo-Saxon countries, trade unions controlled the allocation of work within enterprises and the supply of skilled workers, whereas in Germany, although qualification systems to evaluate skilled labor were well developed, the allocation of work within enterprises was decided by employers. He states that this caused the differences between the UK and Germany even though both of them are classified as the training approach. See Chapter 8 of Marsden (1999).

12. Dore (1973: 411–415).
13. Dore (1990: 448–453).
14. Esping-Andersen (1999: 16).
15. OECD (2019); Müller et al. (ed.) (2019).
16. Japan's Keidanren is an association of large corporations, but it is not an employers' organization that is open to collective labor-management negotiations. In addition, Japan's labor law has a system of extensions of collective agreements to the region or intra-company level, but no system of extensions to the industrial level.
17. Figures for Sweden, Spain and Germany are for 2018, Belgian figures are for 2019, and US figures are for 2020. OECD/AIAS ICTWSS database; https://www.oecd.org/employment/ictwss-database.htm (accessed on 19 January 2023).
18. According to the JILPT (2023), in the US, wages in firms with ten to forty-nine employees were 50.1% of those with 1,000 or more employees in 2021, while in the same year in Japan, wages in firms with five to twenty-nine employees were 55.5% and those with thirty to ninety-nine employees were 64.2% of those with 1,000 or more employees (Japanese data are from the 2021 'Annual Summary of Monthly Labor Survey'). The OECD Entrepreneurship at a Glance 2017 figure 3-7 shows the estimated international comparison gap of compensation per employee by enterprise size in manufacturing in 2014 or latest available year and demonstrates that Japan's firm-size wage gap is relatively moderate (OECD 2017). The number of microenterprises has decreased in Japan since the 1990s, and the wage gap among regular employees by company size has been declining, but the wage gap between regular employees and non-regular workers has attracted more attention.
19. The relationship between collective agreement coverage and the unemployment rate is controversial (Adamopoulou and Villanueva 2022). Studies in South Africa and Portugal have found that when collective agreements are applied, employment in SMEs decreases (Magruder 2012; Guimaraes et al. 2017). On the other hand, some argue that as the rate of application of collective agreements increases, inefficient firms are weeded out, the economy grows, and employment increases as a result (OECD 2019, Chapter 3). Here, I am in line with the theory that a high rate of collective agreement coverage tends to lead to a high unemployment rate, an argument that was common in the 1980s in Europe.
20. OECD (2023). Also see note 104 in Chapter 1.
21. See Esping-Andersen (1990); Gallie (2007); Müller et al. (ed.) (2019); OECD (2023).
22. Müller et al. (ed.) (2019).
23. Gallie (2007: 16–19). Gallie's employment regime theory consists of three models. The first is the market regime, the second is the inclusive regime, and the third is the dualist regime. Using indicators such as the strength of restrictions on layoffs and the labor participation rate of women in Western European countries, Gallie classified the UK as a market regime, the Nordic countries as a inclusive regime, and Germany, France and Spain as dualist regimes. However, he also used the participation rate of official vocational training and the degree of centralization of collective labor-management negotiations as indicators of classification, which are not necessarily suitable for analysis of Japan or the US. Eventually, Gallie limits his classification to only European countries.

Notes

24. See Section 2 of Chapter 2 of OECD (2019).
25. It is unclear why employment at large companies declined in 2002. The recession following the 1997 Asian financial crisis had an impact. In addition, as discussed in Chapter 2, the Japanese government mandated an extension of the retirement age from fifty-five to sixty in 1998. The first regular employees to retire after the five-year extension were retired in 2003, which probably had an impact on the decline.
26. It is not clear to what extent the internal labor market exists in SMEs without labor unions in Japan. However, the MHLW's 'Survey on Labor-Management Communication' asks each business establishment whether or not it has a labor-management consultative body. In the 2018 survey, 16.8% of the establishments that responded that they have no labor union also responded that they have a labor-management consultative body. The matters to be discussed at the labor-management consultative body were 'matters related to working hours, holidays, and vacations' (86.0%), 'matters related to health and safety' (77.3%), and 'matters related to wages and retirement benefits' (69.9%), suggesting that those establishments that have such bodies are likely to have in-house collective agreements on wages and working conditions, even if they do not have labor unions. According to this survey, in 2018, 37.1% of the surveyed companies had a labor-management consultative body. This percentage was 41.8% in 1999 and 40.3% in 2014, which is a slight decrease but not that large a change. Given that larger firms tend to have labor unions, it is likely that a larger percentage of regular employees than this figure work in firms where collective agreements exist. This is consistent with the estimates in Chapter 1 that workers who achieve long-term employment and seniority wages are approximately 50% of regular employees. See the 2018 'Survey on Labor-Management Communications', https://www.mhlw.go.jp/toukei/list/18-r01gaiyou.html (accessed on 30 July 2023).
27. Uys and Blaauw (2006).
28. Michon (2011).
29. E.g., Pellissery and Walker (2007).
30. Gordon (1985) gives credit to the Japanese labor movement for demanding and achieving 'membership' of companies in the postwar period, albeit different from the achievement of the American labor movement. I do not disagree with that assessment. Where he and I differ is that I clarified that this achievement is only one side of the same coin and that it is necessarily related to the dual structure in Japanese society. Nevertheless, the conclusion of this book is the same as the following sentences in the Conclusion of Gordon (1985: 432): 'Cultural values are not the same for all in the culture, and they change with history. They are interpreted and manipulated differently by different groups in a society'. I wrote this book to let people know that they can change their culture and collective norms by knowing themselves.

Bibliography*

Non-Japanese References

Abe, Aya (2006a), 'Empirical analysis of relative deprivation and poverty in Japan', IPSS Discussion Paper Series, No. 2005–07, pp. 1–35. https://www.ipss.go.jp/publication/j/DP/dp2005_07e.pdf (Accessed on 22 June 2022).

Abegglen, James C. (1958), *The Japanese Factory: Aspects of Its Social Organization*, Glencoe, Ill.: Free Press. Translated into Japanese by Kuniyoshi Urabe and published in 1958 under the title *Nihon no keiei* (Japanese Management). Tokyo: Diamond Publishing Co.

Abegglen, James C. (1973), *Management and the Worker*. Tokyo: Sophia University Press.

Abegglen, James C. (2006), *21st-Century Japanese Management: New Systems, Lasting Values*. New York: Palgrave Macmillan.

Adamopoulou, Effrosyni and Ernesto Villanueva (2022), 'Employment and wage effects of extending collective bargaining agreements: Sectoral collective contracts reduce inequality but may lead to job losses among workers with earnings close to the wage floors', *IZA World of Labor*, 136(2), DOI: https://doi.org/10.15185/izawol.136.v2

Ahn, Hie Joo, Bart Hobijn and Aysegül Sahin (2023), 'The dual U.S. labor market uncovered', *Finance and Economics Discussion Series* 2023–031. Washington: Board of Governors of the Federal Reserve System, DOI: https://doi.org/10.17016/FEDS.2023.031

Althauser, Robert P. (1989), 'Internal labor markets', *Annual Review of Sociology*, 15, pp. 143–161.

Aoki, Masahiko (1984), 'Aspects of the Japanese firm', in idem (ed.), *The Economic Analysis of the Japanese Firm*. Amsterdam: North-Holland, pp. 3–43.

Aoyagi, Chie and Giovanni Ganelli (2013), 'The path to higher growth: Does revamping Japan's dual labor market matter?', *IMF Working Papers* 2013(202), International Monetary Fund. DOI: https://doi.org/10.5089/9781484391303.001

Asao, Yutaka (2011), 'Overview of non-regular employment in Japan', in Japan Institute for Labour and Policy Training (ed.), *Non-Regular Employment: Issues and Challenges Common to the Major Developed Countries* (the 2011 JILPT Seminar on Non-regular Employment), Tokyo: JILPT, pp. 1–42.

Baba, Masao, Robert Perloff, Fusako Baba, Mary Lewis and Hiroshi Iwade (1983), *A Comparative Study of the Cultural Climate of American and Japanese Management*. Institute of Business Research, College of Economics, Nihon University.

Bangasser, Paul E. (2000), *The ILO and the Informal Sector: An Institutional History*. Geneva: ILO. https://www.ilo.org/wcmsp5/groups/public/—ed_emp/documents/publication/wcms_142295.pdf (Accessed on 28 October 2023).

Bentolila, Samuel, Juan J. Dolado and Juan F. Jimeno (2019), 'Dual labour markets revisited', *IZA Discussion Papers* 12126. Institute of Labor Economics (IZA).

Berger, Peter L. and Thomas Luckmann (1966), *The Social Construction of Reality: A Treatise in the Sociology of Knowledge*. Garden City, N.Y.: Doubleday.

---

*Unsigned newspaper articles and websites, laws and regulations are referred in notes of chapters and generally excluded from this list of references. Joint publications that refer to more than one article are listed by title only.

Bhatta, Gambhir (2005), *International Dictionary of Public Management and Governance*. Armonk, N.Y.: M.E. Sharpe.

Blossfeld, Hans-Peter and Catherine Hakim (eds.) (1997), *Between Equalization and Marginalization: Women Working Part-Time in Europe and the United States of America*. Oxford and New York: Oxford University Press.

Boltanski, Luc (1987), *The Making of a Class: Cadres in French Society*. Cambridge: Cambridge University Press. Translated from the original French by Arthur Goldhammer. Originally published in 1982 as *Les cadres. La formation d'un groupe social*. Paris: éditions de Minuit.

Bourdieu, Pierre ([1973] 1979), *Distinction: A Social Critique of the Judgement of Taste*. London: Routledge & Kegan Paul. Translated from the original French by Richard Nice. Originally published in 1973 as *La distinction: Critique sociale du jugement*. Paris: éditions de Minuit

Brinton, Mary C. and Takehiko Kariya (1998), 'Institutional embeddedness in Japanese labor markets', in Mary C. Brinton and Victor Nee (eds.), *The New Institutionalism in Sociology*. New York: Russell Sage Foundation, pp. 181–207.

Brinton, Mary C. (2010), *Lost in Transition: Youth, Work, and Instability in Postindustrial Japan*. Cambridge: Cambridge University Press.

Brown, Charles and James Medoff (1989), 'The employer size-wage effect', *Journal of Political Economy*, 97, pp. 1027–1059.

Calder, Kent E. (1988), *Crisis and Compensation: Public Policy and Political Stability in Japan 1949–1986*. Princeton, N.J.: Princeton University Press.

Campbell, John C. (1992), *How Policies Change: The Japanese Government and the Aging Society*. Princeton, N.J.: Princeton University Press.

Campbell, John P. and Robert D. Pritchard (1976), 'Motivation theory in industrial and organizational psychology', in Marvin D. Dunnette (ed.), *Handbook of Industrial and Organizational Psychology*. Chicago: Rand McNally College Publishing Company.

Clark, Burton R. (1995), *Places of Inquiry: Research and Advanced Education in Modern Universities*. Berkeley, Calif.: University of California Press.

Clark, Rodney (1979), *The Japanese Company*. New Haven, Conn.: Yale University Press.

Cole, Robert E. (1979), *Work Mobility and Participation*. Berkeley, Calif.: University of California Press.

Cooke, Fang Lee and Yumei Jiang (2017), 'The growth of non-standard employment in Japan and South Korea: The role of institutional actors and impact on workers and the labour market'. *Asia Pacific Journal of Human Resources*, 55, pp. 155–176. DOI: https://doi.org/10.1111/1744-7941.12138

Creedy, John and Keith Whitfield (1988), 'The economic analysis of internal labor markets', *Bulletin of Economic Research*, 40(4), pp. 247–269.

Dickens, William T. and Kevin Lang (1985), 'A test of dual labor market theory', *The American Economic Review*, 75(4), pp. 792–805.

Dickens, William T. and Kevin Lang (1987), 'Where have all the good jobs gone?: Deindustrialization and labor market segmentation', in K. Lang and J. Leonard (eds.), *Unemployment and the Structure of Labor Markets*. Oxford: Basil Blackwell, pp. 90–102.

Doeringer, Peter B. and Michael J. Piore (1971), *Internal Labor Markets and Manpower Analysis*. Lexington, Mass.: Heath.

Bibliography

461

Dore, Ronald (1973), *British Factory—Japanese Factory: The Origins of National Diversity in Industrial Relations*. Berkeley, Calif.: University of California Press.

Dore, Ronald (1976), *The Diploma Disease: Education Qualification and Development*. Berkeley, Calif.: University of California Press.

Dore, Ronald (1990), 'Afterword to the 1990 edition', in *British Factory—Japanese Factory: The Origins of National Diversity in Industrial Relations*. Berkeley, Calif.: University of California Press, pp. 421–454.

Endo, Koshi (1998), '"Japanization" of a performance appraisal system: A historical comparison of the American and Japanese systems', *Social Science Japan Journal*, 1(2), pp. 247–262.

Esping-Andersen, Gøsta (1990), *The Three Worlds of Welfare Capitalism*. Princeton, N.J.: Princeton University Press.

Esping-Andersen, Gøsta (1999), *Social Foundations of Postindustrial Economies*. Oxford: Oxford University Press.

Estevez-Abe, Margarita (2008), *Welfare and Capitalism in Postwar Japan: Party, Bureaucracy, and Business* (Cambridge Studies in Comparative Politics). Cambridge: Cambridge University Press.

Foucault, Michel ([1966] 1970), *The Order of Things: An Archaeology of the Human Sciences*. London: Tavistock. Translated from the original French by Alan Sheridan. Originally published in 1966 as *Les mots et les choses*. Paris: Éditions Gallimard.

Fu, Huiyan (2012), *An Emerging Non-regular Labour Force in Japan: The Dignity of Dispatched Workers*. Abingdon, Oxon: Routledge.

Gallie, Duncan (2007), 'Production regime, employment regime, and the quality of work', in idem (ed.), *Employment Regimes and the Quality of Work*. New York: Oxford University Press, pp. 1–33.

Gibbs, Jack P. (1965), 'Norms: The problem of definition and classification', *American Journal of Sociology*, 70(5), pp. 586–594.

Goetz, Klaus H. (1999), 'Senior officials in the German federal administration: Institutional change and positional differentiation', in Edward C. Page and Vincent Wright (eds.), *Bureaucratic Elites in Western European States: A Comparative Analysis of Top Officials*. Oxford: Oxford University Press, pp. 147–177.

Gordon, Andrew (1985), *The Evolution of Labor Relations in Japan: Heavy Industry 1853–1955*. Cambridge, Mass.: Harvard University Press.

Gordon, Andrew (1993), 'Contests for the workplace', in idem (ed.), *Postwar Japan as History*. Berkeley, Calif.: University of California Press, pp. 373–394.

Gordon, Andrew (1998), *The Wages of Affluence: Labor and Management in Postwar Japan*. Cambridge, Mass.: Harvard University Press.

Gordon, Andrew (2011), *Fabricating Consumers: The Sewing Machine in Modern Japan*. Berkeley, Calif.: University of California Press.

Gordon, Andrew (2017), 'New and enduring dual structures of employment in Japan: The rise of non-regular labor, 1980s-2010s', *Social Science Japan Journal*, 20(1), pp. 9–36.

Gottshall, Karin (2015), 'A comparison of public employment regimes in Germany, France, Sweden and the United Kingdom,' in Karin Gottschall, Bernhard Kittel, Kendra Briken, Jan-Ocko Heuer, Sylvia Hils, Sebastian Streb and Markus Tepe (2015), *Public Sector Employment Regimes: Transformations of the State as an Employer*. London: Palgrave Macmillan, pp. 107–165.

Green, Francis, Stephen Machin and Alan Manning (1996), 'The employer size-wage effect: Can dynamic monopsony provide an explanation?', *Oxford Economic Papers*, 48, pp. 433–455.

Gregory, Victoria, Guido Menzio and David Wiczer (2021), 'The alpha beta gamma of the labor market', *FRB St. Louis Working Paper* No. 2021-3, DOI: http://dx.doi.org/10.20955/wp.2021.00

Greinert, Wolf-Dietrich (1994), *The "German System" of Vocational Education: History, Organization, Prospects*. Translated from the original German by Mary Carroll. Baden-Baden: Nomos Verlagsgesellschaft.

Guimaraes, Paulo, Fernando Martins and Pedro Portugal (2017), *Upward Nominal Wage Rigidity*. IZA Discussion Paper No. 10510.

Hareven, Tamara K. (2003), *The Silk Weavers of Kyoto: Family and Work in a Changing Traditional Industry*. Berkeley, Calif.: University of California Press.

Hart, Keith (1973), 'Informal income opportunities and urban employment in Ghana', *The Journal of Modern African Studies*, 11(3), pp. 61–89.

Hazama, Hiroshi (1979), 'Japanese labor-management relations and Uno Riemon', *Journal of Japanese Studies*, 5(1), pp. 72–73.

Henry, Nicholas (1999), *Public Administration and Public Affairs 7th edition*. Englewood Cliffs, N.J.: Prentice-Hall.

Hofstede, Geert (1980), *Culture's Consequences: International Differences in Work-Related Values*. Beverly Hills, Calif.: Sage Publications.

Hofstede, Geert (1984), 'Cultural dimensions in management and planning', *Asia Pacific Journal of Management*, 1(2), pp. 81–99.

Houseman, Susan N. and Machiko Ōsawa (2003), 'The growth of nonstandard employment in Japan and the United States: A comparison of causes and consequences', in Susan N. Houseman and Machiko Ōsawa (eds.), *Nonstandard Work in Developed Economies: Causes and Consequences*. Kalamazoo, Mich.: W.E. Upjohn Institute for Employment Research, pp. 175–214.

Idson, Todd L. and Daniel J. Feaster (1990), 'A selectivity model of employer-size wage differentials', *Journal of Labor Economics*, 8, pp. 99–122.

Idson, Todd L. and Walter Y. Oi (1999), 'Firm size and wages', in Orley C. Ashenfelter and David Card (eds.), *Handbook of Labor Economics*, vol. 3, part B. Elsevier, pp. 2165–2214.

Ilgen, Daniel R., Cynthia D. Fisher and Susan M. Taylor (1979), 'Consequences of individual feedback on behavior in organizations', *Journal of Applied Psychology*, 64(4), pp. 349–71.

ILO (International Labor Organization) (2013), *The Informal Economy and Decent Work: A Policy Resource Guide Supporting Transitions to Formality*, Office- Geneva, ILO; URL: https://www.ilo.org/wcmsp5/groups/public/—ed_emp/—emp_policy/documents/publication/wcms_212689.pdf (Accessed on 28 August 2023).

ILO (International Labor Organization) (2016), *Non-Standard Employment around the World: Understanding, Challenges, Shaping Prospects*. Geneva: International Labour Office. URL: https://www.ilo.org/wcmsp5/groups/public/@dgreports/@dcomm/@publ/documents/publication/wcms_534326.pdf (Accessed on 22 June 2022).

ILO (International Labor Organization) (2018), *Women and Men in the Informal Economy: A Statistical Picture Third Edition*. Geneva: International Labour Office. URL: https://www.ilo.org/wcmsp5/groups/public/—dgreports/—dcomm/documents/publication/wcms_626831.pdf (Accessed on 28 August 2022).

Bibliography

Imai, Jun (2011), *The Transformation of Japanese Employment Relations Reform without Labor*. Basingstoke: Palgrave Macmillan.

Jacoby, Sanford M. (1985), *Employing Bureaucracy: Managers, Unions and the Transformation of Work in American Industry 1900-1945*. New York: Columbia University Press.

Jacoby, Sanford M. (1997), *Modern Manors: Welfare Capitalism Since the New Deal*. Princeton, N.J.: Princeton University Press.

Jacoby, Sanford M. (2004), *Employing Bureaucracy: Managers, Unions and the Transformation of Work in American Industry 1900-1945, Revised Edition*. Mahwah, N.J.: Lawrence Erlbaum Associates Publishers.

Jacoby, Sanford M. (2005) *The Embedded Corporation: Corporate Governance and Employment Relations in Japan and the United States*. Princeton, N.J.: Princeton University Press.

JILPT (Japan Institute for Labour Policy and Training) (2012), *Labor Situation in Japan and Its Analysis General Overview 2011/2012*. Tokyo: Japan Institute for Labour Policy and Training. URL: https://www.jil.go.jp/english/lsj/general/2011-2012.html (Accessed on 28 August 2022).

Kambayashi, Ryō and Takao Katō (2016), 'Long-term employment and job security over the past 25 years', *ILR Review*, 70(2), pp. 359–394. DOI: http://dx.doi.org/10.1177/0019793916653956.

Karsh, Bernard (1984), 'Human resources management in Japanese large-scale industry', *Journal of Industrial Relations*, 26(2), pp. 226–245.

Kawanishi, Hirosuke (2005), 'Segmentation of the labor market', in Ross Mouer and Hirosuke Kawanishi, *A Sociology of Work in Japan*. Cambridge: Cambridge University Press, pp. 117–142.

Kerr, Clerk (1954), 'The Balkanization of labor markets', in E. Wight Bakke (ed.), *Labor Mobility and Economic Opportunity*. Cambridge, Mass.: MIT Press, pp. 92–110.

Kocka, Jürgen (1981a), 'Capitalism and bureaucracy in German industrialization before 1914', *The Economic History Review*, 2nd series, 34(3), pp. 453–468.

Kocka, Jürgen ([1981b] 1992), 'Bildung und sozialer Ungleichheit: Entstehung und Diffrenzierung angestellter Mittel-schichten im 19. und frühen 20. Jahrhundert, in *Die Angestellten in der deutschen Geschichte 1850–1980: Vom Privatbeamten zum angestellten Arbeitnehmer*. Göttingen: Vandenhoeck & Ruprecht, pp. 90–115. 'Kyoiku to shakaiteki fubyōdō' (Education and inequality), in *Kōgyō-ka soshiki-ka kanryō-sei: Kindai Doitsu no kigyō to shakai* (Industrialization, organization, and bureaucracy: Enterprise and society in modern Germany). Translated from the German into Japanese by Sachio Kaku. Nagoya: University of Nagoya Press, pp. 73–103.

Koettl-Brodmann, Johannes, Claudio E. Montenegro and Truman G. Packard (2012), *In from the Shadow: Integrating Europe's Informal Labor*. Washington, D.C.: The World Bank. URL: http://documents.worldbank.org/curated/en/458701468035954123/In-from-the-shadow-integrating-Europes-informal-labor (Accessed on 28 August 2022).

Koike, Kazuo (1988), *Understanding Industrial Relations in Modern Japan*. New York: St. Martin's Press.

Koshiro, Kazutoshi (1984), 'Lifetime employment in Japan: Three models of the concept', *Monthly Labor Review*, 107(8), pp. 34–35.

Kracauer, Siegfried (1998), *The Salaried Masses: Duty and Distraction in Weimar Germany*. London: Verso. Translated from the original German by Quintin Hoare. Originally published in 1930 as *Die Angestellten. Aus dem neuesten Deutschland*. Frankfurter Societäts-Druckerei, Frankfurt am Main.

Kumazawa, Makoto (1996), *Portraits of the Japanese Workplace: Labor Movements, Workers, and Managers*. Boulder, C.O.: Westview Press. Translated from the original Japanese by Mikiso Hane and Andrew Gordon. Originally published in 1993 as *Shinpen Nihon no rōdōsha zō* (Portraits of Japanese Workers). Tokyo: Chikuma Gakugei Bunko.

Lange, Matthew, James Mahoney and Matthias vom Hau (2006), 'Colonialism and development: A comparative analysis of Spanish and British colonies', *American Journal of Sociology*, 111(5), pp. 1412–1462.

Lebra, Takie S. (1976), *Japanese Patterns of Behavior*. Honolulu, Hi.: University of Hawaii Press.

Lester, Richard (1967) 'Pay differentials by size of establishment', *Industrial Relations*, 7, pp. 57–67.

Levine, Solomon B. (1958), *Industrial Relations in Postwar Japan*. Urbana, Ill.: University of Illinois Press.

Lewis, William Arthur (1954), 'Economic development with unlimited supplies of labor', *The Manchester School*, 22(2), pp. 139–191.

Locke, Edwin A. and Gary P. Latham (1984), *Goal Setting: A Motivational Technique That Works*. Englewood Cliffs, N.J.: Prentice–Hall.

Magruder, Jeremy (2012), 'High unemployment yet few small firms: The role of centralized bargaining in South Africa', *AEJ: Applied Economics*, 4(3), pp. 138–166.

Marsden, David (1990), 'Institutions and labour mobility: Occupational and internal labour markets in Britain, France, Italy and West Germany', in Renato Brunetta and Carlo Dell'Aringa (eds.), *Labour Relations and Economic Performance*. New York: New York University Press, pp. 414–438.

Marsden, David (1999), *A Theory of Employment Systems*. Oxford: Oxford University Press.

McCreary, Eugene C. (1968), 'Social welfare and business: The Krupp Welfare Program, 1860-1914', *The Business History Review*, 42(1), pp. 24–49.

Michon, François (2011), 'Non-regular employment in France: A profile', in *Non-regular Employment: Issues and Challenges Common to the Major Developed Countries*. Tokyo: JILPT (Japan Institute for Labor Policy and Training), pp. 117–140.

Mills, C. Wright (1951), *White Collar: The American Middle Classes*. Oxford: Oxford University Press.

Miura, Mari (2012), *Welfare through Work: Conservative Ideas, Partisan Dynamics, and Social Protection in Japan*. Ithaca, N.Y.: Cornell University Press.

Moore, Joe (1983), *Japanese Workers and the Struggle for Power*. Madison, Wis.: University of Wisconsin Press.

Moriguchi, Chiaki and Emmanuel Saez (2008), 'The evolution of income concentration in Japan, 1886–2005: Evidence from Income Tax Statistics', *The Review of Economics and Statistics*, 90(4), pp. 713–734.

Mouer, Ross and Yoshio Sugimoto (1986), *Images of Japanese Society*. London: Keegan Paul.

Bibliography

Müller, Torsten, Kurt Vandaele and Jeremy Waddington (ed.) (2019), *Collective Bargaining in Europe: Towards an Endgame*. Volumes I, II, III and IV. Belgium: ETUI-REHS (The European Trade Union Institute for Research, Education and Health and Safety).

Naff, Katherine C., Norma M. Riccucci and Siegrun Fox Freyss (2014), *Personnel Management in Government: Politics and Process, 7th edition*. Boca Raton, Fla.: CRC Press.

Nakane, Chie (1970), *Japanese Society*. Berkeley, Calif.: University of California Press.

Norgren, Tiana (2001), *Abortion Before Birth Control: The Politics of Reproduction in Postwar Japan*. Princeton: Princeton University Press.

Odaka, Kōnosuke (1999), '"Japanese-style" labour relations', in Tetsuji Okazaki and Masahiro Okuno-Fujiwara (eds.), *The Japanese Economic System and Its Historical Origins*. Oxford: Clarendon Press. Originally published in Japanese in 1993.

OECD (Organisation for Economic Co-operation and Development) (2009), *Government at a Glance 2009*. Paris: OECD Publishing. DOI: https://doi.org/10.1787/9789264075061-en. (Accessed on 31 August 2023).

OECD (Organisation for Economic Co-operation and Development) (2013), *OECD Skills Outlook 2013: First Results from the Survey of Adult Skills*. Paris: OECD Publishing. DOI: http://dx.doi.org/10.1787/9789264204256-en (Accessed on 5 July 2022).

OECD (Organisation for Economic Co-operation and Development) (2017), *Entrepreneurship at a Glance*. Paris: OECD Publishing. DOI: https://doi.org/10.1787/entrepreneur_aag-2017-en (Accessed on 5 July 2023).

OECD (Organisation for Economic Co-operation and Development) (2018a), *Social Policy for Shared Prosperity, Embracing the Future: How does your country compare?* URL: https://www.oecd.org/social/ministerial/Compare-your-country.pdf (Accessed on 5 July 2022).

OECD (Organisation for Economic Co-operation and Development) (2018b), *Working Better with Age: Japan, Ageing and Employment Policies*. Paris: OECD Publishing. DOI: https://dx.doi.org/10.1787/9789264201996-en (Accessed on 31 January 2020).

OECD (Organisation for Economic Co-operation and Development) (2018c), *OECD Employment Outlook 2018*. Paris: OECD Publishing. DOI: https://doi.org/10.1787/empl_outlook-2018-en (Accessed on 31 January 2020).

OECD (Organisation for Economic Co-operation and Development) (2019), *Negotiating Our Way Up: Collective Bargaining in a Changing World of Work*. Paris: OECD Publishing. URL: https://www.oecd.org/els/negotiating-our-way-up-1fd2da34-en.htm (Accessed 31 on January 2020).

OECD (Organisation for Economic Co-operation and Development) (2021), *Creating Responsive Adult Learning Opportunities in Japan, Getting Skills Right*. Paris: OECD Publishing. DOI: https://doi.org/10.1787/cfe1ccd2-en (Accessed on 30 August 2022).

OECD (Organisation for Economic Co-operation and Development) (2023), *Government at a Glance 2023*. Paris: OECD Publishing. DOI: https://doi.org/10.1787/3d5c5d31-en (Accessed on 31 August 2023).

OECD (Organisation for Economic Co-operation and Development) Manpower and Social Affairs Directorate (1973), *Manpower Policy in Japan*. OECD Reviews of Manpower and Social Policies, no. 11, Paris: OECD Publishing.

OECD/ADB (2019), *Government at a Glance Southeast Asia 2019*. Paris: OECD Publishing. DOI: https://doi.org/10.1787/9789264305915-en (Accessed on 31 August 2023).

OECD/ILO (2019), 'Definitions of informal economy, informal sector and informal employment', in *Tackling Vulnerability in the Informal Economy*. Paris: OECD Publishing. DOI: https://doi.org/10.1787/103bf23e-en (Accessed on 31 January 2020).

Oguma, Eiji (2002a). *A Genealogy of 'Japanese' Self-Images*. Melbourne: Trans Pacific Press. Translated from the original Japanese by David Askew.

Oguma, Eiji (2014), *The Boundaries of 'The Japanese', Volume 1: Okinawa 1818-1972, Inclusion and Exclusion*. Melbourne: Trans Pacific Press. Translated from the original Japanese by Leonie R. Strickland. See Oguma 1998.

Oguma, Eiji (2015), 'Japan's 1968: A Collective Reaction to Rapid Economic Growth in an Age of Turmoil', *The Asia-Pacific Journal Japan Focus*, 12(1), pp. 1–27.

Oguma, Eiji (2017), *The Boundaries of 'The Japanese', Volume 2, Korea, Taiwan and the Ainu 1868-1945*. Melbourne: Trans Pacific Press. Translated from the original Japanese by Leonie R. Strickland. See Oguma 1998.

Oguma, Eiji (2021), 'The other "post-1968": A socio-historical analysis of the resurgence of the conservatives in Japan's long 1960s', *International Quarterly for Asian Studies*, 52(3–4), pp. 229–252.

Ono, Hiroshi (2006), *Lifetime Employment in Japan: Concepts and Measurements*. SSE/EFI Working Paper Series in Economics and Finance, No. 624, Stockholm: Stockholm School of Economics, The Economic Research Institute (EFI).

Osawa, Mari (2011), *Social Security in Contemporary Japan: A Comparative Analysis*. London and New York: Routledge/University of Tokyo Series.

Ouchi, William (1981), *Theory Z: How American Business Can Meet the Japanese Challenge*. Reading, Mass.: Addison-Wesley.

Pekkanen Robert J. (2006), *Japan's Dual Civil Society: Members without Advocates*. Redwood: Stanford University Press.

Pellissery, Sony and Robert Walker (2007), 'Social security options for informal sector workers in emergent economies and the Asia and Pacific region', *Social Policy and Administration*, 41(4), pp. 401–409.

Player, Mack A. (1992), *Federal Law of Employment Discrimination in a Nutshell (3rd edition)*. St. Paul, Minn.: West Publishing.

Price, James L. and Charles W. Mueller (1986), *Handbook of Organizational Measurement*. Marshfield, Mass.: Pitman.

Räisänen, Heikki (2005), 'Comparative analysis on the job-broking market in Japan and Finland', Discussion Papers 370, VATT Institute for Economic Research. URL: https://www.doria.fi/bitstream/handle/10024/148349/k370.pdf (Accessed on 30 August 2022).

Rebick, Marcus E. (2005), *The Japanese Employment System Adapting to a New Economic Environment*. Oxford: Oxford University Press.

Recruit Works Institute (2018), *Kigyō kibo-kan no chingin kakusa, furukute atarashī kadai* (Wage disparities by company size: Old and new challenges), 19 January. URL: https://www.works-i.com/column/policy/detail008.html (Accessed on 10 May 2022).

Recruit Works Research Institute (2013), *Global Career Survey*, Tokyo: Recruit Works Research Institute. https://www.works-i.com/research/works-report/item/140501_glo_en.pdf (Accessed on 30 August 2022).

Bibliography

Reichard, Christoph and Eckhard Schröter (2021) 'Civil service and public employment', in Sabine Kuhlmann, Isabella Proeller, Dieter Schimanke and Jan Ziekow (ed.), *Public Administration in Germany*. Berlin: Springer, pp. 205–223.

Röhl, Wilhelm (2005), 'Public law', in Wilhelm Röhl (ed.), *History of Law in Japan Since 1868*. Leiden: Brill, pp. 26–165.

Rouban, Luc (1999), 'The senior civil service in France', in Edward C. Page and Vincent Wright (eds.), *Bureaucratic Elites in Western European States: A Comparative Analysis of Top Officials*. Oxford: Oxford University Press.

Saglio, Jean (2000), 'Changing wage orders: France 1900–1995', in Linda Clarke, Peter de Gijsel and Joern Janssen (eds.), *The Dynamics of Wage Relations in the New Europe*. Boston, Mass.: Springer, pp. 44–59.

Schinagl, Mary S. (1966), *History of Efficiency Ratings in the Federal Government*. New York: Bookman Associates.

Schneier, Dena B. (1978), 'The impact of EEO legislation on performance appraisal', *Personnel*, July-August.

Shaeffer, Ruth G. (1983), *Staffing Systems: Managerial and Professional Jobs*. Amsterdam: Elsevier Science.

Shirai, Taishiro (ed.) (1983), *Contemporary Industrial Relations in Japan*. Madison, Wis.: University of Wisconsin Press.

Skocpol, Theda (1984), 'Emerging agendas and recurrent strategies in historical sociology', in idem (ed.), *Vision and Method in Historical Sociology*. Cambridge: Cambridge University Press, pp. 356–391.

Sullivan, Jeremiah J. and Richard B. Peterson (1991), 'A test of theories underlying the Japanese lifetime employment system', *Journal of International Business Studies*, 22(1), pp. 79–97.

Supreme Commander for the Allied Powers, Advisory Committee on Labor (1946), *Final Report: Labor Policies and Programs in Japan*. National Diet Library of Japan, NRS 11842–11844.

Suzuki, Jun (2002), 'Two time systems, three patterns of working hours', *Japan Review*, 14 (The birth of tardiness: The formation of time consciousness in modern Japan), pp. 79–97.

Suzuki, Kyoko (2020), 'The latent structure of the Japanese labor market and the type of employment: Latent class analysis with finite mixture model', *Japan Labor Issues*, 4(22), pp. 42–58.

Tachibanaki, Toshiaki (1996), *Wage Determination and Distribution in Japan*. London: Oxford University Press.

Taira, Koji (1962), 'The characteristics of Japanese labor markets', *Economic Development and Cultural Change*, 10, pp. 150–168.

Taira Koji (1970), 'The labor market origins of employer paternalism', in idem (ed.), *Economic Development and the Labor Market in Japan*. New York: Columbia University Press, pp. 79–127.

Tanaka, Fujio J. (1981), 'Lifetime employment in Japan', *Challenge*, 24(3), pp. 23–29.

Tanaka, Hiroshi (1988), *Personality in Industry*. Philadelphia, Pa.: University of Pennsylvania Press.

Tanimoto, Masayuki (2013), "From peasant economy to urban agglomeration: The transformation of "labour-intensive industrialization" in modern Japan', in Gareth Austin and Kaoru Sugihara (eds.), *Labour-Intensive Industrialization in Global History*. London: Routledge, pp. 144–175.

Taylor, Frederick W. (1911), *The Principles of Scientific Management*. New York: Harper & Brothers.

Tepe, Markus (2015), 'Public employment regimes in OECD countries', in Gottshall et al. *Public Sector Employment Regimes: Transformations of the State as an Employer*. London: Palgrave Macmillan, pp. 69–106.

Thomann, Bernard ([2016] 2023), 'The rationalisation and modernisation of labour organisation and the transformation of coal miners' lives in twentieth-century Japan'. Translated from the original French by Karen Grimwade, *Cipango* 23, pp. 15–62. DOI: https://doi.org/10.4000/cjs.174\4.

Thurow, Lester C. (1975), *Generating Inequality: Mechanisms of Distribution in the U.S. Economy*. New York: Basic Books.

Tominaga, Ken'ichi (1991), 'A theory of modernization and social change of the non-western societies: Toward a generalization from Japan's experiences', *International Review of Sociology*, 2, pp. 95–120.

Troske, Kenneth R. (1999), 'Evidence on the employer size-wage premium from worker-establishment matched data', *The Review of Economics and Statistics*, 81, pp. 15–26.

Tsujinaka, Yutaka, Robert J. Pekkanen and Hidehiro Yamamoto (2014), *Neighborhood Associations and Local Governance in Japan*. London: Routledge.

Uys, M.D. and Phillip F. Blaauw (2006), 'The dual labour market theory and the informal sector in South Africa', *Acta Commercii*, 6(1), pp. 248–257. DOI: https://doi.org/10.4102/ac.v6i1.122

Vogel, Ezra, F. (1963), *Japan's New Middle Class: The Salaryman and His Family in a Tokyo Suburb*. Berkeley, Calif.: University of California Press.

Vogel, Ezra F. (1979), *Japan as Number One: Lessons for America*. Cambridge, Mass: Harvard University Press.

Weber, Max ([1905] 1930), *The Protestant Ethic and the Spirit of Capitalism*. London: George Allen & Unwin. Translated from the original German by Talcott Parsons. Originally published in 1905 as *Die protestantische Ethik und der "Geist" des Kapitalismus*. Tübingen: J.C.B. Mohr.

Weber, Max ([1918] 1994), 'Parliament and government in Germany under a new political order: Towards a political critique of officialdom and the party system', in Peter Lassman and Ronald Speirs (eds.), *Weber: Political Writings*. Cambridge: Cambridge University Press, pp. 130–271. Originally published in German in 1918 as *Parlament und Regierung im neugeordneten Deutschland. Zur politischen Kritik des Beamtentums und Parteiwesens*. Munich and Leipzig.

Werner, Jon M. and Mark C. Bolino (1997), 'Explaining U.S. courts of appeals decisions involving performance appraisal: Accuracy, fairness, and validation', *Personnel Psychology*, 50(1), pp. 1–24.

Yamaguchi, Kazuo (2019), *Gender Inequalities in the Japanese Workplace and Employment: Theories and Empirical Evidence*. Singapore: Springer.

Japanese References

Abe, Aya (2006b), 'Sōtaiteki hakudatsu no jittai to bunseki' (Empirical analysis of relative deprivation in Japan using Japanese microdata), *Shakai seisaku gakkaishi* (Social Policy and Labor Studies), 16, pp. 251–275.

Abe, Etsuo, Ryōichi Iwauchi, Reiko Okamoto and Takeshi Yuzawa (1997), *Igirisu kigyō keiei no rekishi–teki tenkai* (The historical development of British enterprise). Tokyo: Keisō Shobō.

Bibliography

Abegglen, James C. (2004), *Shinyakuban Nihon no Keiei* (*The Japanese Factory: Aspects of Its Social Organization, New Translation Version*). Tokyo: Nihon Keizai Shimbunsha Syuppan.

Ahn, Hee Tak (2015), 'Kankoku kigyō no jinzai keisei no aratana tenkai' (New developments in human resource formation in South Korean companies), *Keieigaku Ronshū* (Business Review), 25(4), pp. 1–23.

Akagi, Suruki (1991), *<Kansei> no keisei: Nihon kanryō–sei no kōzō* (The formation of 'the bureaucracy': Structure of the Japanese bureaucratic system). Tokyo: Nihon Hyōronsha.

Akiyama, Katsuyuki and Tadashi Aoki (1968), *Zengakuren wa nani o kangaeru ka* (What Zengakuren thinks). Tokyo: Jiyū Kokuminsha.

Amano, Ikuo (1986), *Kōtō kyōiku no Nihon-teki kōzō* (The Japanese structure of higher education). Tokyo: Tamagawa University Press.

Amano, Ikuo (1992), *Gakureki no shakai-shi: Kyōiku to Nihon no kindai* (A social history of academic credentials: Education and modern Japan). Tokyo: Shinchōsha.

Amanuma, Yasushi (1982), 'Teinen / teinen' (Retirement age), *Ōtsumajoshidaigaku bungakubu kiyō* (Annual report, Faculty of Literature, Otsuma Women's University), 14, pp. 65–81.

Arahata, Kanson ([1960] 1975), *Kanson jiden* (The autobiography of Arakawa Kanson). Tokyo: Ronsōsha. Iwanami Bunko edition, 2 volumes, published 1975.

Arisawa, Hiromi (1956), 'Nihon shihon-shugi to koyō' (Employment and Japanese capitalism), *Sekai* (World), 121, pp. 23–34.

Asō, Makoto and Morikazu Ushiogi (eds.) (1977), *Gakureki kōyō-ron: Gakureki shakai kara gakuryoku shakai e no michi* (Studies on the effects of academic credentials: The road from a credentialist society to a learned society). Tokyo: Yūhikaku Sensho.

Banno, Junji, Masato Miyachi, Naosuke Takamura, Hiroshi Yasuda and Osamu Watanabe (eds.) (1994), *Shirīzu Nihon kindai-shi dai-4-kan: Sengo kaikaku to gendai shakai no keisei* (Series on modern Japanese history, vol. 4: Postwar reforms and the making of contemporary society). Tokyo: Iwanami Shoten.

Bureau of Statistics, Cabinet Office (Naikaku Tōkeikyoku) (ed.) (1935), *Dai-54-kai Nihon teikoku tōkei nenkan* (54th statistical yearbook of the Empire of Japan). Tokyo: Tōkyō Tōkei Kyōkai.

Cabinet Office (2006), *Annual Economic and Fiscal Report 2006*. URL: https://www5. cao.go.jp/j-j/wp/wp-je06/06.html (Accessed on 31 August 2023).

Cabinet Office Public Relations Department (2003), *Kōteki nenkin seido ni kansuru yoron chōsa* (Public opinion survey on the public pension system). URL: https:// survey.gov-online.go.jp/h14/h14-kouteki/ (Accessed on 31 August 2023).

Cabinet Office Public Relations Department (2019), *Rōgo no seikatsu sekkei to kōteki nenkin ni kansuru yoron chōsa* (Public opinion survey on planning for retirement and public pensions). URL: https://www.mhlw.go.jp/content/12601000/ 000475095.pdf (Accessed on 31 August 2023).

Cabinet Official Gazette Bureau (Naikaku Kanpō-kyoku) (ed.) (1874), *Hōrei zensho* (Statutes-at-large of Japan), 1874 edition.

Cabinet Official Gazette Bureau (Naikaku Kanpō-kyoku) (ed.) (1890), *Hōrei zensho* (Complete book of laws of Japan), 1890 edition.

Cabinet Records Bureau (Naikaku Kiroku-kyoku) (ed.) ([1894] 1979), *Meiji-shokukan enkaku-hyō* (A timeline of Meiji officials), supplementary volume, 'Keio 3-nen ~ Meiji 26-nen / kantō hōkyū' (1867–1893 / official ranks and salaries). Tokyo: Hara Shobō.

470 The System of Japanese Society

Corporate Pension and Wage Research Center (Kigyō Nenkin Chingin Kenkyū Sentā) (ed.) (2007), *Chingin no honshitsu to jinji kakushin: Rekishi ni manabu hito no sodate-kata ikashi-kata* (The essence of wages and personnel system innovation). Tokyo: Sanshusha.

Ebihara, Tsuguo (2012), *Shūshoku ni tsuyoi daigaku gakubu: Hensachi, chimeido de wa wakaranai* (Universities and faculties with strong employment potential: Deviation scores and name recognition don't tell the whole story). Tokyo: Asahi Shinsho.

Ebihara, Tsuguo (2013), 'Nihonjin ga gokai shite iru "Ōbei-gata koyō no honshitsu"' (The 'essence of Western-style employment' so misunderstood by the Japanese)', summary of a lecture delivered on 14 February 2013, *Saiyō seikō nabi* (Recruitment Success Navigator). URL: http://www.direct-recruiting.jp/topics/knowhow/category_010491/detail_0036.html (Accessed on 30 June 2022).

Ebihara, Tsuguo (2015), *Naze 7-wari no entorī shīto wa, yomazu ni suterareru no ka?: Ninki kigyō no 'teguchi' o shireba, shūkatsu no nayami wa 9-wari nakunaru* (Why are 70% of job applications discarded without being read? Learn the 'tricks' that popular companies use and eliminate 90% of your job-seeking woes). Tokyo: Tōyō Keizai.

Economic Deliberation Council (Keizai Shingikai) (ed.) (1960), *Kokumin shotoku baizō keikaku* (National income doubling plan). Tokyo: Ministry of Finance Printing Bureau.

Economic Deliberation Council (Keizai Shingikai) (ed.) (1963), *Keizai hatten ni okeru jinteki nōryoku kaihatsu no kadai to taisaku* (Problems and strategies for labor capacity development in the context of economic growth). Tokyo: Ministry of Finance Printing Bureau.

Economic Planning Agency (Keizai Kikakuchō) (ed.) (1957), 'Keizai no nijū kōzō' (The dual structure of the Japanese economy), in *Nenji keizai hōkoku* (Annual Economic Report). URL: https://www5.cao.go.jp/keizai3/keizaiwp/wp-je57/wp-je57-010402.html.

Economic Planning Agency Planning Bureau (Keizai Kikakuchō Sōgō Keikakukyoku) (ed.) (1985), *21-seiki no sararīman shakai: Gekidō suru Nihon no rōdō shijō* (Salaried workers in the 21st century: Japan's turbulent labor market). Tokyo: Tōyō Keizai.

Endō, Kōshi (1999), *Nihon no jinji satei* (Personnel assessment in Japan). Kyoto: Minerva Shobō.

Enoki, Kazue and Tomoji Onozuka (eds.) (2014), *Rōmu kanri no seisei to shūen* (The genesis and demise of labor management). Tokyo: Nihon Keizai Hyōronsha.

Fujii, Nobuyuki (1991), 'Ryō taisen-kan Nihon ni okeru kōtō kyōiku sotsugyōsha no shūshoku kikai: Daigaku, senmongakkō sotsugyōsha o chūshin ni' (Employment opportunities for higher education graduates in Japan between the two world wars: Focus on university and professional school graduates), *Waseda daigaku kiyō* (Transactions of Waseda University Archives), 23, pp. 97–116.

Fujimura, Satoshi (2014), 'Senzen-ki kigyō, kan'ei kōjō ni okeru jūgyōin no gakureki bunpu: Monbushō "Jūgyōin gakureki chōsa hōkoku" no bunseki' (The distribution of employees' educational backgrounds in prewar corporations and government-owned factories: An analysis of the Ministry of Education's 'Report on the Survey of Employees' Educational Backgrounds'), *Kokumin keizai zasshi* (Journal of Economics and Business Administration), 210(2), pp. 53–73.

Bibliography

471

Fujita, Tei'ichirō (1995), *Kindai nihon dōgyō kumiaishi ron* (A history of modern trade associations). Tokyo, Seibundo.

Fujita, Yoshitaka (2010), 'Nōryoku-shugi kanri kenkyūkai ga mezashita mono' (Aims of the merit-based management study group), in Yashiro et al. (eds.), *Nōryoku-shugi kanri kenkyūkai ōraru hisutorī: Nihon-teki jinji kanri no kiban keisei* (An oral history of the merit-based management study group: The formation of the foundations of Japanese style personnel management). Tokyo: Keio University Press, pp. 25–72.

Fukuda, Kunizō and Hiroshi Sekiguchi (1955), 'Nōsan-mura no tsūkonken ni tsuite' (On matrimonial migration in rural Japanese highland communities), *Minzoku eisei* (Japanese Journal of Health and Human Ecology), 22(2/3), pp. 81–88.

Fukui, Yasutaka (2016), *Rekishi no naka no daisotsu rōdō shijō: Shūshoku saiyō no shakai-gaku* (The university graduate labor market in historical context: The economic sociology of employment and recruitment). Tokyo: Keisō Shobō.

Genda, Yūji (2010), *Ningen ni kaku wa nai: Ishikawa Tsuneo to 2000-nendai no rōdō shijō* (There is no status among people: Tsuneo Ishikawa and the labor market in the 2000s). Kyoto: Minerva Shobō.

Gordon, Andrew (2012), *Nihon rōshi kankei-shi 1853–2010* (A history of labor relations in Japan: Heavy industry 1853–2010). Tokyo: Iwanami Shoten. An updated version of the author's 1985 English-language monograph, translated into Japanese by Kazuo Nimura.

Gotō, Michio (1994), 'Nihon-gata taishū shakai to sono keisei' (Japanese-style mass society and its formation), in Junji Banno, Masato Miyachi, Naosuke Takamura, Hiroshi Yasuda and Osamu Watanabe (eds.), *Shirīzu Nihon kindai-shi dai-4-kan: Sengo kaikaku to gendai shakai no keisei* (Series on modern Japanese history, vol. 4: Postwar reforms and the making of contemporary society). Tokyo: Iwanami Shoten, pp. 252–288.

Gotō, Michio (2004a), 'Nihon-gata shakai hoshō no kōzō' (The structure of Japanese-style social security), in Osamu Watanabe (ed.), *Kōdo seichō to kigyō shakai* (Rapid economic growth and corporate society). Tokyo: Yoshikawa Kōbunkan, pp. 190–221.

Gotō, Michio (ed.) (2004b), *Kiro ni tatsu Nihon* (Japan at a crossroads). Tokyo: Yoshikawa Kōbunkan, pp. 7–94.

Gotō, Michio (2016), '"Karyū-ka" no shosō to shakai hoshō seido no sukima' (Aspects of 'downstreaming' and gaps in the security system), *Posse*, 30, pp. 32–49.

Hamada, Fujio (1994), *Shūgyō kisoku hō no kenkyū* (A study of the work rule laws). Tokyo: Yūhikaku. gyō kisoku.

Hamaguchi, Kei'ichirō (2008), 'Kōmu rōdō no hō seisaku' (Legal policies on public service labor), *Kikan rōdō-hō* (Labor Law Quarterly), no. 220, pp. 138–167.

Hamaguchi, Kei'ichirō (2011), *Nihon no koyō to rōdō-hō* (Employment and labor law in Japan). Tokyo: Nikkei Bunko.

Hamaguchi, Kei'ichirō (2013a), *Wakamono to rōdō: 'Nyūsha' no shikumi kara tokihogusu* (Youth and labor: Unraveling the mechanism of 'joining the workforce'). Tokyo: Chūōkōron-Shinsha.

Hamaguchi, Kei'ichirō (2013b), 'Hi-seiki kōmuin mondai no genten' (The origins of the non-regular civil service problem), *Chihō kōmuin geppō* (Local Civil Service Monthly), 605 (December), pp. 2–15.

Hamaguchi, Kei'ichirō (2014), *Nihon no koyō to chūkōnen* (Employment and middle-age in Japan). Tokyo: Chikuma Shinsho.

Hamaguchi, Kei'ichirō (2018), 'Ōdan-teki ronkō' (A cross-sectional discussion), *Nihon rōdō kenkyū zasshi* (Japanese Journal of Labor Studies), 693, pp. 2–10.

Hashimoto, Kenji (2009), *'Kakusa' no sengo-shi: Kaikyū shakai Nihon no rirekisho* (A postwar history of 'disparity': An overview of Japan's class society). Tokyo: Kawade Shobō Shinsha.

Hayakawa, Seiichirō and Akira Matsui (1979), *Kōmuin no chingin: Sono seido to chingin suijun no mondaiten* (Public service wages: Institutional and wage level issues). Tokyo: Rōdō Junpōsha.

Hayama, Hiroshi (2008), *Furansu no keizai erīto: kādoru kaisō no koyō shisutemu* (France's economic elite: The cadre employment system). Tokyo: Nihon Hyōronsha.

Hazama, Hiroshi (1964), *Nihon rōmu kanri-shi kenkyū: Keiei kazoku-shugi no keisei to tenkai* (A historical study of labor management in Japan: The formation and development of managerial familism). Tokyo: Diamond Sha.

Hirai, Yōichi (2000), *Miike sōgi: Sengo rōdō undō no bunsuirei* (The Miike Dispute: A watershed in the postwar labor movement). Kyoto: Minerva Shobō.

Hiroi, Yoshinori (1999), *Nihon no shakai hoshō* (Social security in Japan). Tokyo: Iwanami Shinsho.

Hisamoto, Norio (1998), *Kigyō-nai rōshi kankei to jinzai keisei* (In-house labor-management relations and personnel development). Tokyo: Yūhikaku.

Hisamoto, Norio (2007), 'Rōdō-sha no "mibun" ni tsuite: Kō-hoku mibun kakusa teppai to kintō shogū' (On workers' 'status': Eliminating status disparities and treating workers equally), *Nihon rōdō kenkyū zasshi* (Japanese Journal of Labor Studies), 49(5; no. 562), pp. 56–64.

Hisamoto, Norio (2008), 'Nōryoku kaihatsu' (Skills development), in Michio Nitta and Norio Hisamoto (eds.), *Nihon-teki koyō shisutemu* (A Japanese-style employment system), Kyoto: Nakanishiya Shuppan, pp. 9–26.

Honda, Isamu (1978), *Kōgakureki-ka shakai no rōmu kanri* (Labor management in an increasingly educated society). Tokyo: Nihon Rōdō Kyōkai.

Honda, Yuki (2005), *Wakamono to shigoto: 'Gakkō keiyu no shūshoku' o koete* (Youth and work: Beyond finding employment through school). Tokyo: University of Tokyo Press.

Honda, Yuki (2009), *Kyōiku no shokugyō-teki igi: Wakamono, gakkō, shakai o tsunagu* (The vocational significance of education: Connecting youth, schools and society). Tokyo: Chikuma Shinsho.

Hyōdō, Tsutomu (1971), *Nihon ni okeru rōshi kankei no tenkai* (The evolution of labor-management relations in Japan). Tokyo: University of Tokyo Press.

Hyōdō, Tsutomu (1997), *Rōdō no sengo-shi* (A postwar history of labor), 2 vols. Tokyo: University of Tokyo Press.

Ichihara, Hiroshi (2012), 'Mitsubishi kōgyō no gijutsu-kei shokuin genba shokuin no hito-teki shigen keisei' (Technical and field staff development at Mitsubishi Mining), *Mitsubishi shiryō-kan ronshū* (Mitusbishi Archives Review), 13, pp. 85–110.

IERC (Chuo University Institute of Economic Research) (ed.) (1976), *Chūsyō Kigyō no Kaisō Kōzō: Hitachi Seisakujo Shitauke Kigyō Kōzō no Jittai Bunseki* (The stratified structure of small and medium enterprises: An analysis of the actual structure of Hitachi's subcontractors). Tokyo: Chūō University Press.

IERC (ed.) (1985), *ME Gijutsu Kakushinka no Shitauke Kigyō to Nōson Henbō* (Subcontracting system under the microelectronics technology innovation). Tokyo: Chūō University Press.

Bibliography

Iida, Hiroyuki (1992), 'Shinsei kōtō gakkō no rinen to jissai' (The philosophy and practice of the new high school system), in Atsushi Kadowaki and Hiroyuki Iida (eds.), *Kōtō gakkō no shakai-shi: Shinsei kōkō no 'yoki senu kiketsu'* (A social history of secondary schooling: The 'unexpected consequences' of Japan's new high school system). Tokyo: Tōshindō, pp. 3–70.

Ikeda, Seihin (1949), *Zaikai kaiko* (Memoirs of the Japanese business circle). Tokyo: Sekai no Nihonsha.

Ikeda, Seihin (1951), *Watakushi no jinseikan* (My views on life). Tokyo: Bungei shunjū shinsha.

Ikeda, Yoshimasa (1994), *Nihon ni okeru shakai fukushi no ayumi* (The development of social welfare in Japan). Kyoto: Hōritsu Bunka-sha.

Imazawa, Hijiri (1978), 'Konishiroku Shashin Kōgyō no kanrisha ninyō kōhosha kensyū seido' (The manager candidate training system at Knishiroku Shashin Kōgyō), in Koyō Shinkō Kyōkai (ed.), *Kōrei kōgakureki-ka jidai no nōryoku kaihatsu: Hōkō to jissai* (Capacity development in the age of aging and the popularization of higher education: Direction and practice). Tokyo: Nikkeiren Kōhōbu, pp. 95–115.

Inatsugu, Hiroaki (2005), *Kōmuin kyūyo josetsu: Kyūyo taikei no rekishi-teki hensen* (An introduction to civil service salaries: Historical changes in salary schemes). Tokyo: Yūhikaku.

Inoue, Yoshikazu (1930), *Daigaku senmon gakkō sotsugyō-sha shūshokumondai no kaiketsu* (Solving the problem of employment of university professional school graduates). Tokyo: Shinkensha.

Institute of Labor Administration (Rōmu Gyōsei Kenkyūjo) (ed.) (1963), 'Yahata seitetsu no shokumu-kyū o kanō ni shita mono: Gijutsu kakushin to gōri-ka suishin no han'ei' (Enabling job-based wages at Yahata Steel: A reflection of technological innovation and the promotion of rationalization), *Rōsei jihō* (Labor Administration Report), no. 1694, pp. 25–27.

Institute of Labor Administration (Rōmu Gyōsei Kenkyūjo) (ed.) (1986), 'Hon'ne zadan-kai sirizu 6: Shōshin shōkaku seido no mondaiten o tsuku' (Real talk series 6: Exploring the problems with the promotion and advancement system), *Rōsei jihō* (Labor Administration Report), no. 2809, pp. 43–53.

Institute of Social Science, the University of Tokyo (Tokyo daigaku shakai Kagaku kenkyūjo) (ed.) (1973), *Sengo kiki ni okeu rōdō sōgi: Yomiuri shimbun sōgi*, Tokyo daigaku shakai kagaku kenkyūjo siryō vol. 6. Tokyo: Institute of Social Science, the University of Tokyo.

Institute of Social Science, the University of Tokyo (ed.) (1979), *Densan 10-gatsu tōsō (1946-nen): Sengo shoki rōdō sōgi shiryō* (The Densan labor dispute, October 1946: Materials on labor disputes in the early postwar period), ISS Materials Collection, no. 9. Tokyo: ISS.

Inui, Akio (1990), *Nihon no kyōiku to kigyō shakai: Ichigen-teki nōryoku-shugi to gendai no kyōiku = shakai kōzō* (Education and corporate society in Japan: Unified meritocracy and contemporary education as social structure). Tokyo: Ōtsuki Shoten.

Irie, Torao (1963), 'Chingin kanri no Nippon-teki kiban' (A Japanese-style basis for wage management), *Keieisha* (Management Monthly), 17(9), pp. 25–27.

Irie, Toshio (1957), 'Atarashii shikaku seido no kangaekata' (The thinking behind the new ranking system), *Keieisha* (Business Leader Monthly), 11(10), pp. 1–3.

474 The System of Japanese Society

Ishida, Keigo and Hide Hamada (2006), 'Kyū Nihon-gun ni okeru jinji hyōka seido: Shōkō no kōka, kōka o chūshin ni' (Personnel evaluation systems in the former Japanese army: Focus on officer evaluations), *Bōei kenkyūjo kiyō* (NIDS Security Studies), 9(1), pp. 43–82.

Ishida, Mitsuo (1990), *Chingin no shakai kagaku: Nihon to Igirisu* (The social science of wages: Japan and the United Kingdom). Tokyo: Chūō Keizaisha.

Ishida, Mitsuo (1992), 'Jūjō seishi no shokumu-kyū no hensen (jō) (ge)' (Changes in Jūjō Paper's Job salaries, parts 1 and 2)', *Hyōron shakaikagaku* (Social Science Review), 44, pp. 37–98 and 45, pp. 43–89.

Ishida, Mitsuo (2014), 'Nihon no chingin kaikaku to rōshi kankei' (Wage reform and labor-management relations in Japan), *Hyōron shakaikagaku* (Social Science Review), 109, pp. 1–12.

Ishida, Mitsuo and Junpei Higuchi (2009), *Jinji seido no Nichi-Bei hikaku: Seika-shugi to Amerika no genjitsu* (A comparison of personnel systems in Japan and the U.S.: Performance-based systems and actual reality in the U.S.). Kyoto: Minerva Shobō.

Ishida, Mitsuo and Motohiro Terai (eds.) (2012), *Rōdō jikan no kettei: Jikan kanri no jittai bunseki* (The determination of working hours: An analysis of the actual situation of time management). Kyoto: Minerva Shobō.

Ishiguro, Itaru, Lee Young-Jun, Sugiura Hiroaki and Yamaguchi Keiko (2011), *'Tokyo' he deru wakamono tachi: shigoto, shakaikankei, chiikikan kakusa* (Young people leaving for 'Tokyo': Work, social relations, and regional disparities). Tokyo: Minerva Shobō.

Ishii, Shigeru (2016), *Hikanri seido no kenkyu: Senzenki nihon ni okeru koin, yōnin, taigukanri, syokutaku seido no seiritsu to hensen* (A study of non-officials: The establishment and change of the system of *koin, yonin, taigukanri, syokutaku* in pre-war Japan). Nagoya: V2 Solution.

Ishikawa, Masumi (1978), *Sengo seiji kōzō shi* (A history of the structure of postwar politics). Tokyo: Nihon Hyōronsha.

Ishikawa, Masumi (1995), *Sengo seiji shi* (A history of postwar politics). Tokyo: Iwanami Syoten.

Ishikawa, Tsuneo and Takahisa Dejima (1994), 'Rōdō shijō no ni-jū kōzō' (The dual structure of the labor market), in Tsuneo Ishikawa (ed.), *Nihon no shotoku to tomi no bunpai* (Income and wealth distribution in Japan). Tokyo: University of Tokyo Press, pp. 169–209.

Itō, Mitsuharu (1978), *Nihon no keizai fūdo* (Japan's economic climate). Tokyo: Nihon Hyōronsha.

Iwasaki, Sodō (1904), *Dai shōten kaisha ginkō chomei kōjō: Kaken tensoku yatoinin saiyō taigū-hō* (Large merchant stores, companies, banks, prominent factories: In-house rules on the hiring and treatment of employees). Tokyo: Daigakukan.

Iwase, Akira ([2006] 2017), *'Gekkyū 100-en sararīman' no jidai: Senzen Nihon no 'futsū' no seikatsu* (The era of the '100 yen-a-month salaryman': 'Regular' life in prewar Japan). Tokyo: Kōdansha. Reprinted in 2017 by Chikuma Bunko.

Japan Business History Institute (Nihon keiei-shi kenkyūjo) (ed.) (1976), *Kaiko-roku: Mitsui Bussan kabushikigaisha* (Memoirs: Mitsui & Co.). Tokyo: Mitsui Bussan.

Japan Employers' Federation Merit-Based Management Study Group (Nikkeiren Nōryoku-Shugi Kanri Kenkyūkai) ([1969] 2001), *Nōryoku-shugi kanri: Sono riron to jissen* (Merit-based management: Theory and practice). Tokyo: Nikkeiren Shuppanbu; New edition 2001.

Bibliography

Japan Employers' Federation Public Relations Department (Nikkeiren Kōhō-bu) (ed.) (1960), *Shikaku seido no kangaekata to jissai* (The rank system in theory and practice). Tokyo: Nikkeiren Kōhō-bu.

Japan Employers' Federation Research Project on the New Japanese-Style Management Systems (Nikkeiren Shin Nihon-teki Keiei Shisutemu-tō Kenkyū Purojekuto) (ed.) (1995), *Shin jidai no 'Nihon-teki keiei': Chōsen subeki hōkō to sono gutai-saku: Shin Nihon-teki keiei shisutemu-tō kenkyū purojekuto hōkoku* ('Japanese-style management' for a new era: Challenging directions and specific measures—Report of the research project on the new Japanese-style management systems). Tokyo: Nikkeiren.

Japan Employers' Federation Special Committee on Labor-Management Relations (Japan Employers' Federation Special International Committee [Nikkeiren Kokusai Tokubetsu Iinkai]) (2000), *Keiei no gurōbaru-ka ni taiō shita Nihon-gata jinji shisutemu no kakushin: Howaitokarā no jinji shisutemu o megutte* (Innovation of Japanese-style personnel systems in response to the globalization of management: On the white-collar personnel system). Tokyo: Nikkeiren.

Japan Employment Development Association (Koyō Shinkō Kyōkai) (1978), *Kōrei kōgakureki-ka jidai no nōryoku kaihatsu: Hōkō to jissai* (Capacity development in the age of aging and the popularization of higher education: Direction and practice). Tokyo: Nikkeiren Kōhōbu.

Japanese National Railways (Nihon Kokuyū Tetsudō) (1997), *Nihon kokuyū tetsudō hyakunen-shi* (A centennial history of Japanese National Railways). Tokyo: Seizandō Shoten.

JJILPT (Japan Institute for Labour Policy and Training) (ed.) (2011), *Sho gaikoku ni okeru nōryoku hyōka seido: Ei Futsu Doku Bei Chū Kan EU ni kan suru chōsa* (Competency assessment systems in other countries: A survey of the U.K., France, Germany, the U.S., China, South Korea and the EU). Tokyo: Japan Institute for Labour Policy and Training.

JILPT (Japan Institute for Labour Policy and Training) (2013), *'Tan Jikan Rōdōsha no Tayō na Jittai ni Kansureu Chōsa' Kekka: Muki Paat no Koyō Kanri no Genjō ha Dounatte Irunoka* (Results of the 'Survey on Various Actual Conditions of Part-Time Workers': What is the current status of employment management for part-time workers with permanent jobs?), JILPT Survey Series No. 105. URL: https://www.jil.go.jp/ institute/research/2012/documents/0105.pdf (Accessed on 4 November 2023).

JILPT (Japan Institute for Labour Policy and Training) (2023), *Deta bukku kokusairōdō hikaku 2023* (Databook of international labour statistics 2023). Tokyo: Japan Institute for Labour Policy and Training. URL: https://www.jil.go.jp/english/lsj/general/2011-2012.html (Accessed on 28 August 2023).

Jō, Shigeyuki (2004), *Uchigawa kara mita Fujitsū: 'Seika-shugi' no hōkai* (The collapse of performance-based management at Fujitsu: An insider's view). Tokyo: Kōbunsha.

Joint Committee of the Japan Employers' Federation Labor Management Committee and Merit-Based Management Study Group (Nikkeiren Rōmu Kanri Iinkai & Nōryoku-shugi Kanri Kenkyūkai Gōdō-kai) (1969 [2010]), 'Nōryoku-shugi kanri o megutte' (Merit-based management), reprinted in Yashiro et al. (eds.) (2010), *Nōryoku-shugi kanri kenkyūkai ōraru hisutorī: Nihon-teki jinji kanri no kiban keisei* (An oral history of the merit-based management study group: The formation of the foundations of Japanese style personnel management). Tokyo: Keio University Press, pp. 333–377.

Kadowaki, Atsushi and Hiroyuki Iida (eds.) (1992), *Kōtō gakkō no shakai-shi: Shinsei kōkō no 'yoki senu kiketsu'* (A social history of secondary schooling: The 'unexpected consequences' of Japan's new high school system). Tokyo: Tōshindō.

Kagiyama, Yoshimitsu (1989), *Shokunō shikaku seido* (Competence ranking systems). Tokyo: Hakutō Shobō.

Kai, Itosuke (1994), 'Kaikei jimu shokuin no benshō sekinin to fuhō kōi sekinin no kankei' (The relationship between tort liability and indemnity liability on the part of accounting clerks), *Kaikei kensa kenkyū* (Government Auditing Review), 9, pp. 77–88.

Kambayashi, Ryō (2017), *Seiki no sekai, hi-seiki no sekai: Gendai Nihon rōdō keizaigaku no kihon mondai* (The world of regular employment, the world of non-regular employment: Fundamental issues in contemporary Japanese labor economics). Tokyo: Keio University Press.

Kamijō, Toshiaki (1979), *'Fu' no nai keizai: Kōgakureki. Kōrei-ka., kō shotoku no otoshiana* (An economy without 'pawns': The pitfalls of high education, aging, and high income). Tokyo: Tōyō Keizai Shinpōsha.

Kamisaka, Fuyuko ([1959] 1981), *Shokuba no gunzō* (Scenes from the workplace). Tokyo: Chūō Kōronsha (Chūkō Bunko edition 1981).

Kamishima, Jirō (1962), *Kindai Nihon no seishin kōzō* (The spiritual structure of modern Japan). Tokyo: Iwanami Shoten.

Kanbayashi, Yōji (2015), *Hiseiki kōmuin no genzai: sinka suru kakusa* (The contemporary situation of non-regular civil servants: The growing disparity). Tokyo: Nihonhyōronsha.

Kanbayashi, Yōji (2021), 'Kaikei nendo ninyō syokuin hakusyo' (A white paper on public officials appointed for a single fiscal year), *Jichisōken*, 514, pp. 26–56.

Kaneko, Ryōji (2013), *Nihon no chingin o rekishi kara kangaeru* (Japanese wages in historical perspective). Tokyo: Junpōsha.

Kaneko, Ryōji and Yōji Tatsui (2017), 'Nenkō-kyū ka shokumu-kyū ka?' (Seniority-based pay or job-based pay?), *Rōdō jōhō* (Japanese Labor Information Journal), 956, pp. 22–29.

Kantō Employers' Association (Kantō Keieisha Kyōkai) (1954), 'Teiki shōkyū seido ni tai suru ichikōsatsu' (A consideration of the regular salary raise system), *Keieisha* (Business Leader Monthly), 8(9), pp. 72–80.

Kantō Employers' Association (Kantō Keieisha Kyōkai) (1976), 'Keieisha dantai ga shimeshita koyō chōsei ni kansuru kenkai' (Management group's view on 'employment adjustment'), *Rōdō keizai junpō* (Labor Economy Bulletin), no. 997, pp. 36–38.

Kariya, Takehiko (1991), *Gakkō shokugyō senbatsu no shakaigaku: Kōsotsu shūshoku no Nihon-teki mekanizumu* (The sociology of schools, jobs, and selection: The Japanese style mechanism of employing high school graduates). Tokyo: University of Tokyo Press.

Kariya, Takehiko (1993), 'Amerika daigaku shūshoku jijō (jō) (ge)' (The state of employment at American colleges and universities, parts 1 and 2), *UP*, 249, pp. 16–19 and 250, pp. 34–38.

Kase, Kazutoshi (1997), *Shūdan shūshoku no jidai: Kōdo seichō no ninaite-tachi* (The era of collective employment: The labor fueling Japan's high-speed growth). Tokyo: Aoki Shoten.

Bibliography

477

Katō, Ei'ichi (2007), *Fukushi kokka shisutemu* (The welfare state system). Kyoto: Minerva Shobō.

Katō, Hidetoshi (1957), 'Sengoha no Chūkanteki Seikaku' (The middle-class consciousness of the post-war generation), *Chūō Kōron*, 72(11), pp. 231–241.

Katō, Kan'ichirō ([1991] 1995), *Reisen no hijutsu* (Secret arts of the zero fighter). Tokyo: Kōdansha; Kōdansha Bunko edition, 1995.

Katsura, Takashi (1930), 'Kōgyō rōdōsha no teinen seido ni kan suru ichikōsatsu – jō' (A study of the retirement system for industrial workers [Part 1]), *Shakai seisaku jihō* (Social Policy Bulletin), no. 121, pp. 60–71.

Kawamura, Hidefumi (1974), 'Kokuho-hō seitei no omoide' (Recollections on the enactment of the National Health Insurance Act), in Ministry of Health and Welfare Health Insurance Bureau (Kōseishō Hokenkyoku) and Social Insurance Agency Medical Insurance Department (Shakai Hokenchō Iryō Hoken-bu) (eds.) (1974), *Iryō hoken han-seiki no kiroku* (A historical account of a half-century of health insurance administration). Tokyo: Shakai Hoken Hōki Kenkyūkai, pp. 238–244.

Kawanishi, Hirosuke (1992), *Kikigaki, densan no gunzō: Densan 10-gatsu tōsō, reddopāj, densan 52-nen sōgi* (Interviews with the Japan Electric Power Industry Labor Union: The October struggle, red purge, and the '52 dispute). Tokyo: Heigensha.

Kawanishi, Hirosuke (1999), *Densan-gata chingin no sekai: Sono keisei to rekishi-teki igi* (The world of the Japan Electric Power Industry Labor Union's wage system: Its formation and historical significance). Tokyo: Waseda University Press.

Kawate, Shō (2005), *Sengo Nihon no kōmuin seido-shi:'Kyaria' shisutemu no seiritsu to tenkai* (A history of postwar Japanese civil service: Establishment and development of the 'career' system). Tokyo: Iwanami Shoten.

Kawate, Shō (2015), 'Shōwa sen-zenki no kanri seido kaikaku kōsō: Kōbun kanryō yūgū no seido-teki kiban (2)' (An initiative to reform the public service in the pre-war Showa period: The institutional foundations of preferential treatment of higher bureaucrats, part 2), *Toshi mondai* (Municipal Problems), 106(7), pp. 95–117.

Keidanren (Japan Business Federation) (2018), '2018-nendo shinsotsu saiyō ni kan suru ankēto chōsa kekka' (Results of survey on new graduate recruitment in FY2018). URL: https://www.keidanren.or.jp/policy/2018/110.pdf (Accessed on 4 June 2019).

Keieishi hensyūshitsu (The management history editorial team) (ed.) (1965), *Nihon keieishi: sengo keiehis* (The history of Japanese business management: Postwar management history). Tokyo: Nihon seisanseihonbu.

Kinoshita, Takeo (1999), *Nihonjin no chingin* (The wages of Japanese people). Tokyo: Heibonsha.

Kinoshita, Takeo (2004a), 'Kigyō-shugi-teki tōgō to rōdō undo' (Enterprise integration and the labor movement), in Osamu Watanabe (ed.), *Kōdo seichō to kigyō shakai* (Rapid economic growth and corporate society). Tokyo: Yoshikawa Kōbunkan, pp. 127–156.

Kinoshita, Takeo (2004b). 'Nihon-gata koyō nenkō chingin no kaitai katei' (The dismantling of Japanese-style employment and seniority-based wages), in Michio Gotō (ed.), *Kiro ni tatsu Nihon* (Japan at a crossroads). Tokyo: Yoshikawa Kōbunkan, pp. 134–161.

Kita, Satakichi (1933), *Kanreki kinen 60-nen kaiko* (A sixty-year retrospective in commemoration of my 60th birthday). Privately printed.

Kiyosawa, Kiyoshi (1960), *Ankoku nikki* (Diary of darkness). Tokyo: Iwanami Shoten.

Kizaki, Hajime (1978), 'Nippon Kōkan no kanrishoku seido to nōryoku hyōka' (The management system and ability assessment at Nippon Kōkan), in Koyō Shinkō Kyōkai (ed.), *Kōrei kōgakureki-ka jidai no nōryoku kaihatsu: Hōkō to jissai* (Capacity development in the age of aging and the popularization of higher education: Direction and practice). Tokyo: Nikkeiren Kōhōbu, pp. 49–94.

Kobayashi, Hideo, Tetsuji Okazaki, Seiichirō Yonekura and NHK News (1995), 'Nihon kabushiki gaisha' no Shōwa-shi: Kanryō shihai no kōzō (The Showa-period history of 'Japan, Inc.': Structures of bureaucratic control). Tokyo: Sōgensha.

Kōda, Hirofumi (2002), 'Sengo wagakuni ni miru chingin taikei gōri-ka no shiteki tenkai (1)' (The historical development of wage system rationalization in postwar Japan, part 1), *Keiei ronshū* (Journal of Business Administration), no. 56, pp. 79–93.

Koike, Kazuo (1977), *Shokuba no rōdō kumiai to sanka: Rō-shi kankei no Nichi-Bei hikaku* (Trade unions and participation in the workplace: A comparison of labor-management relations in the U.S. and Japan). Tokyo: Tōyō Keizai.

Koike, Kazuo (1981), *Nihon no jukuren: Sugureta jinzaikeisei shisutemu* (Skills in Japan: A superior skill formation system). Tokyo: Yūhikaku.

Koike, Kazuo (1993), *Amerika no howaito karā: Nichi-Bei dochira ga yori 'jitsuryoku-shugi' ka* (White collar workers in the U.S.A.: Who is more 'meritocratic', Japan or the U.S.?). Tokyo: Tōyō Keizai.

Koike, Kazuo (2005), *Shigoto no keizaigaku* (The economics of work, 3rd edition). Tokyo: Tōyō Keizai.

Koike, Kazuo (2009), *Nihon sangyō shakai no 'shinwa': Keizai jigyaku shikan o tadasu* (The 'myths' of Japan's industrial society: Debunking economically self-defeating views of history). Tokyo: Nihon Keizai Shimbun Shuppansha.

Koike, Kazuo (2015), *Sengo rōdō-shi kara mita chingin: Kaigai Nihon kigyō ga ikinuku chingin to wa* (Wages in the context of postwar labor history: What wages can overseas Japanese companies abroad endure?). Tokyo: Tōyō Keizai.

Koike, Kazuo and Takenori Inoki (eds.) (2002), *Howaito karā no jinzai keisei: Nichi-Bei-Ei-Doku no hikaku* (White-collar personnel development: A comparison of Japan, the U.S., the U.K., and Germany). Tokyo: Tōyō Keizai.

Koike, Kazuo and Yukirō Watanabe (1979), *Gakureki shakai no kyozō* (The false image of a credentialist society). Tokyo: Tōyō Keizai.

Koike, Shirō (1929), *Hōkuū seikkatsusha-ron* (On salaried workers). Tokyo: Seiunkaku Syobō.

Komatsu, Ryūji (1971), *Kigyōbetsu kumiai no seisei* (The rise of enterprise unions). Tokyo: Ocyanomizu Syobō.

Koyama, Shinjirō (1980), 'Kokumin nenkin seido sōsetsu no butaiura' (Behind the scenes of the creation of the National Pension System), in Japan National Pension Association Public Relations Department (Nihon Kokumin Nenkin Kyōkai Kōhō-bu) (ed.), *Kokumin nenkin 20-nen hishi* (Twenty years of the National Pension System: A secret history). Tokyo: Nihon Kokumin Nenkin Kyōkai, pp. 15–55.

Kumazawa, Makoto ([1989] 1998), *Nihon-teki keiei no meian* (The bright and dark sides of Japanese-style management). Tokyo: Chikuma Shobō; Chikuma Bunko edition, 1998.

Bibliography

Kumazawa, Makoto (1993), *Hatarakimono-tachi naki egao: Gendai Nihon no rōdō kyōiku keizai shakai shisutemu* (The crying and laughing faces of working people: Labor, education, and the economic and social system in contemporary Japan). Tokyo: Yūhikaku.

Kurauchi, Shirō (1963), 'Gijutsu kakushin to ginō rōdō-ryoku no kyūgen: Chūsotsu kara kōsotsu e no ikō o meguru yōin mondai' (Technological innovation and the source of skilled labor: Personnel issues concerning the transition from middle school graduates to high school graduates), *Rōmu kenkyū* (Personnel Management Studies), 16(6), pp. 14–17.

Kurose, Naohiro (2018), *Fukuganteki chūsyō kigyō ron: chūsyō kigyō ha hattensei to mondaisei no tōitsu butsu* (Compound eye SMEs theory: SMEs are a unity of development and problems). Tokyo: Dōyūkan.

Kusuda, Kyū (2004), *Kusuda Kyū ōraru hisutorī—Chingin to wa nani ka: Sengo Nihon no jinji chingin seido-shi* (Kyū Kusuda's oral history—What is a wage? A history of personnel and wage systems in postwar Japan), edited with commentary by Mitsuo Ishida. Tokyo: Chūō Keizaisha.

Labor Capacity Development Center (Ningen Nōryoku Kaihatsu Sentā) (1977), *Kōgakureki-ka no shinkō to rōmu kanri* (Advancement of higher educational attainment and labor management), Nōryoku kaihatsu shirīzu (Series on capacity development), no. 40. Tokyo: Zen Nihon Nōritsu Renmei (All Japan Federation of Management Organizations).

Labor Law Association (Rōdō hōrei kyōkai) (ed.) (1965), *Saiyō kanri no jissai* (Recruitment management in practice). Tokyo: Rōdō hōrei kyōkai.

Labor Policy Bureau, Ministry of Welfare (*Kōseisyō Roōseikyoku*) (1947) *Chingin Chōsa Hōkoku: Kōseisyō Rinji Kinrōsha Kyūyo Chōsa* (Wege Survey Report: Special Workers' Salary Survey by Ministry of Welfare), Tokyo: *Chūō Rōdō Gakuen.*

LDP (Liberal Democratic Party) (1979), *Nihon-gata fukushi shakai* (Japanese-style welfare society). Tokyo: Liberal Democratic Party Public Relations Committee Publication Bureau.

Maeda, Kentarō (2014), *Shimin o yatowanai kokka: Nihon ga kōmuin no sukunai kuni e to itatta michi* (A state without civil servants: Japan's public sector in comparative perspective). Tokyo: University of Tokyo Press.

Makino, Nobuaki (1948), *Kaikoroku* (My retrospectives), 2 vols. Tokyo: Bunkeisyunju shinsha.

Makiuchi, Masashi (1960), 'Nippon keikinzoku ni okeru shikaku seido no jissai' (The facts of the ranking scheme at Nippon Light Metal), in Japan Employers' Federation Public Relations Department (Nikkeiren Kōhō-bu) (ed.) (1960), *Shikaku seido no kangaekata to jissai* (The rank system in theory and practice). Tokyo: Nikkeiren Kōhō-bu, pp. 134–160.

MEXT (Ministry of Education, Culture, Sports, Science and Technology) (2018), *Monbukagaku tōkei yōran (Heisei 30-nenban)* (Statistical digest of education, culture, sports, science and technology, 2018 edition). URL: https://www.mext. go.jp/b_menu/toukei/002/002b/1403130.htm (Accessed on 19 January 2023).

MHLW (Ministry of Health, Labour and Welfare) (2007), '"Paato rōdō-sha no kōsei nenkin tekiyō ni kansuru wākingu gurūpu" gaiyō' (Outline of the 'Working Group on the Application of Employees' Pension to Part-Time Workers'). URL: https://www.mhlw.go.jp/shingi/2007/03/dl/s0306-15b.pdf (Accessed on 19 January 2023).

MHLW (Ministry of Health, Labour and Welfare) (2012), *Kōsei rōdō hakusho* (White paper on health, labor and welfare). URL: https://www.mhlw.go.jp/wp/hakusyo/kousei/12/ (Accessed on 19 January 2023).

MHLW (Ministry of Health, Labour and Welfare) (2018), 'Heisei 30-nendo no nenkingaku kaitei ni tsuite' (On the revision to pension amounts for 2018), 26 January. URL: http://www.mhlw.go.jp/stf/houdou/0000191631.html (Accessed on 19 January 2023).

MHLW (Ministry of Health, Labour and Welfare) (2019a), *2019-nen kokumin seikatsu kiso chōsa no gaikyō* (Overview of the 2019 comprehensive survey of living conditions). URL: https://www.mhlw.go.jp/toukei/saikin/hw/k-tyosa/k-tyosa19/index.html (Accessed on 30 June 2022).

MHLW (Ministry of Health, Labour and Welfare) (2019b), *2019-nen rōdō kumiai kiso chōsa no gaikyō* (Overview of the 2019 basic survey of labor unions). URL: https://www.mhlw.go.jp/toukei/itiran/roudou/roushi/kiso/19/index.html (Accessed on 19 January 2023).

MHLW (Ministry of Health, Labour and Welfare) (2020a), 'Rōdō sōgi tōkei' (Labor dispute statistics). URL: https://www.jil.go.jp/kokunai/statistics/timeseries/html/g0702_01.html (Accessed on 22 June 2022).

MHLW (Ministry of Health, Labour and Welfare) (2020b), *Kōsei rodō hakusyo* (White paper on health and labour). URL: https://www.mhlw.go.jp/content/000735866.pdf (Accessed on 24 July 2023).

MHLW (Ministry of Health, Labour and Welfare) (2022a), *Kōsei rodō hakusyo* (White paper on health and labour). URL: https://www.mhlw.go.jp/wp/hakusyo/kousei/21/dl/1-01.pdf (Accessed on 24 July 2023).

MHLW (Ministry of Health, Labour and Welfare) (2022b), *Kōrei shakai hakusyo* (White paper on health and labour). URL: https://www.mhlw.go.jp/wp/hakusyo/kousei/21/dl/1-01.pdf (Accessed on 24 July 2023).

MHLW Pension Bureau (2017), 'Heisei 28-nendo kōsei nenkin hoken kokumin nenkin jigyō no gaikyō' (FY2016 Overview of Employees' Pension Insurance and National Pension Programs). URL: http://www.mhlw.go.jp/file/06-Seisakujouhou-12500000-Nenkinkyoku/H28.pdf (Accessed on 19 January 2023).

MIAC (Ministry of Internal Affairs and Communications) (2021), 'Ichi jūtaku atari nobe took menseki no todōfuken hikaku' (Prefectural comparison of total floorspace per house), from 'Heisei 29-nendo jūtaku keizai kanren dēta' (Housing and economic-related data for FY2017). URL: http://www.mlit.go.jp/statistics/details/t-jutaku-2_tk_000002.html (Accessed on 19 January 2023).

Minami, Ryōshin (2002), *Nihon no keizai hatten: Dai 3 han* (Japan's economic development, 3rd edition). Tokyo: Tōyō Keizai Shinpōsha.

Ministry of Education (Monbushō) (1961), *Shokuba no gakureki no ima to shōrai: Shokuba ni okeru gakureki kōsei no chōsa hōkoku-sho, daiichibu* (The current state of educational backgrounds in the workplace and future prospects: A survey report on the composition of educational backgrounds in the workplace, part I).

Ministry of Education (Monbushō) (1981), 'Shinsei daigaku no hossoku' (Inauguration of the new university system), in idem (ed.), *Gakusei hyakunenshi* (A centennial history of the Japanese school system). Tokyo: Teikoku Chihō Gyōsei Gakkai. URL: http://www.mext.go.jp/b_menu/hakusho/html/others/detail/1317752.htm (Accessed on 5 June 2019).

Bibliography 481

Ministry of Education (Monbushō) (1999), 'Sengo han seiki no kyōiku no hatten to sono kadai' (Education in the postwar half-century: Developments and challenges), in *Shotō chūtō kyōiku to kōtō kyōiku to no setsuzoku no kaizen ni tsuite (tōshin)* (Improving the link between elementary and secondary education and higher education [Report]). URL: https://www.mext.go.jp/b_menu/shingi/chuuou/toushin/991201b.htm (Accessed on 19 January 2023).

Ministry of Labor (1993), *Rodo Hakusho* (White paper on the labor economy). Tokyo: Ministry of Labor.

Minobe, Tatsukichi (1936), *Nihon gyōsei-hō* (Japan's administrative law), Vol. 1. Tokyo: Yūhikaku.

Mitsubishi Company History Publication Society (Mitsubishi Shashi Kankōkai) (ed.) (1979–1982), *Mitsubishi shashi* (Mitsubishi Company Journal). Tokyo: University of Tokyo Press.

Miura, Shumon (1968), 'Nihon daigaku yo amaeru nakare' (Do not falter, Nihon University!), *Chūō kōron* (Central Review), 83(8), pp. 287–294.

Miyachi, Katsunori (2015), 'Senzen-ki Nihon ni okeru teinen-sei saikō' (Rethinking retirement systems in prewar Japan: The theory and practice of Takashi Katsura), *Keizaigaku zasshi* (Journal of Economics), 115(3), pp. 283–304.

Miyamoto, Mataji (1938), *Kabu-nakama no kenkyū* (A study of Japanese occupational organizations). Tokyo: Yūhikaku.

Miyamoto, Tarō (1994), *Kaisō no Yomiuri sōgi: Aru jānarisuto no jinsei* (Reminiscences of the Yomiuri Dispute: A life in journalism). Tokyo: Shin Nihon Shuppansha.

Miyamoto, Tarō (2008), *Fukushi seiji: nihon no seikatsu hosyō to democrashi* (Politics of welfare: Social security and democracy in Japan). Tokyo: Yūhikaku.

Mizumachi, Yūichirō (2019), *Rōdō hō nyūmon sihnban* (Introduction to labor law, new edition). Tokyo: Iwanami syoten.

Mizutani, Mitsuhiro ([1999] 2013), *Kanryō no fūbō* (Bureaucrats' appearances). Tokyo: Chūōkōron-Shinsha; Chūkō Bunko edition, 2013.

MLIT (Ministry of Land, Infrastructure, Transport and Tourism) (2009), *Kokudo kōtsū hakusho* (White paper on land, infrastructure and transport), Chapter 1, Section 1, 'Chiiki ni sumau' (Dwelling in the community). URL: http://www.mlit.go.jp/hakusyo/mlit/h20/hakusho/h21/html/k1112000.html (Accessed on 19 January 2023).

MLIT (Ministry of Land, Infrastructure, Transport and Tourism) (2015), *Heisei 27-nen Kokudo kōtsū hakusho* (2015 white paper on land, infrastructure, and transport). URL: http://www.mlit.go.jp/hakusyo/mlit/h26/hakusho/h27/pdf/np102100.pdf (Accessed on 19 January 2023).

Mori, Tateshi (2005), 'Kan'ei Yahata Seitetsujo no rōmu kanri (1) (2)' (Labor management at the Yahata Steel Works from the 1890s to the 1930s, parts 1 and 2), *Keizaigaku ronshū* (The Journal of Economics), 71(1), pp. 2–47; 71(2), pp. 79–120.

Mori, Tateshi (2006), 'Kan'ei Yahata Seitetsujo no chingin kanri (1) (2)' (The payment of wages in Yahata Steel Works from the 1900s to 1930s, parts 1 and 2), *Keizaigaku ronshū* (The Journal of Economics), 71(4), pp. 2–47; 72(1), pp. 51–96.

Mori, Tateshi (2007), 'Chingin taikei no 2-sō kōzō' (A two-tiered wage structure), *Nihon rōdō kenkyū zasshi* (Japanese Journal of Labor Studies), 562, pp. 67–76.

Morimoto, Atsukichi (1921), 'Gendai keizai seikatsu no "nihon hyōojun"' (The 'Japanese standard' of modern economic life), *Chūōkōron*, 36(2), pp. 17–38.

Murakami, Yasusuke, Shunpei Kumon and Seizaburō Satō (1979), *Bunmei to shite no ie shakai* (The *ie* society as civilization). Tokyo: Chūō Kōronsha.

Muramatsu, Michio (ed.) (2018), *Kōmuin jinji kaikaku: Saishin Bei Ei Doku Futsu no dōkō o fumaete* (Civil service personnel reform: The latest trends in the U.S., U.K., Germany and France). Tokyo: Gakuyō Shobō.

Muramatsu, Takashi (1965), *Kyōiku no mori 1: Shingaku no arashi* (Forest of education 1: The storm of progress). Tokyo: Mainichi Shimbunsha.

Mynavi (2022), 'Tettei kaisetsu 2023-nendo-sotsu shūkatsu sukejūru to susumekata' (Job hunting schedule and strategies for the class of 2023: A thorough explanation), Mynavi Corporation. URL: https://job.mynavi.jp/conts/2023/susumekata/ (Accessed on 27 June 2022).

Nagashima, Osamu (2008), 'Sōritsu-ki kan'ei Yahata seitetsusho no keiei to soshiki: Shokuin-sō ni tsuite' (The management and organization of the Yahata Steel Works during its founding period: The workforce hierarchy), *Ritsumeikan keizaigaku* (Ritsumeikan Economic Review), 47(4), pp. 191–222.

Nagashima, Osamu (2009), 'Sōritsu-ki kan'ei Yahataseitetsusho ni okeru kakyū hojo-in ni kansuru ichi kōsatsu' (A study of junior staff at the Yahata Steel Works during the founding period), *Ritsumeikan Daigaku jinbun kagaku kenkyūjo kiyō* (Memoirs of the Institute of Humanities, Human and Social Sciences, Ritsumeikan University), 93, pp. 133–175.

Nakajima, Yasutsuna (1988), *Shokugyō antei gyōsei-shi: Edo jidai yori gendai made* (History of the Public Employment Security Administration: From the Edo period to the present). Tokyo: Koyō Mondai Kenkyūkai (Employment Issues Study Group).

Nakane, Chie (1967), *Tateshakai no ningen kankei: Tan'itsu shakai no riron* (Inter-personal relations in a vertical society: Theory of a unitary society). Tokyo: Kōdansha Gendai Shinsho.

Nakanishi, Yō (2003), *Nihon kindai-ka no kiso katei: Nagasaki Zzōsenjo to sono rōshi kankei, 1855–1900-nen* (The fundamental processes of Japanese modernization: The Nagasaki Shipyard and its labor relations, 1855–1900), vol. 1. Tokyo: University of Tokyo Press.

Nakayama, Ichirō (ed.) (1956), *Chingin kihon chōsa: Sono kōzō keitai oyobi taisei* (Basic wage survey: Structure, form and systems). Tokyo: Tōyō Keizai Shinpōsha.

Nakayama, Saburō (1960), 'Sōron' (Introduction), in Japan Employers' Federation Public Relations Department (Nikkeiren Kōhō-bu) (ed.), *Shikaku seido no kangaekata to jissai* (The rank system in theory and practice). Tokyo: Nikkeiren Kōhō-bu, pp. 3–18.

National Federation of Health Insurance Societies (kenko hoken kumiai rengokai) (2022), *Kenko hoken kumiai no gensei, reiwa 3 nen 3 gatsu sue genzai* (The annual report on the Health Insurance Associations, as of the end of March, 2021). Tokyo: National Federation of Health Insurance Societies. URL: https://www.kenporen.com/toukei_data/pdf/chosa_r03_03_03.pdf (Accessed on 19 January 2023).

National Personnel Authority (Jinji-in) (ed.) (1968), *Jinji gyōsei ni jū-nen no ayumi* (Twenty years of personnel administration). Tokyo: Ōkurashō Insatsu-Kyoku.

National Personnel Authority (Jinji-in) (ed.) (2007), *Heisei 19-nendo nenji hōkoku-sho* (Annual Report 2007). URL: https://www.jinji.go.jp/hakusho/h19/front.html (Accessed on 4 June 2019).

Bibliography 483

National Personnel Authority (Jinji-in) (ed.) (2008), *Heisei 20-nendo nenji hōkoku-sho* (Annual Report 2008). URL: https://www.jinji.go.jp/hakusho/h20/front.html (Accessed on 4 June 2019).

Navy Minister's Secretariat (Kaigun daijin kanbō) (ed.) (1939), *Kaigun seido enkaku* (Institutional history of the navy), vol. 4. Tokyo: Kaigun Daijin Kanbō.

NHK Broadcasting Culture Research Institute (NHK Hōsō Seron Chōsa-sho) (ed.) (1975), *Zusetsu sengo yoron-shi* (Illustrated history of postwar public opinion). Tokyo: Japan Broadcasting Publishing Association.

Nikkeiren (ed.) (1955), *Shokumu-kyū no kenkyū* (A study of job salaries). Tokyo: Nikkeiren Kōhōbu.

Nikkeiren Rōshi Kankei Tokubetsu Iinkai (Japan Employers' Federation Special Committee on Labor-Management Relations) (2002), *Taritsu-gata chingin taikei no kōchiku e: Seika-shugi jidai no chingin shisutemu no arikata* (Toward the construction of a multi-tier wage system: Wage systems in the performance-based era). Tokyo: Nikkeiren.

Nimura, Kazuo (1987), 'Nihon rōshi kankei no rekishi-teki tokushitsu' (Historical characteristics of Japanese labor-management relations), *Shakai seisaku gakkai nenpō* (Annals of the Society for the Study of Social Policy), 31, pp. 77–95.

Nimura, Kazuo (1994), 'Sengo shakai no kiten ni okeru rōdō kumiai undo' (The trade union movement at the outset of postwar society), in Junji Banno, Masato Miyachi, Naosuke Takamura, Hiroshi Yasuda and Osamu Watanabe (eds.), *Shirīzu Nihon kindai-shi dai-4-kan: Sengo kaikaku to gendai shakai no keisei* (Series on modern Japanese history, vol. 4: Postwar reforms and the making of contemporary society). Tokyo: Iwanami Shoten, pp. 37–78.

Nishikawa, Tadashi (1964), 'Burū karā no shōshin mondai' (Promotion issues for blue collar workers), *Rōmu kenkyū* (Personnel Management Studies), 17(2), pp. 12–17.

Nishimoto, Katsumi (2004), 'Kigyō shakai no seiritsu to kyōiku no kyōsō kōzō' (Establishment of the corporate society and the competitive structure of education), in Osamu Watanabe (ed.) *Kōdo seichō to kigyō shakai* (Rapid economic growth and corporate society). Tokyo: Yoshikawa Kōbunkan, pp. 157–189.

Nishimura, Itaru (2014a), 'Jobu-gata shain to omowa reru rōdō-sha no shinjō' (Emotions among workers who are considered job-type employees). Tokyo: Japan Institute for Labour Policy and Training (JILPT). URL: http://www.jil. go.jp/column/bn/colum0247.html (Accessed on 31 January 2019).

Nishinarita, Yutaka (1988), *Kindai Nihon rōshi kankeishi no kenkyū* (A study of labor-employer relations in modern Japan). Tokyo: University of Tokyo Press.

Nishinarita, Yutaka (1995a), 'Nihon-teki rōshi kankei no shiteki tenkai: 1870-nendai ~1990-nendai (jo)' (The historical development of Japanese labor-employer relations from the 1870s to the 1990s; Part 1), *Ikkyō ronsō* (The Hitotsubashi Review), 113(6), pp. 69–89 (739–759).

Nishinarita, Yutaka (1995b), 'Nihon-teki rōshi kankei no shiteki tenkai: 1870-nendai ~ 1990-nendai (ge)' (The historical development of Japanese labor-employer relations from the 1870s to the 1990s; Part 2), *Ikkyō ronsō* (The Hitotsubashi Review), 114(6), pp. 17–37 (975–995).

Nishinarita, Yutaka (2004), *Keiei to rōdō no Meiji ishin: Yokosuka seitetsusho zōsensho o chūshin ni* (The Meiji Restoration of management and labor: Focus on the Yokosuka Steel Works and Shipyard). Tokyo: Yoshikawa Kōbunkan.

Nishinarita, Yutaka (2009), *Taishokukin no 140 nen* (140 years of retirement allowance). Tokyo: Aoki syoten.

Nitta, Michio (2009), 'Koyō pōtoforio shisutemu kaikaku no shiten' (Perspectives on employment portfolio and system reform), *Gendai no riron* (Modern Theory Quarterly), 20, pp. 150–160.

Nitta, Michio (2011), 'Hiseikikoyō no ni-jū kōzō' (The dual structure of non-regular employment), *Shakai kagaku kenkyū* (Journal of Social Science), 62(3/4), pp. 3–23.

Nitta, Michio and Norio Hisamoto (eds.) (2008), *Nihon-teki koyō shisutemu* (A Japanese-style employment system). Kyoto: Nakanishiya Shuppan.

NLPB (National Land Planning Bureau) (2006), 'Hitori Atari Kenmin Syotoku no Jini Keisū, Jōi 5 Ken Heikin to Kai 5 Ken Heinki no Hi' (The proportion of gini-coefficients of income per capita of top 5 prefectures and bottom 5 prefectures), National Land Planning Bureau, Ministry of Land, Infrastructure, Transport and Tourism. URL: https://www.mlit.go.jp/kokudokeikaku/monitoring/system/contents/03/3-1-2.pdf (Accessed on 20 May 2020).

Noma, Seiji (1936), *Watakushi no hansei* (Half my life). Tokyo: Chikura Syobō.

Nomura, Kōichi (1995), 'Kanri shikaku no seido to kinō' (Civil service qualifications: Institutions and functions), in Yukio Mochida (ed.), *Kindai Doitsu: 'Shikaku shakai' no seido to kinō* (Modern Germany: Institutions and functions of the 'credentialist society'). Nagoya: Nagoya University Press, pp. 17–46.

Nomura, Masami (1994), *Shūshin koyō* (Lifetime employment). Tokyo: Iwanami Shoten.

Nomura, Masami (1998), *Koyō fuan* (Employment anxiety). Tokyo: Iwanami Shinsho.

Nomura, Masami (2003), *Nihon no rōdō kenkyū: Sono fu no isan* (Labor studies in Japan: Their negative legacies). Kyoto: Minerva Shobō.

Nomura, Masami (2007), *Nihon-teki koyō kankō: Zentai-zō kōchiku no kokoromi* (Japanese employment norms: An attempt to draw a complete picture). Kyoto: Minerva Shobō.

Nomura, Masami (2014), *Gakureki-shugi to rōdō shakai: Kōdo seichō to jieigyō no suitai ga motarashita mono* (Credentialism and labor society: The consequences of rapid growth and the decline of self-employment). Kyoto: Minerva Shobō.

Noro, Saori and Fumio Ohtake (2006), 'Nenrei-kan rōdō daitai-sei to gakureki-kan chingin kakusa' (Labor substitutability between ages and wage gaps due to educational backgrounds), *Nihon rōdō kenkyū zasshi* (The Japanese Journal of Labour Studies), 550, pp. 51–66.

Ōbori, Teruji (1960), 'Ishikawajima Jūkō ni okeru shikaku seido no jissai' (The facts of the qualification scheme at Ishikawajima Heavy Industries), in Japan Employers' Federation Public Relations Department (Nikkeiren Kōhō-bu) (ed.), *Shikaku seido no kangaekata to jissai* (The rank system in theory and practice). Tokyo: Nikkeiren Kōhō-bu, pp. 93–133.

Odaka, Kōnosuke (1984), *Rōdō shijō bunseki: Nijū kōzō no Nihon-teki tenkai* (Labor market analysis: The Japanese-style development of a dual structure). Tokyo: Iwanami Shoten.

Odaka, Kōnosuke (1993), '"Nihon-teki" rōshi kankei' ('Japanese-style' labor-management relations), in Tetsuji Okazaki and Masahiro Okuno (eds.), *Gendai Nihon keizai shisutemu no genryū* (The Japanese economic system and its historical origins). Tokyo: Nihon Keizai Shimbunsha, pp. 145–182.

Bibliography 485

OECD (Organization for Economic Co-operation and Development (Keizai Kyōryoku Kaihatsu Kikō) and Ministry of Labor (Rōdōshō) (eds.) (1972), *OECD tai-Nichi rōdō hōkoku-sho* (OECD labor report on Japan). Tokyo: Nihon Rōdō Kyōkai (Japan Institute of Labor). Japanese Edition of OECD Manpower and Social Affairs Directorate (1973).

Ogata, Takaaki (1981), 'Chūshō jigyōsho ni okeru hi seiki jūgyōin no jittai' (Actual situation of non-regular employees at small and medium-sized business establishments), *Rōdō kenkyū shohō* (Bulletin of the Tokyo Metropolitan Labor Research Institute), 2, pp. 45–51.

Ogawa, Yoshikazu (2002), 'Gakui kara mita Amerika kyōiku daigakuin: sono tokushitsu to mondaiten' (American graduate schools of education from the viewpoint of degrees: Characteristics and problems), *Nagoya kōtō kyōiku kenkyū* (Nagoya Journal of Higher Education), 2, pp. 161–184.

Ogihara, Masaru (1984), *Teinen-sei no rekishi* (A history of the retirement system). Tokyo: Nihon Rōdō Kyōkai (Japan Institute of Labor).

Ogoshi, Yōnosuke (1987), *Nihon saitei chingin-sei-shi kenkyū* (Studies in the history of Japan's minimum wage system). Matsudo, Chiba: Azusa Shuppan.

Oguma, Eiji (1998), *'Nihonjin' no kyōkai: Okinawa Ainu Taiwan Chōsen shokuminchi shihai kara fukki undō made* (Boundaries of the 'Japanese': Okinawa, the Ainu, Taiwan and Korea from colonial rule to the reversion movement). Tokyo: Shin'yōsha.

Oguma, Eiji (2002b), *'Minshu' to 'aikoku': Sengo Nihon no nashonarizumu to kōkyō-sei* ('Democracy' and 'patriotism': Postwar Japanese nationalism and the public sphere). Tokyo: Shin'yōsha.

Oguma, Eiji (2009), *1968 (ge): Hanran no shūen to sono isan* (1968, volume 2: The end of the revolt and its legacies). Tokyo: Shin'yōsha.

Okada, Akira (1994), *Gendai Nihon kanryō-sei no seiritsu: Sengo senryō-ki ni okeru gyōsei seido no sai-hensei* (The establishment of Japan's modern bureaucracy: Reorganization of the administrative system under the post-war occupation). Tokyo: Hosei University Press.

Okada, Mariko (2003), 'Kokka kōmuin no shokkai-sei: Seido dōnyū seitei keigai-ka katei no bunseki kara mieru jinji seido no tokuchō' (The job classification system for national public servants: Characteristics of the personnel system as seen from an analysis of the system's introduction, establishment and formalization), *Rikkyō keizai-gaku kenkyū* (Rikkyo Economic Review), 56(4), pp. 87–111.

Okazaki, Tetsuji (1991), 'Senji keikaku keizai to kigyō' (The planned economy and enterprise in wartime), in ISS (Institute of Social Science, the University of Tokyo) (ed.), *Gendai Nihon shakai 4: Rekishi-teki zentei* (Contemporary Japanese society, 4: Historical premises). Tokyo: University of Tokyo Press, pp. 363–398.

Oki, Sayaka (2018), *Bunkei to rikei wa naze wakareta no ka* (Why did the humanities and sciences diverge?). Tokyo: Seikaisha.

Ōkōchi, Kazuo (ed.) (1956), *Rōdō kumiai no seisei to soshiki: Sengo rōdō kumiai no jittai* (The formation and organization of labor unions: The realities of postwar labor unions). Tokyo: University of Tokyo Press.

Ōmori, Wataru (2006), *Kan no shisutemu* (Continuity and transformation in the Japanese bureaucracy: The 'Kan' system). Tokyo: University of Tokyo Press.

Onozuka, Tomiji (2001), *Kurafuto-teki kisei no kigen: 19 seiki Igirisu kikai sangyō* (The origins of craft regulations: The British machine industry in the nineteenth century).

Orii, Hyūga (1973), *Rōmu kanri ni jū-nen: Nihon Kōkan (kabu) ni miru sengo Nihon no rōmu kanri* (Twenty years of labor management: Postwar Japanese labor management at NKK Corporation). Tokyo: Tōyō Keizai.

Ōsawa, Machiko (1993), *Keizai henka to joshi rōdō: Nichi-Bei no hikaku kenkyū* (Economic change and women's employment: Comparison between Japan and the US). Tokyo: Nihon Keizai Hyōronsha.

Ōsumi, Kiyoharu (1993), 'Kan'the sōtōsei' (Official rank equivalent system), in *Nihon-shi daijiten 2* (Cyclopedia of Japanese history, vol. 2). Tokyo: Heibonsha, pp. 115–116.

Ōta, Takashi (1978), *Sengo Nihon kyōiku-shi* (A history of postwar Japanese education). Tokyo: Iwanami Shoten.

Ōtake, Fumio and Chiaki Moriguchi (2015), 'Nenshū 580 man-en ijō ga jōi 10-pāsento no kuni: Naze Nihon de kakusa o meguru giron ga moriagaru no ka' (A country where the top 10% have an annual income of at least 5.8 million yen: Why is the debate over inequality gaining momentum in Japan?), *Chūō kōron* (Central Review), 129(4; 1577), pp. 32–41.

Ōuchi, Hirokazu and Kōichirō Komikawa (2012), 'Kyaria kyōiku o toinaosu: Kyōiku no uchi to soto o ika ni tsunagu ka' (Rethinking career education: How to connect the inner and outer aspects of education), *Gendai shisō* (Contemporary Thought), 40(5), pp. 61–83.

Policy Research Department, Labor Minister's Secretariat (Rōdō Daijin Kanbō Seisaku Chōsa-bu) (ed.) (1991), *Tenkin to tanshin funin: Tenkin to kinrō-sha seikatsu ni kan suru chōsa kenkyūkai hōkokusho* (Relocation assignment and single-posting transfers: Report of the study group on transfers and workers' lives). Tokyo: Ministry of Finance.

Policy Research Department, Labor Minister's Secretariat (Rōdō Daijin Kanbō Seisaku Chōsa-bu) (ed.) (1992), 'Rōshi kankei sōgō chōsa rōdō kumiai kiso chōsa hōkoku' (Report on the comprehensive survey of labor-management relations and the basic survey of labor unions).

Research and Statistics Division, Minister's Secretariat, Ministry of Education (1978), 'Shinki gakusotsu-sha no saiyō oyobi shūgyō jōkyō-tō ni kan suru chōsa (sokuhō): Shitei-kō-sei o toru kigyō genshō' (Survey on the recruitment and employment status of new graduates [Preliminary report]: A decrease in the number of firms with designated school systems), *Monbu jihō* (The Monthly Journal of the Ministry of Education), 121(3), pp. 83–85.

Research Division, Research Bureau, Ministry of Education (Monbusyō chōsakyoku chōsaka) (ed.) (1957), 'Daigaku to syūshoku: shakaiteki yosei ni motozuku kyōiku keikaku ritsuan no tameno chōsa hōkokusyo' (Universities and employment: A research report for educational planning based on social demands). Tokyo: Ministry of Education.

Saitō, Jun (2010), *Jimintō chōki seiken no seiji keizaigaku: Rieki yūdō seiji no jiko mujun* (The political economy of the LDP regime: The self-contradiction of pork barrel politics). Tokyo: Keisō Shobō.

Saitō, Osamu (1984), 'Zairai orimonogō ni okeru kōjōsei kōgyōka no syoyōin: Senzenki nihon no keiken' (The factors of factory-type industrialization in traditional textile industries: The experience of pre-war Japan), *Shakai Keizai shigaku*, 49(6), pp. 114–131.

Bibliography 487

Sakakura, Shōhei (2021), *Otona no ijime* (Adult bullying). Tokyo: Kōdansha.

Sakurai, Minoru (1985), 'Henka ni chokumen suru kin'yūkikan no jinji rōmu kanri' (Human resource management at financial institutions facing change), *Sōgo ginkō* (Mutual Banking Monthly), 35(10), pp. 16–20.

Sasajima, Yoshio (2012), 'Nihon no chingin seido' (Japan's wage system), *Keizai kenkyū* (The Bulletin of Institute for Research in Business and Economics, Meiji Gakuin University), 145, pp. 31–54.

Sasaki, Takao (1982), 'Fukkatsu shi hajimeta? Rōdō shijō no nijūkōzō' (Is it beginning to revive? The labor market's dual structure), *Nihon Keizai Shimbun*, 21 August, morning edition.

Satō, Atsushi (2016), *Soshiki no naka de hito o sodateru: Kigyō-nai jinzai ikusei to kyariakeisei no hōhō* (Developing people in an organization: Strategies for developing personnel and shaping careers in a company). Tokyo: Yūhikaku.

Satō, Minoru (1970), 'Shin shain jinji seidoni yoru kyūyo shogū kanri' (Managing salary and worker treatment under the new company employee system), *Rōdō hōgaku kenkyū kaihō* (Bulletin of the Labor Law Study Group), 882, pp. 1–21.

Sawai, Minoru and Masayuki Tanimoto (2016), *Nihon keizai-shi: Kinsei kara gendai made* (The economic history of Japan: From the early modern era to the present). Tokyo: Yūhikaku.

Seikō Editorial Team (ed.) (1905), *Gendai shūshoku annai* (Contemporary guide to employment), *Seikō* (Success), 6(1), New Year's Special Issue booklet.

Seki, Mitsuhiro (2017), *Nihon no chūsyō kigyō: syōshi kōreika jidai no kigyō, keiei, keisyō kigyō* (Japan's SMEs: Entrepreneurship, management and succession in the era of low fertility and aging society). Tokyo: Chūō kōronsha.

Senmoto, Akiko (1989), 'Mitsui no chōki kinzoku syōreisaku no siteki kōsatsu' (A historical study of Mitsui's policy for encouraging long-term service), *Keiei Shigaku* (Management History), 23(4), pp. 1–23.

Senmoto, Akiko (1990), 'Nihon ni okeru seibetsu yakuwari bungyō no Keisei' (The emergence of gender roles in Japan), in Ogino Miho et al. (ed.), *Seido to shite no on'na: Sei, San, Kazoku no hikaku shakaishi* (Woman as an institution: A comparative social history of gender, birth and family). Tokyo: Heibonsha, pp. 187–228.

Shimizu, Katsuhiro (2010), 'Dentō-teki, keiken-shugi-teki totei-sei kara taikei-teki, hōhō-teki shokugyō kyōiku e: 1925-nen Furansu shokugyō kyōikukyoku "rōdō shūkan hōkoku" no kentō o chūshin ni' (From a traditional, empiricist apprenticeship system to systematic, methodical vocational education: A study of the French Ministry of Public Instruction and Fine Arts' 1925 'Compte rendu de la Semaine du Travail manuel'), *Ōhara Shakai Mondai Kenkyūjo zasshi* (Journal of the Ohara Institute for Social Research), 619, pp. 34–55.

Shimizu, Yuichirō (2007), *Seitō to kanryō no kindai: Nihon ni okeru rikken tōchi kōzō no sōkoku* (Political parties and the bureaucracy in the modern period: Conflicts in the structure of constitutional governance in Japan). Tokyo: Fujiwara Shoten.

Shimizu, Yuichirō (2009), 'Meiji Nihon no kanryō rikurūtomento: Sono seido, un'yō, jittai' (Recruiting national elites and building the administrative state: A mentality of modern Japan), *Hōgaku kenkyū: Hōritsu, seiji, shakai* (Journal of Legal Studies: Law, Politics and Society), 82(2), pp. 193–219.

Shimizu, Yuichirō (2013), *Kindai Nihon no kanryō: Ishin kanryō kara gakureki erīto e* (Bureaucracy in modern Japan: From restoration bureaucrats to an educational elite). Tokyo: Chūkōshinsho.

Shimoi, Yasushi (2017), *Kōmuin seido no hō riron: Nchihutsu hikaku kōmuin hō kenkyu* (The legal theory of the civil service system: A comparative study of civil service law in Japan and France). Tokyo: Kōbundō.

Shindō, Hyō (2004), '1990-Nendai no kokudo to chiiki no saihen' (Land and regional restructuring in the 1990s), in Michio Gotō (ed.), *Kiro ni tatsu Nihon* (Japan at a crossroads). Tokyo: Yoshikawa Kōbunkan, pp. 268–278.

Shindō, Muneyuki (1992), *Gyōsei shidō: Kanchō to gyōkai no aida* (Administrative guidance: Between agencies and industries). Tokyo: Iwanami Shoten.

Shinozaki, Nobuo (1967), 'Tsūkonken ni kan suru ichi kōsatsu' (A consideration of intermarriage zones), *Jinkō Mondai Kenkyūjo nenpō* (Annual Report of the Institute of Population Problems), 12, pp. 48–52.

Shinozaki, Nobuo (1974), 'Tsūkonken mondai to jinkō seisaku Shōwa 47-nen dai 6-ji shussan-ryoku chōsa hōkoku' (Intermarriage zone issues and population policy: Report of the 6th Fertility Survey of 1972), *Jinkō mondai kenkyū* (Journal of Population Problems), 130, pp. 46–52.

Shintani, Yuriko (2015), 'Kōmu sekutā ni okeru josei no shūgyō jōkyō to kosodate shien kankyō' (Employment status and environment to support childcare for females in the public sector), *Jinkō mondai kenkyū* (Journal of Population Problems), 71(4), pp. 326–350.

Shiomi, Toshiyuki (1994), 'Kigyō shakai to kyōiku' (The corporate society and education), in Junji Banno, Masato Miyachi, Naosuke Takamura, Hiroshi Yasuda and Osamu Watanabe (eds.), *Shirīzu Nihon kindai-shi dai-4-kan: Sengo kaikaku to gendai shakai nokeisei* (Series on modern Japanese history, vol. 4: Postwar reforms and the making of contemporary society). Tokyo: Iwanami Shoten, pp. 289–330.

Shiozawa, Miyoko (1980), *Hitamuki ni ikite: Aru sengo-shi* (A single-minded life: A history of the postwar). Osaka: Sōgensha.

Shōwa Comrades' Association (Shōwa Dōjinkai) (ed.) (1957), *Tōkei kara mita koyō to shitsugyō* (Statistics on employment and unemployment). Tokyo: Shōwa Dōjinkai.

Shōwa Comrades' Association (Shōwa Dōjinkai) (ed.) (1960), *Wagakuni chingin kōzō no shiteki kōsatsu* (A historical study of Japanese wage structure). Tokyo: Shiseidō.

SMEA (Small and Medium Enterprise Agency) (2016), *2016 SME White Paper (Chūshō kigyō hakusho)*. URL: https://www.chusho.meti.go.jp/pamflet/hakusyo/H28/PDF/h28_pdf_mokujityuu.html (Accessed on 25 June 2022).

SMEA (Small and Medium Enterprise Agency) (2017), *2017 White Paper on Small Enterprises in Japan (Shōkibo kigyō hakusho)*, https://www.chusho.meti.go.jp/pamflet/hakusyo/H29/PDF/2017shohaku_eng.pdf (Accessed on 30 July 2023).

SMEA (Small and Medium Enterprise Agency) (2020), *2020 Small Enterprises White Paper (Shōkibo kigyō hakusho)*. URL: https://www.chusho.meti.go.jp/pamflet/hakusyo/2020/shokibo/index.html (Accessed on 25 June 2023).

Staff Welfare Division, Staff Welfare Bureau, National Personnel Authority (Jinji-in Shokuin Fukushi-kyoku Shokuin Fukushi-ka) (2019), 'Heisei 30-nen minkan kigyō no kinmu jōken seido-tō chōsa kekka no gaiyō' (Summary of the results of the 2018 survey on the system of working conditions in the private sector), *Jinji-in geppō* (National Personnel Authority Monthly Newsletter), no. 842, pp. 30–35. URL: https://www.jinji.go.jp/geppou/geppou_pdf/geppou_20191001_kiji5.pdf. (Accessed on 4 November 2023).

Bibliography 489

Statistics Bureau, Ministry of Internal Affairs and Communications (Sōmushō tōkeikyoku) (2014), 'Tōkei kara mita wagakuni no kōrei-sha (65-sai ijō)' (Statistics on the aged in Japan [aged 65 and over]). URL: http://www.stat.go.jp/data/topics/topi843.html (Accessed on 30 January 2019).

Sugawara, Taku (2015), 'Fuantei-ka suru shakai ni taiō dekinai Nihon no senkyo' (Japan's elections fail to respond to an increasingly unstable society), *Chūō kōron* (Central Review), 129(4; 1577), pp. 78–91.

Sugayama, Shinji (2011), *'Shūsha' shakai no tanjō: Howaito karā kara burū karā e* (The birth of corporate society: From white collar to blue collar). Nagoya: Nagoya University Press.

Sugeno, Kazuo and Takashi Araki (eds.) (2017), *Kaiko rūru to funsō kaiketsu: 10-kakoku nokokusai hikaku* (Dismissal rules and dispute resolution systems: A comparative study of 10 countries). Tokyo: Japan Institute for Labour Policy and Training (JILPT).

Sugimoto, Yoshio and Ross E. Mouer (eds.) (1982), *Nihonjinron ni kan suru 12-shō: Tsūsetsu ni igi ari* (Twelve chapters on Nihonjinron: Objections to conventional theories). Tokyo: Gakuyō Shobō.

Sumiya, Mikio (1955), *Nihon chin-rōdō shiron: Meiji zenki ni okeru rōdōs hakai kyū nokeisei* (A treatise on the history of wage labor in Japan: Formation of the working class in the early Meiji era). Tokyo: University of Tokyo Press.

Sumiya, Mikio (1960), 'Nihon shihohnsyugi to rōdō shijō' (The labor market and Japanese capitalism), in Tōbata Sei'ichi (ed.), *Nōson kajō jinkōron* (On rural surplus population). Tokyo: Nihon hyōronsha, pp. 93–115.

Sumiya, Mikio (1976), *Nihon chin-rōdō no shiteki kōsatsu* (A historical study of wage labor in Japan). Tokyo: Ochanomizu Shobō.

Sumiya, Mikio (1980), 'Teinen-sei no keisei to shūshin koyō' (Formation of the retirement system and lifetime employment), *Nenpō: Nihon no rōshi kankei* (Yearbook of Japanese Labor Relations), 1980 edition, pp. 3–28.

Suzuki, Takane (2023), *'Sararīman' no bunkashi: aruiha 'kazoku' to 'antei' no kingendaishi* (A cultural history of 'salaryman': Or a modern history of 'family' and 'security'). Tokyo: Seikyūsha.

Tachibanaki, Toshiaki (2015), *Nihonjin tokeizai: Rōdō seikatsu no shiten kara* (The Japanese people and the economy: Perspectives on labor and daily life). Tokyo: Tōyō Keizai.

Tachibanaki, Toshiaki and Tadashi Yagi (2009), *Kyōiku to kakusa: Naze hito wa burando-kō o mezasu no ka* (Education and inequality: Why do people go to prestigious schools?). Tokyo: Nihon Hyōronsha.

Takabatake, Michitoshi (1969), '"Hatten-koku-gata" gakuseiundō no ronri' (The logic of the 'developing country-type' student movement), *Sekai* (World), 278, pp. 244–250.

Takahashi, Masaki (2001), '"Shakai-teki hyōshō to shite no sararīman" no tōjō: Senzen hōkyūseikatsusha nokumiai undō o dō miru ka' (The emergence of 'salaryman as social representation': Finding a perspective on union movements among salaried workers in the pre-war period), *Ōhara Shakai Mondai Kenkyūjo zasshi* (Journal of the Ohara Institute for Social Research), 511, pp. 16–30.

Takahashi, Takeo (1982), 'Nipponkeizai shin nijū kōzō-ron: Senzai seichō-ryoku o jūshi shi, naiju kakudai' (A new dual structure paradigm for the Japanese economy: Emphasis on growth potential and the expansion of domestic demand), *Ekonomisuto* (Weekly Economist), 60(20), pp. 10–16.

Takano, Tsuyoshi (2018), *Kanai rōdō to zaitaku work no sengo nihon Keizai: jusan naisyoku kara zaitaku syūgyō sien e* (A history of work at home in the postwar Japanese economy: From the encouragement of cottage industry to support for remote work). Tokyo: Minerva Syobō.

Takaragi, Fumihiko (2003), *Shōgen: Sengo rōdōundō-shi* (Testimony: History of the postwar labor movement). Hatano: Tōkai University Press.

Takata, Ryōji (1989), *Gendai chūshō kigyō no kōzō bunseki: Koyō hendō to arata na nijū kōzō* (A structural analysis of modern SMEs: Shifting employment and the new dual structure). Tokyo: Shinhyōron.

Takeda, Kiyoko (1953), 'Kōjō ni mita uso to kaigara-teki ningenzō' (Lies and the shell-like images of men in factories), *Me* (Sprout, formerly *Shisō no kagaku*), August, pp. 38–42.

Takegawa, Shōgo (2007), *Rentai to shōnin: Gurōbaru-ka to kojin-ka no naka no fukushi kokka* (Solidarity and recognition: The welfare state in the context of globalization and individualization). Tokyo: University of Tokyo Press.

Takeuchi, Yō (1995), *Nihon no meritokurashī: Kōzō to shinsei* (Meritocracy in Japan: Structure and mentality). Tokyo: University of Tokyo Press.

Takeuchi, Yō (1999), *Gakureki kizoku no eikō to zasetsu* (The glories and frustrations of Japan's academic aristocracy). Tokyo: Chūōkōron-Shinsha.

Tamano, Kazushi (2005), *Tōkyō no rōkaru komyuniti: Aru machi no monogatari 1900–80* (Tokyo's local communities: The story of a town 1900–1980). Tokyo: University of Tokyo Press.

Tanaka, Hirohide (1980), *Gendai Koyōron* (Contemporary employment theory). Tokyo: Nihon Rōdō Kyōkai (Japan Institute of Labor).

Tanaka, Hirohide (1983), *Nihongata koyō kankō wo kizuita hitotachi sono 3, moto jūjō Seishi huku shachō Tanaka Shin'ichirō shi ni kiku* (The people who established Japanese-style employment No. 3: The former vice-president of Jūjō Seishi, Mr. Tanaka Shin'ichirō). *Nihon Rōdō Kyōkai Zasshi*, 289, pp. 37–45.

Tanaka, Shin'ichirō (1984), *Senzen rōmu kanri no jittai: Seido to rinen* (The realities of prewar labor management: Systems and principles). Tokyo: Nihon Rōdō Kyōkai (Japan Institute of Labor).

Tanaka, Yōko (2001), *Doitsu kigyō shakai nokeisei to hen'yō: Kuruppu-sha ni okeru rōdō seikatsu tōchi* (The formation and transformation of German corporate society: Work, life and governance at Krupp). Kyoto: Minerva Shobō.

Tanaka, Yōko (2003), 'Dai kigyō ni okeru shikaku seido to sono kinō' (Qualification systems and their functions in large companies), in Yukio Mochida (ed.) (2003), *Kindai Doitsu: Shikaku shakai no tenkai* (Modern Germany: Development of the credentialist society), Nagoya: Nagoya University Press, pp. 17–47.

Tōbata, Sei'ichi (1956), 'Nōgyō jinkō no kyō to asu' (The today and tomorrow of the agricultural population), in Arisawa Hiromi, Uno Kōzō and Sakisaka Itsurō (eds.), *Sekai Keizai to Nihon Keizai* (Japanese economy and the world economy). Tokyo: Iwanami Syoten, pp. 211–236.

Tokyo Institute of Technology (Tōkyō kōgyō daigaku) (ed.) (1940), *Tōkyō kōgyō daigaku 60-nen-shi* (Sixty years of history at the Tokyo Institute of Technology). Tokyo: Tokyo Institute of Technology.

Tsuchida, Takeshi (1997), *Doitsu iryō hōken seido no seiritsu* (Establishment of the German health insurance system). Tokyo: Keisō Shobō.

Tsuchida, Takeshi (2011), 'Sengo no Nichi-Doku iryō hoken seisaku no hikaku' (A comparison of postwar Japanese and German health insurance policies), *Seikatsu fukushi kenkyū* (Life and Welfare Studies), 79, pp. 52–76.

Bibliography

Tsuji, Katsuji (2011), 'Sengo Toyota ni okeru jinji idō no teiki-ka katei' (The postwar regularization of personnel changes at Toyota), *Ritsumeikan sangyō shakai ronshū* (Ritsumeikan Review of Industrial Society), 47(3), pp. 59–81.

Uchiyama, Mitsuo (1980), 'Shokuba tōsō to rōdō kumiai no shutai kyōka: Shokuba o rōdō-sha no te ni torimodosu tame ni' (Workplace struggles and strengthening trade union entity: Putting the workplace back in workers' hands), *Gekkan rōdō mondai* (Labor Issues Monthly), no. 279 (October), pp. 86–91.

Ueda, Hirofumi (2004), *Gendai Nihon no chūshōkigō* (Modern Japanese SMEs). Tokyo: Iwanami Shoten.

Ueyama, Yasutoshi (1964), *Doitsu kanryō-sei seiritsu-ron* (A theory on the formation of the German bureaucracy). Tokyo: Yūhikaku.

Ujihara, Shōjirō ([1953] 1966), 'Dai kōjō rōdō-sha no seikaku' (The temperament of workers in large factories), in Nihon Jinbun Kagakukai (Japan Association for Humanities) (ed.), *Shakai-teki kinchō no kenkyū* (Studies in social tension). Tokyo: Yūhikaku. Reprinted in Ujihara (1966), *Nihon rōdō mondai kenkyū* (Contributions to the study of Japanese labor issues). Tokyo: University of Tokyo Press, pp. 351–401.

Ujihara, Shōjirō ([1954a] 1966), 'Nihon nōson to rōdō shijō' (Rural Japan and the labor market), in Seizō Ōtani (ed.), *Nōson mondai kōza, dai-3-kan: Nōson shakai no kōzō* (Lectures on agrarian problems, vol. 3: The structure of rural villages). Tokyo: Kawade Shobō. Reprinted in Ujihara (1966), *Nihon rōdō mondai kenkyū* (Contributions to the study of Japanese labor issues). Tokyo: University of Tokyo Press, pp. 426–456.

Ujihara, Shōjirō ([1954b] 1966), 'Rōdō shijō no mokei' (A model of the labor market), in Kanagawa-ken Chiji Kikaku Shingika (Kanagawa Prefectural Governor's Office, Planning and Review Section) (ed.), *Keihin kōgyō chitai chōsa hōkoku-sho: Sangyō rōdō-hen kakuron* (Report of a survey of the Keihin Industrial Zone: Papers on industrial labor). Kanagawa ken. Reprinted in Ujihara (1966), *Nihon rōdō mondai kenkyū* (Contributions to the study of Japanese labor issues). Tokyo: University of Tokyo Press, pp. 402–425.

Ujihara, Shōjirō ([1959] 1968), 'Sengo rōdō shijō no henbō' (Transformation of the postwar labor market), *Nihon rōdō kyōkai zasshi* (Monthly Journal of the Japan Institute of Labour), May issue. Reprinted in Ujihara (1968), *Nihon no rōshi kankei* (The relationship between labor and management in Japan). Tokyo: University of Tokyo Press, pp. 61–99.

Ujihara, Shōjirō (1966), *Nihon rōdō mondai kenkyū* (Contributions to the study of Japanese labor issues). Tokyo: University of Tokyo Press.

Ujihara, Shōjirō (1968), *Nihon no rōshi kankei* (The relationship between labor and management in Japan). Tokyo: University of Tokyo Press.

Ujihara, Shōjirō and Akira Takanashi (1971), *Nihon rōdō shijō bunseki* (The analysis of Japan's labor market), 2 vols. Tokyo: University of Tokyo Press.

Umemura, Mataji (1957), 'Rōdō-ryoku no kōzō to hendō' (Labor force structure and change), *Keizai kenkyū* (The Economic Review), 8(3), pp. 227–233. Reprinted in Mataji Umemura (1971), *Rōdō-ryoku no kōzō to koyō mondai* (Labor force structure and employment issues). Tokyo: Iwanami Shoten, pp. 3–21.

Usami, Takuzō (1960), 'Nihon semento ni okeru shikaku seido no jissai' (The facts of the ranking scheme at Nippon Cement), in Japan Employers' Federation Public Relations Department (Nikkeiren Kōhō-bu) (ed.) (1960), *Shikaku seido no kangaekata to jissai* (The rank system in theory and practice). Tokyo: Nikkeiren Kōhō-bu, pp. 62–92.

Ushiyama, Keiji (1975), *Nōmin sō bunkai no kōzō: senzenki* (The structure of differentiation of peasantry: Prewar era). Tokyo: Otyanomizu shobō.

Wage Committee of Manager's Association in the Kanto Area (Kantō Keieisha Kyōkai Chingin Iinkai) (ed.) (1962), *Chingin kanri kindai-ka no kihon hōkō: Nenkō chingin kara shokumu-kyū e* (The basic direction of wage management modernization: From seniority-based wages to job-based wages). Tokyo: Nikkeiren Kōhōbu.

Wakabayashi, Yukio (2007), *Mitsui Bussan jinji seisaku-shi 1876~1931-nen: Jōhō kōtsū kyōiku infura to shokuin soshiki* (A history of personnel policies at Mitsui & Co., 1876–1931: Information transport, education infrastructure and employee organization). Kyoto: Minerva Shobō.

Wakabayashi, Yukio (2014), '1920~30-Nendai Mitsui Bussan ni okeru shokuin-sō no chikuseki to kyaria pasu dezain ni kan suru ichi kōsatsu: Shoninkyū-gaku no kettei yōin o chūshin ni shite' (A study of the accumulation of staff hierarchies and career path design at Mitsui & Co in the 1920s and 1930s: Focusing on the factors determining starting salaries), *Meiji Daigaku Shakai Kagaku Kenkyūjo kiyō* (Memoirs of the Institute of Social Sciences, Meiji University), 53(1), pp. 119–138.

Wakabayashi, Yukio (ed.) (2018), *Gakureki to kakusa no keieishi: Atarashī rekishi-zō o motomete* (A business history from the perspective of differences in educational backgrounds: In search of a new historical view). Tokyo: Nihon Keizai Hyōronsha.

Wakisaka, Akira (2004), 'Shinki gakusotsusha no rōdō shijō: Hyōgo ken no chōsa kara mita rōdō idō' (The labor market for new graduates: Survey on labor migration in Hyogo prefecture), in Kingo Tamai and Norio Hisamoto (eds.), *Kōdo seichō no naka no shakai seisaku: Nihon ni okeru rōdō kazoku shisutemu no tanjō* (Social policy in the midst of rapid growth: The birth of the working family system in Japan). Kyoto: Minerva Shobō, pp. 63–86.

Watanabe, Hiroto (2016), 'Kyōiku-hi futan no kon'nan to fainansharu puran'nā: Fainansharu puran o tsūjita shakai hoshō yōkyū no fūjikome' (Difficulties in paying for education and financial planners: Moderating social security demands through financial planning), *Posse*, 32, pp. 98–111.

Watanabe, Osamu (2004), 'Kōdo seichō to kigyō shakai' (Rapid economic growth and corporate society), in Osamu Watanabe (ed.) (2004), *Kōdo seichō to kigyō shakai* (Rapid economic growth and corporate society). Tokyo: Yoshikawa Kōbunkan, pp. 7–126.

Watanabe, Yukio, Masahiro Ogawa, Naohiro Kurose and Masao Mukoyama (2022), *21-seiki chūshōkigō-ron: Tayō-sei to kanōsei o saguru* (Small and medium-sized enterprises in the twenty-first century: Exploring diversity and possibilities), 4th edition. Tokyo: Yūhikaku.

Women and Youth Bureau, Ministry of Labor (Rōdōshō fujin shōnen-kyoku) (ed.) (1951), *Danjo dōitsu rōdō dōitsu chingin ni tsuite* (Equal pay for equal work for men and women alike). Tokyo: Rōdōshō fujin shōnen-kyoku.

Women and Youth Bureau, Ministry of Labor (Rōdōshō Fujin Shōnen-kyoku) (ed.) (1966), *Nobiyuku chikara: Hataraku seishōnen no seikatkiroku, Syowa 41 nen ban* (Growing power: Essays on the lives of working youths, 1966 version). Tokyo: Shibun syoin.

Women and Youth Bureau, Ministry of Labor (Rōdōshō Fujin Shōnen-kyoku) (ed.) (1969), *Nobiyuku chikara: Hataraku seishōnen no seikatkiroku, Syowa 44 nen ban* (Growing power: Essays on the lives of working youths, 1969 version). Tokyo: Rōmu gyōsei kenkyujo.

Bibliography

Woo, Jong-won (2003), *'Mibun no torihiki' to Nihon no koyō kankō: Kokutetsu no jirei kenkyū* ('Status transactions' and Japanese employment norms: A case study of Japanese National Railways). Tokyo: Nihon Keizai Hyōronsha.

Woo, Jong-won (2009), 'Nihon no rōdō-sha ni totte no kaisha: "Mibun" to "hoshō" o chūshin ni' (The significance of the *kaisha* [corporation] for Japanese workers: Considered from the perspective of their status and welfare), *Rekishi to keizai* (The Journal of Political Economy and Economic History), 51(3), pp. 3–13. Reprinted in Enoki and Onozuka (eds.) (2014), *Rōmu kanri no seisei to shūen* (The genesis and demise of labor management). Tokyo: Nihon Keizai Hyōronsha, pp. 317–340.

Woo, Jong-won (2016), 'Sengo ni okeru shikaku-kyū no keisei' (The postwar formation of qualification-based wage scales), *Ōhara Shakai Mondai Kenkyūjo zasshi* (Journal of the Ohara Institute for Social Research), 688, pp. 5–28.

Yamada, Moritarō (1934), *Nihon Shihon-shugi bunseki* (An analysis of Japanese capitalism). Tokyo: Iwanami Shoten.

Yamafuji, Ryūtarō (2018), 'Mitsuibussan no jinzai saiyō shisutemu to gakkō kyōiku shisutemu no hensen' (Changes in Mitsui & Co.'s recruitment and school-based education systems), in Yukio Wakabayashi (ed.), *Gakureki to kakusa no keieishi: Atarashī rekishi-zō o motomete* (A business history from the perspective of differences in educational backgrounds: In search of a new historical view). Tokyo: Nihon Keizai Hyōronsha, pp. 161–195.

Yamamoto, Keimei and Hirohide Tanaka (1982), 'Nihon-teki koyō kankō o kizuita hitotachi - 2 - moto Toyota jidōsha kōgyō senmu torishimariyaku Yamamoto Keimei-shi ni kiku (2)' (People who established Japanese-style employment norms, part 2: Interview with Mr. Keimei Yamamoto, former senior managing director of Toyota Motor Corporation [2]), *Nihon rōdō kyōkai zasshi* (Monthly Journal of the Japan Institute of Labour), 24(8), pp. 64–81.

Yamamoto, Masayoshi (1974), 'Kokuho zaisei saiken jidai no kaiko' (Looking back on the National Health Insurance reform era), in Ministry of Health and Welfare Health Insurance Bureau (Kōseishō Hokenkyoku) and Social Insurance Agency Medical Insurance Department (Shakai Hokenchō Iryō Hoken-bu) (eds.) (1974), *Iryō hoken han-seiki no kiroku* (A historical account of a half-century of health insurance administration). Tokyo: Shakai Hoken Hōki Kenkyūkai, pp. 269–272.

Yamazaki, Kiyoshi (1988), *Nihon no taishokukin seido* (Japan's retirement benefits system). Tokyo: Nihon Rōdō Kyōkai (Japan Institute of Labor).

Yano, Shigenori (1982), *Shōshaman konjaku jijō* (Trading company man, past and present). Tokyo: Tōyō Keizai Shinpōsha.

Yashiro, Atsushi, Osamu Umezaki, Tomoki Shimanishi, Chiaki Nagumo and Toshiaki Ushijima (eds.) (2015), *Shin jidai no 'Nihon-teki keiei' ōraru hisutorī: Koyō tayō-ka-ron no kigen* (An oral history of 'Japanese-style management' in the new era: Origins of the theory of employment diversification). Tokyo: Keio University Press.

Yashiro, Atsushi, Osamu Umezaki, Tomoki Shimanishi, Chiaki Nagumo and Toshiaki Ushijima (eds.) (2010), *Nōryoku-shugi kanri kenkyūkai ōraru hisutorī: Nihon-teki jinji kanri no kiban keisei* (An oral history of the merit-based management study group: The formation of the foundations of Japanese-style personnel management). Tokyo: Keio University Press.

Yashiro, Naohiro (1980), *Gendai Nihon no byōri kaimei: Kyōiku sabetsu fukushi iryō no keizaigaku* (Understanding the pathology of contemporary Japan: The economics of education, welfare and medical care). Tokyo: Tōyō Keizai.

Yashiro, Naohiro (1997), *Nihon-teki koyō kankō no keizaigaku: Rōdō shijō no ryūdō-ka to Nihon keizai* (The economics of Japan's employment norms: A mobilized labor market and the Japanese economy). Tokyo: Nihon Keizai Shimbunsha.

Yonekura, Seiichirō (1995), 'Nihon-gata shisutemu to kōdo keizai seichō' (The Japanese-style system and rapid economic growth), in Hideo Kobayashi, Tetsuji Okazaki, Seiichirō Yonekura and NHK News (1995), *'Nihon kabushiki gaisha' no Shōwa-shi: Kanryō shihai no kōzō* (The Showa-period history of 'Japan, Inc'.: Structures of bureaucratic control). Tokyo: Sōgensha, pp. 199–219.

Yoshida, Kōji and Hiroyuki Okamuro (2016), 'Senzen-ki howaito karā no shōshin senbatsu katei: Mitsubishi zōsen no shokuin dēta ni motodzuku jisshō bunseki' (The promotion and selection of white-collar workers in the prewar period: An empirical analysis using employee micro data from Mitsubishi Shipbuilding), *Keiei shigaku* (Japan Business History Review), 50(4), pp. 3–26.

Yoshida, Makoto (2007), *Satei kisei to rōshi kankei no hen'yō: Zenji no chingin gensoku to Nissan bunkai no tatakai* (Changes in assessment regulations and labor-management relations: The Automobile Workers' Union wage principle and the Nissan branch's struggle). Okayama: Daigaku Kyōiku Shuppan.

Yoshikawa, Hiroshi (2013), *Defuresyon: 'nihon no manseibyō' no zenbō wo kaimei suru* (Deflation: A whole picture and its analysis of 'Japan's chronical disease'). Tokyo: Nikkei BP.

Yoshino, Kōsaku (1997), *Bunka nashonarizumu no shakaigaku: Gendai Nihon no aidentiti no yukue* (The sociology of cultural nationalism: Situating contemporary Japanese identity). Nagoya: Nagoya University Press.

Index

Personal Names

Abe, Aya, 53–54, 416
Abegglen, James, 73, 122–127, 130, 169, 197, 268, 289, 291–292, 299, 301, 303, 306, 312–313, 341, 391, 407, 425–426, 445–447
Arisawa, Hiromi, 280, 414, 444

Berger, Peter, 14, 410
Bourdieu, Pierre, 14–15, 115, 410
Brinton, Mary, 376, 407, 413, 452, 454

Calder, Kent, 64, 66, 418

Doeringer, Peter, 70, 72, 386, 418–419, 443, 455
Dore, Ronald, 110–112, 117–118, 147–148, 166, 195, 278, 329, 334, 389–392, 407, 412, 422, 424, 428–429, 431, 444, 449–450, 456
Drucker, Peter, 341

Ebihara, Tsuguo, 35, 98, 414, 419, 421–422
Endō, Kōshi, 188, 236, 241, 296, 433, 439–440, 444
Enomoto, Takeaki, 160
Esping-Andersen, Gøsta, 15, 38, 47, 385, 393, 410, 414–415, 455–456

Foucault, Michel, 17, 410
Fukui, Yasutaka, 199, 203, 205, 208, 430, 435–436

Gallie, Duncan, 396, 411, 456
Gibbs, Jack P., 14, 410
Godō, Takuo, 236
Gordon, Andrew, 6–7, 116, 229, 237, 407, 411, 424, 430, 436–440, 449–450, 453, 457
Guillain, Robert, 341

Hamaguchi, Kei'ichirō, 92, 380, 420, 422, 426, 428, 437, 441, 449, 454
Hashimoto, Kenji, 350, 410, 440, 447, 451–452
Hazama, Hiroshi, 162, 407, 430
Hoover, Blaine, 252–255
Hyōdō, Tsutomu, 86, 229, 236, 331, 407, 421, 438–440, 443, 448–453

Ikeda, Seihin (Shigeaki), 156–157, 429
Imai, Kazuo, 254, 313–314, 447
Inui, Akio, 346–348, 376, 437, 446, 450–451, 454
Ishida, Mitsuo, 333, 381, 430, 439, 440, 442, 449–450, 454
Ishikawa, Masumi, 351–352, 452
Ishikawa, Tsuneo, 30–31, 70, 410, 412–413

Jacoby, Sanford, 12, 165, 206, 410, 419, 422, 424, 431, 435–436, 444, 455

Kahn, Herman, 341
Kambayashi, Ryō, 34, 40, 407, 410–411, 413–414, 451–452
Kamisaka, Fuyuko, 248, 440
Kamishima, Jirō, 185–186, 433
Kaneko, Yoshio, 93, 429
Kariya, Takehiko, 362–363, 452
Katayama, Tetsu, 254
Katsura, Takashi, 194, 434
Kawai, Yoshinari, 200
Kawate, Shō, 131, 176, 178, 426, 428, 432, 434, 441
Kerr, Clark, 109–110, 141, 386, 424
Kinoshita, Takeo, 380, 431, 441–442, 450, 454
Kita, Sadakichi, 136, 138, 427
Kiyosawa, Kiyoshi, 226, 438

Kocka, Jürgen, 214–216, 422, 424, 436–437
Koike, Kazuo, 30–32, 63–64, 98, 315, 343, 407, 410, 413, 418, 421–422, 424, 427, 429, 447–450, 455
Kumazawa, Makoto, 347–348, 350, 359, 362, 420, 449–452, 455
Kurauchi, Shirō, 291, 445
Kusuda, Kyū, 93, 422

Lewis, William Arthur, 43, 414
Luckmann, Thomas, 14, 410

Makino, Nobuaki, 138, 427
Marsden, David, 12, 244–245, 388, 410–411, 422, 424, 440, 448, 455
Marx, Karl, 9
Mills, C. Wright, 309, 447
Mizutani, Mitsuhiro, 135, 184–185, 314, 426–427, 429, 431, 433, 447
Mori, Tateshi, 165, 381, 426, 430, 452, 454
Moriguchi, Chiaki, 52, 416

Nagashima, Osamu, 131, 426, 434
Nakamigawa, Hikojirō, 157
Nakane, Chie, 18–19, 410
Naruse, Takeo, 147, 454
Nasmyth, James, 221
Nimura, Kazuo, 116, 166, 229–230, 332, 424, 426, 431, 437–440, 450
Nishikawa, Tadashi, 315–319, 323, 445–446, 448
Nishinarita, Yutaka, 243–244, 266–267, 425, 428, 430, 434, 439–440, 443, 450
Noma, Seiji, 201, 435
Nomura, Masami, 41–43, 54, 57, 61, 239, 352, 407, 410, 414, 418, 423, 429, 430, 433–434, 436, 439–441, 447, 449, 452–453, 455

Ogihara, Masaru, 191, 434
Ogura, Masatsune, 156

Ōmori, Wataru, 88, 183, 421, 433
Ōsawa, Machiko, 89, 421
Ōtsuki, Bunpei, 342
Ōuchi, Hirokazu, 376, 454
Ōya, Sōichi, 346

Peterson, Richard B., 3, 13, 407
Piore, Michael, 70, 72, 386, 418–419, 443, 455

Saez, Emmanuel, 52, 416
Saitō, Jun, 351, 452
Shibusawa, Eiichi, 156
Shindō, Muneyuki, 89, 421
Skocpol, Theda, 18, 410
Sugayama, Shinji, 128, 163, 291, 407, 425–426, 428, 430–431, 435, 437–440, 445–446
Sullivan, Jeremiah J., 3, 13, 407

Takabatake, Michitoshi, 308, 447
Takaragi, Fumihiko, 232, 239–240, 439–440
Takata, Ryōji, 370, 453
Takeuchi, Yō, 98, 422, 432–433, 435, 447
Tamano, Kazushi, 349, 451
Tanaka, Hirohide, 96–98, 110, 344, 420, 424, 430, 451
Thurow, Lester, 309, 447
Tōbata, Sei'ichi, 44, 280, 414, 444
Tsuji, Katsuji, 325, 432, 449

Ujihara, Shōjirō, 9, 70–72, 169, 207, 209–210, 270–271, 280–281, 302, 329, 409, 418–419, 428, 431, 436, 443–444, 446
Umemura, Mataji, 44, 414

Vogel, Ezra F., 334, 355, 450, 452

Wakabayashi, Yukio, 158, 160, 201, 210, 429–430, 435–436, 447

Index

497

Weber, Max, 13–16, 18, 181, 216, 410, 432, 436

Woo, Jong-won, 165, 262, 328, 428, 431, 439–442, 444, 448–449

Yashiro, Naohiro, 94, 347, 362, 422, 451

Yoshida, Shigeru, 253–254, 255

Company

English Electric (UK), 110–112, 147, 166

Fuji Steel, 318, 327

Fukushima Bōseki, 194

Hitachi, Ltd., 111, 113, 117, 147–148, 161–162, 164, 167, 225, 247, 249–250, 329, 334, 364, 372, 449

Hitachi Works, 161–164, 167, 225, 234–235, 247, 431

Inabata Dyestuffs Factory, 193

Ishikawajima Heavy Industries (later Ishikawajima-Harima Heavy Industries), 148–155, 179, 249–250, 306, 429

Japanese National Railways (JNR) / Japanese Government Railways (JGR), 143, 165, 196, 233, 238, 257, 261–262, 271, 277, 332, 405, 428

Jūjō Paper (formerly Oji Paper), 276, 439

Kanegafuchi Cotton Spinning Company (or 'Kanebō' for short), 271

Kantō Metal, 240

Kawasaki Electric, 277

Kawasaki Steel Works, 230

Konishiroku Photo Industry (later Konica), 145–146

Krupp, 217, 219, 272

Matsushita Electric (later Panasonic), 297, 327

Matsuyama Bōseki, 192

Misawa Homes Co., Ltd., 361, 452

Mitsubishi (Mitsubishi Corporation), 145, 157, 428, 433, 442

Mitsubishi (Mitsubishi Joint-Stock Company), 129, 144, 188, 192, 429

Mitsubishi Electric, 327

Mitsubishi Heavy Industries, 327

Mitsubishi industrial conglomerate (*zaibatsu*), 144, 155, 189, 193, 258

Mitsui & Co., 157–160, 165, 196, 199–202, 208, 210–211, 246, 331, 430, 435, 442

Mitsui Bank, 156–157, 192, 211

Mitsui Engineering & Shipbuilding, 327

NEC, 247

Nippon Cement, 155

Nippon Express, 284, 331

Nippon Kōkan (NKK), 230, 232, 290, 297, 315–316, 318, 321–324, 327, 333, 356–357, 365, 449

Nippon Light Metal, 259–260, 276

Nippon Yūsen, 196

Nissan Motor, 246–247, 263–265, 277, 327, 420

Oji Paper (later Jūjō Paper), 162–163, 224–226, 234, 247, 430, 438, 442–443

Seikosha (later Seiko), 312

Shibaura Seisakusho (later Toshiba), 194

Shikoku Machinery Industries (later Sumitomo Heavy Industries, Ltd.), 238

Sumitomo Bank, 156, 193
Sumitomo Cement, 326, 449
Sumitomo *zaibatsu* (conglomerate),
156, 200

Toho Gas, 276
Tokyo Express Electric Railway
(Tōkyū) Corporation, 276
Tokyo Gas, 193–194
Tōkyū Kikan Kōgyō (Tokyu Engine
Industry, later Nissan Engine
Industry), 326

Toyota Motor Company, 81, 179,
247–248, 325, 327, 343–344, 354,
372–373, 383, 399, 420, 454–455

Yahata Steel Works, 128–132, 143,
155, 161, 164–165, 192, 196,
202, 207, 249, 258, 318–319, 324,
327–328, 330, 332, 381, 428–430,
434, 440, 446, 448–449, 454
Yasuda Mutual Life Insurance
Company, 193
Yokohama Specie Bank, 192–193

Act/Law/Policy

Act for Securing the Proper
Operation of Worker Dispatching
Undertakings and Improved
Working Conditions for
Dispatched Workers (*Rōdōsha
haken hō*), 365
Act on Pensions for Civil Officials
(*Kanri onkyū hō*), 190
Act on Subsidies for Private Schools
(*Shiritsu gakkō shinkō josei-hō*),
345–346

Basic Act on the Reform of the
National Public Service (*Kokka
kōmuin seido kaikaku kihon-hō*),
441

Classification Act (for the US Federal
Government), 180
Companies Act (*Kaisha hō*), 195, 434

Edict on Pensions for Civil Officials
(*Kanri onkyū rei*), 190
Employment Insurance Act (*Koyō
hoken-hō*), 342
Employment Placement Act
(*Shokugyō shōkai-hō*), 300
Employment Security Act (*Shokugyō
antei-hō*), 300, 446

Equal Employment Opportunity Law
(*Danjo koyō kikai kintō hō*), 365
Eugenic Protection Law (*Yūsei hogo
hō*), 37

Factory Act (*Kōjō-hō*), 272, 420
Fair Labor Standards Act (FLSA, US),
96

Health Insurance Act (*Kenkō hoken-
hō*), 272
Housing Construction Planning Act
(*Jūtaku kensetsu keikaku-hō*), 284

Japan Workers' Housing Association
Act (*Nihon kinrō-sha jūtaku
kyōkai-hō*), 284

Labor Contracts Act (*Rōdō keiyaku-
hō*), 423
Labor Standards Act (*Rōdō kijun-hō*),
75, 102, 367, 419, 423
Labor Union Act (*Rōdō kumiai-hō*),
248, 367, 396

Mining Act (*Kōgyō-hō*), 272

National Labor Relations Act (US),
110, 285, 388

Index

499

National Public Service Act (*Kokka kōmuin-hō*), 190, 255, 276, 314

Naval Construction Regulations (*Kaigun kōmu kisoku*), 191

Naval Factory Workers' Regulations (*Kaigun shokkō kisoku*), 191

New Salary Implementation Act (*Shin kyūyo jisshi-hō*), 255

Ordinance on the Promotion of Army Officers (*Rikugun shinkyū jōrei*), 176–177, 189

Part-Time Labor Law (*Paat taimu rōdō hō*), 411

Regulations Concerning Examination, Probation and Training of Civil Officials (*Bunkan shiken shiho oyobi minarai kisoku*), 172

Servicemen's Pension Law (*Gunjin onkyū hō*), 193

Severance and Retirement Allowance Reserve Law (*Taishoku tsumitate-kin oyobi taishoku teate hō*), 194

Total Personnel Act (*Sōteiin-hō*), 62, 354, 377, 452

University Edict (*Daigaku rei*), 200–201, 203

Versicherungsgesetz für Angestellte (Law Relating to Insurance of Salaried Employees, Germany), 220, 272

Welfare Pension Act (*Kōsei nenkin-hō*), 274

Worker's Relief Program (*Shokkō kyūgo hō*), 193

Other Subjects

accumulation of skills, 4, 6, 405, 420

aging, 29, 53, 69, 193–194, 355–356, 374, 414–415

agricultural/agriculture, 11, 13, 27, 30, 42, 44–45, 49, 55–57, 61, 63–64, 67–70, 107, 207, 270, 272, 292, 294, 304, 339, 343, 350–354, 395, 398, 401–402, 412, 418, 432, 443

Allied Occupation, 224, 273, 275

all-middle-class society (*sōchūryū shakai*), 339, 350, 355, 402

assignment after appointment (*ninkan hoshoku*), 121, 139–140, 146, 320

baby boomer, 37–39, 42, 65–67, 303, 376, 414

baby boomer junior, 37–38, 40, 68, 375

blue-collar, 6–7, 20, 79, 94, 98, 105, 108, 110, 121–123, 161, 172, 287–288, 317, 328, 390–392, 404, 425, 432, 438, 445, 449

bulk recruitment of new graduates, 20, 35, 73–74, 92, 103–104, 130, 169, 171–172, 175, 178–180, 192, 200–201, 216, 288, 298, 301–302, 325, 387, 389, 420, 424

bureaucracy/bureaucracies/ bureaucratic system, 5–7, 18–20, 109, 116–119, 121, 130–131, 133–135, 139, 141–144, 148, 154, 156–158, 167, 169, 171–173, 179–184, 190, 214–217, 251–252, 256, 387–392, 403, 424–425, 427–429, 431–432

career advancement, 1, 81, 185

career-based system, 5, 20, 117–118

career-track (*sōgō-shoku*), 35, 365

China, 74, 373, 427, 433

civil servant (*kanri*), 57, 131–132, 135–137, 139–140, 142, 156–158, 161, 165, 172–174, 176, 178, 181–182, 190, 195–196, 215, 219–220, 222, 251, 253, 256, 271, 313, 433–434, 441

   hannin/hanninkan (lower-civil officials), 130, 132–133, 135–139, 142–143, 145, 156, 163, 165, 172, 176, 186, 207, 251, 253, 257, 262, 426–430, 433, 442

   Higher Examination for Civil Officials (*kōbun*), 134, 137, 314

   kōbun-gumi (those who passed the higher civil service examinations), 134, 177–178, 184, 314

   kōtōkan (higher-civil officials), 130, 131, 132, 136, 137, 251

      chokunin/chokuninkan, 132–138, 140, 142, 145, 157, 178, 185, 314

      sōnin/sōninkan, 132–135, 137–138, 142–143, 145, 156–157, 163, 172, 175, 178, 257, 426, 430, 433

   non-regular civil servant, 176

      koin (*yatoi*), 132–133, 135, 142–143, 150, 161, 165, 176, 207, 222, 234, 251, 253, 255–257, 262, 326–327, 354, 426, 428, 442

      yōnin, 132, 135, 142–143, 150, 207, 251, 253, 255–257, 327, 426, 428

   shiho (probationary officers), 172, 174

civil service, 117–118, 121–122, 131–135, 137, 142, 148, 158, 167, 171, 173–180, 183–186, 189–190, 193, 195, 196, 200–202, 207, 214–215, 221, 224, 251–253, 255, 257, 263, 271, 287, 313–314, 387, 399, 403, 426, 435, 442, 446, 452

clerical/clerk, 31, 81, 96, 99, 104, 113, 121, 126, 129, 131, 135, 140, 142, 144–145, 154, 161, 165, 171–172, 196–197, 202, 210–212, 215, 218–219, 222, 249–251, 256–257, 259–260, 272, 288, 297, 311, 313, 323, 325–326, 334, 344, 358, 380, 387, 413, 426, 428–429, 432, 448, 451

collective norms, 1–2, 13–15, 17–18, 122, 171, 193, 201, 242, 380, 383, 385, 406, 457

company employee (*shain*), 57, 100, 104, 106, 108, 112, 116, 127, 144, 146, 149–151, 153, 158, 161, 163–165, 169, 172, 192, 195, 198, 213, 222–224, 231, 234–236, 242, 246–249, 256–258, 260–261, 268–269, 287–288, 293, 301–302, 318, 321–325, 328, 334, 337, 345, 355, 360–363, 365, 372, 377, 382–383, 391, 402, 405, 437, 445, 447–448

contract employees, 25–26, 408–409, 416

cross-firm labor market, 218, 295–296, 380–381

cross-firm standard, 20, 282, 284, 340

Danish/Denmark, 9, 80, 103, 109, 394

diploma, 37, 99, 126, 168, 218, 289, 305, 319, 326

discriminating/discrimination/ discriminatory, 75, 99, 122, 131, 142, 148, 165–166, 168, 172, 187, 195, 220–226, 231, 233–235, 245, 250, 263–264, 296, 305, 317, 318, 323–324, 326, 362, 365, 390–401, 404, 419, 431, 438, 442

dismiss/dismissal, 26, 34, 52, 81–82, 102–103, 107, 125, 166, 190–195, 233, 246, 248, 281, 299, 331, 339–340, 366–370, 386, 392, 399–401, 412, 420, 423, 425, 453

disparity, 8, 25, 52, 55, 72, 99, 131, 163, 224, 277, 374–375, 377, 411, 429

Index

501

dualization, 1
dual structure, ix–x, 2, 7–9, 12,
16–17, 19–21, 23–25, 31, 41,
43–47, 67, 69–70, 72–73, 107,
116, 169, 224, 269–271, 275,
280, 339–340, 369–372, 385,
390, 392–393, 395–396, 400,
403–406, 410–411, 441, 457
dual structure paradigm, 269–271,
369–370
dual structure theory, 9, 43, 410
dualist regime, 456
new dual structure, 21, 45–46, 337,
339, 369–371, 414, 450

education reform/educational
reform, 150, 203, 288, 289
educational background/academic
background, 30, 67–68, 70, 80,
84–85, 93, 95, 99, 121, 123–125,
130–131, 143, 148, 151, 157–158,
160, 162, 164, 166–169, 176,
207, 210, 233–234, 236–237, 249,
251, 260–262, 289–291, 293, 296,
302, 306, 309–312, 315–321, 323,
328–329, 331–334, 347–348, 350,
356–357, 360, 362, 366, 381, 405,
412, 422–423, 431, 440, 445, 448,
451–452
employers' organizations, 386, 393,
456
Kantō Employers' Association,
328, 364, 368, 449, 453
Keidanren (Japan Business
Federation), 1, 75, 383, 407,
419, 456
Keizai Dōyūkai (Association of
Corporate Executives), 364, 365
Nikkeiren (Japan Federation of
Employers' Associations),
83, 126, 147–148, 249, 257,
275–279, 282, 284, 294, 311,
320, 328, 330, 332, 335,
342, 356, 363, 377–379, 437,
444–445, 454

employment regime, 10, 12, 23–25,
34, 41, 43, 107, 386, 392, 396, 400,
403–404, 410–411, 456
equal pay for equal work, 106, 220,
263–264, 275, 277–278, 280–282,
404

factory workers (*shokkō, kōin*),
6, 71, 81, 95–96, 105, 114, 128,
130, 143–144, 151, 160–167, 169,
191–192, 207, 211–212, 218, 222,
224–226, 229, 231–236, 239,
247–249, 258–260, 268, 291–292,
297–300, 302, 315, 317–319, 321,
323–325, 331, 333–334, 344, 366,
381, 390–391, 399, 428, 430–431,
437–440, 442–443, 446, 448, 451
family allowance, 236–237, 241, 253, 261
family size, 223, 236, 242, 266, 391
family worker, 8, 23–24, 27–30, 32–34,
41–43, 49, 61–62, 64, 67–68, 91,
274, 327, 350–351, 353, 375,
401–402, 408–409
firm size/company size, 29–30, 46,
51, 62–63, 71, 104–105, 243, 269,
369–370, 394, 398, 409, 411, 424,
456
firm-size wage gap, 104–105, 394, 456
fixed-term contract/employment/
worker, 25–26, 400, 409, 411
four explanatory models, 5
Control Model, 3–4, 6–7, 13, 108,
391–392, 407
Cultural Model, 3–4, 108
Economic Model, 3–4, 6–7, 108,
391–392, 407
Motivation Model, 4, 6–7, 13, 108
France/French, 14, 16, 42–43, 51,
56, 90, 94, 98, 103, 115–116,
118–119, 141, 172, 180, 195–196,
214, 220–221, 239, 295, 347, 387,
393–394, 400, 409, 416, 421, 424,
428, 437, 455–456
cadre, 98, 115–116, 118, 214, 220, 437
corps, 141, 428

gender, 4, 10, 17, 26, 29, 95, 195, 221, 237, 245, 264, 268, 281, 326, 365, 370, 405, 414

    female, 10, 28–29, 31, 39, 42, 52, 54, 61, 64, 71, 90–91, 95, 126–127, 136, 151, 153, 210–213, 243, 244, 267–268, 271, 280–281, 312, 326–327, 351, 357, 365, 370–372, 374, 395, 414, 416, 421–422, 443, 447

    female office staff, 210–211

    male, 10, 28–31, 39–40, 42, 52, 70, 86–87, 90, 95, 100–101, 108, 126, 136, 212–213, 243–244, 267–268, 291, 303, 306, 312, 326, 334, 356–357, 364, 365, 396, 411, 413, 421, 443, 447

    M-shape, 91–92, 327, 422

    status of women, x, 88, 126

    woman/women, x, 1–2, 8, 10, 26, 29–30, 38, 40–44, 46, 50, 54, 57–59, 62, 68, 70, 81, 89–91, 94, 101–102, 126–127, 150–151, 165, 171, 210–213, 221–222, 227, 243, 266–268, 277, 297, 300, 311, 325–327, 340, 346, 352–353, 363–366, 370–372, 374, 377, 402, 405, 412–414, 422, 436, 444, 446–447, 450–451, 456

general office positions (*ippan-shoku*), 365–366

German/Germany, 6, 10, 12–14, 16, 20, 43, 47–48, 51, 56, 64, 74, 80, 84–85, 90, 92, 96, 103, 109, 113–115, 118–119, 128, 141, 171–176, 180–182, 214–222, 234, 239, 245, 251–253, 256, 272, 287, 295, 333–334, 387–389, 394–396, 404–405, 409–411, 416, 421, 424, 428, 431–432, 436, 443, 455–456

    Angestellte, 97, 215, 219–220, 251, 272, 436–437, 441

    Arbeiter, 97, 215, 219, 251, 441

    Beamte, 97, 173, 215, 219, 234, 251, 441

    Krankenkasse, 272, 443

    Öffentliches Recht, 173, 251

    Privatrecht, 251

    Prussia/Prussian, 172–173, 180–182, 184

graduate school, ix, 78–79, 310–311, 441

graduate student, 158, 347

hierarchical, 18, 96, 143, 160, 173, 210, 215–216, 231, 234, 310, 320, 378

higher education, 36, 38, 58, 97, 129, 137, 144, 148, 150, 158, 160–161, 173–174, 198–201, 205–208, 210, 212, 219, 239, 241, 251, 262, 287–290, 292–295, 303–306, 310, 312, 314–315, 323, 339, 345–346, 348, 350, 356, 375–377, 391, 397, 430, 435, 445–446, 448, 451, 454

high-growth period, 20, 64, 66, 210, 310, 330, 342, 344, 354, 358, 365, 379

household, 41–42, 44, 47, 49, 53–55, 59–62, 68, 212–213, 239, 264, 298–299, 307, 320, 332, 350–351, 353–355, 364, 372, 374, 401–403, 405, 415, 436

housewife, 25–26, 41, 49, 415

ILO (International Labor Organization), 1, 26, 407–409, 411

inequality, xi, 2, 4, 9, 17, 24, 26, 46, 50, 55, 118, 268, 339, 393

insurance system, 47–48, 51, 60, 224, 272–273, 392, 402, 409, 415–416, 443

    health insurance association, 60, 272–273, 417–418

    National Health Insurance (*kokumin kenkō hoken*), 273–275, 416, 418, 443

internal labor market, 4, 20, 39, 45–46, 69, 72–73, 107, 109–110, 119, 371, 376, 385–388, 392–393, 399–401, 403, 405, 424, 443, 455, 457

Index 503

craft market, 386, 388, 455
enterprise market, 386–388, 404, 455
external labor market, 39, 45–46,
70, 371, 376, 386, 393, 400–401,
403, 405
guild system, 109–110, 141, 386
manorial system, 109–110, 141, 386
primary labor market, 30–31, 70, 412
secondary labor market, 30, 70, 412

Japanese-style employment system,
x, 2–8, 11–13, 18–20, 24–25, 27, 29,
34–35, 40, 73, 87, 91–92, 94–95,
98, 100–101, 104, 106–110, 113,
116–117, 121–122, 127, 154, 171,
287–288, 339–340, 354, 373, 378,
385, 389–392, 400–401, 403–404,
407, 410, 419, 422, 437, 441, 443,
455
Japanese-style management, 148,
377, 454

Korea, ix, 42–43, 50–51, 74, 80, 90, 103,
118, 394, 409, 422, 436

Labor Capacity Development Center
(Ningen Nōryoku Kaihatsu Sentā),
421, 423, 447, 449, 452, 453
labor force, 10, 26, 42, 44, 50–51, 61,
66, 68, 70–71, 91, 225, 270, 281,
327, 350, 356, 365, 370, 375, 401,
408, 412, 414, 449
labor movement/workers' movement, 3–4, 6, 13, 20, 71, 73, 80, 95,
99, 108–112, 114–116, 118–119,
122, 148, 167, 219–223, 228–229,
234, 236–237, 239–240, 245–246,
249, 253–255, 258, 264, 266,
275, 281–283, 288, 293, 391–392,
403–405, 407, 437–438, 440, 457
length of service, 29, 84, 111, 128,
147, 149, 151–153, 158–159, 167,
236, 245, 249, 262, 266–268, 271,
276, 293, 329, 332, 357, 370, 381,
404–405, 411, 422–423, 442

lifetime commitment, 126, 139, 268, 425
lifetime employment, 1, 30, 46, 73, 81,
83, 122, 126, 193, 302, 330–331,
335, 342, 363–364, 379, 412, 425
livelihood wage/living wage, 223,
236–240, 243–244, 246–247,
253–254, 261–262, 264, 266, 268,
276–277, 329, 332, 391, 443
long-term employment, 5, 7, 8, 11,
19, 23–24, 29, 34, 40, 57, 60, 95,
101–102, 106, 122, 128, 130, 166,
169, 206, 288, 301–302, 325–326,
330, 335, 339–340, 344, 349,
366–368, 378, 381, 387, 391–392,
399–400, 403–405, 437, 439,
443, 457

mandatory retirement (*teinen*), 20,
35, 74, 81–83, 94, 97–98, 101, 171,
189–195, 201, 211–212, 215, 314,
321, 325–326, 419, 421, 434, 438
manual labor/manual worker, 97, 114,
142, 166, 218–219, 247, 251, 256,
288, 327, 426, 428, 438, 440, 452
Meiji, 20, 121–122, 127–131, 139, 141,
144, 154–155, 157, 172, 174–175,
181–186, 189, 196–200, 203–204,
320, 327, 334, 383, 389–390,
426–427, 431, 433–435
microenterprise, x, 43–44, 269, 398, 456
migration, 65–68, 330, 334, 339,
351–353, 402
military, 17, 84, 115, 118, 121, 134–137,
140–142, 146–147, 155–156, 158,
160–161, 171–172, 174, 176,
186–191, 193, 195, 214–216,
220–221, 223, 226, 239–241, 265,
287, 300, 313, 319, 335–336,
387–388, 426–428, 430, 432–434,
436, 438, 441
Army War College
(*rikugun daigakkō*), 186–187
commissioned officer, 160, 336
Military Academy
(*rikugun shikangakkō*), 186

military experience, 135, 239, 335
military industry, 220
military-type, 158, 161, 287, 430
Naval Academy (*kaigun heigakkō*),
336
non-commissioned officer, 132, 135,
160, 191, 211, 308, 427
warrant officer, 133, 177, 321, 426
ministries/agencies, 7, 16, 25, 43, 58,
88, 117, 119, 130, 133–134, 139,
141–142, 155, 174–175, 179, 182,
200–201, 222, 251–254, 300–301,
313–314, 363, 408, 416, 426, 428,
446
Advisory Council on Social
Security (*shakai hoshō seido
shingikai*), 194, 443
Economic Deliberation Council
(EDC), 280–283, 285, 295–296,
437, 444–445
Headquarters for Economic
Stabilization (*Keizai antei
honbu*), 276
Japan Institute for Labour Policy
and Training (JILPT), 25, 52,
73, 84, 90, 100, 104, 394–395,
416, 419–421, 423–424, 456
Ministry of Education, 162, 294,
301, 306, 345, 429, 435, 445–447
Ministry of Education, Culture,
Sports, Science and
Technology (MEXT), 36–37,
53, 290, 304, 454
Ministry of Finance, 155–157, 182,
184, 202, 254–255, 274, 283,
313, 429, 433
Ministry of Health, Labour and
Welfare (MHLW), 25, 35, 48–49,
51, 53–54, 75, 85, 101–102, 397,
407, 409, 411, 415–416, 457
Ministry of Home Affairs, 134–135,
156, 202, 204–205, 208, 212,
314, 352

Ministry of Internal Affairs and
Communications (MIAC), 28,
33, 49–50, 56, 62–63, 352, 377,
398, 451
Ministry of Labor, 30, 93, 96, 244,
251, 267, 277–278, 297, 305,
311, 327, 340, 364–365, 412,
429, 444, 446–447, 450
Ministry of Land, Infrastructure,
Transport and Tourism
(MLIT), 58, 416–417
Ministry of the Navy, 143, 155
Ministry of Welfare, 243
National Personnel Authority
(NPA), 82–83, 189, 252,
254–255, 421, 427, 434, 441
SME Agency, 101, 374
Supreme Court, 75, 81–82, 133,
368, 419–421, 423
Tokyo High Court, 81, 367, 420, 423
mobility, 6, 20, 71, 92, 97, 107, 141, 266,
269, 280–282, 366, 403, 431, 444
mutual assistance, 55, 401–402, 418

National Income Doubling Plan,
280, 294
nationalism, 224, 226, 231, 390,
437–438
neighborhood associations/NHAs
(*Jichikai* or *Chōnaikai*), 59–60,
349, 352, 355, 403, 410
new graduate, 8, 20, 35–36, 38, 40, 66,
69–70, 73–75, 78, 81–82, 84–85,
87–92, 94, 97–98, 103–104, 106,
111, 119, 128, 130, 153, 169,
171–172, 175, 178–180, 192, 196,
199–206, 210, 216, 288, 292, 298,
301–302, 306, 311, 313, 315, 325,
343–344, 346–347, 362, 365,
368–369, 379, 383, 387, 389,
402–403, 414, 420, 424, 446
non-regular employment, 5, 20, 23,
29, 34, 43, 45, 50, 61, 65, 67–69,
91, 106–107, 327, 364, 366, 371,
374–376, 378, 397, 400, 422

Index

non-regular worker, 1–3, 5, 8, 11, 21,
23–29, 32–35, 38–39, 42, 45–53,
55, 61, 63–64, 67–70, 81, 91, 101,
106–107, 135, 142, 165, 288, 340,
343, 345, 354–355, 360, 363,
365–369, 371, 374–375, 377–378,
397, 400–402, 406, 408–409,
411–413, 416, 418, 450–451,
453, 456
  arubaito, 25–26, 39, 371, 408, 415–416
  dispatched worker, 25–26, 366,
    408–409, 416, 428
  entrusted worker, 82
  non-standard, 1
  paat, 25–26, 327, 371, 408, 415–416
  part-time/part-time worker, 1, 25–26,
    39, 42, 46, 51, 54, 91, 106, 327,
    351, 353–354, 364–365, 368, 371,
    400, 408–409, 411–412, 415–416
norm, 2, 14–19, 26, 68, 102, 105, 107,
115, 119, 169, 171, 176–179, 182,
185, 189, 195–196, 200–201, 214,
222, 229, 246, 249, 251, 255, 258,
268, 270, 274–275, 282, 292–293,
298, 301–302, 305, 312, 317, 325,
331, 334–335, 339–343, 356, 362,
366–367, 377, 380, 387, 389, 399,
405, 423, 429, 432, 434, 441, 443,
444, 446

occupational organization, 6, 10,
20, 109–110, 113–116, 122, 127–128,
130, 142, 154, 158–159, 197, 205,
299, 386–389, 392, 401, 403
  guild, 47, 109, 113–115, 141, 218
  kabu-nakama, 127
  trade associations (*dōgyō Kumiai*),
    128
OECD (Organisation for Economic
Co-operation and Development),
42–43, 51, 54–55, 62, 73, 87,
102–103, 117, 341, 355, 394, 396,
405, 408, 414, 416, 418–424, 450,
456–457
open plan office, 88, 168, 171,
182–183, 216, 278, 332, 421

patriotism, 224, 232, 240
pension, 8, 47–50, 54, 61, 82, 115, 140,
173, 190, 194, 216, 220, 256, 271,
274, 280, 314, 365, 367, 371, 415,
441
  employee's pension (*kōsei nenkin*),
    48, 416
  national pension (*kokumin nenkin*),
    48–49, 51, 69, 274, 280, 416
  public pension, 48, 50
peripheral workforce/labor force,
44, 68, 70, 370
personnel evaluation (*kōka*), 7, 78,
109, 171, 188, 241–242, 315, 328,
340, 358–359, 361–363, 366, 386,
388–389, 403, 433
political party, 10
  Japan Socialist Party (JSP), 351
  Japanese Communist Party (JCP),
    228
  Liberal Democratic Party (LDP),
    55, 57, 64, 351, 416
postwar education system
  elementary school, 150, 294
  high school, 36–37, 39–40, 68,
    99–101, 123–127, 146, 150, 260,
    287, 289–294, 296–303, 306–307,
    309–312, 315–319, 321, 323, 326,
    331–332, 343–348, 350, 363, 369,
    376, 399, 412, 414, 422–423, 441,
    445–446, 448, 451–452
  junior college, 37, 40, 146, 303–304,
    321–322, 326, 345–346, 348,
    375, 414, 451
  junior high school, 53, 64, 123–126,
    146, 149–150, 153, 260, 289–296,
    298–302, 306, 316, 319, 323,
    331–332, 369, 425, 445
  miscellaneous school, 348, 376
  training school, 37, 40, 348, 376
prewar education system, 212, 289
  elementary school, 129, 133, 138,
    143, 148–150, 163, 168, 190,
    208, 289, 301

girls' high school, 211, 293

high school, 432

higher elementary school, 148–151, 153, 301

professional school, 149–153, 162, 168, 205–206, 208, 212, 218, 289–290, 303, 429–430, 446

secondary school, 121, 129–131, 133, 136, 138, 143, 150–151, 153, 156, 204, 208–209, 212, 289, 293, 300–301

vocational school, 37, 149–152, 161, 163, 197–198, 203–205, 293, 348, 429

private law, 173, 251–253, 256

private sector, 5–7, 20, 29, 47, 57, 73, 93, 115, 118, 121–122, 136, 142, 154–156, 158–159, 171, 179–180, 186, 188, 192, 196, 201–202, 207, 211, 214, 220, 224, 251, 252–253, 256–257, 331, 366, 377, 388–390, 399, 441

public law, 173, 219, 251

public sector, 30, 118, 214, 251, 253, 255, 257–258, 354–355, 377, 395, 412, 434

public servant (kōmuin), 60, 117, 140–141, 214, 252–257, 276, 307, 314, 354–355, 377, 417–418, 426, 441, 454

non-regular public servant (hiseiki-kōmuin), 257

public service, 10, 23, 117, 139, 142, 252–254, 283, 354, 450

qalification system, 104–105, 113, 455

cross-firm qualification system, 6–7, 72, 107

ranking system, 5, 107, 146, 148, 154, 161, 237, 250, 262, 319–324, 327–328, 330, 332, 334, 357–358, 438, 448–449

bureaucratic ranking system, 131, 161

competence ranking system, 122, 146, 319–322, 324–325, 327–331, 333, 335–336, 357–358, 366, 378, 422, 445, 448, 455

in-house ranking system, 5–6, 12, 18, 73–74, 92, 94, 413

official rank (kantō), 131–135, 140–141, 143, 155, 176, 184, 426–427

ranking scheme, 193, 201, 224, 249, 251, 254, 257–260, 288, 323–324, 381–383, 431, 438, 442, 448

regular employee, 1–2, 21, 23–36, 38–41, 45, 47–53, 55, 57–58, 60–61, 63, 65, 66–70, 78–82, 84, 86–87, 90–91, 94, 101, 104–107, 135, 223, 266, 271, 274, 337, 339–340, 343, 345, 349–350, 354, 360, 362, 368–371, 373, 375, 379–381, 390, 396, 397–403, 405, 408, 411–413, 415, 421–422, 428, 447, 450, 456–457

regular employment, 8, 25, 35–36, 38, 40–41, 68, 375, 382, 400, 407, 411–413

retention rate (of workers), 29, 40, 88, 421

self-employed, ix–x, 8, 11, 23–24, 27–30, 32–34, 41–45, 47–51, 55, 57, 61–64, 68–69, 72, 91, 207, 334, 339, 349, 351, 353–355, 374–375, 401–405, 409, 416, 418, 422, 432, 435–436

self-employment sector, 5, 20, 24, 27, 31–32, 44, 67–68, 72, 107, 375, 403, 409, 411

seniority-based promotion, 46, 169, 176, 344, 366

Index 507

seniority-based wage/seniority wage/
seniority-based pay, 3, 5, 7–8, 11,
19, 23–24, 29–34, 41–42, 46, 55, 57,
60–61, 73, 80, 84, 87, 95, 99, 106,
110, 113, 121–122, 135, 159, 163,
166, 169, 211–212, 223, 258, 262,
266, 275, 288, 302, 326, 335, 340,
342, 349, 356, 358, 366–368, 377,
379, 381, 387, 399–400, 403–404,
422, 437, 439, 443, 450, 457
shop-floor worker, 96, 100, 108, 110,
113, 130, 144, 161, 168–169, 222,
288, 291, 293, 302, 310–312, 316,
323–324, 328, 358, 362–363, 367,
391, 399, 408, 437, 449
Sino-Japanese War, 174, 177, 188, 206
small and medium-sized enterprises
(SMEs), 7–8, 23–24, 29, 31–34,
41–42, 44–46, 54, 57, 62–66, 68,
70–72, 101, 103–104, 106–107,
122, 126, 135, 224, 269, 291,
298, 311, 339–340, 352, 354, 364,
367–375, 378, 392, 397–400, 402,
404, 412–413, 417–418, 423, 440,
445, 453, 456–457
social capital, 24–25, 55–57, 59, 61,
65, 405, 410
social security, x, 8–11, 17–18, 24–26,
38, 47–49, 55–57, 113–114, 116,
194, 224, 271–275, 279, 282–283,
295–296, 314, 380, 385, 395,
400–401, 403–404, 408–409,
411, 415, 437, 443
solidarity, 19, 112, 219, 233, 248, 273,
333, 390
staff employee (*syoku-in*), 108, 128,
144, 161–164, 167, 195–197,
204–205, 207, 217, 223–226,
228–229, 231, 233–236, 238–239,
243–244, 246, 248–251, 258–259,
262, 266, 269, 271–272, 277,
287–289, 292, 297–299, 301–303,
307, 312, 314–321, 323, 325–326,
332–334, 344, 349, 356–357, 360,
362, 366, 390–391, 399, 404, 428,
431–435, 437–438, 447, 451–452

standard worker, 1, 101, 350, 412, 421
state-owned enterprise (SOE), 5, 20,
121, 143–144, 154–156, 165, 196,
390, 425, 429
status system, 123, 226, 228, 231, 234,
247, 249–250, 443
surveys
Basic School Survey (*gakkō kihon
chōsa*), 36–37, 290, 306, 414
Current Population Survey
(CPS, the US), 31
Employment Status Survey
(*shūgyō kōzō kihon chōsa*,
Basic Survey on Employment
Structure), 27, 30–31, 33–34,
40, 63, 364, 398, 407–408,
411–413, 450
Labor Force Survey (*rōdōryoku
chōsa*), 25–30, 61–62, 90–91,
373, 408, 411
Longitudinal Employer Household
Dynamics (LEHD, the US), 31
Wage Census (*chingin kōzō kihon
tōkei chōsa*, Basic Survey on
Wage Structure), 30, 40, 79,
84–87, 101, 244, 350, 412,
421, 424
Sweden/Swedish, 10, 43, 51, 80, 90,
92, 100, 103, 394–395, 405, 456

Taishō, 128, 272
three-tier structure, 96–97, 100,
121–122, 124, 127, 130–132, 144,
155, 161, 165–166, 169, 207, 210,
215, 247, 287–289, 291–292, 302,
315, 317–319, 323, 334, 391, 428,
445, 448
three types of employment
informal employment type, 8, 23,
34, 413, 422
large company type, 8, 23–24,
33, 53, 55, 60–61, 63, 67–69,
417–418
SME type, 8, 23, 33

total war, 225, 334, 336, 390–391

transfer (idō), 78, 432

    external transfer (shukkō), 83, 363–365, 421

    regular personnel transfers/regular (periodic) personnel transfers, 20, 78–80, 169, 171–172, 176, 178–180, 314, 325, 357, 424

    relocation assignment (tenkin), 59, 81, 94, 364, 368, 419

    single-posting transfer (tanshin funin), 81, 90, 364

UK/British, 11–12, 43–44, 51, 59, 64, 80, 90, 92, 96, 103, 110–114, 117–118, 147–148, 165–166, 168, 218, 248, 278, 334, 341, 347, 363, 388, 394, 396, 410–411, 415–416, 424, 455–456

union

    company union, 110, 285, 388, 437

    craft union, 6, 18, 20, 73, 110, 112–114, 116, 127, 221, 229, 341, 386–387, 424, 443

    Densan (the Japan Electric Power Industry Labor Union), 232, 237, 239–240, 250

    enterprise union, 6, 73, 110, 112, 172, 222–223, 228, 232, 245, 250, 269, 277, 285, 334, 342, 367, 391, 396–397

    Salarymen's Union (SMU), 221–222, 390, 437

    Sōdōmei (Japan Confederation of Labor), 229

    Sōhyō (the General Council of Trade Unions of Japan), 277, 296, 332, 444

    Tekkōrōren (the Japan Federation of Steel Workers' Unions), 332, 448

    trade union, 110, 112, 115, 162, 198, 229, 277, 282, 333, 386, 389, 393, 437, 455

World Federation of Trade Unions (WFTU), 276

Zenji (the All-Japan Automobile Workers' Union), 246, 263–265, 442

Zentei (the Japan Postal Workers' Union), 232, 240

university, 2, 8, 34–40, 53, 65, 67–68, 72, 74–75, 77, 79, 81, 85, 87, 93, 98–101, 104, 107, 121, 123, 126, 138, 146, 149–152, 157, 160, 166–168, 171, 173–175, 179–180, 184–186, 197–199, 202–203, 205–209, 212, 215, 236, 250–251, 260, 287–288, 290, 292, 294, 299, 302–303, 305–313, 315–317, 320–321, 323, 325–328, 332–333, 339, 346–347, 349–350, 355–356, 358, 363, 375–376, 383, 387, 405, 412, 414, 417, 419–420, 422–423, 425–426, 441, 447–448, 451

    Hitotsubashi University/Tokyo Higher Commercial School, 124, 157, 197, 199, 200, 429

    imperial university, 132–134, 137–138, 140, 149, 151–152, 157, 175–177, 185, 190, 196–197, 200–202, 239, 426, 433, 435–436

    Keio University, 124, 199, 204

    Kyoto University/Kyoto Imperial University, 124, 197, 239, 436

    national university, 53, 295, 304–305, 446

    private university, 149, 151, 199, 305

    public university, 376

    the University of Tokyo/Tokyo Imperial University, 1, 124, 156, 158, 174, 179, 185–186, 196–197, 202, 204, 228–229, 231, 234, 333, 347, 429, 431–432, 436, 439, 444

    Waseda University, 124, 204, 436

Index   **509**

US/American, 6, 9–10, 12–14, 16, 18, 20, 30–31, 42–44, 47–48, 51–52, 56, 64, 70, 74, 84–85, 88–90, 92–94, 96, 98–100, 105, 110, 112, 117–118, 122, 165–167, 180, 182, 184, 189, 195, 198, 206, 212, 214–216, 218, 220–221, 224, 229, 241–242, 245, 252–254, 256, 264, 275–276, 278–279, 281–282, 285, 287–289, 309–310, 316–317, 333–334, 341, 345, 347, 362–363, 372–373, 387–389, 392–395, 400, 404–405, 409, 411, 416, 424, 431, 433, 436, 440, 455–457

U-turn/U-turners, 58, 416–417

vertical (*tate*), 18, 55, 110, 254, 348

welfare capitalism, 110

welfare regime, 9–11, 15, 47, 411

white-collar, 6–7, 72, 84, 94, 98, 108, 110, 123–125, 161, 165–166, 172, 215, 219, 287, 303, 317, 324, 328, 347, 379, 390, 397, 404, 412, 420, 425, 438, 449

work experience, 75, 77, 92, 96, 98, 100, 128, 198, 395, 412

workforce, 26, 46, 91, 107, 125, 143, 157, 161, 163, 184, 193, 202, 204, 207, 222, 247, 251, 281, 291, 295, 301, 312, 334–335, 355–356, 367, 372, 375, 396, 399–400, 402–403, 405, 411–412, 423

working hours, 1, 51–52, 57, 73, 83, 88–89, 94, 97, 139, 143, 161, 235, 253, 280, 340, 377, 411, 415, 428, 451, 457

working people, x, 2, 7–8, 19, 23, 29, 31–33, 49, 53, 55, 60, 236, 343, 400, 403, 407–408, 411

working population, 272

World War I, 6, 118, 139, 162, 165, 167, 180, 192–193, 197, 200, 214, 220, 241, 285, 387

World War II, 3–4, 37, 67, 92, 94, 99–100, 108, 116, 118, 131, 145, 150, 179, 194, 212, 223, 252, 268, 273–275, 293, 367, 390, 401, 405, 427, 429

years of experience, 84, 263–265, 267, 277

years of service, 40, 80, 84–87, 93, 99, 100–101, 104, 106, 109, 121, 135, 140, 148, 150–151, 163, 176, 178–179, 184, 190, 223, 235–236, 242–244, 256–258, 260–262, 265–268, 270–271, 354, 360, 370, 411–412, 421, 426, 442